MW01200622

UNIVERSITY CASEBOOK SERIES®

ADVANCED CORPORATION LAW

A PRACTICAL APPROACH TO CORPORATE GOVERNANCE

STEPHEN M. BAINBRIDGE
William D. Warren Distinguished Professor of Law
UCLA School of Law

FOUNDATION
PRESS

University Casebook Series is a trademark registered in the U.S. Patent and Trademark Office.

© 2021 LEG, Inc. d/b/a West Academic
    444 Cedar Street, Suite 700
    St. Paul, MN 55101
    1-877-888-1330

Printed in the United States of America

ISBN: 978-1-68328-622-6

PREFACE

This text is designed for use in an advanced course in corporate law and governance. It assumes that students have taken a basic course in Corporations or Business Associations.

Corporate governance has been much in the news in recent years and lawyers are devoting increasing amount of attention to it. The passage of major federal legislation in 2002 (the Sarbanes-Oxley Act a.k.a. SOX) and 2010 (the Dodd-Frank Act) were particularly important developments, generating much new law and, as a result, much new legal work. Curiously, however, the law school casebook market has largely ignored these trends.

Corporate governance is regulated by many of the same laws covered in the basic Business Associations course, but increasingly is also regulated by laws—such as SOX and Dodd-Frank—that get short shrift in the typical Business Associations casebook and course. In contrast, those laws are the core focus of this text.

Unlike the more basic topics that dominate Business Associations, which are a product of state corporate law with a minor federal overlay, corporate governance is regulated by a much more complex body of law that emanates from multiple regulators. Many of the rules of corporate governance come from traditional state corporate and federal securities law sources, but many more come from sources such as stock exchange listing standards or rules issued by the Public Company Accounting Oversight Board and similar quasi-governmental bodies. All of these are grist for the mill in this text.

Importantly, however, lawyers practicing in the corporate governance space must be knowledgeable not only about the law but also best practice. As Sir Adrian Cadbury observed in connection with the United Kingdom's adoption of the so-called Cadbury Code, it is tempting for managers to obey the letter of law while ignoring the deeper purposes behind it. Sound corporate governance structures thus must be informed as much by best practices as well as formal legal rules.

Likewise, this text assumes that mastering the relevant law requires situating it in an understanding of the contemporary business environment. The legal issues governing executive compensation makes little sense, for example, if one does not understand the political and economic debate over CEO pay. Similarly, to cite just one more example, mastering the high-profile issues respecting shareholder rights will be much easier if the students are familiarized with the changing demographics of shareholders and the rise of activist hedge funds.

Notice that I refer to this book as a text rather than a casebook. Although the text includes many canonical cases presented in the traditional format, the case method is not the only—or even always the best—way of teaching students to draft workable contracts and disclosure documents, conduct due diligence, or counsel clients on issues that require business savvy as well as knowing the law. Accordingly, the book also relies on textual explication, sample documents, and problems to build student transactional skills.

This approach is driven by my belief that, because lawyers plan at least as often as they litigate, advanced business law course texts need to adopt a transaction planner's perspective. Most law school casebooks—even in the corporate law area, where the authors ought to know better—have an inherent bias towards litigation perspectives due to their emphasis on cases. I avoid that by using additional sources, such as law review articles and regulatory materials, and by including numerous problems—typically at the start of a block of material—requiring students to think about how the materials will affect real world transactions and planning.

The text assumes familiarity with some basic law and economics tools—such as transaction costs and agency costs—that are commonly used in many business law classes. Indeed, the central theme of this text is the agency costs resulting from the separation of ownership and control in public corporations. The appendix offers a brief overview of these tools for the benefit of those students who have not encountered them previously.

STEPHEN M. BAINBRIDGE

September 2020

EDITORIAL NOTE

Editorial footnotes run consecutively, starting over at 1 at the beginning of each chapter, except that footnotes in excerpted materials retain their numbering from the original source, with no renumbering to take account of omitted footnotes. Editorial footnotes in excerpted materials are indicated using an asterisk and have the footnote text in brackets.

Citations and footnotes in cases and other excerpts are generally omitted without indication thereof, except where they provide the source of quoted language or otherwise seemed noteworthy.

A number of abbreviations are used throughout the text, as follows:

- DGCL: Delaware General Corporation Law
- Dodd-Frank: Dodd-Frank Act of 2010
- MBCA: Model Business Corporation Act
- Rule: A rule promulgated by the SEC under either the Securities Act or the Securities Exchange Act
- SEC: Securities and Exchange Commission
- Securities Act: Securities Act of 1933
- Securities Exchange Act: Securities Exchange Act of 1934
- SOX: Sarbanes-Oxley Act of 2002

The text makes active use of text boxes to highlight certain materials:

- Case in Point. These boxes offer a concise summary of cases that illustrate the point being made in the text.
- For More Information. These boxes point students to additional resources to consult for more information on a subject.
- FYI. A self-explanatory category that shares useful or simply interesting information relevant to material in the text.
- Think About It. These boxes pose questions that prompt students to pause to think about various issues presented by the material or raise critical reading questions designed to focus student attention on the key issues.
- What's That? These boxes explain the meaning of special legal terms that appear in the main text.

SUMMARY OF CONTENTS

TABLE OF CONTENTS

PART III. EXECUTIVES

TABLE OF CASES

The principal cases are in bold type.

UNIVERSITY CASEBOOK SERIES®

ADVANCED CORPORATION LAW

A PRACTICAL APPROACH TO CORPORATE GOVERNANCE

PART I

INTRODUCTION

CHAPTER 1

REGULATING CORPORATE GOVERNANCE IN A FEDERAL SYSTEM

One of the most widely cited definitions of corporate governance was set out in 1992 by the UK's Cadbury Commission report: "Corporate governance is the system by which companies are directed and controlled."[1] The Cadbury definition is certainly correct, but it turns the virtue of succinctness into a vice. It is simply too concise to tell us very much.

A more detailed definition offered by former Delaware Chief Justice Norman Veasey states that corporate governance encompasses "the structure, relationships, norms, control mechanisms, and objectives of the corporate enterprise."[2] Yet, while more detailed than the Cadbury definition, the Chief Justice's statement sweeps far too broadly for the concept to be useful.

Properly understood, corporate governance consists of the legal rules, private contracts, and best practices that create, maintain, and respond to the separation of ownership and control that is the defining characteristic of the U.S. public corporation.

In the U.S.A.'s federal system, the legal rules creating and constraining corporate governance traditionally came from the states. To be sure, the federal securities laws long have regulated some aspects of corporate governance—such as shareholder voting procedures and trading by a corporation's officers and directors in the company's stock—but these rules were never intended to form a comprehensive federal law of corporations. Instead, they placed a limited gloss on the underlying body of state law. As we shall see, however, over the last several decades the federal role in corporate governance has dramatically increased.

> **FYI**
>
> The separation of ownership and control, of course, is not the corporation's only critical feature. The others include formal creation as prescribed by state law; legal personality; separation of ownership and control; freely alienable ownership interests; indefinite duration; and limited liability.

---

[1]   Adrian Cadbury, Report of the Committee on the Financial Aspects of Corporate Governance 15 (1992).

[2]   E. Norman Veasey & Christine T. Di Guglielmo, What Happened in Delaware Corporate Law and Governance from 1992–2004? A Retrospective on Some Key Developments, 153 U. Pa. L. Rev. 1399, 1411 (2005).

Lastly, it is critical to remember that corporate governance consists not only of legal rules, but also an ever-growing body of private contracts and best practice guides. Many of the rules we will study herein, for example, are embedded in stock exchange listing standards. Many more are not really rules at all, but rather recommendations and guidelines promulgated by quasi-governmental bodies and professional organizations.

A. THE MEANS AND ENDS OF CORPORATE GOVERNANCE

Two basic questions lie at the heart of corporate governance: (1) Who decides? In other words, when push comes to shove, who controls the corporation? (2) Whose interests prevail? When the ultimate decision maker is presented with a zero-sum game, in which it must prefer the interests of one constituency class over those of all others, whose interests prevail?

FOR MORE INFORMATION

HG.org offers a useful collection of internet links to materials about corporate governance at https://www.hg.org/corporate-governance-law.html

Any organization needs a governance system that facilitates efficient decision making. Although firms can choose amongst a wide array of options, most decision-making structures fall into one of two categories: "consensus" and "authority."[3] Consensus is utilized where each member of the organization has comparable information and interests. Under such conditions, assuming no serious collective action problems, decision maker preferences can be aggregated at low cost. In contrast, authority-based decision-making structures arise where team members have different interests and amounts of information. Such structures are characterized by the existence of a central agency to which all relevant information is transmitted and which is empowered to make decisions binding on the whole.

American business law allows one to choose between off-the-rack governance systems ranging from an almost purely consensus-based model to an almost purely authority-based model. At one extreme, the decision-making structure provided by partnership law is largely a consensus model. Partners, for example, have equal rights to participate in management of the firm on a one-vote per partner basis.[4] The selection of this one person-one vote standard as the default rule makes sense because all partners are also entitled to share equally in profits and losses,[5] giving them essentially identical interests (namely higher profits), and are entitled to equal access to information,[6] giving them

---

[3]   Kenneth J. Arrow, The Limits of Organization 68–70 (1974).

[4]   As with most partnership rules, the off-the-rack rule is subject to contrary agreement among the parties. UPA (1914) § 18(e).

[5]   UPA (1914) § 18(a).

[6]   UPA (1914) §§ 19 and 20.

essentially identical levels of information. In addition, the small size characteristic of most partnerships means that collective action problems generally are not serious in this setting. (Large multi-jurisdiction law firms are a prominent exception to this rule, which explains why many such firms have created corporation-like governance structures in their partnership agreement.)

At the other extreme, a publicly held corporation's decision-making structure is principally an authority-based one. As a practical matter, most public corporations are marked by a separation of ownership and control.[7] Shareholders, who are said to "own" the firm, have virtually no power to control either its day-to-day operation or its long-term policies. In contrast, the board of directors and senior management, whose equity stake often is small, effectively controls both. As a doctrinal matter, moreover, corporate law essentially carves this separation into stone. Under all corporation statutes, the board of directors is the key player in the formal decision-making structure. As the Delaware code puts it, for example, the corporation's business and affairs "shall be managed by or under the direction of a board of directors."[8]

Having said that, however, several qualifications must be introduced immediately. First, we will use "decision" as a shorthand for a process that often is much less discrete in practice. Second, operational decisions are normally delegated by the board to subordinate employees. The board, however, retains the power to hire and fire firm employees and to define the limits of their authority. Moreover, certain extraordinary acts may not be delegated, but are instead reserved for the board's exclusive determination.

In any case, the statutory separation of ownership and control means that shareholders have essentially no power to initiate corporate action and, moreover, are entitled to approve or disapprove only a very few board actions.[9] The statutory decision-making model thus is one in which the board acts and shareholders, at most, react.[10]

---

[7]   Adolf A. Berle & Gardiner C. Means, The Modern Corporation and Private Property 84–89 (1932).

[8]   DGCL § 141(a). See In re CNX Gas Corp. Shareholders Litig., 2010 WL 2705147, at *10 (Del. Ch. July 5, 2010) ("Delaware law would seem to call for a consistently board-centric approach.").

[9]   Under the Delaware code, for example, shareholder voting rights are essentially limited to the election of directors and approval of charter or bylaw amendments, mergers, sales of substantially all of the corporation's assets, and voluntary dissolution. As a formal matter, only the election of directors and amending the bylaws do not require board approval before shareholder action is possible. See DGCL §§ 109 and 211. In practice, of course, even the election of directors (absent a proxy contest) is predetermined by the existing board nominating the next year's board.

[10]   To be sure, the shareholders' right to elect the board of directors can give the former de facto control even though the statute assigns de jure control to the latter. Consequently, we can speak of a "control block," i.e., shares held by one or more shareholders whose stockownership gives them effective control. In their classic study, Berle and Means in fact found that relatively small blocks of stock could give their owners effective control of the enterprise. Berle and Means identified such firms as minority-controlled corporations. These firms exhibit a partial separation of ownership and control. The dominant shareholder controls the firm, despite

Of course, the knowledgeable student will point out that the statutory board-centric model doesn't match up to the real world. True, in practice, most corporate actions are actually taken by corporate officers and subordinate employees pursuant to delegated authority. Yet, even a board that has been thoroughly captured by senior management typically retains at least some formal functions.

Accordingly, it is possible to identify several basic roles that most boards perform most of the time. First, and foremost, the board monitors and disciplines senior management. In other words, the board acts to constrain the agency costs that result from giving management the power to run the firm on a day-by-day basis. Second, while boards almost never get involved in making day-to-day operational decision making, most boards have some managerial functions. Broad policymaking is commonly a board prerogative, for example. Even more commonly, however, individual board members provide advice and guidance to senior managers with respect to operational and/or policy decisions. Finally, the board provides access to a network of contacts useful in gathering resources and/or obtaining business.[11]

FYI

The titles of top managers tend to start with the word "Chief": Chief Executive Officer (CEO), Chief Operating Officer (COO), Chief Financial Officer (CFO), Chief Legal Officer (CLO), etc. As a result, the top management team is often referred to as the "C-suite."

Among these functions, the board's monitoring role reigns supreme. To be sure, at one time, corporation statutes affirmatively required the board to manage the corporation. Delaware's statute, for example, formerly provided: "The business and affairs of every corporation organized under this chapter shall be managed by a board of directors."[12] It was only when the legislature added the phrase "or under the direction of" that the statute expressly contemplated the delegation of managerial functions to corporate officers.

In practice, of course, the old statutory formulation did not preclude the board from delegating management responsibility. Indeed, as early as 1922, the Delaware Chancery Court held that the directors' role was

---

owning less than 50% of the outstanding voting shares, leaving the minority shareholders without significant control power. Adolf A. Berle & Gardiner C. Means, The Modern Corporation and Private Property 80–84 (1932). Majority controlled firms, in which a dominant shareholder (or group of shareholders acting together) owns more than 50% of the outstanding voting shares, likewise exhibit a partial separation of ownership and control. Id. at 70–72. Where no such control block exists, however, Berle and Means found that control passes from the firm's shareholders to its managers. Although shareholders of such firms retain the right to elect directors, management controls the election process, and thus the firm. Id. at 86–87. At the time they wrote, about half of the 200 largest U.S. corporations exhibited total separation of ownership and control. Id. at 94.

[11] Lynne L. Dallas, The Relational Board: Three Theories of Corporate Boards of Directors, 22 J. Corp. L. 1, 10–16 (1996).

[12] Delaware General Corporation Law § 141(a), quoted in Ernest L. Folk III, The Delaware General Corporation Law: A Commentary and Analysis 50 (1972).

one of supervision and control, with the detailed conduct of the business being a matter that properly could be delegated to subordinate employees.[13] The modern statutory formulation that the firm shall be "managed by or under the direction of" the board of directors simply codifies this understanding.

But towards what end should the board run the corporation? Put another way, what is the purpose of the corporation? One important school of thought contends corporations should be run so as to maximize shareholder wealth. The other major school of thought argues that directors and managers should consider the interests of all corporate stakeholders in making corporate decisions.[14] Judges and scholars in the latter camp advocate what they call "corporate social responsibility." Hence, they define the "socially responsible firm" as "one that becomes deeply involved in the solution of society's major problems."[15] In particular, they emphasize the corporation's obligation to consider the impact of its actions on nonshareholder corporate constituents, such as employees, customers, suppliers, and local communities. We consider this debate in further detail in Chapter 13.

We thus have an organization in which decisions are made by one body—the board—that is supposed to put the interests of its members to one side in pursuit of the interests of others, whether those others be shareholders or stakeholders. How can we assure that the directors use their powers responsibly? This has been the central problem of corporate governance at least since either the 1932 publication of Adolf Berle and Gardiner Means' famous book THE MODERN CORPORATION AND PRIVATE PROPERTY, which began the modern era of corporate governance scholarship.

Berle and Means demonstrated that public corporations were characterized by a separation of ownership and control—the firm's nominal owners, the shareholders, exercised virtually no control over either day-to-day operations or long-term policy. Instead, control was vested in the hands of professional managers, who typically owned only a small portion of the firm's shares. Separation of ownership and control occurred, they argued, because stock ownership was dispersed amongst many shareholders, no one of whom owned enough shares to materially affect the corporation's management.[16]

According to Berle and Means, "separation of ownership from control produces a condition where the interests of owner and of ultimate

[13]   Cahall v. Lofland, 114 A. 224, 229 (Del. Ch. 1921), aff'd, 118 A. 1 (Del. 1922).

[14]   The term "stakeholders" reportedly originated in a 1963 Stanford Research Institute memorandum as a descriptive term for "those groups without whose support the organization would cease to exist." R. Edward Freeman & David L. Reed, Stockholders and Stakeholders: A New Perspective on Corporate Governance, 25 Cal. Mgmt. Rev. 88, 89 (1983).

[15]   Robert Hay and Ed Gray, Social Responsibilities of Business Managers, in Managing Corporate Social Responsibility 8, 11 (Archie B. Carroll ed. 1977).

[16]   Adolf A. Berle & Gardiner C. Means, The Modern Corporation and Private Property 6–7 (1932).

manager may, and often do, diverge."[17] Will the board of directors use its control of the corporation to further the selfish interest of the board members rather than the best interests of the corporation's shareholders and other constituencies? To ask the question is to answer it. Given human nature, it would be surprising indeed if directors did not sometimes shirk or self-deal. Consequently, much of corporate law is best understood as a mechanism for constraining agency costs.

Organizing production within a firm creates certain costs, of which the class known as agency costs is the most important for our purposes. Agency costs are defined as the sum of the monitoring and bonding costs, plus any residual loss, incurred to prevent shirking by agents.[18] In turn, shirking is defined to include any action by a member of a production team that diverges from the interests of the team as a whole. As such, shirking includes not only culpable cheating, but also negligence, oversight, incapacity, and even honest mistakes. In other words, shirking is simply the inevitable consequence of bounded rationality and opportunism within agency relationships.[19]

A sole proprietorship with no agents will internalize all costs of shirking, because the proprietor's optimal trade-off between labor and leisure is, by definition, the same as the firm's optimal trade-off. Agents of a firm, however, will not internalize all of the costs of shirking: the principal reaps part of the value of hard work by the agent, but the agent receives all of the value of shirking. In a classic article, Professors Alchian and Demsetz offered the useful example of two workers who jointly lift heavy boxes into a truck.[20] The marginal productivity of each worker is difficult to measure and their joint output cannot be separated easily into individual components. In such situations, obtaining information about a team member's productivity and appropriately rewarding each team member are very difficult and costly. In the absence of such information, however, the disutility of labor gives each team

---

[17]   Id. at 6.

[18]   Michael C. Jensen & William H. Meckling, Theory of the Firm: Managerial Behavior, Agency Costs and Ownership Structure, 3 J. Fin. Econ. 305 (1976).

[19]   A simple example of the agency cost problem is provided by the bail upon which alleged criminals are released from jail while they await trial. The defendant promises to appear for trial. But that promise is not very credible: The defendant will be tempted to flee the country. The court could keep track of the defendant—monitor him—by keeping him in jail or perhaps by means of some electronic device permanently attached to the defendant's person. Yet, such monitoring efforts are not free—indeed, keeping someone in jail is quite expensive (food, guards, building the jail, etc.). Alternatively, the defendant could give his promise credibility by bonding it, which is exactly what bail does. The defendant puts up a sum of money that he will forfeit if he fails to appear for trial. (Notice that the common use of bail bonds and the employment of bounty hunters to track fugitives further enhances the credibility of bail as a deterrent against flight.) Of course, despite these precautions, some defendants will escape jail and/or jump bail. Hence, there will always be some residual loss in the form of defendants who escape punishment. Notice, by the way, that this example illustrates how the economic analysis can be extended beyond the traditional agency relationship.

[20]   Armen A. Alchian & Harold Demsetz, Production, Information Costs, and Economic Organization, 62 Am. Econ. Rev. 777 (1972).

member an incentive to shirk because the individual's reward is unlikely to be closely related to conscientiousness.

Although agents ex post have strong incentives to shirk, ex ante they have equally strong incentives to agree to a corporate contract containing terms designed to prevent shirking. Bounded rationality, however, precludes firms and agents from entering into the complete contract necessary to prevent shirking by the latter. Instead, there must be some system of ex post governance: some mechanism for detecting and punishing shirking. Accordingly, an essential economic function of management is monitoring the various inputs into the team effort: management meters the marginal productivity of each team member and then takes steps to reduce shirking. (No implication is intended that ex post governance structures are noncontractual.)

The process just described, of course, raises a new question: who will monitor the monitors? In any organization, one must have some ultimate monitor who has sufficient incentives to ensure firm productivity without himself having to be monitored. Otherwise, one ends up with a never-ending series of monitors monitoring lower level monitors. Alchian and Demsetz solved this dilemma by consolidating the roles of ultimate monitor and residual claimant. According to Alchian and Demsetz, if the constituent entitled to the firm's residual income is given final monitoring authority, he is encouraged to detect and punish shirking by the firm's other inputs because his reward will vary exactly with his success as a monitor.

Unfortunately, this elegant theory breaks down precisely where it would be most useful. Because of the separation of ownership and control, it simply does not describe the modern publicly held corporation. As the corporation's residual claimants, the shareholders should act as the firm's ultimate monitors. But while the law provides shareholders with some enforcement and electoral rights, these are reserved for fairly extraordinary situations. In general, shareholders of public corporation have neither the legal right, the practical ability, nor the desire to exercise the kind of control necessary for meaningful monitoring of the corporation's agents.

The apparent lack of managerial accountability inherent in the modern corporate structure has troubled legal commentators since at least Adolf Berle's time.[21] To be sure, agency costs are an important component of any viable theory of the firm. A narrow focus on agency costs, however, easily can distort one's understanding. In the first instance, corporate managers operate within a pervasive web of accountability mechanisms that substitute for monitoring by residual claimants. The capital and product markets, the internal and external

---

[21]   Adolf A. Berle, Jr. & Gardiner C. Means, The Modern Corporation and Private Property 6 (1932) ("The separation of ownership from control produces a condition where the interests of owner and of ultimate manager may, and often do, diverge, and where many of the checks which formerly operated to limit the use of power disappear.").

employment markets, and the market for corporate control all constrain shirking by firm agents.

In the second, agency costs are the inescapable result of placing ultimate decision-making authority in the hands of someone other than the residual claimant. Because we could substantially reduce agency costs by eliminating discretion, but do not do so, one infers that discretion has substantial virtues. In a complete theory of the firm, neither discretion nor accountability can be ignored, because both promote values essential to the survival of business organizations.[22] At the same time, however, the power to hold to account is ultimately the power to decide.[23] Managers cannot be made more accountable without undermining their discretionary authority. Establishing the proper mix of discretion and accountability therefore is critical.

The separation of ownership and control thus emerges as the overarching organizational principle around which this text is organized. How can we align the incentives of directors and managers with shareholders? How can we help directors do a better job of monitoring management and shareholders to do a better job of managing both directors and managers? What alternative constraints can we devise besides monitoring and bonding? These are the central corporate governance questions.

QUESTIONS

1. Cathy Capitalist recently purchased a farm in California's Central Valley. Cathy is a hedge fund manager who lives and works in another part of the state and thus is unable to run the farm herself on a day to day basis. Cathy recently met Oliver Douglas, a young, enterprising farmer in the area. Oliver has the necessary equipment and expertise to run the farm on a daily basis. Cathy is considering two options with regard to Oliver: (1) leasing the farm to him in return for a fairly sizable rent or (2) hiring Oliver as an employee to manage the farm. In the first scenario, Cathy is engaged in a market transaction; in the second, she will have formed what we can describe as firm with herself as employer and Smith as employee. Why is some economic activity conducted across markets and some within firms? What are the economic costs and benefits of each? What factors is Cathy likely to consider most important?

2. Which of the following statements is more accurate?

A. Investors are more likely to lose money because managers are incompetent and make too many mistakes.

B. Investors are more likely to lose money because managers are self-interested and put their preferences ahead of the best interests of the company.

---

[22] Michael P. Dooley, Two Models of Corporate Governance, 47 Bus. Law. 461 (1992).

[23] Kenneth J. Arrow, The Limits of Organization 78 (1974).

3.   Shareholders are the corporation's residual claimants. Whatever assets and profits are left over after all other claimants—such as creditors and employees—have been paid belong to the shareholders. It is the separation of ownership and control that causes agency costs, because shareholders have very little say over what happens to those residual assets and profits. Instead, control over them is vested in the board of directors and the top managers in the C-suite. It would seem logical to reduce agency costs by increasing shareholder control, but that has not happened. Why not?

B. THE FEDERAL ROLE IN REGULATING CORPORATE GOVERNANCE

As we have seen, corporate governance consists not just of laws and regulations but also norms and practices. Having said that, however, law obviously matters a lot. But whose law? Historically, the answer was the states. Today, the answer is much more complex.

1) THE RACE TO THE BOTTOM DEBATE

Although Congress has never seen fit to promulgate a federal law of corporations, no one seriously doubts its powers under the Commerce Clause of the Constitution to do so. Instead, Congress and the Securities and Exchange Commission (SEC) have nibbled around the edges of corporate governance, regulating various aspects of it without preempting the field. Much of this book is devoted to those regulations. We begin, however, with the fundamental question: Should Congress nationalize corporate law?

William L. Cary, Federalism and Corporate Law: Reflections Upon Delaware
83 Yale LJ 663 (1974)[24]

Delaware is both the sponsor and the victim of a system contributing to the deterioration of corporation standards. This unhappy state of affairs, stemming in great part from the movement toward the least common denominator, Delaware, seems to be developing on both the legislative and judicial fronts. In the management of corporate affairs, state statutory and case law has always been supreme, with federal intrusion limited to the field of securities regulation. Perhaps now is the time to reconsider the federal role.

I.   The History of State Corporation Laws

A.   Legislative Developments

. . .

In 1896 New Jersey adopted what is regarded as the first of the modern liberal corporation statutes. As Mr. Justice Brandeis pointed out

---

[24]   Reprinted by permission of the Yale Law Journal.

. . ., this act is commonly credited with attracting the incorporation of the New Jersey trusts, such as the old Standard Oil Company, which were not trusts at all but corporations operating as consolidated or holding companies. While corporation statutes had been restrictive, the leading industrial states began removing the limits upon both the size and powers of business units. The states, realizing that local restriction would be circumvented by foreign incorporation and eager for the revenue derived from the traffic in charters, joined in advertising their wares. In Brandeis' words, the race was not one of diligence but of laxity.

Shortly afterwards, Delaware, seeking new sources of revenue, copied very largely from the New Jersey act to establish its own statute. Then in 1913, at the insistence of Governor Woodrow Wilson, New Jersey drastically tightened its law relating to corporations and trusts with a series of provisions known as the seven sisters. Since Delaware did not amend its statute, it took the lead at that time and has never lost it . . . .

B.   The Primacy of Delaware

. . . With some justification Delaware corporate counsel take pride in their role and enjoy the fees that flow from it. The system "engenders a volume of business for the bar which tends to be regarded as a vested interest, so that any attempt to retrace steps would encounter opposition in powerful quarters."[39] Most important, the *raison d'etre* behind the whole system has been achieved—revenue for the state of Delaware.

> **FYI**
>
> Today, more than a million corporations and limited liability companies are domiciled in Delaware, including 60 percent of the Fortune 500 corporations.

Stimulating incorporation in Delaware has some of the flavor of a community chest drive. According to a state official, "The response 'has greatly exceeded our expectations.' So far this year 6,556 companies have incorporated themselves in Delaware . . . . The total may hit 9,000 by Dec. 31 . . . . The influx boosted the state's incorporation tax take by $2.9 million in fiscal 1968 . . . ."[40] In 1971 corporation franchise taxes represented $52 million out of a total of $222 million in state tax collections, approximately one-quarter of the total.[41] For revenue reasons, "creating a favorable climate" is declared to be the public policy of the state.

Some of the features of Delaware law demonstrating liberality have been recited in publications for practitioners. These include:

> greater freedom to pay dividends and make distributions; greater ease of charter amendment and less restrictions upon selling assets, mortgaging, leasing, and merging . . . freedom from mandatory cumulative voting; permission to have staggered boards of directors; lesser pre-emptive rights for

---

[39]   [E. Dodd & R. Baker, Cases and Materials on Corporations 38 n.7 (1951).]

[40]   Wall St. J., Nov. 21, 1968, at 1, col. 5.

[41]   State Tax Collections in 1972, at 16 (Dep't of Commerce, Dec. 1972).

shareholders; [and] clearer rights of indemnification for directors and officers . . . .[43]

. . .

A few illustrations of the legislative approach reveal the Delaware position. For example, shareholders meetings may now be dispensed with if a consent is signed by the number of votes necessary to take the intended action, thus offering a technique to avoid disclosure. Protection from this abuse is provided through the proxy rules under federal law but they do not apply to firms that are [registered with the SEC under the Exchange Act]. Under § 109 of the Delaware law any corporation may in its certificate of incorporation confer the power to amend or repeal by-law provisions upon the directors and thus possibly foreclose any initiative outside the management.

> **THINK ABOUT IT**
>
> Do any of these provisions seem objectionable as a matter of public policy? Do any of them seem contrary to shareholder interests?

. . .

II.   Judicial Developments

> **THINK ABOUT IT**
>
> What incentives, if any, do Delaware judges have to encourage incorporation in Delaware? Do Delaware judges have incentives to pursue some other policy? If so, what?

Judicial decisions in Delaware illustrate that the courts have undertaken to carry out the "public policy" of the state and create a "favorable climate" for management. Consciously or unconsciously, fiduciary standards and the standards of fairness generally have been relaxed. In general, the judicial decisions can best be reconciled on the basis of a desire to foster incorporation in Delaware. . . .

. . . The necessary high standards of conduct cannot be maintained by courts shackled to public policy based upon the production of revenue, pride in being "number one," and the creation of a "favorable climate" for new incorporations. The view is widely held that Delaware corporate decisions lean toward the status quo and adhere to minimal standards of director responsibility both to the corporation and its shareholders. Although these generalizations are difficult to prove absolutely, a series of cases illustrates that this reputation is based upon an accurate analysis of the courts' decisions and that Gresham's law applies. One of the striking aspects of these opinions is that among the three supreme court justices there is rarely a dissent.

[Professor Cary next reviewed seven doctrines, as to each of whom he concluded that Delaware law favored managers over shareholders. We

---

[43]   [Kaplan, Foreign Corporations and Local Corporate Policy, 21 Vand. L. Rev. 433, 436 (1968).]

will excerpt selected portions of this section of the article at appropriate places later in the text.]

III. Hypothetical Tests of Public Policy

Perhaps there is no public policy left in Delaware corporate law except the objective of raising revenue. . . .

IV. The Freedom to Litigate in Delaware— The Other Side of the Coin

In response to such criticisms of Delaware's policy approach, counsel may point to the relative ease of entry into Delaware courts for suits against corporate directors. . . .

Delaware's approach to litigation, both legislatively and judicially, appears clearly contrary to its general attitude presented in the preceding sections of this article. Although there is no legislative history to support it, the concept of a competing interest in the Delaware bar, members of which draft the statutes and constitute the court, seems to provide a reasonable explanation. To summarize in the salty words of Professor Bishop, "Delaware's general approach to stockholder litigation . . . is to make it easy to sue the executives of Delaware corporations, no matter where they reside or where the corporation does business, so long as the suit is in Delaware Courts, and conducted by Delaware counsel."[145]

. . .

VII. Up from Delaware—Federal Standards of Corporate Responsibility

A.   Underlying Premises

Even if it is assumed that the Delaware courts have contributed to shrinking the concept of fiduciary responsibility and fairness, and indeed have followed the lead of the Delaware legislature in watering down shareholders' rights, the question is whether anything should be done about it. The principle of states' rights and the idea that each state is a laboratory are strong in this country.

On the other hand, one can fairly hope that the growth of the law in a civilized society should be evolutionary. It therefore seems reasonable to suggest several principles on which we should proceed. The first is to recognize the importance of an independent and impartial judiciary. The second is to preserve public policy as a standard to be observed by the courts. The third is to emphasize the need for uniformity, so that states shall not compete with each other by lowering standards for competitive reasons or for the purpose of generating revenue. Finally, there should be as much federal concern about the management of the public issue company and about its share owners as about the investor engaged in the purchase and sale of its stock.

---

[145] [See Bishop, Sitting Ducks and Decoy Ducks: New Trends in the Indemnification of Corporate Directors and Officers, 77 YALE L.J. 1078, 1084 (1968).]

With respect to public policy, the question arises whether the policy of a single state occupying a critical position should be permitted to grant management unilateral control untrammeled by other interests. Should one state set social policy in the corporate field when a corner-stone of that policy is to stay ahead of (or behind) the rest? It is understandable that Delaware would choose not to let its premier position in American corporate law go by default, but it must also be understood that the generic reason for attaining it was revenue.

. . .

B.   The Need for Federal Standards

The discussion thus far might seem to lead to the recommendation of federal incorporation. In my opinion, however, this is politically unrealistic. It has been raised many times in Congress and in the literature but has no public appeal. American business would unanimously reject such a convenient vehicle for government control of the major industries of this country. . . .

However, in order to remedy the Delaware syndrome it does appear that federal standards of corporate responsibility are called for. This can best be achieved by prescribing minimum corporation law provisions which shall be applicable to companies doing business in interstate commerce and construed by federal judicial standards. Uniformity is of the essence. Efforts must be made to insure that provisions are not interpreted differently owing to varying state interpretations of public policy. There should also be wide-ranging service of process upon directors and officers of corporations. The participation of a government agency such as the Securities and Exchange Commission is not contemplated in this proposal.

. . .

C.   A Proposed Federal Corporate Uniformity Act

. . . I propose a Federal Corporate Uniformity Act applying to all corporations having more than $1 million of assets and 500 shareholders. . . . To prevent disparity in the law, however, it might be preferable to make such an act apply to all public companies engaged in or affecting interstate commerce. . . .

The proposal is to continue allowing companies to incorporate in the jurisdiction of their choosing but to remove much of the incentive to organize in Delaware or its rival states. Such companies, nevertheless, must be subject to the jurisdiction of the federal courts under certain general standards. To illustrate, some of the major provisions of such a federal statute might include (1) federal fiduciary standards with respect to directors and officers and controlling shareholders; (2) an "interested directors" provision prescribing fairness as a prerequisite to any transaction; (3) a requirement of certain uniform provisions to be incorporated in the certificate of incorporation: for example, authority to amend by-laws, initiate corporate action, or draw up the agenda of shareholders' meetings shall not be vested exclusively in management; (4) a more frequent requirement of shareholder approval of corporate transactions, with limits placed upon the number of shares authorized at any one time; (5) abolition of nonvoting shares; (6) the scope of indemnification of directors specifically prescribed and made exclusive; (7) adoption of a long-arm provision comparable to § 27 of the Securities Exchange Act to apply to all transactions within the corporate structure involving shareholders, directors, and officers.

The foregoing suggestions do not pretend to offer a complete model for a minimum standards act. . . .

Conclusion

THINK ABOUT IT

What other provisions would be necessary or appropriate to create a complete minimum standards act under today's conditions?

In summary, as long as we operate within a capitalist society and as long as confidence in management is prerequisite to its continuance, there should be a federal interest in the proper conduct of the corporation itself as much as in the market for its securities. A civilizing jurisprudence should import lifting standards; certainly there is no justification for permitting them to deteriorate. The absurdity of this race for the bottom, with Delaware in the lead— tolerated and indeed fostered by corporate counsel—should arrest the conscience of the American bar when its current reputation is in low estate.

NOTES AND QUESTIONS

1.   Cary's article is the classic articulation of the so-called "race to the bottom" hypothesis, which contends that managers rather than shareholders choose the state of incorporation and to attract incorporations states will therefore cater to the interests of managers in making corporate law. In response to Cary, Yale corporate law professor and later U.S. Circuit Court of Appeals Judge Ralph Winter argued that state competition for corporate charters produced a race to the top:

> Owners of firms going public will want to maximize revenues from initial public offerings, and managers will be constrained by their need to ensure that the company performs successfully in the marketplace. Thus, they will choose the state that is likely to produce the greatest profit for the firm over time. States will recognize that to attract firms, they must worry not about attracting managers but about attracting the owners of firms undergoing initial public offerings. Thus, the states will adopt corporate law structures that maximize shareholder wealth. These structures will also maximize the returns from initial public offerings, because bidders will be willing to pay more for shares in companies with shareholder-maximizing corporate law than for

shares in companies that allow managers to expropriate superoptimal private benefits.[25]

Which version strikes you as more plausible?

2.   Both Cary's and Winter's argument depends on an assumption that states compete to attract incorporations. When a firm incorporates in a state it pays, among other things, annual franchise taxes to that state for the privilege of being incorporated in it. In Delaware's admittedly extreme case, those franchise taxes typically amount to around one-fifth of the state's annual revenues. Accordingly, or so the argument goes, because states can raise substantial revenues for providing a service—i.e., incorporation—that costs the state almost nothing, the states have strong incentives to attract as many incorporations as possible. Race to the bottom proponents think this leads states to favor management over investors, while race to the top believe the opposite.

But do states really compete? Scholars have run various empirical analyses of the problem, which have failed to put the issue to rest. Nevertheless, there does seem to be an emerging consensus that while states do compete, that competition is more of a brisk walk than a 100-yard dash. As Judge Winter explained in a subsequent article:

First, . . . state legislatures are political bodies and may be governed by a variety of motives. A race to the top argument applies only when a state legislature is guided solely by a desire to maximize franchise taxes. Other motives may well prevail, however.

Second, . . . there are cases in which management may seek legal rules allowing side payments where those payments outweigh the negative effects of the capital market. These cases seem limited to changes in legal rules, including charter amendments or reincorporation in a new state, that occur after investors have become locked in and that involve, or are accompanied by, measures that impede takeovers. States that offer such impediments to takeovers may thus attract some chartering business. Of course, . . . the purpose of impediments to takeovers is precisely to reduce the discipline of the capital market and that may well seem attractive to inefficient managers.

Third, the race to the top may be slow because Delaware is the only state devoted exclusively to maximizing franchise taxes and may need only to offer a code marginally more efficient than other states which may be influenced by law professors, the American Law Institute or management. It thus may not be difficult for Delaware to compete with such states for franchise taxes. In fact, the history of state antitakeover statutes may support the view that the race to the top is a leisurely walk. In both the first and second generation of takeover statutes, Delaware waited until its principal competitors had passed such legislation and then enacted a

---

[25]   Michael Abramowicz, Speeding Up the Crawl to the Top, 20 Yale J. on Reg. 139, 161–62 (2003).

relatively mild statute. It may thus be that what we need is not a federal chartering statute but rather a second Delaware that pursues franchise taxes and nothing else.[26]

Could a leisurely walk still result in corporate law rules that systematically trend either towards the bottom or the top?

3.   Setting aside the question of how fast Delaware is racing and the direction of that race, there are numerous other reasons Delaware dominates the market for incorporations:

> [P]ublicly traded companies incorporate in Delaware (and pay its high franchise taxes) at least in part because of its high-quality and specialized courts and, as a general matter, want important and high-profile cases to be decided by Delaware judges. The Delaware court system rests on a highly respected Chancery Court that decides cases without juries and specializes in corporate law adjudication, combined with a Supreme Court that offers quick review and brings its own considerable expertise—three of the five current Delaware Supreme Court justices are former members of the Chancery Court, and all regularly hear appeals from the Chancery Court on corporate law issues. The Delaware Supreme Court and Chancery Court judges are not only experts, but are few in number and communicate regularly with each other and members of the corporate bar. In such a system, much of the shared understanding of Delaware doctrine resides between the lines of the judicial opinions.[27]

4.   Some products become more valuable as the number of persons using them increases. Each person who adopts the product thus confers positive externalities on other users. Personal computers (PCs) are a commonly cited example of this phenomenon. The value of Microsoft's Windows operating system, for example, depends in part on how many people use it and thus create markets for compatible hardware and software. The more people who use Windows, the larger the market for ancillary products becomes, thus encouraging the development of more ancillary products of higher quality and lower price. This phenomenon is known as a "network effect" or "network benefit." How might network effects help explain Delaware's dominance of the market for charters?

5.   What is the purpose of laws regulating corporate governance? To benefit society? To benefit shareholders? Or something else?

---

[26]   Ralph K. Winter, The "Race for the Top" Revisited: A Comment on Eisenberg, 89 Colum. L. Rev. 1526, 1528–29 (1989).

[27]   Marcel Kahan & Edward Rock, How to Prevent Hard Cases from Making Bad Law: Bear Stearns, Delaware, and the Strategic Use of Comity, 58 Emory L.J. 713, 748–49 (2009).

2) A BRIEF HISTORY OF FEDERAL CORPORATE GOVERNANCE REGULATION

Until the 1930s, corporate law and governance were exclusively the province of state law. In the wake of the stock market crash of 1929 and the Great Depression that followed, however, President Franklin Delano Roosevelt's New Deal program included a series of laws designed to regulate the stock markets and securities transactions. The second of those statutes—the Securities Exchange Act of 1934—contained a number of provisions that, for the first time, involved the federal government in corporate governance.

On its face, of course, the Exchange Act said nothing about regulation of corporate governance. Instead, the Act's basic focus was trading of securities on the secondary market and securities pricing. Virtually all of its provisions are addressed to such matters as the production and distribution of information about issuers and their securities, the flow of funds in the market, and the basic structure of the market.

> **FYI**
>
> The New Deal was not the first time a federal law of corporations was considered. James Madison, for example, proposed that the Constitution give the federal government power to grant charters of incorporation, which presumably would have led to the development of a detailed body of federal statutory and common law. More recently, just 20 years prior to the adoption of the Exchange Act, the Pujo Committee suggested that "much-needed reforms in the organization and methods of our corporations" could be affected through stock exchange listing standards. H.R. Rep. NO. 1593, 62d Cong., 3d Sess. 114–15 (1913).

When the bill that became the Exchange Act was pending before Congress, moreover, the bill's supporters strenuously denied that they intended to regulate corporate management. The Senate Banking and Currency Committee went to the length of adding a proposed section 13(d) to the bill, which would have provided: "Nothing in this Act shall be construed as authorizing the Commission to interfere with the management of the affairs of an issuer."[28] The conference committee deleted the provision because it was seen "as unnecessary, since it is not believed that the bill is open to misconstruction in this respect."[29]

Subsequently, however, there were a number of direct efforts to create a federal corporate law. While the Exchange Act was being drafted, the Roosevelt administration considered developing a comprehensive federal corporation law. The Senate Banking and Currency Committee's report on stock exchange practices also suggested that the cure for the nation's "corporate ailments . . . may lie in a national

---

[28] S. 3420, 73d Cong., 2d Sess. § 13(d) (1934).

[29] H.R. Conf. Rep. No. 1838, 73d Cong., 2d Sess. 35 (1934).

incorporation act."[30] In the late 1930s, then SEC Chairman William O. Douglas orchestrated yet another effort to replace state corporate law with a set of federal rules administered by the SEC.[31]

Although none of these efforts came to fruition, judicial and regulatory interpretations of the Exchange Act gradually expanded the SEC's role in corporate governance. The proxy rules play a dominant role in shareholder voting. A federal prohibition of insider trading created by judicial interpretations of Rule 10b–5 essentially displaced state fiduciary duty law governing such trading. We will see numerous other examples throughout this text.

Congress and the SEC have created a dual system in which federal and state law uneasily coexist. The recurring question we will address throughout this text thus is where to draw the line.

NOTE ON CORPORATE FEDERALISM IN THE SUPREME COURT

As the D.C. Circuit observed in *Business Roundtable v. SEC*, validating rule 19c–4 would "overturn or at least impinge severely on the tradition of state regulation of corporate law."[32] In a series of cases, the Supreme Court has made clear that this is not a step to be taken lightly.

In the early 1970s, courts gave SEC Rule 10b–5, designed originally as a catch-all anti-fraud provision, an increasingly expansive reading that in time might have led to a federal common law of corporations. The Supreme Court applied the brakes in a series of cases, most notably *Santa Fe Industries v. Green*.[33] Santa Fe attempted to freeze out minority shareholders of one of its subsidiaries by means of a statutory short-form merger. The plaintiffs had state law appraisal rights available, but chose to seek redress under Rule 10b–5. Plaintiffs claimed a Rule 10b–5 violation arose because the minority shareholders did not receive prior notice and the merger lacked any legitimate business purpose. They also claimed that their shares had been fraudulently undervalued.

The Supreme Court held that plaintiffs had not stated a cause of action under rule 10b–5.[34] For present purposes, however, *Santa Fe*'s significance

---

[30]   S. Rep. No. 1455, 73d Cong., 2d Sess. 391 (1934).

[31]   Joseph C. O'Mahoney, Federal Charters to Save Free Enterprise, 1949 Wis. L. Rev. 407. Proposals for a federal corporation statute did not stop when the New Deal ended. E.g., Protection of Shareholders' Rights Act of 1980: Hearing Before the Subcomm. on Securities of the Sen. Comm. on Banking, Housing, and Urban Affairs, 96th Cong., 2d Sess. (1980); The Role of the Shareholder in the Corporate World: Hearings Before the Subcomm. on Citizens and Shareholders Rights and Remedies of the Sen. Comm. on the Judiciary, 95th Cong., 1st Sess. (1977). In the 1970s, the Commission considered imposing a variety of corporate governance reforms, including various proposed new proxy rules. Exchange Act Release No. 14970 (July 18, 1978). After vigorous objections that the Commission had exceeded its statutory authority, the rules were substantially modified before adoption. Exchange Act Release No. 15384 (Dec. 6, 1978). See generally Homer Kripke, The SEC, Corporate Governance, and the Real Issues, 36 Bus. Law. 173 (1981).

[32]   Bus. Roundtable v. SEC, 905 F.2d 406, 412 (D.C. Cir. 1990).

[33]   430 U.S. 462 (1977).

[34]   Id. at 470–71. The Court rested its holding on several bases. First, section 10(b) and rule 10b–5 were only intended to reach deception and manipulation. Neither was present on

derives from its recognition that the fundamental purpose of the Exchange Act is to assure full disclosure. Once complete disclosure is made, the transaction's fairness and terms do not become issues under federal law, instead they are a matter for state corporate law. The Court was seemingly concerned that a decision in favor of plaintiffs would result in federalizing much of state corporate law; in many cases, overriding well-established state policies of corporate regulation. This concern was well-founded, for if the Court gave these plaintiffs a federal cause of action, it could not meaningfully justify denying a federal claim in any breach of fiduciary duty case. The Court simply refused to give rule 10b–5 such an expansive reach.[35]

In the 1980s, the Court once again faced the need to draw lines between the state and federal roles in regulating public corporations. At about the same time as Congress adopted the Williams Act to regulate cash tender offers, the states also began adopting tender offer statutes. This first generation of state takeover laws placed significant obstacles in the bidder's path. The Supreme Court's decision in *Edgar v. MITE Corp.,* 457 U.S. 624 (1982), however, rendered these laws invalid. The *MITE* decision, nevertheless, suggested one loophole through which state

> **WHAT'S THAT?**
>
> TENDER OFFER, Black's Law Dictionary (10th ed. 2014): A public offer to buy a minimum number of shares directly from a corporation's shareholders at a fixed price, usually at a substantial premium over the market price, in an effort to take control of the corporation. — Also termed takeover offer; takeover bid."

regulation might pass constitutional muster: the internal affairs doctrine. The states picked up on this hint and quickly began adopting a second generation of takeover laws, this time focusing on matters traditionally viewed as falling within the sphere of state corporate governance regulation: shareholder voting rights, shareholder approval of changes in corporate control, the fairness of post-tender offer mergers, and the like.

In *CTS Corp. v. Dynamics Corp.,*[36] the Supreme Court upheld one of these statutes as valid. When Dynamics made a tender offer for CTS, it challenged the Indiana control share acquisition statute on both preemption and commerce clause grounds. The Seventh Circuit struck down the Indiana Act on both grounds, but a majority of the Supreme Court reversed. In doing so, the Court made a number of observations directly relevant to the later Rule 19c–4 controversy. The Court recognized that states have a legitimate interest in defining the attributes of their corporations and protecting shareholders of their corporations. It also strongly indicated that the substance of corporate voting rights is solely a matter of state concern: "No principle of corporation law and practice is more firmly established than a

---

these facts. Id. at 471–77. Second, the implied private right of action under rule 10b–5 should not be extended to cases that do not involve deception or manipulation. Id. at 477–80.

[35]   It is, of course, still possible to state a federal claim in some breach of duty cases. However, the correct allegation in such cases derives not from the breach itself, but rather from the failure to disclose the breach. E.g., Goldberg v. Meridor, 567 F.2d 209 (2d Cir. 1977), cert. denied, 434 U.S. 1069 (1978).

[36]   481 U.S. 69 (1987).

State's authority to regulate domestic corporations, including the authority to define the voting rights of shareholders."[37]

These two lines of cases suggest that the Supreme Court views the states as the principal regulators of corporate governance. Federal law is seen as placing a gloss on the underlying background of state corporate law, but not as replacing it. Absent a clear expression of congressional intent, the Court has been reluctant to federalize questions traditionally within the state sphere.

3) SOX

As we have seen, although it has never opted to preempt the field of corporate governance, Congress long has been in the business of piecemeal federalization of corporate governance.

> Washington makes corporate law. From 1933 to 2002, that is, from the passage of the securities laws to the passage of Sarbanes-Oxley, Washington has made rules governing the voting of stock and the solicitation of proxies to elect directors. It has made the main rules governing insider trading, stock buybacks, how institutional investors can interact in corporate governance, the structure of key board committees, board composition (how independent some board members must be), how far states could go in making merger law, how attentive institutional investors must be in voting their proxies, what business issues and transactional information public firms must disclose (which often affect the structure and duties of insiders and managers to shareholders in a myriad of transactions), the rules on dual class common stock recapitalizations, the duties and liabilities of gatekeepers like accountants and lawyers, and more.[38]

In this sense, both the Sarbanes-Oxley Act of 2002 and the Dodd-Frank Act of 2010 simply represent additional milestones in a process of gradual federalization. In another sense, however, they represent a significant departure. Unlike past federal corporate governance regulations, many of those in the two post-crisis laws cross the traditional boundary between state and federal law to directly regulate substantive aspects of corporate governance.

---

[37] *CTS,* 481 U.S. at 89. The Supreme Court also has consistently recognized that state law governs the rights and duties of corporate directors. See, e.g., Burks v. Lasker, 441 U.S. 471, 478 (1979) ("As we have said in the past, the first place one must look to determine the powers of corporate directors is in the relevant State's corporation law. 'Corporations are creatures of state law' and it is state law which is the font of corporate directors' powers.").

[38] Mark J. Roe, Washington and Delaware as Corporate Lawmakers, 34 Del. J. Corp. L. 1, 10 (2009).

In response to the scandals that followed in the wake of the dotcom bubble, Congress passed the Public Company Accounting Reform and Investor Protection Act of 2002 ("Sarbanes-Oxley" or SOX), which President Bush praised at its signing for having made "the most far-reaching reforms of American business practices since the time of Franklin Delano Roosevelt."[39]

Those reforms included:

- The creation of the Public Company Accounting Oversight Board to oversee the accounting profession.

- A number of mandates requiring companies to adopt more effective internal controls—i.e., the processes the company uses to ensure the reliability of its public financial disclosures and to make sure that it complies with applicable laws and regulations.

- A requirement that the chief executive officer and chief financial officer of a company must certify its financial statements and disclosure reports.

- A number of rules designed to ensure that a company's auditor is truly independent of company management.

- A related requirement that companies have an audit committee consisting of independent directors to deal with the auditor and oversee the company's financial processes.

- New restrictions on loans to insiders and stock trading by insiders.

- Changes in rules governing how corporations disclose information to the public, so as to increase the speed and transparency of such disclosures.

- Protections for whistle blowers and restrictions on document destruction, designed to prevent the sort of obstruction of justice witnessed at Enron.

FYI

"U.S. institutional investors are not a homogenous or monolithic group. In addition to pension funds, which themselves are divided into public, union, and private funds, institutional investors include mutual funds, private investment funds (including hedge funds), insurance companies, banks, endowments, sovereign wealth funds, and other types of institutions, subject to regulation in varying degrees. Institutional investors are usually intermediaries who hold shares for the benefit of someone else." Report of the Task Force of the ABA Section of Business Law Corporate Governance Committee on Delineation of Governance Roles and Responsibilities, 65 Bus. Law. 107, 140 (2009).

---

[39] The Public Company Accounting Reform and Investor Protection Act, Pub. L. No. 107–204, 2002 U.S.C.C.A.N. (116 Stat.) 745 (codified in scattered sections of 15 and 18 U.S.C.) [hereinafter cited as SOX].

- New and severe criminal and civil penalties for corporate misconduct.

WHAT'S THAT?

CHIEF EXECUTIVE OFFICER, Black's Law Dictionary (10th ed. 2014): A corporation's highest-ranking administrator or manager, who reports to the board of directors. — Abbr. CEO.

CHIEF FINANCIAL OFFICER, Black's Law Dictionary (10th ed. 2014): The executive in charge of making a company's accounting and fiscal decisions. — Abbr. CFO.

We will look at most of these provisions in the chapters that follow.

4)   DODD-FRANK

After the financial crisis of 2007–08, when the economy suffered through one of the worst downturns in U.S. history following the bursting of the housing bubble and the subprime mortgage crisis, populist outrage motivated Congress to pass The Wall Street Reform and Consumer Protection Act of 2010 ("Dodd-Frank").[40] Although Dodd-Frank's 2319 pages dwarfed SOX in both size and scope, most of Dodd-Frank deals with issues other the corporate governance. We will focus on 6 key provisions in the chapters that follow:

1. Section 951's "say on pay" mandate, requiring periodic shareholder advisory votes on executive compensation.

2. Section 952's mandate that the compensation committees of reporting companies must be fully independent and that those committees be given certain specified oversight responsibilities.

3. Section 953's direction that the SEC require companies to provide additional disclosures with respect to executive compensation.

4. Section 954's expansion of SOX's rules regarding clawbacks of executive compensation.

5. Section 971's affirmation that the SEC has authority to promulgate a so-called "shareholder access" rule pursuant to which shareholders would be allowed to use the company's proxy statement to nominate candidates to the board of directors.

6. Section 972's requirement that companies disclose whether the same person holds both the CEO and Chairman of the Board positions and why they either do or do not do so.

---

[40]   The Wall Street Reform and Consumer Protection Act of 2010, Pub. L. No. 111–203, 124 Stat. 1376 (2010) (hereinafter cited as "The Dodd-Frank Act").

NOTE ON SEC PERIODIC REPORTING REQUIREMENTS

If a corporation is required to register under the Securities Exchange Act,[41] it becomes subject to the Act's periodic disclosure rules. In addition, the corporation also becomes subject to the proxy rules under § 14, the tender offer rules under §§ 13 and 14, and certain of the Act's anti-fraud provisions. Finally, the company becomes subject to the extensive rules under the Sarbanes-Oxley Act of 2002 and the Dodd-Frank Act of 2010.

There are three basic categories of companies subject to the Securities Exchange Act's requirements. The first two are identified by §§ 12 and 13(a) of the Act. Section 13(a) requires periodic reports from any company registered with the SEC under Section 12 of the Act. In turn, § 12(a) requires that any class of securities listed and traded on a national securities exchange (such as the New York or American Stock Exchanges) must be registered under the Securities Exchange Act. In addition, as amended by the Jumpstart Our Business Startups Act (the "JOBS Act"), § 12(g) and the rules thereunder require all other companies with assets exceeding $10 million and a class of equity securities held of record by either (1) 2,000 or more persons or (2) 500 or more persons who are not accredited investors to register that class of equity securities with the SEC. The third and final group of companies subject to the Securities Exchange Act is identified by § 15(d), which picks up any issuer that made a public offering of securities under the Securities Act. Issuers with less than 1,200 record shareholders, however, are not subject to this requirement except during the fiscal year in which they made the offering.

> **WHAT'S THAT?**
>
> STOCKHOLDER OF RECORD, Black's Law Dictionary (11th ed. 2019): The person who is listed in the issuer's books as the owner of stock on the record date.
>
> RECORD DATE, Black's Law Dictionary (11th ed. 2019): The date on which a stockholder must own shares to be entitled to vote or receive a dividend.

The periodic reports required by the Securities Exchange Act include: (1) Form 10, the initial Securities Exchange Act registration statement. It is only filed once with respect to a particular class of securities. It closely resembles a Securities Act registration statement. (2) Form 10-K, an annual report containing full audited financial statements and management's report of the previous year's activities. It usually incorporates the annual report sent to shareholders. (3) Form 10-Q, filed for each of first three quarters of the year. The issuer does not file a Form 10-Q for the last quarter of the year, which is covered by the Form 10-K. Form 10-Q contains unaudited financial statements and management's report of material recent developments. (4) Form 8-K, which must be filed within 4 business days after certain important

---

[41]   It is sometimes said that the Securities Exchange Act registers companies, while the Securities Act registers securities. In fact, the former registers classes of securities, but the point is otherwise well-taken. A corporation that has registered a class of securities under the Securities Exchange Act must nevertheless register a particular offering of securities of that class under the Securities Act.

events affecting the corporation's operations or financial condition, such as bankruptcy, sales of significant assets, or a change in control of the company.

To assess your understanding of the material in this chapter, click here to take a quiz.

PART II

THE BOARD OF DIRECTORS

CHAPTER 2

THE ROLES AND DUTIES OF THE BOARD OF DIRECTORS

A. WHY A BOARD?

As noted above, the formal statutory model contemplates a corporation run by its board of directors: "All corporate powers shall be exercised by or under the authority of, and the business and affairs of the corporation managed by or under the direction of, its board of directors . . . ."[1] At the apex of the corporate hierarchy thus stands not a single individual but a collective—the board of directors. The legal rules governing the board of directors, moreover, put considerable emphasis on the need for collective rather than individual action.[2] As the Restatement (Second) of Agency puts it, for example, a director "has no power of his own to act on the corporation's behalf, but only as one of a body of directors acting as a board."[3] Why this emphasis on collective action? Put another way, why not vest the ultimate power of fiat in an individual autocrat rather than a collegial group?

Although these may seem like esoteric questions more appropriate for philosophers or economists, the answers will help us understand both the legal rules governing boards and the real-world functions of boards.

The commentary to the MBCA's provisions on board meetings provides one answer to the question of why a board:

> A well-established principle of corporate common law accepted by implication in the Model Act is that directors may act only at a meeting unless otherwise expressly authorized by statute. The underlying theory is that the consultation and exchange of views is an integral part of the functioning of the board.[4]

The drafters' argument runs afoul of the old joke that a camel is a horse designed by a committee, yet their "underlying theory" is pervasively reflected in the statutory rules governing corporate boards. The implicit preference for group decision making also finds support in two basic economic principles: bounded rationality and agency costs.

Vesting decision-making authority in a group rather than a single individual is a high value-added adaptive response to the problem of

---

[1] MBCA § 8.01(b).

[2] At one time, many states in fact required that the board have at least three members, although most have eliminated that requirement. MBCA § 8.03(a) cmt.

[3] Restatement (Second) of the Law of Agency § 14C cmt.

[4] MBCA § 8.20 cmt.

bounded rationality. Decision making requires the use of scarce resources for four purposes: (1) observation, or the gathering of information; (2) memory, or the storage of information; (3) computation, or the manipulation of information; and (4) communication, or the transmission of information.[5] How do groups minimize these transaction costs vis-à-vis individual decision makers? Multiple sources of information may make it less costly to gather information, but it seems unlikely that directors qua directors do much to facilitate the observation process. Any such savings, moreover, likely are off-set by increased communication costs. By decentralizing both access to information and decision-making power, group decision making requires additional resources and imposes additional delays on the decision-making process.

CASE IN POINT

"Vice Chancellor Hartnett's common sense intuition that two heads are better than one in the context of special board committees has since been bolstered, in some sense, by economic and empirical research. See, e.g., Stephen M. Bainbridge, Why a Board? Group Decisionmaking in Corporate Governance, 55 Vand. L.Rev. 1, 12 (2002) ("In sum, groups appear to outperform their average member consistently, even at relatively complex tasks requiring exercise of evaluative judgment. . . . Corporate law's strong emphasis on collective decisionmaking by the board thus seems to have a compelling efficiency rationale.")." *Gesoff v. IIC Indus., Inc.*, 902 A.2d 1130, 1146 (Del. Ch. 2006).

The relevant advantages of group decision making therefore likely arise with respect to either memory and/or computation. As to the former, groups develop a sort of collective memory that consists not only of the sum of individual memories, but also an awareness of who knows what. Consequently, institutional memory is superior when the organization is structured as a set of teams rather than as a mere aggregate of individuals. There is some laboratory evidence, moreover, that the collective memory of groups leads to higher quality output.[6] Group members, for example, seem to specialize in memorizing specific aspects of complex repetitive tasks.

As to the relationship between group decision making and computation-based costs, an actor can economize limited cognitive resources in two ways. First, by adopting institutional governance structures designed to promote more efficient decision making. Second, by invoking shortcuts; i.e., heuristic problem-solving decision-making processes. Here we focus on the former approach, positing that group decision making provides a mechanism for aggregating the inputs of multiple individuals with differing knowledge, interests, and skills. Numerous studies suggest that groups benefit from both by pooling of

---

[5]   Roy Radner, Bounded Rationality, Indeterminacy, and the Theory of the Firm, 106 Econ. J. 1360, 1363 (1996).

[6]   Susan G. Cohen & Diane E. Bailey, What Makes Teams Work: Group Effectiveness Research from the Shop Floor to the Executive Suite, 23 J. Mgmt. 239, 259 (1997).

information and from providing opportunities for one member to correct another's errors.[7] In the corporate context, the board of directors thus may have emerged as an institutional governance mechanism to constrain the deleterious effect of bounded rationality on the organizational decision-making process.

The validity of this theoretical work is confirmed by empirical evidence generated by experimental psychologists, who have found that group decision making, under certain circumstances, can be superior to decision making by individuals. Where evaluation of complex problems requiring the exercise of critical judgment is concerned, the evidence is clear that the performance of a group will be superior to that of the group's average member. This result has been confirmed by experiments requiring performance of a wide variety of tasks.[8]

The board of directors, however, also plays an important role in constraining agency costs. Individuals are subject to the temptations to shirk or self-deal. The internal dynamics of group governance, however, constrain self-dealing and shirking by individual team members. In this regard, group decision making has a bi-directional structure. In the vertical dimension, a group may be superior to an individual autocrat as a monitor of subordinates in the corporate hierarchy. In the horizontal dimension, intra-group governance structures help constrain shirking and self-dealing at the apex of the hierarchy.

Recall that agency cost theory tells us that because all members of the corporate hierarchy have incentives to shirk, a mechanism to monitor

---

[7]   See Gayle W. Hill, Group Versus Individual Performance: Are N + 1 Heads Better than One?, 91 Psych. Bull. 517, 533 (1982).

[8]   See, e.g., Larry K. Michaelsen et al., A Realistic Test of Individual Versus Group Consensus Decision Making, 74 J. App. Psych. 834 (1989) (test taking in team learning settings); Marjorie E. Shaw, A Comparison of Individuals and Small Groups in the Rational Solution of Complex Problems, 44 Am. J. Psych. 491 (1932) (puzzle solving); see generally Gayle W. Hill, Group Versus Individual Performance: Are N + 1 Heads Better than One?, 91 Psych. Bull. 517 (1982).

There may also be a behavioral explanation for the board. Research in behavioral economics has identified a number of pervasive cognitive errors that bias decision making. Several of the identified decision-making biases seem especially pertinent to managerial decision making, especially the so-called overconfidence bias. Research on brainstorming as a decision-making process, for example, confirms that individuals working alone generate a greater number of ideas than do groups, especially when the assigned task is "fanciful" rather than "realistic." Gayle W. Hill, Group Versus Individual Performance: Are N + 1 Heads Better than One?, 91 Psych. Bull. 517, 527 (1982). Individuals often become wedded to their ideas, however, and fail to recognize flaws that others might identify. Peter M. Blau & W. Richard Scott, Formal Organizations 116–21 (1962). In contrast, there is a widely-shared view that groups are superior at evaluative tasks. Group decision making presumably checks individual overconfidence by providing critical assessment and alternative viewpoints, which is consistent with the standard account of the board's function. Recall that our taxonomy identified three basic board roles: monitoring, service, and resource gathering. At the core of the board's service role is providing advice and counsel to the senior management team, especially the CEO. At the intersection of the board's service and monitoring roles is the provision of alternative points of view. Put another way, most of what boards do requires the exercise of critical evaluative judgment but not creativity. Even the board's policymaking role entails judgment more than creativity, as the board is usually selecting between a range of options presented by subordinates. The board serves to constrain subordinates who have become wedded to their plans and ideas, rather than developing such plans in the first instance.

their productivity and reduce their incentive to shirk must be created or one ends up with a never-ending series of monitors monitoring lower level monitors. As noted above, Armen Alchian and Harold Demsetz solved this dilemma by requiring that the monitor be given the residual income left after all other workers have been paid.[9] This arrangement encourages the monitor to promote the most efficient use of the other inputs and to reduce shirking because his reward will depend upon the efficacy of his monitoring efforts. Unfortunately, their otherwise quite useful model has limited relevance to the public corporation. Although common stockholders are the corporation's residual claimants, they also are the corporate constituency perhaps least able to meaningfully monitor management behavior.

Consequently, corporate law and governance must provide alternatives to monitoring by the residual claimants. A hierarchy of individuals whose governance structures contemplate only vertical monitoring, such as that hypothesized above, cannot resolve the problem of who watches the watchers. By adding the dimension of horizontal monitoring, however, placing a group at the apex of the hierarchy provides a solution to that problem. Where an individual autocrat would have substantial freedom to shirk or self-deal, the internal dynamics of group governance constrain self-dealing and shirking by individual team members and, perhaps, even by the group as a whole. Within a production team, for example, mutual monitoring and peer pressure provide a coercive backstop for a set of interpersonal relationships founded on trust and other noncontractual social norms. Of particular relevance here are effort and cooperation norms.[10]

While the old adage opines "familiarity breeds contempt," personal proximity to others in fact deeply affects behavior. As people become closer, their behavior tends to improve: "something in us makes it all but impossible to justify our acts as mere self-interest whenever those acts are seen by others as violating a moral principle"; rather, "[w]e want our actions to be seen by others—and by ourselves—as arising out of appropriate motives."[11] Small groups strengthen this instinct in several ways. First, they provide a network of reputational and other social sanctions that shape incentives. Because membership in close knit groups satisfies the human need for belongingness, the threat of expulsion gives the group a strong sanction by which to enforce compliance with group norms. Because close knit groups involve a continuing relationship, the threat of punishment in future interactions

---

[9]   Armen A. Alchian & Harold Demsetz, Production, Information Costs, and Economic Organization, 62 Am. Econ. Rev. 777 (1972).

[10]   Social norms are relevant to other aspects of decision making besides agency costs. Group norms of reciprocity, for example, facilitate the process of achieving consensus within groups.

[11]   James Q. Wilson, What is Moral and How do we Know It?, Commentary, June 1993, at 37, 39. See also Kenneth L. Bettenhausen, Five Years of Groups Research: What have we Learned and What Needs to be Addressed?, 17 J. Mgmt. 345, 348 (1991).

deters the sort of cheating possible in one-time transactions.[12] Second, because people care about how they are perceived by those close to them, communal life provides a cloud of witnesses whose good opinion we value. We hesitate to disappoint those people and thus strive to comport ourselves in accordance with communal norms. Effort norms will thus tend to discourage board members from simply going through the motions, but instead to devote greater cognitive effort to their tasks. Finally, there is a transaction costs economics explanation for the importance of closeness in trust relationships. Close knit groups know a lot about one another, which reduces monitoring costs and thus further encourages compliance with group norms. Members of close-knit groups therefore tend to internalize group norms.

Taken together, these factors suggest that group decision making is a potentially powerful constraint on agency costs. It creates a set of high-powered incentives to comply with both effort and cooperation norms. This analysis thus goes a long way towards explaining the formalistic rules of state corporate law governing board decision making.[13]

QUESTIONS

1.   What is/are the role(s) of the board of directors of public corporations? Put another way, what services does the board provide public corporations?

---

[12]   See generally Oliver E. Williamson, The Economic Institutions of Capitalism 48 (1985) ("Informal peer group pressures can be mobilized to check malingering. . . . The most casual involves cajoling or ribbing. If this fails, rational appeals to persuade the deviant to conform are employed. The group then resorts to penalties by withdrawing the social benefits that affiliation affords. Finally, overt coercion and ostracism are resorted to.")

[13]   The case should not be overstated. Cohesive groups are subject to inherent cognitive biases that limit their effectiveness. A widely-cited example is the so-called risky shift phenomenon. There seems to be a polarizing effect in group decisionmaking, so that post-discussion consensus is more extreme than the individual pre-test results. See Norbert L. Kerr, Group Decision Making at a Multialternative Task: Extremity, Interfaction Distance, Pluralities, and Issue Importance, 52 Org. Behav. and Human Decision Processes 64 (1992). The most significant group bias for our purposes, however, is the "group think" phenomenon. Highly cohesive groups with strong civility and cooperation norms value consensus more greatly than they do a realistic appraisal of alternatives. Irving Janis, Victims of Groupthink (1972). In such groups, groupthink is an adaptive response to the stresses generated by challenges to group solidarity. To avoid those stresses, groups may strive for unanimity even at the expense of quality decision making. To the extent groupthink promotes the development of social norms, it facilitates the board's monitoring function (see the next section). It may also be relevant to other board functions, such as resource acquisition, to the extent that it promotes a sort of esprit de corps. Yet, the downside is an erosion in the quality of decision making. The desire to maintain group cohesion trumps the exercise of critical judgment. Adverse consequences of groupthink thus include not examining alternatives, being selective in gathering information, and failing to be either self-critical or evaluative of others. Studies of meeting behavior, for example, conclude that people tend to prefer options that have obvious popularity. Sara Kiesler & Lee Sproull, Group Decision Making and Communication Technology, 52 Org. Behav. & Human Decision Processes 96 (1992). In the corporate setting, board culture often encourages groupthink. Boards emphasize politeness and courtesy at the expense of oversight. CEOs can foster and channel groupthink through their power to control information flows, reward consensus, and discourage reelection of troublemakers. The groupthink phenomenon therefore demands close attention with respect to a variety of corporate governance issues, but is most directly relevant to the board composition debate discussed below.

2.   Why are those services provided by boards of directors rather than the top management team and/or outside consultants?

3.   How might the role(s) of/services provided by the board of directors differ in:

A.   Public corporations with a controlling shareholder

B.   Large closely held corporations

C.   Startup/venture capital financed corporations

D.   "Mom and pop" close corporations

4.   In social norm research, a concept known as "pluralistic ignorance" has been derived from the Abilene Paradox, which describes an account of a family's decision to travel to Abilene for dinner when, individually, no single person wanted to go:

> On a hot afternoon visiting in Coleman, Texas, the family is comfortably playing dominoes on a porch, until the father-in-law suggests that they take a trip to Abilene [53 miles north] for dinner. The wife says, "Sounds like a great idea." The husband, despite having reservations because the drive is long and hot, thinks that his preferences must be out-of-step with the group and says, "Sounds good to me. I just hope your mother wants to go." The mother-in-law then says, "Of course I want to go. I haven't been to Abilene in a long time." The drive is hot, dusty, and long. When they arrive at the cafeteria, the food is as bad as the drive. They arrive back home four hours later, exhausted. One of them dishonestly says, "It was a great trip, wasn't it?" The mother-in-law says that, actually, she would rather have stayed home, but went along since the other three were so enthusiastic. The husband says, "I wasn't delighted to be doing what we were doing. I only went to satisfy the rest of you." The wife says, "I just went along to keep you happy. I would have had to be crazy to want to go out in the heat like that." The father-in-law then says that he only suggested it because he thought the others might be bored. The group sits back, perplexed that they together decided to take a trip which none of them wanted. They each would have preferred to sit comfortably, but did not admit to it when they still had time to enjoy the afternoon.

Give examples of how the Abilene Paradox might occur in boards of directors. Explain how social norms encourage or discourage it.

5.   What impact might the following changes have on board cultures and norms?

A.   Increasing the proportion of independent members of the board relative to insiders (employees)?

B.   Compensating directors in stock rather than cash?

C.   Judicial opinions imposing liability on directors who are inattentive or engage in self-dealing?

    D.   Increasing board diversity with respect to:

        i.   Race/ethnicity

        ii.   Gender

        iii.   Educational background

        iv.   Profession

        v.   Social class

    6.   Would you expect board appointees who lack the demographic, social, and educational credentials of the "power elite" to be more or less beholden to the CEO than those with such credentials?

B. BOARD OF DIRECTORS HOUSEKEEPING RULES

Many of the rules discussed in this case book can be understood as reactions to the real-world dominance of the CEO. Put another way, although the statutory model is predicated on rule by committee, in the real world we more often see one-person rule. In that sense, the rules of corporate governance that have evolved in the last two decades can be seen as attempts to restore rule by committee. As a simple example that also may serve as a useful review of corporate governance's most basic principles, consider the housekeeping rules that govern board decision making.

The Requirement That Boards Act Collectively by Meeting. The board of directors is a collegial body that, for the most part, makes decisions by consensus. Accordingly, an individual director acting alone generally has neither rights nor powers.[14] Instead, unless otherwise authorized by statute, only collective decisions taken at a meeting of the board at which a quorum is present are binding on the corporation.[15] This common law principle is reflected, albeit by negative implication, in DGCL § 141(b)'s statement that "[t]he vote of the majority of the directors present at a meeting at which a quorum is present shall be the act of the board of directors . . . ."[16]

Board Size. Corporate statutes historically required that boards consist of at least three members, who had to be shareholders of the

---

[14]   This general statement is subject to the caveat that individual directors do have rights to inspect corporate books and records. See, e.g., Cohen v. Cocoline Products, Inc., 150 N.Y.S.2d 815 (1956).

[15]   See, e.g., Greenberg v. Harrison, 124 A.2d 216 (Conn. 1956) (directors cannot vote by proxy); Baldwin v. Canfield, 1 N.W. 261 (Minn. 1879) (corporation not bound by a sale of land where the board never met to vote, even though all directors individually executed the deed). But see, e.g., Myhre v. Myrhe, 554 P.2d 276 (Mont. 1976) (board could act informally in a close corporation in which all shareholders were also directors); Gerard v. Empire Square Realty Co., 187 N.Y.S. 306 (N.Y. App. Div. 1921) (informal approval of a contract by the board of a close corporation, all of whose shareholders were represented on the board, and all of whom had consented, was binding on the corporation); Remillong v. Schneider, 185 N.W.2d 493 (N.D. 1971) (close corporation board with long-standing practice of acting informally could bind corporation by informal act); Baker v. Smith, 102 A. 721 (R.I. 1918) (same).

[16]   DGCL § 141(b). MBCA § 8.21 and DGCL § 141(f) authorize boards to act without a meeting by means of written consents, but require unanimity.

corporation and, under some statutes, residents of the state of incorporation.[17] Today these requirements have largely disappeared. DGCL § 141(b) authorizes boards to have one or more members and mandates no qualifications for board membership. MBCA §§ 8.02 and 8.03 are comparable. As a default rule, allowing single member boards probably makes sense. It gives promoters maximum flexibility, while allowing the creation of multi-member boards at low cost. In light of the apparent advantages of group decision making, however, it is hardly surprising that multi-member boards are the norm for corporations of any significant size.[18]

Is there an optimal board size? One meta-analysis found a statistically significant correlation between increased board size and improved financial performance.[19] Given the potential influence of moderating variables, however, it does not seem safe to draw firm conclusions from that survey. Other studies, moreover, are to the contrary.[20]

In theory, larger boards may facilitate the board's resource-gathering function by providing interlocking relationships with potential customers, suppliers, and other strategic partners. Large boards also provide more opportunities to create insurgent coalitions that constrain agency costs with respect to senior management. On the other hand, however, large boards likely will be contentious and fragmented, which reduces their ability to collectively monitor and discipline senior management. In such cases, the senior managers can affirmatively take advantage of the board through coalition building, selective channeling of information, and dividing and conquering. In sum, the question of whether there is an optimum board size lacks a parsimonious answer. As is so often the case, one size likely will not fit all.

Electronic Participation in Board Meetings. Modern statutes typically provide that directors may participate in board meetings by conference call or speakerphone, provided that all participants can hear one another.[21] The requirement that members be able to "hear" one another seems quaint in an era of electronic mail, instant messaging, and so forth. Interestingly, however, research on decision making has found

---

[17] MBCA § 8.03(a) cmt.

[18] Board sizes vary widely. A 1999 survey found that slightly less than half of had 7 to 9 members, with the remaining boards scattered evenly on either side of that range. National Association of Corporate Directors, Public Company Governance Survey 1999–2000 7 (Oct. 2000) (44 percent between 7 and 9).

[19] Dan R. Dalton, Number of Directors and Financial Performance: A Meta-Analysis, 42 Acad. Mgmt. J. 674, 676 (1999).

[20] See, e.g., Theodore Eisenberg et al., Larger Board Size and Decreasing Firm Value in Small Firms, 48 J. Fin. Econ. 35 (1998) (finding a significant negative correlation between board size and firm profitability in small and medium Finnish firms); see generally Sanjai Bhagat & Bernard Black, The Uncertain Relationship Between Board Composition and Firm Performance, 54 Bus. Law. 921, 941–42 (1999) (summarizing studies).

[21] See, e.g., DGCL § 141(i); MBCA § 8.20(b).

that groups linked by computer make fewer remarks and take longer to reach decisions than do groups meeting face to face.[22]

As with other aspects of the rules governing board meetings, accordingly, there seems to be a legitimate basis for otherwise formalistic rules. Electronic communication takes place mostly through text-based mediums. Reading and typing, for many people, are slower and require greater effort than verbal communication. Text-based communication also deprives participants of social cues, such as body language and tone of voice, that may be important signals. Social norms constraining behavior apparently function less well in text-based communication, as demonstrated by the flaming phenomenon in Usenet discussion groups.

Notice of Board Meetings. Unless the articles of incorporation require otherwise, no notice of regularly scheduled board meetings is required.[23] Special meetings require at least two days' notice.[24] As a matter of statutory law, the requisite notice need not announce the purpose of the meeting. Because the directors' duty of care requires them to make an informed decision, however, it is advisable to provide directors of advance notice of the reason for calling a meeting and any relevant documentation.[25] Notice may be waived in writing, either before or after the meeting.[26] Attendance at a meeting also constitutes waiver of notice, unless the director objects to the lack of notice at the beginning of the meeting and thereafter refrains from voting.[27] Any party may challenge the adequacy of notice in any context in which the validity of the board's actions are challenged.[28] As with other requirements relating to board meetings, the notice rules are intended to ensure that the board functions as a collegial body, all of whose members participate and get the benefit of the participation by all other members.

---

[22] Starr Roxanne Hiltz et al., Experiments in Group Decision Making: Communication Process and Outcome in Face-to-Face versus Computerized Conferences, 13 Human Communication Research 225, 243–44 (1986); Jane Siegel et al., Group Processes in Computer-Mediated Communication, 37 Org. Behavior & Human Decision Processes 157 (1986).

[23] MBCA § 8.22(a).

[24] MBCA § 8.22(b).

[25] See, e.g., Smith v. Van Gorkom, 488 A.2d 858 (Del. 1985), in which the court held that the board breached its fiduciary duty of care by "approving the 'sale' of the Company upon two hours' consideration, without prior notice, and without the exigency of a crisis or emergency." Id. at 874. The court went on to note: "None of the directors, other than Van Gorkom and Chelberg [two insiders], had any prior knowledge that the purpose of the meeting was to propose a cash-out merger of Trans Union. . . . Without any documents before them concerning the proposed transaction, the members of the Board were required to rely entirely upon Van Gorkom's 20-minute oral presentation of the proposal." Id. See also Gimbel v. Signal Companies, Inc., 316 A.2d 599 (Del. Ch.), aff'd per curiam, 316 A.2d 619 (Del. 1974), in which the court criticized the facts that (1) the "board meeting was called on only one-and-a-half days' notice" and (2) that the company's "outside directors were not notified of the meeting's purpose," which were cited as factors in the court's determination that the company's management had failed to give the board "the opportunity to make a reasonable and reasoned decision." Id. at 615.

[26] MBCA § 8.23(a).

[27] MBCA § 8.23(b).

[28] Schroder v. Scotten, Dillon Co., 299 A.2d 431 (Del. Ch. 1972).

Quorum and Voting. The statutory default for a quorum is a majority of the directors, although the articles or bylaws may provide for either a greater or lesser number.[29] As for voting, the statute further provides: "If a quorum is present when a vote is taken, the affirmative vote of a majority of directors present is the act of the board of directors unless the articles of incorporation or bylaws require the vote of a greater number of directors."[30] Note that the effectively treats abstentions as no votes, because abstaining directors are "present." By negative implication, this provision also ensures "that the board of directors may act only when a quorum is present."[31] If the quorum is broken by departing directors, the board may not act. Directors who are present at the meeting are deemed to assent to any actions taken unless they, inter alia, ensure that their dissent is noted on the minutes of the meeting.[32] This provision reinforces the notion of the board as a collegial body, "forcefully bringing the position of the dissenting member to the attention of the balance of the board of directors."[33]

Board Term Limits. Corporate law statutes generally limit directors to one-year terms of office, although the Delaware code provides that directors shall serve until their successor is elected and qualified.[34] Where the corporation has adopted a classified board, the directors' term of office is either two or three years, depending on whether the board was divided into two or three classes respectively. In any case, the statutes are silent as to the number of terms a director may serve. Because corporation statutes broadly authorize corporations to adopt articles of incorporation specifying director qualifications, however, corporations may adopt charter provisions limiting the number of times someone may serve as a director.

Some commentators contend that such limits are an emerging best practice. After the Enron scandal, the American Bar Association set up a task force to study corporate governance issues. The task force recommended that boards should at least "[c]onsider whether to establish term limits or policies governing rotation of the chair and membership of the Board of Directors and its Corporate Governance, Audit and Compensation Committees, and the number of board and committee memberships."[35]

---

[29] See, e.g., DGCL § 141(b) (providing a minimum quorum of 1/3 of the directors); MBCA § 8.24(b) (same).

[30] MBCA § 8.24(c).

[31] MBCA § 8.24 cmt.

[32] MBCA § 8.24(d).

[33] MBCA § 8.24 cmt.

[34] DGCL § 141(b).

[35] James H. Cheek, III et al., Preliminary Report of the American Bar Association Task Force on Corporate Responsibility, 54 Mercer L. Rev. 789, 805 (2003).

C. THE BOARD'S FIDUCIARY DUTIES

This text assumes that the reader has had the benefit of a basic Business Associations or Corporations course. The reader thus is assumed to have a working familiarity with the duties of care and loyalty, the business judgment rule, and the direct and derivative suits by which those duties are enforced. Even so, before delving into advanced topics in this area, a quick review of these topics may be helpful.

Vice Chancellor Travis Laster's opinion, *In re Trados Inc. S'holder Litig.*,[36] explained that:

> When determining whether directors have breached their fiduciary duties, Delaware corporate law distinguishes between the standard of conduct and the standard of review. The standard of conduct describes what directors are expected to do and is defined by the content of the duties of loyalty and care. The standard of review is the test that a court applies when evaluating whether directors have met the standard of conduct. It describes what a plaintiff must first plead and later prove to prevail.
>
> Under Delaware law, the standard of review depends initially on whether the board members (i) were disinterested and independent (the business judgment rule), (ii) faced potential conflicts of interest because of the decisional dynamics present in particular recurring and recognizable situations (enhanced scrutiny), or (iii) confronted actual conflicts of interest such that the directors making the decision did not comprise a disinterested and independent board majority (entire fairness). The standard of review may change further depending on whether the directors took steps to address the potential or actual conflict, such as by creating an independent committee, conditioning the transaction on approval by disinterested stockholders, or both.[37]

Lyman P.Q. Johnson & Mark A. Sides, The Sarbanes-Oxley Act and Fiduciary Duties
30 Wm. Mitchell L. Rev. 1149 (2004)[38]

Courts have long recognized that corporate officers and directors are fiduciaries and that equity, not law, is the source of their fiduciary obligations. As stated by former Delaware Chancellor William Allen:

> The duties [corporate officers and directors] owe to shareholders with respect to the exercise of their legal power

---

[36] 73 A.3d 17 (Del. Ch. 2013).

[37] Id. at 35–36.

[38] Reprinted by permission of Lyman P.Q. Johnson, Mark A. Sides, and the William Mitchell Law Review.

over corporate property supervene their legal rights, are imposed by equity and are recognized and enforced exclusively by a court of equity. Chancery takes jurisdiction over "fiduciary" relationships because equity, not law, is the source of the right asserted.[218]

. . .

A. Director Fiduciary Duties

On several occasions, the Delaware Supreme Court has stated that corporate directors owe "fiduciary duties of care, loyalty and good faith."[226] However, Vice Chancellor Leo Strine, upon closely examining supreme court language, concluded that the obligation of good faith, although a fiduciary requirement, is, in fact, an aspect of the duty of loyalty.[227] . . .

1. Duty of Due Care

. . . In the decision-making setting—whether it involves directors making a routine business decision or responding to a high-stakes unsolicited bid for corporate control—the duty of care inquiry clearly focuses on a board's "decision-making process."[230] Directors in that setting are under an obligation to obtain and act with due care on all material information reasonably available. The most famous case involving breach of the duty of care in the decision-making context *is Smith v. Van Gorkom,*[232] where directors were held to have been grossly negligent in discharging that facet of the duty of due care requiring them to be fully informed before making a business decision. After the *Van Gorkom* decision, however, Delaware amended its corporation statute to permit an amendment to a company's certificate of incorporation either to limit or eliminate director liability for breaches of the duty of due care.[234] The vast majority of public companies in Delaware have adopted an exculpation provision eliminating director liability in this way.

Directors also may be liable for breach of the duty of care if they fail to properly monitor and oversee the business affairs of a corporation. . . .

2. Duty of Loyalty

The duty of loyalty requires directors to act in the best interest of the corporation. The duty of loyalty has a well-recognized dimension

---

[218] McMahon v. New Castle Assocs., 532 A. 2d 601, 604 (Del. Ch. 1987) (citations omitted).

[226] See, e.g., Malone v. Brincat, 722 A.2d 5, 11 (Del. 1998); Cinerama, Inc. v. Technicolor, Inc., 663 A.2d 1156 (Del. 1995).

[227] In re Gaylord Container Corp. S'holders Litig., 753 A.2d 462, 475–76 n.41 (Del. Ch. 2000). [Ed.: The Delaware Supreme Court subsequently confirmed that "the fiduciary duty violated by [bad faith] conduct is the duty of loyalty." Stone ex rel. AmSouth Bancorporation v. Ritter, 911 A.2d 362, 370 (Del. 2006).]

[230] See Citron v. Fairchild Camera & Instrument Corp., 569 A.2d 53, 66 (Del. 1989); Brehm v. Eisner, 746 A.2d 244, 264 (Del. 2000) ("Due care in the decisionmaking context is process due care only.").

[232] 488 A.2d 858 (Del. 1985).

[234] Del. Code Ann. tit. 8, § 102 (b)(7) (2003).

prohibiting a director from preferring his or her own interests over the interests of the corporation. Accordingly, a director may not engage in an unfair self-dealing ("conflict of interest") transaction, wrongly usurp a corporate opportunity, improperly compete with the corporation, or use corporate assets or confidential company information for personal gain. Mere absence of a personal, conflicting interest by a director, however, is insufficient, by itself, to fulfill the affirmative aspect of the duty of loyalty. The Delaware Chancery Court has observed that a breach of loyalty can be unintended and can occur even when board action is taken in good faith, and even where self-interest is absent. As the chancery court has noted, "a fiduciary may act disloyally for a variety of reasons other than personal pecuniary interest; and . . . regardless of his motive, a director who consciously disregards his duties to the corporation and its stockholders may suffer a personal judgment for monetary damages for any harm he causes."[251]

NOTES AND QUESTIONS

1.   Your author has elsewhere suggested that:

Two conceptions of the business judgment rule compete in the case law. One treats the rule as a standard of liability. Hence, for example, some courts and commentators argue that the business judgment rule shields directors from liability so long as they act in good faith. Others contend that the rule simply raises the liability bar from mere negligence to, say, gross negligence or recklessness.

Alternatively, however, the business judgment rule can be seen as an abstention doctrine. In this conception, the rule's presumption of good faith does not state a standard of liability but rather establishes a presumption against judicial review of duty of care claims. The court therefore abstains from reviewing the substantive merits of the directors' conduct unless the plaintiff can rebut the business judgment rule's presumption of good faith.[39]

He contends that the latter is the correct view, explaining that:

The claim is not that courts rubberstamp the board's decision. Conceptualizing the business judgment rule as a principle of judicial abstention means that the rule is not a standard of liability; it does not preclude the rule from having some aspects of a standard of review. As the quoted passages from [*Shlensky*] make clear, the business judgment rule does not prevent judicial review of director conduct involving fraud or self-dealing. In addition, before the rule comes into play, various prerequisites must be satisfied. It is well established, for example, that directors may only invoke the

---

[251]   Nagy v. Bistricer, 770 A.2d 43, 49 n.2 (Del. Ch. 2000). See also Hoover Indus., Inc. v. Chase, 1988 WL 73758, at *2 (Del. Ch. July 13, 1988) ("A director does breach his duty of loyalty if he knows that the company has been defrauded and does not report what he knows to the board. . . .").

[39]   Stephen M. Bainbridge, The Business Judgment Rule as Abstention Doctrine, 57 Vand. L. Rev. 83, 89 (2004).

business judgment rule when they have made a conscious decision. Hence, the business judgment rule does not prevent judicial review of a board's failure to exercise proper oversight of the corporation's management. The good faith and disinterested independence of the directors are also often identified as conditions on which the rule is predicated. Finally, some courts and commentators contend that the business judgment rule does not protect an irrational decision.101 Instead, what the abstention conception contemplates is that, if the requisite preconditions are satisfied, there is no remaining scope for judicial review of the substantive merits of the board's decision.

The Delaware Supreme Court expressed this point well in *Brehm v. Eisner*, in which the court explicitly rejected, as "foreign to the business judgment rule," the plaintiffs' argument that the rule could be rebutted by a showing that the directors failed to exercise "substantive due care":

> Courts do not measure, weigh or quantify directors' judgments. We do not even decide if they are reasonable in this context. Due care in the decisionmaking context is process due care only. . . .

> Thus, directors' decisions will be respected by courts unless the directors are interested or lack independence relative to the decision, do not act in good faith, act in a manner that cannot be attributed to a rational business purpose or reach their decision by a grossly negligent process that includes the failure to consider all material facts reasonably available. Perhaps Brehm was not as pure an abstention decision as was Shlensky, but note that none of the preconditions set forth by Brehm contemplate substantive review of the merits of the board's decision. Even the reference to a rational business purpose requires only the possibility that the decision was actuated by a legitimate business reason, not that directors must prove the existence of such a reason. Absent self dealing or other conflicted interests, or truly egregious process failures, the court will abstain.[40]

Why would courts abstain from reviewing director decisions provided the requisite preconditions are satisfied?

2.   Both the duty of care and the duty of loyalty come into play where the board has made a decision.

> When courts say that they will not interfere in matters of business judgment, it is presupposed that judgment—reasonable diligence—has in fact been exercised. . . . Courts have properly decided to give directors a wide latitude in the management of the affairs of a corporation provided always that judgment, and that means an honest, unbiased judgment, is reasonably exercised by them.[41]

---

[40]   Id. at 98–100.

[41]   Burt v. Irvine Co., 237 Cal. App. 2d 828, 852–53, 47 Cal. Rptr. 392, 408 (Ct. App. 1965).

The difficulty is that most board of director activity "does not consist of taking affirmative action on individual matters; it is instead a continuing flow of supervisory process, punctuated only occasionally by a discrete transactional decision."[42] The business judgment rule clearly does not apply to such activities, because there is no exercise of judgment.

> [The] business judgment rule does not protect a director if he abdicated his responsibility and failed to exercise his judgment as a director. As the Second Circuit has stated:
>
>> Whatever its merit, however, the business judgment rule extends only as far as the reasons which justify its existence. Thus, it does not apply in cases, e.g., in which the corporate decision lacks a business purpose, is tainted by a conflict of interest, is so egregious as to amount to a no-win decision, or results from an obvious and prolonged failure to exercise oversight or supervision. Other examples may occur.
>
> Other courts have also concluded that directors who "abdicate their managerial responsibilities" are not entitled to the business judgment rule's protection from liability. The [plaintiff] has alleged the type of "prolonged failure to exercise oversight or supervision" that falls outside the business judgment rule as a failure to exercise any judgment.[43]

If the business judgment rule is inapplicable, what standard of review should to claims that the board has failed to properly monitor management? We will return to that question in the discussion of board oversight duties.

3.   Why do we have fiduciary duties? According to Judge Frank Easterbrook and Professor Daniel Fischel it is because ex ante monitoring of agents is, at best, an imperfect solution to the problem of agency costs:

> The fiduciary principle is an alternative to direct monitoring. It replaces prior supervision with deterrence, much as the criminal law uses penalties for bank robbery rather than pat-down searches of everyone entering banks. Acting as a standard-form penalty clause in every agency contract, the elastic contours of the fiduciary principle reflect the difficulty that contracting parties have in anticipating when and how their interests may diverge.[44]

Put another way, fiduciary duties are "a corporate governance device uniquely crafted to fill in the massive gap in this open-ended bargain between shareholders and corporate officers and directors."[45]

In other words, neither ex ante statutes nor contracts can anticipate all of the ways in which agency costs might affect the management—

---

[42]   Bayless Manning, The Business Judgment Rule and the Director's Duty of Attention: Time for Reality, 39 Bus. Law. 1477, 1494 (1984).

[43]   Resolution Tr. Corp. v. Norris, 830 F. Supp. 351, 359–60 (S.D. Tex. 1993) (citations omitted).

[44]   Frank H. Easterbrook, Corporate Control Transactions, 91 Yale L.J. 698, 702 (1982)

[45]   Jonathan R. Macey, An Economic Analysis of the Various Rationales for Making Shareholders the Exclusive Beneficiaries of Corporate Fiduciary Duties, 21 Stetson L. Rev. 23, 41 (1991).

shareholder relationship. Where statutes and contracts are silent, fiduciary duties fill in the gaps. But what happens when the corporation has multiple classes of stockholders, with differing rights and priorities? If the board is faced with a zero-sum decision that will inevitably leave some classes of shareholders worse off and some worse off, how does the board choose between those classes?

Just as the shareholder—corporation contact is inevitably incomplete, so are the relationships between a corporation and its creditors. Accordingly, like any long-term relational contract, bond indentures inevitably prove incomplete. In a world characterized by uncertainty, complexity, and bounded rationality, it cannot be otherwise. Where the bond indenture is silent, should the law invoke fiduciary duties or other extra-contractual rights as gap fillers?

4.   Your author has argued that:

> The insistence that the firm is a real entity is a form of reification—i.e., treating an abstraction as if it has material existence. Reification is often useful, or even necessary, because it permits us to utilize a form of shorthand—it is easier to say General Motors did so and so than to attempt in conversation to describe the complex process that actually may have taken place. Indeed, it is very difficult to think about large firms without reifying them. Reification, however, can be dangerous. It becomes easy to lose sight of the fact that firms do not do things, people do things.

In other words, the corporation is not a thing to which duties can be owed, except as a useful legal fiction.[46]

In *Trenwick Am. Litig. Trust v. Ernst & Young, L.L.P.*,[47] then-Vice Chancellor Leo Strine explained that:

> Professor Bainbridge is critical of jurisprudence that expresses the view that directors owe fiduciary duties to the corporation itself, rather than a particular constituency of the corporation. When a corporation is solvent, Professor Bainbridge believes that fiduciary duties are owed by the directors to the stockholders. When a corporation is insolvent, he accepts the notion that the directors owe their fiduciary duties to the creditors, because the creditors are now the residual claimants. That does not mean, however, that Professor Bainbridge believes that all claims against directors of insolvent corporations are direct claims belonging to the creditors individually. To the contrary, he recognizes that if the directors of an insolvent firm commit a breach of fiduciary duty reducing the value of the firm, any claim belongs to the entity and that creditors would benefit from the recovery derivatively, based on their claim on the firm's assets. Supporting his view that owing fiduciary duties to a firm is an unhelpful concept, Professor

---

[46]   Stephen M. Bainbridge, Much Ado About Little? Directors' Fiduciary Duties in the Vicinity of Insolvency, 1 J. Bus. & Tech. L. 335, 352–53 (2007).

[47]   906 A.2d 168, 195 n.75 (Del. Ch. 2006), aff'd sub nom. Trenwick Am. Litig. Trust v. Billett, 931 A.2d 438 (Del. 2007).

Bainbridge relies heavily on the idea of the corporation as a nexus of contracts [under] which it is silly to think duties can be owed. His concern is that telling directors that they owe fiduciary duties to a "nexus of contracts" provides no concrete objective against which to measure their conduct; thus, he favors clarity that the directors' obligation is to maximize returns for the corporation's residual claimants, who in the case of insolvency, are its creditors.

Although Professor Bainbridge's views regarding the substantive effect the question of insolvency should have on directors' ability to rely upon the business judgment rule and on the application of the derivative/direct claim distinction is identical to mine—short answer: none—I am not as critical as he of references to the directors owing duties to the insolvent corporation itself. That expression might be short-hand that elides the rich academic debates about what corporations are but the expression seems to be used to advance an end that Bainbridge supports. Even when a corporation is solvent, the notion that the directors should pursue the best interests of the equityholders does not prevent them from making a myriad of judgments about how generous or stingy to be to other corporate constituencies in areas where there is no precise legal obligation to those constituencies. I do not understand this complexity to diminish when a firm is insolvent simply because the residual claimants are now creditors. Indeed, it is not immediately apparent to me why, if the common law were to begin to dole out in insolvency special, non-contractual "ward" rights to certain constituencies that transformed in a material way the obligations of directors, creditors would be the primary object of that (difficult to legitimize) act of judicial invention. Better for society that those who manage them see them as something more importantly human, as societal institutions freighted with the goal of responsible wealth creation. In the insolvency context, directors have, in my view, no less discretion, for example, to decide to accord respectful and considerate treatment to the company's workers (who as Bainbridge admits, may have made more of a non-diversifiable risk with less opportunity to use the tool of contract as a shield) if they believe that will improve the firm's value and the return to its creditors.

In other words, insolvency does not suddenly turn directors into mere collection agents. Rather, the creditors become the enforcement agents of fiduciary duties because the corporation's wallet cannot handle the legal obligations owed. Theft from the firm remains theft from the firm, even if the firm as seen by academics is a legal fiction. In other words, the fiduciary duty tool is transferred to the creditors when the firm is insolvent in aid of the creditor's contract rights. Because, by contract, the creditors have the right to benefit from the firm's operations until they are fully repaid, it is they who have an interest in ensuring that the directors comply with their traditional fiduciary duties of loyalty and care. Any wrongful self-dealing, for example, injures creditors as a class by reducing the assets of the firm available to satisfy creditors.

To ensure that the directors manage the enterprise to maximize its value so that the firm can meet as many of its obligations to creditors as possible—the new goal of the firm—the jurisprudence refers to the directors as owing fiduciary duties to the firm and its creditors. The judicial decisions indicating that directors owe fiduciary duties to the firm when it is insolvent are not, in my view, at odds with Bainbridge's fundamental perspective; indeed, they seem to me more a judicial method of attempting to reinforce the idea that the business judgment rule protects the directors of solvent, barely solvent, and insolvent corporations, and that the creditors of an insolvent firm have no greater right to challenge a disinterested, good faith business decision than the stockholders of a solvent firm. To this point, many firm life cycles have involved an emergence from bankruptcy with the firms' former creditors emerging in the form of the firms' new equityholders.

D. THE BOARD'S REAL-WORLD FUNCTIONS

As we have just seen, the board has fiduciary duties to the shareholders, with which the board must comply when it acts and, in some cases, when it fails to act. But those duties do not define the board's functions. So, what does the board actually do?

The board of directors has many functions, but they fall into three basic categories. These are management, oversight, and service. The balance between them has varied over time and from firm to firm. In recent decades, however, the trend has been to elevate the importance of monitoring at the expense of the others. Sarbanes-Oxley and Dodd-Frank did much to further that trend.

Management. As we've seen, if one looked solely to corporation statutes for guidance, one would assume that the board of directors plays a very active role in the corporation's management. Besides the general allocation of the conduct of the corporation's business and affairs to the board, corporation statutes include many specific mandates that only the board can fulfill. Approval by the board of directors is a statutory prerequisite, for example, to mergers and related transactions such as sales of all or substantially all corporate assets, the issuance of stock, distribution of dividends, and amendments to the articles of incorporation. Approval by the board of directors of related party transactions involving top managers or board members is a statutory option for substantially insulating such transactions from judicial review for fairness. The board typically has non-exclusive power to amend bylaws. And so on.

In fact, however, the typical modern public corporation is too big for the board to manage on anything resembling a day-to-day basis. As we'll discuss in the next Chapter, these days most board members are outsiders who have full-time jobs elsewhere and therefore can devote relatively little time to the running of the business for which they act as directors.

The formulation of typical modern corporation statutes reflects this shift. Section 8.01(b) of the Model Business Corporation Act (MBCA) reflects these basic truisms in two respects. First, the statute provides that the "business and affairs of the corporation" shall be "managed under the direction of" the board. This formulation is intended to make clear that the board's role is to formulate broad policy and oversee the subordinates who actually conduct the business day-to-day.[48] Second, the statute also provides that corporate powers may be exercised "under the [board's] authority." This formulation allows the board to delegate virtually all management functions to senior corporate officers, who in turn of course will delegate most decisions to subordinate employees.

Even so, modern boards typically retain some managerial functions that go beyond the statutory mandates discussed above. Indeed, courts have held that some decisions are so important that the board of directors must make them.[49] In some states, such basic matters as filing a lawsuit[50] or executing a guarantee of another corporation's debts are extraordinary matters reserved to the board.[51] In recent years, courts also have imposed substantial managerial responsibilities on the board of directors—especially its independent members—in connection with shareholder derivative litigation, conflict of interest transactions, and mergers and acquisitions.

Best practice also assigns important managerial roles to the board. Broad policymaking or, at least, review and approval of major policies, for example, are board prerogatives. Boards are also responsible for hiring the top management team, especially the CEO, and setting their compensation.

Monitoring Managers. Although it is a "fundamental precept of Delaware corporation law" that the board "has ultimate responsibility for the management of the enterprise," that law also recognizes that "modern multi-function business corporations" are "large, complex

---

[48] MBCA § 8.01 cmt.

[49] See Lee v. Sentina Bros., 268 F.2d 357, 365–66 (2d Cir. 1959) (officers have no apparent authority with respect to extraordinary matters, which are reserved to the board).

[50] Compare Custer Channel Wing Corp. v. Frazer, 181 F. Supp. 197 (S.D.N.Y. 1959) (president had authority to do so) with Lloydona Peters Enter., Inc. v. Dorius, 658 P.2d 1209 (Utah 1983) (no authority to do so); Ney v. Eastern Iowa Tel. Co., 144 N.W. 383 (Iowa 1913) (no authority to do so with respect to the corporation's largest shareholder).

[51] Compare Sperti Products, Inc. v. Container Corp. of Am., 481 S.W.2d 43 (Ken. App. 1972) (president had authority) with First Nat'l Bank v. Cement Products Co., 227 N.W. 908 (Iowa 1929) (no authority to do so); Burlington Indus., Inc. v. Foil, 202 S.E.2d 591 (N.C. 1974) (president lacked authority, inter alia, because making such guarantees was not part of the corporations' ordinary business).

organizations" and that modern boards are comprised mainly "of persons dedicating less than all of their attention to that role."[52] Accordingly, directors "satisfy their obligations by thoughtfully appointing officers, establishing or approving goals and plans and monitoring performance."[53]

> **THINK ABOUT IT**
>
> How does a board monitor the C-suite?

Service. A diverse board that includes outsiders can provide a number of services to the top management team. Outsiders can provide access to networks to which insiders do not belong, thereby assisting the firm in gathering resources and obtaining business. Outside directors affiliated with financial institutions, for example, facilitate the firm's access to capital. In addition to simply providing a contact between the firm and the lender, the financial institution's representative can use his board membership to protect the lender's interests by more closely monitoring the firm than would be possible for an outsider. In turn, that reduction of risk should result in the lender accepting a lower return on its loans, thereby reducing the firm's cost of capital.

Another example is the politically connected board member, whose access to legislators and regulators may aid the firm in dealing with the government. Such board members not only assist with obtaining government contracts, but also with clearing red tape and providing the firm with political cover in times of trouble.

A core service provided by boards of directors, especially its outside members, is providing advice and counsel to the CEO. By virtue of being outsiders, the board members can offer the CEO alternative points of view. In particular, the board can serve as a source of outside expertise. Complex business decisions require knowledge in such areas as accounting, finance, management, and law. Members who possess expertise themselves or have access to credible external experts play an important role in the board's service function.

Shifting Priorities. The relative balance between these functions has shifted over time. Survey data and other forms of fieldwork in the 1970s suggested that boards had a mainly advisory role. Survey data from the 1990s, by contrast, shows an emphasis on managerial functions in the sense of broad policy making and setting strategy. By the end of the 1990s, survey data showed that boards were becoming active and independent monitors of the top management team.[54] What drove this shift?

Boards historically have had a bad press. In the 18th Century, Adam Smith famously complained that one could not expect the directors of a

---

[52]   Chapin v. Benwood Foundation, 402 A.2d 1205, 1211 (Del. Ch. 1979).

[53]   Id.

[54]   Renee B. Adams et al., The Role of Boards of Directors in Corporate Governance: A Conceptual Framework and Survey, 48 J. Econ. Lit. 58, 64–65 (2010).

joint stock company, "being the managers rather of other people's money than of their own, . . . should watch over it with the same anxious vigilance with which the partners in a private copartnery frequently watch over their own."[55] Almost two centuries later, William O. Douglas complained that there were too many boards whose members did "not direct"[56] and dismissed directors as "business colonels of the honorary type—honorary colonels who are ornamental in parade but fairly useless in battle."[57]

Although much of the criticism was merited, little was done in the first two-thirds of the 20th Century. In the 1970s, however, a crisis of confidence threatened not just the comfortable world of the board of directors but the very foundations of corporate capitalism. The triggering event was the collapse of Penn Central "in 1970 amidst personality clashes, mismanagement, and lax board oversight."[58] Subsequent investigations revealed that Penn Central's board had been mere figureheads who were wholly unaware of the company's deteriorating financial condition and passively rubberstamped such transactions as paying over $100 million in dividends to shareholders even as the company was going down the tubes.[59]

Penn Central was followed in short order by the widespread corrupt payments scandal in which hundreds of prominent public corporations were implicated. The scandal was an offshoot of the Watergate investigations. The probes brought to light numerous illegal corporate contributions to the Nixon campaign. Investigation of those violations then revealed an even broader pattern of both domestic and foreign corporations making illegal campaign contributions, bribes to government officials, kickbacks on contracts, and the like. Eventually the government targeted some 50 corporations for criminal prosecution or SEC civil litigation. Another 400 voluntarily disclosed having made

---

[55]   2 Adam Smith, An Inquiry into the Nature and Causes of the Wealth of Nations 264–65 (Edwin Cannan ed., Univ. of Chicago Press 1976) (1776).

[56]   William O. Douglas, Directors Who Do Not Direct, 47 Harv. L. Rev. 1305 (1934).

[57]   William O. Douglas, Democracy and Finance 46 (1940). A well-known British judicial opinion from the early 20th Century, describing the selection of a rubber corporation's board, provides an amusing illustration of the basic problem:

> The directors of the company, Sir Arthur Aylmer Bart., Henry William Tugwell, Edward Barber and Edward Henry Hancock were all induced to become directors by Harboard or persons acting with him in the promotion of the company. Sir Arthur Aylmer was absolutely ignorant of business. He only consented to act because he was told the office would give him a little pleasant employment without his incurring any responsibility. H.W. Tugwell was partner in a firm of bankers in a good position in Bath; he was seventy-five years of age and very deaf; he was induced to join the board by representations made to him in January, 1906. Barber was a rubber broker and was told that all he would have to do would be to give an opinion as to the value of rubber when it arrived in England. Hancock was a man of business who said he was induced to join by seeing the names of Tugwell and Barber, whom he considered good men.

In re Brazilian Rubber Plantations & Estates Ltd., [1911] 1 Ch. 425.

[58]   Brian R. Cheffins, Did Corporate Governance "Fail" During the 2008 Stock Market Meltdown? The Case of the S&P 500, 65 Bus. Law. 1, 7 (2009).

[59]   Jeffrey N. Gordon, The Rise of Independent Directors in the United States, 1950–2005: Of Shareholder Value and Stock Market Prices, 59 Stan. L. Rev. 1465, 1515 (2007).

improper payments.[60] By the end, it was clear that senior management at many of these companies had been well aware of the corrupt payments, but their boards had been too far out of the loop to prevent them.[61]

The scandals swept the legitimacy of the corporate form itself into the tumultuous political battles of the day. The period was one in which multiple progressive movements—including the anti-war movement, civil rights, feminism, gay rights, consumer protection, and environmentalism—intertwined in a constantly shifting flux of activism. A number of these groups came to see the institution of the corporation as being a root cause of social problems.

This view found a classic expression in Ralph Nader's philippic *Taming the Giant Corporation*. Nader and his co-authors claimed that public confidence in American corporations was declining precipitously in the face of antisocial corporate behavior.[62] They blamed a myriad of social ills—pollution, workplace hazards, discrimination, unsafe products, and corporate crime—on corporate managers accountable to neither boards, shareholders, nor society.[63]

Consistent with the generally accepted diagnosis of the Penn central collapse and the questionable payments scandal, Nader and his coauthors laid much of the blame at the feet of boards of directors. In turn, they blamed the board's impotence in large part on state corporate law, which purportedly had been "reduced to reflecting the preferences of the managers of the largest corporations."[64] Accordingly, Nader called for a federal corporation law, displacing state law, whose precepts would ensure greater management accountability both to shareholders and to society.

Although Nader was an outlier, at least in terms of the ferocity of his attacks and the radical nature of his proposals, many mainstream regulators and scholars of the period likewise concluded that state corporate law was moving away from, not towards, greater managerial accountability. Former SEC Chairman William Cary famously argued, for example, that competition among states for incorporations produced a "race to the bottom" in which shareholder interests were sacrificed.[65]

In order to arrest those trends, Cary urged adoption of a federal statute designed to promote greater management accountability to shareholders, although not going so far as to require federal incorporation.[66] Like Nader's more ambitious scheme, Cary's proposal for partially federalizing corporation law ultimately went nowhere. Along

---

[60]   Id. at 1516.

[61]   Cheffins, supra note 58, at 7.

[62]   Ralph Nader et al., Taming the Giant Corporation 17–32 (1976).

[63]   Id. at 62–65.

[64]   Id. at 60.

[65]   William L. Cary, Federalism and Corporate Law: Reflections Upon Delaware, 83 Yale L.J. 663 (1974).

[66]   Id. at 696–703.

with other similar proposals, however, they contributed to a shift in best practices and ultimately laid the groundwork for the creeping federalization of corporate law exemplified by Sarbanes-Oxley and Dodd-Frank.

Although such proposals for sweeping changes failed, the ferment of the 1970s did produce one lasting change; namely, the rise of the so-called monitoring board. Much of the credit (or blame, depending on your point of view) for this development must go to Professor Melvin Eisenberg. In *The Structure of the Corporation*, "perhaps the most important work on corporate law since Berle and Means's *The Modern Corporation and Private Property*,"[67] Eisenberg argued that boards were essentially passive, with most of their functions captured by senior executives.[68] According to Eisenberg, the board's principal remaining function was selection and supervision of the firm's chief executive, but most boards failed adequately to perform even that residual task.[69]

As a solution, Eisenberg articulated a corporate governance model that explicitly separated the task of managing large publicly held corporations from that of monitoring those who do the managing. In this monitoring model, directors did not undertake decision making or policymaking, which were assigned to senior management. Instead, the board's principal function was to monitor the performance of the company's senior executives. Other functions such as advising the CEO, authorizing major corporate actions, and exercising control over decision making were of minor importance or were merely pro forma.[70]

Eisenberg perhaps came closest to enshrining the monitoring model in corporate law in the First Tentative Draft of what ultimately became the American Law Institute's *Principles of Corporate Governance: Analysis and Recommendations*. Eisenberg served as Reporter for Parts I through III of the *Principles*, which gave him chief drafting responsibility for the board composition and role standards. In 1984, moreover, Eisenberg succeeded Stanley Kaplan as Chief Reporter for the entire project.

In monitoring management, the board was to do more than just look at results. Rather, the board was to establish mechanisms by which it could closely oversee management performance.[71] At the heart of these

---

[67]   Dalia Tsuk Mitchell, Status Bound: The Twentieth-Century Evolution of Directors' Liability, 5 N.Y.U. J.L. & Bus. 63 (2009).

[68]   Melvin Aron Eisenberg, The Structure of the Corporation 139–41 (1976).

[69]   Id. at 162–72.

[70]   Id. at 157–62.

[71]   American Law Institute, Principles of Corporate Governance: Analysis and Recommendations 65 (Tent. Draft No. 1 1982) [hereinafter "TD No. 1"] ("the concept of monitoring requires the employment of sophisticated and independent systems designed to gather and disseminate information concerning management performance, and independent directors who are sophisticated in interpreting both financial and nonfinancial data."). The Principles divide corporations into three categories. The "large publicly held corporation" has two thousand or more record stockholders and $ 100 million in total assets. "Publicly held corporation" has five hundred or more record stockholders and $5 million in total assets. "Small

mechanisms were three oversight committees: audit, nomination, and compensation.

Because financial data is the basic metric for management performance, Eisenberg argued that the board should have an audit committee comprised of independent directors. The committee was to select the corporation's independent auditor and, among other things, review the corporation's financial results in consultation with the auditor. Shifting responsibility for selecting the auditor from management to an independent board committee would reduce management's ability to influence the presentation of financial data to its benefit. Shifting responsibility for interacting with the auditor from management to the audit committee would address the information asymmetry between management and the board by giving the latter access to an independent source of key information.[72]

Tentative Draft No. 1 of the *Principles* also envisioned a nominating committee to be comprised exclusively of outside directors, including at least a majority of independent directors, and was charged with, among other things, recommending candidates for director positions.[73] The exclusion of officers or employees from membership on the nominating committee was intended to ensure that senior executives did not play a significant role in the selection of board members. In addition, it seems likely that the drafters expected that a nominating committee comprised of independent directors would screen

---

publicly held corporation" are those companies that fall within the definition of publicly held corporation, but do not qualify as a large publicly held corporation. In general, the board composition and function provisions of Tentative Draft No. 1 applied only to large publicly held corporations. For small publicly held corporations, these provisions generally were recommended as rules of good corporate practice. See, e.g., TD No.1 at 89 (audit committees).

[72]   Eisenberg, supra note 68, at 210–11.

[73]   TD No.1 at § 3.06(a). Not all outside directors qualified as independent under the Principles, because the Principles set out an elaborate standard for determining whether a director is independent, which looked to whether the director has a significant relationship with the corporation's senior executives. Tentative Draft No. 1 defined significant relationship very broadly. It included employment, prior employment within the two preceding years, family relationships, and various economic relationships. The final Principles define "significant relationship" to include the same basic types of relationships as did Tentative Draft No. 1, although some of the details differ in minor ways.

out individuals who in fact are biased towards the incumbent senior executives even though those individuals might otherwise meet the *Principles'* definition of an independent director.

The recommended compensation committee, like the nominating committee, was to be comprised solely of outside directors, including at least a majority of independent directors.[74] As the name suggests, it was to review and approve (or recommend to the full board) the compensation of senior executives and generally oversee the corporation's compensation policies. A separate compensation committee was recommended because of concerns that inside directors, even if recused from considering their own compensation, would not be able to objectively evaluate the compensation of other senior executives in light of the close relationship between one executive's compensation and that of another.

Eisenberg's proposals underwent substantial modification in subsequent drafts. Some of the changes were merely cosmetic. For example, while the word monitoring no long appears in the *Principles'* description of the board's function, the basic division between monitoring and management functions was retained under new terminology. The *Principles* thus still urge that the company be managed by its principal senior executives, as well as arguing that the selection and oversight of those executives is the board's basic function.

A more meaningful change was the conversion of virtually all of the proposed mandatory board composition and function rules into mere recommendations of corporate practice. Where Tentative Draft No. 1 prohibited the board of a large publicly held corporation from managing the firm on a regular basis, for example, the *Principles* restore the board's traditional power to do so. Where Tentative Draft No. 1 required that independent directors make up a majority of a large publicly held corporation's board, the *Principles* merely recommend such a composition as a matter of corporate practice. The ALI further explicitly made clear that such recommendations concerning corporate practice were "not intended as legal rules, noncompliance with which would impose liability."[75]

As it turned out, however, the monitoring model quickly "became conventional wisdom, endorsed by the Chairman of the SEC, the corporate bar, and even the Business Roundtable."[76] Several key sources of best practice embraced the model. In 1978, for example, the American Bar Association's Section of Business Law promulgated a Corporate Director's Guidebook that embraced an Eisenberg-like model in which the management and monitoring of management roles were separated with the latter task being assigned to a board comprised mainly of

---

[74] Id. at § 3.07(a).
[75] See TD No. 2 at 83.
[76] Gordon, supra note 59, at 1518.

outside directors.[77] A formal statement by the Business Roundtable likewise adopted the monitoring model.[78]

The absorption of the monitoring model into generally accepted best practice continued throughout the 1990s.[79] By 1997, Eisenberg thus was able to declare that "key structural elements of the monitoring model—including a board that has at least a majority of independent directors, and audit, nominating, and compensation committees—[were] already well-established."[80] A board of directors' failure to comply with best practices is not a violation of corporate law, however, a point the Delaware Supreme Court has taken pains to drive home.[81]

E. CODIFYING THE MONITORING MODEL

The first steps towards transforming the monitoring model into law came in 1977 when the NYSE amended its listing standards to require the board of directors of a domestic listed company to have an audit committee comprised solely of directors independent of management. This requirement grew directly out of the same ferment that prompted the ALI to begin work on the *Principles*. As the SEC noted in approving the NYSE rule change, "support for audit committees independent of management" had grown "in the wake of recent revelations of questionable and illegal corporate payments."[82]

Finding the Monitoring Model in the Sarbanes-Oxley Act. After the Enron scandal broke, its board of directors appointed a special investigative committee whose report concluded that senior managers "were enriched, in the aggregate, by tens of millions of dollars they should never have received."[83] The report laid much of the blame at the feet of Enron's board of directors, which "failed . . . in its oversight duties" with "serious consequences for Enron, its employees, and its shareholders."[84] Unfortunately, Enron was not alone. As a NYSE report opined, the post-dotcom bubble period had seen a " 'meltdown' of significant companies

---

[77] ABA Section of Corporation, Banking and Business Law, Corporate Director's Guidebook, 33 Bus. Law. 1591, 1619–28 (1978).

[78] Statement of the Business Roundtable: The Role and Composition of the Board of Directors of the Large Publicly Owned Corporation, 33 Bus. Law. 2083 (1978).

[79] See Ira M. Millstein & Paul W. MacAvoy, The Active Board of Directors and Performance of the Large Publicly Traded Corporation, 98 Colum. L. Rev. 1283, 1288–89 (1998) (reviewing best practice guidelines).

[80] Melvin A. Eisenberg, The Board of Directors and Internal Control, 19 Cardozo L. Rev. 237, 239 (1997).

[81] See, e.g., Brehm v. Eisner, 746 A.2d 244, 256 (Del. 2000) ("Aspirational ideals of good corporate governance practices . . . are highly desirable, [and] often tend to benefit stockholders . . . . But they are not required by the corporation law and do not define standards of liability.").

[82] In re NYSE, Exchange Act Release No. 13,346, 11 SEC Docket 1945 (Mar. 9, 1977).

[83] William C. Powers, Jr., et al., Report of Investigation by the Special Investigative Committee of the Board of Directors of Enron Corp. 3 (Feb. 1, 2002).

[84] Id. at 22.

due to failures of diligence, ethics and controls" on the part of directors and senior managers.[85]

The Sarbanes-Oxley Act's legislative history makes clear that Congress shared these concerns. Pre-SOX congressional investigations regarding Enron and WorldCom, for example, "found that directors had extensive social and professional ties with corporate officers and their fellow directors that compromised their ability to be impartial and undermined their ability to provide an adequate check on directors' and officers' conduct."[86] Even the most cursory glance at the text of the statute, moreover, reveals a slew of new federal rules relating to corporate governance, including director and officer duties, responsibilities of auditors, and obligations for corporate lawyers, many of which were expressly intended to empower the board of directors—especially independent directors—vis-à-vis management.[87] Many of these provisions "seem designed to reduce conflicts of interest or interpersonal pressures in order to make it more likely that the directors will act as judgmental monitors of management rather than as reciprocating colleagues."[88] Still others "require directors to engage in processes that may increase their self-awareness and diligence, or because they increase the ability and incentives to directors to act diligently on behalf of public shareholders."[89]

Among the former are such mandates as a majority of independent directors on the board, an audit committee comprised solely of independent directors, new ethics codes and committee charters, and financial literacy requirements. Among the latter are provisions intended to redress the information asymmetry between management and the board, such as the new rules on the auditor-board and legal counsel-board relationships, and the board's new obligations with respect to internal controls. Viewed collectively, these provisions leave little doubt that Congress intended that the Sarbanes-Oxley Act change the dynamics that allegedly allowed independent board members to be mere management cuckolds. The monitoring model thus lies at the heart of the Sarbanes-Oxley Act.

Finding the Monitoring Model in Dodd-Frank. Unlike Sarbanes-Oxley, the Dodd-Frank back story is not one in which failures by Main Street boards of directors figure prominently. The statute nevertheless ended up including a number of governance provisions. Most of these

---

[85] NYSE, Corporate Governance Rule Proposals Reflecting Recommendations from the NYSE Corporate Accountability and Listing Standards Committee, as Approved by the NYSE Board of Directors (August 1, 2002).

[86] Lisa M. Fairfax, The Uneasy Case for the Inside Director, 96 Iowa L. Rev. 127, 149 (2010).

[87] See Larry E. Ribstein, Market vs. Regulatory Responses to Corporate Fraud: A Critique of the Sarbanes-Oxley Act of 2002, 28 J. Corp. L. 1, 26 (2002) (explaining that "corporate reformers have emphasized independent directors as a way to curb insider abuse").

[88] Robert Charles Clark, Corporate Governance Changes in the Wake of the Sarbanes-Oxley Act: A Morality Tale for the Policymakers Too, 22 Ga. St. U. L. Rev. 251, 267 (2005).

[89] Id.

were intended to empower shareholders at the expense of both boards and managers.

The requirement for independent compensation committees, for example, mandates longstanding best practices that emerged directly from Eisenberg's work on the monitoring model. The separation of the CEO and board chairman positions likewise is an outgrowth of that work. Perhaps most notably, Eisenberg's *The Structure of the Corporation* advocated as long ago as 1976 that shareholder access to the corporation's proxy machinery was a necessary corollary of the shareholders' undoubted right to nominate directors.[90] Dodd-Frank's proxy access provision provides the statutory framework for implementing that part of Eisenberg's model.

NOTE ON INTERNAL CONTROLS

Although internal control originated as an accounting concept, it evolved to take on a broader meaning. A 1949 American Institute of Certified Public Accountants (AICPA) committee report defined internal control as "the plan of organization and all of the coordinate methods and measures adopted within a business to safeguard its assets, check the accuracy and reliability of its accounting data, promote operational efficiency, and encourage adherence to prescribed managerial policies."[91]

By 1992, however, the Committee of Sponsoring Organizations of the Treadway Commission (COSO), a group comprised from five major accounting professional associations, issued a broader definition of internal control, which stated it is as "a process, effected by an entity's board of directors, management and other personnel, designed to provide reasonable assurance regarding the achievement of objectives" in the areas of "effectiveness and efficiency of operations, reliability of financial reporting, and compliance with applicable laws and regulations."[92] COSO further opined that internal control consists of five interrelated components: the control environment, risk assessment, control activities, information and communication, and monitoring. All five components must be functioning properly for the internal control to be deemed satisfactory.

In simpler terms, we can loosely divide internal controls into two main categories. First, preventative controls seek to deter misconduct and prevent errors or irregularities that could cause the organization to break the law, issue inaccurate or fraudulent disclosures, or otherwise fail to operate at maximum efficiency. Requiring two signatures for checks over a certain amount is a simple example of such a control. Second, curative controls seek to identify and remediate misconduct and errors that do occur. Auditing

---

[90]   Eisenberg, supra note 68, at 114.

[91]   American Institute of Certified Public Accountants Committee on Auditing Procedure, Internal Control—Elements of a Coordinated System and Its Importance to Management and the Independent Public Accountant 5, 6 (1949).

[92]   Committee of Sponsoring Organizations of the Treadway Commission, Internal Control—Integrated Framework 9 (1992).

expense accounts to identify personal expenditures is a simple example of a control in this category.

F. BOARDS TODAY

There seems little doubt that the monitoring model has influenced board behavior. In 1995, only one in eight CEOs was fired or resigned under board pressure. By 2006, however, almost a third of CEOs were terminated involuntarily.[93] Over the last several decades, the average CEO tenure has decreased, which also has been attributed to more active board oversight.[94] In sum, boards of directors, "which once served largely as rubber stamps for powerful CEOs, have become more independent, more powerful, and under more pressure to dump leaders who perform poorly."[95]

At the same time, however, directors themselves recognize that one size does not fit all. Instead, they understand their role to be much broader than mere monitoring. According to a survey by the National Association of Corporate Directors (NACD), for example, boards believe their key roles include such issues as planning for CEO succession, strategic business planning, and risk management.[96]

Whatever boards do, they are spending more time doing it. The average number of board meetings per year increased from seven in 1998 to nine in 2008.[97] The average number of board committee meetings likewise increased significantly after Sarbanes-Oxley became law in 2002.[98] More meetings, of course, meant more time and, presumably, effort. A 2005 survey found that directors spent an average of more than 200 hours per year on firm business, which was a significant increase from the 100 to 150 hours per year typical of boards prior to the passage of Sarbanes-Oxley.[99] A closer look at the data is even more informative. A 2006 survey found that prior to Sarbanes-Oxley, 66 percent of board members reported they worked less than 200 hours per year on firm business. After Sarbanes-Oxley became law, 65 percent of board members reported working more than 200 hours per year and 30 percent claimed to work more than 300 hours per year on firm business.[100] At the

---

[93]   Chuck Lucier et al., The Era of the Inclusive Leader, Strategy & Bus., Summer 2007, at 3.

[94]   Denis B.K. Lyons, CEO Casualties: A Battlefront Report, Directors & Boards, Summer 1999, at 43.

[95]   Lauren Etter, Why Corporate Boardrooms Are in Turmoil, Wall St. J., Sept. 16, 2006, at A7.

[96]   Nat'l Ass'n Corp. Directors, Public Company Governance Survey (2008).

[97]   Report of the Task Force of the ABA Section of Business Law Corporate Governance Committee on Delineation of Governance Roles and Responsibilities, 65 Bus. Law. 107, 130–31 (2009) (footnotes omitted).

[98]   James S. Linck et al., Effects and Unintended Consequences of the Sarbanes-Oxley Act on Corporate Boards (May 16, 2006).

[99]   Ed Speidel & Rob Surdel, High Technology Board Compensation, Boardroom Briefing, Spring 2008, at 25.

[100]   Peter D. Hart Research Associates, A Survey of Corporate Directors (Feb. 2006).

same time, the average number of boards on which directors serve has declined post-SOX.[101]

While the data do not establish a causal relationship, they do suggest at least a correlation between the passage of Sarbanes-Oxley and the time commitment required of board members. Much of the additional time appears to be devoted to oversight activities, which is consistent with the assumption that the Sarbanes-Oxley Act reinforced the monitoring model's influence. If so, the additional time and effort being expended by directors may have important costs. Recall the risk that monitoring can morph into unproductive adversarial conflict between boards and management. As Peter Wallison observes, the "congressional imprimatur" Sarbanes-Oxley put on the monitoring model therefore "may have set up an adversarial relationship between managements and boards that will, over time, impair corporate risk-taking and thus economic growth."[102]

Even if a firm's board and management maintain an appropriately balanced relationship, the additional time and effort elicited by the Sarbanes-Oxley Act may not be directed productively. Wallison argues that boards today "are more focused on compliance with standards and regulations than they are on obtaining a competitive advantage."[103] If directors in fact are spending much of their time complying with their obligations under the Sarbanes-Oxley Act and much of the rest overseeing the corporation's compliance with Sarbanes-Oxley, there is comparatively less time available for the board to spend on its traditional functions.

It thus may not be unreasonable to speculate that the unrelenting need to focus on compliance post-SOX may have contributed in some small measure to the financial crisis at the end of the decade. Financial institution directors distracted by the emphasis on internal controls and disclosure may have let slide tasks like risk management oversight. If so, the law of unintended consequences will truly have claimed an epic victim.

QUESTIONS

1.   Which of the following functions is typically carried out by modern boards and which by the top managers?

    A.   Approving strategic decisions.

    B.   Approving the company's budget.

    C.   Monitors the performance of the CEO.

    D.   Monitors the performance of members of the C-suite other than the CEO.

---

[101]   Linck et al., supra note 98, at 16–17.

[102]   Peter J. Wallison, Capital Punishment, Wall St. J., Nov. 4–5, 2006, at A7.

[103]   Id.

E.   Developing strategic decisions.

F.   Implements corporate strategy.

2.   What is the difference between monitoring and managing?

3.   Why do people want to be on boards of directors? What are the personal and professional benefits of being on a corporate board?

4.   What qualities, skills, knowledge, and values would be appropriate for a candidate to join a corporate board of directors?

5.   What advantages, if any, would be provided by board term limits? What disadvantages, if any, would be result from board term limits?

6.   Twelve has often been regarded as an optimal number for decision making groups. In the federal system and those of most states, for example, juries have 12 members. Indeed, twelve is the number that many "deliberative democrats argue is the optimal size for meaningful deliberation."[104] Is twelve also an optimal size for corporate boards? If so, why does the law not mandate that all boards have twelve members?

7.   How are the advantages of group versus individual decision making pertinent to the board's monitoring function?

To assess your understanding of the material in this chapter, click here to take a quiz.

---

[104] Robyn Eckersley, Moving Forward in the Climate Negotiations: Multilateralism or Minilateralism?, 12 Global Envtl. Pol., May 2012, at 35.

CHAPTER 3

DIRECTOR INDEPENDENCE

Corporate statutes historically required that directors be shareholders of the corporation and, under some statutes, residents of the state of incorporation. Today these requirements have largely disappeared. DGCL § 141(b) mandates no qualifications for board membership, nor does MBCA § 8.02. Critics of state corporate law therefore have complained that it is both descriptively and normatively deficient because state corporate codes do so little to define either the composition or function of the board, its committees, and its subordinates.

As the monitoring model came to dominate thinking about the board's role, reforming the rules governing the board's composition inevitably became the subject of much debate. A board comprised of insiders is poorly positioned to monitor the CEO. Research on group decision making shows that in mixed status groups, higher status persons talk more than lower status members.[1] Managers, for example, talk more than subordinates in business meetings. Such disparities result in higher status group members being more inclined to propound initiatives and having greater influence over the group's ultimate decision. Group dynamics thus help ensure the CEO's dominance over inside directors. As a practical matter, moreover, the CEO typically served as the chairman of the board, giving him substantial control over both the selection of new directors and the board's agenda. Not surprisingly, director independence therefore is a longstanding goal of corporate reformers, especially those affiliated with the monitoring model school of thought.

Even before the Sarbanes-Oxley Act and the concomitant stock exchange listing standard changes mandated that most public companies have a majority independent board, the increasing emphasis on monitoring contributed to a long-term decline the percentage of insiders on boards.

---

[1]   Sara Kiesler and Lee Sproul, Group Decision Making and Communication Technology, 52 Org. Beh. & Human Decision Processes 96 (1992).

Year	Mean Percentage of Inside Directors	Decade to Decade % Change
1950	49%	
1955	47%	
1960	43%	−12%
1965	42%	
1970	41%	−5%
1975	39%	
1980	33%	−20%
1985	30%	
1990	26%	−21%
1995	21%	
2000	16%	−38%

Table 1. **Change in Percentage of Inside Directors 1950–2000.** Source: Jeffrey N. Gordon, The Rise of Independent Directors in the United States, 1950–2005: Of Shareholder Value and Stock Market Prices, 59 Stanford Law Review 1465, 1473 n.9 (2007). Used by permission of Jeffrey N. Gordon and the Board of Trustees of the Leland Stanford Junior University.

As we'll see below, the trend towards director independence accelerated even further with the adoption of SOX and Dodd-Frank in 2002 and 2010, respectively, because both contained new mandates requiring increased director independence.

A. STATE LAW

State corporation statutes are silent on the issue of board composition. Issues such as board size, director qualifications, and independence are left to private ordering. If state statutory law were all that mattered, firms would thus be free to select the board structure and composition optimal to their unique circumstances.

The state common law of corporations, however, provides some incentives for corporations to include at least some independent directors on the board. It has long been the case, for example, that approval of related party and other conflicted interest transactions by vote of a majority of the disinterested and independent directors effectively immunizes such transactions from judicial review by invoking the defendant-friendly business judgment rule as the standard of review.[2] In connection with going private transactions initiated by a controlling

---

[2]   Marciano v. Nakash, 535 A.2d 400, 405 n.3 (Del. 1987) (opining that "approval by fully-informed disinterested directors under section 144(a)(1) . . . permits invocation of the business judgment rule and limits judicial review to issues of gift or waste with the burden of proof upon the party attacking the transaction").

shareholder, the Delaware Supreme Court called upon boards to create "an independent negotiating committee of its outside directors to deal with [the buyer] at arm's length."[3] Indeed, the Court went on to equate "fairness in this context" to the conduct that might be expected from "a theoretical, wholly independent, board of directors acting upon the matter before them." Similarly, with respect to antitakeover defenses, the Court has held that the validity of such defenses is "materially enhanced ... where, as here, a majority of the board favoring the proposal consisted of outside independent directors."[4] Taken together with similar decisions in other areas of corporate law, these judicially created safe harbors provide substantial incentives for both boards and managers to favor director independence.

But what constitutes independence?

The *Sanchez* case excerpted below arose in the context of derivative litigation. We will discuss derivative litigation in somewhat greater detail below. For now, suffice it to say that when plaintiffs file derivative suits on behalf of the corporations in which they are investors, the shareholder-plaintiffs often opt not to make demand on the corporation's board of director before filing suit. Although demand is required both by statute and civil procedure rules, plaintiffs often argue that it should be excused as futile. In *Aronson v. Lewis*[5] and its progeny, the Delaware Supreme Court laid out a two-pronged test for determining whether demand should be excused, which requires "that the plaintiff allege particularized facts creating a reason to doubt that '(1) the directors are disinterested and independent [or that] (2) the challenged transaction was otherwise the product of a valid exercise of business judgment.' "[6] It was the independence prong that was at issue in *Sanchez*.

Until recently, the test for whether someone was independent of the alleged wrongdoer focused almost exclusively on the nature and extent of the business relationships between them.[7] The trouble with a standard that focuses exclusively on business relationships is that it fails to capture the myriad of other ways in which individuals can be biased towards others. Many nominally independent directors have full-time jobs as executives at other firms or as partners in business service companies such as law firms or financial institutions. Directors tend to be white males, educated at top 20 schools, and share a host of other social ties. When their fellow directors get into trouble, the reaction of

---

[3]   Weinberger v. UOP, Inc., 457 A.2d 701, 709 n.7 (Del. 1983).

[4]   Moran v. Household Intern., Inc., 500 A.2d 1346, 1356 (Del. 1985).

[5]   473 A.2d 805 (Del.1984).

[6]   Wood v. Baum, 953 A.2d 136, 140 (Del. 2008).

[7]   See Abrams v. Koether, 766 F.Supp. 237, 256 (D.N.J.1991) (holding that, under Delaware law, demand was not excused despite the fact that the directors would have to sue "their friends, family and business associates").

these nominally independent directors may be one of leniency, motivated by a " 'there but for the grace of God go I' empathy."[8]

The problem is not just one of undue empathy, however. Social ties have a deterrent effect on director behavior that can be just as important, if not more so, than economic relationships. As then-Delaware Vice Chancellor Leo Strine observed:

> [C]orporate directors are generally the sort of people deeply enmeshed in social institutions. Such institutions have norms, expectations that, explicitly and implicitly, influence and channel the behavior of those who participate in their operation. Some things are "just not done," or only at a cost, which might not be so severe as a loss of position, but may involve a loss of standing in the institution. In being appropriately sensitive to this factor, our law also cannot assume-absent some proof of the point-that corporate directors are, as a general matter, persons of unusual social bravery, who operate heedless to the inhibitions that social norms generate for ordinary folk.[9]

Delaware County Employees
Retirement Fund v. Sanchez
124 A.3d 1017 (Del. 2015)

I.   INTRODUCTION

. . . In this case, the plaintiffs pled not only that the director had a close friendship of over half a century with the interested party, but that consistent with that deep friendship, the director's primary employment (and that of his brother) was as an executive of a company over which the interested party had substantial influence. These, and other facts of a similar nature, when taken together, support an inference that the director could not act independently of the interested party. Because of that, the plaintiffs pled facts supporting an inference that a majority of the board who approved the interested transaction they challenged could not consider a demand impartially. . . .

II.   BACKGROUND

This case involves an appeal from a complicated transaction between a private company whose equity is wholly owned by the family of A.R. Sanchez, Jr., Sanchez Resources, LLC (hereinafter, the "Private Sanchez Company"), and a public company in which the Sanchez family constitutes the largest stockholder bloc with some 16% of the shares and that is dependent on the Private Sanchez Company for all of its management services, Sanchez Energy Corporation (the "Sanchez Public Company"). The transaction at issue required the Sanchez Public Company to pay $78 million to: i) help the Private Sanchez Company buy

---

[8]   Zapata Corp. v. Maldonado, 430 A.2d 779, 787 (Del. 1981).

[9]   In re Oracle Corp. Derivative Litigation, 824 A.2d 917, 938 (Del. Ch. 2003).

out the interests of a private equity investor; ii) acquire an interest in certain properties with energy-producing potential from the Private Sanchez Company; iii) facilitate the joint production of 80,000 acres of property between the Sanchez Private and Public Companies; and iv) fund a cash payment of $14.4 million to the Private Sanchez Company. In this derivative action, the plaintiffs allege that this transaction involved a gross overpayment by the Sanchez Public Company, which unfairly benefited the Private Sanchez Company by allowing it to use the Sanchez Public Company's funds to buy out their private equity partner, obtain a large cash payment for itself, and obtain a contractual right to a lucrative royalty stream that was unduly favorable to the Private Sanchez Company and thus unfairly onerous to the Sanchez Public Company. As to the latter, the plaintiffs allege that the royalty payment was not only unfair, but was undisclosed to the Sanchez Public Company stockholders, and that it was the Sanchez family's desire to conceal the royalty obligation that led to what can be fairly described as a convoluted transaction structure.

. . . The parties agree that two of the five directors on the Sanchez Public Company board were not disinterested in the transaction: A.R. Sanchez, Jr., the Public Company's Chairman; and his son, Antonio R. Sanchez, III, the Sanchez Public Company's President and CEO. For the sake of clarity, we refer to the patriarch of the Sanchez family, A.R. Sanchez, Jr., as Chairman Sanchez.

The question for *Aronson* purposes was therefore whether the plaintiffs had pled particularized facts raising a pleading-stage doubt about the independence of one of the other Sanchez Public Company directors. . . .

III. ANALYSIS

. . .

The closest question below centered on director Alan Jackson. The complaint bases its challenge to Jackson's independence on two related grounds. First, it pleads that "[Chairman] Sanchez and Jackson have been close friends for more than five decades." Consistent with this allegation, the complaint indicates that when Chairman Sanchez ran for Governor of Texas in 2012, Jackson donated $12,500 to his campaign.

Second, the complaint pleads facts supporting an inference that Jackson's personal wealth is largely attributable to business interests over which Chairman Sanchez has substantial influence. According to the complaint, Jackson's full-time job and primary source of income is as an executive at IBC Insurance Agency, Ltd. IBC Insurance provides insurance brokerage services to the Sanchez Public Company and other Sanchez affiliates. But even more importantly, IBC Insurance is a wholly owned subsidiary of International Bancshares Corporation ("IBC"), a company of which Chairman Sanchez is the largest stockholder and a director who IBC's board has determined is not independent under the

NASDAQ Marketplace Rules. Not only does Jackson work full-time for
IBC Insurance, so too does his brother. Both of them service the work
that IBC Insurance does for the Sanchez Public and Private Companies.
The complaint also alleges that the approximately $165,000 Jackson
earned as a Sanchez Public Company director constituted "30–40% of
Jackson's total income for 2012."

The plaintiffs contend that these pled facts support an inference that
Jackson cannot act independently of Chairman Sanchez . . . .

. . . [O]ur law requires that all the pled facts regarding a director's
relationship to the interested party be considered in full context in
making the, admittedly imprecise, pleading stage determination of
independence. . . .

Here, the plaintiffs did not plead the kind of thin social-circle
friendship, for want of a better way to put it, which was at issue in *Beam*.*
In that case, we held that allegations that directors "moved in the same
social circles, attended the same weddings, developed business
relationships before joining the board, and described each other as
'friends,' . . . are insufficient, without more, to rebut the presumption of
independence."[22] In saying that, we did not suggest that deeper human
friendships could not exist that would have the effect of compromising a
director's independence. When, as here, a plaintiff has pled that a
director has been close friends with an interested party for a half century,
the plaintiff has pled facts quite different from those at issue in *Beam*.
Close friendships of that duration are likely considered precious by many
people, and are rare. People drift apart for many reasons, and when a
close relationship endures for that long, a pleading stage inference arises
that it is important to the parties.

The plaintiffs did not rely simply on that proposition, however. They
pled facts regarding the economic relations of Jackson and Chairman
Sanchez that buttress their contention that they are confidantes and that
there is a reasonable doubt that Jackson can act impartially in a matter
of economic importance to Sanchez personally. It may be that it is
entirely coincidental that Jackson's full-time job is as an executive at a
subsidiary of a corporation over which Chairman Sanchez has
substantial influence, as the largest stockholder, director, and the
Chairman of an important source of brokerage work. It may be that it is
also coincidental that Jackson's brother also works there. It may be
coincidental that Jackson and his brother both work on insurance
brokerage work for the Sanchez Public and Private Companies there.
And it may be coincidental that Jackson finds himself a director of the
Sanchez Public Company. But rather certainly, there arises a pleading

---

*   [Ed.: Beam ex rel. Martha Stewart Living Omnimedia, Inc. v. Stewart, 845 A.2d 1040
(Del. 2004).]

[22]   *Beam*, 845 A.2d at 1051; see also id. at 1051–52 ("Mere allegations that they move in
the same business and social circles, *or* a characterization that they are close friends, is not
enough to negate independence for demand excusal purposes.") (emphasis added).

stage inference that Jackson's economic positions derive in large measure from his 50-year close friendship with Chairman Sanchez, and that he is in these positions because Sanchez trusts, cares for, and respects him.[24] If that is true, there is of course nothing wrong with that. Human relationships of that kind are valuable. In this context, however, where the question is whether the plaintiffs have met their pleading burden to plead facts suggesting that Jackson cannot act independently of Chairman Sanchez, these obvious inferences that arise from the pled facts require that the defendants' motion to dismiss be denied. . . .

NOTES AND QUESTIONS

1.   Would the *Sanchez* court have treated Jackson as independent if he and Chairman Sanchez had simply shared their long-term friendship without any of the business relationships that also bound the two? Should it do so?

2.   In *Sandys v. Pincus*,[10] the Court concluded that director Ellen Siminoff was not independent of defendant Mark Pincus:

> The Siminoff and Pincus families own an airplane together. . . . [O]wning an airplane together is not a common thing, and suggests that the Pincus and Siminoff families are extremely close to each other and are among each other's most important and intimate friends. Co-ownership of a private plane involves a partnership in a personal asset that is not only very expensive, but that also requires close cooperation in use, which is suggestive of detailed planning indicative of a continuing, close personal friendship. In fact, it is suggestive of the type of very close personal relationship that, like family ties, one would expect to heavily influence a human's ability to exercise impartial judgment.

In a footnote, the Court favorably cited *In re MFW S'holders Litig.*,[11] which explained that a friendship in which "the parties had served as each other's maids of honor, had been each other's college roommates, shared a beach house with their families each summer for a decade, and are as thick as blood relations," differs significantly from one in which the parties "occasionally

---

[24]   On a motion to dismiss in *Harbor Financial Partners v. Huizenga*, the defendants argued that the brother-in-law of the CEO and Chairman should be deemed to be an independent director because the plaintiffs had not pled facts that the brothers-in-law were in fact loving family members. Harbor Fin. Partners v. Huizenga, 751 A.2d 879, 886–87 (Del. Ch.1999). The Court of Chancery rejected that argument for two reasons. First, it noted that there was not only a familial relationship between the CEO and the brother-in-law, but a business one, and that the fact that the brother-in-law was on not just the board of the company that was the focus of the litigation, but others controlled by the CEO, supported a pleading stage inference that the two were in fact close. Id. at 889. In so ruling, the Court noted that it remained the rule that plaintiffs were entitled to have reasonable inferences drawn in their favor from the pled facts. Id. Second, the Court of Chancery noted that there were limits to the extent to which a plaintiff could use books and records to explore such a relationship between a director and an interested party before filing: "In this regard, one wonders how a plaintiff could use tools such as 8 Del. C. § 220 or public filings to generate such facts." Id. at 889 n.32.

[10]   152 A.3d 124 (Del. 2016).

[11]   67 A.3d 496, 509 n.37 (Del. Ch. 2013), aff'd sub nom. Kahn v. M & F Worldwide Corp., 88 A.3d 635 (Del. 2014).

had dinner over the years, go to some of the same parties and gatherings annually, and call themselves 'friends.' ''

3.   The determination of whether directors are independent of the defendants is typically made on the pleadings before the plaintiff has had the benefit of discovery. How then might plaintiff determine whether the director and defendant share a sufficiently close friendship or economic relationship?

4.   A director will not be deemed independent if the wrongdoer has the power to deprive the director of a material benefit, but the fact that "a director sits on a controlled company board is not, and cannot of course, be determinative of director independence at the pleading stage, as that would make the question of independence tautological." *Sandys v. Pincus*, 152 A.3d 124, 133 (Del. 2016). Does that seem sensible?

5.   Is there a difference between a director who is disinterested and one who is independent?

PROBLEMS

1.   Dana Whitaker is a director of Quo Vadimus, Inc. ("QV"), and its founder, chairman, chief executive officer, and its majority shareholder. QV owns and operates a cable sports network. QV has approximately 1 billion shares of stock outstanding. Assess whether the following individuals would be deemed independent under state law.

    A.   Isaac Jaffe is a director of QV and its president and chief operating officer. Last year QV paid Jaffe a director's fee of $200,000, a salary as president and CEO of $700,000, a $280,000 employment bonus, and granted him options for 130,000 shares. Jaffe and Whitaker are longtime personal friends. Their spouses are also best friends who play golf together every Saturday. Whitaker and Jaffe frequently vacation with one another and their families. When Jaffe contracted suffered a stroke some years ago, Whitaker visited him in the hospital daily. In addition, they meet for coffee at least once a week and lunch at least once a month.

> **WHAT'S THAT?**
>
> CHIEF OPERATING OFFICER, Black's Law Dictionary (10th ed. 2014): A manager who supervises a company's day-to-day operations and who usu. reports to the chief executive officer. — Abbr. COO.

    B.   Casey McCall is a director of QV and the host of Sports Hour, QV's top-rated and flagship program. McCall receives a director's fee of $200,000 per year. He also receives $5 million per year in his capacity as a QV employee.

    C.   Dan Rydell is a director of QV but has no other ties to the company. Rydell went to college with Allen Grubman. Grubman now serves as both Whitaker and Rydell's personal tax lawyer. They occasionally encounter one another at social events. Most recently, in November of last year, Rydell attended a wedding reception hosted by Grubman for his daughter, who was marrying Whitaker's nephew, at which Whitaker was present.

D.   Jeremy Goodwin is a director of QV and serves as chair of QV's Board of Directors Compensation Committee, which sets Whitaker's salary. Goodwin is the former dean of the University of Burbank School of Law and is currently President of the University of Burbank. Whitaker's undergraduate degree is from Burbank and she also has a joint J.D./M.B.A. degree from Burbank. Over the years, Whitaker has encouraged QV's board of directors to make substantial contributions to Burbank. Over the last five years, QV's contributions to Burbank have averaged $10 million per year, amounting to five percent of Burbank's annual donations, and representing ten percent of QV's annual charitable giving. Burbank has an annual budget of $1.5 billion.

2.   Natalie Hurley is the founder, CEO, and Chair of the Board of Directors of Acme, Inc. Hurley owns approximately10% of the company's stock. Acme's principal asset is a chain of stores selling inexpensive ready-to-wear clothing. You are Acme's general counsel. The board has asked you to advise them as to which of the following directors, if any, are not independent of Hurley.

A.   Marty Martinez is the President and CEO of Supplier, Inc., which manufactures inexpensive ready-to-wear clothing. Acme is Supplier's biggest customer. Over the last five years, Acme has purchased on average 55% of Supplier's output. Martinez is a director of Acme but has no other relationship with Hurley or Acme.

B.   Randy Redstone is the President and Chief Operating Officer of Phoenix Real Estate Investment Trust. Phoenix owns shopping centers and rents stores therein to companies like Acme. About five prevent of Acme's stores are located in Phoenix malls. Phoenix receives about three percent of its annual revenues in rent from Acme. Hurley sits on the board of Phoenix and serves as the Chair of Phoenix's Compensation Committee, which sets the compensation for top Phoenix managers, including Redstone.

B. STOCK EXCHANGE LISTING STANDARDS

NYSE listing standards require that all listed companies "must have a majority of independent directors.[12] In addition, as we will see below, the NYSE has mandated the use of several board committees consisting of independent directors. Finally, the NYSE's Listed Company Manual provides that: "To empower non-management directors to serve as a more effective check on management, the non-management directors of each

---

[12]   NYSE Listed Company Manual § 303A.01.

listed company must meet at regularly scheduled executive sessions without management."[13] The listed company's Form 10-K must disclose the identity of the independent director who chairs the mandatory executive sessions. Although the rule does not indicate how many times per year the outside directors must meet to satisfy this requirement, emerging best practice suggests that there should be such a meeting held in conjunction with every regularly scheduled meeting of the entire board of directors.

The NASDAQ standard is substantially similar. One wrinkle is that NASDAQ expressly states an expectation that executive sessions of the outside directors will be held at least twice a year. Note that both the NYSE and NADAQ exempt controlled companies—those in which a shareholder or group of shareholders acting together control 50 percent or more of the voting power of the company's stock—from the obligation to have a majority independent board.

NOTE ON STOCK EXCHANGE LISTING STANDARDS

Listing of a company's equity securities for trading on a prestigious stock market, such as the NYSE, confers significant benefits on the company and its management. The greater liquidity of listed securities relative to those sold in the over-the counter (OTC) market reduces listed issuers' cost of capital. Listing also confers considerable prestige on the firm and its managers. Listed companies therefore desire to remain so, while many unlisted firms pursue eligibility for listing as their primary goal. By virtue of their power to set listing standards with which listed companies must comply, the exchanges thus wield considerable power over the governance of public corporations. Indeed, in many respects, many of the mandatory details of corporate governance now come from exchange listing standards rather than the more vague and enabling state law.

Listing standards are subject to approval by the SEC under § 19(b) of the Securities Exchange Act of 1934, as amended. 15 U.S.C. § 78s (2001). In addition, by virtue of the unique relationship between the SEC and the exchanges, the Commission naturally exercises considerable informal influence over exchange rulemaking. The late Donald Schwartz aptly referred to this influence as the SEC's "raised eyebrow" power.[14]

NYSE Listed Company Manual § 303A.02
Independence Tests

(a)(i)   No director qualifies as "independent" unless the board of directors affirmatively determines that the director has no material relationship with the listed company (either directly or as

---

[13]   Id., § 303A.03.

[14]   Donald E. Schwartz, Federalism and Corporate Governance, 45 Ohio St. L.J. 545, 571 (1984). In the mid-1990s, the SEC used that power to coerce the exchanges into adopting uniform voting rights listing standards. See Stephen M. Bainbridge, Revisiting the One-Share/One-Vote Controversy: The Exchanges' Uniform Voting Rights Policy, 22 Sec. Reg. L.J. 175, 183–86 (1994) (criticizing the role played by SEC Chairman Arthur Levitt in the exchanges' adoption of voting rights listing standards).

a partner, shareholder or officer of an organization that has a relationship with the company).

(ii) In addition, in affirmatively determining the independence of any director who will serve on the compensation committee of the listed company's board of directors, the board of directors must consider all factors specifically relevant to determining whether a director has a relationship to the listed company which is material to that director's ability to be independent from management in connection with the duties of a compensation committee member, including, but not limited to:

(A) the source of compensation of such director, including any consulting, advisory or other compensatory fee paid by the listed company to such director; and

(B) whether such director is affiliated with the listed company, a subsidiary of the listed company or an affiliate of a subsidiary of the listed company.

Commentary: It is not possible to anticipate, or explicitly to provide for, all circumstances that might signal potential conflicts of interest, or that might bear on the materiality of a director's relationship to a listed company (references to "listed company" would include any parent or subsidiary in a consolidated group with the listed company). Accordingly, it is best that boards making "independence" determinations broadly consider all relevant facts and circumstances. In particular, when assessing the materiality of a director's relationship with the listed company, the board should consider the issue not merely from the standpoint of the director, but also from that of persons or organizations with which the director has an affiliation. Material relationships can include commercial, industrial, banking, consulting, legal, accounting, charitable and familial relationships, among others. However, as the concern is independence from management, the Exchange does not view ownership of even a significant amount of stock, by itself, as a bar to an independence finding.

When considering the sources of a director's compensation in determining his independence for purposes of compensation committee service, the board should consider whether the director receives compensation from any person or entity that would impair his ability to make independent judgments about the listed company's executive compensation. Similarly, when considering any affiliate relationship a director has with the company, a subsidiary of the company, or an affiliate of a subsidiary of the company, in determining his independence for purposes of compensation committee service, the board should consider whether the affiliate relationship places the director under the direct or indirect control of the listed company or its senior management, or creates a direct relationship between the director and members of senior management, in each case of a nature that would impair his ability to make independent judgments about the listed company's executive compensation.

Disclosure Requirement: The listed company must comply with the disclosure requirements set forth in Item 407(a) of Regulation S–K.

(b)   In addition, a director is not independent if:

(i)   The director is, or has been within the last three years, an employee of the listed company, or an immediate family member is, or has been within the last three years, an executive officer, 1 of the listed company.

Commentary: Employment as an interim Chairman or CEO or other executive officer shall not disqualify a director from being considered independent following that employment.

(ii)   The director has received, or has an immediate family member who has received, during any twelve-month period within the last three years, more than $120,000 in direct compensation from the listed company, other than director and committee fees and pension or other forms of deferred compensation for prior service (provided such compensation is not contingent in any way on continued service).

Commentary: Compensation received by a director for former service as an interim Chairman or CEO or other executive officer need not be considered in determining independence under this test. Compensation received by an immediate family member for service as an employee of the listed company (other than an executive officer) need not be considered in determining independence under this test.

(iii)   (A) The director is a current partner or employee of a firm that is the listed company's internal or external auditor; (B) the director has an immediate family member who is a current partner of such a firm; (C) the director has an immediate family member who is a current employee of such a firm and personally works on the listed company's audit; or (D) the director or an immediate family member was within the last three years a partner or employee of such a firm and personally worked on the listed company's audit within that time.

(iv)   The director or an immediate family member is, or has been with the last three years, employed as an executive officer of another company where any of the listed company's present executive officers at the same time serves or served on that company's compensation committee.

(v)   The director is a current employee, or an immediate family member is a current executive officer, of a company that has made payments to, or received payments from, the listed company for property or services in an amount which, in any of the last three fiscal years, exceeds the greater of $1 million, or 2% of such other company's consolidated gross revenues.

Commentary: In applying the test in Section 303A.02(b)(v), both the payments and the consolidated gross revenues to be measured shall be those reported in the last completed fiscal year of such other company. The look-back provision for this test applies solely to the financial relationship between the listed company and the director or immediate family member's current employer; a listed company need not consider former employment of the director or immediate family member.

Disclosure Requirement: Contributions to tax exempt organizations shall not be considered payments for purposes of Section 303A.02(b)(v), provided however that a listed company shall disclose either on or through its website or in its annual proxy statement, or if the listed company does not file an annual proxy statement, in the listed company's annual report on Form 10-K filed with the SEC, any such contributions made by the listed company to any tax exempt organization in which any independent director serves as an executive officer if, within the preceding three years, contributions in any single fiscal year from the listed company to the organization exceeded the greater of $1 million, or 2% of such tax exempt organization's consolidated gross revenues. If this disclosure is made on or through the listed company's website, the listed company must disclose that fact in its annual proxy statement or annual report, as applicable, and provide the website address. Listed company boards are reminded of their obligations to consider the materiality of any such relationship in accordance with Section 303A.02(a) above.

General Commentary to Section 303A.02(b): An "immediate family member" includes a person's spouse, parents, children, siblings, mothers and fathers-in-law, sons and daughters-in-law, brothers and sisters-in-law, and anyone (other than domestic employees) who shares such person's home. When applying the look-back provisions in Section 303A.02(b), listed companies need not consider individuals who are no longer immediate family members as a result of legal separation or divorce, or those who have died or become incapacitated.

In addition, references to the "listed company" or "company" include any parent or subsidiary in a consolidated group with the listed company or such other company as is relevant to any determination under the independent standards set forth in this Section 303A.02(b).

Schedule 14A, the SEC's proxy statement disclosure form, requires that the issuer include in its annual proxy statement the information required in Reg S–K Item 407(a).

Regulation S–K Item 407

(a) Director independence. Identify each director and, when the disclosure called for by this paragraph is being presented in a proxy or information statement relating to the election of directors, each nominee for director, that is independent under the independence standards applicable to the registrant under paragraph (a)(1) of this Item. In addition, if such independence standards contain independence requirements for committees of the board of directors, identify each director that is a member of the compensation, nominating or audit committee that is not independent under such committee independence standards. If the registrant does not have a separately designated audit, nominating or compensation committee or committee performing similar functions, the registrant must provide the disclosure of directors that are not independent with respect to all members of the board of directors applying such committee independence standards.

(1) In determining whether or not the director or nominee for director is independent for the purposes of paragraph (a) of this Item, the registrant shall use the applicable definition of independence, as follows:

> **WHAT'S THAT?**
>
> Regulation S–K (a.k.a. Reg S–K) is a set of standard instructions for providing disclosures required by various SEC forms. Each instruction—which may have many subparts—is referred to as an Item. In this example, when counsel is preparing a proxy statement, the instructions for the form—Schedule 14A—direct counsel to include the information set out in paragraph (a) of Item 407.

(i) If the registrant is a listed issuer whose securities are listed on a national securities exchange or in an inter-dealer quotation system which has requirements that a majority of the board of directors be independent, the registrant's definition of independence that it uses for determining if a majority of the board of directors is independent in compliance with the listing standards applicable to the registrant. When determining whether the members of a committee of the board of directors are independent, the registrant's definition of independence that it uses for determining if the members of that specific committee are independent in compliance with the independence standards applicable for the members of the specific committee in the listing standards of the national securities exchange or inter-dealer quotation system that the registrant uses for determining if a majority of the board of directors are independent. If the registrant does not have independence standards for a committee, the independence standards for that specific committee in the listing standards of the national securities exchange or inter-dealer quotation system that the registrant uses for determining if a majority of the board of directors are independent.

(ii) If the registrant is not a listed issuer, a definition of independence of a national securities exchange or of an inter-dealer quotation system which has requirements that a majority of the board of directors be independent, and state which definition is used. Whatever such definition the registrant chooses, it must use the same definition with respect to all directors and nominees for director. When determining whether the members of a specific committee of the board of directors are independent, if the national securities exchange or national securities association whose standards are used has independence standards for the members of a specific committee, use those committee specific standards.

(iii) If the information called for by paragraph (a) of this Item is being presented in a registration statement on Form S-1 (§ 239.11 of this chapter) under the Securities Act or on a Form 10 (§ 249.210 of this chapter) under the Exchange Act where the registrant has applied for listing with a national securities exchange or in an inter-dealer quotation system that has requirements that a majority of the board of directors be independent, the definition of independence that the registrant uses for determining if a majority of the board of directors is independent, and the definition of independence that the registrant uses for determining if members of the specific committee of the board of directors are independent, that is in compliance with the independence listing standards of the national securities exchange or inter-dealer quotation system on which it has applied for listing, or if the registrant has not adopted such definitions, the independence standards for determining if the majority of the board of directors is independent and if members of the committee of the board of directors are independent of that national securities exchange or inter-dealer quotation system.

(2) If the registrant uses its own definitions for determining whether its directors and nominees for director, and members of specific committees of the board of directors, are independent, disclose whether these definitions are available to security holders on the registrant's Web site. If so, provide the registrant's Web site address. If not, include a copy of these policies in an appendix to the registrant's proxy statement or information statement that is provided to security holders at least once every three fiscal years or if the policies have been materially amended since the beginning of the registrant's last fiscal year. If a current copy of the policies is not available to security holders on the registrant's Web site, and is not included as an appendix to the registrant's proxy statement or information statement, identify the most recent fiscal year in which the policies were so included in satisfaction of this requirement.

(3) For each director and nominee for director that is identified as independent, describe, by specific category or type, any transactions, relationships or arrangements not disclosed

pursuant to Item 404(a) (§ 229.404(a)), or for investment companies, Item 22(b) of Schedule 14A (§ 240.14a–101 of this chapter), that were considered by the board of directors under the applicable independence definitions in determining that the director is independent.

Instructions to Item 407(a). 1. If the registrant is a listed issuer whose securities are listed on a national securities exchange or in an inter-dealer quotation system which has requirements that a majority of the board of directors be independent, and also has exemptions to those requirements (for independence of a majority of the board of directors or committee member independence) upon which the registrant relied, disclose the exemption relied upon and explain the basis for the registrant's conclusion that such exemption is applicable. The same disclosure should be provided if the registrant is not a listed issuer and the national securities exchange or inter-dealer quotation system selected by the registrant has exemptions that are applicable to the registrant. Any national securities exchange or inter-dealer quotation system which has requirements that at least 50 percent of the members of a small business issuer's board of directors must be independent shall be considered a national securities exchange or inter-dealer quotation system which has requirements that a majority of the board of directors be independent for the purposes of the disclosure required by paragraph (a) of this Item.

2. Registrants shall provide the disclosure required by paragraph (a) of this Item for any person who served as a director during any part of the last completed fiscal year, except that no information called for by paragraph (a) of this Item need be given in a registration statement filed at a time when the registrant is not subject to the reporting requirements of section 13(a) or 15(d) of the Exchange Act (15 U.S.C. 78m(a) or 78o(d)) respecting any director who is no longer a director at the time of effectiveness of the registration statement.

3. The description of the specific categories or types of transactions, relationships or arrangements required by paragraph (a)(3) of this Item must be provided in such detail as is necessary to fully describe the nature of the transactions, relationships or arrangements.

PROBLEMS

1. Wolfgang is a world-famous chef. Wolfgang is a member of the board of directors of DAA, a publicly traded Hollywood talent agency. He is paid $200,000/year in directors fees and also receives $50,000 for each board and committee meeting he attends. DAA annually contributes $100,000 to a retirement fund for Wolfgang. Wolfgang annually cooks the meals for DAA's Oscar and Golden Globe parties, for which he is paid $125,000 plus expenses by DAA. Is Wolfgang independent of DAA?

A.   Wolfgang's domestic partner John is a chef who is employed by DAA to run the company's in-house cafeteria and is paid a salary of $125,000 plus expenses by DAA to develop menus for the company's in-house cafeteria. Is John independent of DAA? Does his relationship with John affect Wolfgang's independence status? Should DAA board have approved John's hiring anyway?

B.   Wolfgang's domestic partner John is an independent contractor who is paid $125,000 plus expenses by DAA to develop menus for the company's in-house cafeteria. Is John independent of DAA? Does his relationship with John affect Wolfgang's independence status? Should DAA board have approved John's hiring anyway?

C.   Would your answers to A or B change if John had his own residence?

2.   Sven is a director of Norse, Inc. Sven's daughter Ingrid is a junior human resources manager in the Swedish affiliate of PWC. PWC is Norse's independent auditor. Is Sven independent vis-à-vis Norse?

3.   Jane is a director of Ajax Corporation. Jane is also the CFO of Zeus Corporation. Donna is Ajax's CLO (a.k.a., general counsel), a member of Zeus' board of directors, and a member of Zeus' compensation committee. Is Jane independent vis-à-vis Ajax? Is Donna independent vis-à-vis Zeus?

4.   Over the years, Acme Corporation has frequently donated money to your alma mater, Big State University School of Business. In recent years, the amount in question consistently exceeded $1 million. Acme is considering adding the dean of BSU's business school to the board of directors. If appointed, will the Dean be independent under NYSE standards?

5.   Jane is a director of Acme Corporation. Jane is a partner with Dewey, Cheatem & Howe. DCH is Acme's principal outside law firm and Jane is its principal outside lawyer. In each of the last three years, DCH has billed Acme in excess of $5 million. Is Jane independent vis-à-vis Acme?

6.   Jane Hurley is the founder, CEO, and Chair of the Board of Directors of Acme, Inc. Hurley owns approximately 10% of the company's stock. Acme's principal asset is a chain of stores selling inexpensive ready-to-wear clothing. You are Acme's general counsel. The board has asked you to advise them as to which of the following directors, if any, are not independent of Hurley.

A.   Marty Martinez is the President and CEO of Supplier, Inc., which manufactures inexpensive ready-to-wear clothing. Acme is Supplier's biggest customer. Over the last five years, Acme has purchased on average 55% of Supplier's output. Martinez is a director of Acme but has no other relationship with Hurley or Acme.

B.   Randy Redstone is the President and Chief Operating Officer of Phoenix Real Estate Investment Trust. Phoenix owns shopping centers and rents stores therein to companies like

Acme. About five prevent of Acme's stores are located in
Phoenix malls. Phoenix receives about three percent of its
annual revenues in rent from Acme. Hurley sits on the board
of Phoenix and serves as the Chair of Phoenix's Compensation
Committee, which sets the compensation for top Phoenix
managers, including Redstone.

C. EVALUATING DIRECTOR INDEPENDENCE

As we have seen, the board of directors has three basic functions.
First, while boards rarely are involved in day-to-day operational decision
making, most boards have at least some managerial functions. Second,
the board provides networking and other services. Finally, the board
monitors and disciplines top management.

Independence is potentially relevant to all three board functions. As
to the former two, outside directors provide both their own expertise and
interlocks with diverse contact networks. As to the latter, at least
according to conventional wisdom, board independence is an important
device for constraining agency costs. On close examination, however,
neither rationale for board independence justifies the sort of one size fits
all mandates adopted by the exchanges at the behest of Congress and the
SEC.

Putting outside directors on the board can create valuable
relationships with a variety of potential strategic partners. This is
relevant not only to the board's resource gathering function, but also to
its monitoring and service functions. Complex business decisions require
knowledge in such areas as accounting, finance, management, and law.
Providing access to such knowledge is part of the board's resource
gathering function. Outside board members may either possess such
specialized knowledge themselves or have access to credible external
sources thereof.[15]

---

[15] Reliance on outside specialists is a rational response to bounded rationality. The expert
in a field makes the most of his limited capacity to absorb and master information by limiting
the amount of information that must be processed by limiting the breadth of the field in which
the expert specializes. As applied to the corporate context, more diverse boards with strong
outsider representation likely contain more specialists, and therefore should get greater benefits
from specialization.

Conversely, however, note that, because their decisions are publicly observable, board
members have a strong incentive to defer to expert opinion. Because even a good decision maker
is subject to the proverbial "act of God," the market for reputation evaluates decision makers by
looking at both the outcome and the action before forming a judgment. If a bad outcome occurs,
but the action was consistent with approved expert opinion, the hit to the decision maker's
reputation is reduced. In effect, by deferring to specialists, a decision maker operating under
conditions of bounded rationality is buying insurance against a bad outcome. In a collegial,
multi-actor setting, the potential for log rolling further encourages deference. A specialist in a
given field is far more likely to have strong feelings about the outcome of a particular case than
a non-expert. By deferring to the specialist, the non-expert may win the specialist's vote in other
cases as to which the non-expert has a stronger stake. Such log rolling need not be explicit,
although it doubtless is at least sometimes, but rather can be a form of the tit-for-tat cooperative
game. In board decision making, deference thus invokes a norm of reciprocation that allows the
non-expert to count on the specialist's vote on other matters.

Having said that, however, a full-time senior employee has important informational advantages over outsiders who devote but a small portion of their time and effort to the firm. At the minimum, the presence of outsiders on the board increases decision-making costs simply because the process takes longer. Outsiders need more information and are likely to take longer to persuade than are insiders. More subtly, and perhaps more importantly, long-term employees make significant investments in firm-specific human capital. Any employee who advances to senior management levels necessarily invests considerable time and effort in learning how to do his job more effectively. Much of this knowledge will be specific to the firm for which he works, such as when other firms do not do comparable work or his firm has a unique corporate culture. In either case, the longer he works for the firm, the more firm specific his human capital becomes. Such an employee is likely to make better decisions for the firm than an outsider, even assuming equal levels of information relating to the decision at hand. The insider can put the decision in a broader context, seeing the relationships and connections the decision has to the firm as whole.

Insider access to information is particularly significant due to the nature of decision making within large corporations. Recall that the corporation is a classic example of an authority-based decision-making structure characterized by the existence of a central agency to which all relevant information is transmitted and which is empowered to make decisions binding on the whole. Unlike many other organizations, the corporation's central agency is not a single autocrat, but rather a multi-member body—the board of directors—that usually functions by consensus. Put another way, the board of directors is best understood as a collegial body using consensus-based decision making. Because consensus works best where team members have equal information and comparable interests, insiders may find it easier to reach consensus than would a diverse body of outsiders. Insiders are more likely to have comparable access to information and similar interests than are outsiders. Insiders have many informal contacts within the organization, which both promote team formation and provide them with better access to information. Hence, insofar as efficient decision making is the goal of corporate governance, independence may not be desirable. To the contrary, these factors suggest that an all-insider board might be preferable.

Turning to the problem of ensuring accountability, corporate law provides a number of accountability mechanisms designed to constrain agency costs. Chief among them is the board of directors, especially the independent directors. To be sure, outsiders have neither the time nor the information necessary to be involved in the minutiae of day-to-day firm management. What outsiders can do, however, is monitor senior managers and replace those whose performance is sub-par. Accordingly, proponents of the monitoring model have always been among the strongest proponents of director independence.

It is not clear, however, why one would expect independent directors to be an effective constraint on shirking or self-dealing by management. Monitoring the performance of the firm's officers and employees is hard, time-consuming work. Moreover, most outside directors have full-time employment elsewhere, which commands the bulk of their attention and provides the bulk of their pecuniary and psychic income. Independent directors therefore may prefer leisure or working on their primary vocation to monitoring management.

Other factors impede an independent director from monitoring management, even if he wishes to do so. Although boards meet more often and longer now than they did pre-SOX, board meetings are still few and short relative to the amount of time insiders spend with one another. Moreover, outside directors are generally dependent upon management for information.

Collective action problems also impede the board's ability to effectively monitor and discipline managers. Even though faithful monitoring may be in an individual director's interest, he or she may assume that other directors will do the hard work of identifying sub-par performances, permitting the free rider to shirk. As in any free riding situation, this will tend to result in sub-optimal levels of monitoring. Even in cases of clearly sub-par management performance, moreover, other collective action problems may prevent the board from taking necessary remedial steps. Some director must step forward to begin building a majority in favor of replacing the incumbent managers, which again raises a free rider problem. Furthermore, if an active director steps forward, he or she must not only overcome the forces of inertia and bias, but also must likely do so in the face of active opposition from the threatened managers who will try to cut off the flow of information to the board, co-opt key board members, and otherwise undermine the disciplinary process. Board members are likely to have developed warm personal relationships with the CEO and other managers, who will in turn have cultivated that type of sentiment. Those relationships make it hard for boards to fire senior managers, especially when personal friendships of long standing are in play. Lastly, at some board members will have been responsible for hiring the managers and will need to make the cognitively difficult admission of their error in order to fire the managers.

Finally, the insiders may effectively control nominally independent directors. As we've seen, it has long been common practice for a corporation's outside directors to include lawyers and bankers (of both the investment and commercial varieties) who are currently providing services to the corporation or may wish to provide services in the future. University faculty or administrators, to take another common example, may be beholden to insiders who control corporate donations to their home institutions. None of these outsiders are likely to bite the hand that feeds them.

Even if the independent directors are not actually biased in favor of the insiders, moreover, they often are predisposed to favor the latter. As noted above, outside directors tend to be corporate officers or retirees who share the same views and values as the insiders. Because outside directors are nominated by the incumbent board members and passively elected by the shareholders, structural bias remains one of the key insoluble riddles of corporate governance.

Despite these concerns, the driving logic of the Sarbanes-Oxley Act and the stock exchange board composition rules was that independent directors will be an effective constraint on the agency costs inherent in the corporate separation of ownership and control. Does the evidence support that belief? In fact, the empirical evidence on the relationship between board composition and firm performance available when Sarbanes-Oxley was adopted was inconclusive, at best. If independent directors effectively constrain agency costs, one would have expected the evidence to show a correlation between the presence of independent outsiders on the board and firm performance. But it did not.

True, some early studies found positive correlations between independence and performance. Rosenstein and Wyatt, for example, found that shareholder wealth increased when management appointed independent directors.[16] Weisbach studied board decisions to remove a CEO, finding that boards comprised mainly of independent directors were more likely to base the removal decision on poor performance, as well as being more likely to remove an under-performing CEO, than were insider dominated boards. He also found that CEO removals by outsider dominated boards added to firm value, while CEO removals by insider-dominated boards did not.[17] Baysinger and Butler found that corporate financial performance tends to increase (up to a point) as the percentage of independent directors increases.[18] Cotter found that boards dominated by outsiders generate higher shareholder gains from tender offers.[19]

Other studies, however, such as that by MacAvoy, found that board composition had no effect on profitability.[20] Klein likewise found little evidence of a general association between firm performance and board composition, but found a positive correlation between the presence of

[16]   Stuart Rosenstein & Jeffrey G. Wyatt, Outside Directors, Board Independence, and Shareholder Wealth, 26 J. Fin. Econ. 175 (1990).

[17]   Michael S. Weisbach, Outside Directors and CEO Turnover, 20 J. Fin Econ. 431 (1988).

[18]   Barry D. Baysinger & Henry N. Butler, Revolution Versus Evolution in Corporation Law: The ALI's Project and the Independent Director, 52 Geo. Wash. L. Rev. 557, 572 (1984).

[19]   James F. Cotter et al., Do Independent Directors Enhance Target Shareholder Wealth During Tender Offers?, 43 J. Fin. Econ. 195 (1997).

[20]   Paul MacAvoy, et al., ALI Proposals for Increased Control of the Corporation by the Board of Directors, in Statement of the Business Roundtable on the American Law Institute's Proposed "Principles of Corporate Governance and Structure: Restatement and Recommendations" C-1 (Feb. 1983).

insiders on board finance and investment committees and firm performance.[21] Rosenstein and Wyatt found that the stock market experienced a significantly positive price reaction to announcements that insiders had been appointed to the board when insiders owned more than 5% of the firm's stock.[22]

A 1999 meta-analysis of numerous studies in this area concluded that there was no convincing evidence that firms with a majority of independent directors outperform other firms. It further concluded that there was some evidence that a "moderate number" of insiders correlates with higher performance.[23]

A literature review by Wagner et al. further complicated the empirical landscape by effectively splitting the baby.[24] Their meta-analysis of 63 correlations found that, on average, increasing the number of outsiders on the board is positively associated with higher firm performance. On the other hand, increasing the number of insiders on the board had the same effect. In other words, greater board homogeneity was positively associated with higher firm performance, which is not what the Sarbanes-Oxley Act's proponents would have predicted.

But what about more recent evidence, especially based on data from the post-SOX period? There is some evidence that the post-SOX regulatory changes and the new market forces affecting independent directors have had an impact. Robert Felton's review of studies of post-SOX boards of directors found that the average number of companies on whose board a director sits has gone down, presumably because boards and committees meet more often and have to process more information. The amount of time required for board service has especially gone up for members of audit committees, who have a host of new duties. Overall, "the average commitment of a director of a U.S. listed company increased from 13 hours a month in 2001 to 19 hours in 2003 (and then fell to 18 hours in 2004)."[25]

Somewhat stronger evidence that the fetish for independence has had at least some beneficial effects is provided by Michael Useem and

---

[21]   April Klein, Firm Performance and Board Committee Structure, 41 J. L. & Econ. 275 (1998).

[22]   Stuart Rosenstein & Jeffrey G. Wyatt, Outside Directors, Board Independence, and Shareholder Wealth, 26 J. Fin. Econ. 175 (1990).

[23]   Sanjai Bhagat & Bernard Black, The Uncertain Relationship Between Board Composition and Firm Performance, 54 Bus. Law. 921, 922 (1999). A 1998 meta-analysis likewise found no evidence that board composition affects financial performance. Dan R. Dalton et al., Meta-Analytic Reviews of Board Composition, Leadership Structure, and Financial Performance, 19 Strategic Mgmt. J. 269 (1998).

A more recent study of Australian firms found that corporate boards "chaired by non-executives and dominated by non-executive directors at the full board and compensation committee levels are no more adept at enforcing CEO pay-for-firm-performance than are executive-dominated boards." Alessandra Capezio et al., Too Good to be True: Board Structural Independence as a Moderator of CEO Pay-for-Firm-Performance, 48 J. Mgmt. Stud. 487 (2011).

[24]   John A. Wagner et al., Board Composition and Organizational Performance: Two Studies of Insider/Outsider Effects, 35 J. Mgmt. Stud. 655 (1998).

[25]   Robert F. Felton, A New Era in Corporate Governance, McKinsey Q., 2004 No.2, 28, 60.

Andy Zelleke's survey of governance practices. They found that boards of directors increasingly view delegation of authority to management as properly the subject of careful and self-conscious decision making. The surveyed board members acknowledged that they do not run the company on a day-by-day basis, but rather are seeking to provide stronger oversight and supervision. Increasingly, boards are establishing written protocols to allocate decision-making rights between the board and management, although the protocols vary widely, ranging from detailed and comprehensive to skeletal and limited in scope. Useem and Zelleke conclude that executives still set much of the board's decision-making agenda. At the same time, they found that boards are increasingly asserting their sovereignty in recent years and that an emergent norm requires management to be mindful of what information boards want to hear and what decisions boards believe they should make.[26]

A critical issue, of course, has always been board access to information. Indirect evidence that independent directors now have good access to information is provided by a study by Enrichetta Ravina and Paola Sapienza of independent directors' trading results. The authors found that independent directors earn substantial positive abnormal returns when trading in their corporation's stock. Even more interestingly, the difference between their results and those of the same firm's executive officers is relatively small, although it widens in firms with weaker governance regimes.[27] It seems reasonable to infer from this evidence that outsiders now have good access to material information about firm performance; indeed, that their access to such information is comparable to that of executive officers.[28]

So where does this leave us? The post-SOX regulatory environment rests on the conventional wisdom that board independence is an unalloyed good. As the preceding discussion demonstrated, however, the empirical evidence on the merits of board independence is mixed. Accordingly, even though there is some reason to think independent board members are finally becoming properly incentivized and, as a result, more effective, the clearest take-home lesson from the preceding analysis is still that one size does not fit all.

WHAT'S THAT?

Information "is material if there is a substantial likelihood that a reasonable shareholder would consider it important . . . ." *TSC Industries, Inc. v. Northway, Inc.,* 426 U.S. 438, 449 (1976).

---

[26] Michael Useem & Andy Zelleke, Oversight and Delegation in Corporate Governance: Deciding What the Board Should Decide, 14 Corp. Gov.: An Int'l Rev. 2 (2006).

[27] Enrichetta Ravina & Paola Sapienza, What do Independent Directors Know? Evidence from Their Trading (December 2006), available at http://ssrn.com/abstract=928246.

[28] Note that this raises doubts about the extent to which independent directors are relying on stock price based metrics. If independent directors are performing as well as insiders, it may be assumed that the former—like the latter—have access to material nonpublic information.

In addition, the fetish for board independence has costs. Two are already on the table; namely, those associated with the information asymmetry between outsiders and insiders and those occasioned by the need to incent outsiders to perform. A third is the lost value of insider representation.

Economist Oliver Williamson suggests that one of the board's functions is to "safeguard the contractual relation between the firm and its management."[29] Insider board representation may be necessary to carry out that function. Many adverse firm outcomes are beyond management's control. If the board is limited to monitoring management, and especially if it is limited to objective measures of performance, however, the board may be unable to differentiate between acts of god, bad luck, ineptitude, and self-dealing. As a result, risk averse managers may demand a higher return to compensate them for the risk that the board will be unable to make such distinctions. Alternatively, managers may reduce the extent of their investments in firm-specific human capital, so as to minimize non-diversifiable employment risk. Insider representation on the board may avoid those problems by providing better information and insight into the causes of adverse outcomes.

Insider representation on the board also will encourage learned trust between insiders and outsiders. Insider representation on the board thus provides the board with a credible source of information necessary to accurate subjective assessment of managerial performance. In addition, however, it also serves as a bond between the firm and the top management team. Insider directors presumably will look out for their own interests and those of their fellow managers. Board representation thus offers some protection against dismissal for adverse outcomes outside management's control.

Such considerations likely explain the finding by Klein of a positive correlation between the presence of insiders on board committees and firm performance.[30] They also help explain the finding by Wagner et al. that increasing the number of insiders on the board is positively correlated with firm performance.[31]

D. CHOOSING DIRECTORS

Directors are elected by shareholders. But who nominates the candidates that will stand for election?

Until relatively recently, CEOs effectively controlled the process for selecting new board members:

---

[29]   Oliver E. Williamson, The Economic Institutions of Capitalism 298 (1985).

[30]   See April Klein, Firm Performance and Board Committee Structure, 41 J. L. & Econ. 275 (1998).

[31]   See John A. Wagner et al., Board Composition and Organizational Performance: Two Studies of Insider/Outsider Effects, 35 J. Mgmt. Stud. 655 (1998).

This is a consequence of state judicial decision that permit incumbent corporate management to use corporate funds to pay the proxy election campaign expenses of their directorical candidates while requiring all other shareholders to bear the costs of proxy solicitations for opposition nominees, with reimbursement possible only if the opposition candidates win control of the board. As the number of shareholders in giant corporations and the costs of proxy elections increased, the nomination of directors by anyone other than incumbent management became virtually impossible. In fiscal year 1974, for example, the SEC supervised 6,615 proxy solicitations. Management ran unopposed in 6,600 elections, or 99.8% of the elections. In 6,606 elections, or 99.9% of the elections, management's entire slate was elected.

Chief executives consistently used their control to select board members who would not 'rock the boat.' As one corporate president explained . . ., 'What would you do, if you were president? You control the company and you control the board. You want to perpetuate this control. You certainly don't want anyone on your board who even slightly might be a challenge or a question to your tenure . . . .'[32]

Today, however, most public corporations (excepting those with a controlling shareholder) must have a nominating committee comprised of independent directors who are charged with selecting new board members.

In theory, having a separate committee of independent directors who are in charge of the nomination process should weaken the CEO's grip on power. There is some evidence to support this theory. Business school professors James Westphal and Edward Zajac demonstrated that as board power increases relative to the CEO—measured by such factors as the percentage of insiders and whether the CEO also served as chairman—newly appointed directors become more demographically similar to the board.[33] In other words, instead of replicating the CEO and staffing the board with his cronies, independent directors controlling the nomination process tend to replicate themselves.

1) THE NOMINATING COMMITTEE

NYSE Listed Company Manual § 303A.04

(a) Listed companies must have a nominating/corporate governance committee composed entirely of independent directors.

---

[32] Joel Seligman, A Sheep in Wolf's Clothing: The American Law Institute Principles of Corporate Governance Project, 55 Geo. Wash. L. Rev. 325, 331–32 (1987).

[33] James D. Westphal & Edward J. Zajac, Who Shall Govern? CEO/Board Power, Demographic Similarity, and New Director Selection, 40 Admin. Sci. Q. 60 (1995).

(b) The nominating/corporate governance committee must have a written charter that addresses:

(i) the committee's purpose and responsibilities— which, at minimum, must be to: identify individuals qualified to become board members, consistent with criteria approved by the board, and to select, or to recommend that the board select, the director nominees for the next annual meeting of shareholders; develop and recommend to the board a set of corporate governance guidelines applicable to the corporation; and oversee the evaluation of the board and management; and

(ii) an annual performance evaluation of the committee.

Commentary: A nominating/corporate governance committee is central to the effective functioning of the board. New director and board committee nominations are among a board's most important functions. Placing this responsibility in the hands of an independent nominating/corporate governance committee can enhance the independence and quality of nominees. The committee is also responsible for taking a leadership role in shaping the corporate governance of a corporation.

If a listed company is legally required by contract or otherwise to provide third parties with the ability to nominate directors (for example, preferred stock rights to elect directors upon a dividend default, shareholder agreements, and management agreements), the selection and nomination of such directors need not be subject to the nominating committee process.

The nominating/corporate governance committee charter should also address the following items: committee member qualifications; committee member appointment and removal; committee structure and operations (including authority to delegate to subcommittees); and committee reporting to the board. In addition, the charter should give the nominating/corporate governance committee sole authority to retain and terminate any search firm to be used to identify director candidates, including sole authority to approve the search firm's fees and other retention terms.

Boards may allocate the responsibilities of the nominating/corporate governance committee to committees of their own denomination, provided that the committees are composed entirely of independent directors. Any such committee must have a committee charter.

Website Posting Requirement: A listed company must make its nominating/corporate governance committee charter available on or through its website. If any function of the nominating/corporate governance committee has been delegated to another committee, the charter of that committee must also be made available on or through the listed company's website.

Disclosure Requirements: A listed company must disclose in its annual proxy statement or, if it does not file an annual proxy statement, in its annual report on Form 10-K filed with the SEC that its nominating/corporate governance committee charter is available on or through its website and provide the website address.

Regulation S–K Item 407(c)

(1) If the registrant does not have a standing nominating committee or committee performing similar functions, state the basis for the view of the board of directors that it is appropriate for the registrant not to have such a committee and identify each director who participates in the consideration of director nominees.

(2) Provide the following information regarding the registrant's director nomination process:

(i) State whether or not the nominating committee has a charter. If the nominating committee has a charter, provide the disclosure required by Instruction 2 to this Item regarding the nominating committee charter;

(ii) If the nominating committee has a policy with regard to the consideration of any director candidates recommended by security holders, provide a description of the material elements of that policy, which shall include, but need not be limited to, a statement as to whether the committee will consider director candidates recommended by security holders;

(iii) If the nominating committee does not have a policy with regard to the consideration of any director candidates recommended by security holders, state that fact and state the basis for the view of the board of directors that it is appropriate for the registrant not to have such a policy;

(iv) If the nominating committee will consider candidates recommended by security holders, describe the procedures to be followed by security holders in submitting such recommendations;

(v) Describe any specific minimum qualifications that the nominating committee believes must be met by a nominating committee-recommended nominee for a position on the registrant's board of directors, and describe any specific qualities or skills that the nominating committee believes are necessary for one or more of the registrant's directors to possess;

(vi) Describe the nominating committee's process for identifying and evaluating nominees for director, including nominees recommended by security holders, and any differences in the manner in which the nominating committee evaluates nominees for director based on whether the nominee is recommended by a security holder, and whether, and if so how, the nominating committee (or the board) considers diversity in identifying nominees for director. If the nominating committee (or the board) has a policy with regard to the consideration of diversity in identifying director nominees, describe how this policy is implemented, as well as how the nominating committee (or the board) assesses the effectiveness of its policy;

(vii) With regard to each nominee approved by the nominating committee for inclusion on the registrant's proxy card (other than nominees who are executive officers or who are directors standing for re-election), state which one or more of the following categories of persons or entities recommended that nominee: Security holder, non-management director, chief executive officer, other executive officer, third-party search firm, or other specified source. With regard to each such nominee approved by a nominating committee of an investment company, state which one or more of the following additional categories of persons or entities recommended that nominee: Security holder, director, chief executive officer, other executive officer, or employee of the investment company's investment adviser, principal underwriter, or any affiliated person of the investment adviser or principal underwriter;

(viii)If the registrant pays a fee to any third party or parties to identify or evaluate or assist in identifying or evaluating potential nominees, disclose the function performed by each such third party; and

(ix) If the registrant's nominating committee received, by a date not later than the 120th calendar day before the date of the registrant's proxy statement released to security holders in connection with the previous year's annual meeting, a recommended nominee from a security holder that beneficially owned more than 5% of the registrant's voting common stock for at least one year as of the date the recommendation was made, or from a group of security holders that beneficially owned, in the aggregate, more than 5% of the registrant's voting common stock, with each of the securities used to calculate that ownership held for at least one year as of the date the recommendation was made, identify the candidate and the security holder or security holder group that recommended the candidate and disclose whether the nominating committee chose to nominate the candidate, provided, however, that no such identification or disclosure is required without the written consent of both the security holder or security holder group and the candidate to be so identified.

(3)   Describe any material changes to the procedures by which security holders may recommend nominees to the registrant's board of directors, where those changes were implemented after the registrant last provided disclosure in response to the requirements of paragraph (c)(2)(iv) of this Item, or paragraph (c)(3) of this Item.

Instructions to Item 407(c)(2)(ix). 1. For purposes of paragraph (c)(2)(ix) of this Item, the percentage of securities held by a nominating security holder may be determined using information set forth in the registrant's most recent quarterly or annual report, and any current report subsequent thereto, filed with the Commission pursuant to the Exchange Act (or, in the case of a registrant that is an investment company registered under the Investment Company Act of 1940, the registrant's most recent report on Form N-CSR (§§ 249.331 and 274.128 of this chapter)), unless the party relying on such report knows or has reason to believe that the information contained therein is inaccurate.

2.   For purposes of the registrant's obligation to provide the disclosure specified in paragraph (c)(2)(ix) of this Item, where the date of the annual meeting has been changed by more than 30 days from the date of the previous year's meeting, the obligation under that Item will arise where the registrant receives the security holder recommendation a reasonable time before the registrant begins to print and mail its proxy materials.

3.   For purposes of paragraph (c)(2)(ix) of this Item, the percentage of securities held by a recommending security holder, as well as the holding period of those securities, may be determined by the registrant if the security holder is the registered holder of the securities. If the security holder is not the registered owner of the securities, he or she can submit one of the following to the registrant to evidence the required ownership percentage and holding period:

a.   A written statement from the "record" holder of the securities (usually a broker or bank) verifying that, at the time the security holder made the recommendation, he or she had held the required securities for at least one year; or

b.   If the security holder has filed a Schedule 13D (§ 240.13d–101 of this chapter), Schedule 13G (§ 240.13d–102 of this chapter), Form 3 (§ 249.103 of this chapter), Form 4 (§ 249.104 of this chapter), and/or Form 5 (§ 249.105 of this chapter), or amendments to those documents or updated forms, reflecting ownership of the securities as of or before the date of the recommendation, a copy of the schedule and/or form, and any subsequent amendments reporting a change in ownership level, as well as a written statement that the security holder continuously held the securities for the one-year period as of the date of the recommendation.

4.   For purposes of the registrant's obligation to provide the disclosure specified in paragraph (c)(2)(ix) of this Item, the security holder or group must have provided to the registrant, at the time of the recommendation, the written consent of all parties to be identified and, where the security holder or group members are not registered holders, proof that the security holder or group satisfied the required ownership percentage and holding period as of the date of the recommendation.

Instruction to Item 407(c)(2). For purposes of paragraph (c)(2) of this Item, the term nominating committee refers not only to nominating committees and committees performing similar functions, but also to groups of directors fulfilling the role of a nominating committee, including the entire board of directors.

Instructions to Item 407(c)(3). 1. The disclosure required in paragraph (c)(3) of this Item need only be provided in a registrant's quarterly or annual reports.

2.   For purposes of paragraph (c)(3) of this Item, adoption of procedures by which security holders may recommend nominees to the registrant's board of directors, where the registrant's most recent disclosure in response to the requirements of paragraph (c)(2)(iv) of this Item, or paragraph (c)(3) of this Item, indicated that the registrant did not have in place such procedures, will constitute a material change.

NOTES AND QUESTIONS

1.   NYSE Listed Company Manual § 303A.00 provides that a controlled company, which is defined as one in "which more than 50% of the voting power for the election of directors is held by an individual, a group or another company," is not required to have a nominating committee. What does Reg S-K require controlled companies to do if they lack a nominating committee?

2.   In addition to nominating director candidates, many companies assign responsibility for selecting new CEOs to the nominating committee. In cooperation with the compensation committee, the nominating committee may take the lead in negotiating the terms of a newly appointed CEO's employment agreement. Finally, the nominating committee may be tasked with setting director compensation, although many firms assign that job to the compensation committee.

3.   Note that the NYSE listing requirement includes "corporate governance" as part of the nominating committee's job. This aspect of the committee's duties remains relatively poorly defined. In general, however, the intent seems to be that the nominating committee should serve as the board of directors' principal point of contact with shareholders. As a practical matter, one common task given this committee is assigning directors to other board committees (typically subject to approval by the entire board).

4.   Who chooses the members of the nominating committee? Does it matter?

5.   Does the nominating committee or the board as a whole determine which directors are independent?

6.   What relevance does the existence and use of a NYSE listing standard compliant nominating committee have with respect to the determination of whether directors are independent for purposes of state law?

7.   The general counsel can be a key advisor to the nominating committee:

> The Governance/Nominating Committee would benefit from the general counsel's regular involvement and advice on matters such as evolving standards of director conduct, a definition of independence, nomination/qualification standards, director [change in status] procedures, expectations of directors, the appropriate extent of outside board service, and similar topics with clear legal implications.
>
> A related topic on which the impact of the general counsel would be particularly valuable is conflicts of interest management—which has dramatically increased in importance in the corporate responsibility environment. The general counsel could advise the Governance/Nominating (or other applicable) Committee on such important matters as (a) the continued effectiveness of the conflicts questionnaire; (b) issues raised by individual responses thereto; (c) processing and evaluation of disclosed potential conflicts; and (d) dealing with director conduct and participation when an actual conflict is determined to exist.[34]

In some cases, however, CEOs have tried to limit contact between the board (or board committees) and senior executives, so that the CEO serves as the sole contact point between the board and management. Why might CEOs do so? Should boards accept such a limitation?

8.   What role, if any, may a CEO play in the nominating process under the exchange listing standard? To the extent such a role is permitted, should the CEO in fact so participate?

2)   THE NOMINATING COMMITTEE CHARTER

Exercise: Evaluate the Nominating and Corporate Governance Committee Charter of Apple, Inc. (2018)

There shall be a Committee of the Board of Directors (the "Board") of Apple Inc. (the "Corporation") to be known as the Nominating and Corporate Governance Committee (the "Committee") with purpose, composition, authority, duties and responsibilities, as follows:

---

[34] Legal Ethics: In-House Counsel as Chief Governance Officer, AHLA-PAPERS P06260502 (June 26, 2005).

A.   Purpose of the Committee

The purpose of the Committee is to:

  1.   Consider and report periodically to the Board on matters relating to the identification, selection and qualification of Board members and candidates nominated to the Board; and

  2.   Advise and make recommendations to the Board of Directors with respect to corporate governance matters.

B.   Composition of the Committee

The members of the Committee shall be appointed by the Board. The Committee will be composed of not less than two Board members. Each member shall be "independent" in accordance with applicable law, including the rules and regulations of the Securities and Exchange Commission and the rules of the NASDAQ Stock Market. The Chair of the Committee shall be designated by the Board.

Members of the Committee shall serve until their successors are duly elected and qualified or their earlier resignation or removal. The Board may replace any member of the Committee.

Questions

1.   Is it a good idea to have the committee appointed by the Board? What alternative method might be chosen for nominating and appointing committee members?

2.   Is there any reason not to have a nominating committee with a single member?

3.   Is there any reason to have a nominating committee with an odd number of members?

4.   Should members of the nominating committee be subject to a more stringent independence test than that of the stock exchange? If so, what additional criteria would you suggest?

5.   Should the board select the chair? If not, who should?

C.   Committee Meetings

The Committee shall meet as often as it deems appropriate to perform its duties and responsibilities under this charter. The Chair of the Board, any member of the Committee or the Secretary of the Corporation may call meetings of the Committee. The Chair of the Committee, in consultation with the Committee members and members of management, will determine the frequency and length of Committee meetings and develop the Committee's agenda. At the beginning of the year, the Committee will establish a schedule of agenda subjects to be discussed during the year (to the extent these can be foreseen). The

Committee shall maintain written minutes of its meetings which will be filed with the meeting minutes of the Board.

Questions

6.   Is it appropriate to have the committee chair consult with management about the timing of and agenda for committee meetings?

7.   Part of becoming a good lawyer is learning not to trust form documents. They frequently contain errors. For example, did you spot the grammatical errors in the text?

D.   Authority and Resources

The Committee may request any officer or employee of the Corporation or the Corporation's outside counsel to attend a Committee meeting or to meet with any members of, or consultants to, the Committee. The Committee has the right at any time to obtain advice, reports or opinions from internal and external counsel and expert advisors and has the authority to hire and terminate independent legal, financial and other advisors as it may deem necessary, at the Corporation's expense, without consulting with, or obtaining approval from, any officer of the Corporation in advance.

Question

8.   Is the provision giving the committee the right to hire outside advisors at company expense required under the NYSE listing standard? Is such a provision wise?

E.   Duties and Responsibilities

The Committee shall:

1.   Screen and recommend the selection of nominees to the Board to fill vacancies and newly created directorships based on, among other things, their independence, character, ability to exercise sound judgment, diversity, age, demonstrated leadership, skills, including financial literacy, and experience in the context of the needs of the Board. The Committee is committed to actively seeking out highly qualified women and individuals from minority groups to include in the pool from which Board nominees are chosen.

Questions

9.   It is common for nominating committee charters to authorize the committee to "identify and screen" nominees. Is that phrasing preferable to the phrasing of the Apple committee charter?

10. Should the list of criteria to be used be more specific (e.g., should it specify what skills are desirable besides financial literacy)?

11. As you understand this provision, who chooses the nominees that will be included on the company's proxy statement? The board or the committee? In either case, rewrite the first sentence to ensure that the charter gives the committee sole power to nominate directors. Now rewrite it to ensure that the charter gives the board sole power to nominate directors.

12. Should the provision address the issue of whether the CEO or other top managers are permitted to make recommendations to the committee of possible nominees? In either case, should they be allowed to make such recommendations?

2.   Develop a pool of potential director candidates for consideration in the event of a vacancy on the Board.

Questions

13. The charter does not address how or by whom a vacancy will be filled. Is that consistent with the NYSE rule? What other corporate document, if any, likely would contain instructions on filling vacancies? Should the charter give the committee power to fill a vacancy?

14. Do the criteria and statement of intent vis-à-vis diversity set out in paragraph 1 carry over to this paragraph? In either case, should you make it explicit?

3.   Oversee the annual Board performance evaluation process, including conducting surveys of director observations, suggestions and preferences.

> **Task**
>
> Devise a strategy for evaluating the board. What metrics should be used? Should metrics be purely quantitative (e.g., how did the company's return on assets (ROA) do last year?), purely qualitative (how easy is Dan Director to work with?), or a mix of both? Who should conduct the evaluation? Who should be asked to give their views on board performance? Are there advantages and disadvantages to hiring an outside advisor or facilitator?

4.　Consider the performance of incumbent members of the Board in determining whether to recommend that they be nominated for reelection.

5.　Evaluate and recommend termination of membership of individual directors in accordance with the Corporation's Bylaws, for cause or for other appropriate reasons.

6.　Make recommendations to the Board concerning the size, structure and composition of the Board and its committees.

7.　Consider shareholder nominees for election to the Board.

8.　Monitor compliance with the Corporation's Business Conduct Policy and the Guidelines regarding Director Conflicts of Interest.

9.　Consider matters of corporate governance and periodically review the Corporation's corporate governance policies and recommend to the Board modifications to the policies as appropriate.

> **Question**
>
> 15. Some companies authorize the nominating committee to periodically review their bylaws and make recommendations to the board for changes. Does this paragraph grant Apple's committee such authority? If not, should it?

10.　Review the Committee's charter, structure, processes, and membership requirements and submit any recommended changes to the Board at least once a year.

11.　Review the Corporate Governance Guidelines annually and submit any recommended changes to the Board.

12.　Report to the Board concerning the Committee's activities with such recommendations as the Committee deems appropriate at least once a year.

13.　Perform such other functions as assigned by law, the Corporation's charter or bylaws, or the Board.

Questions

16. Should the committee be given authority to review and approve the relevant portions of the company's Reg S-K Item 407 disclosures relating to director independence and the director nomination process?

17. What responsibilities, if any, should the committee have with respect to issues such as political contributions and lobbying expenses, sustainability and other social responsibility initiatives, compensation of directors, selection of the CEO and other top managers, CEO succession planning, and director education?

---

3) DIVERSITY

Note that the SEC does not require that boards be diverse or inclusive. Instead, Item 407(c) of Reg S-K simply requires that the issuer disclose "whether, and if so how, the nominating committee (or the board) considers diversity in identifying nominees for director. If the nominating committee (or the board) has a policy with regard to the consideration of diversity in identifying director nominees, describe how this policy is implemented, as well as how the nominating committee (or the board) assesses the effectiveness of its policy." Should the SEC do more?

Deborah L. Rhode & Amanda K. Packel, Diversity on Corporate Boards: How Much Difference Does Difference Make?

39 Del. J. Corp. L. 377 (2014)[35]

. . .

II. THE CURRENT STATE OF DIVERSITY ON CORPORATE BOARDS

A. *Female and Minority Representation on Corporate Boards*

Close to three-quarters of members of corporate boards of the largest American companies are white men. According to the most recent data, women hold only 16.9% of the seats on Fortune 500 boards. Women occupy 14.8% of Fortune 501–1000 board seats and only 11.9% of board seats in Russell 3000 companies. The situation in other nations is not markedly better, with the exception of those countries that have mandated quotas.

In the U.S., people of color also occupy a very small percentage of board seats. Among the Standard and Poor's (S&P) 200, 13% of the companies have no minorities on their boards, and more than two thirds

---

[35] Reprinted by permission of Deborah L. Rhode, Amanda K. Packel, and The Delaware General Corporation Law.

of the Fortune 500 have no women of color. Only 3.2% of directors are women of color. Within the S&P 100 companies, only 37% have minority women on their boards.

B. *Progress or Plateau?*

Although the overall percentage of women and minorities on corporate boards remains small, the actual number has been growing. By some measures, diversity has increased substantially over the last three decades. In 1973, only 7% of Fortune 1000 boards had any minority directors; thirty-five years later, 76% had at least one minority director. Over the same period, the number of Fortune 100 boards with at least one woman increased from 11% to 97% in 2006. In 2004, the majority of Fortune 100 companies had 0–30% board diversity; by 2012, the majority had 31% or more board diversity. For certain minority groups, the progress has been particularly striking. In the last decade, Asian-American board representation has tripled and Latino board representation has doubled. Among S&P 100 companies, 71% "have achieved [a] critical mass of three or more diverse directors[—]a 4% increase since 2010[;]" only 2% lack any diversity on their boards.

By other measures, however, progress—especially in the past decade—has stalled. For S&P 1500 companies, the share of board seats held by women has only grown from 11% in 2006 to 14% in 2012. Women are also underrepresented as chairs of compensation, audit, and nominating committees, which are among the most influential board positions. At current rates of change, it would take almost seventy years before women's representation on corporate boards reached parity with that of men.

Increases in minority representation pose still greater challenges. Total minority seats on Fortune 100 boards have barely increased since 2003, and the representation of women of color has grown less than 1% since 2003. African-American representation declined from 2010 to 2012. Outside of the largest, most high-profile corporations, progress has been harder to achieve, in part, "because [smaller] companies do not receive as much scrutiny from those promoting gender diversity in the boardroom . . . ."

FOR MORE INFORMATION

DirectWomen.org "is a national non-profit that works to increase the representation of women lawyers on corporate boards." "DirectWomen hosts its Board Institute, Sandra Day O'Connor Board Excellence Award Luncheon, Annual Alumnae Conference, and many regional programs. These events provide education and networking opportunities around the issue of women on boards." http://www.directwomen.org/

Moreover, some of the most encouraging numbers on board diversity may conceal less promising trends. The Sarbanes-Oxley Act led many corporations to reduce overall board size, meaning that the same number of women and minority directors may comprise a greater percentage of a now smaller board. In addition, much of the increase in women and minority directors over the last decade may reflect the same individuals sitting on more boards rather than the appointment of new individuals as directors. Many commentators worry that these "trophy directors," who may serve on as many as seven boards, are spread too thin to provide adequate oversight. Another concern is that the appointment of one or two token female or minority members will decrease pressure for continued diversity efforts.

III. THE CASE FOR DIVERSITY
ON CORPORATE BOARDS

The growing consensus within the corporate community is that diversity is an important goal. The case for diversity rests on two primary claims. The first is that diversity provides equal opportunity to groups historically excluded from positions of power. The public has a "strong [ ] interest in ensuring that opportunities are available to all, . . . that women [and minorities] entering the labour market are able to fulfil their potential, and that we make full use of the wealth of talented women . . ." and minorities available for board service.[38] The second claim is that diversity will improve organizational processes and performance. This "business case for diversity" tends to dominate debates in part because it appeals to a culture steeped in shareholder value as the metric for corporate decision making. This is also the claim on which controversy centers, so it is the focus of the discussion below.

A. *Diversity and Firm Performance*

Despite increasing references to acceptance of the business case for diversity, empirical evidence on the issue is mixed. While some studies have found positive correlations between board diversity and various measures of firm performance, others have found the opposite or no significant relationship. The discussion below reviews these findings, as well as their methodological limitations. One of the most significant constraints is the shortage of studies on racial and ethnic diversity. Most of the modern research focuses on gender, from which commentators often generalize without qualification.

1. Studies Finding a Positive Relationship

FYI

"It is axiomatic in logic and in science that correlation is not causation." *Craig v. Oakwood Hosp.*, 684 N.W.2d 296, 312 (Mich. 2004).

One of the most frequently cited studies in support of board diversity is a 2007 Catalyst study. It ranked Fortune 500 companies according to the percentage of women on their boards and found that, from 2001 to 2004, companies in the highest quartile outperformed companies in the lowest quartile by 53% in return on equity (ROE), 42% in return on sales (ROS), and 66% in return on

---

[38] HOUSE OF LORDS [H.L.], EUR. UNION COMM., WOMEN ON BOARDS: REPORT 13–14 (Nov. 9, 2012) (U.K.).

invested capital (ROIC). This study was a univariate analysis, which compares the means of two groups but does not include any control variables that might explain a correlation. The results of such a means comparison can also be skewed by any extreme values in the group. Further, the study did not specify whether the reported differences in means were statistically significant, which could also distort results. In addition, the strength of these relationships did not hold up in Catalyst's follow-up study covering 2004 to 2008, which found no significant difference in ROE.

More recently, advocates of increasing the representation of women on corporate boards have cited a Credit Suisse Research Institute study as evidence that the presence of women leads to better performance. This analysis of 2,360 companies from around the world found that companies with at least one female director had higher net income growth during a six-year period than companies with no women directors (14% versus 10%); companies with a market capitalization of more than $10 billion that have women on their boards had share price performance 26% higher than comparable businesses with all-male boards. This study also used a means comparison of groups of companies and thus is subject to many of the same criticisms as the Catalyst study.

Other studies, using regression analyses, have also found a positive relationship between board diversity and various measures of firm performance in samples of U.S. companies. Erhardt, Werbel, and Shrader examined five years of data for 112 large companies and found a significant positive correlation between gender and minority representation on boards and return on assets (ROA) and return on investment (ROI).[52] Adams and Ferreira also found a positive significant relationship between the proportion of female directors and financial performance in 1,066 publicly traded companies as measured by Tobin's Q (the ratio of the market value of a firm divided by the replacement cost of its assets), but they found no relationship or a negative relationship between board gender diversity and ROA. Carter, D'Souza, Simkins, and Simpson's study of major U.S. corporations listed in the S&P 500 index, found that gender and ethnic diversity on the board had a significant positive effect on ROA, although it found no effect on Tobin's Q. Another study by Carter et al. found a significant relationship between the percentages of women and minorities on the board and return on assets and equity.

---

[52] Niclas L. Erhardt, James D. Werbel & Charles B. Shrader, Board of Director Diversity and Firm Financial Performance, 11 CORP. GOVERNANCE: AN INT'L REV. 102, 106–07 (2003). ROA measures net income divided by the total value of assets, while ROI measures net income divided by investment capital. Id. at 106. The authors recognized that they could be observing reverse causation: firms with better financial performance may be more open to appointing diverse boards. Id. at 108.

Studies in other countries have also found a positive correlation between gender diversity on boards and measures of financial performance. In Australian firms, Bonn found a positive relationship between the proportion of female directors and book-to-market ratio,

> **WHAT'S THAT?**
>
> Tobin's q is the ratio of the market value of a company's assets (as measured by the market value of its outstanding stock and debt) divided by the replacement cost of the company's assets (book value).

while Nguyen and Faff found a positive link between gender diversity and Tobin's Q. Campbell and Minguez-Vera found a significant and positive relationship in Spanish firms between the gender composition on boards and Tobin's Q. In a study of Dutch companies, Luckerath-Rovers found a significant positive relationship between female board representation and return on equity. In a study of Israeli companies in which the government owned a substantial equity interest and required relative gender balance on boards, Schwartz-Ziv found that the ROE and net profit margin were significantly higher in companies with at least three women on their boards.

. . . A few studies have claimed to show that board diversity leads to improved financial performance, but causal linkages are extremely difficult to prove. As other studies have suggested, it could be that better firm performance leads to increased board diversity rather than the reverse. More successful firms may be better positioned to attract the female and minority candidates in high demand for board service. Larger and better-performing organizations may have more resources to devote to pursuing diversity and may face more pressure from the public and large institutional investors to increase diversity on the board. Finally, some third factor could be causing both improved performance and greater board diversity.[64]

2. Studies Finding a Negative Relationship or No Significant Relationship

Several other studies of U.S. firms found no relationship or a negative relationship between board diversity and firm performance. Looking at a random sample of one hundred Fortune 500 corporations, Zahra and Stanton found the ratio of board member minorities, including women, was inversely related to the organization's financial performance in terms of profitability and efficiency. They found no relationship between diversity and ROE, profit margin, sales to equity, earnings per share, or dividends per share. Another early study by Shrader et al. concluded that although the proportion of female managers was

---

[64] See, e.g., Amy J. Hillman et al., Organizational Predictors of Women on Corporate Boards, 50 ACAD. OF MGMT. J. 941, 944–45 (2007) (finding that organizational size, industry type, firm diversification strategy, and network effects, i.e., links to other boards with women directors, have significant effects on the likelihood of board gender diversity). These and other exogenous variables for which many studies do not control could account for an apparent correlation.

significantly and positively related to return on sales, ROA, ROE, and ROIC, the proportion of female directors was not significant. Carter et al. found no significant relationship between financial performance, as measured by Tobin's Q, and the number of women or minority directors on the board or on certain board committees. In a study of 250 listed companies from 2000–2006, Hussein and Kiwia found no relationship between female board representation and Tobin's Q. Miller and Triana's 2009 research found no significant relationship between board gender diversity and return on investment or return on sales. O'Reilly and Main's analysis of 2000 firms found no positive association "between either the number of women outside directors on the board or the addition of a woman to the board on [return on assets]." In addition, a meta-analysis of 85 studies of board composition found little evidence that it has any effect on firm performance.

In 2009, Adams and Ferreira studied a sample of firms from 1996–2003 and found a negative relationship between gender diversity and both ROA and Tobin's Q. The authors concluded "the positive correlation between performance and gender diversity shown in prior literature is not robust to any method of addressing the endogeneity of gender diversity. If anything, the relation appears to be negative." In well-governed firms, increased gender diversity on boards seemed to decrease profitability and stock prices. A study of 400 leading U.S. corporations between 1997 and 2005, by Dobbin and Jung, found that increases in board gender diversity had no effect on subsequent profitability but were followed by marginally significant decreases in stock value. The authors concluded that non-blockholding institutional investor bias—rather than changes in the board's behavior or capabilities—may explain the negative effects.

Studies of board diversity in other countries have also found no link to various measures of firm performance. For Canadian firms, Francoeur et al. found a positive correlation between female officers and financial performance, but no relationship between women directors and performance. In a recent study of UK listed companies, Gregory-Smith, Main, and O'Reilly found no significant relationship between the proportion of women directors and ROA, ROE, total shareholder return, or the price to book ratio. Wang and Clift's 2009 study of non-financial Australian firms revealed no significant relationship between gender or racial diversity on boards and ROA, ROE, or shareholder return. A study by Rose and a study by Smith et al. both failed to find a significant link between female board representation and various measures of firm performance for Danish corporations. A study of Norwegian firms found a negative effect of quotas on performance. Other research on Scandinavian firms has found no relationship between board diversity and organizational performance.

3.   Explanations for the Inconclusive Results

In sum, the empirical research on the effect of board diversity on firm performance is inconclusive, and the results are highly dependent on methodology. The mixed results reflect the different time periods, countries, economic environments, types of companies, and measures of diversity and financial performance. The relationship between board characteristics and firm performance likely varies by country because of the different regulatory and governance structures, economic climate and culture, and size of capital markets. Some researchers attribute the varied findings to the methodological shortcomings in many of the studies, including small sample size, short-term observations of performance, and the difficulty of controlling for reverse causation, endogeneity, and other omitted variables that may be affecting both board diversity and firm performance. Moreover, with so many different measures of firm performance from which to choose, researchers are likely to find some values that show a positive relationship with board diversity and others that show a negative relationship. Scholars also question whether focusing on short-term accounting measures of financial performance is the best way to measure the impact of diversity. Research is lacking on the relationship between board diversity and long-term stock price performance, which is the "gold standard" measure of shareholder value.

These mixed quantitative results may reflect not only differences in research methodology, but also differences in the context in which diversification occurs. For example, some studies suggest that the influence of minority directors on corporate boards is heavily shaped not only by the prior experience of the directors, but also by the "larger social structural context in which demographic differences are imbedded." The failure to include a critical mass of women or minorities may in some cases prevent the potential benefits of diversity. Those benefits may also be dampened by corporations' well-documented tendency to appoint women and minorities who are least likely to challenge the status quo, or who are "trophy directors," with too many board positions to provide adequate oversight.

Perhaps it should not be surprising that studies of the relationship between board diversity and financial performance are inconclusive, given that a direct relationship between various other aspects of board composition and performance has been similarly difficult to establish. Empirical studies of board characteristics usually considered significant and in some cases undesirable, such as large board size, few outside directors, little or no investment by directors, and the CEO serving as board chair, "ha[ve] not yielded much evidence that these 'usual suspects' have any meaningful connection to firm performance." The relationship between board characteristics, including diversity, and company performance may be "complex and indirect." Because boards perform multiple and varied tasks, diversity may affect different functions in different ways, making it difficult to establish any consistent relationship between board diversity and firm performance.

Although empirical research has drawn much-needed attention to the underrepresentation of women and minorities on corporate boards, it has not convincingly established that board diversity leads to improved financial performance. Given the limitations of these studies, many commentators believe that the "business case for diversity" rests on other grounds, particularly its effects on board decision-making processes, corporate reputation, and governance capacities.

B. *Diversity and Board Process, Corporate Reputation and Good Governance*

A common argument by scholars, as well as board members of both sexes, is that diversity enhances board decision-making and monitoring functions. This assertion draws on social science research on small-group decision making, as well as studies of board process and members' experiences. The basic premise is that diversity may lessen the tendency for boards to engage in groupthink—a phenomenon in which members' efforts to achieve consensus override their ability to "realistically appraise alternative courses of action."

The literature on board decision making reflects three different theories about the process through which diversity enhances performance. The first theory is that women and men have different strengths, and that greater inclusion can ensure representation of valuable capabilities. For instance, some empirical evidence suggests that women generally are more financially risk averse than men. For that reason, many commentators have speculated that women's increased participation in corporate financial decision making could have helped to curb tendencies that caused the most recent financial crisis. A widely discussed panel at a World Economic Forum in Davos put the question: "Would the world be in this financial mess if it had been Lehman Sisters?" Many Davos participants believed that the answer was no, and cited evidence suggesting that women were " "more prudent" and less "ego driven" than men in financial management contexts. One study found presence of at least one woman on a company's board was associated with a reduction of almost 40% in the likelihood of a financial restatement. Other research pointed in similar directions, including studies from researchers at Harvard and Cambridge Universities, which found a correlation between high levels of testosterone and an appetite for risk.

Some commentators also cite evidence indicating women have higher levels of trustworthiness or collaborative styles that can improve board dynamics. As one female director put it, "[w]omen are more cooperative and less competitive in tone and approach. When there's an issue, men are ready to slash and burn, while women are ready to approach . . . . Women often provide a type of leadership that helps boards do their jobs better." Women's experience with uncomfortable situations may give them particular capabilities in championing difficult issues. Similarly, racial and ethnic minorities' experience of needing to relate to both dominant and subordinate groups provides a form of bicultural fluency that may enhance decision making.

A second theory of how diversity enhances performance is that women and minorities have different life experiences than white men, and bringing different concerns and questions to the table allows the board to consider "a wider range of options and solutions to corporate issues." Diversity is productive by generating cognitive conflict: "conflicting opinions, knowledge, and perspectives that result in a more thorough consideration of a wide range of interpretations, alternatives, and consequences." For example, Phillips et al.'s study of group decision making found that when new members were "socially similar" to existing team members, subjective satisfaction was high but actual problem solving results were not. Although team members rated productivity much lower when newcomers were socially dissimilar, the more heterogeneous group was much better at accomplishing the problem-solving task. A diverse board can also enhance the quality of a board's decision-making and monitoring functions because diverse groups are less likely to take extreme positions and more likely to engage in higher-quality analysis.

Some scholars have also suggested that diverse boards can help prevent corporate corruption because they are "bold enough to ask management the tough questions." According to one study, female directors expanded the content of board discussions and were more likely than their male counterparts to raise issues concerning multiple stakeholders. Research has found that heterogeneous groups are associated with broader information networks as well as increased creativity and innovation. One study concluded that board racial diversity increased innovation by expanding access to information and networks, and prompting more thorough evaluation. Overall, studies on the relationship between board diversity and its capacity for strategic change have reached conflicting results.

. . .

Given the competing findings and methodological limitations of these studies, the financial benefits of board diversity should not be overstated. But neither should boards understate other justifications for diversity, including values such as fairness, justice, and equal opportunity, as well as the symbolic message it sends to corporate stakeholders. A diverse board signals that women's perspectives are important to the organization, and that the organization is committed to gender equity not only in principle but also in practice. Further, corporations with a commitment to diversity have access to a wider pool of talent and a broader mix of leadership skills than corporations that lack such a commitment. For example, the adverse publicity that Twitter received when it went public with a board of all white men is a case study in the reputational costs of a leadership structure that fails to reflect the diversity of the user community it serves.

NOTES AND QUESTIONS

1.   If the business case for diverse boards has not been made, is it appropriate for a nominating committee to take consideration of "other justifications for diversity" in selecting directors?

2.   Whether or not the business case for diverse boards has been made, is it appropriate for the SEC to mandate disclosure in this area?

3.   A number of European countries have adopted quotas requiring that public companies have a statutorily specified minimum percentage of women. What are the pros and cons of such requirements?

Sample Diversity Disclosures

Former SEC Chair Mary Jo White wrote in 2016 that:

The SEC does not have the authority to mandate board diversity, but, in 2009, the Commission adopted a rule requiring companies to disclose whether, and if so, how their nominating committees consider diversity and, if they have a policy on diversity, how its effectiveness is assessed. The rule does not define diversity and the adopting release made clear that there was no single way required to define the term. It left it to companies to say what they mean by diversity in their policies and disclosures.

What has been the impact of our rule? Companies' disclosures on board diversity in reporting under our current requirements have generally been vague and have changed little since the rule was adopted. Very few companies have disclosed a formal diversity policy and, as a result, there is very little disclosure on how companies are assessing the effectiveness of their policies. Companies' definitions of diversity differ greatly, bringing in life and work experience, living abroad, relevant expertise and sometimes race, gender, ethnicity, and sexual orientation.[36]

Consider the following examples:

Apple (2017 proxy statement):

In evaluating potential nominees to the Board, the Nominating Committee considers, among other things, independence, character, ability to exercise sound judgment, diversity, age, demonstrated leadership, skills, including financial literacy, and experience in the context

---

[36]   Mary Jo White, Keynote Address, International Corporate Governance Network Annual Conference: Focusing the Lens of Disclosure to Set the Path Forward on Board Diversity, Non-GAAP, and Sustainability (June 27, 2016).

of the needs of the Board. The Nominating Committee is committed to actively seeking out highly qualified women and individuals from minority groups to include in the pool from which Board nominees are chosen.

Berkshire Hathaway (2015 proxy statement):

> Berkshire does not have a policy regarding the consideration of diversity in identifying nominees for director. In identifying director nominees, the Governance Committee does not seek diversity, however defined. Instead, as previously discussed, the Governance Committee looks for individuals who have very high integrity, business savvy, an owner-oriented attitude and a deep genuine interest in the Company.

Prudential Financial (2016 proxy statement):

> While the Company does not have a formal policy on Board diversity, our Corporate Governance Principles and Practices place great emphasis on diversity, and the [Corporate Governance and Business Ethics] Committee actively considers diversity in recruitment and nominations of directors. The current composition of our Board reflects those efforts and the importance of diversity to the Board:

> Over 60% of our Board is diverse:

> - 4 director nominees have worked outside the United States
> - 2 director nominees are African-American
> - 1 director nominee is Asian-American
> - 2 director nominees are Hispanic
> - 3 director nominees are Women
> - 1 director nominee is LGBT

QUESTIONS

1. How much information and of what kinds do investors need to assess board diversity efforts?

2. Should the SEC define diversity? If so, how?

3. Should disclosure statements such as Berkshire Hathaway's be permissible?

4. Is there any potential disadvantage to being as forthcoming a Prudential Financial?

PROBLEM

You are Chief Legal Officer of a major NYSE corporation. The corporation is a diversified financial services company with a primary focus

system depends at its core upon the fact that a corporation—
except in the rarest situations—is organized under, and
governed by, the law of a single jurisdiction, traditionally the
corporate law of the State of its incorporation.

To be sure, the Court here may be referring not to constitutional
principle, but rather to the conflict of laws principle known as the
internal affairs doctrine, "which recognizes that only one State should
have the authority to regulate a corporation's internal affairs—matters
peculiar to the relationships among or between the corporation and its
current officers, directors, and shareholders—because otherwise a
corporation could be faced with conflicting demands" from different
states.[37]

But while the Supreme Court has not held that it is unconstitutional
for a state other than the state of incorporation to attempt to regulate a
corporation's internal affairs,[2] a number of commentators have concluded
that the internal affairs rule rises to the level of a constitutional
doctrine.[3]

Admittedly, there is not much case law on this issue, and the leading
case comes from a very interesting party—i.e., the Delaware Supreme
Court—but that case held that attempted application of California's
§ 2115 to a company incorporated in Delaware violated the U.S.
Constitution's Due Process and Commerce Clauses:

> Pursuant to the Fourteenth Amendment Due Process
> Clause, directors and officers of corporations "have a significant
> right . . . to know what law will be applied to their actions" and
> "[s]tockholders . . . have a right to know by what standards of
> accountability they may hold those managing the corporation's
> business and affairs." Under the Commerce Clause, a state "has
> no interest in regulating the internal affairs of foreign
> corporations." Therefore, this Court has held that an
> "application of the internal affairs doctrine is mandated by
> constitutional principles, except in the 'rarest situations,'" e.g.,
> when "the law of the state of incorporation is inconsistent with
> a national policy on foreign or interstate commerce."

Assuming Delaware to be correct on the constitutional status of the
internal affairs doctrine, SB 826 is unlikely to survive judicial scrutiny.
As Professor Grundfest explains:

> A board's gender diversity is a matter of internal corporate
> governance, as is shareholder voting, and SB 826 interferes with
> both. SB 826 would establish the first and only demographic test

---

[37] Edgar v. MITE Corp., 457 U.S. 624, 645 (1982).

[2] Erin A. O'Hara & Larry E. Ribstein, The Law Market 124 (2009) ("The Supreme Court has not spoken definitively on whether the courts in the United States are constitutionally compelled to apply the IAD.").

[3] See, e.g., Alan R. Palmitier, The CTS Gambit: Stanching the Federalization of Corporate Law, 69 Wash. U. L.Q. 445, 501–10 (1991).

for board membership. It thereby constrains a board's ability to designate directors in the event of a vacancy and interferes with the shareholder franchise by imposing a financial penalty if shareholders refuse to elect the minimum number of women directors mandated by SB 826.

California therefore cannot require that corporations headquartered in California but chartered in Delaware have a minimum number of women directors while Delaware simultaneously permits its chartered corporations to have any number of women directors that is consistent with the board's business judgment, subject to shareholder approval and constraints imposed by the corporation's charter and bylaws. The conflict between California law and Delaware law is apparent. Indeed, because SB 826 would be the first and only mandatory board diversity requirement in the United States, the bill creates a conflict between California and the chartering laws of every other state in the nation.

He therefore concludes "Delaware wins. California loses. End of story." Which seems the most likely outcome.

NOTE AND QUESTIONS

The Delaware Supreme Court has stated that:

Corporations and individuals alike enter into contracts, commit torts, and deal in personal and real property. Choice of law decisions relating to such corporate activities are usually determined after consideration of the facts of each transaction. In such cases, the choice of law determination often turns on whether the corporation had sufficient contacts with the forum state, in relation to the act or transaction in question, to satisfy the constitutional requirements of due process. The internal affairs doctrine has no applicability in these situations. Rather, this doctrine governs the choice of law determinations involving matters peculiar to corporations, that is, those activities concerning the relationships inter se of the corporation, its directors, officers and shareholders.[38]

1. Is board diversity an internal corporate affair? Does it matter whether one is applying the internal affairs doctrine as a rule of conflicts of law or one of constitutional law?

2. Is electing directors an internal corporate affair?

3. Is filling board vacancies an internal corporate affair?

---

[38] McDermott Inc. v. Lewis, 531 A.2d 206, 214–15 (Del. 1987).

PROBLEM

Alice Ludlow was Vice President of International Resistors Corporation (IR), which is incorporated in Delaware and has its principal executive office in El Segundo, California. IR is a semiconductor company founded by Ludlow's father. Ludlow began working for IR in 1997 after graduating from Stanford University. At no point in time did Ludlow have a written employment contract with IR. IR's bylaws provided at all relevant times that the corporation's officers (including the CEO) "shall be chosen annually by, and shall serve at the pleasure of, the Board, and shall hold their respective offices until their resignation, removal, or other disqualification from service." Removal of an officer, according to IR's bylaws, may be "with or without cause, by the Board at any time."

In early 2020, Ludlow complained to the board of directors that she had been harassed by the CEO. In late August 2020, the Board placed Ludlow on paid administrative leave. Prior to being placed on administrative leave, Ludlow had not received any negative criticisms or negative reviews about her performance as CEO. Ludlow resigned in October 2007 pursuant to a negotiated separation agreement she entered into with IR. The separation agreement did not include a release of liability for either party.

Approximately 18 months later, Ludlow sued IR, alleging breach of contract, wrongful termination in violation of public policy, and various other causes of action. IR moved for summary adjudication of Ludlow's cause of action for wrongful termination. Under Delaware law, a CEO serves at the pleasure of the corporation's board of directors and is barred from bringing a wrongful termination claim as a matter of law. Under California law, however, a CEO may bring a wrongful termination claim if the reasons for her termination violate public policy. Ludlow claimed she was fired in retaliation for filing the harassment complaint. California law further provides that a retaliatory termination violates important state policies.

Was Ludlow's termination a matter of internal corporate affairs?

E. SHOULD THE CEO ALSO SERVE AS CHAIRMAN OF THE BOARD?

Dodd-Frank § 972

The Securities Exchange Act of 1934 (15 U.S. C. 78a et seq.) is amended by inserting after section 14A, as added by this title, the following:

"SEC. 14B.   CORPORATE GOVERNANCE.

"Not later than 180 days after the date of enactment of this subsection, the Commission shall issue rules that require an issuer to disclose in the annual proxy sent to investors the reasons why the issuer has chosen—

'(1) the same person to serve as chairman of the board of directors and chief executive officer (or in equivalent positions); or

'(2) different individuals to serve as chairman of the board of directors and chief executive officer (or in equivalent positions of the issuer).'.

Regulation S–K Item 407

(h) Board leadership structure and role in risk oversight. Briefly describe the leadership structure of the registrant's board, such as whether the same person serves as both principal executive officer and chairman of the board, or whether two individuals serve in those positions .... If one person serves as both principal executive officer and chairman of the board, ... disclose whether the registrant has a lead independent director and what specific role the lead independent director plays in the leadership of the board. This disclosure should indicate why the registrant has determined that its leadership structure is appropriate given the specific characteristics or circumstances of the registrant. In addition, disclose the extent of the board's role in the risk oversight of the registrant, such as how the board administers its oversight function, and the effect that this has on the board's leadership structure.

NYSE Listed Company Manual § 303A.03

To empower non-management directors to serve as a more effective check on management, the non-management directors of each listed company must meet at regularly scheduled executive sessions without management.

Commentary: To promote open discussion among the non-management directors, companies must schedule regular executive sessions in which those directors meet without management participation. "Non-management" directors are all those who are not executive officers, and includes such directors who are not independent by virtue of a material relationship, former status or family membership, or for any other reason.

Regular scheduling of such meetings is important not only to foster better communication among non-management directors, but also to prevent any negative inference from attaching to the calling of executive sessions. A non-management director must preside over each executive session, although the same director is not required to preside at all executive sessions.

While this Section 303A.03 refers to meetings of non-management directors, listed companies may instead choose to hold regular executive sessions of independent directors only. An independent director must preside over each executive session of the independent directors, although the same director is not required to preside at all executive sessions of the independent directors.

If a listed company chooses to hold regular meetings of all non-management directors, such listed company should hold an executive session including only independent directors at least once a year.

If one director is chosen to preside at all of these executive sessions, his or her name must be disclosed either on or through the listed company's website or in its annual proxy statement or, if the listed company does not file an annual proxy statement, in its annual report on Form 10-K filed with the SEC. If this disclosure is made on or through the listed company's website, the listed company must disclose that fact in its annual proxy statement or annual report, as applicable, and provide the website address. Alternatively, if the same individual is not the presiding director at every meeting, a listed company must disclose the procedure by which a presiding director is selected for each executive session. For example, a listed company may wish to rotate the presiding position among the chairs of board committees.

In order that all interested parties (not just shareholders) may be able to make their concerns known to the non-management or independent directors, a listed company must also disclose a method for such parties to communicate directly with the presiding director or with those directors as a group either on or through the listed company's website or in its annual proxy statement or, if the listed company does not file an annual proxy statement, in its annual report on Form 10-K filed with the SEC. If this disclosure is made on or through the listed company's website, the listed company must disclose that fact in its annual proxy statement or annual report, as applicable, and provide the website address. . . .

PROBLEMS

1.   Does the following disclosure comply with Item 407?

Our Corporate Governance Guidelines currently provide that our board leadership structure shall consist of a Chairman of the Board who is also our Chief Executive Officer. At least every two years, the Nominating and Corporate Governance Committee of our Board of Directors assesses this board leadership structure to ensure the interests of the Company and its stockholders are best served.

A.   You are a law firm partner who represents the Company. One of your junior associates has recommended inserting the words ", subject to the authority of the Board of Directors," in the first sentence of the disclosure statement between the words "provide that" and "our leadership structure." Assess that recommendation.

2.   The Company has asked you to advise it on whether it should establish a lead director and, if so, what authorities and responsibilities the lead director should be assigned.[39] What does the NYSE Listed Company Manual require with respect to such a "lead director"?

---

[39]   Professor Jeff Gordon explains:

3.   The Company's chief legal officer has asked you to revise the current disclosure to include a list of reasons justifying the current leadership structure. Draft it.

4.   The Company's board of directors has decided to separate the position of board chairman and CEO. Pursuant thereto, the board has amended its Corporate Governance Guidelines to adopt a policy that the Chairman of the Board may not have been an officer of the Company during the previous three years. Revise the disclosure statement to reflect this change.

A.   The board asks your advice as to whether the policy ensures adequate independence on the part of the board's chairman.

B.   The board asks your advice as to whether the policy should permit the board to waive the policy so that the CEO may also serve as the board chairman.

C.   The board asks your advice as to whether the Company should appoint a lead independent director even though it has separated the CEO and chairman positions.

NOTE

A study by Olubunmi Faleye finds support for the hypothesis that firms actively weigh the costs and benefits of alternative leadership structures in their unique circumstances and concludes that requiring a one size fits all model separating the CEO and Chairman positions may be counterproductive.[40] A study by James Brickley, Jeffrey Coles, and Gregg A. Jarrell found little evidence that combining or separating the two titles affected corporate performance.[41] A subsequent study by the same authors found "preliminary support for the hypothesis that the costs of separation are larger than the benefits for most firms."[42]

As John Coates summarizes the field, the evidence is mixed, at best:

> At least 34 separate studies of the differences in the performance of companies with split vs. unified chair/CEO positions have been conducted over the last 20 years, including two "meta-studies." . . . The only clear lesson from these studies is that

The naming of a "lead director"—an independent director who convenes the board, where the chair is a senior executive, typically the CEO—. . .represented a compromise between those who . . . wanted to separate the roles of chair and CEO by making a non-executive director the chair, and those who felt that such separation would undermine the CEO's authority. Lead directors [have come] to play an increasingly important role in U.S. corporate governance practice, providing an organizational focal point for crises where the CEO's actions have been challenged.

Jeffrey N. Gordon, The Rise of Independent Directors in the United States, 1950–2005: Of Shareholder Value and Stock Market Prices, 59 Stan. L. Rev. 1465, 1495 (2007).

[40]   Olubunmi Faleye, Does One Hat fit All? The Case of Corporate Leadership Structure (January 2003).

[41]   James A. Brickey et al., Leadership Structure: Separating the CEO and Chairman of the Board, 3 J. Corp. Fin. 189 (1997).

[42]   James A. Brickley et al., Corporate Leadership Structure: On the Separation of the Positions of CEO and Chairman of the Board, Simon School of Business Working Paper FR 95-02 (Aug. 29, 2000), http://ssrn.com/abstract=6124.

there has been no long-term trend or convergence on a split chair/CEO structure, and that variation in board leadership structure has persisted for decades, even in the UK, where a split chair/CEO structure is the norm.[43]

Although Coates concludes that splitting the CEO and Chairman positions by legislation "may well be a good idea for larger companies," he further concludes that mandating such a split "is not clearly a good idea for all public companies."[44]

Proponents of a mandatory non-executive Chairman of the Board have overstated the benefits of splitting the positions, while understating or even ignoring the costs of doing so. Michael Jensen identified the potential benefits in his 1993 Presidential Address to the American Finance Association, arguing that: "The function of the chairman is to run the board meetings and oversee the process of hiring, firing, evaluation, and compensating the CEO. . . . Therefore, for the board to be effective, it is important to separate the CEO and Chairman positions."[45] In fact, however, overseeing the "hiring, firing, evaluation, and compensating the CEO," is the job of the board of directors as a whole, not just the Chairman of the Board.

To be sure, in many corporations, the Chairman of the Board is given unique powers to call special meetings, set the board agenda, and the like.[46] In such companies, a dual CEO-Chairman does wield powers that may impede board oversight of his or her performance. Yet, in such companies, the problem is not that one person holds both posts; the problem is that the independent members of the board of directors have delegated too much power to the Chairman. The solution is to adopt bylaws that allow the independent board members to call special meetings, require them to meet periodically outside the presence of managers, and the like.

Indeed, the influence of an executive chairman may not even be a problem. Brickley, Coles, and Jarrell concluded that the separation and combination of titles is part of the natural succession process. A successful CEO receives a variety of rewards from the company, one of which may be a fancier title. If the power that comes with the combined title came as a reward for sustained high performance, that power may actually redound to the company's benefit.

Turning from the benefit side to the cost side of the equation, even if splitting the posts makes it easier for the board to monitor the CEO, the board now has the new problem of monitoring a powerful non-executive Chairman. The board now must expend effort to ensure that such a Chairman does not use the position to extract rents from the company and,

---

[43]   John Coates, Protecting Shareholders and Enhancing Public Confidence through Corporate Governance (July 30, 2009), http://blogs.law.harvard.edu/corpgov/2009/07/30/protecting-shareholders-and-enhancing-public-confidence-through-corporate-governance/.

[44]   Id.

[45]   Michael C. Jensen, Presidential Address: The Modern Industrial Revolution, Exit and the Failure of Internal Control Systems, 48 J. of Fin. 831, 866 (1993).

[46]   James Verdonik and Kirby Happer, Role of the Chairman of the Board 2 (explaining that "one of the duties of the Chairman is to call meetings of the Board of Directors and the shareholders. . . . Chairmen often set the agenda for Board meetings").

moreover, that the Chairman expends the effort necessary to carry out the post's duties effectively. The board also must ensure that a dysfunctional rivalry does not arise between the Chairman and the CEO, both of whom presumably will be ambitious and highly capable individuals. In other words, if the problem is "who watches the watchers?," splitting the two posts simply creates a second watcher who also must be watched.

Regardless of the merits of splitting the two positions, the trend has been towards doing so. More than half of the companies in the S&P 500 index now have an independent chairman, where as only 35% did in 2009. Another trend has been a steady rise in the number of executive chairmen; i.e., a chairman who is not the CEO but nevertheless does not qualify as an independent director for purposes of the stock exchange listing standards. In most of these cases, a founder or a long-serving CEO steps down as CEO but remains the chairman of the board.

To assess your understanding of the material in this chapter, click here to take a quiz.

CHAPTER 4

OPERATIONALIZING THE MONITORING MODEL: STATE CORPORATE LAW

As Professor Elizabeth Noicki explains, director inattention is a pervasive problem that undermines the board's monitoring function:

> The modern board of directors is . . . a "monitoring" board, with the business of the corporation in the hands of senior corporate officers whose performance is monitored by the board. This monitoring structure removes directors from the daily operations of the corporation and limits the board in two obvious ways: (1) boards do not possess first-hand information on the day-to-day machinations of their corporate charge; and (2) corporate officers, who provide the directors information regarding the corporation's operations, become informational gatekeepers with the power to limit or skew the information they relay to the board.

> Because the modern board is a monitoring board and boards manage "other people's money," a director's ability and incentive to be an outstanding director are compromised. It is not surprising, then, that over the past two decades, many boards have proved themselves to be poor monitors. Many have failed to detect and squelch corporate fraud, allowing serious product failings to mar corporate reputations. In addition to a board's inability to detect corporate fraud, boards have tacitly approved a range of questionable accounting, financing, and disclosure practices. Recent corporate scandals dealing with vulgar and inexplicable executive compensation, stock option backdating, and overt looting make manifest the fact that the monitoring board may not be monitoring quite so well. Some corporate boards appear plagued by inattention, and some directors are asleep at the wheel.

> Director inattention is troubling at both micro and macro levels. On an individual level, director inattention is a problem because, to the extent that corporations suffer damage due to director inattention, shareholders who hold stock in those corporations lose money when the value of their investment decreases. From a broader perspective, director inattention is a problem because it undermines investor confidence. When investors lose confidence in the management of the modern corporation, they stop investing in stocks and corporations,

which tightens capital market liquidity and limits corporate expansion. Further, as an academic matter, director inattention throws into question the utility of the corporation as a business entity. One of the key benefits to the corporate form is that it allows for passive investment because management is the responsibility of directors. If the directors are inattentive, this undermines the utility of passive investment.[1]

Can the law force directors to pay attention? If so, should it try?

A. OVERSIGHT DUTIES: SUBSTANTIVE LAW

As a preliminary matter, what is the pertinent fiduciary duty when the board of directors allegedly fails adequately to monitor management? Is it the duty of care or the duty of loyalty? In either case, does the business judgment protect directors whose alleged breach of duty consists of inadequate supervision as opposed to making a bad decision?

> When courts say that they will not interfere in matters of business judgment, it is presupposed that judgment— reasonable diligence—has in fact been exercised. . . . Courts have properly decided to give directors a wide latitude in the management of the affairs of a corporation provided always that judgment, and that means an honest, unbiased judgment, is reasonably exercised by them.[2]

The difficulty is that most board of director activity "does not consist of taking affirmative action on individual matters; it is instead a continuing flow of supervisory process, punctuated only occasionally by a discrete transactional decision."[3] The business judgment rule does not apply to the ongoing supervisory process, because there is no exercise of judgment:

> [The] business judgment rule does not protect a director if he abdicated his responsibility and failed to exercise his judgment as a director. As the Second Circuit has stated:

> > Whatever its merit, however, the business judgment rule extends only as far as the reasons which justify its existence. Thus, it does not apply in cases, e.g., in which the corporate decision lacks a business purpose, is tainted by a conflict of interest, is so egregious as to amount to a no-win decision, or results from an obvious and prolonged failure to exercise oversight or supervision. Other examples may occur.

---

[1]   Elizabeth A. Nowicki, Director Inattention and Director Protection Under Delaware General Corporation Law Section 102(b)(7): A Proposal for Legislative Reform, 33 Del. J. Corp. L. 695, 699–701 (2008).

[2]   Burt v. Irvine Co., 237 Cal. App. 2d 828, 852–53, 47 Cal. Rptr. 392, 408 (Ct. App. 1965).

[3]   Bayless Manning, The Business Judgment Rule and the Director's Duty of Attention: Time for Reality, 39 Bus. Law. 1477, 1494 (1984).

Other courts have also concluded that directors who "abdicate their managerial responsibilities" are not entitled to the business judgment rule's protection from liability. The [plaintiff] has alleged the type of "prolonged failure to exercise oversight or supervision" that falls outside the business judgment rule as a failure to exercise any judgment.[4]

If the business judgment rule is inapplicable, what standard of review applies to claims that the board has failed to properly monitor management?

William L. Cary, Federalism and Corporate Law: Reflections Upon Delaware
83 Yale L.J. 663, 683–84 (1974)[5]

Graham v. Allis-Chalmers Manufacturing Co.[111] is an example of the low standard that Delaware shares with most other jurisdictions as to the duty of care on the part of directors. *Graham* involved a derivative action on behalf of Allis-Chalmers in connection with the much publicized price-fixing conspiracy involving electric equipment in the late 1950's. The company, together with four nondirector defendants, pleaded guilty to the indictments and as a result had been subjected not only to fines and penalties but to treble damage actions brought by purchasers of the equipment.

In this case it was impossible to establish actual knowledge on the part of any officers, but it was claimed that they should have had notice, or constructive knowledge, of what was happening. One reason why a duty might arise here is that in 1937 (19 years before the illegal action) the Federal Trade Commission had issued a cease and desist order from alleged price-fixing in connection with the sale of many of the same items. However, the point was made by the vice-chancellor that such an order was "entered at a time when none of the Allis-Chalmers directors here charged held a position of responsibility with the company."[112]

The supreme court upheld the lower court's ruling for the defendants, finding that since the company's directors could not investigate personally all of the company's employees they were entitled to rely on summaries, reports, and corporate records.[113] No one would expect the directors to have personal knowledge of all corporate activities. However, a . . . state less hospitable than Delaware might have imposed upon directors the duty of installing an internal control system to prevent repeated antitrust violations. There had been ample warning.

---

[4]   Resolution Tr. Corp. v. Norris, 830 F. Supp. 351, 359–60 (S.D. Tex. 1993) (citations omitted).

[5]   Reprinted by permission of the Yale Law Journal.

[111]   40 Del. Ch. 335, 182 A.2d 328 (Ch. 1962), aff'd, 41 Del. Ch. 78, 188 A.2d 125 (1963).

[112]   40 Del. Ch. at 341, 182 A.2d at 331.

[113]   41 Del. Ch. at 85, 188 A.2d at 130.

And directors of financial institutions, particularly banks, have been expected—indeed required—to provide a proper system of supervision. Even if a court should refuse to impose such a duty on all the directors, certainly where almost the same action previously had been found in violation of law at a time when the present senior officers had been employees the inside directors should be held responsible.

NOTE AND QUESTIONS

In *Graham*, the Delaware Supreme Court held that:

> The precise charge made against these director defendants is that, even though they had no knowledge of any suspicion of wrongdoing on the part of the company's employees, they still should have put into effect a system of watchfulness which would have brought such misconduct to their attention in ample time to have brought it to an end. However, the Briggs case expressly rejects such an idea. On the contrary, it appears that directors are entitled to rely on the honesty and integrity of their subordinates until something occurs to put them on suspicion that something is wrong. If such occurs and goes unheeded, then liability of the directors might well follow, but absent cause for suspicion there is no duty upon the directors to install and operate a corporate system of espionage to ferret out wrongdoing which they have no reason to suspect exists.
>
> . . .
>
> In the last analysis, the question of whether a corporate director has become liable for losses to the corporation through neglect of duty is determined by the circumstances. If he has recklessly reposed confidence in an obviously untrustworthy employee, has refused or neglected cavalierly to perform his duty as a director, or has ignored either willfully or through inattention obvious danger signs of employee wrongdoing, the law will cast the burden of liability upon him. This is not the case at bar, however, for as soon as it became evident that there were grounds for suspicion, the Board acted promptly to end it and prevent its recurrence.[6]

Consider the old saying: "every dog gets one bite." This saying was based on the common law principle that a dog's master was only liable for bites if the master knew or had reason to know the dog had a propensity to bite. Such knowledge could be based either on the breed's inherently violent propensities or a prior bite.

1. Is the rule in *Graham* analogous to the dog bite rule?

2. What was the policy rationale behind the common law dog bite rule?

---

[6]   Graham v. Allis-Chalmers Mfg. Co., 188 A.2d 125, 130 (1963).

3. Does the policy argument for the dog bite rule suggest a policy argument for *Graham*?

NOTE ON RISK MANAGEMENT

A large public corporation these days faces "a myriad of risks . . . ranging from complex financial risk to quality control."[7] In general, however, the risks corporations face can be broadly categorized as operational, market, and credit. Operational risk encompasses such concerns as "inadequate systems, management failure, faulty controls, fraud, and human error."[8] Related concerns include failure to comply with applicable legal rules, accounting irregularities, bad business models, and strategic planning errors.

Market risk can be broadly defined as changes in firm valuation linked to asset performance. For example, financial risk management views market risk as the expected variance of a portfolio's rate of return. In contrast, the Basel Accords define market risk "as the risks (a) 'in the trading book of debt and equity instruments and related off-balance-sheet contracts and (b) foreign exchange and commodities risks.' "[9] In either case, market risks are identified and evaluated by financial models that predict changes in prices, interest rates, liquidity, and foreign exchange rates.

Credit risk is defined as the possibility that a change in the credit quality of a counterparty will affect the firm's value.[10] It thus includes not only the risk of default, but also such risks as the possibility a credit-rating agency might downgrade the counterparty's creditworthiness. The financial crisis revealed that the existing models for measuring and predicting consumer credit risk are poorly developed.

Enterprise risk management is a subset of internal control, falling into mainly into the first COSO category. It is commonly defined as the process by which the board of directors and executives of a corporation define the firm's strategies and objectives so as "to strike an optimal balance between growth and return goals and related risks."[11] It encompasses determining an appetite for risk consistent with the interests of the firm's equity owners and identifying, preparing for, and responding to risks.

Risk management tools include (1) avoiding risk by choosing to refrain from certain business activities, (2) transferring risk to third parties through hedging and insurance, (3) mitigating operational risk through preventive and responsive control measures, and (4) accepting that certain risks are necessary to generate the appropriate level of return. Although primary

---

[7]   Betty Simkins & Steven A. Ramirez, Enterprise-Wide Risk Management and Corporate Governance, 39 Loy. U. Chi. L. J. 571 (2008).

[8]   Michel Crouhy et al., The Essentials of Risk Management 30–31 (2006).

[9]   W. Ronald Gard, George Bailey in the Twenty-First Century: Are We Moving to the Postmodern Era in International Financial Regulation With Basel II?, 8 Transactions 161, 183 (2006).

[10]   Crouhy et al., supra note 8, at 29.

[11]   Committee of Sponsoring Organizations of the Treadway Commission, Enterprise Risk Management—Integrated Framework: Executive Summary 1 (2004) [hereinafter COSO Framework].

responsibility for adopting and adapting these tools to the corporation's needs rests with the corporation's top management team, the board of directors is responsible for ensuring that the corporation has established appropriate risk management programs and for overseeing management's implementation of such programs.[12]

The financial crisis of 2008 revealed serious risk management failures on an almost systemic basis throughout the business community. At some firms, the problem was the absence of any system for managing risk. According to a 2002 survey of corporate directors, 43 percent said that their boards had either an ineffective risk management process or no process for identifying and managing risk at all.[13] According to the same survey, 36 percent of directors felt they had an incomplete understanding of the risks faced by their companies.[14]

A 2008 Towers Perrin survey of CFOs suggests that risk management remained underdeveloped when the financial crisis hit. Seventy-two percent of the respondents, for example, "expressed concern about their own companies' risk management practices and ability to meet strategic plans."[15] Instructively, 42% "foresaw more energized involvement by boards of directors in risk management policies, processes and systems,"[16] which implies that pre-crisis boards were inadequately engaged with risk management. This inference finds support in a 2006 observation that risk management was still "a work in progress at many boards."[17]

Among firms that had undertaken risk management programs prior to the crisis, many used a silo approach in which different types of risk were managed by different teams within the firm using different processes. This sizeable group of firms thus failed to adopt an enterprise management approach in which all risk areas are brought into a single, integrated, firm-wide process. Indeed, according to a 2007 survey, only about 10% of respondent firms had adopted such a holistic approach to risk management.[18]

The significance of these failures as a causal factor in the financial crisis is highlighted by the Towers Perrin CFO survey. Sixty two percent of respondents blamed "poor or lax risk management at financial institutions as a major contributor to the current financial mess," a higher figure than either the complexity of financial instruments or speculation (55% and 57%, respectively).[19] Accordingly, "more than half (55%) of the CFOs" surveyed planned "to put their risk management practices under a microscope" in an

[12] See American Bar Association Committee on Corporation Laws, Corporate Director's Guidebook 27–28 (5th ed. 2007) (setting out board obligations for risk management and compliance programs).

[13] Carolyn Kay Brancato & Christian A. Plath, Corporate Governance Handbook 2005 75 (2005).

[14] Id. at 75.

[15] Towers Perrin, Financial Crisis Intensifies Interest in Risk Management Among CFOs (Sept. 2008).

[16] Id.

[17] Crouhy et al., supra note 8, at 85.

[18] Simkins & Ramirez, supra note 7, at 584.

[19] Towers Perrin, supra note 15.

investigation that "will in many instances reach all levels of the organization, from the board down and from the shop floor up."[20]

To be sure, some argue that even effective risk management programs could not have anticipated the financial crisis that struck in 2008. As the argument goes, risks fall into three broad categories: known problems, known unknowns, and unknown unknowns. "There is a view that the financial crisis—while clearly a high-impact; rare-event risk—was unpredictable and possibly unmanageable, an unknown unknown."[21] In fact, however, there were warning signs of an approaching crisis in the housing market, including "easy home-mortgage credit terms combined with rapidly accelerating home prices and reportedly lax credit standards,"[22] which in turn signaled risks for the financial services industry and then the economy as a whole.

Evaluating such extremely low probability but very high magnitude risks is challenging because the outcomes associated with such risks do not follow a normal distribution. Instead, they tend to have long or fat tails.[23] Because risk management focuses on extreme events, requiring one to quantify the probability and magnitude of severe loss events, an uncertainty generating such a fat- or long-tailed distribution poses "a severe problem for risk managers."[24] Indeed, there is considerable evidence that such risks are approached in "a sort of lax, undisciplined way" that results in them being "undermanaged before they first occur and overmanaged afterward."[25] Nonetheless, "it is simply unacceptable to chalk such an event up to 'not manageable' and focus on the more predictable, tameable and probably less-severe risks."[26]

Writing off efforts to enhance risk management so as to anticipate future crises is especially unacceptable when one considers the price shareholders paid for management failures in the most recent crisis. In 2008 alone, declining stock prices caused investors to lose $6.9 trillion. Curiously, however, Dodd-Frank did very little to change risk management practices. Instead, risk management remains mainly with the domain of state corporate law.

---

[20] Id.

[21] Thomas L. Barton et al., Managing an Unthinkable Event, Fin. Exec., Dec. 1, 2008, at 24.

[22] Id.

[23] A fat tail distribution has a mean and variance similar to the normal distribution but different probability masses at the tails. Linda Allen et al., Understanding Market, Credit, and Operational Risk: The Value at Risk Approach 25 (2004). As such the probability of an extreme outcome is higher in a fat tailed distribution than the normal distribution. Id. In a long tail distribution, a small number of high frequency outcomes is followed by a large set of low frequency outcomes that gradually tail off asymptotically. Outcomes at the far end of the tail thus have a very low probability of occurrence. Robert Sandy, Statistics for Business and Economics 47 (1989).

[24] Allen et al., supra note 23, at 26.

[25] Barton et al., supra note 21.

[26] Id.

In re Citigroup Inc. Shareholder
Derivative Litigation

964 A.2d 106 (Del. Ch. 2009)

This is a shareholder derivative action brought on behalf of Citigroup Inc. ("Citigroup" or the "Company"), seeking to recover for the Company its losses arising from exposure to the subprime lending market. Plaintiffs, shareholders of Citigroup, brought this action against current and former directors and officers of Citigroup, alleging, in essence, . . . that since as early as 2006, defendants have caused and allowed Citigroup to engage in subprime lending[2] that ultimately left the Company exposed to massive losses by late 2007. Beginning in late 2005, house prices, which many believe were artificially inflated by speculation and easily available credit, began to plateau, and then deflate. Adjustable rate mortgages issued earlier in the decade began to reset, leaving many homeowners with significantly increased monthly payments. Defaults and foreclosures increased, and assets backed by income from residential mortgages began to decrease in value. By February 2007, subprime mortgage lenders began filing for bankruptcy and subprime mortgages packaged into securities began experiencing increasing levels of delinquency. In mid-2007, rating agencies downgraded bonds backed by subprime mortgages.

Much of Citigroup's exposure to the subprime lending market arose from its involvement with collateralized debt obligations ("CDOs")— repackaged pools of lower rated securities that Citigroup created by acquiring asset-backed securities, including residential mortgage backed securities ("RMBSs"),[4] and then selling rights to the cash flows from the securities in classes, or tranches, with different levels of risk and return. Included with at least some of the CDOs created by Citigroup was a "liquidity put"—an option that allowed the purchasers of the CDOs to sell them back to Citigroup at original value.

By late 2007, it was apparent that Citigroup faced significant losses on its subprime-related assets . . . .

Plaintiffs allege that defendants are liable to the Company for breach of fiduciary duty for . . . failing to adequately oversee and manage Citigroup's exposure to the problems in the subprime mortgage market, even in the face of alleged "red flags" . . . . [T]he "red flags" alleged . . . are generally statements from public documents that reflect worsening conditions in the financial markets, including the subprime and credit markets, and the effects those worsening conditions had on market participants, including Citigroup's peers. By way of example only, plaintiffs' "red flags" include the following:

---

[2] "Subprime" generally refers to borrowers who do not qualify for prime interest rates, typically due to weak credit histories, low credit scores, high debt-burden ratios, or high loan-to-value ratios.

[4] RMBSs are securities whose cash flows come from residential debt such as mortgages.

- *May 27, 2005:* Economist Paul Krugman of the *New York Times* said he saw "signs that America's housing market, like the stock market at the end of the last decade, is approaching the final, feverish stages of a speculative bubble."

- *May 2006:* Ameriquest Mortgage, one of the United States' leading wholesale subprime lenders, announced the closing of each of its 229 retail offices and reduction of 3,800 employees.

- *February 12, 2007:* ResMae Mortgage, a subprime lender, filed for bankruptcy. According to *Bloomberg,* in its Chapter 11 filing, ResMae stated that "[t]he subprime mortgage market has recently been crippled and a number of companies stopped originating loans and United States housing sales have slowed and defaults by borrowers have risen."

- *April 18, 2007:* Freddie Mac announced plans to refinance up to $20 billion of loans held by subprime borrowers who would be unable to afford their adjustable-rate mortgages at the reset rate.

- *July 10, 2007:* Standard and Poor's and Moody's downgraded bonds backed by subprime mortgages.

- *August 1, 2007:* Two hedge funds managed by Bear Stearns that invested heavily in subprime mortgages declared bankruptcy.

- *August 9, 2007:* American International Group, one of the largest United States mortgage lenders, warned that mortgage defaults were spreading beyond the subprime sector, with delinquencies becoming more common among borrowers in the category just above subprime.

- *October 18, 2007:* Standard & Poor's cut the credit ratings on $23.35 billion of securities backed by pools of home loans that were offered to borrowers during the first half of the year. The downgrades even hit securities rated AAA, which was the highest of the ten investment-grade ratings and the rating of government debt.

. . .

Plaintiffs' argument is based on a theory of director liability famously articulated by former-Chancellor Allen in *In re Caremark.*[37] . . . In *Caremark*, the plaintiffs alleged that the directors were liable because they should have known that certain officers and employees were violating the federal Anti-Referral Payments Law. . . .

---

[37]   In re Caremark Int'l Inc. Derivative Litig., 698 A.2d 959 (Del.Ch.1996).

With regard to director liability standards, the Court distinguished between (1) "*a board decision* that results in a loss because that decision was ill advised or 'negligent' " and (2) "an *unconsidered failure of the board to act* in circumstances in which due attention would, arguably, have prevented the loss."[40] In the former class of cases, director action is analyzed under the business judgment rule, which prevents judicial second guessing of the decision if the directors employed a rational process and considered all material information reasonably available—a standard measured by concepts of gross negligence. As former-Chancellor Allen explained:

> What should be understood, but may not widely be understood by courts or commentators who are not often required to face such questions, is that compliance with a director's duty of care can never appropriately be judicially determined by reference to *the content of the board decision* that leads to a corporate loss, apart from consideration of the good faith *or* rationality of the process employed. That is, whether a judge or jury considering the matter after the fact, believes a decision substantively wrong, or degrees of wrong extending through "stupid" to "egregious" or "irrational", provides no ground for director liability, so long as the court determines that the process employed was either rational or employed in *a good faith* effort to advance corporate interests. To employ a different rule—one that permitted an "objective" evaluation of the decision—would expose directors to substantive second guessing by ill-equipped judges or juries, which would, in the long-run, be injurious to investor interests. Thus, the business judgment rule is process oriented and informed by a deep respect for all *good faith* board decisions.[42]

In the latter class of cases, where directors are alleged to be liable for a failure to monitor liability creating activities, the *Caremark* Court, in a reassessment of the holding in *Graham*, stated that while directors could be liable for a failure to monitor, "only a sustained or systematic failure of the board to exercise oversight—such as an utter failure to attempt to assure a reasonable information and reporting system

---

40   *Caremark*, 698 A.2d at 967 [emphasis supplied].

42   *Caremark*, 698 A.2d at 967–68 (footnotes omitted).

exists—will establish the lack of good faith that is a necessary condition to liability."[43]

In *Stone v. Ritter,* the Delaware Supreme Court approved the *Caremark* standard for director oversight liability and made clear that liability was based on the concept of good faith, which the *Stone* Court held was embedded in the fiduciary duty of loyalty and did not constitute a freestanding fiduciary duty that could independently give rise to liability. As the *Stone* Court explained:

> *Caremark* articulates the necessary conditions predicate for director oversight liability: (a) the directors utterly failed to implement any reporting or information system or controls; *or* (b) having implemented such a system or controls, consciously failed to monitor or oversee its operations thus disabling themselves from being informed of risks or problems requiring their attention. In either case, imposition of liability requires a showing that the directors knew that they were not discharging their fiduciary obligations. Where directors fail to act in the face of a known duty to act, thereby demonstrating a conscious disregard for their responsibilities, they breach their duty of loyalty by failing to discharge that fiduciary obligation in good faith.[45]
>
> . . .

Plaintiffs' theory of how the director defendants will face personal liability is a bit of a twist on the traditional *Caremark* claim. In a typical *Caremark* case, plaintiffs argue that the defendants are liable for damages that arise from a failure to properly monitor or oversee employee misconduct or violations of law. For example, in *Caremark* the board allegedly failed to monitor employee actions in violation of the federal Anti-Referral Payments Law; in *Stone,* the directors were charged with a failure of oversight that resulted in liability for the company because of employee violations of the federal Bank Secrecy Act.

In contrast, plaintiffs' *Caremark* claims are based on defendants' alleged failure to properly monitor Citigroup's *business risk,* specifically its exposure to the subprime mortgage market. In their answering brief, plaintiffs allege that the director defendants are personally liable under *Caremark* for failing to "make a good faith attempt to follow the procedures put in place or fail[ing] to assure that adequate and proper corporate information and reporting systems existed that would enable them to be fully informed regarding Citigroup's risk to the subprime mortgage market."

. . .

---

[43] Id. at 971.

[45] [Stone v. Ritter, 911 A.2d 362, 370 (Del.2006).]

The Delaware Supreme Court made clear in *Stone* that directors of Delaware corporations have certain responsibilities to implement and monitor a system of oversight; however, this obligation does not eviscerate the core protections of the business judgment rule— protections designed to allow corporate managers and directors to pursue risky transactions without the specter of being held personally liable if those decisions turn out poorly. Accordingly, . . . as former-Chancellor Allen noted in *Caremark,* director liability based on the duty of oversight "is possibly the most difficult theory in corporation law upon which a plaintiff might hope to win a judgment."[57]

To the extent the Court allows shareholder plaintiffs to succeed on a theory that a director is liable for a failure to monitor business risk, the Court risks undermining the well settled policy of Delaware law by inviting Courts to perform a hindsight evaluation of the reasonableness or prudence of directors' business decisions. Risk has been defined as the chance that a return on an investment will be different that expected. The essence of the business judgment of managers and directors is deciding how the company will evaluate the trade-off between risk and return. Businesses—and particularly financial institutions—make returns by taking on risk; a company or investor that is willing to take on more risk can earn a higher return. Thus, in almost any business transaction, the parties go into the deal with the knowledge that, even if they have evaluated the situation correctly, the return could be different than they expected.

It is almost impossible for a court, in hindsight, to determine whether the directors of a company properly evaluated risk and thus made the "right" business decision.[58] In any investment there is a chance that returns will turn out lower than expected, and generally a smaller chance that they will be far lower than expected. When investments turn out poorly, it is possible that the decision-maker evaluated the deal correctly but got "unlucky" in that a huge loss—the probability of which was very small—actually happened. It is also possible that the decision-maker improperly evaluated the risk posed by an investment and that the company suffered large losses as a result.

Business decision-makers must operate in the real world, with imperfect information, limited resources, and an uncertain future. To impose liability on directors for making a "wrong" business decision would cripple their ability to earn returns for investors by taking business risks. Indeed, this kind of judicial second guessing is what the

---

[57]   *Caremark*, 698 A.2d at 967.

[58]   *See* Stephen M. Bainbridge, The Business Judgment Rule as Abstention Doctrine, 57 VAND. L.REV. 83, 114–15 (2004) ("[T]here is a substantial risk that suing shareholders and reviewing judges will be unable to distinguish between competent and negligent management because bad outcomes often will be regarded, ex post, as having been foreseeable and, therefore, preventable ex ante. If liability results from bad outcomes, without regard to the ex ante quality of the decision or the decision-making process, however, managers will be discouraged from taking risks.") (footnotes omitted).

business judgment rule was designed to prevent, and even if a complaint is framed under a *Caremark* theory, this Court will not abandon such bedrock principles of Delaware fiduciary duty law. With these considerations and the difficult standard required to show director oversight liability in mind, I turn to an evaluation of the allegations in the Complaint.

. . .

The allegations in the Complaint amount essentially to a claim that Citigroup suffered large losses and that there were certain warning signs that could or should have put defendants on notice of the business risks related to Citigroup's investments in subprime assets. Plaintiffs then conclude that because defendants failed to prevent the Company's losses associated with certain business risks, they must have consciously ignored these warning signs or knowingly failed to monitor the Company's risk in accordance with their fiduciary duties. Such conclusory allegations, however, are not sufficient to state a claim for failure of oversight that would give rise to a substantial likelihood of personal liability, which would require particularized factual allegations demonstrating bad faith by the director defendants.

Plaintiffs do not contest that Citigroup had procedures and controls in place that were designed to monitor risk. Plaintiffs admit that Citigroup established the ARM Committee and in 2004 amended the ARM Committee charter to include the fact that one of the purposes of the ARM Committee was to assist the board in fulfilling its oversight responsibility relating to policy standards and guidelines for risk assessment and risk management. The ARM Committee was also charged with, among other things, (1) discussing with management and independent auditors the annual audited financial statements, (2) reviewing with management an evaluation of Citigroup's internal control structure, and (3) discussing with management Citigroup's major credit, market, liquidity, and operational risk exposures and the steps taken by management to monitor and control such exposures, including Citigroup's risk assessment and risk management policies. According to plaintiffs' own allegations, the ARM Committee met eleven times in 2006 and twelve times in 2007.

Plaintiffs nevertheless argue that the director defendants breached their duty of oversight either because the oversight mechanisms were not adequate or because the director defendants did not make a good faith effort to comply with the established oversight procedures. . . .

The warning signs alleged by plaintiffs are not evidence that the directors consciously disregarded their duties or otherwise acted in bad faith; at most they evidence that the directors made bad business decisions. The "red flags" in the Complaint amount to little more than portions of public documents that reflected the worsening conditions in the subprime mortgage market and in the economy generally. . . .That the director defendants knew of signs of a deterioration in the subprime mortgage market, or even signs suggesting that conditions could decline further, is not sufficient to show that the directors were or should have been aware of any wrongdoing at the Company or were consciously disregarding a duty somehow to prevent Citigroup from suffering losses. . . .

. . . These types of conclusory allegations are exactly the kinds of allegations that do not state a claim for relief under *Caremark.*

To recognize such claims under a theory of director oversight liability would undermine the long established protections of the business judgment rule. It is well established that the mere fact that a company takes on business risk and suffers losses—even catastrophic losses—does not evidence misconduct, and without more, is not a basis for personal director liability.[72]

. . .

NOTES AND QUESTIONS

1.   In this section, we are focused exclusively on the substantive law of director oversight. In actual litigation, however, these cases are subject to the further substantial complications caused by the fact that oversight litigation is almost exclusively brought as shareholder derivative suits. For a discussion of the derivative suit aspects of oversight cases, see below.

2.   In a subsequent decision, the Delaware Chancery Court reaffirmed that board oversight of law compliance with positive law is distinguishable from "management of business risk."[27] In contrast, your author has argued that:

> In fact, risk management and law compliance are not "fundamentally different." First, there are no reasonable grounds in the Caremark opinion for limiting the obligations created therein to legal and accounting compliance. Granted, Chancellor Allen made much of the benefits that law compliance programs offered corporations under the federal sentencing guidelines. Yet, that was only one of the three justifications Chancellor Allen offered. The necessity for the board to ensure that it is provided with sufficient information to carry out its obligations, which drove Chancellor Allen's other rationales, seems just as relevant to risk management as to legal and accounting compliance. . . .
>
> Second, the risk management role assigned to the board of directors by emergent corporate best practice guides is comparable to the role assigned to boards with respect to law compliance and accounting controls. The Corporate Director's Guidebook, for example, conflates risk and compliance oversight into a single

---

[72]   *See* Gagliardi v. TriFoods Int'l, Inc., 683 A.2d 1049, 1051 (Del.Ch.1996) ("The business outcome of an investment project that is unaffected by director self-interest or bad faith, cannot itself be an occasion for director liability.") (footnote omitted).

[27]   In re Clovis Oncology, Inc. Derivative Litig., CV 2017-0222-JRS, 2019 WL 4850188, at *12 (Del. Ch. Oct. 1, 2019).

topic. . . . Likewise, the Committee of Sponsoring Organizations of the Treadway Commission (COSO) lists "compliance with applicable laws and regulations" as one of four broad categories of enterprise risk management, along with ensuring that the corporation is pursuing appropriate strategic goals, making effective and efficient operational use of resources, and providing reliable disclosures.

Third, the board's role in risk management has been described as one of ensuring that the corporation has put into place an effective risk management program with procedures "for identifying, assessing, and managing all types of risk, i.e. business risk, operational risk, market risk, liquidity risk, and credit risk." The board's role thus includes "making sure that all the appropriate policies, methodologies, and infrastructure are in place." Notice the rather precise parallel to Caremark's description of the board's obligation to ensure that effective reporting structures exist with respect to law compliance.

Finally, risk management failures raise concerns about board-management relations comparable to those raised by law compliance or accounting irregularities. . . . In particular, a corporation's failure to adopt effective enterprise risk management may often be attributable to resistance by the CEO and top management.[28]

Do you agree with the court or your author? Why?

3.   By some estimates, there are at least 4,500 federal criminal statutes, which obviously omits federal statutes giving rise to civil sanctions and both state criminal and civil laws. Given that enormous volume of laws with which corporations must comply, how does a board decide what law compliance programs their corporation should adopt?

4.   How would the *Citigroup* court have decided the following cases?

A.   The board of directors adopts an effective law compliance program and effectively monitors the program, but a subordinate employee nevertheless causes the corporation to commit serious criminal violations for which the corporation is indicted and ultimately required to pay a substantial fine.

B.   The board of directors failed to adopt any law compliance program because the board was simply unaware of the need for such a program.

C.   Counsel advised the board that the nature of the company's business created a risk that company employees might violate a certain federal regulation. The board of directors carefully considered adopting a law compliance program, receiving expert advice on the relevant laws, the likelihood of violations, and other pertinent concerns. After lengthy deliberations, the

---

[28]   Stephen M. Bainbridge, Caremark and Enterprise Risk Management, 34 J. Corp. L. 967, 979–81 (2009).

board concluded that the costs associated with creating and maintaining an effective compliance program outweighed the benefits such a program offered. The board therefore decided not to adopt the law compliance program. Company employees subsequently violate the regulation. The company is convicted and required to pay a substantial fine that has a materially adverse impact on its earnings.

5. An interesting version of the *Caremark* duty was raised in *Beam ex rel. Martha Stewart Living Omnimedia, Inc. v. Stewart*,[29] involving Martha Stewart's alleged insider trading:

Defendant Martha Stewart ("Stewart") is a director of the company and its founder, chairman, chief executive officer, and by far its majority shareholder. . . . Stewart, a former stockbroker, has in the past twenty years become a household icon, known for her advice and expertise on virtually all aspects of cooking, decorating, entertaining, and household affairs generally.

The market for [Martha Stewart Living Omnimedia, Inc. ("MSO")] products is uniquely tied to the personal image and reputation of its founder, Stewart. MSO retains "an exclusive, worldwide, perpetual royalty-free license to use [Stewart's] name, likeness, image, voice and signature for its products and services." In its initial public offering prospectus, MSO recognized that impairment of Stewart's services to the company, including the tarnishing of her public reputation, would have a material adverse effect on its business. . . . In fact, under the terms of her employment agreement, Stewart may be terminated for gross misconduct or felony conviction that results in harm to MSO's business or reputation but is permitted discretion over the management of her personal, financial, and legal affairs to the extent that Stewart's management of her own life does not compromise her ability to serve the company.

Stewart's alleged misadventures with ImClone arise in part out of a longstanding personal friendship with Samuel D. Waksal ("Waksal"). Waksal is the former chief executive officer of ImClone. . . . Waksal and Stewart have provided one another with reciprocal investment advice and assistance, and they share a stockbroker, Peter E. Bacanovic ("Bacanovic") of Merrill Lynch. . . . The speculative value of ImClone stock was tied quite directly to the likely success of its application for FDA approval to market the cancer treatment drug Erbitux. On December 26, Waksal received information that the FDA was rejecting the application to market Erbitux. The following day, December 27, he tried to sell his own shares and tipped his father and daughter to do the same. Stewart also sold her shares on December 27. . . . After the close of trading on December 28, ImClone publicly announced the rejection of its application to market Erbitux. The following day the trading price

---

[29]　833 A.2d 961 (Del. Ch. 2003), aff'd, 845 A.2d 1040 (Del. 2004).

closed slightly more than 20% lower than the closing price on the date that Stewart had sold her shares. By mid-2002, this convergence of events had attracted the interest of the New York Times and other news agencies, federal prosecutors, and a committee of the United States House of Representatives. Stewart's publicized attempts to quell any suspicion were ineffective at best because they were undermined by additional information as it came to light and by the other parties' accounts of the events. Ultimately Stewart's prompt efforts to turn away unwanted media and investigative attention failed. Stewart eventually had to discontinue her regular guest appearances on CBS' The Early Show because of questioning during the show about her sale of ImClone shares. After barely two months of such adverse publicity, MSO's stock price had declined by slightly more than 65%. In August 2002, James Follo, MSO's chief financial officer, cited uncertainty stemming from the investigation of Stewart in response to questions about earnings prospects in the future. . . .

Count II of the amended complaint alleges that the director defendants and defendant Patrick breached their fiduciary duties by failing to ensure that Stewart would not conduct her personal, financial, and legal affairs in a manner that would harm the Company, its intellectual property, or its business.[30]

The *Stewart* case was heard by the same judge—Chancellor William Chandler—who later decided the *Citigroup* case. How do you think he ruled in *Stewart* and why?

6.   The Federal Sentencing Guidelines provide that the punishment to be imposed on a corporation that violates federal law may be reduced if the corporation has an effective law compliance program. Guidelines § 8B2.1 provides that:

(a) To have an effective compliance and ethics program . . . an organization shall (1) exercise due diligence to prevent and detect criminal conduct; and (2) otherwise promote an organizational culture that encourages ethical conduct and a commitment to compliance with the law.

Such compliance and ethics program shall be reasonably designed, implemented, and enforced so that the program is generally effective in preventing and detecting criminal conduct. The failure to prevent or detect the instant offense does not necessarily mean that the program is not generally effective in preventing and detecting criminal conduct.

(b) Due diligence and the promotion of an organizational culture that encourages ethical conduct and a commitment to compliance with the law within the meaning of subsection (a) minimally require the following:

---

[30]   Id. at 966–71. Stewart eventually was convicted not of insider trading but rather of obstruction of justice and jailed for five months. She later settled SEC insider trading allegations.

(1) The organization shall establish standards and procedures to prevent and detect criminal conduct.

(2) (A)   The organization's governing authority shall be knowledgeable about the content and operation of the compliance and ethics program and shall exercise reasonable oversight with respect to the implementation and effectiveness of the compliance and ethics program.

(B)   High-level personnel of the organization shall ensure that the organization has an effective compliance and ethics program, as described in this guideline. Specific individual(s) within high-level personnel shall be assigned overall responsibility for the compliance and ethics program.

(C)   Specific individual(s) within the organization shall be delegated day-to-day operational responsibility for the compliance and ethics program. Individual(s) with operational responsibility shall report periodically to high-level personnel and, as appropriate, to the governing authority, or an appropriate subgroup of the governing authority, on the effectiveness of the compliance and ethics program. To carry out such operational responsibility, such individual(s) shall be given adequate resources, appropriate authority, and direct access to the governing authority or an appropriate subgroup of the governing authority.

(3)   The organization shall use reasonable efforts not to include within the substantial authority personnel of the organization any individual whom the organization knew, or should have known through the exercise of due diligence, has engaged in illegal activities or other conduct inconsistent with an effective compliance and ethics program.

(4) (A)   The organization shall take reasonable steps to communicate periodically and in a practical manner its standards and procedures, and other aspects of the compliance and ethics program, to the individuals referred to in subparagraph (B) by conducting effective training programs and otherwise disseminating information appropriate to such individuals' respective roles and responsibilities.

(B)   The individuals referred to in subparagraph (A) are the members of the governing authority, high-level personnel, substantial authority personnel, the organization's employees, and, as appropriate, the organization's agents.

(5)   The organization shall take reasonable steps—

(A)   to ensure that the organization's compliance and ethics program is followed, including monitoring and auditing to detect criminal conduct;

(B)   to evaluate periodically the effectiveness of the organization's compliance and ethics program; and

(C) to have and publicize a system, which may include mechanisms that allow for anonymity or confidentiality, whereby the organization's employees and agents may report or seek guidance regarding potential or actual criminal conduct without fear of retaliation.

(6) The organization's compliance and ethics program shall be promoted and enforced consistently throughout the organization through (A) appropriate incentives to perform in accordance with the compliance and ethics program; and (B) appropriate disciplinary measures for engaging in criminal conduct and for failing to take reasonable steps to prevent or detect criminal conduct.

(7) After criminal conduct has been detected, the organization shall take reasonable steps to respond appropriately to the criminal conduct and to prevent further similar criminal conduct, including making any necessary modifications to the organization's compliance and ethics program.

Must a compliance program meet all of these criteria in order for a board of directors to satisfy its state law *Caremark* duty?

7. In *Stone*, the Delaware Supreme Court held that, absent "red flags, good faith in the context of oversight must be measured by the directors' actions to assure a reasonable information and reporting system exists and not by second-guessing after the occurrence of employee conduct that results in an unintended adverse outcome."[31]

In *In re Citigroup Inc. Shareholders Litig.*, the Chancery Court held that:

> Plaintiff's red flags consisted "of a series of internal corporate memoranda and e-mails disseminated at the level of Citigroup's operating subsidiaries. There is nothing . . . to suggest or to permit the court to infer that any of these ever came to the attention of the board of directors or any committee of the board. How, exactly, a member of the Citigroup board of directors was supposed to be put on inquiry notice by something he or she never saw or heard of is not explained. . . . 'Red flags' are only useful when they are either waved in one's face or displayed so that they are visible to the careful observer."[32]

Finally, in *Iron Workers Mid-S. Pension Fund v. Davis,* a federal district court held that the requisite "red flags must show that the director defendants knew that there were material weaknesses in [the company]'s internal controls, not simply that directors knew that mortgage-backed securities were receiving intense scrutiny."[33]

What are these mysterious red flags? Can you give examples?

---

[31]   Stone ex rel. AmSouth Bancorporation v. Ritter, 911 A.2d 362, 373 (Del. 2006).

[32]   2003 WL 21384599, at *2 (Del. Ch. June 5, 2003).

[33]   93 F. Supp. 3d 1092, 1099 (D. Minn. 2015) [internal quotation marks omitted].

8.   Should directors with specialized expertise be held to a higher standard?

9.   Although most of Dodd-Frank's corporate governance provisions applied equally to Main Street and Wall Street, this is not the case with respect to risk management. Instead, Dodd-Frank § 165 mandates creation of board-level risk management committees only for bank holding companies and those non-bank financial services companies supervised by the Federal Reserve.

Likewise, the SEC has refrained from substantive regulation of risk management, which likely is beyond the scope of its regulatory authority in any case. Instead, the Commission amended its proxy disclosure rules in 2009 to require risk management-related disclosures in two contexts. First, if "risks arising from a company's compensation policies and practices for employees are reasonably likely to have a material adverse effect on the company," the proxy statement must discuss those policies and practices. As originally proposed, the rule would have required disclosure of risks that "may have a material effect" on the company. The higher standard included in the rule as adopted is expected to result in fewer disclosures and to confine disclosure mainly to financial services firms.[34]

Second, the proxy statement must include a discussion of how the board of directors administers its risk management oversight. The new rule assumes a board role in risk management but does not attempt to define substantively what that role ought to be. It seems likely that disclosures will focus on those risks identified in the MD&A section of the corporation's annual report, since those are the ones most likely to have a material impact on the company. The disclosures also likely will focus on such issues as whether the board has a separate risk management committee and how the board interacts with those managers responsible for risk management on an operational basis.

10.   Does *Citigroup* mean that the monitoring model has no legal teeth? If so, should the Delaware courts rethink the rules that make successful *Caremark* claims so rare?

In thinking about that question, consider *Marchand v. Barnhill*,[35] in which shareholders of Blue Bell Creameries USA, Inc., a major ice cream manufacturer, brought *Caremark* claims against Blue Bell's board after listeria—a bacterium capable of causing a potentially fatal food borne illness—contaminated the company's manufacturing facilities and, as a result, its products. Three people died from eating contaminated ice cream and many were struck ill. The company had to shut down its facilities, recall all of its products, lay off a third of its workers, and suffered a serious liquidity crisis. The Supreme Court held that "the complaint alleges particularized facts that support a reasonable inference that the Blue Bell board failed to implement any system to monitor Blue Bell's food safety performance or compliance." The court further explained that:

---

[34]   Proxy Disclosure Enhancements, Exchange Act Rel. No. 61,675 (Dec. 16, 2009).

[35]   212 A.3d 805 (Del. 2019).

As a monoline company that makes a single product—ice cream—Blue Bell can only thrive if its consumers enjoyed its products and were confident that its products were safe to eat. That is, one of Blue Bell's central compliance issues is food safety. Despite this fact, the complaint alleges that Blue Bell's board had no committee overseeing food safety, no full board-level process to address food safety issues, and no protocol by which the board was expected to be advised of food safety reports and developments. Consistent with this dearth of any board-level effort at monitoring, the complaint pleads particular facts supporting an inference that during a crucial period when yellow and red flags about food safety were presented to management, there was no equivalent reporting to the board and the board was not presented with any material information about food safety.

The court rejected the defendants' arguments that Blue Bell was subject to state and federal food safety regulations, its facilities were periodically inspected by government officials with the results being reported to management, management periodically audited the company's safety procedures, and employees were provided with policy manuals detailing safety procedures. According to the court, the fact "that Blue Bell is in a highly regulated industry and complied with some of the applicable regulations does not foreclose any pleading-stage inference that the directors' lack of attentiveness rose to the level of bad faith indifference required to state a *Caremark* claim." For the court, that there was no board-level monitoring system was especially problematic since food safety was "essential and mission critical" for a monoline food producer like Blue Bell.

PROBLEM

You are counsel to Serenity Biologics, Inc., a startup pharmaceutical company that has a drug called Clearlung under development. Clearlung is a potential treatment for lung cancer that performed well in animal trials. Clearlung is currently undergoing human trials pursuant to the extensive regulatory regime administered by the Food and Drug Administration. If approved, Clearlung will be Serenity's first product to go to market. Because of the estimated $3 billion annual market for drugs of its type, Serenity expects Clearlung to generate large profits if Serenity can secure FDA approval for the drug and bring it to market.

To obtain FDA approval, new drugs like Clearlung must prove their efficacy and safety in clinical trials. Before commencing a clinical trial, the FDA requires a drug's sponsor to agree to certain standards that define how the trial will be conducted, how the data generated by the trial will be analyzed, and the criteria by which success or failure in the trial will be measured. If the manufacturer fails to adhere to these clinical trial protocols, the FDA will not approve the new drug for market.

Minutes of Serenity's board of directors meetings show that the board was closely involved in supervising the clinical trials. Management gave the board a report on the trials at each quarterly board meeting and the board conducted extensive question and answer sessions with management. In addition, Serenity's board of directors created a Development Oversight Committee (DOC) comprised of independent directors specifically charged with oversight of the development process. The committee met monthly with management to receive detailed reports on the trial's progress. All three members of the Committee have extensive experience in the pharmaceutical industry. One is a physician who has conducted dozens of clinical trials of other drugs. Another is a former FDA official who oversaw hundreds of clinical trials. The third is a Professor of Oncology at a leading medical school.

In the fall of 202X, management of Serenity learned that a much larger drug company had begun clinical trials on a potential competitor to Clearlung. Knowing that the first product to reach the market would have significant competitive advantages, management began taking shortcuts in the trial. The agreed upon trial protocol allowed Serenity to report a positive patient result only if two successive MRI scans conducted two months apart both showed that the patient's tumors had shrunk. Serenity management nevertheless began reporting positive results based on a single scan. The reports given the DOC did not disclose that fact. The raw data on which those reports was based would have disclosed the improper trial procedures but that data was neither provided to the DOC nor requested by it.

Shortly before the clinical trial was to end the FDA discovered the shortcuts Serenity management had been taking. The FDA declared the clinical trial to be a failure and banned Clearlung from sale until a new clinical trial could be conducted by a new team of researchers.

You are counsel to Serenity's board of directors. The board has asked you to prepare a report on whether the board of directors faces any potential liability for breach of their fiduciary duties to the company and its shareholders in connection with the failed trial.[36]

PROBLEM

Gotham City is a major metropolis on the East Coast of the United States. Its city street layout was designed in the late 1800s long before cars became commonplace. As a result, the streets are quite narrow. In addition, large sections of the city were built prior to the Second World War, when cars were rare. As a result, many buildings—in both residential and business sections of the city—lack off-street parking and loading docks. In turn, the lack of off-street parking means that the limited amount of available on-street parking is typically fully occupied. The parking issues significantly complicate the work of parcel delivery services, which is becoming even worse as internet-based home delivery services have multiplied to include products such as meals, groceries, and a host of other products. Drivers are often unable to find parking at or near the building to which they must make a delivery. In such circumstances, drivers routinely double park while dashing inside a building to make a delivery.

---

[36] This problem is loosely based on the facts of In re Clovis Oncology, Inc. Derivative Litigation, 2019 WL 4850188 (Del.Ch.).

To combat the increasing wave of traffic congestion, the Gotham City Council recently passed a new law significantly increasing the fine for double parking.

You are General Counsel and Chief Legal Officer of Federal Package Services, a leading parcel delivery service corporation. The Chairman of the Board has called a meeting of the board of directors to consider a response to the new law. The Chief Logistics Officer reports to the board that drivers complying with the new law are expending significant amounts of time circling blocks looking for legal parking spaces and, if they can be found, are parking significantly further away from delivery locations. She tells the board that drivers are making 50% fewer deliveries per day, while fuel and related costs are up by 40%. If the company continues to comply with new law, it will need to hire a significant number of new drivers and add a substantial number of new delivery vehicles, since the search for parking means each truck will make fewer deliveries. The corporation's Head of Human resources reports that driver morale is extremely low. The board member who chairs the board's Committee on Sustainability and Social Responsibility Initiatives chimes in with an observation that compliance with the law has increased the corporation's global carbon footprint by 5 percent.

The corporation's Chief Financial Officer reports calculations that the new drivers, additional vehicles, and lost time necessary for compliance with the law will cost the company $30 million per year (out of revenues of $1.5 billion and profits of $115 million), not including social costs of increased carbon output and so on. If the corporation orders its drivers to disobey the law, double park as needed, and have the company pay any parking tickets, the company not incur any of those expenses but will pay about $4 million per year in traffic fines, resulting in a net savings of $26 million.

The Chairman of the Board asks you to advise the board as to whether adopting a corporate policy instructing drivers to violate the parking ordinance when and as necessary would expose the board of directors to any risk of personal liability. What advice to you give the board? In thinking about that question, bear in mind that Model Rule of Professional Responsibility 2.1 provides, in pertinent part, that "[i]n rendering advice, a lawyer may refer not only to law but to other considerations such as moral, economic, social and political factors, that may be relevant to the client's situation."

The Corporation is incorporated in Maine, which has no law on point. Your research turned up the following potentially relevant sources from other jurisdictions:

In re Walt Disney Co. Derivative Litig., 907 A.2d 693, 755 (Del. Ch. 2005), aff'd, 906 A.2d 27 (Del. 2006):

> A failure to act in good faith may be shown, for instance, where the fiduciary intentionally acts with a purpose other than that of advancing the best interests of the corporation, where the fiduciary acts with the intent to violate applicable positive law, or where the

fiduciary intentionally fails to act in the face of a known duty to act, demonstrating a conscious disregard for his duties.

Desimone v. Barrows, 924 A.2d 908, 934–35 (Del. Ch. 2007):

In short, by consciously causing the corporation to violate the law, a director would be disloyal to the corporation and could be forced to answer for the harm he has caused. Although directors have wide authority to take lawful action on behalf of the corporation, they have no authority knowingly to cause the corporation to become a rogue, exposing the corporation to penalties from criminal and civil regulators. Delaware corporate law has long been clear on this rather obvious notion; namely, that it is utterly inconsistent with one's duty of fidelity to the corporation to consciously cause the corporation to act unlawfully. The knowing use of illegal means to pursue profit for the corporation is director misconduct.

American Law Institute, Principles of Corporate Governance § 2.01:

(b) Even if corporate profit and shareholder gain are not thereby enhanced, the corporation, in the conduct of its business: (1) Is obliged, to the same extent as a natural person, to act within the boundaries set by law . . . .

Comment g. Under § 2.01(b)(1), the corporation is obliged, to the same extent as a natural person, to act within the boundaries set by law. It is sometimes maintained that whether a corporation should adhere to a given legal rule may properly depend on a kind of cost-benefit analysis, in which probable corporate gains are weighed against either probable social costs, measured by the dollar liability imposed for engaging in such conduct, or probable corporate losses, measured by potential dollar liability discounted for likelihood of detection. Section 2.01 does not adopt this position. With few exceptions, dollar liability is not a "price" that can properly be paid for the privilege of engaging in legally wrongful conduct. Cost-benefit analysis may have a place in the state's determination whether a given type of conduct should be deemed legally wrongful. Once that determination has been made, however, the resulting legal rule normally represents a community decision that the conduct is wrongful as such, so that cost-benefit analysis whether to obey the rule is out of place.

Accordingly, in conducting its business, the corporation, like all other citizens, is under an obligation to act within the boundaries set by law. . . .

Section 2.01(b)(1) is based on the moral norm of obedience to law. . . .

In this connection, there are certain limited exceptions where the norm of obedience to law is usually deemed inapplicable or counterbalanced by other norms. Thus notwithstanding the norm of obedience to law, noncompliance with law may be justified under the concept of necessity in extraordinary situations where compliance would inflict substantial harm on third parties, and noncompliance would not. This might occur, for example, if despite all efforts a public utility was unable to complete a modification of its plant in time to meet a statutory clean-air deadline, and the failure posed no imminent danger to health and safety, while plant shutdown would black out the local community. Similarly, noncompliance with law might be justified under the concept of desuetude (that is, disuse) where a departure from a legal rule is condoned by both social morality and relevant government authorities. The norm of obedience to law also is usually deemed counterbalanced where, under appropriate conditions, a rule is violated openly for the purpose of testing its validity or interpretation. Similarly, although a breach of contract may violate the moral norm that promises should be kept, the obligation of contract does not necessarily derive independent support from the norm of obedience to law.

These exceptions are not exhaustive: for example, the de minimis principle applies here as elsewhere in the law. Similarly, there may be isolated cases in which it is widely understood that liability is properly viewed as a price of noncompliance. In general, knowing noncompliance by a corporation should be treated no differently than knowing noncompliance by a natural person. Where a natural person would not be considered to be acting in a manner that violates the norm of obedience to law, neither should the corporation be deemed to be in violation of § 2.01(b)(1).

DGCL § 102(b)(7):

[T]he certificate of incorporation may also contain . . . [a] provision eliminating or limiting the personal liability of a director to the corporation or its stockholders for monetary damages for breach of fiduciary duty as a director, provided that such provision shall not eliminate or limit the liability of a director: (i) For any breach of the director's duty of loyalty to the corporation or its stockholders; (ii) for acts or omissions not in good faith or which involve intentional misconduct or a knowing violation of law; (iii) under § 174 of this title; or (iv) for any transaction from which the director derived an improper personal benefit.

DGCL § 145(a):

A corporation shall have power to indemnify any person who was or is a party or is threatened to be made a party to any threatened, pending or completed action, suit or proceeding, whether civil, criminal, administrative or investigative (other than an action by or in the right of the corporation) by reason of the fact that the person is or was a director, officer, employee or agent of the corporation, or is or was serving at the request of the corporation as a director, officer, employee or agent of another corporation, partnership, joint venture, trust or other enterprise, against expenses (including attorneys' fees), judgments, fines and amounts paid in settlement actually and reasonably incurred by the person in connection with such action, suit or proceeding if the person acted in good faith and in a manner the person reasonably believed to be in or not opposed to the best interests of the corporation, and, with respect to any criminal action or proceeding, had no reasonable cause to believe the person's conduct was unlawful.

B. OVERSIGHT DUTIES: PROCEDURAL RULES

There are two basic types of shareholder lawsuits. "Direct" shareholder suits arise out of causes of action belonging to the shareholders in their individual capacity. They are typically premised on an injury directly affecting the shareholders and must be brought by the shareholders in their own name. In contrast, a "derivative" suit is one brought by the shareholder on behalf of the corporation. The cause of action belongs to the corporation as an entity and arises out of an injury done to the corporation as an entity. The shareholder is merely acting as the firm's representative.

Lawsuits posing *Caremark*-based claims typically are derivative suits, because the directors' oversight duty runs to the corporation and because any recovery would go to the corporation.[37] As such, *Caremark* claims are subject to the extensive and unique procedural rules applicable to derivative litigation. For present purposes, the key requirement is the rule that shareholder either make demand on the board of directors before filing a derivative suit or convince the court that demand should be excused because making it would be futile.

City of Birmingham Ret. and Relief System v. Good
177 A.3d 47 (Del. 2017)

■ SEITZ, JUSTICE, for the Majority:

A stormwater pipe ruptured beneath a coal ash pond at Duke Energy Corporation's Dan River Steam Station in North Carolina. The spill sent a slurry of coal ash and wastewater—containing lead, mercury, and arsenic—into the Dan River, fouling the river for many miles downstream. In May 2015, Duke Energy pled guilty to nine misdemeanor criminal violations of the Federal Clean Water Act and paid a fine exceeding $100 million. The plaintiffs, stockholders of Duke Energy, filed a derivative suit in the Court of Chancery against certain of Duke Energy's directors and officers. On behalf of the Company, they sought to hold the directors—a majority of whom were outside directors and were

---

[37] See Tooley v. Donaldson, Lufkin & Jenrette, Inc., 845 A.2d 1031, 1033 (Del. 2004) (holding that whether a fiduciary duty claim is direct or derivative turns on: "(1) who suffered the alleged harm (the corporation or the suing stockholders, individually); and (2) who would receive the benefit of any recovery or other remedy (the corporation or the stockholders, individually)?").

not named in the criminal proceedings—personally liable for the damages the Company suffered from the spill.

. . .

I.

In 2013, several citizens' environmental groups filed a notice of intent to sue three of Duke Energy's subsidiaries under the CWA for coal ash seepages at ponds in North Carolina. In response, the North Carolina Department of Environmental Quality ("DEQ") filed an enforcement action, which preempted the suits. DEQ and Duke Energy negotiated a consent decree that would require Duke Energy to pay a $99,000 fine and create a compliance schedule. The consent decree also required Duke Energy to "identify[ ] and characteriz[e] seeps" and conduct "[g]roundwater studies." The Company planned to use the decree as a "model for resolving litigation" at twelve other sites, and estimated that enforcing the decree at all of its North Carolina locations would cost between $4 and $5 million. The consent decree was subject to a public comment period and court approval.

. . .

On April 22, 2016, the plaintiffs filed derivative suits in the Court of Chancery,32 alleging that the directors breached their fiduciary duties because they knew of and disregarded Duke Energy's CWA violations and allowed Duke Energy to collude with DEQ to evade compliance with environmental regulations. . . .

The directors moved to dismiss the complaint for failure to plead demand futility, claiming that the plaintiffs did not allege the particularized facts required by Court of Chancery Rule 23.1 to show that the directors faced a substantial likelihood of personal liability.* The Court of Chancery . . . dismissed the complaint under Court of Chancery Rule 23.1 for failure to make a demand on the board. This appeal followed. We review the Court of Chancery's dismissal of a stockholder derivative complaint de novo.

II.

The board of directors, exercising its statutory authority to manage the business and affairs of the corporation, ordinarily decides whether to initiate a lawsuit on behalf of the corporation. Stockholders cannot shortcut the board's control over the corporation's litigation decisions

---

* [Ed.: Delaware Rule of Chancery 23.1 governing derivative actions provides, in pertinent part:

(a) In a derivative action brought by one or more shareholders or members to enforce a right of a corporation or of an unincorporated association, the corporation or association having failed to enforce a right which may properly be asserted by it, the complaint shall allege that the plaintiff was a shareholder or member at the time of the transaction of which the plaintiff complains or that the plaintiff's share or membership thereafter devolved on the plaintiff by operation of law. The complaint shall also allege with particularity the efforts, if any, made by the plaintiff to obtain the action the plaintiff desires from the directors or comparable authority and the reasons for the plaintiff's failure to obtain the action or for not making the effort.]

without first complying with Court of Chancery Rule 23.1. Before stockholders can assert a claim belonging to the corporation, they must first demand that the directors pursue the claim and, if the directors decline, attempt to demonstrate that the directors wrongfully refused the demand. Alternatively, stockholders can allege with sufficient particularity that demand is futile and should be excused due to a disabling conflict by a majority of the directors to consider the demand.

For alleged violations of the board's oversight duties under *Caremark*, the test articulated in *Rales v. Blasband*** applies to assess demand futility. Under *Rales*, the plaintiffs must plead particularized facts raising "reasonable doubt of the board's independence and disinterestedness when the demand would reveal board inaction of a nature that would expose the board to 'a substantial likelihood' of personal liability."[40]

When, like here, the directors are protected from liability for due care violations under § 102(b)(7) of the Delaware General Corporation Law, the plaintiff must allege with particularity that the directors acted with scienter, meaning "they had 'actual or constructive knowledge' that their conduct was legally improper."[41] In other words, the stockholders must allege "that a director acted inconsistent with his fiduciary duties and, most importantly, that the director *knew* he was so acting."[42] This is because a *Caremark* claim "is rooted in concepts of bad faith; indeed, a showing of bad faith is a *necessary condition* to director oversight liability."[43] A specific example of bad faith is when the director engages in an "intentional dereliction of duty" or "conscious disregard for one's responsibilities,"[44] or acted "with the intent to violate applicable positive law."[45] Because of the difficulties in proving bad faith director action, a *Caremark* claim is "possibly the most difficult theory in corporation law upon which a plaintiff might hope to win a judgment."[46]

A. *The Board Presentations*

The Court of Chancery reviewed the board presentations addressing the ash ponds at Duke Energy's power generation sites, and concluded that the board was both "aware of environmental problems [and] what the company was doing to attempt to address those situations."

[**]   [Ed.: Rales v. Blasband, 634 A.2d 927 (Del. 1993).]

[40]   Horman v. Abney, 2017 WL 242571, at *6 (Del. Ch. Jan. 19, 2017) (quoting Rales, 634 A.2d at 936); see also In re Citigroup Inc. S'holder Derivative Litig., 964 A.2d 106, 121 (Del. Ch. 2009) (explaining demand is futile "in the rare case when a plaintiff is able to show director conduct that is so egregious on its face that board approval cannot meet the test of business judgment, and a substantial likelihood of director liability therefore exists").

[41]   [Ed.: Wood v. Baum, 953 A.2d 136, 141 (Del. 2008).]

[42]   [Ed.: In re Massey Energy Co., 2011 WL 2176479, at *22 (Del. Ch. May 31, 2011) (emphasis in original).]

[43]   In re Citigroup Inc. S'holder Derivative Litig., 964 A.2d at 123 (emphasis in original).

[44]   In re Walt Disney Co. Derivative Litig., 906 A.2d 27, 66 (Del. 2006).

[45]   In re Citigroup Inc. S'holder Derivative Litig., 964 A.2d at 125 (emphasis in original).

[46]   In re Caremark Int'l Inc. Derivative Litig., 698 A.2d at 967. . . .

According to the court, the directors did not consciously disregard the environmental problems. Rather, the presentations informed the board that Duke Energy was working with DEQ "to achieve regulatory compliance in a cost-effective way with limited liability." The court found the board presentations an insufficient basis to raise a reasonable inference of bad faith by the board.

On appeal, the plaintiffs challenge the Court of Chancery's conclusion, pointing to specific information in the board presentations and minutes that they argue suggested longstanding knowledge and disregard of environmental violations. The plaintiffs first highlight the December 12, 2012 Coal Combustion Residuals presentation, which stated that "[s]ome metals have leached to groundwater from unlined landfills and surface impoundments." Thus, the plaintiffs argue, the board knew Duke Energy was violating the law but did nothing to remedy it.

The plaintiffs unfairly describe the overall presentation, which we are not required to accept on a motion to dismiss. Jeff Lyash, Executive Vice President of Energy Supply, presented to the board's Regulatory Policy and Operations Committee on the Company's exposure (liability) from coal combustion residuals ("CCR's"), which are different kinds of coal ash. . . . The presentation is fairly described as a status update to the board committee of the proposed EPA regulations' impact on Duke Energy's ash disposal practices, and its "work underway" for "risk mitigation." As the Court of Chancery found, the board was not only informed of environmental problems, but also the steps being taken to address them. It does not support plaintiffs' central theory that a majority of the board consciously ignored or intentionally violated positive law.

The plaintiffs next point to the August 27, 2013 Environmental Review Presentation to the board of directors. In the twenty-two pages of slides, Keith Trent, Executive Vice President and Chief Operating Officer of Regulated Utilities, presented a comprehensive review of the history of coal ash ponds and environmental regulation, on-going litigation, and steps Duke Energy was taking to mitigate the financial and environmental risks posed by ash ponds at various Duke Energy sites.

The plaintiffs focus on one line in a slide stating "[s]eeps are unpermitted discharges; [groundwater] violations." The statement they refer to, however, was reporting allegations against Duke Energy in pending lawsuits. But more to the point, the . . . Presentation is fairly characterized as another update on environmental problems associated with coal ash disposal sites, and steps Duke Energy was taking to address the environmental concerns. It does not lead to a reasonable inference of the board's bad faith conduct by consciously ignoring environmental problems.

The plaintiffs' allegations here are like those in *Stone v. Ritter*.[66] In Stone, this Court considered whether a board of directors failed to discharge its oversight duties regarding compliance with the Federal Bank Secrecy Act. Although "[n]either party dispute[d] that the lack of internal controls resulted in a huge fine," the reports to the board showed that the board "exercised oversight by relying on periodic reports" from the officers.[68] Thus, the court found plaintiffs' complaint unsuccessfully attempted "to equate a bad outcome with bad faith."[69] Similarly, the plaintiffs here conflate the bad outcome of the criminal proceedings with the actions of the board. As in *Stone*, the board "exercised oversight" by receiving management presentations on the status of environmental problems. The presentations identified issues with the coal ash disposal ponds, but also informed the board of the actions taken to address the regulatory concerns. Thus, we agree with the Vice Chancellor that the board presentations do not lead to the inference that the board consciously disregarded its oversight responsibility by ignoring environmental concerns

B. *Collusion with Regulators*

To overcome the motion to dismiss, plaintiffs concede that they must plead sufficient facts showing that the board knew DEQ was a "captive regulator" with whom Duke Energy was "colluding." The Court of Chancery rejected this argument, finding it "a theory at once creative and unsustainable on the facts plead." According to the court, even if DEQ's prosecution of environmental violations was "insufficiently rigorous, or even wholly inadequate," it fell short of leading to a reasonable inference that Duke Energy illegally colluded with regulators.

On appeal, the plaintiffs claim the Court of Chancery made several errors in reaching this conclusion. Before addressing the details of these arguments, however, it is important to keep in mind the target the plaintiffs must hit to defeat the motion to dismiss. As the Court of Chancery found, it is not enough to allege cooperation with what plaintiffs describe as a too-friendly regulator. Instead, the plaintiffs must allege in sufficient detail that Duke Energy illegally colluded with a corrupt regulator. And then, plaintiffs must tie the improper conduct to an intentional oversight failure by the board. The complaint falls short of these pleading requirements.

1. *The Consent Decree*

The plaintiffs first argue the consent decree negotiated with DEQ was a fig leaf because it only imposed a $99,000 fine and did not require remediation. They allege that the fine was a "meaningless amount" in light of Duke Energy's $2.5 billion yearly earnings and that remediation

---

[66] 911 A.2d 362.

[68] Id. at 372–73.

[69] Id. at 373.

would not occur because the compliance schedule was not yet established, but was to be "further delineat[ed]." . . .

Like their characterization of the board presentations, the plaintiffs isolate one part of a much bigger picture. In addition to the fine, Duke Energy estimated spending $4 to $5 million to enforce the consent decree at all its North Carolina sites, $100,000 to identify and characterize seeps, and $300,000 to $500,000 to conduct groundwater studies and reroute flows or treatment. Duke Energy also expected to negotiate a compliance schedule with regulators. Further, the presentations show the EPA had still not finalized rules regulating CCR, and there were "[i]ndications that final rule may be non-hazardous," which would impact remediation costs. Regardless, even though DEQ imposed a relatively small fine and gave Duke Energy time to establish a compliance schedule, which was not as aggressive as the plaintiffs would have preferred, those facts do not lead to an inference that the board should have been alerted to corrupt activities between Duke Energy and its regulator. Nor does it lead to a reasonable inference that the board ignored evidence of alleged misconduct with a state regulator.

Finally, the collusion argument loses its force when another undisputed fact is considered—the consent decree was subject to approval by the North Carolina court. The public and environmental groups who intervened in the enforcement action had the opportunity to comment on and object to the consent decree before a court gave it the force of law. Thus, if the consent decree was as deficient as the plaintiffs claim and resulted from improper collusion with regulatory authorities, the court was in a position to make that judgment, and refuse to approve it.

2. *Lax Environmental Law Enforcement*

Next, plaintiffs argue that the board should have known DEQ was a captive regulator because DEQ was not a "particularly vigorous enforcer of environmental laws," and became "particularly friendly" when Patrick McCrory was elected governor. . . .

Although the plaintiffs have alleged that DEQ in general did not aggressively enforce environmental laws, DEQ's lack of aggressiveness does not lead to an inference in this case that Duke Energy illegally colluded with DEQ, and that the board was complicit in such illegal activities. We agree with the Court of Chancery that general allegations regarding a regulator's business-friendly policies are insufficient to lead to an inference that the board knew Duke Energy was colluding with a corrupt regulator.

. . .

III.

Duke Energy was responsible for fouling the Dan River with a slurry of toxic coal ash, causing major environmental damage many miles downstream. The Company pled guilty to environmental crimes and faced stiff fines and costly remediation expenses. The backlash for its poor environmental stewardship was severe. The EPA and the State of North Carolina responded by enacting stricter laws and proposing rules governing coal ash pond maintenance and closure.

None of this reflected well on Duke Energy. But, the question before us is not whether Duke Energy should be punished for its actions. That has already happened. What is before us is whether a majority of Duke Energy directors face a substantial likelihood that they will be found personally liable for intentionally causing Duke Energy to violate the law or consciously disregarding the law. We find, as the Court of Chancery did, that the plaintiffs failed to meet this pleading requirement. Thus, the plaintiffs were required to first demand that the board of directors address the claims they wished to pursue on behalf of the Company.

We therefore affirm the Court of Chancery's December 14, 2016 judgment dismissing the plaintiffs' derivative complaint.

■ STRINE, CHIEF JUSTICE, dissenting:

With regret, I respectfully dissent from the well-stated decision of my colleagues, which affirms a thoughtful decision of the Court of Chancery. I do so because I find that the facts pled raise a pleading stage inference that it was the business strategy of Duke Energy, accepted and supported by its board of directors, to run the company in a manner that purposely skirted, and in many ways consciously violated, important environmental laws. Being skilled at running an energy company whose conduct presented environmental hazards, but whose operations provided an important source of employment, Duke's executives, advisors, and directors used all the tools in their large box to cause Duke to flout its environmental responsibilities, therefore reduce its costs of operations, and by that means, increase its profitability. This, fiduciaries of a Delaware corporation, may not do.

My primary disagreement with my friends in the majority and the Court of Chancery involves the application of the procedural posture to the facts as pled. Even though we are in a context when particularized pleading is required, that does not mean that the plaintiffs must have conclusive proof of all their contentions. Instead, they must plead particularized facts that support a rational inference of non-exculpated breaches of fiduciary duty by a majority of the Duke Energy board. Rarely will such evidence involve admissions by experienced managers and board advisors that the strategy they are undertaking involves a conscious decision to violate the laws, against the backdrop of a regulatory environment heavily influenced by the company's own lobbying and political contributions.

. . . What [the plaintiffs] have to do [at this stage] is plead facts supporting an inference that Duke consciously was violating the law, taking steps that it knew were not sufficient to come into good faith compliance, but which it believed would be given a blessing by a regulatory agency whose fidelity to the law, the environment, and public health, seemed to be outweighed by its desire to be seen as protecting Duke and the jobs it creates.

The pled facts that support this inference at this stage include:

- Duke's board knew that Duke illegally discharged highly toxic water from its coal ash ponds into the groundwater, sometimes intentionally through manmade channels, in violation of both state and federal environmental law. Duke's 760 daily violations of environmental regulations dated back to at least January 2012: the earliest time period from which the state regulator could assess liability under the statute of limitations.

- Duke knew its coal ash ponds were contaminating groundwater at illegal levels, as confirmed by testing dating back to at least 2007 conducted by Duke itself, regulators, and environmental groups.

- Duke's board knew that Duke had to procure discharge permits for its many coal ash ponds, but continued to operate them illegally and, in some cases, without any permit at all, in violation of state law and the Clean Water Act, even after trying, but failing, to secure a less restrictive type of permit.

- Duke and its affiliated donors spent over $1.4 million dollars to influence its home state political process to secure the election of officials who would be lax in their enforcement of federal and state environmental laws that applied to Duke's operations, including a Governor who had been a Duke employee for twenty-eight years.

- Duke's board was aware of and supported the strategy to enlist the state regulator, which had done little to cause Duke to come into compliance with law in the past and which was now overseen by the Governor who had been a Duke employee for twenty-eight years and was supported by Duke in his campaign, to file complaints against Duke and thereby preempt the citizen suits that sought substantial remediation. The regulator then proposed a consent order that involved a trifle of a civil penalty and that did not require remediation or a change in Duke's coal ash storage practices.

- Four days after being court-ordered to immediately eliminate all sources of contamination from its coal ash ponds, Duke "was caught illegally and deliberately dumping toxic coal ash wastewater into the Cape Fear River, a practice that had been ongoing for several months and which resulted in 61 million gallons of wastewater discharged in the river." Confronted with aerial photographs of this illegal activity, a Duke spokesman attributed the pumping to routine maintenance—an assertion rejected by DEQ because the pumping activity "far exceeded what would reasonably be considered routine maintenance."

As can be seen, in one respect, I share a key assumption with my colleagues in the majority. I do not rest my dissent on the notion that the board of Duke, under the pled facts, was ignorant of the company's practices. Sadly, my dissent rests on my reluctant conclusion that the facts as pled support a fair inference that the board was all too aware that Duke's business strategy involved flouting important laws, while employing a strategy of political influence-seeking and cajolement to reduce the risk that the company would be called to fair account. Under the facts as pled, the only surprising thing about the Dan River spill that gave rise to the state regulator's issuance of a $6.8 million fine, twenty-three Notice of Violation letters, twenty-six Notice of Deficiency letters, and a finding that Duke committed more than 760 daily violations of environmental regulations, in addition to other severe civil and criminal penalties related to Duke's operations at other sites, is that something like it did not happen years earlier. And the fact that the local regulator that had been so compliant and cooperative in shaping easy conditions for Duke that the plaintiffs from the environmental community Duke sought to avoid would not have accepted, so rapidly turned tail and ran in the face of public sentiment supports, rather than contradicts, the complaint's allegation that Duke knew it was dealing with a regulator that was not focused on its legal duties. When the deal they cut was put under the spotlight of public scrutiny, its friendly regulator abandoned it, consistent with the behavior one would expect of a regulator that did not, let's say, run straight. The company then experienced the predictable: the serious financial and reputational consequences that come when an offender is caught out, and those complicit in turning a blind eye to the past misbehavior tries to distance itself from responsibility by slapping its old buddy hard.

NOTES AND QUESTIONS

1.   There are several ways in which a board may be found to have violated its *Caremark* duties. First, where "(1) the directors knew or should have known that a violation of the law was occurring and, (2) 'the directors took no steps in a good faith effort to prevent or remedy that situation.' "[38] This was the issue in *Good*. Alternatively, liability may arise where "(a) the directors utterly failed to implement any reporting or information system or controls; or (b) having implemented such a system or controls, consciously

---

[38]   Beam ex rel. Martha Stewart Living Omnimedia, Inc. v. Stewart, 833 A.2d 961, 976 (Del. Ch. 2003), aff'd, 845 A.2d 1040 (Del. 2004).

failed to monitor or oversee its operations thus disabling themselves from being informed of risks or problems requiring their attention."[39]

2.   Where plaintiffs are unable to show that directors knew a violation of law was occurring, they often seek to show that the directors should have known by pointing to so-called red flags. Information may constitute a red flag where there is a "clear warning" that should put defendants on notice, "alerting [them] to potential misconduct at the Company."[40] Because red flags "are only useful when they are either waved in one's face or displayed so that they are visible to the careful observer," plaintiffs must allege and prove that defendants were aware of the red flags.[41]

In *Rich v. Chong*,[42] Fuqi International, Inc., had accessed the US capital markets via a reverse merger into a US shell company listed on NASDAQ. A reverse merger is one in which the target rather than acquiring corporation survives. When that target is listed on an exchange like NASDAQ, the technique lets the acquirer go public without the expense of an initial public offering.

In 2009, Fuqi announced that it would be unable to file its quarterly and annual SEC disclosure statements due to "certain errors related to the accounting of the Company's inventory and cost of sales." In 2010, Fuqi disclosed that the SEC had begun an investigation of Fuqi's failures to file SEC reports on a timely basis and other potential violations. Thereafter, Fuqi disclosed accounting errors, internal control failures, and other management problems.

Plaintiff Rich brought a derivative suit alleging that Fuqi's board of directors had violated its *Caremark* duties. The court explained that:

> One way a plaintiff may successfully plead a *Caremark* claim is to plead facts showing that a corporation had no internal controls in place. Fuqi had some sort of compliance system in place. For example, it had an Audit Committee and submitted financial statements to the SEC in 2009. However, accepting the Plaintiff's allegations as true, the mechanisms Fuqi had in place appear to have been woefully inadequate. In its press releases, Fuqi has detailed its extensive problems with internal controls. . . . These disclosures lead me to believe that Fuqi had no *meaningful* controls in place. The board of directors may have had regular meetings, and an Audit Committee may have existed, but there does not seem to have been any regulation of the company's operations *in China*.[43]

What is the rule for liability? Is it that any information system suffices or that there must be a meaningful one?

---

[39]   Stone ex rel. AmSouth Bancorporation v. Ritter, 911 A.2d 362, 370 (Del. 2006).

[40]   In re Citigroup Inc. S'holder Derivative Litig., 964 A.2d 106, 128 (Del.Ch.2009).

[41]   Wood v. Baum, 953 A.2d 136, 143 (Del. 2008).

[42]   66 A.3d 963 (Del. Ch. 2013).

[43]   Id. at 982–83 (footnotes omitted) (emphasis in original).

The *Rich* court further explained that:

> As the Supreme Court held in *Stone v. Ritter*, if the directors have implemented a system of controls, a finding of liability is predicated on the directors' having "consciously failed to monitor or oversee [the system's] operations thus disabling themselves from being informed of risks or problems requiring their attention." One way that the plaintiff may plead such a conscious failure to monitor is to identify "red flags," obvious and problematic occurrences, that support an inference that the Fuqi directors knew that there were material weaknesses in Fuqi's internal controls and failed to correct such weaknesses. . . .

> First, Fuqi was a preexisting Chinese company that gained access to the U.S. capital markets through the Reverse Merger. Thus, Fuqi's directors were aware that there may be challenges in bringing Fuqi's internal controls into harmony with the U.S. securities reporting systems. Notwithstanding that fact, according to the Complaint, the directors did nothing to ensure that its reporting mechanisms were accurate. Second, the board knew that it had problems with its accounting and inventory processes by March 2010 at the latest, because it announced that the 2009 financial statements would need restatement at that time. In the same press release, Fuqi also acknowledged the likelihood of material weaknesses in its internal controls. Third, Fuqi received a letter from NASDAQ in April 2010 warning Fuqi that it would face delisting if Fuqi did not bring its reporting requirements up to date with the SEC.

> It seems reasonable to infer that, because of these "red flags," the directors knew that there were deficiencies in Fuqi's internal controls.[44]

Why was the defendant directors' knowledge of illegality sufficient in *Rich* but not in *Good*?

3.   In *Good*, plaintiffs contended that Duke Energy worked with DEQ so as to minimize Duke Energy's liability and maximize the time it had to bring its facilities into compliance with environmental regulations. Do you agree with plaintiffs that that constituted bad faith as defined by Delaware law?

4.   Does former Chief Justice Strine's dissent imply that all corporate lobbying efforts to obtain favorable laws and regulatory actions constitute bad faith? If so, do you agree that that constitutes bad faith as defined by Delaware law?

5.   Assume Duke Energy was violating the law. Further assume that Duke Energy's board of directors knew about the violations. Why is that not enough for them to have *Caremark* liability?

---

[44]   Id. at 983–84 (footnotes omitted).

6. *Caremark* claims are not exculpable under § 102(b)(7) clauses. Why not? Should they be exculpable?

PROBLEM

In 202X, Amennyy Ugol, a Russian corporation, effected a reverse merger with Allison Coal, Inc., a small coal mining company incorporated in Delaware and whose common stock is listed for trading on the Chicago Stock Exchange. Because Allison was the surviving company, the newly combined entity remains a Delaware corporation and remains listed on the Chicago exchange.

Ten of Allison's twelve directors are Russian nationals. Gabriel Romans is a United States national who agreed to serve on Allison's board of directors and audit committee. Romans recently retired from his position as CEO of Alabama Coal, Inc., a coal mining firm with operations in the South Eastern United States. Romans does not speak Russian. Romans has never visited Russia.

Romans participates in board and committee meetings by video conferencing from his home. He has noticed that when he asks a question, the Russian board members often converse among themselves in Russian before answering him.

Upon joining Allison's board, Romans was provided with a balance sheet and various other documents indicating that Allison owned three coal mines in Siberia that collectively produced approximately 23 million tons of coal per year. Romans made no independent effort to verify those claims.

Allison's audit committee did not hire independent financial or legal advisors, instead relying on the company's independent auditor and legal counsel.

Almost all of the company's documents provided to Romans in connection with his board and committee service were in Russian. One such document was a corporate registry filing with the Russian Ministry of Finance, which indicated that Allison's chairman had transferred ownership of one of the company's mines to himself in return for consideration of $1 US. The chairman had then sold the mine to a Russian coal oligarch for $175 million, which he had retained. Due to the lack of a translation, however, Romans remained unaware of the sale.

A report published in a Russian language mining trade magazine noted serious problems with one of Allison's remaining mines, which had reduced its output by 55%. Romans received a copy of the magazine from a fellow director, accompanied by a note saying "this is worrisome," but Romans failed to inquire as to why the other director found it worrisome or to have the article translated.

Has Romans breached his fiduciary duty to the company and its shareholders? What should Romans have done both before and after becoming a director?

To assess your understanding of the material in this chapter, click here to take a quiz.

CHAPTER 5

OPERATIONALIZING THE MONITORING MODEL: FEDERAL LAW

Corporate gatekeepers help solve one of corporate governance's most basic agency cost problems. Companies want investors to purchase their securities, but investors may doubt the accuracy and completeness of the disclosures provided by the firm. As a form of bonding the credibility of their disclosures, the company hires various outsiders—such as independent directors, an outside auditor, underwriters, and legal counsel—to function as reputational intermediaries. Because the gatekeeper's business depends on its reputation for honesty, probity, and accuracy, it will not ruin that reputation to aid one client to cheat. These outsiders thereby function as gatekeepers, policing access to the capital markets.

In the period prior to adoption of the Sarbanes-Oxley Act in 2002, these gatekeepers failed rather miserably. As a result, much of the Act "can be seen as a consistent effort to enhance the awareness of gatekeepers to their duty to investors."[1] In particular, the Act paid great attention to the role of the corporation's independent auditors and the directors on the audit committee that supervise them.

A. INDEPENDENT AUDITORS

SEC regulations under the Securities Act require that issuers selling securities to the public include audited financial statements in their registration statements and prospectuses. In addition, regulations under the Exchange Act require registered companies to include audited financial statements in their annual report on Form 10-K.

Since those acts became law in 1933 and 1934 respectively, companies have therefore been obliged to annually select an independent certified public accounting company to conduct the requisite financial statement audits. Shareholders must approve the board of directors' choice of outside accounting firm at the company's annual meeting.

Until SOX came into force in 2002, the accounting profession was

> **FOR MORE INFORMATION**
>
> The SEC provides an overview of the work of independent auditors at https://www.sec.gov/reportspubs/investor-publications/investorpubs aboutauditorshtm.html

---

[1] Remarks at Advanced ALI-ABA Course of Study by SEC Commissioner Paul S. Atkins, 2003 WL 134882, at *2.

largely self-regulating. Although the Securities Exchange Act authorized the SEC to impose financial accounting standards, the SEC had never done so. Instead, it allowed private sector organizations—especially the Financial Accounting Standards Board (FASB) and the American Institute of Certified Public Accountants (AICPA)—to take the lead in developing the standards by which corporate audits are conducted (Generally Accepted Auditing Standards or GAAS) and the way in which financial statements are presented (Generally Accepted Accounting Principles or GAAP).

But then came the Enron scandal. Enron was primarily an accounting scandal, little different from the 150-plus other accounting fraud cases that the SEC investigates in most years. Indeed, this was true not just of Enron, but also most of the dotcom era corporate scandals. Management relied upon the substantial flexibility inherent in GAAP to manage earnings and manipulate financial data so that operating results conformed to forecasts. The goal was to keep the firm's stock price high so that the managers could profit from their stock options. Because a standard accounting audit is not a true forensic audit designed to uncover wrongdoing, but rather only a sampling audit that may entirely miss the problem, many managers thought they could get away with cooking the books. The willingness of some accountants to turn a blind eye to questionable practices meant that some managers did get away with doing so, at least for a while.

Auditing firms attracted the attention of SOX's drafters because while the frauds at Enron, Global Crossing, and WorldCom differed in many details, they had at least one common element. All three had used Arthur Andersen as their outside auditor. Indeed, Arthur Andersen's name figured prominently in many other cases of accounting fraud in the 1990s and early 2000s, including the scandals at Sunbeam, Waste Management, Qwest, and the Baptist Foundation of Arizona.

The government had brought both criminal and civil suits against Arthur Andersen and many companies or their shareholders sued Andersen for securities fraud. In 2002, Arthur Andersen was convicted of obstruction of justice charges arising out of destruction of Enron documents. Although the U.S. Supreme Court later overturned the conviction on technical grounds relating to the jury instructions, the verdict sounded Arthur Andersen's death knell. Its sole remaining legacy is the regulatory edifice erected by SOX to govern the accounting profession and the auditing process.

Many of the key SOX provisions in fact are concerned with auditing and accounting. Congress set out to reform the accounting industry by establishing the Public Company Accounting Oversight Board (PCAOB) as a new regulator with real teeth. Congress also sought to remake the relationship between auditor and corporate client to reduce the conflicts of interest inherent in that relationship. Finally, Congress sought to reshape the intrafirm accounting process, by imposing new rules on the audit process and the firm's internal control systems.

1) THE PCAOB

As noted, before SOX, the accounting profession was largely self-regulating. The key actors—FASB and the AICPA—were private sector entities subject to minimal SEC oversight. FASB set accounting standards, while the AICPA provided guidance and contributed to the development of generally accepted principles and standards.

SOX shook up that cozy little world. Section 101 established the Public Company Accounting Oversight Board (PCAOB) as a nonprofit corporation to "oversee the audit of public companies that are subject to the securities laws." Funding for its operations comes from a special tax—called an "accounting support fee—on public corporations. The fee varies with company size, specifically with the company's "average monthly U.S. equity market capitalization," so that larger firms bear a higher share of the burden.

The five members of the PCAOB's board must be "prominent individuals of integrity and reputation who have a demonstrated commitment to the interests of investors and the public," no more than two of whom can be CPAs. The SEC appoints the board members, in consultation with the chairman of the Federal Reserve Board and the Secretary of the Treasury. The members serve five-year terms. The SEC can remove board members for good cause. The chairman of the board may not have been a practicing CPA within the five years prior to his or her appointment. While serving as a PCAOB board member, no one may receive payments from a public accounting firm other than fixed retirement income.

SOX § 101(c) specifies the PCAOB's duties, the most important of which are:

1. Develop a system for registration of public accounting firms that prepare audit reports for reporting companies. Per SOX § 102, only registered accounting firms can audit the books of reporting companies. In order to register, an accounting firm must make extensive disclosures about its clients, fees, and practices, as well as consent to cooperate in any PCAOB investigation.

2. Establish standards governing auditing, quality control, ethics, independence, and other matters relating to the preparation of audit reports for reporting companies.

3. Conduct regular inspections of registered public accounting firms to ensure that the firms are complying with PCAOB and SEC rules. Large accounting firms (with more than 100 reporting company clients) get inspected annually, while smaller ones are inspected every three years. If the PCAOB

finds any violations, it reports them to the SEC and any relevant state accountant licensing board. Even if the PCAOB finds no violations, it still must send a written report to the SEC and the relevant state agencies.

4. Conduct investigations and disciplinary proceedings of misconduct by registered public accounting firms and any individuals associated with such firms. The PCAOB can impose a wide range of sanctions on violators, up to and including permanent revocation of the right to conduct audits of reporting companies.

Sarbanes-Oxley § 103 gave the PCAOB what the Senate committee report on the act called "plenary authority" to set accounting standards. The PCAOB thus can adopt, amend, or preempt guidance issued by the AICPA and other private sector groups. To date, except where SOX clearly requires otherwise, the PCAOB mostly has simply adopted the preexisting standards set by the AICPA. In effect, however, the act downgrades the AICPA's role in the standard-setting process to merely advisory.

A mid-2004 change in how audit reports are drafted forcefully illustrated the PCAOB's new predominance in the standard-setting area. In the past, a reporting company's auditors would certify that the audit was conducted in accordance with GAAS and that the financial statements fairly and accurately represented the company's condition in accordance with GAAP. Since May 2004, however, the PCAOB requires audit reports to state that the audit and financial statements comply with "the standards of the Public Company Accounting Oversight Board."

The PCAOB doesn't have the field entirely to itself, however. SOX § 108 authorizes the SEC to "recognize, as 'generally accepted' for purposes of the securities laws, any accounting principles established by a standard setting body" that meets the following conditions:

- The body is a private entity.

- The body is governed by a board of trustees, the majority of whom are not, or have not been during the past two years, associated with any registered public accounting firm.

- The body "has adopted procedures to ensure prompt consideration, by majority vote of its members, of changes to accounting principles necessary to reflect emerging accounting issues and changing business practices" and "considers, in adopting accounting principles, the need to keep standards current in order to reflect changes in the business environment, the extent to which international convergence on high quality accounting standards is necessary or appropriate in the public interest and for the protection of investors."

- The SEC determines that the body has the capacity to assist the commission in carrying out its duties "because, at a minimum, the standard setting body is capable of improving the accuracy and effectiveness of financial reporting and the protection of investors under the securities laws."

In April 2003, the SEC recognized FASB as such a standard-setting body. Accordingly, FASB now receives funding from the same user fees that support the PCAOB. In addition, FASB functions as a separate standard setter working in parallel with the PCAOB.

The relationships between the SEC, PCAOB, FASB, and AICPA are fraught with the potential for conflict. To date, the three private sector entities have managed to work together in a reasonably cooperative manner. In general, the PCAOB has primary responsibility for GAAS, the FASB for GAAP, and the AICPA for nonreporting company accounting rules, but there seems to be a good deal of mutual consultation. In the event of conflict, of course, the SEC's oversight role gives it the last word.

Like lawyers, physicians, dentists, and various other professionals, accountants traditionally are licensed for practice by states rather than the federal government. The PCAOB does not displace this system of state licensing and regulation. Instead, the two work in tandem. A CPA thus must be licensed by the state to practice accounting; if the CPA's practice includes auditing the books of reporting companies, the CPA's accounting firm also must be registered with the PCAOB.

PCAOB standards governing auditing of reporting companies will preempt any contrary state regulations, but this leaves the states as the primary regulator for audits of non-reporting companies. In general, of course, states simply mandate compliance with GAAS and GAAP.

There's clearly a need for effective coordination between the PCAOB and state licensing bodies, both so that accounting practices and auditing standards remain reasonably uniform across all types of companies and so that individuals or firms disciplined at one level are also investigated at the other. Here, again, is a role for the SEC to use its oversight authority to encourage such cooperation.

In 2006, the Free Enterprise Fund, an activist think tank, sued to challenge the PCAOB's constitutionality. The Fund argued that SOX vests the PCAOB with extensive governmental functions and powers, including a quasi-law enforcement investigatory power and a quasi-judicial power to impose substantial fines for violations of its rules. Accordingly, the Fund contended, the PCAOB violated several constitutional provisions, most notably the Appointments Clause.

The Appointments Clause of Article II, section 2 of the Constitution provides that:

[The President] shall have Power, by and with the Advice and Consent of the Senate, to make Treaties, provided two thirds of the Senators present concur; and he shall nominate, and by and with the Advice and Consent of the Senate, shall appoint Ambassadors, other public Ministers and Consuls, Judges of the supreme Court, and all other Officers of the United States, whose Appointments are not herein otherwise provided for, and which shall be established by Law: but the Congress may by Law vest the Appointment of such inferior Officers, as they think proper, in the President alone, in the Courts of Law, or in the Heads of Departments.

Because the SEC rather than the President appoints the PCAOB's members, the statute presented three key constitutional questions. First, were the members of the PCAOB "Officers of the United States" and thus subject to the Appointments Clause? Second, if so, were the members of the PCAOB "inferior Officers" whose appointment Congress "may by Law vest" in one of the specified alternative mechanisms other than the advice and consent process? Third, if so, did the SEC Commissioners collectively qualify as a Head of Department for this purpose?

There was surprisingly little guidance on these questions, but there nevertheless was a strong argument in favor of the Fund's position. Although putatively private, the PCAOB in fact is a regulatory agency in all but name. It has an enormously broad Congressional mandate to create and enforce rules for the accounting profession and the auditing process. It can fine accounting firms up to $2 million and individual accountants up to $100,000 for violations.

While it thus wields extensive quasi-governmental powers, the PCAOB is almost immune from direct Congressional or Presidential oversight. The board is funded by a general power to tax all public companies. Compared to other regulatory agencies, which are limited in their reach by the amount of money appropriated to them by Congress, the PCAOB's independent power to tax as needed means there is very little Congressional or Presidential control on the power of the PCAOB.

The lack of de facto institutional control via the budgetary process is compounded by the formal lack of control created by the statutory structure. The President can neither appoint nor remove PCAOB members. Instead, it is the SEC acting collectively that appoints those members. Likewise, the President has no removal power. Only the SEC can remove board members, and only if they can be shown to have willfully violated federal laws.

All of this seemed highly problematic under the relevant precedents. In *Edmond v. United States*, for example, the Court wrote:

By vesting the President with the exclusive power to select the principal (noninferior) officers of the United States, the Appointments Clause prevents congressional encroachment upon the Executive and Judicial Branches. . . . This disposition was also designed to assure a higher quality of appointments: The Framers anticipated that the President would be less vulnerable to interest-group pressure and personal favoritism than would a collective body. . . . The President's power to select principal officers of the United States was not left unguarded, however, as Article II further requires the "Advice and Consent of the Senate." This serves both to curb Executive abuses of the appointment power . . . and "to promote a judicious choice of [persons] for filling the offices of the union. . . ." By requiring the joint participation of the President and the Senate, the Appointments Clause was designed to ensure public accountability for both the making of a bad appointment and the rejection of a good one.[2]

Instead, the PCAOB seems to have been designed to avoid public accountability.

In *Edmond*, the court also held that:

Generally speaking, the term "inferior officer" connotes a relationship with some higher ranking officer or officers below the President: Whether one is an "inferior" officer depends on whether he has a superior. It is not enough that other officers may be identified who formally maintain a higher rank, or possess responsibilities of a greater magnitude. If that were the intention, the Constitution might have used the phrase "lesser officer." Rather, in the context of a Clause designed to preserve political accountability relative to important Government assignments, we think it evident that "inferior officers" are officers whose work is directed and supervised at some level by others who were appointed by Presidential nomination with the advice and consent of the Senate.[3]

Because the members of the PCAOB are not subject to such oversight except to the very limited extent they are overseen by the SEC, it would seem that the members of the PCAOB are not inferior officers.

Likewise, the Fund could draw support from *Freytag v. CIR*, in which the Court opined that:

The Framers understood . . . that by limiting the appointment power, they could ensure that those who wielded it were accountable to political force and the will of the people . . . . The Appointments Clause prevents Congress from distributing power too widely by limiting the actors in whom Congress may vest the power to appoint. The Clause reflects our Framers' conclusion that widely distributed appointment power subverts democratic government. Given the inexorable presence

---

[2]   Edmond v. United States, 520 U.S. 651, 659–60 (1997).

[3]   Id. at 662–63.

of the administrative state, a holding that every organ in the executive Branch is a department would multiply the number of actors eligible to appoint.[4]

Holding that the SEC is a Department empowered to appoint the PCAOB would threaten precisely the democratic values the Founders intended the Appointments Clause to protect.

The Fund thus had a very strong case that the provisions of Sarbanes-Oxley creating the PCAOB are unconstitutional. Because Congress in its rush to adopt Sarbanes-Oxley failed to include a clear severability provision, moreover, the Fund might well have been able to persuade a reviewing court that the entire Sarbanes-Oxley law had to be thrown out.

The Supreme Court dismissed these arguments almost out of hand, expressing "no hesitation in concluding that under *Edmond* the Board members are inferior officers whose appointment Congress may permissibly vest in a 'Hea[d] of Departmen[t].' "[5] Next, the majority held that the SEC is a Department and that the 5 commissioners acting collectively constitute a Head of said Department. "Because the Commission is a freestanding component of the Executive Branch, not subordinate to or contained within any other such component, it constitutes a 'Departmen[t]' for the purposes of the Appointments Clause."[6] The trouble, of course, is that the SEC really is part of the so-called Fourth Branch; i.e., the independent agencies. The President's powers to remove members of the SEC are far more limited than his powers to remove, say, a Cabinet Secretary. The independent agencies are, in Scalia's apt phrase, a "headless fourth branch."[7]

With the constitutionality of the PCAOB—and thus of the Sarbanes-Oxley Act itself—assured by Supreme Court fiat, attention can turn to how effective the board has been in regulating the accounting profession. In the material that follows, we will see that the PCAOB has struggled at great length with making § 404 compliance less burdensome and more informative. Despite those struggles, the PCAOB has failed to ameliorate § 404 costs sufficiently to make U.S. capital markets globally competitive.

The PCAOB also has failed in making audit firm quality more transparent. Recall that the PCAOB is charged with making regular inspections of registered public accounting firms and with investigating misconduct by such firms. A study by Clive Lennox and Jeffrey Pittman, however, found that less is now known about audit firm quality than was the case under the pre-SOX regime. PCAOB inspection reports disclose an auditor's engagement weaknesses but not its quality control problems.

---

[4]   Freytag v. CIR, 501 U.S. 868, 884–885 (1991),

[5]   Free Enterprise Fund v. Public Co. Accounting Oversight Bd., 561 U.S. 477, 510 (2010).

[6]   Id. at 511.

[7]   Freytag v. Commissioner, 501 U.S. 868, 921 (1991) (Scalia, J., concurring).

The report also fails to provide an overall assessment of the auditor's quality. As a result, the study found no evidence that corporations "view PCAOB reports as being informative about differences in audit firm quality."[8] In contrast, the pre-SOX peer review system provided precisely such information.

A more recent study by a team of economists found that the PCAOB's inspection reports for large auditors consist mainly of anecdotal evidence of deficiencies. The lack of any statistical context makes it difficult for consumers of the PCAOB reports to determine the quality of auditing firms.[9]

2) THE AUDITOR'S REPORT

Audited financial statements long have been accompanied by a report from the independent auditor attesting that, in its opinion, the financial statements are presented fairly in all material respects.[10] In 2017, the PCAOB adopted Auditing Standard 3101, governing the information an independent auditor must include in its report:

> The final standard retains the pass/fail opinion of the existing auditor's report but makes significant changes to the existing auditor's report, including the following:
>
> - Critical audit matters ... requires the auditor to communicate in the auditor's report any critical audit matters arising from the current period's audit of the financial statements or state that the auditor determined that there are no critical audit matters:
>
>   o A critical audit matter is defined as a matter that was communicated or required to be communicated to the audit committee and that: (1) relates to accounts or disclosures that are material to the financial statements and (2) involved especially challenging, subjective, or complex auditor judgment.
>
>   o In determining whether a matter involved especially challenging, subjective, or complex

---

[8]   Clive Lennox & Jeffrey Pittman, Auditing the Auditors: Evidence on the Recent Reforms to the External Monitoring of Audit Firms 4 (Oct. 2008).

[9]   James Wainberg et al., An Investigation into PCAOB Reporting Deficiencies (Feb. 2010).

[10]   Where the auditor determines that the issuer's financial statements are not fairly presented in accordance with GAAP, the auditor may issue a qualified opinion, an adverse opinion, or a disclaimer of opinion. Under PCAOB Auditing Standard 3105, a "qualified opinion states that, except for the effects of the matter(s) to which the qualification relates, the financial statements present fairly, in all material respects, the financial position, results of operations, and cash flows of the entity in conformity with generally accepted accounting principles. . . . An adverse opinion states that the financial statements do not present fairly the financial position, results of operations, or cash flows of the entity in conformity with generally accepted accounting principles. . . . A disclaimer of opinion states that the auditor does not express an opinion on the financial statements."

auditor judgment, the auditor takes into account, alone or in combination, certain factors, including, but not limited to:

- The auditor's assessment of the risks of material misstatement, including significant risks;

- The degree of auditor judgment related to areas in the financial statements that involved the application of significant judgment or estimation by management, including estimates with significant measurement uncertainty;

- The nature and timing of significant unusual transactions and the extent of audit effort and judgment related to these transactions;

- The degree of auditor subjectivity in applying audit procedures to address the matter or in evaluating the results of those procedures;

- The nature and extent of audit effort required to address the matter, including the extent of specialized skill or knowledge needed or the nature of consultations outside the engagement team regarding the matter; and

- The nature of audit evidence obtained regarding the matter.

o The communication of each critical audit matter includes:

- Identifying the critical audit matter;

- Describing the principal considerations that led the auditor to determine that the matter is a critical audit matter;

- Describing how the critical audit matter was addressed in the audit; and

- Referring to the relevant financial statement accounts or disclosures.

o The documentation of critical audit matters requires that for each matter arising from the audit of the financial statements that (a) was communicated or required to be communicated to the audit committee, and (b) relates to accounts or disclosures that are material to the financial statements, the auditor documents whether or not the matter was determined to be a critical audit matter (i.e., involved especially challenging, subjective, or complex auditor judgment) and the basis for such determination.

- Additional Improvements to the Auditor's Report—the final standard also includes a number of other improvements to the auditor's report that are primarily intended to clarify the auditor's role and responsibilities related to the audit of the financial statements, provide additional information about the auditor, and make the auditor's report easier to read:

  o Auditor tenure—a statement disclosing the year in which the auditor began serving consecutively as the company's auditor;

  o Independence—a statement that the auditor is required to be independent;

  o Addressee—the auditor's report will be addressed to the company's shareholders and board of directors or equivalents (additional addressees are also permitted);

  o Enhancements to basic elements—certain standardized language in the auditor's report has been changed, including adding the phrase whether due to error or fraud, when describing the auditor's responsibility under PCAOB standards to obtain reasonable assurance about whether the financial statements are free of material misstatements; and

  o Standardized form of the auditor's report—the opinion will appear in the first section of the auditor's report and section titles have been added to guide the reader.[11]

3) LIMITS ON NON-AUDIT SERVICES

A key concern motivating SOX's drafters was the conflict of interest inherent when accounting firms sell other services to the corporations whose books they audit. Title II of the act therefore limited the extent to which accountants may provide consulting services to their audit clients. Some non-audit services were banned outright. The outside auditor, for example, may not provide bookkeeping or related services, design or implement financial information systems, provide fairness opinions in connection with corporate transactions, conduct internal audits on an outsourced basis, provide humans relations services, or act as an

---

[11] PCAOB Release No. 2017–001 (June 1, 2017).

investment banker or legal expert. In addition, the PCAOB is authorized to ban other non-audit services as it deems fit.

Contrary to conventional wisdom, however, SOX did not completely ban all such services. Provided the client's audit committee approves the retention in advance, in fact, the auditor may perform any non-audit services not banned by SOX or the PCAOB. For example, a corporation's outside auditor can also prepare its corporate tax returns. It's advisable, however, to check with legal counsel before asking the auditor to perform any non-audit services.

The SEC requires disclosure of any "fees paid to the independent accountant for (1) audit services, (2) audit-related services, (3) tax services, and (4) other services" in the annual report on Form 10-K. The SEC has also cautioned companies that there are "some circumstances where providing certain tax services to an audit client would impair the independence of an accountant, such as representing an audit client in tax court or other situations involving public advocacy."

The SEC did create an exception for *de minimis* non-audit services, pursuant to which a registered accounting firm still is independent even if it provides non-approved, non-audit services. The aggregate compensation for all such services may constitute no more than 5 percent of the total fees paid the auditor by the client during the relevant fiscal year. Once the company recognizes that it is compensating its auditor for non-audit services without prior approval by the audit committee, the management promptly must bring the oversight to the audit committee's attention and have the services approved by the committee.

QUESTION

Were there any benefits to companies, investors, or society when accounting firms provided both audit and non-audit services to the same client?

4) AUDITORS WORK FOR THE AUDIT COMMITTEE

As we shall see below, SOX significantly expanded the role of the audit committee of the board of directors. Many of these new rules directly affect the reporting company's outside auditor. It is now the audit committee, for example, that must select the reporting company's outside auditor and negotiate the auditor's fees. The audit committee must approve (typically in advance) any non-banned, non-audit services the auditor provides to the corporation.

SOX clarified that the outside auditor is responsible to the audit committee, rather than management. The outside auditors must periodically meet with the audit committee outside the presence of management. At least annually, the outside auditor of a NYSE-listed company must give the audit committee a report detailing: (1) the firm's internal control procedures; (2) any material problems identified in the most recent internal control review, or by any government or other regulatory body investigation; (3) any steps taken to deal with any such problems; and (4) all relationships between the independent auditor and the listed company. Obtaining such a report has become best practice for non-NYSE firms, as well.

The auditor should report to the audit committee any disagreement between management and the auditor as to financial reporting. If the disagreement is resolved, the auditor still must report it to the audit committee, and also report on the manner in which it was dealt with. If a dispute is not resolved between management and the auditor, it is up to the audit committee to solve the problem.

Where GAAP provides options as to how to disclose information, the auditor should flag the issue for the audit committee. The auditor should discuss the alternatives with the audit committee and identify the disclosure it preferred.

5) ANTI-COERCION RULES

SOX § 303 makes it unlawful for an officer or director of a reporting company, or anyone acting under their orders, to "fraudulently influence, coerce, manipulate, or mislead any independent" CPA "engaged in the performance of an audit" of the company's financial statements "for the purpose of rendering such financial statements materially misleading." The SEC defines officer for this purpose as including "the company's 'president, vice president, secretary, treasurer or principal financial officer, comptroller or principal accounting officer, and any person routinely performing corresponding functions.'"

Per the SEC rules implementing § 303, the prohibition does not apply solely to employees of the reporting company acting under orders from directors or officers of the company:

> In other words, someone may be "acting under the direction" of an officer or director even if they are not under the supervision or control of that officer or director. Such persons might include not only the issuer's employees but also, for example, customers, vendors or creditors who, under the direction of an officer or director, provide false or misleading confirmations or other false or misleading information to auditors, or who enter into "side agreements" that enable the issuer to mislead the auditor. In appropriate circumstances, persons acting under the direction of officers and directors also may include not only lower level employees of the issuer but also other partners or employees of the accounting firm (such as consultants or forensic accounting specialists retained by counsel for the issuer) and attorneys, securities professionals, or other advisors who, for example, pressure an auditor to limit the scope of the audit, to issue an unqualified report on the financial

statements when such a report would be unwarranted, to not object to an inappropriate accounting treatment, or not to withdraw an issued audit report on the issuer's financial statements.[12]

The SEC likewise has provided guidance as to the kinds of conduct deemed improper influence:

- Offering or paying bribes or other financial incentives, including offering future employment or contracts for non-audit services

- Providing an auditor with an inaccurate or misleading legal analysis

- Threatening to cancel or canceling existing non-audit or audit engagements if the auditor objects to the issuer's accounting

- Seeking to have a partner removed from the audit engagement because the partner objects to the issuer's accounting

- Blackmailing or making physical threats

This list is not exclusive and under appropriate circumstances other conduct could be a violation. Among other potentially prohibited conduct is "knowingly providing to the auditor inadequate or misleading information that is key to the audit, transferring managers or principals from the audit engagement, and when predicated by an intent to defraud, verbal abuse, creating undue time pressure on the auditors, not providing information to auditors on a timely basis, and not being available to discuss matters with auditors on a timely basis." As the following excerpt suggests, this broad language potentially poses problems for both lawyers and their clients.

Rule 13b2–2

(a) No director or officer of an issuer shall, directly or indirectly:

(1) Make or cause to be made a materially false or misleading statement to an accountant in connection with; or

(2) Omit to state, or cause another person to omit to state, any material fact necessary in order to make statements made, in light of the circumstances under which such statements were made, not misleading, to an accountant in connection with:

(i) Any audit, review or examination of the financial statements of the issuer required to be made pursuant to this subpart; or

---

[12]   SEC, In Re Improper Influence on Conduct of Audits, Release No. 26050 (May 20, 2003).

(ii) The preparation or filing of any document or report required to be filed with the Commission pursuant to this subpart or otherwise.

(b) (1)   No officer or director of an issuer, or any other person acting under the direction thereof, shall directly or indirectly take any action to coerce, manipulate, mislead, or fraudulently influence any independent public or certified public accountant engaged in the performance of an audit or review of the financial statements of that issuer that are required to be filed with the Commission pursuant to this subpart or otherwise if that person knew or should have known that such action, if successful, could result in rendering the issuer's financial statements materially misleading.

(2) For purposes of paragraphs (b)(1) and (c)(2) of this section, actions that, "if successful, could result in rendering the issuer's financial statements materially misleading" include, but are not limited to, actions taken at any time with respect to the professional engagement period to coerce, manipulate, mislead, or fraudulently influence an auditor:

(i) To issue or reissue a report on an issuer's financial statements that is not warranted in the circumstances (due to material violations of generally accepted accounting principles, the standards of the PCAOB, or other professional or regulatory standards);

(ii) Not to perform audit, review or other procedures required by the standards of the PCAOB or other professional standards;

(iii) Not to withdraw an issued report; or

(iv) Not to communicate matters to an issuer's audit committee.

Peter Irot, Sarbanes-Oxley and "The Treaty"
Why Litigators Must Communicate
Carefully With Auditors

36 The Advoc. (Texas) 52 (2006)[13]

I.   Introduction: Public Accounting and Legal Secrets

. . .

Relations between attorneys and auditors have long been governed by a set of documents commonly referred to as "the Treaty," which was designed with an eye toward preserving client confidentiality while still allowing auditors to perform their vital duties. Sarbanes-Oxley, meanwhile, was passed in an atmosphere of intense suspicion of corporate executives. Accordingly, the new law restructures many of the

---

[13]   Reprinted by permission of Peter Irot and The Advocate.

rules concerning what information auditors are given and the manner in which the information is given.

. . .

II. The Treaty: Reconciling Confidentiality with Auditors' Requests for Information

A. The Treaty's Key Words: "Probable" and "Remote"

Every year, a public company must file a form 10-K with the SEC. As part of the 10-K, its independent auditor, an accountant, must certify the company's financial statement. During this certification process, the auditor must investigate to determine whether the company is in a financial position to pay out in any current lawsuits against it, and it must also determine if the company is aware of any potential claims against it that have not yet been filed as lawsuits. The obvious source of information for this aspect of an auditor's job is the company's counsel, and the vehicle by which counsel responds to such requests is known as the "audit response letter."

Such communication between an attorney and an auditor is rife with potential for impacting attorney-client confidentiality. In response to the problems such communication caused, in the mid-1970s the ABA and the American Institute of Certified Public Accountants (AICPA) negotiated what is now referred to as "the Treaty," which governs auditors' letters and the responses thereto. The Treaty consists of two documents: the ABA's Statement of Policy Regarding Lawyers' Responses to Auditors' Requests for Information (dated December 1975) and the AICPA's Statement on Auditing Standards No. 12 (dated January 1976). The ABA document is an interpretation of the terms of the Treaty directed at lawyers[8] and the AICPA document is a set of instructions based on the Treaty directed at auditors.[9]

The crux of the ABA document is in Paragraph 5, where attorneys are directed to only comment on suits whose favorable prospects they consider to be either "probable" or "remote." That is, as long as the likelihood of a given claim succeeding is not "extremely doubtful," and the likelihood of the company's defense succeeding is not "judged to be slight," the attorney does not have to comment directly on the case's chances. The Statement of Policy makes it clear that the ABA considers "probable" and "remote" to be very limiting on the number of cases that

---

[8] See AM. BAR ASS'N, STATEMENT OF POLICY REGARDING LAWYERS' RESPONSES TO AUDITORS' REQUESTS FOR INFORMATION, available at http://www.abanet.org/buslaw/attorneyclient/policies/aicpa.pdf (1975) (comprising the part of the Treaty directed at lawyers).

[9] See INQUIRY OF A CLIENT'S LAWYER CONCERNING LITIGATION, CLAIMS, AND ASSESSMENTS, Statement on Auditing Standards No. 12 (Am. Inst. of Certified Pub. Accountants 1976), available at http://www.abanet.org/buslaw/attorneyclient/policies/aicpa.pdf (comprising the part of the Treaty directed at auditors).

can be commented upon: it notes that they really only apply to "relatively few clear cases."[12]

. . .

B. Precedent Supporting the Treaty

. . . In *Tew v. Arky, Freed, Stearns, Watson, Greer, Weaver, & Harris, P.A.*,[18] the plaintiff, a receiver for a corporation, sued a law firm because it had not informed its client's auditors of its client's insolvency. The defendant law firm moved for partial summary judgment in its favor on the argument that it had properly answered all the questions put to it by the auditor under the Treaty, and that, having received no questions regarding any unasserted claims, it could not address that information. The court in the Southern District of Florida granted the motion, relying to a significant degree on the Treaty. The court even explicitly noted that "[a]n attorney's responsibility with respect to auditor's [sic] inquiries is governed by" the Treaty.[22] . . .

III. Sarbanes-Oxley and the New SEC Rules: The Treaty Enters a New Age

A. Language of the Statute and the Rule

. . . [SOX] § 303(a) . . . states:

> It shall be unlawful, in contravention of such rules or regulations as the Commission shall prescribe as necessary and appropriate in the public interest or for the protection of investors, for any officer or director of an issuer, or any other person acting under the direction thereof, to take any action to *fraudulently influence, coerce, manipulate, or mislead* any independent public or certified accountant engaged in the performance of an audit of the financial statements of that issuer for the purpose of rendering such financial statements materially misleading (emphasis added).

This portion of the act clearly has direct bearing on attorneys' responses to auditor letters.

But of even greater interest are the SEC Rules written at the direction of this section. SEC Rule 13b2–2 takes the words "fraudulently influence" which are at the beginning of the list of prohibited actions in the Act and moves them to the end such that the prohibited verbs now read as follows: "coerce, manipulate, mislead, or fraudulently influence."[29] Because the phrase containing the modifier "fraudulently" has been moved to the end of the list, it is clear that the SEC does not

---

12   [STATEMENT OF POLICY REGARDING LAWYERS' RESPONSES TO AUDITORS' REQUESTS FOR INFORMATION, supra note 8, at 9–10.]

18   655 F. Supp. 1573 (S.D. Fla. 1987).

22   Id. at 1574.

29   17 C.F.R. § 240.13b2–2(b)(1) (2005).

believe that a person's coercion, manipulation, or misleading in the course of an audit must be fraudulent. . . .

B. The SEC's Discussion of the Final Rules

1. How the Rule Was Expanded to Apply to Attorneys

. . . An SEC Release from 2003 . . . tackles the words "coerce" and "manipulate" first, stating that they cover actions like "pressure, threats, trickery, intimidation or some other form of purposeful action."[31] That is, there is a scienter requirement: the actor must have "purpose" to his actions.

But the calculus changes when it comes to the word "mislead." In the release, the SEC states that there is actually no change in the "mislead" requirement from the previous incarnation of Rule 13b2–2. "Directly or indirectly making or causing to be made materially misleading statements to auditors" was prohibited before 2003, and according to the release, is still prohibited. What is not made explicit in the release's discussion, however, is the fact that the older version of Rule 13b2–2 applies only to "director[s] or officer[s]," while the pertinent part of the newer version applies to "officer[s] or director[s] . . . or any other person acting under the direction thereof."[35] It is the "any other person" phrase, of course, that affects attorneys.

In the same release, the SEC goes on to explicitly consider the scienter requirement, or lack thereof, when it explains its decision to include the phrase "knew or should have known" in part (b)(1) of the Rule. Paragraph (b)(1) is the operative portion of the Rule that covers "coercing" and "misleading" an auditor, and in relevant part it states that a person is liable if he or she "knew or should have known that such action, if successful, could result in rendering the issuer's financial statements materially misleading."[37] The SEC indicates in the release that it decided to go with the phrase "knew or should have known" because it "historically has indicated the existence of a negligence standard."[38] . . . In other words, SEC Rule 13b2–2 has completely done away with a scienter requirement, at least so far as the word "mislead" is concerned, and it has done so not only for officers and directors of public companies, but also for "any other person" acting at the direction of those officers or directors. . . .

2. Actions Prohibited by the Rule

The SEC's release even lists some specific actions that it would consider potentially prohibited by the Rule, including . . . "Providing an auditor with an inaccurate or misleading legal analysis."[43] Thus, in the

---

[31]   [Improper Influence on Conduct of Audits, Sarbanes-Oxley Act of 2002 Release No. 34–47890, 68 Fed. Reg. 31,820, at 31,823 (May 28, 2003).]

[35]   17 C.F.R. § 240.13b2–2(b)(1) (2005).

[37]   [Id.]

[38]   Improper Influence on Conduct of Audits, 68 Fed. Reg. at 31,826.

[43]   [Id. at 31,823.]

SEC's eyes, a lawyer who gives an auditor a legal analysis that is inaccurate in such a way that the auditor's financial statement becomes materially misleading can be liable, so long as the lawyer knew or should have known that his or her analysis would have such an effect.

Because the release does *not* list "withholding a legal analysis" as a specific type of conduct that can be considered prohibited under the Rule, it is tempting to suppose that simply giving no information to auditors is the proper solution to this problem. That would likely be a mistake for two reasons. First, the release makes it clear that the list of types of conduct is by no means an exclusive one, and many other types of behavior or actions could also be subject to the Rule. Second, it can be just as easy to mislead an auditor by omitting information as it can to mislead him or her through some bad information.

IV. Conclusion: What This Means for Attorneys

. . . A search for criminal prosecutions under SEC Rule 13b2–2 reveals only a handful of cases, and none against attorneys. But the prudent attorney should keep Sarbanes-Oxley in mind when drafting an auditor response letter, as the events that precipitated the new law could easily happen again. For lawyers, another major public accounting scandal could mean the difference between an unenforced rule and a significant conflict with client confidentiality.

NOTES AND QUESTIONS

1. Three distinct issues are in play here. First, as suggested by the reference to the *Tew* case, a lawyer who fails to disclose confidential client information to the client's auditor may subsequently face liability on a variety of theories ranging from securities fraud to legal malpractice. Second, disclosure of confidential client information by counsel to the client's auditor likely will be deemed a waiver of the attorney-client privilege, allowing discovery of such communications in government investigations or litigation. The Treaty was intended to reduce these risks by substantially limiting the amount of information that counsel must disclose to auditors.

> **CASE IN POINT**
>
> "Waiver of a privilege may occur when there is a breach of confidentiality. For example, disclosure of attorney-client communications to a third party lacking a common legal interest will result in a waiver of the attorney-client privilege. . . . Even disclosure of privileged information directly to a client's independent auditor, accountant, or tax analyst destroys confidentiality." *SEC v. Brady*, 238 F.R.D. 429, 439 (N.D. Tex. 2006)."

The third consideration follows from SOX § 303(a) and the SEC rules thereunder. As the excerpt makes clear, there is a non-trivial risk that a lawyer could be accused of breaching the anti-coercion provisions by withholding information from the auditor. Presumably, this is the case even if the lawyer does so in order to protect the attorney-client privilege.

2.   Simon Lorne reports that:

It seems clear that a lawyer, in responding to an audit inquiry letter from a client's auditors, is acting at the direction of the client's officers and directors within the meaning of Rule 13b2–2, as newly revised in response to SOX 303. As such, while the dimensions of the Accord may be reasonably carefully circumscribed, the revised Rule 13b2–2 raises the question whether a response to auditors in careful consistency with the Accord might not, under at least some circumstances, be viewed as misleading to the auditors and hence violative.[14]

3.   Could a law firm be held liable under Rule 13b2–2 in any of the following cases?

A.   The client requests that the law firm's audit response letter minimize the risk of liability created by a pending lawsuit. The law firm cooperates by knowingly drafting a letter that omits material facts relating to the lawsuit.

B.   The audit response letter stated that there were no pending material lawsuits against the client. The law firm knew that there is a material unasserted possible claim against the client, but failed to inform the auditor of that claim because the auditor did not make a specific request for information about that claim but rather only made a general inquiry regarding possible unasserted claims.

C.   The law firm fails to exercise reasonable care in preparing the audit response letter, as result of which the letter materially understates the risk of liability associated with a major pending lawsuit.

6) MISCELLANEOUS RULES

Congress considered requiring reporting companies to rotate their outside auditor periodically, but ultimately decided not to go that route. Instead, SOX § 203 requires registered public accounting firms to rotate (1) the partner having primary responsibility for the audit and (2) the partner responsible for reviewing the audit every five years. The audit committee must ensure that the requisite rotation actually takes place.

As a matter of good practice, a company ought to consider rotating audit firms periodically so as to get the benefit of a fresh set of eyes. Some corporate governance experts recommend doing so at least every ten years. In addition, governance experts recommend rotating audit firms if a substantial number of former company employees have gone to work for the audit firm or vice-versa.

---

[14]   Simon M. Lorne, An Issue-Annotated Version of the SOX Rules for Lawyer Conduct [A Work-in-Process], in Gatekeepers Under Scrutiny: What Attorneys, Accountants and Directors Need to Know Now: Pre-Conference Briefing at the 37th Annual Institute on Securities Regulation 585, 597 (Practicing Law Inst. ed., 2005).

A separate rule imposes a cooling-off period, pursuant to which an employee of a registered accounting firm may not go to work for a client on whose audit team the employee served until one year after ceasing to be a member of the audit team.

The registered accounting firm may not compensate an audit partner based on the amount of non-audit services the client purchases.

The auditor and its employees may not have any financial interest in the client or any business relationship with the client excepting, of course, the audit relationship and any authorized non-audit services.

Finally, SOX requires that registered accounting firms retain records relating to audits of reporting companies for at least seven years. The prohibition applies to both shredding of physical documents and purging of electronic records. It also applies to all work papers and other interim documentation, as well as final reports.

7) AUDITOR LIABILITY FOR MANAGEMENT FRAUD

Cenco Inc. v. Seidman & Seidman
686 F.2d 449 (7th Cir. 1982)

Between 1970 and 1975, managerial employees of Cenco Incorporated engaged in a massive fraud. The fraud began in Cenco's Medical/Health Division but eventually spread to the top management of Cenco, and by the time it was unmasked the chairman and president of Cenco plus a number of vice-presidents and other top managers were deeply involved. Not all the managers of Cenco were corrupt, however. Seven of the nine members of the board of directors were not in on the fraud, although there is evidence that they were negligent in allowing it to flourish undetected beneath their noses. The fraud was eventually discovered by a newly hired financial officer at Cenco who reported his suspicions to the Securities and Exchange Commission. Cenco's independent auditor throughout the period of the fraud, the accounting partnership of Seidman & Seidman, either never discovered the fraud or if it did failed to report it.

The fraud primarily involved the inflating of inventories in the Medical/Health Division far above their actual value. This increased the apparent worth of Cenco and greatly increased the market price of its stock (when the fraud was unmasked, the market price plummeted by more than 75 percent). The inflated stock was used to buy up other companies on the cheap. Cenco further benefited from the fraud by being able to borrow money at lower rates than if its inventories had been honestly stated and by getting its insurers to pay inflated claims for inventory lost or destroyed, since Cenco's insurance claims were based on inflated rather than actual inventory values. Thus, those involved in the fraud were not stealing from the company, as in the usual corporate fraud case, but were instead aggrandizing the company (and themselves) at the expense of outsiders, such as the owners of the companies that Cenco bought with its inflated stock, the banks that loaned Cenco money, and the insurance companies that insured its inventories.

. . .

[The procedural history of the case is complex, but it eventually went to trial on three claims brought by Cenco against Seidman & Seidman, which respectively allege breach of contract, professional malpractice (negligence) and fraud.] Cenco's evidence tended to show that in the early stages of the fraud Seidman had been careless in checking Cenco's inventory figures and its carelessness had prevented the fraud from being nipped in the bud; that as the fraud expanded, Seidman's auditors became suspicious, but, perhaps to protect the very high fees that Seidman was getting from Cenco (about $1 million a year, which was 70 percent of Seidman's total billings), concealed their suspicions and kept giving Cenco a clean bill of health at their audit reports; that one partner in Seidman, asked by Cenco's general counsel (who was not in on the fraud) whether Seidman suspected anything, answered: "No one suspects fraud. Dismiss that." Seidman's evidence tended to show, to the contrary, that Seidman had diligently attempted to follow up all signs of fraud but had been thwarted by the efforts of the large group of managers at all levels at Cenco who were in on the fraud to prevent Seidman from learning about it.

The jury found for Seidman on all three counts. . . .

This brings us to the main issue in the case—whether the district judge gave erroneous instructions to the jury. The challenged instructions relate to the question whether Seidman was entitled to use the wrongdoing of Cenco's managers as a defense against the charges of breach of contract, professional malpractice, and fraud. Despite the plurality of charges it is one question because breach of contract, negligence, and fraud, when committed by auditors, are a single form of wrongdoing under different names. The contract in question here (really a series of contracts) consists of the letters between Seidman and Cenco outlining the terms of Seidman's annual retention to audit Cenco's books. The material part of the letters is the incorporation by reference of general accounting standards which, so far as pertinent to this case, require the auditor to use his professional skill to follow up any signs of fraud that he discovers in the audit. The tort of negligence in the context of auditing is likewise a failure to use professional care and skill in carrying out an audit. And if such care and skill are not used, then the audit reports to the client will contain misrepresentations, either negligent or, if the auditor knows that the representations in the reports are untruthful or is indifferent to whether or not they are truthful, fraudulent.

Because these theories of auditors' misconduct are so alike, the defenses based on misconduct of the audited firm or its employees are also alike, though verbalized differently. A breach of contract is excused if the promisee's hindrance or failure to cooperate prevented the promisor from performing the contract. The corresponding defense in the case of negligence is, of course, contributory negligence. . . .

Negligence is not a defense to an intentional tort such as fraud. But a participant in a fraud cannot also be a victim entitled to recover damages, for he cannot have relied on the truth of the fraudulent representations, and such reliance is an essential element in a case of fraud. If the misrepresentation is negligent rather than intentional, contributory negligence plays the same role it would play in an ordinary negligence case.

The jury instructions in this case stated these defenses accurately, but Cenco contends that the instructions should not have been given, because they related not to Cenco's conduct but to that of its managers. The judge was aware of the distinction but instructed the jury that the acts of a corporation's employees are the acts of the corporation itself if the employees were acting on the corporation's behalf. If this instruction was correct, then the instructions which allowed the jury to consider Cenco's misconduct as a defense to Seidman's alleged wrongdoing were proper.

To determine the correctness of the instruction requires us to decide in what circumstances, if any, fraud by corporate employees is a defense in a suit by the corporation against its auditors for failure to prevent the fraud. Illinois precedent allows us to reject one extreme position on this question, which is that the employee's fraud is always attributed to the corporation by the principle of respondeat superior. This position, which would exonerate auditors from all liability for failing to detect and prevent frauds by employees of the audited company, was rejected in *Cereal Byproducts Co. v. Hall*, 8 Ill.App.2d 331, 132 N.E.2d 27 (1956), where a company's independent auditors were held liable for negligently failing to detect embezzlement by the company's bookkeeper. Auditors are not detectives hired to ferret out fraud, but if they chance on signs of fraud they may not avert their eyes-they must investigate. The references to keeping an eye out for fraud that appear in the accounting standards incorporated (by reference) in the retention letters between Cenco and Seidman would have little point if not interpreted to impose a duty on auditors to follow up any signs of fraud that come to their attention.

But this does not tell us what the result should be if the fraud permeates the top management of the company and if, moreover, the managers are not stealing from the company—that is, from its current stockholders—but instead are turning the company into an engine of theft against outsiders—creditors, prospective stockholders, insurers, etc. On this question the Illinois cases on auditors' liability provide no guidance. In fact, to our knowledge the question has never been the subject of a reported case. . . .

In predicting how the Illinois courts might decide the present case, we assume they would be guided by the underlying objectives of tort liability. Those objectives are to compensate the victims of wrongdoing and to deter future wrongdoing. With regard to the first, we must refine our earlier statement that the "victim" of Seidman's alleged laxity was Cenco Incorporated. A corporation is a legal fiction. The people who will receive the benefits of any judgment rendered in favor of Cenco on its cross-claim against Seidman are Cenco's stockholders, comprising people who bought stock in Cenco before the fraud began, people who bought during the fraud period and either sold afterwards when the stock price fell or continue to hold the stock at a loss, and people who bought after the fraud was unmasked. A judgment in favor of Cenco on its claim against Seidman would not differentiate among these classes, but would benefit every stockholder as of the date of the judgment (or the date when a judgment was anticipated with some precision) in proportion to the number of shares he owned.

Once the real beneficiaries of any judgment in favor of Cenco are identified, it is apparent that such a judgment would be perverse from the standpoint of compensating the victims of wrongdoing. Among the people who bought stock in Cenco before the fraud began are the corrupt officers themselves. To the extent they are still stockholders in the company, they would benefit pro rata from a judgment in favor of Cenco. The other stockholders in this class are innocent in a sense, but of course it is they who elected the board of directors that managed Cenco during the fraud. The people who bought during the fraud period and either sold at a loss or continue to hold at a loss are the plaintiffs in the recently settled class action in which both Cenco and Seidman were defendants. Seidman has already paid $3.5 million to them. Those who continue to own stock in Cenco (as distinct from those who sold at a loss) would receive additional compensation if Cenco prevailed in this action against Seidman. This is not to say they would be overcompensated; but it seems odd that the same shareholders should be able to recover damages from Seidman twice for the same wrong-once directly and once, in this suit, indirectly. Finally, the shareholders who bought after the fraud was unmasked lost nothing. The unmasking of the fraud caused the price of Cenco's stock to be bid down to reflect not only the true value of its inventories but also any anticipated injury to the company as a result of the fraud.

Because of shareholder turnover, there is always a potential mismatch between the recovery of damages by a corporation and the compensation of the shareholders actually injured by the wrong for which the damages were awarded. It is simply a more dramatic mismatch in this case than usual.

From the standpoint of deterrence, the question is whether the type of fraud that engulfed Cenco between 1970 and 1975 will be deterred more effectively if Cenco can shift the entire cost of the fraud from itself (which is to say, from its stockholders' pockets) to the independent auditor who failed to prevent the fraud. We think not. Cenco's owners—the stockholders—hired managers (directly, in the case of the president and chairman, who were both members of the board of directors, indirectly in the case of the others) who turned out to be thoroughly corrupt and to corrupt the corporation so thoroughly that it caused widespread harm to outsiders. If Seidman had been a more diligent auditor, conceivably if it had been a more honest auditor, the fraud might have been nipped in the bud; and liability to Cenco would make Seidman, and firms like it, more diligent and honest in the future. But if the owners of the corrupt enterprise are allowed to shift the costs of its wrongdoing entirely to the auditor, their incentives to hire honest managers and monitor their behavior will be reduced. While it is true that in a publicly held corporation such as Cenco most shareholders do not have a large enough stake to want to play an active role in hiring and supervising managers, the shareholders delegate this role to a board of directors, which in this case failed in its responsibility. . . .

Thus, not only were some of Cenco's owners dishonest (and, to repeat, to the extent they still own stock in Cenco they would benefit from any judgment in Cenco's favor against Seidman), but the honest owners, and their delegates—a board of directors on which dishonesty and carelessness were well represented—were slipshod in their oversight and so share responsibility for the fraud that Seidman also failed to detect. In addition, the scale of the fraud—the number and high rank of the managers involved—both complicated the task of discovery for Seidman and makes the failure of oversight by Cenco's shareholders and board of directors harder to condone.

Cenco tries to draw a sharp contrast between an innocent Cenco and a Seidman that was (or so the jury could have found) an intentional tortfeasor. But if Cenco may be divorced from its corrupt managers, so may Seidman from the members and employees of the firm who suspected the fraud. If Seidman failed to police its people, Cenco failed as or more dramatically to police its own.

Furthermore, we must assume that Cenco's corrupt managers were acting for the benefit of the company, not against it as in the *Cereal Byproducts* case. The jury was instructed that it could attribute the fraud of Cenco's managers to Cenco only if it found that the managers had been acting on Cenco's behalf, and the verdict for Seidman implies that the jury either so found or found that Seidman had not even committed a prima facie breach of duty to Cenco. The former assumption is more favorable to Cenco.

Fraud on behalf of a corporation is not the same thing as fraud against it. Fraud against the corporation usually hurts just the corporation; the stockholders are the principal if not only victims; their equities vis-a-vis a careless or reckless auditor are therefore strong. But the stockholders of a corporation whose officers commit fraud for the benefit of the corporation are beneficiaries of the fraud. Maybe not net beneficiaries, after the fraud is unmasked and the corporation is sued—that is a question of damages, and is not before us. But the primary costs of a fraud on the corporation's behalf are borne not by the stockholders but by outsiders to the corporation, and the stockholders should not be allowed to escape all responsibility for such a fraud, as they are trying to do in this case.

We need not go so far as to predict that the Illinois courts would hold that in any action by a corporation against its auditors an employee's fraud intended to benefit the company rather than the employee at the company's expense will be attributed to the corporation, however lowly the employee. It is true that the lower down the employee is in the company hierarchy, the less likely he is to commit fraud for rather than against the company. But there are overzealous employees at every level—many a corporation has paid heavy damages for antitrust violations committed by low-level sales managers who thought they were acting in the company's best interests as well as their own—and we think it premature as well as unnecessary to decide that an auditor is never liable for the frauds of loyal but misguided company employees that he could have prevented by taking care. But here the uncontested facts show fraud permeating the top management of Cenco. In such a case the corporation should not be allowed to shift the entire responsibility for the fraud to its auditors.

NOTES AND QUESTIONS

1. Was there a common issue in all three counts that went to the jury? What did Cenco's evidence tend to show as it relates to that common issue?

2. What was Seidman's defense? What did Seidman's evidence tend to show as it relates to that defense?

3. What did Judge Posner hold?

4. Was the fraud in this case considered to "stealing for" the firm and, if so, why?

5. Is Posner's critique of the role of Cenco's shareholders valid?

6. Would Cenco's board have liability under *Caremark* for not detecting the fraud?

PROBLEM

In *Vitellone v. Evans*,[15] shareholder Joseph Vitellone brought a derivative suit on behalf of Magnum Hunter Resources Corporation ("Magnum Hunter" or the "Company against Gary C. Evans, Ronald D. Ormand, Fred J. Smith, Jr., H.C. Ferguson, III, James W. Denny, III, J. Raleigh Bailes, Sr., Brad Bynum, Stephen C. Hurley, Joe L. McClaugherty, Victor G. Carrillo, Steven A. Pfeifer, Jeff Swanson, and David S. Kreuger

---

[15] 2013 WL 6806179 (S.D. Tex. 2013).

(collectively, "Defendants"), and nominal Defendant Magnum Hunter, a publicly-traded energy company incorporated in Delaware, for breach of fiduciary duty, as well as other federal and state violations. Plaintiff's claims arise out of the alleged failure of Defendants, who are past or present officers and directors of Magnum Hunter, to ensure adequate financial controls during a period of rapid growth from 2010 to 2012 when, with a series of about a half dozen acquisitions in 2011 and 2012, Magnum Hunter's assets grew from $249 million to $2.19 billion.

According to Plaintiff's Complaint, current management took control of a much smaller Magnum Hunter in 2009. Defendant Gary C. Evans became Magnum Hunter's Chief Executive Officer, Chairman of the Board, and a director in May 2009, and since then has continuously held those offices. Magnum Hunter's new management in 2009 also retained Hein & Associates, LLP ("Hein") as Magnum Hunter's external auditor.

In November 2010, Magnum Hunter announced plans to evaluate a number of joint venture and acquisition opportunities, and by February, 2011, the Company told investors that it anticipated substantial growth in 2011. The Complaint alleges that with the Company's new acquisitions its revenues and capital expenditures significantly increased in 2011. Indeed, the Complaint describes the Company as growing at a "breakneck pace" in 2011, which continued in 2012. By October 1, 2011, Magnum Hunter began using its own internal accounting and financial services and dismissed Hein as the Company's independent auditor for fiscal 2012. In the Form 8-K announcing the change, Magnum Hunter had "concluded that it would be in the Company's best interest for the Company to engage a new independent registered public accounting firm for 2012 with a greater depth of resources . . . ." Magnum Hunter replaced Hein with Pricewaterhouse Coopers LLP ("PwC") as its external auditor.

PwC discovered previously unreported material weaknesses at Magnum Hunter, and on November 14, 2012, Magnum Hunter restated its second quarter 2012 Form 10-Q/A financial results, which increased its quarterly loss and disclosed certain accounting errors and material weaknesses in its internal controls over financial reporting. In portions of its November 14, 2012 restated Form 10-Q/A quoted in the Complaint, Magnum Hunter described multiple remediation actions, including that it had on October 23, 2012, hired a new Chief Accounting Officer who had the appropriate knowledge and experience to establish and maintain a desired control environment, was implementing more formalized processes and controls, was expanding its accounting department to respond to the Company's growth, and added an Assistant Controller, a Division Controller, an Internal Audit Manager, and other accounting personnel, all hired between July and November, 2012.

On November 15, 2012, according to the Complaint, Magnum Hunter filed with the SEC its Quarterly Report on Form 10-Q for the third quarter ending September 30, 2012. The Company acknowledged that as of September 30, 2012, the Company had material weaknesses in its disclosure controls and procedures, and that management was making changes to establish an environment necessary to prevent or detect potential deficiencies as also detailed in the restated second quarter 2012 Form 10-Q/A filed the previous day.

Defendants have filed a motion to dismiss. How should the court rule?

B. THE AUDIT COMMITTEE

CASE IN POINT

Morefield v. Bailey, 959 F.Supp.2d 887 (Ed. Va. 2013): "The existence of deficiencies in the internal audit practice does not equate to the Board members being conscious of a failure to do their jobs. Nor will the Board's acknowledgement of such errors preclude dismissal of a *Caremark* claim; *Caremark* liability here requires a conscious failure to monitor of the sort that' "disabl[es] themselves from being informed of risks or problems requiring their attention.' . . . Unlike one who knowingly and consciously turns a blind eye to their duties, the Board imposed a thorough review of their financial and accounting practices . . . ."

The data contained in a corporation's financial statements is the market's best tool for evaluating how well a firm's managers perform. Because management prepares the financial statements, however, how can the market trust those statements to represent fairly and accurately the company's true financial picture? Would managers really tell the truth if it meant losing their jobs?

To ensure that the financial statements are accurate and complete, the SEC requires corporations to have those statements audited by an independent firm of certified public accountants. In order to prevent management and the outside auditor from getting too cozy with one another, it has long been considered good practice for the corporation's board of directors to have an audit committee. As defined by SOX § 2(a)(3), that committee is "established by and amongst the board of directors of an issuer for the purpose of overseeing the accounting and financial reporting processes of the issuer and audits of the financial statements of the issuer."

For decades, the NYSE required listed companies to have an audit committee consisting solely of independent directors. The committee had to have at least three members, all of whom were "financially literate." At least one committee member had to have expertise in accounting or financial management. When Sarbanes-Oxley was under consideration by Congress, a consensus quickly formed in favor of imposing a tougher version of the NYSE requirements on all public corporations.

SOX § 301

Section 10A of the Securities Exchange Act of 1934 (15 U.S.C. 78f) is amended by adding at the end the following:

'(m) STANDARDS RELATING TO AUDIT COMMITTEES.—

"(1) COMMISSION RULES.—

"(A) IN GENERAL.—Effective not later than 270 days after the date of enactment of this subsection, the Commission shall, by rule, direct the national securities exchanges and national securities associations to prohibit the listing of any security of an issuer that is not in compliance with the requirements of any portion of paragraphs (2) through (6).

'(B) OPPORTUNITY TO CURE DEFECTS.—The rules of the Commission under subparagraph (A) shall provide for appropriate procedures for an issuer to have an opportunity to cure any defects that would be the basis for a prohibition under subparagraph (A), before the imposition of such prohibition.

'(2) RESPONSIBILITIES   RELATING   TO REGISTERED PUBLIC ACCOUNTING FIRMS.—The audit committee of each issuer, in its capacity as a committee of the board of directors, shall be directly responsible for the appointment, compensation, and oversight of the work of any registered public accounting firm employed by that issuer (including resolution of disagreements between management and the auditor regarding financial reporting) for the purpose of preparing or issuing an audit report or related work, and each such registered public accounting firm shall report directly to the audit committee.

'(3) INDEPENDENCE.—

'(A) IN GENERAL.—Each member of the audit committee of the issuer shall be a member of the board of directors of the issuer, and shall otherwise be independent.

"(B) CRITERIA.—In order to be considered to be independent for purposes of this paragraph, a member of an audit committee of an issuer may not, other than in his or her capacity as a member of the audit committee, the board of directors, or any other board committee—

'(i) accept any consulting, advisory, or other compensatory fee from the issuer; or

'(ii) be an affiliated person of the issuer or any subsidiary thereof.

'(C) EXEMPTION AUTHORITY.—The Commission may exempt from the requirements of subparagraph (B) a particular relationship with respect to audit committee members, as the Commission determines appropriate in light of the circumstances.

'(4) COMPLAINTS.—Each   audit   committee   shall establish procedures for—

'(A) the receipt, retention, and treatment of complaints received by the issuer regarding accounting, internal accounting controls, or auditing matters; and

'(B) the confidential, anonymous submission by employees of the issuer of concerns regarding questionable accounting or auditing matters.

'(5) AUTHORITY TO ENGAGE ADVISERS.—Each audit committee shall have the authority to engage independent counsel and other advisers, as it determines necessary to carry out its duties.

'(6) FUNDING.—Each issuer shall provide for appropriate funding, as determined by the audit committee, in its capacity as a committee of the board of directors, for payment of compensation—

'(A) to the registered public accounting firm employed by the issuer for the purpose of rendering or issuing an audit report; and

'(B) to any advisers employed by the audit committee under paragraph (5).'.

SEC Exchange Act Rule 10A–3

(a) Pursuant to section 10A(m) of the Act (15 U.S.C. 78j–1(m)) and section 3 of the Sarbanes-Oxley Act of 2002 (15 U.S.C. 7202):

(1) National securities exchanges. The rules of each national securities exchange registered pursuant to section 6 of the Act (15 U.S.C. 78f) must, in accordance with the provisions of this section, prohibit the initial or continued listing of any security of an issuer that is not in compliance with the requirements of any portion of paragraph (b) or (c) of this section.

(2) National securities associations. The rules of each national securities association registered pursuant to section 15A of the Act (15 U.S.C. 78o–3) must, in accordance with the provisions of this section, prohibit the initial or continued listing in an automated inter-dealer quotation system of any security of an issuer that is not in compliance with the requirements of any portion of paragraph (b) or (c) of this section.

(3) Opportunity to cure defects. The rules required by paragraphs (a)(1) and (a)(2) of this section must provide for appropriate procedures for a listed issuer to have an opportunity to cure any defects that would be the basis for a prohibition under paragraph (a) of this section, before the imposition of such prohibition. Such rules also may provide that if a member of an audit committee ceases to be independent in accordance with the requirements of this

section for reasons outside the member's reasonable control, that person, with notice by the issuer to the applicable national securities exchange or national securities association, may remain an audit committee member of the listed issuer until the earlier of the next annual shareholders meeting of the listed issuer or one year from the occurrence of the event that caused the member to be no longer independent.

(4) Notification of noncompliance. The rules required by paragraphs (a)(1) and (a)(2) of this section must include a requirement that a listed issuer must notify the applicable national securities exchange or national securities association promptly after an executive officer of the listed issuer becomes aware of any material noncompliance by the listed issuer with the requirements of this section.

. . .

(b) Required standards—

(1) Independence.

(i) Each member of the audit committee must be a member of the board of directors of the listed issuer, and must otherwise be independent; provided that, where a listed issuer is one of two dual holding companies, those companies may designate one audit committee for both companies so long as each member of the audit committee is a member of the board of directors of at least one of such dual holding companies.

(ii) Independence requirements for non-investment company issuers. In order to be considered to be independent for purposes of this paragraph (b)(1), a member of an audit committee of a listed issuer that is not an investment company may not, other than in his or her capacity as a member of the audit committee, the board of directors, or any other board committee:

(A) Accept directly or indirectly any consulting, advisory, or other compensatory fee from the issuer or any subsidiary thereof, provided that, unless the rules of the national securities exchange or national securities association provide otherwise, compensatory fees do not include the receipt of fixed amounts of compensation under a retirement plan (including deferred compensation) for prior service with the listed issuer (provided that such compensation is not contingent in any way on continued service); or

(B) Be an affiliated person of the issuer or any subsidiary thereof.

(iii) Independence requirements for investment company issuers. In order to be considered to be independent for purposes of this paragraph (b)(1), a member of an audit committee of a listed issuer that is an investment company may not, other than in his or her capacity as a member of the audit committee, the board of directors, or any other board committee:

(A) Accept directly or indirectly any consulting, advisory, or other compensatory fee from the issuer or any subsidiary thereof, provided that, unless the rules of the national securities exchange or national securities association provide otherwise, compensatory fees do not include the receipt of fixed amounts of compensation under a retirement plan (including deferred compensation) for prior service with the listed issuer (provided that such compensation is not contingent in any way on continued service); or

(B) Be an "interested person" of the issuer as defined in section 2(a)(19) of the Investment Company Act of 1940 (15 U.S.C. 80a–2(a)(19)).

(iv) Exemptions from the independence requirements.

(A) For an issuer listing securities pursuant to a registration statement under section 12 of the Act (15 U.S.C. 78*l*), or for an issuer that has a registration statement under the Securities Act of 1933 (15 U.S.C. 77aet seq.) covering an initial public offering of securities to be listed by the issuer, where in each case the listed issuer was not, immediately prior to the effective date of such registration statement, required to file reports with the Commission pursuant to section 13(a) or 15(d) of the Act (15 U.S.C. 78m(a) or 78*o*(d)):

(1) All but one of the members of the listed issuer's audit committee may be exempt from the independence requirements of paragraph (b)(1)(ii) of this section for 90 days from the date of effectiveness of such registration statement; and

(2) A minority of the members of the listed issuer's audit committee may be exempt from the independence requirements of paragraph (b)(1)(ii) of this section for one year from the date of effectiveness of such registration statement.

(B) An audit committee member that sits on the board of directors of a listed issuer and an affiliate of the listed issuer is exempt from the requirements of paragraph (b)(1)(ii)(B) of this section if the member, except for being a director on each such board of directors, otherwise meets the independence requirements of paragraph (b)(1)(ii) of this section for each such entity, including the receipt of only ordinary-course compensation for serving as a member of the board of directors, audit committee or any other board committee of each such entity.

(C) An employee of a foreign private issuer who is not an executive officer of the foreign private issuer is exempt from the requirements of paragraph (b)(1)(ii) of this section if the employee is elected or named to the board of directors or audit committee of the foreign private issuer pursuant to the issuer's governing law or documents, an employee collective bargaining or similar agreement or other home country legal or listing requirements.

(D) An audit committee member of a foreign private issuer may be exempt from the requirements of paragraph (b)(1)(ii)(B) of this section if that member meets the following requirements:

(1) The member is an affiliate of the foreign private issuer or a representative of such an affiliate;

(2) The member has only observer status on, and is not a voting member or the chair of, the audit committee; and

(3) Neither the member nor the affiliate is an executive officer of the foreign private issuer.

(E) An audit committee member of a foreign private issuer may be exempt from the requirements of paragraph (b)(1)(ii)(B) of this section if that member meets the following requirements:

(1) The member is a representative or designee of a foreign government or foreign governmental entity that is an affiliate of the foreign private issuer; and

(2) The member is not an executive officer of the foreign private issuer.

(F) In addition to paragraphs (b)(1)(iv)(A) through (E) of this section, the Commission may exempt from the requirements of paragraphs (b)(1)(ii) or (b)(1)(iii) of this section a particular relationship with respect to audit committee members,   as   the   Commission   determines appropriate in light of the circumstances.

(2) Responsibilities relating to registered public accounting firms. The audit committee of each listed issuer, in its capacity as a committee of the board of directors, must be directly responsible for the appointment, compensation, retention and oversight of the work of any registered public accounting firm engaged (including resolution of disagreements between management and the auditor regarding financial reporting) for the purpose of preparing or issuing an audit report or performing other audit, review or attest services for the listed issuer, and each such registered public accounting firm must report directly to the audit committee.

(3) Complaints. Each audit committee must establish procedures for:

(i) The receipt, retention, and treatment of complaints received by the listed issuer regarding accounting, internal accounting controls, or auditing matters; and

(ii) The confidential, anonymous submission by employees of the listed issuer of concerns regarding questionable accounting or auditing matters.

(4) Authority to engage advisers. Each audit committee must have the authority to engage independent counsel and other advisers, as it determines necessary to carry out its duties.

(5) Funding. Each listed issuer must provide for appropriate funding, as determined by the audit committee, in its capacity as a committee of the board of directors, for payment of:

(i) Compensation to any registered public accounting firm engaged for the purpose of preparing or issuing an audit report or performing other audit, review or attest services for the listed issuer;

(ii) Compensation to any advisers employed by the audit committee under paragraph (b)(4) of this section; and

(iii) Ordinary administrative expenses of the audit committee that are necessary or appropriate in carrying out its duties.

(c) General exemptions.

(1) At any time when an issuer has a class of securities that is listed on a national securities exchange or national securities association subject to the requirements of this section, the listing of other classes of securities of the listed

issuer on a national securities exchange or national securities association is not subject to the requirements of this section.

(2) At any time when an issuer has a class of common equity securities (or similar securities) that is listed on a national securities exchange or national securities association subject to the requirements of this section, the listing of classes of securities of a direct or indirect consolidated subsidiary or an at least 50% beneficially owned subsidiary of the issuer (except classes of equity securities, other than non-convertible, non-participating preferred securities, of such subsidiary) is not subject to the requirements of this section.

(3) The listing of securities of a foreign private issuer is not subject to the requirements of paragraphs (b)(1) through (b)(5) of this section if the foreign private issuer meets the following requirements:

(i) The foreign private issuer has a board of auditors (or similar body), or has statutory auditors, established and selected pursuant to home country legal or listing provisions expressly requiring or permitting such a board or similar body;

(ii) The board or body, or statutory auditors is required under home country legal or listing requirements to be either:

(A) Separate from the board of directors; or

(B) Composed of one or more members of the board of directors and one or more members that are not also members of the board of directors;

(iii) The board or body, or statutory auditors, are not elected by management of such issuer and no executive officer of the foreign private issuer is a member of such board or body, or statutory auditors;

(iv) Home country legal or listing provisions set forth or provide for standards for the independence of such board or body, or statutory auditors, from the foreign private issuer or the management of such issuer;

(v) Such board or body, or statutory auditors, in accordance with any applicable home country legal or listing requirements or the issuer's governing documents, are responsible, to the extent permitted by law, for the appointment, retention and oversight of the work of any registered public accounting firm engaged (including, to the extent permitted by law, the resolution of disagreements between management and the auditor regarding financial reporting) for the purpose of preparing or issuing an audit report or performing other audit, review or attest services for the issuer; and

(vi) The audit committee requirements of paragraphs (b)(3), (b)(4) and (b)(5) of this section apply to such board or body, or statutory auditors, to the extent permitted by law.

(4) The listing of a security futures product cleared by a clearing agency that is registered pursuant to section 17A of the Act (15 U.S.C. 78q–1) or that is exempt from the registration requirements of section 17A pursuant to paragraph (b)(7)(A) of such section is not subject to the requirements of this section.

(5) The listing of a standardized option, as defined in § 240.9b–1(a)(4), issued by a clearing agency that is registered pursuant to section 17A of the Act (15 U.S.C. 78q–1) is not subject to the requirements of this section.

(6) The listing of securities of the following listed issuers are not subject to the requirements of this section:

(i) Asset-Backed Issuers (as defined in § 229.1101 of this chapter);

(ii) Unit investment trusts (as defined in 15 U.S.C. 80a–4(2)); and

(iii) Foreign governments (as defined in § 240.3b–4(a)).

(7) The listing of securities of a listed issuer is not subject to the requirements of this section if:

(i) The listed issuer, as reflected in the applicable listing application, is organized as a trust or other unincorporated association that does not have a board of directors or persons acting in a similar capacity; and

(ii) The activities of the listed issuer that is described in paragraph (c)(7)(i) of this section are limited to passively owning or holding (as well as administering and distributing amounts in respect of) securities, rights, collateral or other assets on behalf of or for the benefit of the holders of the listed securities.

(d) Disclosure. Any listed issuer availing itself of an exemption from the independence standards contained in paragraph (b)(1)(iv) of this section (except paragraph (b)(1)(iv)(B) of this section), the general exemption contained in paragraph (c)(3) of this section or the last sentence of paragraph (a)(3) of this section, must:

(1) Disclose its reliance on the exemption and its assessment of whether, and if so, how, such reliance would materially adversely affect the ability of the audit committee to act independently and to satisfy the other requirements of this section in any proxy or information statement for a meeting of shareholders at which directors are elected that is

filed with the Commission pursuant to the requirements of section 14 of the Act (15 U.S.C. 78n); and

(2) Disclose the information specified in paragraph (d)(1) of this section in, or incorporate such information by reference from such proxy or information statement filed with the Commission into, its annual report filed with the Commission pursuant to the requirements of section 13(a) or 15(d) of the Act (15 U.S.C. 78m(a) or 78o(d)).

(e) Definitions. Unless the context otherwise requires, all terms used in this section have the same meaning as in the Act. In addition, unless the context otherwise requires, the following definitions apply for purposes of this section:

(1)(i)   The term affiliate of, or a person affiliated with, a specified person, means a person that directly, or indirectly through one or more intermediaries, controls, or is controlled by, or is under common control with, the person specified.

(ii)(A)   A person will be deemed not to be in control of a specified person for purposes of this section if the person:

(1) Is not the beneficial owner, directly or indirectly, of more than 10% of any class of voting equity securities of the specified person; and

(2) Is not an executive officer of the specified person.

(B) Paragraph (e)(1)(ii)(A) of this section only creates a safe harbor position that a person does not control a specified person. The existence of the safe harbor does not create a presumption in any way that a person exceeding the ownership requirement in paragraph (e)(1)(ii)(A)(1) of this section controls or is otherwise an affiliate of a specified person.

(iii) The following will be deemed to be affiliates:

(A) An executive officer of an affiliate;

(B) A director who also is an employee of an affiliate;

(C) A general partner of an affiliate; and

(D) A managing member of an affiliate.

(iv) For purposes of paragraph (e)(1)(i) of this section, dual holding companies will not be deemed to be affiliates of or persons affiliated with each other by virtue of their dual holding company arrangements with each other, including where directors of one dual holding company are also directors of the other dual holding company, or where directors of one or both dual holding companies are also directors of the businesses jointly controlled, directly or indirectly, by the dual holding companies (and, in each case, receive only ordinary-course compensation for serving as a member of the board of directors, audit committee or any other board committee of the dual holding companies or any entity that is jointly controlled, directly or indirectly, by the dual holding companies).

(2) In the case of foreign private issuers with a two-tier board system, the term board of directors means the supervisory or non-management board.

(3) In the case of a listed issuer that is a limited partnership or limited liability company where such entity does not have a board of directors or equivalent body, the term board of directors means the board of directors of the managing general partner, managing member or equivalent body.

(4) The term control (including the terms controlling, controlled by and under common control with) means the possession, direct or indirect, of the power to direct or cause the direction of the management and policies of a person, whether through the ownership of voting securities, by contract, or otherwise.

(5) The term dual holding companies means two foreign private issuers that:

(i) Are organized in different national jurisdictions;

(ii) Collectively own and supervise the management of one or more businesses which are conducted as a single economic enterprise; and

(iii) Do not conduct any business other than collectively owning and supervising such businesses and activities reasonably incidental thereto.

(6) The term executive officer has the meaning set forth in § 240.3b–7.

(7) The term foreign private issuer has the meaning set forth in § 240.3b–4(c).

(8) The term indirect acceptance by a member of an audit committee of any consulting, advisory or other compensatory fee includes acceptance of such a fee by a spouse, a minor child or stepchild or a child or stepchild sharing a home with the member or by an entity in which such member is a partner, member, an officer such as a managing director occupying a comparable position or executive officer, or occupies a similar position (except limited partners, non-managing members and those occupying similar positions who, in each case, have no active role in providing services to

the entity) and which provides accounting, consulting, legal, investment banking or financial advisory services to the issuer or any subsidiary of the issuer.

(9)   The terms listed and listing refer to securities listed on a national securities exchange or listed in an automated inter-dealer quotation system of a national securities association or to issuers of such securities.

Instructions to § 240.10A–3:

1.   The requirements in paragraphs (b)(2) through (b)(5), (c)(3)(v) and (c)(3)(vi) of this section do not conflict with, and do not affect the application of, any requirement or ability under a listed issuer's governing law or documents or other home country legal or listing provisions that requires or permits shareholders to ultimately vote on, approve or ratify such requirements. The requirements instead relate to the assignment of responsibility as between the audit committee and management. In such an instance, however, if the listed issuer provides a recommendation or nomination regarding such responsibilities to shareholders, the audit committee of the listed issuer, or body performing similar functions, must be responsible for making the recommendation or nomination.

2.   The requirements in paragraphs (b)(2) through (b)(5), (c)(3)(v), (c)(3)(vi) and Instruction 1 of this section do not conflict with any legal or listing requirement in a listed issuer's home jurisdiction that prohibits the full board of directors from delegating such responsibilities to the listed issuer's audit committee or limits the degree of such delegation. In that case, the audit committee, or body performing similar functions, must be granted such responsibilities, which can include advisory powers, with respect to such matters to the extent permitted by law, including submitting nominations or recommendations to the full board.

3.   The requirements in paragraphs (b)(2) through (b)(5), (c)(3)(v) and (c)(3)(vi) of this section do not conflict with any legal or listing requirement in a listed issuer's home jurisdiction that vests such responsibilities with a government entity or tribunal. In that case, the audit committee, or body performing similar functions, must be granted such responsibilities, which can include advisory powers, with respect to such matters to the extent permitted by law.

4.   For purposes of this section, the determination of a person's beneficial ownership must be made in accordance with § 240.13d–3.

NYSE Listed Company Manual § 303A.06

Listed companies must have an audit committee that satisfies the requirements of Rule 10A–3 under the Exchange Act.

Commentary: The Exchange will apply the requirements of Rule 10A–3 in a manner consistent with the guidance provided by the Securities and Exchange Commission in SEC Release No. 34–47654 (April 1, 2003). Without limiting the generality of the foregoing, the Exchange will provide companies the opportunity to cure defects provided in Rule 10A–3(a)(3) under the Exchange Act.

Disclosure Requirement: Please note that Rule 10A–3(d)(1) and (2) require listed companies to disclose reliance on certain exceptions from Rule 10A–3 and to disclose an assessment of whether, and if so, how, such reliance would materially adversely affect the ability of the audit committee to act independently and to satisfy the other requirements of Rule 10A–3.

NYSE Listed Company Manual § 303A.07

(a) The audit committee must have a minimum of three members. All audit committee members must satisfy the requirements for independence set out in Section 303A.02 and, in the absence of an applicable exemption, Rule 10A–3(b)(1).

Commentary: Each member of the audit committee must be financially literate, as such qualification is interpreted by the listed company's board in its business judgment, or must become financially literate within a reasonable period of time after his or her appointment to the audit committee. In addition, at least one member of the audit committee must have accounting or related financial management expertise, as the listed company's board interprets such qualification in its business judgment. While the Exchange does not require that a listed company's audit committee include a person who satisfies the definition of audit committee financial expert set out in Item 407(d)(5)(ii) of Regulation S–K, a board may presume that such a person has accounting or related financial management expertise.

Because of the audit committee's demanding role and responsibilities, and the time commitment attendant to committee membership, each prospective audit committee member should evaluate carefully the existing demands on his or her time before accepting this important assignment.

Disclosure Requirement: If an audit committee member simultaneously serves on the audit committees of more than three public companies, the board must determine that such simultaneous service would not impair the ability of such member to effectively serve on the listed company's audit committee and must disclose such determination either on or through the listed company's website or in its annual proxy statement or, if the listed company does not file an annual proxy statement, in its annual report on Form 10-K filed with the SEC. If this disclosure is made on or through the listed company's website, the listed company must disclose that fact in its annual proxy statement or annual report, as applicable, and provide the website address.

(b) The audit committee must have a written charter that addresses:

(i) the committee's purpose—which, at minimum, must be to:

(A) assist board oversight of (1) the integrity of the listed company's financial statements, (2) the listed company's compliance with legal and regulatory requirements, (3) the independent auditor's qualifications and independence, and (4) the performance of the listed company's internal audit function and independent auditors (if the listed company does not yet have an internal audit function because it is availing itself of a transition period pursuant to Section 303A.00, the charter must provide that the committee will assist board oversight of the design and implementation of the internal audit function); and

(B) prepare the disclosure required by Item 407(d)(3)(i) of Regulation S–K;

(ii) an annual performance evaluation of the audit committee; and

(iii) the duties and responsibilities of the audit committee—which, at a minimum, must include those set out in Rule 10A–3(b)(2), (3), (4) and (5) of the Exchange Act, as well as to:

(A) at least annually, obtain and review a report by the independent auditor describing: the firm's internal quality-control procedures; any material issues raised by the most recent internal quality-control review, or peer review, of the firm, or by any inquiry or investigation by governmental or professional authorities, within the preceding five years, respecting one or more independent audits carried out by the firm, and any steps taken to deal with any such issues; and (to assess the auditor's independence) all relationships between the independent auditor and the listed company;

Commentary: After reviewing the foregoing report and the independent auditor's work throughout the year, the audit committee will be in a position to evaluate the auditor's qualifications, performance and independence. This evaluation should include the review and evaluation of the lead partner of the independent auditor. In making its evaluation, the audit committee should take into account the opinions of management and the listed company's internal auditors (or other personnel responsible for the internal audit function). In addition to assuring the regular rotation of the lead audit partner as required by law, the audit committee should further consider whether, in order to assure continuing auditor independence, there should be regular rotation of the audit firm itself. The audit committee should present its conclusions with respect to the independent auditor to the full board.

> (B) meet to review and discuss the listed company's annual audited financial statements and quarterly financial statements with management and the independent auditor, including reviewing the listed company's specific disclosures under "Management's Discussion and Analysis of Financial Condition and Results of Operations";

Commentary: Meetings may be telephonic if permitted under applicable corporate law; polling of audit committee members, however, is not permitted in lieu of meetings.

With respect to closed-end funds, Section 303A.07(b)(iii)(B) requires that the audit committee meet to review and discuss the fund's annual audited financial statements and semi-annual financial statements. In addition, if a closed-end fund chooses to voluntarily include the section "Management's Discussion of Fund Performance" in its Form N-CSR, then the audit committee is required to meet to review and discuss it.

> (C) discuss the listed company's earnings press releases, as well as financial information and earnings guidance provided to analysts and rating agencies;

Commentary: The audit committee's responsibility to discuss earnings releases, as well as financial information and earnings guidance, may be done generally (i.e., discussion of the types of information to be disclosed and the type of presentation to be made). The audit committee need not discuss in advance each earnings release or each instance in which a listed company may provide earnings guidance.

> (D) discuss policies with respect to risk assessment and risk management;

Commentary: While it is the job of the CEO and senior management to assess and manage the listed company's exposure to risk, the audit committee must discuss guidelines and policies to govern the process by which this is handled. The audit committee should discuss the listed company's major financial risk exposures and the steps management has taken to monitor and control such exposures. The audit committee is not required to be the sole body responsible for risk assessment and management, but, as stated above, the committee must discuss guidelines and policies to govern the process by which risk assessment and management is undertaken. Many companies, particularly financial companies, manage and assess their risk through mechanisms other than the audit committee. The processes these companies have in place should be reviewed in a general manner by the audit committee, but they need not be replaced by the audit committee.

(E) meet separately, periodically, with management, with internal auditors (or other personnel responsible for the internal audit function) and with independent auditors;

Commentary: To perform its oversight functions most effectively, the audit committee must have the benefit of separate sessions with management, the independent auditors and those responsible for the internal audit function. As noted herein, all listed companies must have an internal audit function. These separate sessions may be more productive than joint sessions in surfacing issues warranting committee attention. If the listed company does not yet have an internal audit function because it is availing itself of a transition period pursuant to Section 303A.00, the committee must meet periodically with the company personnel primarily responsible for the design and implementation of the internal audit function.

(F) review with the independent auditor any audit problems or difficulties and management's response;

Commentary: The audit committee must regularly review with the independent auditor any difficulties the auditor encountered in the course of the audit work, including any restrictions on the scope of the independent auditor's activities or on access to requested information, and any significant disagreements with management. Among the items the audit committee may want to review with the auditor are: any accounting adjustments that were noted or proposed by the auditor but were "passed" (as immaterial or otherwise); any communications between the audit team and the audit firm's national office respecting auditing or accounting issues presented by the engagement; and any "management" or "internal control" letter issued, or proposed to be issued, by the audit firm to the listed company. The review should also include discussion of the responsibilities, budget and staffing of the listed company's internal audit function. If the listed company does not yet have an internal audit function because it is availing itself of a transition period pursuant to Section 303A.00, the review should include discussion of management's plans with respect to the responsibilities, budget and staffing of the internal audit function and its plans for the implementation of the internal audit function.

(G) set clear hiring policies for employees or former employees of the independent auditors; and

Commentary: Employees or former employees of the independent auditor are often valuable additions to corporate management. Such individuals' familiarity with the business, and personal rapport with the employees, may be attractive qualities when filling a key opening. However, the audit committee should set hiring policies taking into account the pressures that may exist for auditors consciously or subconsciously seeking a job with the listed company they audit.

(H) report regularly to the board of directors.

Commentary: The audit committee should review with the full board any issues that arise with respect to the quality or integrity of the listed company's financial statements, the listed company's compliance with legal or regulatory requirements, the performance and independence of the listed company's independent auditors, or the performance of the internal audit function. If the listed company does not yet have an internal audit function because it is availing itself of a transition period pursuant to Section 303A.00, the committee should review with the board management's activities with respect to the design and implementation of the internal audit function.

General Commentary to Section 303A.07(b): While the fundamental responsibility for the listed company's financial statements and disclosures rests with management and the independent auditor, the audit committee must review: (A) major issues regarding accounting principles and financial statement presentations, including any significant changes in the listed company's selection or application of accounting principles, and major issues as to the adequacy of the listed company's internal controls and any special audit steps adopted in light of material control deficiencies; (B) analyses prepared by management and/or the independent auditor setting forth significant financial reporting issues and judgments made in connection with the preparation of the financial statements, including analyses of the effects of alternative GAAP methods on the financial statements; (C) the effect of regulatory and accounting initiatives, as well as off-balance sheet structures, on the financial statements of the listed company; and (D) the type and presentation of information to be included in earnings press releases (paying particular attention to any use of "pro forma," or "adjusted" non-GAAP, information), as well as review any financial information and earnings guidance provided to analysts and rating agencies.

Website Posting Requirement: A listed company must make its audit committee charter available on or through its website. A closed-end fund is not required to comply with this website posting requirement.

Disclosure Requirements: A listed company must disclose in its annual proxy statement or, if it does not file an annual proxy statement, in its annual report on Form 10-K filed with the SEC that its audit committee charter is available on or through its website and provide the website address.

(c) Each listed company must have an internal audit function.

Commentary: Listed companies must maintain an internal audit function to provide management and the audit committee with ongoing assessments of the listed company's risk management processes and system of internal control. A listed company may choose to outsource this function to a third party service provider other than its independent auditor. While Section 303A.00 permits certain categories of newly-listed companies to avail themselves of a transition period to comply with the internal audit function requirement, all listed companies must have an internal audit function in place no later than the first anniversary of the company's listing date.

General Commentary to Section 303A.07: To avoid any confusion, note that the audit committee functions specified in Section 303A.07 are the sole responsibility of the audit committee and may not be allocated to a different committee.

QUESTIONS

1.   What would be a reasonable definition of the required financial literacy?

2.   Should the listing standard be amended to require that an audit committee member have financial literacy at the time of their appointment?

3.   What would be a reasonable definition of "accounting or related financial management expertise"?

4.   Should all members of the audit committee have "accounting or related financial management expertise"?

5.   Expertise is no guarantee of success. Members of the Enron board of directors at the time of its collapse included a Stanford accounting professor, two former CEOs of financial institutions, a hedge fund manager, and an economist who had previously served as chair of the federal Commodity Futures Trading Commission. Why might such skilled experts have failed to detect Enron's many problems?

6.   Should members of the audit committee receive higher compensation than other board members?

7.   Should state law impose higher fiduciary duties on audit committee members than ordinary board members?

8.   Pauline is a well-known motivational speaker. In each of the last 5 years, Pauline has been paid $10,000 by Ajax, Inc., a NYSE-listed public company, to give a motivational speech to top management. Ajax now wishes to appoint Pauline to the board of directors and have her serve on Ajax's audit committee. Both Ajax and Pauline anticipate that she will continue to provide motivational speeches and continue to be paid $10,000 per year for those services, which will be in addition to any director fees she is paid. If appointed, will Pauline qualify as an independent director? If so, is Pauline eligible to serve on Ajax's audit committee?

NOTE

The idea for a mandatory audit committee has been around for a long time. The American Law Institute's Principles of Corporate Governance, for example, proposed back in 1994 that large public corporations should have an "audit committee to implement and support the oversight function of the board . . . by reviewing on a periodic basis the corporation's processes for producing financial data, its internal controls, and the independence of the corporation's external auditor."[16] The commentary to that requirement explained the rationale for doing so as follows:

(i)   Such a committee provides a means for review of the corporation's processes for producing financial data, its internal controls, and the independence of the corporation's external auditor, and a forum for dialogue with the corporation's external and internal auditors. In theory, the full board might execute these functions itself, because the board is obliged in any event to be conversant with those matters. In practice, however, there are several reasons why an audit committee would normally constitute a preferable location for these functions. For one thing, a focused review and detailed discussion of the corporation's processes for producing financial data, its internal controls, and the independence of its external auditor might be too time-consuming for the full board. For another, because the corporation's financial data concerns the performance of management, it is important to have a forum for discussing this data, and the manner of its preparation, in which management participates only on request.

(ii)   An independent audit committee reinforces the independence of the corporation's external auditor, and thereby helps assure that the auditor will have free rein in the audit process. This reinforcement is achieved in part by conferring, on an organ that is independent of the management whose financial results are being audited, a vital role in the retention, discharge, and compensation of the external auditor. In addition, such a committee provides tangible embodiment of the concept that, within the framework of corporate relationships, the external auditor is responsible to the board and to the shareholders.

(iii)   An independent audit committee provides a forum for regular, informal, and private discussion between the external auditor and directors who have no significant relationships with management. In the absence of such a forum, an external auditor would often be reluctant to call for a meeting at the board level unless a problem of great magnitude had arisen. In contrast, the provision of an institutionalized forum facilitates and indeed encourages the external auditor to raise potentially troublesome issues at a relatively early stage, allows the auditor to broach sensitive problems in an uninhibited and private fashion, and gives

---

[16]   Principles of Corp. Governance § 3.05 (1994).

the auditor assurance that it can readily get a hearing in the event of a disagreement with management.

(iv) An independent audit committee reinforces the objectivity of the internal auditing department. If that department reports primarily to management (as is normally the case), and has no regular access to the board or to a board committee, it may encounter resistance to recommendations that do not meet with management's approval. Regular access to an audit committee may help ameliorate such resistance. A working relationship with an audit committee is also likely to increase the status and therefore the effectiveness of the internal auditing department.[17]

Eight years later, Congress mandated public company audit committees and turned those committees into the Act's central player. The audit committee must approve any non-audit services performed by the company's outside certified public accounting firm. The audit committee supervises the company's whistle-blower policies. The audit committee is required to ensure that the outside auditor can perform its audit unimpeded by management. The audit committee acts as a liaison between management and the outside auditor, especially with respect to any disagreements between them or any other problems that arise during the audit. The audit committee should review the CEO and CFO's certifications with the outside auditor. The audit committee must ensure that every five years the outside auditor rotates both the partner principally responsible for conducting the audit and the partner responsible for reviewing the audit.

The SEC put additional teeth into the exchange's audit committee requirements by mandating that corporate proxy statements include a report from that committee containing a variety of disclosures. The report, for example, must state whether the committee reviewed and discussed the company's audited financial statements with management and the firm's independent auditors. The report also must state whether the audit committee recommended to the board of directors that the audited financial statements be included in the company's annual report on Form 10-K.

As a matter of good corporate practice, an audit committee should establish a "tone at the top" that encourages honesty, integrity, and compliance with legal requirements. In particular, members of an audit committee should not passively rely on management and the outside auditors. While members of the audit committee are not private investigators charged with conducting corporate espionage to detect wrongdoing, they are obliged to make a candid inquiry before accepting the reports they receive from management and outside auditors. As the Delaware Supreme Court observed in *Smith v. Van Gorkom*, the board must "proceed with a critical eye in assessing information" provided by others.[18]

As with the other post-SOX federal and stock exchange listing standards governing board composition, the audit committee rules preempt state corporate law. The post-SOX audit committee rules have had other

---

[17]   Id.
[18]   Smith v. Van Gorkom, 488 A.2d 858, 872 (Del. 1985).

unforeseen consequences. There are important conflicts between § 301's mandate that the audit committee establish and oversee a corporate whistle blowing program and EU directives with respect to data protection, for example. As a result, the French data protection authority struck down whistle blowing systems proposed by two subsidiaries of U.S. corporations subject to both § 301 and French data protection law.[19]

As was true of the other post-SOX federal and stock exchange listing standards governing board composition, the new audit committee rules were imposed despite a lack of compelling empirical justification. Roberta Romano identified and summarized 16 pre-SOX studies of independent audit committees. Four of the studies tried to find a correlation between audit committee independence and firm performance as measured by both accounting and stock market metrics. None found a statistically significant relationship between the two using any metric.[20]

Other studies tried to find a link between audit committee independence and the probability of financial statement misconduct, as measured by such indicia as "abnormal accruals, financial statement restatements and fraud, SEC actions, third-party or contract fraud allegations, and stock market responses to unexpected earnings."[21] Ten of the studies found no such link, with one reporting inconsistent results depending on the empirical model being tested.

Studies finding a correlation between audit committee independence and firm performance on some metric must be taken with a grain of salt. It is difficult to draw causality conclusions from these studies. Firms with high quality disclosure practices opted for an active, fully independent audit committee. Firms that created such a committee may have done so as part of a broader package of accounting and

> **THINK ABOUT IT**
>
> "Requiring audit committees to be directly responsible for all matters related to the audit engagement has created an adversarial model of corporate governance that pits the audit committee against the CEO and CFO, who would typically be the front-line players with respect to such matters. This adversarial relationship will likely result in a decline in the overall competitiveness of the U.S. capital markets, as boards of directors are concerned with additional responsibilities placed on them by the Act as well as coping with the new corporate governance dynamic that results from the Commission's emphasis on investor protection." Peter Ferola, The Role of Audit Committees in the Wake of Corporate Federalism: Sarbanes-Oxley's Creep into State Corporate Law, 7 J. Bus. & Sec. L. 143, 160 (2007). Does concern about an adversarial relationship between managers and auditors seem significant?

---

[19]   Michael Delikat, Developments Under Sarbanes-Oxley Whistleblower Law, in Internal Investigations 2007: Legal, Ethical & Strategic Issues (June 2007), available on Westlaw at 1609 PLI/Corp 19.

[20]   Roberta Romano, The Sarbanes-Oxley Act and the Making of Quack Corporate Governance, 114 Yale L.J. 1521, 1530 (2005).

[21]   Id. at 1531 (footnote omitted).

disclosure enhancements. Accordingly, the studies inherently suffer from a serious endogeneity problem.

In so far as post-SOX evidence is available, there appears to be little connection between audit committee independence prompted by the Sarbanes-Oxley law and avoidance of earnings restatements. A study of the relation between the probability of financial misstatements by a firm and various corporate governance features found no statistically significant correlation between the former and audit committee independence. The study did find a negative correlation between financial expertise on the part of audit committee members and the probability of financial misstatements.[22] That result is hardly surprising. An expert director should do a better job of monitoring corporate performance in his area of expertise than a layperson. All that finding supports is an expertise requirement, however, not the elaborate apparatus erected by the Sarbanes-Oxley Act and the exchange standards.

The additional audit committee responsibilities imposed by that apparatus have been a prime factor in the increased workload of corporate directors and, as a result, the increase in director compensation.[23] On average, the number of times per year an audit committee met rose from five in 2002 to nine in 2005.[24]

Small firms were especially affected because they were less likely to have sufficient independent directors to satisfy the new exchange listing standards. Many of them therefore had to add new independent directors who not only met the heightened standards of independence but also satisfied the new expertise requirements for audit committee membership. In addition, because director compensation does not scale on a one-to-one basis as firm size increases, the increase in director compensation necessary to compensate these new directors for the perceived rise in workload and liability exposure post-SOX also disproportionately affected small firms. A post-SOX empirical study confirms both that director compensation costs rose dramatically after Sarbanes-Oxley passed and that those costs disproportionally burdened smaller public corporations.[25]

The world of nonprofit governance provides an interesting insight on the cost-benefit ratio of an independent audit committee. Only two of Sarbanes-Oxley's provisions apply directly to nonprofits: (1) The protections for whistle blowers and (2) the prohibition of destroying, altering, or falsifying documents so as to prevent their use or discovery in any official proceeding.[26] After Sarbanes-Oxley came into law, however, nonprofits undertook an

---

[22]   Anup Agrawal & Sahiba Chadha, Corporate Governance and Accounting Scandals, 48 J.L. & Econ. 371, 375 (2005).

[23]   Judith Burns, Corporate Governance (A Special Report)—Everything you Wanted to Know About Corporate Governance But Didn't Know to Ask, Wall St. J., Oct. 27, 2003, at R6.

[24]   Jo Lynne Koehn & Stephen C. DelVecchio, Revisiting the Ripple Effects of the Sarbanes-Oxley Act, CPA J. Online, May 2006.

[25]   James S. Linck et al., The Effects and Unintended Consequences of the Sarbanes-Oxley Act, and Its Era, on the Supply and Demand for Directors (2009), http://ssrn.com/abstract= 902665.

[26]   See generally Stephen M. Bainbridge, The Complete Guide to Sarbanes-Oxley 96–108 (2005) (discussing these requirements).

assessment of whether they should voluntarily comply with Sarbanes-Oxley rules. An Urban Institute study of governance practices at 5,000 nonprofits found varying degrees of Sarbanes-Oxley compliance. Most nonprofits, for example, had an independent outside auditor. Indeed, the practice was almost universal (97%) at large nonprofits with annual expenses exceeding $2 million. In contrast, a "separate audit committee was the least commonly adopted practice related to Sarbanes-Oxley issues in all size groups."[27] Even among very large nonprofits, with over $40 million in annual expenses, only 58% had an SOX-like independent audit committee. Nonprofits face considerable pressure from key stakeholders, such as outside auditors, major donors, and government regulators to have effective corporate governance practices. The striking absence of audit committees among nonprofits therefore suggests that the benefits of such a committee do not outweigh the costs.

Exercise: Evaluating the Audit Committee Charter of Walmart Stores, Inc.

Purpose

The Audit Committee is appointed by the Board to: (1) assist the Board in monitoring (a) the integrity of the financial reporting process, systems of internal controls and financial statements and reports of the Company, (b) the performance of the Company's global internal audit function, (c) the compliance by the Company with legal and regulatory requirements, and (d) the qualifications, independence and performance of the Company's independent auditor employed by the Company for the purpose of preparing or issuing an audit report or related work (the "Outside Auditor"); and (2) be directly responsible for the appointment, compensation and oversight of the Outside Auditor.

Question

1. Is this statement of purpose required by the NYSE listing standards?

Committee Membership

The Audit Committee should consist of no fewer than three members, as determined annually by the Board on the recommendation of the Nominating and Governance Committee; provided, however, that the Audit Committee may operate with fewer than three members as long as such composition complies with applicable laws, rules, regulations, and securities exchange listing standards. The members of the Audit Committee shall meet the independence and expertise requirements of the New York Stock Exchange, any other exchange on which the Company's securities are traded, Section 10A(m)(3) of the

---

[27] Francie Ostrower & Marla J. Bobowick, Urban Institute, Nonprofit Governance and the Sarbanes-Oxley Act 2 (2006).

Securities Exchange Act of 1934, as amended (the "Exchange Act") and the rules and regulations of the Securities and Exchange Commission (the "Commission"). Audit Committee members shall not serve simultaneously on the audit committees of more than two other public companies without the approval of the full Board.

Questions

2.   Does the second sentence comply with the NYSE listing standard?

3.   In either case, should it be revised to be more specific about the questions of committee member independence and expertise? If so, how?

4.   Should a serial comma (a.k.a. an Oxford comma) have been used in the second sentence?

5.   The last sentence allows audit committee members to serve on a total of three audit committees (Walmart plus two others), in addition to serving on as many other boards of directors as the member wishes. Is that consistent with the NYSE listing standard?

6.   Given the demands on the time and effort of an audit committee member, should Walmart have imposed stricter limits on audit committee members?

The members of the Audit Committee shall be appointed annually by the Board on the recommendation of the Nominating and Governance Committee. Audit Committee members may be replaced by the Board at any time. The Board shall designate the Chairman or Chairwoman (the "Chairperson") of the Audit Committee. Committee members may resign by giving written notice to the Board. A Committee member may resign Committee membership without resigning from the Board, but a member shall cease automatically to be a member of the Committee upon either ceasing to be a member of the Board or ceasing to be "independent" as required above.

Questions

7.   Is the statement of how the committee members shall be appointed required by the NYSE listing standard?

8.   Does the charter requirement that the committee members be "appointed annually" present any potential difficulties? Is there a better alternative wording?

9.   Should the appointment power with respect to audit committee members and/or the committee chair be vested exclusively in the nominating committee?

Committee Authority and Responsibilities

The basic responsibility of the members of the Audit Committee is to exercise their business judgment to act in what they reasonably believe to be in the best interests of the Company and its shareholders. In discharging that obligation, members should be entitled to rely on the honesty and integrity of the Company's senior executives and its outside advisors and auditors, to the fullest extent permitted by law.

The Audit Committee shall prepare the report required by the rules of the Commission to be included in the Company's annual proxy statement.

The Audit Committee shall be responsible directly for the appointment (subject, if applicable, to shareholder ratification), retention, termination, compensation and terms of engagement, evaluation, and oversight of the work of the Outside Auditor (including resolution of disagreements between management and the Outside Auditor regarding financial reporting). The Outside Auditor shall report directly to the Audit Committee.

> **Question**
>
> 10. Should the word "solely" be inserted in the first sentence between the words "shall be" and "responsible"? If so, what other changes should be made to this provision?

The Audit Committee shall oversee the integrity of the audit process, financial reporting and internal accounting controls of the Company, oversee the work of the Company's management, global internal auditors (the "Internal Auditors") and the Outside Auditor in these areas, oversee management's development of, and adherence to, a sound system of internal accounting and financial controls, review whether the Internal Auditors and the Outside Auditor objectively assess the Company's financial reporting, accounting practices and internal controls, and provide an open avenue of communication among the Outside Auditor, the Internal Auditors and the Board. It is the responsibility of: (i) management of the Company and the Outside Auditor, under the oversight of the Audit Committee and the Board, to plan and conduct financial audits and to determine that the Company's financial statements and disclosures are complete and accurate in accordance with accounting principles generally accepted in the United States ("US GAAP") and applicable rules and regulations and fairly present, in all material respects, the financial condition of the Company; (ii) management of the Company, under the oversight of the Audit Committee and the Board, to assure compliance by the Company with applicable legal and regulatory requirements; and (iii) the Internal Auditors, under the oversight of the Audit Committee and the Board, to review the Company's internal transactions and accounting which do not require involvement in the detailed presentation of the Company's financial statements.

The Audit Committee shall pre-approve all audit services and non-audit services (including the fees and terms thereof) to be performed for the Company by the Outside Auditor to the extent required by and in a manner consistent with applicable law.

Question

11. If the company hires additional accounting firms to conduct non-audit services, such as tax preparation, should the audit committee be given responsibility for selecting, compensating, and terminating those accountants?

The Audit Committee shall meet as often as it determines necessary or appropriate, but not less frequently than quarterly. The Chairperson shall preside at each meeting and, in the absence of the Chairperson, one of the other members of the Audit Committee shall be designated as the acting chair of the meeting. The Chairperson (or acting chair) may direct appropriate members of management and staff to prepare draft agendas and related background information for each Audit Committee meeting. The draft agenda shall be reviewed and approved by the Audit Committee Chairperson (or acting chair) in advance of distribution to the other Audit Committee members. Any background materials, together with the agenda, should be distributed to the Audit Committee members in advance of the meeting. All meetings of the Audit Committee shall be held pursuant to the amended and restated bylaws of the Company with regard to notice and waiver thereof, and written minutes of each meeting, in the form approved by the Audit Committee, shall be duly filed in the Company records. Reports of meetings of the Audit Committee shall be made to the Board at its next regularly scheduled meeting following the Audit Committee meeting accompanied by any recommendations to the Board approved by the Audit Committee.

Question

12. Best practice recommendations typically advise that the audit committee should control the agenda for committee meetings, especially with respect to internal controls, the scope of the audit, and the competence, compensation, and independence of the auditors. Why? Is the Walmart audit charter's treatment of the agenda a reasonable alternative?

The Audit Committee may form and delegate authority to subcommittees consisting of one or more members when appropriate.

> **Question**
>
> 13. Does this provision authorize the committee to delegate to its chair such tasks as reviewing and discussing with management and the independent auditors such items as press releases relating to earnings or other accounting information, financial information and earnings guidance furnished to analysts and rating agencies, or Walmart's financial statements? If so, is that consistent with the NYSE listing standard?

The Audit Committee shall have the authority, to the extent it deems necessary or appropriate, to retain independent legal, accounting or other advisers. The Company shall provide for appropriate funding, as determined by the Audit Committee, for payment of compensation to the Outside Auditor for the purpose of rendering or issuing an audit report and to any advisers employed by the Audit Committee, subject only to any limitations imposed by applicable rules and regulations. The Audit Committee may request any officer or associate of the Company or the Company's outside counsel or Outside Auditor to attend a meeting of the Audit Committee or to meet with any members of, or consultants to, the Audit Committee. The Audit Committee shall meet with management, the Internal Auditors and the Outside Auditor in separate executive sessions at least quarterly to discuss matters for which the Audit Committee has responsibility.

The Audit Committee shall make regular reports to the Board. The Audit Committee and the Nominating and Governance Committee shall review and reassess the adequacy of this Charter annually and recommend any proposed changes to the Board for approval. The Audit Committee shall annually review its own performance.

In performing its functions, the Audit Committee shall undertake those tasks and responsibilities that, in its judgment, would contribute most effectively to and implement the purposes of the Audit Committee. In addition to the general tasks and responsibilities noted above, the following are the specific functions of the Audit Committee:

Financial Statement and Disclosure Matters

Review and discuss with management, and to the extent the Audit Committee deems necessary or appropriate, the Internal Auditors and the Outside Auditor, the Company's disclosure controls and procedures that are designed to ensure that the reports the Company files with the Commission comply with the Commission's rules and forms.

Review and discuss with management, the Internal Auditors and the Outside Auditor the annual audited financial statements, including disclosures made in management's discussion and analysis, and recommend to the Board whether the audited financial statements should be included in the Company's Form 10-K.

Review and discuss with management, the Internal Auditors and the Outside Auditor the Company's quarterly financial statements, including disclosures made in management's discussion and analysis, prior to the filing of its Form 10-Q, including the results of the Outside Auditor's reviews of the quarterly financial statements.

Review and discuss quarterly reports from the Outside Auditor on:

- All critical accounting policies and practices to be used;

- All alternative treatments within US GAAP for policies and practices related to material items that have been discussed with management, including ramifications of the use of such alternative disclosures and treatments, and the treatment preferred by the Outside Auditor;

- The internal controls adhered to by the Company, management, and the Company's financial, accounting and internal auditing personnel, and the impact of each on the quality and reliability of the Company's financial reporting; and

- Other material written communications between the Outside Auditor and management, such as any management letter or schedule of unadjusted differences.

Discuss in advance with management the Company's practice with respect to the types of information to be disclosed and the types of presentations to be made in earnings press releases, including the use, if any, of "pro forma" or "adjusted" non-US GAAP information, as well as financial information and earnings guidance provided to analysts and rating agencies.

Review and discuss with management, the Internal Auditors and the Outside Auditor:

- Significant financial reporting issues and judgments made in connection with the preparation of the Company's financial statements;

- The clarity of the financial disclosures made by the Company;

- The development, selection and disclosure of critical accounting estimates and the analyses of alternative assumptions or estimates, and the effect of such estimates on the Company's financial statements;

- Potential changes in US GAAP and the effect such changes would have on the Company's financial statements;

- Significant changes in accounting principles, financial reporting policies and internal controls implemented by the Company;

- Significant litigation, contingencies and claims against the Company and material accounting issues that require disclosure in the Company's financial statements;

- Information regarding any "second" opinions sought by management from an independent auditor with respect to the accounting treatment of a particular event or transaction;

- Management's compliance with the Company's processes, procedures and internal controls;

- The adequacy and effectiveness of the Company's internal accounting and financial controls and the recommendations of management, the Internal Auditors and the Outside Auditor for the improvement of accounting practices and internal controls; and

- Any difficulties encountered by the Outside Auditor or the Internal Auditors in the course of their audit work, including any restrictions on the scope of activities or access to requested information, and any significant disagreements with management.

Discuss with management and the Outside Auditor the effect of regulatory and accounting initiatives as well as off-balance sheet structures and aggregate contractual obligations on the Company's financial statements.

Review and discuss with management: (i) the Company's risk assessment and risk management process and policies; and (ii) the Company's major financial and other risk exposures and the steps management has taken to monitor and control such exposures.

Discuss with the Outside Auditor the matters required to be discussed by the Public Company Accounting Oversight Board's Auditing Standard No. 16 relating to the conduct of the audit. In particular, discuss:

- The adoption of, or changes to, the Company's significant internal auditing and accounting principles and practices as suggested by the Outside Auditor, Internal Auditors or management; and

- The management letter provided by the Outside Auditor and the Company's response to that letter.

Receive and review disclosures made to the Audit Committee by the Company's Chief Executive Officer and Chief Financial Officer during their certification process for the Company's Form 10-K and Form 10-Q about (a) any significant deficiencies in the design or operation of internal controls or material weakness therein, (b) any fraud involving management or other associates who have a significant role in the Company's internal controls, and (c) any significant changes in internal controls or in other factors that could significantly affect internal controls subsequent to the date of their evaluation.

Review and discuss with management (including the senior internal auditing executive) and the Outside Auditor the Company's internal controls report and the Outside Auditor's attestation of the report prior to the filing of the Company's Annual Report on Form 10-K.

Oversight of the Company's Relationship with the Outside Auditor

Review the experience and qualifications of the senior members of the Outside Auditor team.

Obtain and review a report from the Outside Auditor at least annually regarding (a) the Outside Auditor's internal quality-control procedures, (b) any material issues raised by the most recent internal quality-control review, or peer review, of the firm, or by any inquiry or investigation by governmental or professional authorities, within the preceding five years respecting one or more independent audits carried out by the firm, (c) any steps taken to deal with any such issues, and (d) all relationships between the Outside Auditor and the Company, including the written disclosures and the letter required by applicable independence standards, rules and regulations.

Evaluate the qualifications, performance and independence of the Outside Auditor, including considering whether the Outside Auditor's quality controls are adequate and the provision of non-audit services is compatible with maintaining the Outside Auditor's independence, and taking into account the opinions of management and the Internal Auditor. The Audit Committee shall present its conclusions to the Board.

Question

14. This provision does not explicitly require the audit committee to evaluate the performance of the lead audit partner. Is that consistent with the NYSE listed company manual?

Oversee the rotation of the lead (or coordinating) audit partner having primary responsibility for the audit and the audit partner responsible for reviewing the audit at least once every five years, and oversee the rotation of other audit partners, in accordance with the rules of the Commission.

Question

15. Should the words "and assure" be inserted after the word "oversee" in one or both places it appears in the foregoing provision?

Develop and periodically review policies for the Company's hiring of present and former employees of the Outside Auditor.

To the extent the Audit Committee deems necessary or appropriate, discuss with the national office of the Outside Auditor issues on which they were consulted by the Company's audit team and matters of audit quality and consistency.

Discuss with management, the Internal Auditors and the Outside Auditor any accounting adjustments that were noted or proposed by the Outside Auditor, but were not adopted or reflected.

Meet with management, the Internal Auditors and the Outside Auditor prior to the audit to discuss and review the scope, planning and staffing of the audit.

Obtain from the Outside Auditor the information required to be disclosed to the Company by generally accepted auditing standards in connection with the conduct of an audit, including topics covered by applicable Statements on Auditing Standards.

Require the Outside Auditor to review the financial information included in the Company's Form 10-Q in accordance with Rule 10–01(d) of Regulation S–X of the Commission prior to the Company filing such reports with the Commission and to provide to the Company for inclusion in the Company's Form 10-Q any reports of the Outside Auditor required by Rule 10–01(d).

Oversight of the Company's Internal Audit Function

Ensure that the Company has an internal audit function.

Review and concur in the appointment, replacement, reassignment or dismissal of the senior internal auditing executive, and the compensation package for such person.

Review the significant reports to management prepared by the internal auditing department and management's responses.

Communicate with management and the Internal Auditors to obtain information concerning internal audits, accounting principles adopted by the Company, internal controls of the Company, management, and the Company's financial and accounting personnel, and review the impact of each on the quality and reliability of the Company's financial statements.

Evaluate the internal auditing department and its impact on the accounting practices, internal controls and financial reporting of the Company.

Discuss with the Outside Auditor and the senior internal auditing executive the internal audit department's responsibilities, budget and staffing and any recommended changes in the planned scope of the internal audit.

Ethics and Compliance Oversight Responsibilities

Obtain from the Outside Auditor the reports required to be furnished to the Audit Committee under Section 10A of the Exchange Act and obtain from the Outside Auditor any information with respect to illegal acts in accordance with Section 10A.

Discuss with management and the Outside Auditor, and advise the Board with respect to, the Company's policies, processes and procedures regarding compliance with applicable laws and regulations and the Statement of Ethics, and instances of non-compliance therewith. Obtain and review reports and disclosures of insider and affiliated party transactions.

Question

16. Is it appropriate under state law for the board to effectively delegate its *Caremark*-based oversight duties to the audit committee?

Review and approve any requested waivers by executive officers and directors of the Company's Statement of Ethics and recommend to the Board, when appropriate, whether a particular waiver should be granted.

Question

17. Could these ethical responsibilities be assigned to the nominating committee? If so, should they?

Establish procedures for (a) the receipt, retention and treatment of complaints received by the Company regarding accounting, internal accounting controls or auditing matters, and (b) the confidential, anonymous submission by associates of the Company of concerns regarding questionable accounting, internal accounting controls or auditing matters.

Discuss with management and the Outside Auditor any correspondence between the Company and regulators or governmental agencies and any associate complaints or published reports that raise material issues regarding the Company's financial statements or accounting policies.

Discuss with the Company's Chief Legal Officer legal matters that may have a material impact on the financial statements or the Company's ethics and compliance policies.

Meet no less than annually with the senior executive(s) of the Company with primary responsibility for ethics and compliance regarding the implementation and effectiveness of the Company's ethics and compliance programs and at such other times as such officer(s) may request.

Review and concur in the appointment, replacement, reassignment or dismissal of the senior executive(s) of the Company with primary responsibility for the Company's ethics and compliance function, and the compensation package for such executive(s).

Additional Responsibilities

Prepare annually a report for inclusion in the Company's proxy statement relating to its annual shareholders' meeting, in accordance with applicable Commission rules and regulations.

Conduct or authorize investigations into any matters within the Audit Committee's scope of responsibilities.

Review the Company's Transaction Review Policy and recommend any changes to the Nominating and Governance Committee and then to the Board for approval. Review and determine whether to approve or ratify transactions covered by such policy, as appropriate.

A Digression on the Internal Audit Function

The Institute of Internal Auditors, a trade association, explains that: "Although they are independent of the activities they audit, internal auditors are integral to the organization and provide ongoing monitoring and assessment of all activities. On the contrary, external auditors are independent of the organization, and provide an annual opinion on the financial statements." In other words, unlike the company's independent auditor, the internal audit function typically is part of the company and staffed corporate employees rather than outside consultants. Having said that, however, it is permissible for companies to outsource their internal audit function to an outside firm, typically a certified public accounting firm.

NYSE Listing Standard § 303A.07(c) provides that:

> Each listed company must have an internal audit function.
>
> *Commentary*: Listed companies must maintain an internal audit function to provide management and the audit committee with ongoing assessments of the listed company's risk management processes and system of internal control. A listed company may choose to outsource this function to a third party service provider other than its independent auditor. . . .[28]

Listing Standard § 303A.07(b)(1)(A) further provides that the audit committee's duties include assisting with "board oversight of . . . the performance of the listed company's internal audit function."

> The internal audit function within an organization is a department that tests the effectiveness of internal control over financial reporting. Internal audit is one of the monitoring

---

[28] Recall that the SEC's rules on the independence of outside auditors forbid outsourcing the internal audit function to the company's independent auditor and prohibit the outside auditor from designing or testing a company's internal controls.

functions within the five components of internal control. Internal audit may or may not get involved in designing controls. Ideally, the internal audit function should report directly to the audit committee or jointly to the management and the audit committee.

The overall objective of the internal audit function is to provide assurance, usually to management and the audit committee, that the organization's principal interests are being met. According to the Institute of Internal Auditors:

Internal auditing is an independent, objective assurance and consulting activity designed to add value and improve an organization's operations. It helps an organization accomplish its objectives by bringing a systematic and disciplined approach to evaluate and improve the effectiveness of risk management, control, and governance processes.

Internal audit is responsible for analysis and testing of internal controls, to provide assurance that:

- Financial reporting and other information systems are free of error, and provide timely information;

- Company resources are used efficiently, and assets are safeguarded; and

- That the company's goals for ethical business practice are being met.[29]

The audit committee should meet with the director of internal auditor on a regular basis to assess the effectiveness of the internal audit department's oversight of the company's financial controls. At least a portion of these meetings should be conducted outside the presence of other management officials.

Careful thought should be given to the placement of the audit function in the institution's management structure. The internal audit function should be positioned so that the board has confidence that the internal audit function will perform its duties with impartiality and not be unduly influenced by managers of day-to-day operations. The audit committee, using objective criteria it has established, should oversee the internal audit function and evaluate its performance. The audit committee should assign responsibility for the internal audit function to a member of management (hereafter referred to as the manager of internal audit or internal audit manager) who understands the function and has no responsibility for operating the system of internal control. The ideal organizational arrangement is for this manager to report directly and solely to

---

[29]   Practical Guide to Corporate Governance and Accounting: Implementing the Requirements of the Sarbanes-Oxley Act, ¶ 1609 Internal Audit Function, 2005 WL 487838.

the audit committee regarding both audit issues and administrative matters, e.g., resources, budget, appraisals, and compensation.[30]

A Digression on Whistle Blowers

Part of the Enron mythology is that former Enron VP Sherron Watkins blew the whistle on Ken Lay, Jeff Skilling, and their fellow miscreants. In fact, however, Watkins was not a whistle blower. She wrote a "cover your ass" letter to Enron CEO Ken Lay, mainly to warn him of potential whistle blowers among the company's increasingly disgruntled employees.

Nevertheless, by the time Congress started work on SOX, this myth of the brave employee bringing down an evil corporate empire had taken root. To protect those who blew the whistle on firms like Enron and WorldCom, as well as to encourage future whistle blowers, Congress included two sets of protections for whistle blowers in SOX: (1) Criminal penalties for those who retaliate against whistle blowers and (2) civil remedies for whistle blowers who are fired or otherwise suffer some form of retaliation by their employer.

SOX § 1107 creates a criminal penalty of up to ten years imprisonment and/or a fine of up to $250,000 on anyone who intentionally retaliates against a whistle blower by taking "any action harmful to any person, including interference with the lawful employment or livelihood of any person." This is one of the few SOX provisions directly applicable to nonprofit organizations and closely held corporations.

SOX § 806 authorizes whistle blowers who suffer retaliation to seek back pay, reinstatement, and compensatory damages from the company. Unlike the criminal sanctions, the civil remedies under § 806 are limited mainly to employees of reporting companies. In addition, however, privately held companies providing services to a reporting company as a contractor, subcontractor, or agent are subject to § 806.

Lawyers typically do not use the term whistle blowing. Instead, they talk about "protected activity." In other words, what actions by an employee may an employer not properly punish?

SOX § 806 identifies a number of actions that employers may not retaliate against or otherwise punish an employee for taking, including:

- Providing information to, or otherwise assisting, an investigation of wire, mail, or bank fraud, or any other federal law on fraud against shareholders, or other securities law violations. Investigations by the SEC, other federal regulatory or law enforcement agencies, and

Congress are covered by this provision. It also applies, however, to internal investigations by the employee's supervisors or any company employee having responsibility for investigating misconduct. In particular, the provision thus covers the company's internal audit personnel and members of the audit committee of the board of directors. Note that there need not be a preexisting investigation for the employee to be engaged in protected activity. An employee who makes an internal or external complaint about alleged fraud violations is protected.

- Filing, testifying, participating in, or otherwise assisting in any legal proceeding involving fraud or other securities violations by the company.

An employee who reports conduct he or she reasonably believes is a violation of one of the covered federal fraud or securities laws is engaged in protected activity even if subsequent investigation proves the employee was wrong. This makes sense, of course. Would employees come forward with charges of serious misconduct if they know they can be fired if they turn out to have made a mistake?

The employee need not specify which laws he or she thinks are being broken. Instead, it is enough that the employee generically allege fraud or other securities misconduct. On the other hand, as one court explained, there must be "allegations of conduct that would alert" the employer that the employee "believed the company was violating any federal rule or law related to fraud on shareholders."[31] Note that the employee's belief that laws are being violated has both an objective and a subjective component. In other words, the employee must actually believe one or more of the requisite laws is being violated and that belief must be reasonable.

Lawyers also don't talk about retaliation or punishment. Instead, they talk about adverse employment action (or adverse action, for short). This is so because the range of prohibited employer conduct taken against those who engage in protected activity is so broad. Adverse actions clearly include threats, reprimands, job transfers, pay cuts, or other actions having a negative effect on employment conditions. When an employee claims that she suffered retaliation for whistleblowing, the employee must show by clear and convincing evidence that he had engaged in protected activity, that the employer knew or suspected that the employee had engaged in protected activity, there had been an unfavorable personnel action directed at the employee, and the circumstances were sufficient to raise inference that protected activity was a contributing factor.

---

[31]   Fraser v. Fiduciary Trust Co. Int'l, 417 F. Supp. 2d 310, 322 (S.D.N.Y. 2006).

C. INTERNAL CONTROLS

1) WHAT ARE "INTERNAL CONTROLS"?

A 1949 American Institute of Certified Public Accountants (AICPA) committee report defined internal control as "the plan of organization and all of the coordinate methods and measures adopted within a business to safeguard its assets, check the accuracy and reliability of its accounting data, promote operational efficiency, and encourage adherence to prescribed managerial policies."[32] Although internal control thus originated as an accounting concept, it evolved to take on a broader meaning. As a result, by 1992, the Committee of Sponsoring Organizations of the Treadway Commission (COSO), a group comprised from five major accounting professional associations, issued a definition of internal control as "a process, effected by an entity's board of directors, management and other personnel, designed to provide reasonable assurance regarding the achievement of objectives" in the areas of "effectiveness and efficiency of operations, reliability of financial reporting, and compliance with applicable laws and regulations."[33] COSO further opined that internal control consists of five interrelated components: the control environment, risk assessment, control activities, information and communication, and monitoring. All five components must be functioning properly for the internal control to be deemed satisfactory. In turn, those components are further broken down into twenty even more jargon-heavy principles, which we shall pass over.

In simpler terms, as explained in Table 2 below, we can identify five general areas into which internal controls fall.

In even simpler terms, we can loosely divide internal controls into two main categories. First, preventative controls seek to deter misconduct and prevent errors or irregularities that could cause the organization to break the law, issue inaccurate or fraudulent disclosures, or otherwise fail to operate at maximum efficiency. Requiring two signatures for checks over a certain amount is a simple example of such a control. Second, curative controls seek to identify and remediate misconduct and errors that do occur. Auditing expense accounts to identify personal expenditures is a simple example of a control in this category.

---

[32] American Institute of Certified Public Accountants Committee on Auditing Procedure, Internal Control—Elements of a Coordinated System and Its Importance to Management and the Independent Public Accountant 5, 6 (1949).

[33] Committee of Sponsoring Organizations of the Treadway Commission, Internal Control—Integrated Framework 9 (1992).

Table 2. **Internal Controls**

Control Activities	Policies	Implementation
Authorization	Identify which corporate actors are authorized to approve, conduct, and review an action. Establish policies for documenting who carried out each task.	Timely review documentation to ensure properly authorized persons conducted each phase of the process.
Documentation	Develop policies on how documentation is submitted, reviewed and verified, and stored.	Ensure that documentation of corporate actions is completed on a timely and accurate basis.
Reconciliation	Establish procedures for comparing activities and transactions to the supporting documentations and for reconciling any discrepancies.	The oversight of any transaction is strengthened by the process of matching source documentation of the transaction to the appropriate reporting documentation or reporting tool.
Security	Establish policies for protection of records.	Limit access to records to authorized personnel. Redundant copies of records should be maintained.
Separation of Duties	Policy should state that no single person can effect a material transaction. Ideally, the tasks of initiating, recording, authorizing, and reconciling a transaction should be assigned to at least two and preferably 4 distinct persons none of whom are subordinate to the others.	Separation of duties should be clearly defined, assigned and documented.

The internal control concept began working its way into corporate law through the efforts of Melvin Eisenberg, who saw assigning responsibility for internal controls to the board of directors as a key component in institutionalizing his monitoring model.[34] Eisenberg recognized that the information asymmetry between the board and management impeded the board's ability to effectively monitor the top management team. A properly functioning system of internal controls with the board would help redress that imbalance in two ways. First, it catches and corrects distortions in the information flowing to the board. Second, the corporate personnel charged with effecting internal control become an alternative source of information for the board, which no longer is reliant solely on top management.

> ### CASE IN POINT
>
> "A contributing factor that allowed the books to be deliberately falsified without attracting much notice was that the Company's internal controls over the preparation and publication of its financial results were dysfunctional at best, and in some areas controls were missing entirely. WorldCom's accounting systems had not kept pace with the growth in the Company due to its feverish pace of acquisitions and management neglect. Numerous legacy financial systems were being operated by different WorldCom units, and producing consolidated financial statements required patchwork software and significant manual processing." *SEC v. Worldcom, Inc.*, 2003 WL 22004827 (S.D.N.Y., Aug 26, 2003).

2) SOX SECTION 404

During the Congressional hearings that led up to Sarbanes-Oxley, much attention was devoted to the internal control failures at Enron, WorldCom, and the like. Congress determined that the state law regime failed adequately to channel board attention to the problem. Accordingly, some of the Sarbanes-Oxley Act's critical provisions were intended to federalize internal control regulation, the most critical of which is SOX § 404.

SOX § 404

(a) RULES REQUIRED.—The Commission shall prescribe rules requiring each annual report required by section 13(a) or 15(d) of the Securities Exchange Act of 1934 (15 U.S.C. 78m or 78o(d)) to contain an internal control report, which shall—

(1) state the responsibility of management for establishing and maintaining an adequate internal control structure and procedures for financial reporting; and

(2) contain an assessment, as of the end of the most recent fiscal year of the issuer, of the effectiveness of the

---

[34]   Melvin A. Eisenberg, The Board of Directors and Internal Control, 19 Cardozo L. Rev. 237 (1997).

internal control structure and procedures of the issuer for financial reporting.

(b) INTERNAL CONTROL EVALUATION AND REPORTING.—With respect to the internal control assessment required by subsection (a), each registered public accounting firm that prepares or issues the audit report for the issuer shall attest to, and report on, the assessment made by the management of the issuer. An attestation made under this subsection shall be made in accordance with standards for attestation engagements issued or adopted by the Board. Any such attestation shall not be the subject of a separate engagement.

Note that § 404 does not encompass the full scope of internal controls, as that term was defined by COSO. Instead, the SEC defines "internal control" for purposes of § 404 as:

A process designed by, or under the supervision of, the registrant's principal executive and principal financial officers, or persons performing similar functions, and effected by the registrant's board of directors, management and other personnel, to provide reasonable assurance regarding the reliability of financial reporting and the preparation of financial statements for external purposes in accordance with generally accepted accounting principles and includes those policies and procedures that

- pertain to the maintenance of records that in reasonable detail accurately and fairly reflect the transactions and dispositions of the assets of the registrant;

- provide reasonable assurance that transactions are recorded as necessary to permit preparation of financial statements in accordance with generally accepted accounting principles, and receipts and expenditures of the registrant are being made only in accordance with authorizations of management and directors of the registrant; and

- provide reasonable assurance regarding prevention or timely detection of unauthorized acquisition, use or disposition of the registrant's assets that could have a material effect on the financial statements.

In other words, the term *internal controls* as used in § 404 refers to the processes the company uses to ensure that its financial statements comply with GAAP and are free from material misrepresentations and omissions.

At first glance, § 404 looks like a mere disclosure requirement. It requires inclusion of internal control disclosures in each public corporation's annual report. This disclosure statement must include: (1)

a written confirmation by which firm management acknowledges its responsibility for establishing and maintaining a system of internal controls and procedures for financial reporting; (2) an assessment by management, as of the end of the most recent fiscal year, of the effectiveness of the firm's internal controls; and (3) a written attestation by the firm's outside auditor confirming the adequacy and accuracy of those controls and procedures.

It is not the disclosure itself that makes § 404 significant, of course; instead, it is the high costs imposed by the need to assess and test the company's internal controls in order to be able to make the required disclosures. These costs have two major components. First, there are the internal costs incurred by the corporation in conducting the requisite management assessment. Second, there are the fees the corporation must pay the auditor for carrying out its assessment.

In the years immediately after SOX became law, these costs include average expenditures of 35,000 staff hours on § 404 compliance alone, which proved to be almost 100 times the SEC's estimate. In addition, firms spent an average of $1.3 million on external consultants and software. Finally, on average, they incurred an extra $1.5 million (a jump of 35%) in audit fees.[35]

To be sure, some of these costs were one-time expenses incurred to bring firms' internal controls up to snuff. Yet, many other Sarbanes-Oxley compliance costs recur year after year. For example, the internal control process required by § 404 relies heavily on on-going documentation. As a result, firms must constantly ensure that they are creating the requisite paper trail. Accordingly, while second year compliance costs dropped, those costs remained many times greater than the SEC's estimate of first year costs.

Recognizing the considerably greater burden § 404 imposed on companies than had been expected, both Congress and the SEC over time have made various tweaks designed to reduce that burden. The most important effort to provide § 404 relief came in the 2010 Dodd-Frank Act. Non-accelerated filers had been required to comply with the management assessment provision of § 404(a) for several years, but the SEC had repeatedly delayed implementation with respect to such corporations of the auditor assessment required by § 404(b). Dodd-Frank permanently exempted non-accelerated filers from compliance with § 404(b).

In 2020, the SEC adopted amendments to the definitions of an accelerated filer and large accelerated filer to exempt from them any issuer that is eligible to be a smaller reporting company[36] and that had

---

[35] Stephen M. Bainbridge, The Complete Guide to Sarbanes-Oxley 4 (2007).

[36] SEC Rule 405 defines "smaller reporting company" as one that, subject to various qualifications and exclusions, "(1) Had a public float of less than $250 million; or (2) Had annual revenues of less than $100 million and either: (i) No public float; or (ii) A public float of less than $700 million," "as of the last business day of the issuer's most recently completed second fiscal quarter."

annual revenues of less than $100 million in the most recent fiscal year for which audited financial statements are available. The SEC estimated that the additional firms thereby exempted from § 404(b)'s auditor assessment requirement "would save approximately $210,000 per year comprised of approximately $110,000 per year reduction in audit fees and an additional reduction in non-audit costs of approximately $100,000. . . . Although the average annual cost savings may represent a small percentage of the average affected issuer's revenues and market capitalization, we believe those savings may be meaningful given that affected issuers have, on average, negative net income and negative net cash flows from operations.[37]

Despite the best of intentions and these efforts at remediation, however, there is no doubt that § 404—along with the rest of the Sarbanes-Oxley Act and the broader U.S. regulatory regime— has had and continues to have a deleterious effect on the U.S. capital markets. As The Financial Economists Roundtable observed, there is "little reason to believe that . . . the benefits of § 404 will exceed the costs."[38] Even former Congressman Michael Oxley, for whom the Sarbanes-Oxley Act is named in part, has admitted that both he and Senator Sarbanes "would have written it differently" if they had known at the time that the Sarbanes-Oxley Act would prove so costly.[39]

WHAT'S THAT?

The SEC divides the universe of public corporations that must file periodic disclosure reports, such as annual and quarterly reports, into three categories:

1.   "Large accelerated filers" are companies with a public float of $700 million or more (i.e., the total market value of their outstanding publicly traded shares). They must file their 10-Q quarterly reports within 40 days after the end of the quarter and their annual report on Form 10-K within 60 days after the end of the year.

2.   "Accelerated filers" are companies with a public float of at least $75 million, but less than $700 million. They must file their 10-Q within 40 days and the 10-K within 75 days after the ends of the quarters and year respectively.

3.   "Non-accelerated filers" are companies with a public float of less than $75 million. They have 45 days and 90 days to file their 10-Q and 10-K, respectively.

3)   PREPARING A § 404(a) MANAGEMENT REPORT

Although some lawyers work for accounting firms and assist with auditors' § 404(b) compliance processes, the vast majority of corporate lawyers who work on § 4040 compliance work for corporations and the

---

[37]   Accelerated Filer and Large Accelerated Filer Definitions, Exchange Act Rel. No. 88,365 (Mar. 12, 2020).

[38]   Statement of the Financial Economists Roundtable on the International Competitiveness of U.S. Capital Markets, 19 J. Applied Corp. Fin. 54, 57 (2007).

[39]   Liz Alderman, Spotlight: Michael Oxley, N.Y. Times, Mar. 2, 2007, http://www.nytimes.com/2007/03/02/business/worldbusiness/02iht-wbspot03.4773621.html.

vast majority of legal work is generated by preparing § 404(a) reports. Accordingly, it is on the latter process that we will focus.

Both the SEC and the PCAOB emphasize that § 404(a) requires a top down approach. The § 404 compliance process therefore usually starts with formation of a cross-function, multi-disciplinary compliance team consisting of senior professionals. Such a team will typically include representatives from the corporation's internal audit department, the controller's office, information technology, human resources, and key business segments. The team commonly begins with review of those controls that apply company wide. The compliance team will then evaluate controls that apply to particular business units or functions. Next, the team looks at how particular business units handle significant accounts. Finally, the team evaluates how transactions in those accounts are processed.

Both the SEC and PCAOB insist that companies should devote most attention to those high-risk areas most likely to result in financial reporting problems. Because over 50% of financial fraud in the pre-SOX period involved overstating revenues either by prematurely recognizing revenue or by booking fictitious revenue, companies must devote considerable attention to the internal controls they use to monitor revenue recognition. In addition, four other areas have proven especially common sources of financial fraud: (1) stock options and other issuance of equity securities, (2) accounting for reserves, accruals, and contingencies, (3) capitalization of expenses, and (4) inventory levels. All of these are areas where emergent best practice dictates that considerable attention should be devoted during the § 404 assessment process.

In light of the narrow definition given internal controls for purposes of § 404, the SEC has also indicated that management should evaluate the company's existing internal controls over financial reporting to determine whether there is a reasonable possibility that those controls would not prevent or detect a material misstatement in the financial statements. Management need not assess all of the various internal controls or other law compliance programs the company may have implemented, but rather should focus on those controls intended or necessary to prevent or detect such a material misstatement.

The SEC has periodically issued guidance to assist companies in complying with these requirements. Nevertheless, the SEC continues to insist that "it is impractical to prescribe a single methodology that meets the needs of every company." As a result, the SEC declines to create safe harbors by which compliant firms are insulated from liability. Indeed, the SEC refuses even to "provide a checklist of steps management should perform in completing its evaluation" of the company's internal controls. Instead, the SEC advises that:

> Management should implement and conduct an evaluation that is sufficient to provide it with a reasonable basis for its

annual assessment. Management should use its own experience and informed judgment in designing an evaluation process that aligns with the operations, financial reporting risks and processes of the company. If the evaluation process identifies material weaknesses that exist as of the end of the fiscal year, such weaknesses must be disclosed in management's annual report with a statement that ICFR [i.e., internal controls over financial reporting] is ineffective. If the evaluation identifies no internal control deficiencies that constitute a material weakness, management assesses ICFR as effective.[40]

The SEC's guidance is inherently vague and ambiguous, leaving plenty of room for interpretation and disagreement. Terms like "reasonable" and "material" are standards, which by their very nature fail to offer bright lines between lawful and unlawful conduct. Indeed, the SEC admitted that "there is a range of judgments that an issuer might make as to what is 'reasonable' in implementing Section 404 and the Commission's rules." As a result, determination of whether a firm has complied with its Sarbanes-Oxley obligations is highly fact-specific and contextual. Accordingly, the company and its management cannot be certain that they've fully complied with Section 404 until the SEC or a court, with the benefit and bias of hindsight, decides that they've done so.

Mere guidance, moreover, does not change the incentives of corporate officers and directors. The best way for directors and officers to avoid the new liability risks created by Sarbanes-Oxley is to pump a lot of corporate resources into ensuring compliance with § 404 and the rest of SOX. Because it is a corporation's directors and officers who control the purse strings, they get to decide how much money and time the corporation spends on Sarbanes-Oxley compliance. Because the money spent on compliance programs comes out of the corporation's bottom-line, however, that money comes out of the stockholders' pockets not those of management. As a result, it remains certain that corporations will over invest in Sarbanes-Oxley compliance efforts.

While it is thus impossible to specify a single compliance process applicable to all companies, SEC guidance and accumulated best practices provide a general framework within which companies may develop their own idiosyncratic processes. There are four basic components of the § 404(a) compliance process. In the first phase, as noted above, management should identify the principal risks to accurate financial disclosures posed by its business and the existing controls, if any, designed to address those risks. Implementing that principle requires management to exercise judgment in separating those areas of its accounting and financial reporting operations that are both material and by their nature present a risk of intentional or negligent errors in

---

[40]   Management's Report on Internal Control Over Financial Reporting, available at www. sec.gov/rules/proposed/2006/33-8762.pdf.

financial reporting. The SEC explains that "financial reporting elements would generally have higher risk when they include transactions, account balances or other supporting information that is prone to misstatement. For example, elements which: (1) involve judgment in determining the recorded amounts; (2) are susceptible to fraud; (3) have complexity in the underlying accounting requirements; or (4) are subject to environmental factors, such as technological and/or economic developments, would generally be assessed as higher risk." The SEC calls attention to those areas "involving significant accounting estimates, related party transactions, or critical accounting policies," which generally should be assessed as having "higher risk for both the risk of material misstatement to the financial reporting element and the risk of control failure." Having identified the areas of high risk, management then must identify the existing controls designed to reduce the risk of a material misstatement these areas. Only those controls must be included in management's § 404(a) assessment report.

In the second phase, once management has identified the controls that must be assessed, management then gathers and analyzes evidence as to whether those controls are effective in preventing or timely detecting financial reporting fraud or errors. Although management's § 404(a) assessment report is based on whether any material weaknesses exist as of the end of the fiscal year, the SEC's guidance encourages management to exercise informed judgment in adapting its existing daily business, self-assessment, and other monitoring activities to provide the basis for its § 404(a) assessment report. According to the SEC, tying the § 404(a) assessment to existing compliance activities will reduce costs by obviating the need for an annual internal § 404(a) audit.

Revenue recognition offers a good example of how management assesses internal controls. At the company-wide control level, controls for revenue recognition would start with distribution of written policy manuals setting out the rules by which the company recognizes revenue and the procedures for doing so. In addition, the company should mandate regular training of both sales and accounting personnel.

Documentation is an essential part of the internal control assessment. Accordingly, not only copies of the policy manual, but also records of attendance at training sessions should be maintained. There's a growing array of software packages available designed to assist with § 404 compliance, most of which include some sort of database system for maintaining electronic copies of the requisite documentation.

Moving down the ladder from the company-wide to the business-unit level, one next would look at large, one-time, or otherwise unique contracts that account for a material share of the company's revenues. An adequate system of internal control requires that the company's internal auditors review the terms of the contract to determine when and how revenues from it should be recognized. In addition, internal audit should double-check the work of the business unit, by confirming the details of the contract with the other party.

The next step down will involve looking at how the company handles routine transactions. Suppose you are on the § 404 compliance team at Acme, a manufacturing company. Like most companies, Acme provides quarterly revenue forecasts for stock market analysts. Acme's top management puts a lot of pressure on employees to "make the number." Suppose Acme is basically healthy, but internal projections suggest that it may not meet its earnings forecasts for the first quarter of the year. Quarterly revenue numbers could be tweaked to help the company meet its earnings forecast in a variety of ways. Acme could backdate shipping records, for example, so that revenue for products actually shipped in the second quarter is recognized in the first quarter. Alternatively, products returned in the first quarter might not be booked until the second quarter, so as to delay the resulting hit to earnings. In the worst case, Acme management might actually report fictitious revenue by claiming to have shipped products that never existed.

An effective system of internal controls will include procedures for ensuring that the responsible personnel treat these sort of routine transactions properly from an accounting perspective. One important control is a walkthrough, by which the internal auditors (or their equivalent) observe how a sample transaction is processed. In a manufacturing company, there should be mechanisms in place for internal audit to meet with the personnel in charge of shipping and receiving to check on shipments and returns, dating of shipping and return documents, and the like. Similarly, internal audit should check inventory levels.

In the third phase, based on the evidence it gathers in the second phase, management must determine whether there are any deficiencies in its internal controls. If so, management must decide whether the identified deficiencies are material weaknesses or significant deficiencies. Those terms are defined by the PCAOB's Auditing Standard No. 5:

> A3. A **deficiency** in internal control over financial reporting exists when the design or operation of a control does not allow management or employees, in the normal course of performing their assigned functions, to prevent or detect misstatements on a timely basis.
>
> - A deficiency in design exists when (a) a control necessary to meet the control objective is missing or (b) an existing control is not properly designed so that, even if the control operates as designed, the control objective would not be met.
> - A deficiency in operation exists when a properly designed control does not operate as designed, or when

the person performing the control does not possess the necessary authority or competence to perform the control effectively.

. . .

A5. **Internal control over financial reporting** is a process designed by, or under the supervision of, the company's principal executive and principal financial officers, or persons performing similar functions, and effected by the company's board of directors, management, and other personnel, to provide reasonable assurance regarding the reliability of financial reporting and the preparation of financial statements for external purposes in accordance with GAAP and includes those policies and procedures that—

1) Pertain to the maintenance of records that, in reasonable detail, accurately and fairly reflect the transactions and dispositions of the assets of the company;

2) Provide reasonable assurance that transactions are recorded as necessary to permit preparation of financial statements in accordance with generally accepted accounting principles, and that receipts and expenditures of the company are being made only in accordance with authorizations of management and directors of the company; and

3) Provide reasonable assurance regarding prevention or timely detection of unauthorized acquisition, use, or disposition of the company's assets that could have a material effect on the financial statements.

Note: The auditor's procedures as part of either the audit of internal control over financial reporting or the audit of the financial statements are not part of a company's internal control over financial reporting.

Note: Internal control over financial reporting has inherent limitations. Internal control over financial reporting is a process that involves human diligence and compliance and is subject to lapses in judgment and breakdowns resulting from human failures. Internal control over financial reporting also can be circumvented by collusion or improper management override. Because of such limitations, there is a risk that material misstatements will not be prevented or detected on a timely basis by internal control over financial reporting. However, these inherent limitations are known features of the financial reporting process. Therefore, it is possible to design into the process safeguards to reduce, though not eliminate, this risk.

. . .

A7. A **material weakness** is a deficiency, or a combination of deficiencies, in internal control over financial reporting, such that there is a **reasonable possibility** that a material misstatement of the company's annual or interim financial statements will not be prevented or detected on a timely basis.

Note: There is a **reasonable possibility** of an event, as used in this standard, when the likelihood of the event is either "reasonably possible" or "probable" . . . .

A11. A **significant deficiency** is a deficiency, or a combination of deficiencies, in internal control over financial reporting that is less severe than a material weakness, yet important enough to merit attention by those responsible for oversight of the company's financial reporting.

As suggested by the Auditing Standard, if a deficiency merely rises to the level of a significant deficiency, it need not be disclosed in management's § 404(a) report. Only a deficiency rising to the level of a material weakness must be included in management's assessment report, which must state that the company's internal control over financial reporting are not effective. But while a significant deficiency need not be disclosed, it is expected that it will be remediated forthwith.

In order not to be deemed deficient, internal controls must be effective as to both their design and operation. Accountant Jack Paul explains the difference between the two as follows:

> Whereas design effectiveness pertains to whether a control is properly crafted, operating effectiveness deals with use of a properly designed control to prevent, detect, or correct misstatements or irregularities on a timely basis. For example, a daily reconciliation of cash receipts is not effectively designed when the cashier performs the reconciliation. But if an independent person is designated to perform the reconciliation and the other procedures are properly documented, the control is effectively designed. The control is not operating effectively when the independent reconciler either fails to perform the reconciliation daily or does so in a perfunctory manner. Design effectiveness of this control could be tested by reviewing documentation to ensure that the procedures are satisfactory. Operating effectiveness could be tested by examining the reconciler's initials on the daily reconciliation sheet.[41]

Internal controls can also be divided between those relating to how transactions flow within a company and those that deal with static data, such as account balances. Again, Jack Paul explains:

---

[41] Jack W. Paul, Exploring PCAOB Auditing Standard 2: Audits of Internal Control, CPA J., May 2005.

Examples of controls relating to transaction flows include approving cash disbursements; prelisting cash receipts; approving credit sales; and matching purchase orders, vendor invoices, and receiving reports when booking accounts payable. Controls over balances (stocks) include periodic reconciliation of bank accounts; reconciliation of subsidiary ledgers with control accounts; procedures for physical inventory counts; and controls governing the periodic preparation of financial statements. Overarching controls include the factors comprising the control environment. Overarching controls and those pertaining to flows operate continuously throughout the fiscal period; controls relating to balances typically operate less frequently. Thus bank accounts are reconciled monthly, whereas controls over cash flows are continuous.[42]

In the final phase, management must document the processes by which its assessment report was prepared and the evidence it gathered and evaluated in the course of its assessment. The SEC encourages management to exercise informed judgment in deciding the form the documentation will take. In practice, most companies rely on the emerging suites of § 404 compliance software tools to provide the requisite documentation.

Although § 404 refers to management's responsibility, the audit committee should be an active player in § 404 compliance. KPMG partner Kenneth Daly recommends that:

> [T]he audit committee must understand where the company is in the process, as well as the critical elements of the plan that will move the company's compliance program forward. The audit committee should monitor management's progress and ask key questions to help evaluate the state of the section 404 compliance process. It is important to ensure that the right questions are directed to the appropriate management personnel. For example, if the audit committee wants to know whether internal audit's resources are adequate, it should ask the director of internal audit, as well as the CFO. Posing the same question to different levels of management and to different managers also may reveal areas of the compliance process that require attention. Questions that audit committees might ask should revolve around process optimization, technology, organization and people, and risk and control.[43]

---

[42] Id.

[43] Kenneth Daly, Audit Committees Drive Section 404: Sustainable Compliance Oversight, 53 Risk Mgmt. 2 (2006).

NOTE AND QUESTION ON THE RULE OF THUMB

A critical part of the § 404 compliance process is selecting those processes that are at high risk of failure and, if they fail, would result in large losses. For instance, more attention should be given to ensuring an account with $100,000 value is accurate rather ensuring petty cash with $250 is accounted for properly.

The Big 4 auditing firms start by identifying material processes. As a rule of thumb, they generally use 5% of the issuer's pre-tax earnings as the materiality threshold. If the client does not have pre-tax income, they may use (+/−) 5% of another metric such as fixed assets, accounts payable, or revenue.

Let's assume the issuer's pre-tax earnings for the most recent fiscal year were $20,000,000. Five percent thereof is $1,000,000. If the process in question has an identified deficiency that results in a loss of 80% of more of the materiality threshold, the deficiency will be characterized as a material weakness. If the process in question has an identified deficiency that results in a loss of more than 30% but less than 80% of the materiality threshold, the deficiency will be characterized as a significant deficiency. If the deficiency falls below 30%, it is a mere deficiency.

Suppose, for example, that the issue has identified an internal control that failed to prevent an overpayment to a vendor in the amount of $475,000. Is that a mere deficiency, a significant deficiency, or a material weakness?

Note that in cases involving matters such as potential over payments, untimely revenue recognition, and so on, it is often possible to assign a precise dollar value to the deficiency. In other cases, where it is not possible to do so, one must fall back on a more qualitative analysis of the deficiency's significance.

NOTES AND QUESTIONS

1.   Increasingly, companies rely on comprehensive software packages both to document and test their internal controls. Many of these packages integrate § 404 compliance with the § 302 certification process, so as to help contain costs.

Using a single software platform/electronic repository to coordinate and document all controls, documentation, test results, and other relevant supporting materials is useful for several reasons.

First, it reduces audit fees. You can simply point your outside auditor at a single repository rather than requiring the auditor to check multiple programs across multiple departments. Second, it ensures adequate documentation in case the SEC challenges the company's compliance. Third, it helps ensure that the company retains key financial reporting documents in accordance with SOX's document retention rules. Finally, a common software platform can provide a central enterprise-wide set of controls. Why might the increasing automation of compliance processes be an area of concern for regulators? What risks does automation pose?

2.   Would finding material weaknesses in the company's internal controls give rise to state law liability under *Caremark* and its progeny?

3.   What two aspects of internal control must management assess to comply with Section 404 of the Sarbanes-Oxley Act?

4.   What benefits might accrue to a company as a result of effective SOX § 404 compliance?

5.   SOX § 404 requires the chief executive and financial officers of a corporation registered with the SEC to certify each periodic report filed with the SEC. True or False?

PROBLEMS

1.   Andrew Alda was CEO of Polycarp, Inc., a manufacturer of ball bearings created hundreds of false expense reports with bogus business descriptions for his personal use of company dollars to pay for meals, entertainment, and gifts. In total over the last two years, Alda received $200,000 from Polycarp that was used to pay personal expenses. The amounts in question should have been disclosed in Polycarp's annual proxy statements as part of Alda's compensation (they would be considered perquisites), but were not so disclosed. Alda hid his misappropriation of corporate funds by:

- Submitting credit card charge slips for reimbursement without supporting documentation to demonstrate the amounts had been spent on corporate expenses.

- Having the company purchase gift cards purportedly to be given clients when Alda entertained them, but which Alda used for personal purchases.

Polycarp has asked you to recommend internal controls that would prevent its officers from engaging in future conduct of this sort. Polycarp has also asked you whether Alda's ability to perpetrate this scheme revealed material weaknesses in its internal controls. Polycarp's market float is $1 billion. Its pre-tax earnings last year were $57,000,000 on revenues of $1.2 billion.

2.   Franco, Inc. CFO Zoey Alleyne created a shell corporation named Niska Inc. Alleyne then added Niska to the corporation's approved list of vendors. Alleyne then caused Niska to submit false invoices to Franco. All the invoices from Niska were for amounts under $2,500. This had two consequences. First, although invoices for amounts less than $2,500 ordinarily would be handled by a deputy treasurer who reported directly to Alleyne, Alleyne told her that Alleyne would handle Niska invoices. Second, Franco's agreement with its bank allows company checks to be issued in amounts up to $2,500 without a counter signature. Alleyne would sign the checks made out to Niska and mail them to a P.O. box specified on the invoice. After retrieving the checks from the P.O. box, Alleyne's husband would sign the checks on Niska's behalf and deposit them in a bank account he and Alleyne had set up for the fake company. In total, over a nine-month period, Alleyne used this scheme to embezzle $1,000,000. Franco's annual

revenues average $75,000,000 and its annual pre-tax income averages $6 million.

Franco's board asked you to recommend internal controls that would prevent its officers from engaging in future conduct of this sort. Franco's board has also asked you whether Alleyne's ability to perpetrate this scheme revealed material weaknesses in its internal controls.

3.   Parent Corporation has 10 operating subsidiaries. Each month Parent processes a significant number of routine intercompany transactions between those subsidiaries. For example, if one subsidiary has a temporary case shortfall, another subsidiary may extend a short-term loan, which the borrower will repay with interest at the end of the month. Historically, these individual intercompany transactions have not been material in amount and, as noted, primarily relate to balance sheet activity, such as, cash transfers between business units to finance normal operations.

> **FYI**
>
> "Reconciliation is an accounting process that uses two sets of records to ensure figures are correct and in agreement. It confirms whether the money leaving an account matches the amount that's been spent, and makes sure the two are balanced at the end of the recording period."
> https://www.investopedia.com/terms/r/reconciliation.asp

A formal Parent policy requires monthly reconciliation of intercompany accounts and confirmation of balances between business units. However, there is not a process in place to ensure performance of these procedures. As a result, detailed reconciliations of intercompany accounts often are not performed on a timely basis. Management does perform monthly procedures to investigate selected large-dollar intercompany account differences. In addition, management prepares a detailed monthly variance analysis of operating expenses to assess their reasonableness.

On these facts, is this process a deficiency, a significant deficiency, or a material weakness? Explain.[44]

4.   A similar question (to # 3) has arisen at Acme, Inc., but remember that each set of facts is unique. Acme also has a number of operational subsidiaries. Acme monthly processes a significant number of intercompany transactions. Acme's intercompany transactions relate to a wide range of activities, including transfers of inventory with intercompany profit between business units, allocation of research and development costs to business units and corporate charges. Individual intercompany transactions are frequently material.

A formal management policy requires monthly reconciliation of intercompany accounts and confirmation of balances between business units. However, there is not a process in place to ensure that these procedures are performed on a consistent basis. As a result, reconciliations of intercompany accounts are not performed on a timely basis, and differences in

---

[44]   https://www.sec.gov/rules/pcaob/34-49544-appendixd.pdf.

intercompany accounts are frequent and significant. Management does not perform any alternative controls to investigate significant intercompany account differences.

On these facts, is this process a deficiency, a significant deficiency, or a material weakness? Explain.[45]

> To assess your understanding of the material in this chapter, <u>click here</u> to take a quiz.

---

[45] https://www.sec.gov/rules/pcaob/34-49544-appendixd.pdf.

PART III

EXECUTIVES

CHAPTER 6

EXECUTIVE COMPENSATION

Executive pay serves two purposes. First, it compensates the executive for the value of time he or she devotes to work. Second, and for our purposes more importantly, a well-designed executive pay program should reduce agency costs by aligning management's interests with those of the shareholders and incentivizing management to maximize shareholder gains. Unfortunately, executive compensation schemes often fall short of that latter goal.

A. INTRODUCTION AND OVERVIEW

Executive compensation generally consists of a package comprised of a mix of salary, cash bonuses, stock options, grants of restricted stock, perquisites, and retirement benefits. In addition to the state and federal corporate governance rules discussed in this chapter, these components are subject to complex regulatory schemes under the tax laws and the Employee Retirement Income Security Act of 1974 (ERISA). Our focus here is on salary and stock options.

> **FYI**
>
> ERISA is a federal statute administered by the Department of Labor that sets minimum standards for most voluntarily established pension and health plans in private industry to provide protection for individuals in these plans.

Salary and any "applicable employee remuneration" are effectively limited to $1 million per year by § 162(m) of the Internal Revenue Code, which precludes publicly traded companies from taking a tax deduction for any compensation paid to a "covered employee" in excess of that amount. Covered employees include the company's CEO, CFO, and the company's other three most highly compensated officers.

As initially adopted in 1993, the $1 million limitation did not apply to "any remuneration payable solely on account of the attainment of one or more performance goals," provided that:

(i) the performance goals are determined by a compensation committee of the board of directors of the taxpayer which is comprised solely of 2 or more outside directors,

(ii) the material terms under which the remuneration is to be paid, including the performance goals, are disclosed to shareholders and approved by a majority of the vote in a separate shareholder vote before the payment of such remuneration, and

(iii) before any payment of such remuneration, the compensation committee referred to in clause (i) certifies that the performance goals and any other material terms were in fact satisfied.

As adopted § 162(m) and its exemptions led to a dramatic shift in the form of executive compensation from cash salary and bonuses to stock options and restricted stock grants inked to performance.

The following shows how stock options are granted and exercised:

- ABC, Inc., hires employee John Smith.

- As part of his employment package, ABC grants John options to acquire 40,000 shares of ABC's common stock at 25 cents per share (the fair market value of a share of ABC common stock at the time of grant).

- The options are subject to a four-year vesting with one year cliff vesting, which means that John has to stay employed with ABC for one year before he gets the right to exercise 10,000 of the options and then he vests the remaining 30,000 options at the rate of 1/36 a month over the next 36 months of employment.

- If John leaves ABC or is fired before the end of his first year, he doesn't get any of the options.

- After his options are "vested" (become exercisable), he has the option to buy the stock at 25 cents per share, even if the share value has gone up dramatically.

- After four years, all 40,000 of his option shares are vested if he has continued to work for ABC.

- ABC becomes successful and goes public. Its stock trades at $20 per share.

- John exercises his options and buys 40,000 shares for $10,000 (40,000 × 25 cents).

- John turns around and sells all 40,000 shares for $800,000 (40,000 × the $20 per share publicly traded price), making a nice profit of $790,000[1]

Such options typically did not count towards the $1 million limit imposed by § 162(m):

An example of a stock option grant that is not subject to the $1 million cap of § 162(m) would be a grant to an executive for the right to buy 5,000 shares of the company at $25 a share. If shares of the company currently trade at $25 a share, the executive will not actually realize any compensation from the

---

[1]   Richard Harroch, How Employee Stock Options Work In Startup Companies, Forbes.com (Feb, 27, 2016).

grant until the shares increase in value to $26 a share. At that point, if the executive exercises his right to buy the shares, then the executive will end up with $1 of profit per share (or $5,000 total). Section 162(m) excludes this type of compensation from the cap because it is implicitly performance-based; the executive only profits from the grant of stock options if the stock price actually increases. The executive will therefore try to increase the stock price in the corporation by performing well. Because the shareholders also want to have the stock price in the corporation increased, the shareholders' and the executive's interests are aligned and the executive has an added incentive to perform well for the corporation.

Stock options that have an exercise price below the current price of shares (referred to as in-the money options) are not exempt from the $1 million cap. An in-the money stock option, for example, would be if our executive in the previous example was granted an option to purchase stock at $20 when the market share price was $25. The executive does not have to perform well (or perform at all) to profit from the grant. As soon as the options are granted the executive will profit $5 per share. Therefore, the performance-based exception does not apply.[2]

All of this significantly changed in for tax years after 2017 as a result of the Tax Cuts and Jobs Act of 2017. It amended § 162(m)(4) to define applicable employee remuneration to include any compensation including benefits, including compensation paid in "any medium other than cash," except for certain pension or retirement benefits. The amendment thereby eliminated the exemption for qualified performance-based compensation. As a result, effectively all pay and benefits in excess of $1 million are now nondeductible. Despite this change the amount of stock-based compensation paid covered executives in 2018 actually increased in 2018. For the first time, the majority of S&P 500 CEOs received more than 50% of their compensation in the form of stock. Including cash bonuses and

> **FYI**
>
> "Stock appreciation rights (SARs) are also a prevalent form of long-term incentives. Similar to a stock option, a SAR gives the executive the ability over an extended period of time to realize the appreciation in value of his employer's stock from the grant date to the date of exercise. However, with a SAR, the executive does not actually purchase the stock. Rather, the corporation simply pays the spread at the date of exercise in cash or shares, or both." Gregory K. Brown, What the Matrimonial Lawyer Needs to Know About Non-ERISA Plans, Executive Compensation, and Other Related Plans, 26 J. Am. Acad. Matrim. Law. 291. 293 (2014).

---

[2]   Meredith R. Conway, Money for Nothing and the Stocks for Free: Taxing Executive Compensation, 17 Cornell J.L. & Pub. Pol'y 383, 398–99 (2008).

similar non-stock compensation, performance-based compensation for such CEOs now approaches 60% of their total pay.[3]

Setting aside tax considerations, the justification for using performance-based stock options as compensation is that it aligns shareholder and management incentives. Managers who make significant non-diversifiable investments in firm-specific human capital and hold undiversified investment portfolios in which equity of their employer is substantially over-represented will seek to minimize firm-specific risks that shareholders eliminate through diversification. As a result, managers generally are more risk averse than shareholders would prefer. By offering managers increased compensation when they take risks that realize returns to the shareholders through higher stock prices, options thus bring management's interests into line with those of the shareholders.

Although options are intended to align shareholder and managerial interests, they can have perverse effects:

> The practice of timing refers to granting options when the stock price appears to be at a low or the CEO has reason to know that the price is likely to rise in the future. If the CEO knows material nonpublic facts that are ripe for disclosure, a grant of options at such a time—spring loading—may be equivalent to insider trading or misappropriation of existing stockholder wealth. . . .

> The practice of backdating refers to granting options as if the grant occurred on an earlier date when stock price was lower. For example, a company might grant an option today when the stock is trading at 30 and record the option as granted a month earlier when the market price was 25. In effect, backdating constitutes grant of an option at a below market price. . . .

> Following the dotcom bust and the demise of Enron, WorldCom, and other corporations, stock options have been criticized as inducing CEOs to pursue overly risky business strategies. The usual argument is that options induce CEOs to take big chances to increase stock price. . . .

> The real problem is overvalued equity. Options can create perverse incentives if stock price becomes too high. CEOs may be tempted to undertake questionable tactics designed to maintain stock price until options can be exercised and option stock can be sold. If stock price is too high, the CEO will

---

[3]   John Roe & Kosmas Papadopoulos, ISS Discusses Trends in 2019 U.S. Executive Compensation, The CLS Blue Sky Blog (April 16, 2019), http://clsbluesky.law.columbia.edu/2019/04/16/iss-discusses-trends-in-2019-u-s-executive-compensation/.

naturally seek to keep it from falling in order to maintain paper gains.[4]

B. THE POLICY DEBATE

Complaints about executive pay are hardly new. In the 1930s, during the Great Depression, for example, a lawsuit challenging executive bonuses as corporate waste gave rise to the aphorism "no man can be worth $1,000,000 per year."[5] This complaint rested, at least in part, not on a belief that executives were being paid too much relative to their company's performance but on the belief that the amounts they were being paid were simply too high.

Over seven decades later, William McDonough, the then-Chairman of the Public Company Accounting Oversight Board (PCAOB), complained that:

> We saw . . . an explosion in compensation that made those superstar CEOs actually believe that they were worth more than 400 times the pay of their average workers. Twenty years before, they had been paid an average of forty times the average worker, so the multiple went from forty to 400—an increase of ten times in twenty years. That was thoroughly unjustified by all economic reasoning, and in addition, in my view, it is grotesquely immoral.[6]

Fat cat CEOs thus "have become poster boys for" the dramatic increase in "inequality in income and wealth in this country."[7]

Growing inequalities of wealth doubtless are a highly significant social issue, but such large policy questions lie outside the purview of corporate governance. Instead, the key question for our purposes is whether high executive pay is inimical to shareholder interests.

THINK ABOUT IT

Would limiting CEO pay solve the problem of wealth inequalities?

---

[4]   Richard A. Booth, Why Stock Options Are the Best Form of Executive Compensation (and How to Make Them Even Better), 6 N.Y.U. J.L. & Bus. 281, 340–47 (2010).

[5]   Harwell Wells, "No Man Can Be Worth $1,000,000 a Year": The Fight Over Executive Compensation in 1930s America, 44 U. Rich. L. Rev. 689, 726 (2010).

[6]   William J. McDonough, The Fourth Annual A.A. Sommer, Jr. Lecture on Corporate, Securities & Financial Law, 9 Fordham J. Corp. & Fin. L. 583, 590 (2004).

[7]   Brett H. McDonnell, Two Goals for Executive Compensation Reform, 52 N.Y.L. Sch. L. Rev. 586, 587 (2008).

Lucian A. Bebchuk & Jesse M. Fried, Pay Without Performance: Overview of the Issues
30 J. Corp. L. 647 (2005)[8]

I.   Introduction

The dramatic rise in CEO pay during the last two decades has been the subject of much public criticism, which intensified following the corporate governance scandals that began erupting in late 2001. The wave of corporate scandals shook confidence in the performance of public company boards and drew attention to possible flaws in their executive compensation practices. . . .

. . . The study of executive compensation opens a window through which we can examine our current reliance on boards to act as guardians of shareholders' interests. Our corporate governance system gives boards substantial power and counts on them to monitor and supervise company managers. As long as corporate directors are believed to carry out their tasks for the benefit of shareholders, current governance arrangements, which insulate boards from intervention by shareholders, appear acceptable. Our analysis of the executive pay landscape casts doubt on the validity of this belief and on the wisdom of insulating boards from shareholders.

II. The Stakes

What is at stake in the debate over executive pay? Some might question whether executive compensation has a significant economic impact on shareholders and the economy. The problems with executive compensation, it might be argued, do not much affect shareholders' bottom line, but instead are mainly symbolic. However, the question of whether and to what extent pay arrangements are flawed is important for shareholders and policymakers because defects in these arrangements can impose substantial costs on shareholders.

. . . [I]f compensation levels could be cut without weakening managerial incentives, the gain to investors would not be merely symbolic. It would have a discernible effect on corporate earnings. But excess pay is unlikely to be the only or even main cost of current compensation practices. Managers' influence over their compensation arrangements can result in the weakening and distortion of managerial incentives. In our view, the dilution and distortion of incentives could well impose a larger cost on shareholders than excessive compensation per se.

Existing pay arrangements have been producing two types of incentive problems. First, compensation arrangements have provided weaker incentives to increase shareholder value than would have been provided under arm's-length contracting. Both the non-equity and equity

---

8   Reprinted by permission of Lucian A. Bebchuk, Jesse M. fried, and The Journal of Corporation Law.

components of managerial compensation have been more severely decoupled from managers' contributions to company performance than appearances might suggest. Making pay more sensitive to performance could therefore have substantial benefits for shareholders.

Second, prevailing practices not only fail to provide cost-effective incentives to increase value, but also create perverse incentives. For example, managers' broad freedom to unload company options and stock can lead them to act in ways that reduce shareholder value. Executives who expect to unload shares have incentives to report misleading results, suppress bad news, and choose projects and strategies that are less transparent to the market. The efficiency costs of such distortions may well exceed—possibly by a large margin—whatever liquidity or risk-bearing benefits executives obtain from being able to unload their options and shares at will. Similarly, because existing pay practices often reward managers for increasing firm size, they provide executives with incentives to pursue expansion through acquisitions or other means, even when that strategy is value-reducing.

III. The Arm's-Length Contracting View

According to the "official" view of executive compensation, corporate boards setting pay arrangements are guided solely by shareholder interests and operate at arm's-length from the executives whose pay they set. The premise that boards contract at arm's-length with executives has long been and remains a central tenet in the corporate world and in most research on executive compensation by financial economists. In the corporate world, the official view serves as the practical basis for legal rules and public policy. It is used to justify directors' compensation decisions to shareholders, policymakers, and courts. These decisions are portrayed as being made largely with shareholders' interests at heart and therefore deserving of deference.

. . .

Financial economists, both theorists and empiricists, have largely worked within the arm's-length model in attempting to explain common compensation arrangements as well as differences in compensation practices among companies. In fact, upon discovering practices that appear inconsistent with the cost-effective provision of incentives, financial economists have labored to come up with clever explanations for how such practices might be consistent with arm's-length contracting after all. Practices for which no explanation has been found have been described as "anomalies" or "puzzles" that will ultimately either be explained within the paradigm or disappear.

. . .

IV. Limits of the Arm's-Length View

The official arm's-length story is neat, tractable, and reassuring. But it fails to account for the realities of executive compensation. The arm's-length contracting view recognizes that managers are subject to an agency problem and do not automatically seek to maximize shareholder value. The potential divergence between managers' and shareholders' interests makes it important to provide managers with adequate incentives. Under the arm's-length contracting view, the board attempts to provide such incentives cost-effectively through managers' compensation packages. But just as there is no reason to assume that managers automatically seek to maximize shareholder value, there is no reason to expect that directors will either. Indeed, an analysis of directors' incentives and circumstances suggests that director behavior is also subject to an agency problem.

Directors have had and continue to have various economic incentives to support, or at least go along with, arrangements that favor the company's top executives. A variety of social and psychological factors—collegiality, team spirit, a natural desire to avoid conflict within the board, friendship and loyalty, and cognitive dissonance—exert additional pull in that direction. Although many directors own some stock in their companies, their ownership positions are too small to give them a financial incentive to take the personally costly, or at the very least unpleasant, route of resisting compensation arrangements sought by executives. In addition, limitations on time and resources have made it difficult for even well-intentioned directors to do their pay-setting job properly. Finally, the market constraints within which directors operate are far from tight and do not prevent deviations from arm's-length contracting outcomes in favor of executives. Below we briefly discuss each of these factors.

A. Incentives to be Re-elected

Besides an attractive salary, a directorship is also likely to provide prestige and valuable business and social connections. The financial and non-financial benefits of holding a board seat naturally give directors an interest in keeping their positions.

In a world where shareholders select individual directors, board members might have an incentive to develop reputations as shareholder-serving. Typically, however, the director slate proposed by management is the only one offered. The key to retaining a board position is thus being placed on the company's slate. And because the CEO has had significant influence over the nomination process, displeasing the CEO has been likely to hurt one's chances of being put on the company slate. Directors thus have an incentive to "go along" with the CEO's pay arrangement, a matter dear to the CEO's heart, at least as long as the compensation package remains within the range of what can plausibly be defended and justified. In addition, developing a reputation as a director

> **THINK ABOUT IT**
>
> Is Bebchuk and Fried's claim about the CEO's influence still valid after the changes in the director nomination process effected by SOX and Dodd-Frank?

who blocks compensation arrangements sought by executives can only hurt a director's chances of being invited to join other boards.

. . .

B.   CEO Power to Benefit Directors

There are a variety of ways in which CEOs can benefit individual directors or board members as a group. For one thing, CEOs have influence over director compensation. As the company leader, usually as a board member, and often as board chairman, the CEO can choose to either discourage or encourage director pay increases. Independent directors who are generous toward the CEO might reasonably expect the CEO to use his or her bully pulpit to support higher director compensation. . . .

C.   Friendship and Loyalty

Many independent directors have some prior social connection to the company's CEO or other senior executives. Even directors who did not know the CEO before their appointment may well have begun their service with a sense of obligation and loyalty to the CEO. . . . As a result, directors often start serving with a reservoir of good will toward the CEO, which will contribute to a tendency to favor the CEO in compensation matters. . . .

F.   The Small Cost of Favoring Executives

Directors typically own only a small fraction of the firm's shares. As a result, the direct personal cost to board members of approving compensation arrangements that are too favorable to executives—the reduction in the value of their shareholdings—is small. This cost is therefore unlikely to outweigh the economic incentives and social and psychological factors that induce directors to go along with pay schemes that favor executives.

THINK ABOUT IT

Is the relevant question what percentage of the company's outstanding stock a director owns? Or is the relevant question what percentage of the director's net worth is comprised of her holdings of company stock? In either case, is it clear that stock ownership does not adequately incentivize directors?

. . .

H.   Limits of Market Forces

. . . The markets for capital, corporate control, and managerial labor do impose some constraints on executive compensation. But these constraints are by no means stringent and they permit substantial deviations from arm's-length contracting.

Consider, for example, the market for corporate control—the threat of a takeover. Most companies have substantial defenses against takeovers. For example, a majority of companies have a staggered board, which prevents a hostile acquirer from gaining control before two annual elections are held, and often enables incumbent managers to block hostile bids that are attractive to shareholders. To overcome incumbent opposition, a hostile bidder must be prepared to pay a substantial premium. The disciplinary force of the market for corporate control is further weakened by the prevalence of golden parachute provisions, as well as by payoffs made by acquirers to target managers to facilitate the acquisition. The market for corporate control thus exerts little disciplining force on managers and boards, leaving them with considerable slack and the ability to negotiate manager-favoring pay arrangements.

. . .

V.   Power and Pay

. . . In our view, high absolute levels of pay do not by themselves imply that compensation arrangements deviate from arm's-length contracting. . . . For us, the "smoking gun" of managerial influence over pay is not high levels of pay, but rather such things as the correlation between power and pay, the systematic use of compensation practices that obscure the amount and performance insensitivity of pay, and the showering of gratuitous benefits on departing executives.

A.   Power-Pay Relationships

. . . The managerial power approach predicts that executives who have more power should receive higher pay—or pay that is less sensitive to performance—than their less powerful counterparts. A substantial body of evidence does indeed indicate that pay is higher, and less sensitive to performance, when executives have more power.

First, there is evidence that executive compensation is higher when the board is relatively weak or ineffectual vis-à-vis the CEO. In particular, CEO compensation is higher (1) when the board is large, which makes it more difficult for directors to organize in opposition to the CEO; (2) when more of the outside directors have been appointed by the CEO, which could cause them to feel gratitude or obligation to the CEO; and (3) when outside directors serve on three or more boards, and thus are more likely to be distracted. Also, CEO pay is 20% to 40% higher if the CEO is the chairman of the board, and it is negatively correlated with the stock ownership of compensation committee members.

> **THINK ABOUT IT**
>
> Is the negative correlation of stock ownership by compensation committee members and CEO pay consistent with Bebchuk and Fried's claim that director stock ownership does not constrain executive pay?

Second, studies find a negative correlation between the presence of a large outside shareholder and pay arrangements that favor executives. . . .

Third, there is evidence linking executive pay to the concentration of institutional shareholders, which are more likely to monitor the CEO and the board. One study finds that more concentrated institutional ownership leads to lower and more performance-sensitive compensation. . . .

Finally, studies find a connection between pay and anti-takeover provisions, arrangements that make CEOs and their boards less vulnerable to a hostile takeover. . . .

B.   Limits of Managerial Influence

There are, of course, limits to the arrangements that directors will approve and executives will seek. Although market forces are not sufficiently powerful to prevent significant deviations from arm's-length outcomes, they do impose some constraints on executive compensation. If a board were to approve a pay arrangement viewed as egregious, for example, shareholders would be less willing to support incumbents in a hostile takeover or a proxy fight.

In addition, directors and executives adopting such an arrangement might bear social costs. Directors approving a clearly inflated and distorted pay package might be subject to ridicule or scorn in the media or in their social and business circles. Most directors would wish to avoid such treatment, even if their board positions were not at risk, and these potential social costs reinforce the constraints imposed by market forces. . . .

One important building block of the managerial power approach is, therefore, "outrage" costs. . . .

C.   Camouflage and Stealth Compensation

The critical role of outsiders' perception of executives' compensation and the significance of outrage costs explain the importance of yet another component of the managerial power approach: "camouflage." The desire to minimize outrage gives designers of compensation arrangements a strong incentive to try to legitimize, justify, obscure, or, more generally, to camouflage—the amount and performance-insensitivity of executive compensation.

. . .

VI. The Decoupling of Pay from Performance

In the early 1990s, prominent financial economists such as Michael Jensen and Kevin Murphy urged shareholders to be more accepting of large pay packages that would provide high-powered incentives. Shareholders, it was argued, should care much more about providing managers with sufficiently strong incentives than about the amounts spent on executive pay. Defenders of current pay arrangements view the rise in pay over the past fifteen years as the necessary price—and one worth paying—for improving executives' incentives.

The problem, however, is that executives' large compensation packages have been much less sensitive to their own performance than has been commonly recognized. Shareholders have not received the most bang for their buck. Companies could have generated the same increase in incentives at a much lower cost to their shareholders, or they could have used the amount spent to obtain more powerful incentives.

. . .

1. Rewards for Market-Wide and Industry-Wide Movements

Conventional stock options enable executives to gain from any increase in the nominal stock price above the grant-date market value. This in turn means that executives can profit even when their companies' performance significantly lags that of their peers, as long as market-wide and industry-wide movements provide sufficient lift for the stock price. A substantial fraction of stock price increases is due to such movements, rather than to firm-specific factors that might reflect the manager's own performance.

Although there are a variety of ways in which market and industry-driven windfalls could be filtered out, very few companies have adopted equity-based plans that even attempt to filter out such windfalls. . . .

2. Rewards for Short-Term Spikes

Option plans have been designed, and largely continue to be designed, in ways that enable executives to make considerable gains from temporary spikes in the company's stock price, even when long-term stock performance is poor. . . . In addition to being granted the freedom to exercise their options as soon as they vest and sell the underlying stock, executives often have considerable control over the timing of sales, enabling them to benefit from their inside information. . . .

VII. Improving Transparency

We now consider ways of improving pay arrangements and the governance processes that produce those arrangements. We start with a reform that could be viewed as a "no-brainer," one for which there seems to be no reasonable basis for opposition. Specifically, the SEC should require public companies to make the amount and structure of their executive pay packages more transparent.

> **FYI**
>
> Since this article was written in 2005, several changes have been made in the federal disclosure rules. See Section D below.

. . . The purpose of executive compensation disclosure is not merely to enable accurate pricing of corporate securities. Its purpose is also to provide some check on arrangements that are too favorable to executives. This goal is not well served by disseminating information in a way that makes the information understandable to a small number of market professionals but opaque to others.

Public officials, governance reformers, and investors should examine how to ensure that compensation arrangements are and remain transparent. Transparency would provide shareholders with a more accurate picture of total pay and its relationship to performance, thereby providing some check on departures from arrangements that serve shareholder interests. Furthermore, transparency would eliminate the distortions that currently arise when pay designers choose particular forms of compensation for their camouflage value rather than for their efficiency. Finally, transparency would impose little cost on companies because it would simply require them to clearly disclose information they have or can obtain at negligible cost.

A.   Place a Dollar Value on All Forms of Compensation

Companies could be required to place a dollar value on all forms of compensation and to include these amounts in the summary compensation tables contained in company SEC filings. Executives routinely receive substantial "stealth compensation" in the form of pensions, deferred compensation, and post-retirement perks and consulting contracts. . . .

To address this issue, companies could be required to place a monetary value on each benefit provided or promised to an executive, and to include this value in the summary compensation table for the year in which the executive becomes entitled to it. . . .

> **FYI**
>
> The SEC adopted a form of this proposal in 2006. See SEC, Exec. Comp. & Related Party Disclosure, Release No. 8655 (Jan. 27, 2006).

C.   Report the Relationship Between Pay and Performance

Companies could be required to report to their shareholders how much of their executives' profits from equity and non-equity compensation is attributable to general market and industry movements. This could be done by requiring firms to calculate and report the gains made by managers from the exercise of options (or the vesting of restricted shares, in the case of restricted share grants) and to report what fraction, if any, reflects the company's success in outperforming its industry peers. Such disclosure would help clarify the extent to which the company's equity-based plans reward the managers for good relative performance.

D.   Disclose Option and Share Unloading

Companies could be required to make transparent to shareholders on a regular basis the extent to which their top five executives have unloaded any equity instruments received as part of their compensation. Although a diligent and dedicated researcher can obtain this information by sifting through stacks of executive trading reports filed with the SEC, requiring the firm to compile and report such information would highlight for all investors the extent to which managers have used their freedom to unwind incentives.

VIII. Improving Pay Arrangements

A. Reduce Windfalls in Equity-Based Compensation

Firms would do well to consider adopting equity compensation plans that filter out at least some of the gains in the stock price that are due to general market or industry movements. . . . This can be done not only by indexing the exercise price of stock options, but in other ways as well. For example, by linking the exercise price of options to changes in the stock price of the worst-performing firms in the industry, market-wide movement can be filtered out without imposing excessive risk on executives.

. . .

B. Reduce Windfalls in Bonus Plans

For similar reasons, companies should consider designing bonus plans that filter out improvements in financial performance due to economy- or industry-wide movements. . . .

D. Tie Bonuses to Long-Term Performance

Even assuming it were desirable to reward managers for improvements in accounting results, it might be desirable to give such rewards not for short-term results but only for improvements that are sustained over a considerable period of time. Rewarding executives for short-term improvements is not an effective way to provide beneficial incentives and indeed might create incentives to manipulate short-term accounting results.

It also might be desirable for compensation contracts to include general "clawback" provisions that require managers to return payments based on accounting numbers that are subsequently restated. Such return of payments is warranted, regardless of whether the executive was in any way responsible for the misreporting. When the board believes it is desirable to tie executive payoffs to a formula involving a metric whose value turns out to have been inflated, correctly applying the formula requires reversing payments that were based on erroneous values. The governing principle should be: "What wasn't earned must be returned."

E. Be Wary of Paying for Expansion

Because running a larger company increases managers' power, prestige, and perquisites, executives might have an incentive to expand the company at the expense of shareholder value. Executive compensation arrangements should seek to counter rather than reinforce this incentive. . . .

. . .

IX. Improving Board Accountability

Past and current flaws in executive pay arrangements have resulted from underlying problems within the corporate governance system:

specifically, directors' lack of sufficient incentives to focus solely on shareholder interests when setting pay. If directors could be relied on to focus on shareholder interests, the pay-setting process, and board oversight of executives more generally, would be greatly improved. . . .

To begin, it might be desirable to turn shareholders' power to replace directors from myth into reality. Even in the wake of poor performance and shareholder dissatisfaction, directors now face very little risk of being ousted. . . .

To improve the performance of corporate boards, it might be desirable to reduce impediments to director removal. As a first step, shareholders could be given the power to place director candidates on the corporate ballot. In addition, proxy contest challengers that attract sufficient support could be given reimbursement of their expenses from the company. Furthermore, it might be desirable to limit the use of staggered boards, a feature of most public companies, to impede director removal. Staggered boards provide powerful protection from removal in either a proxy fight or a hostile takeover. . . .

> **WHAT'S THAT?**
>
> PROXY CONTEST, Black's Law Dictionary (10th ed. 2014): A struggle between two corporate factions to obtain the votes of uncommitted shareholders. A proxy contest usually occurs when a group of dissident shareholders mounts a battle against the corporation's managers. — Also termed proxy fight."

In addition to making shareholder power to remove directors viable, it might be undesirable for boards to have veto power, which current corporate law grants them, over proposed changes to governance arrangements in the company's charter. Shareholders could be given the power, which they now lack, to initiate and adopt changes in the corporate charter. . . .

To fully address the existing problems in executive compensation and corporate governance, structural reforms in the allocation of power between boards and shareholders could well be necessary. Given political realities, such reforms would not be easy to pass. But the corporate governance flaws that we have discussed—and have shown to be pervasive, systemic, and costly—make considering such reforms worthwhile.

NOTES AND QUESTIONS

1.   To what extent does risk aversion explain high executive pay levels?

2.   There is evidence that firms with more hierarchical organizations lavish more perks on their executives than firms with flatter structures. Does that evidence support or rebut Bebchuk and Fried's argument?

3.   There is evidence that the pay practices criticized by Bebchuk and Fried are also present in firms with controlling shareholders. Does that evidence support or rebut Bebchuk and Fried's argument?

4.   Do executive compensation practices encourage managers to take fewer risks than optimal or more risks than optimal?

5.   Do current CEO pay practices encourage managers to focus on long-term strategy or short-term profit maximization?

6.   Should the government regulate executive pay? If so, how?

C. STATE LAW

In re Walt Disney Co. Derivative Litig.
906 A.2d 27 (Del.2006)

In August 1995, Michael Ovitz ("Ovitz") and The Walt Disney Company ("Disney" or the "Company") entered into an employment agreement under which Ovitz would serve as President of Disney for five years. In December 1996, only fourteen months after he commenced employment, Ovitz was terminated without cause, resulting in a severance payout to Ovitz valued at approximately $130 million.

In January 1997, several Disney shareholders brought derivative actions in the Court of Chancery, on behalf of Disney, against Ovitz and the directors of Disney who served at the time of the events complained of (the "Disney defendants"). The plaintiffs claimed that the $130 million severance payout was the product of fiduciary duty and contractual breaches by Ovitz, and breaches of fiduciary duty by the Disney defendants, and a waste of assets. . . .The Court entered judgment in favor of all defendants on all claims alleged in the amended complaint.

. . .

I.   *THE FACTS*

. . . The critical events flow from what turned out to be an unfortunate hiring decision at Disney, a company that for over half a century has been one of America's leading film and entertainment enterprises.

In 1994 Disney lost in a tragic helicopter crash its President and Chief Operating Officer, Frank Wells, who together with Michael Eisner, Disney's Chairman and Chief Executive Officer, had enjoyed remarkable success at the Company's helm. Eisner temporarily assumed Disney's presidency, but only three months later, heart disease required Eisner to undergo quadruple bypass surgery. Those two events persuaded Eisner and Disney's board of directors that the time had come to identify a successor to Eisner.

Eisner's prime candidate for the position was Michael Ovitz, who was the leading partner and one of the founders of Creative Artists

Agency ("CAA"), the premier talent agency whose business model had reshaped the entire industry. By 1995, CAA . . . generated about $150 million in annual revenues and an annual income of over $20 million for Ovitz, who was regarded as one of the most powerful figures in Hollywood.

Eisner and Ovitz had enjoyed a social and professional relationship that spanned nearly 25 years. Although in the past the two men had casually discussed possibly working together, in 1995, when Ovitz began negotiations to leave CAA and join Music Corporation of America ("MCA"), Eisner became seriously interested in recruiting Ovitz to join Disney. Eisner shared that desire with Disney's board members on an individual basis.

A. *Negotiation of The Ovitz Employment Agreement*

Eisner and Irwin Russell, who was a Disney director and chairman of the compensation committee, first approached Ovitz about joining Disney. . . . By mid-July 1995, those negotiations were in full swing.

Both Russell and Eisner negotiated with Ovitz, over separate issues and concerns. From his talks with Eisner, . . . Ovitz came to believe that he and Eisner would run Disney, and would work together in a relation akin to that of junior and senior partner. Unfortunately, Ovitz's belief was mistaken, as Eisner had a radically different view of what their respective roles at Disney should be.

Russell assumed the lead in negotiating the financial terms of the Ovitz employment contract. . . . From the beginning Ovitz made it clear that he would not give up his 55% interest in CAA without "downside protection." Considerable negotiation then ensued over downside protection issues. During the summer of 1995, the parties agreed to a draft version of Ovitz's employment agreement (the "OEA") modeled after Eisner's and the late Mr. Wells' employment contracts. As described by the Chancellor, the draft agreement included the following terms:

> Under the proposed OEA, Ovitz would receive a five-year contract with two tranches of options. The first tranche consisted of three million options vesting in equal parts in the third, fourth, and fifth years, and if the value of those options at the end of the five years had not appreciated to $50 million, Disney would make up the difference. The second tranche consisted of two million options that would vest immediately if Disney and Ovitz opted to renew the contract.

> The proposed OEA sought to protect both parties in the event that Ovitz's employment ended prematurely, and provided that absent defined causes, neither party could terminate the agreement without penalty. If Ovitz, for example, walked away, for any reason other than those permitted under the OEA, he would forfeit any benefits remaining under the OEA and could be enjoined from working for a competitor.

Likewise, if Disney fired Ovitz for any reason other than gross negligence or malfeasance, Ovitz would be entitled to a non-fault payment (Non-Fault Termination or "NFT"), which consisted of his remaining salary, $7.5 million a year for unaccrued bonuses, the immediate vesting of his first tranche of options and a $10 million cash out payment for the second tranche of options.

As the basic terms of the OEA were crystallizing, Russell prepared and gave Ovitz and Eisner a "case study" to explain those terms. In that study, Russell also expressed his concern that the negotiated terms represented an extraordinary level of executive compensation. Russell acknowledged, however, that Ovitz was an "exceptional corporate executive" and "highly successful and unique entrepreneur" who merited "downside protection and upside opportunity." Both would be required to enable Ovitz to adjust to the reduced cash compensation he would receive from a public company, in contrast to the greater cash distributions and other perquisites more typically available from a privately held business. But, Russell did caution that Ovitz's salary would be at the top level for any corporate officer and significantly above that of the Disney CEO. Moreover, the stock options granted under the OEA would exceed the standards applied within Disney and corporate America and would "raise very strong criticism." Russell shared this original case study only with Eisner and Ovitz. . . .

To assist in evaluating the financial terms of the OEA, Russell recruited Graef Crystal, an executive compensation consultant, and Raymond Watson, a member of Disney's compensation committee and a past Disney board chairman who had helped structure Wells' and Eisner's compensation packages. Before the three met, Crystal prepared a comprehensive executive compensation database to accept various inputs and to conduct Black-Scholes analyses to output a range of values for the options.[8] Watson also prepared similar computations on spreadsheets, but without using the Black-Scholes method.

. . . Crystal faxed to Russell a memorandum concluding that the OEA would provide Ovitz with approximately $23.6 million per year for the first five years, or $23.9 million a year over seven years if Ovitz exercised a two year renewal option. Those sums, Crystal opined, would approximate Ovitz's current annual compensation at CAA.

. . .

While Russell, Watson and Crystal were finalizing their analysis of the OEA, Eisner and Ovitz reached a separate agreement. Eisner told Ovitz that: (1) the number of options would be reduced from a single grant of five million to two separate grants, the first being three million options for the first five years and the second consisting of two million

---

[8]   The Black-Scholes method is a formula for option valuation that is widely used and accepted in the industry and by regulators.

more options if the contract was renewed; and (2) Ovitz would join Disney only as President, not as a co-CEO with Eisner. . . .

. . . The next day, August 13, Eisner met with Ovitz, Russell, Sanford Litvack (an Executive Vice President and Disney's General Counsel), and Stephen Bollenbach (Disney's Chief Financial Officer) to discuss the decision to hire Ovitz. Litvack and Bollenbach were unhappy with that decision, and voiced concerns that Ovitz would disrupt the cohesion that existed between Eisner, Litvack and Bollenbach. Litvack and Bollenbach were emphatic that they would not report to Ovitz, but would continue to report to Eisner. Despite Ovitz's concern about his "shrinking authority" as Disney's future President, Eisner was able to provide sufficient reassurance so that ultimately Ovitz acceded to Litvack's and Bollenbach's terms.

On August 14, Eisner and Ovitz signed a letter agreement (the "OLA"), which outlined the basic terms of Ovitz's employment, and stated that the agreement (which would ultimately be embodied in a formal contract) was subject to approval by Disney's compensation committee and board of directors. . . .

That same day, a press release made the news of Ovitz's hiring public. The reaction was extremely positive: Disney was applauded for the decision, and Disney's stock price rose 4.4 % in a single day, thereby increasing Disney's market capitalization by over $1 billion.

Once the OLA was signed, Joseph Santaniello, a Vice President and counsel in Disney's legal department, began to embody in a draft OEA the terms that Russell and Goldman had agreed upon and had been memorialized in the OLA. In the process, Santaniello concluded that the $50 million guarantee created negative tax implications for Disney, because it might not be deductible. Concluding that the guarantee should be eliminated, Russell initiated discussions on how to compensate Ovitz for this change. What resulted were several amendments to the OEA to replace the back-end guarantee. The (to-be-eliminated) $50 million guarantee would be replaced by: (i) a reduction in the option strike price from 115% to 100% of the Company's stock price on the day of the grant for the two million options that would become exercisable in the sixth and seventh year of Ovitz's employment; (ii) a $10 million severance payment if the Company did not renew Ovitz's contract; and (iii) an alteration of the renewal option to provide for a five-year extension, a $1.25 million annual salary, the same bonus structure as the first five years of the contract, and a grant of three million additional options. To assess the potential consequences of the proposed changes, Watson worked with Russell and Crystal, who applied the Black-Scholes method to evaluate the extended exercisability features of the options. Watson also generated his own separate analysis.

On September 26, 1995, the Disney compensation committee (which consisted of Messrs. Russell, Watson, Poitier and Lozano) met for one hour to consider, among other agenda items, the proposed terms of the

OEA. A term sheet was distributed at the meeting, although a draft of the OEA was not. The topics discussed were historical comparables, such as Eisner's and Wells' option grants, and also the factors that Russell, Watson and Crystal had considered in setting the size of the option grants and the termination provisions of the contract. Watson testified that he provided the compensation committee with the spreadsheet analysis that he had performed in August, and discussed his findings with the committee. Crystal did not attend the meeting, although he was available by telephone to respond to questions if needed, but no one from the committee called. . . . The committee voted unanimously to approve the OEA terms, subject to "reasonable further negotiations within the framework of the terms and conditions" described in the OEA.

Immediately after the compensation committee meeting, the Disney board met in executive session. The board was told about the reporting structure to which Ovitz had agreed, but the initial negative reaction of Litvack and Bollenbach to the hiring was not recounted. Eisner led the discussion relating to Ovitz, and Watson then explained his analysis, and both Watson and Russell responded to questions from the board. After further deliberation, the board voted unanimously to elect Ovitz as President.

. . .

B. *Ovitz's Performance as President of Disney*

Ovitz's tenure as President of the Walt Disney Company officially began on October 1, 1995, the date that the OEA was executed. When Ovitz took office, the initial reaction was optimistic, and Ovitz did make some positive contributions while serving as President of the Company. By the fall of 1996, however, it had become clear that Ovitz was "a poor fit with his fellow executives." By then the Disney directors were discussing that the disconnect between Ovitz and the Company was likely irreparable and that Ovitz would have to be terminated.

The Court of Chancery identified three competing theories as to why Ovitz did not succeed:

> First, plaintiffs argue that Ovitz failed to follow Eisner's directives, especially in regard to acquisitions, and that generally, Ovitz did very little. Second, Ovitz contends Eisner's micromanaging prevented Ovitz from having the authority necessary to make the changes that Ovitz thought were appropriate. In addition, Ovitz believes he was not given enough time for his efforts to bear fruit. Third, the remaining defendants simply posit that Ovitz failed to transition from a private to a public company, from the "sell side to the buy side," and otherwise did not adapt to the Company culture or fit in with other executives. . . .

Although the plaintiffs attempted to show that Ovitz acted improperly (*i.e.,* with gross negligence or malfeasance) while in office, the

Chancellor found that the trial record did not support those accusations. . . .

Nonetheless, Ovitz's relationship with the Disney executives did continue to deteriorate through September 1996. In mid-September, Litvack, with Eisner's approval, told Ovitz that he was not working out at Disney and that he should start looking for a graceful exit from Disney and a new job. . . .

On September 30, 1996, the Disney board met. During an executive session of that meeting, and in small group discussions where Ovitz was not present, Eisner told the other board members of the continuing problems with Ovitz's performance. . . .

C. *Ovitz's Termination at Disney*

. . .

During this period Eisner was also working with Litvack to explore whether they could terminate Ovitz under the OEA for cause. If so, Disney would not owe Ovitz the NFT payment. From the very beginning, Litvack advised Eisner that he did not believe there was cause to terminate Ovitz under the OEA. Litvack's advice never changed.

. . .

A December 27, 1996 letter from Litvack to Ovitz, which Ovitz signed, memorialized the termination, accelerated Ovitz's departure date from January 31, 1997 to December 31, 1996, and informed Ovitz that he would receive roughly $38 million in cash and that the first tranche of three million options would vest immediately. By the terms of that letter agreement, Ovitz's tenure as an executive and a director of Disney officially ended on December 27, 1996. Shortly thereafter, Disney paid Ovitz what was owed under the OEA for an NFT, minus a holdback of $1 million pending final settlement of Ovitz's accounts. One month after Disney paid Ovitz, the plaintiffs filed this action.

. . .

IV. *THE CLAIMS AGAINST THE DISNEY DEFENDANTS*

. . .

A. *Claims Arising From The Approval Of The OEA And Ovitz's Election As President*

. . .

1. *The Due Care Determinations*

. . .

(a) TREATING DUE CARE AND BAD FAITH AS SEPARATE GROUNDS FOR DENYING BUSINESS JUDGMENT RULE REVIEW

... Our law presumes that "in making a business decision the directors of a corporation acted on an informed basis, in good faith, and in the honest belief that the action taken was in the best interests of the company."[61] Those presumptions can be rebutted if the plaintiff shows that the directors breached their fiduciary duty of care or of loyalty or acted in bad faith. If that is shown, the burden then shifts to the director defendants to demonstrate that the challenged act or transaction was entirely fair to the corporation and its shareholders.

Because no duty of loyalty claim was asserted against the Disney defendants, the only way to rebut the business judgment rule presumptions would be to show that the Disney defendants had either breached their duty of care or had not acted in good faith. At trial, the plaintiff-appellants attempted to establish both grounds, but the Chancellor determined that the plaintiffs had failed to prove either.

. . .

Even if the trial court's analytical approach were improper, the appellants have failed to demonstrate any prejudice. . . .

(b) RULING THAT THE FULL DISNEY BOARD WAS NOT REQUIRED TO CONSIDER AND APPROVE THE OEA

The appellants next challenge the Court of Chancery's determination that the full Disney board was not required to consider and approve the OEA, because the Company's governing instruments allocated that decision to the compensation committee. This challenge also cannot survive scrutiny.

As the Chancellor found, under the Company's governing documents the board of directors was responsible for selecting the corporation's officers, but under the compensation committee charter, the committee was responsible for establishing and approving the salaries, together with benefits and stock options, of the Company's CEO and President. The compensation committee also had the charter-imposed duty to "approve employment contracts, or contracts at will" for "all corporate officers who are members of the Board of Directors regardless of salary." That is exactly what occurred here. The full board ultimately selected Ovitz as President, and the compensation committee considered and ultimately approved the OEA, which embodied the terms of Ovitz's employment, including his compensation.

The Delaware General Corporation Law (DGCL) expressly empowers a board of directors to appoint committees and to delegate to them a broad range of responsibilities, which may include setting

---

[61] Aronson v. Lewis, 473 A.2d 805, 812 (Del.1984).

executive compensation. Nothing in the DGCL mandates that the entire board must make those decisions. . . .

   (d) HOLDING THAT THE COMPENSATION COMMITTEE
       MEMBERS DID NOT FAIL TO EXERCISE DUE CARE IN
       APPROVING THE OEA

The appellants next challenge the Chancellor's determination that although the compensation committee's decision-making process fell far short of corporate governance "best practices," the committee members breached no duty of care in considering and approving the NFT terms of the OEA. . . .

Although the appellants have balkanized their due care claim into several fragmented parts, the overall thrust of that claim is that the compensation committee approved the OEA with NFT provisions that could potentially result in an enormous payout, without informing themselves of what the full magnitude of that payout could be. . . .

In our view, a helpful approach is to compare what actually happened here to what would have occurred had the committee followed a "best practices" (or "best case") scenario, from a process standpoint. In a "best case" scenario, all committee members would have received, before or at the committee's first meeting on September 26, 1995, a spreadsheet or similar document prepared by (or with the assistance of) a compensation expert (in this case, Graef Crystal). Making different, alternative assumptions, the spreadsheet would disclose the amounts that Ovitz could receive under the OEA in each circumstance that might foreseeably arise. One variable in that matrix of possibilities would be the cost to Disney of a non-fault termination for each of the five years of the initial term of the OEA. The contents of the spreadsheet would be explained to the committee members, either by the expert who prepared it or by a fellow committee member similarly knowledgeable about the subject. That spreadsheet, which ultimately would become an exhibit to the minutes of the compensation committee meeting, would form the basis of the committee's deliberations and decision.

Had that scenario been followed, there would be no dispute (and no basis for litigation) over what information was furnished to the committee members or when it was furnished. Regrettably, the committee's informational and decisionmaking process used here was not so tidy. That is one reason why the Chancellor found that although the committee's process did not fall below the level required for a proper exercise of due care, it did fall short of what best practices would have counseled.

The Disney compensation committee met twice: on September 26 and October 16, 1995. The minutes of the September 26 meeting reflect that the committee approved the terms of the OEA (at that time embodied in the form of a letter agreement), except for the option grants, which were not approved until October 16—after the Disney stock incentive plan had been amended to provide for those options. At the September 26 meeting, the compensation committee considered a "term sheet" which, in summarizing the material terms of the OEA, relevantly disclosed that in the event of a non-fault termination, Ovitz would receive: (i) the present value of his salary ($1 million per year) for the balance of the contract term, (ii) the present value of his annual bonus payments (computed at $7.5 million) for the balance of the contract term, (iii) a $10 million termination fee, and (iv) the acceleration of his options for 3 million shares, which would become immediately exercisable at market price.

Thus, the compensation committee knew that in the event of an NFT, Ovitz's severance payment alone could be in the range of $40 million cash,[77] plus the value of the accelerated options. Because the actual payout to Ovitz was approximately $130 million, of which roughly $38.5 million was cash, the value of the options at the time of the NFT payout would have been about $91.5 million.[78] Thus, the issue may be framed as whether the compensation committee members knew, at the time they approved the OEA, that the value of the option component of the severance package could reach the $92 million order of magnitude if they terminated Ovitz without cause after one year. The evidentiary record shows that the committee members were so informed.

On this question the documentation is far less than what best practices would have dictated. There is no exhibit to the minutes that discloses, in a single document, the estimated value of the accelerated options in the event of an NFT termination after one year. The information imparted to the committee members on that subject is, however, supported by other evidence, most notably the trial testimony of various witnesses about spreadsheets that were prepared for the compensation committee meetings.

The compensation committee members derived their information about the potential magnitude of an NFT payout from two sources. The first was the value of the "benchmark" options previously granted to Eisner and Wells and the valuations by Watson of the proposed Ovitz options. Ovitz's options were set at 75% of parity with the options previously granted to Eisner and to Frank Wells. Because the compensation committee had established those earlier benchmark option grants to Eisner and Wells and were aware of their value, a simple

---

[77] The cash portion of the NFT payout after one year would be the sum of: (i) the present value of Ovitz's remaining salary over the life of the contract (4 years × $1 million/yr = $4 million, reduced to present value), plus (ii) the present value of his unpaid annual bonus payments ($7.5 million/yr × 4 years = $30 million, discounted to present value), plus (iii) $10 million cash for the second tranche of options. These amounts total $44 million before discounting the $34 million of annual salaries and bonuses to present value. The actual cash payment to Ovitz was $38.5 million, which, it would appear, reflects the then-present value of the $34 million of salaries and bonuses.

[78] Or, if it is assumed that the compensation committee would have estimated the cash portion of an NFT payout after one year at $40 million, then the value of the option portion would have been $90 million.

mathematical calculation would have informed them of the potential value range of Ovitz's options. Also, in August and September 1995, Watson and Russell met with Graef Crystal to determine (among other things) the value of the potential Ovitz options, assuming different scenarios. Crystal valued the options under the Black-Scholes method, while Watson used a different valuation metric. Watson recorded his calculations and the resulting values on a set of spreadsheets that reflected what option profits Ovitz might receive, based upon a range of different assumptions about stock market price increases. Those spreadsheets were shared with, and explained to, the committee members at the September meeting.

The committee's second source of information was the amount of "downside protection" that Ovitz was demanding. Ovitz required financial protection from the risk of leaving a very lucrative and secure position at CAA, of which he was a controlling partner, to join a publicly held corporation to which Ovitz was a stranger, and that had a very different culture and an environment which prevented him from completely controlling his destiny. The committee members knew that by leaving CAA and coming to Disney, Ovitz would be sacrificing "booked" CAA commissions of $150 to $200 million-an amount that Ovitz demanded as protection against the risk that his employment relationship with Disney might not work out. Ovitz wanted at least $50 million of that compensation to take the form of an "up-front" signing bonus. Had the $50 million bonus been paid, the size of the option grant would have been lower. Because it was contrary to Disney policy, the compensation committee rejected the up-front signing bonus demand, and elected instead to compensate Ovitz at the "back end," by awarding him options that would be phased in over the five-year term of the OEA.

It is on this record that the Chancellor found that the compensation committee was informed of the material facts relating to an NFT payout. If measured in terms of the documentation that would have been generated if "best practices" had been followed, that record leaves much to be desired. The Chancellor acknowledged that, and so do we. But, the Chancellor also found that despite its imperfections, the evidentiary record was sufficient to support the conclusion that the compensation committee had adequately informed itself of the potential magnitude of the entire severance package, including the options, that Ovitz would receive in the event of an early NFT.

The OEA was specifically structured to compensate Ovitz for walking away from $150 million to $200 million of anticipated commissions from CAA over the five-year OEA contract term. This meant that if Ovitz was terminated without cause, the earlier in the contract term the termination occurred the larger the severance amount would be to replace the lost commissions. Indeed, because Ovitz was terminated after only one year, the total amount of his severance payment (about $130 million) closely approximated the lower end of the range of Ovitz's forfeited commissions ($150 million), less the compensation Ovitz received during his first and only year as Disney's President. Accordingly, the Court of Chancery had a sufficient evidentiary basis in the record from which to find that, at the time they approved the OEA, the compensation committee members were adequately informed of the potential magnitude of an early NFT severance payout.

Exposing the lack of merit in appellants' core due care claim enables us to address more cogently (and expeditiously) the appellants' fragmented subsidiary arguments. First, the appellants argue that not all members of the compensation committee reviewed the then-existing draft of the OEA. The Chancellor properly found that that was not required, because in this case the compensation committee was informed of the substance of the OEA.

. . .

For these reasons, we uphold the Chancellor's determination that the compensation committee members did not breach their fiduciary duty of care in approving the OEA.

. . .

2. *The Good Faith Determinations*

The Court of Chancery held that the business judgment rule presumptions protected the decisions of the compensation committee and the remaining Disney directors, not only because they had acted with due care but also because they had not acted in bad faith. That latter ruling, the appellants claim, was reversible error because the Chancellor formulated and then applied an incorrect definition of bad faith.

In its Opinion the Court of Chancery defined bad faith as follows:

> Upon long and careful consideration, I am of the opinion that the concept of *intentional dereliction of duty,* a *conscious disregard for one's responsibilities,* is an appropriate (although not the only) standard for determining whether fiduciaries have acted in good faith. Deliberate indifference and inaction *in the face of a duty to act* is, in my mind, conduct that is clearly disloyal to the corporation. It is the epitome of faithless conduct.*

. . . This case . . . is one in which the duty to act in good faith has played a prominent role, yet to date is not a well-developed area of our corporate fiduciary law. . . . Because of the increased recognition of the importance of good faith, some conceptual guidance to the corporate community may be helpful. For that reason we proceed to address the merits of the appellants' . . . argument.

The precise question is whether the Chancellor's articulated standard for bad faith corporate fiduciary conduct—intentional

---

*   [Ed.: Emphasis in original.]

dereliction of duty, a conscious disregard for one's responsibilities—is legally correct. In approaching that question, we note that the Chancellor characterized that definition as *"an* appropriate *(although not the only)* standard for determining whether fiduciaries have acted in good faith."* That observation is accurate and helpful, because as a matter of simple logic, at least three different categories of fiduciary behavior are candidates for the "bad faith" pejorative label.

The first category involves so-called "subjective bad faith," that is, fiduciary conduct motivated by an actual intent to do harm. That such conduct constitutes classic, quintessential bad faith is a proposition so well accepted in the liturgy of fiduciary law that it borders on axiomatic. We need not dwell further on this category, because no such conduct is claimed to have occurred, or did occur, in this case.

The second category of conduct, which is at the opposite end of the spectrum, involves lack of due care—that is, fiduciary action taken solely by reason of gross negligence and without any malevolent intent. In this case, appellants assert claims of gross negligence to establish breaches not only of director due care but also of the directors' duty to act in good faith. Although the Chancellor found, and we agree, that the appellants failed to establish gross negligence, to afford guidance we address the issue of whether gross negligence (including a failure to inform one's self of available material facts), without more, can also constitute bad faith. The answer is clearly no.

From a broad philosophical standpoint, that question is more complex than would appear, if only because (as the Chancellor and others have observed) "issues of good faith are (to a certain degree) inseparably and necessarily intertwined with the duties of care and loyalty. . . ." But, in the pragmatic, conduct-regulating legal realm which calls for more precise conceptual line drawing, the answer is that grossly negligent conduct, without more, does not and cannot constitute a breach of the fiduciary duty to act in good faith. The conduct that is the subject of due care may overlap with the conduct that comes within the rubric of good faith in a psychological sense,[104] but from a legal standpoint those duties are and must remain quite distinct. Both our legislative history and our common law jurisprudence distinguish sharply between the duties to exercise due care and to act in good faith, and highly significant consequences flow from that distinction.

---

*   [Ed.: Emphasis in original.]

[104] An example of such overlap might be the hypothetical case where a director, because of subjective hostility to the corporation on whose board he serves, fails to inform himself of, or to devote sufficient attention to, the matters on which he is making decisions as a fiduciary. In such a case, two states of mind coexist in the same person: subjective bad intent (which would lead to a finding of bad faith) and gross negligence (which would lead to a finding of a breach of the duty of care). Although the coexistence of both states of mind may make them indistinguishable from a psychological standpoint, the fiduciary duties that they cause the director to violate-care and good faith-are legally separate and distinct.

The Delaware General Assembly has addressed the distinction between bad faith and a failure to exercise due care (*i.e.*, gross negligence) in two separate contexts. The first is Section 102(b)(7) of the DGCL, which authorizes Delaware corporations, by a provision in the certificate of incorporation, to exculpate their directors from monetary damage liability for a breach of the duty of care. That exculpatory provision affords significant protection to directors of Delaware corporations. The statute carves out several exceptions, however, including most relevantly, "for acts or omissions not in good faith. . . ." Thus, a corporation can exculpate its directors from monetary liability for a breach of the duty of care, but not for conduct that is not in good faith. To adopt a definition of bad faith that would cause a violation of the duty of care automatically to become an act or omission "not in good faith," would eviscerate the protections accorded to directors by the General Assembly's adoption of Section 102(b)(7).

A second legislative recognition of the distinction between fiduciary conduct that is grossly negligent and conduct that is not in good faith, is Delaware's indemnification statute, found at 8 *Del. C.* § 145. To oversimplify, subsections (a) and (b) of that statute permit a corporation to indemnify *(inter alia)* any person who is or was a director, officer, employee or agent of the corporation against expenses (including attorneys' fees), judgments, fines and amounts paid in settlement of specified actions, suits or proceedings, where (among other things): (i) that person is, was, or is threatened to be made a party to that action, suit or proceeding, and (ii) that person "acted in good faith and in a manner the person reasonably believed to be in or not opposed to the best interests of the corporation. . . ." Thus, under Delaware statutory law a director or officer of a corporation can be indemnified for liability (and litigation expenses) incurred by reason of a violation of the duty of care, but not for a violation of the duty to act in good faith.

Section 145, like Section 102(b)(7), evidences the intent of the Delaware General Assembly to afford significant protections to directors (and, in the case of Section 145, other fiduciaries) of Delaware corporations. To adopt a definition that conflates the duty of care with the duty to act in good faith by making a violation of the former an automatic violation of the latter, would nullify those legislative protections and defeat the General Assembly's intent. There is no basis in policy, precedent or common sense that would justify dismantling the distinction between gross negligence and bad faith.

That leaves the third category of fiduciary conduct, which falls in between the first two categories of (1) conduct motivated by subjective bad intent and (2) conduct resulting from gross negligence. This third category is what the Chancellor's definition of bad faith—intentional dereliction of duty, a conscious disregard for one's responsibilities—is intended to capture. The question is whether such misconduct is properly treated as a non-exculpable, nonindemnifiable violation of the fiduciary duty to act in good faith. In our view it must be, for at least two reasons.

First, the universe of fiduciary misconduct is not limited to either disloyalty in the classic sense (*i.e.,* preferring the adverse self-interest of the fiduciary or of a related person to the interest of the corporation) or gross negligence. Cases have arisen where corporate directors have no conflicting self-interest in a decision, yet engage in misconduct that is more culpable than simple inattention or failure to be informed of all facts material to the decision. To protect the interests of the corporation and its shareholders, fiduciary conduct of this kind, which does not involve disloyalty (as traditionally defined) but is qualitatively more culpable than gross negligence, should be proscribed. A vehicle is needed to address such violations doctrinally, and that doctrinal vehicle is the duty to act in good faith. . . .

Second, the legislature has also recognized this intermediate category of fiduciary misconduct, which ranks between conduct involving subjective bad faith and gross negligence. Section 102(b)(7)(ii) of the DGCL expressly denies money damage exculpation for "acts or omissions not in good faith or which involve intentional misconduct or a knowing violation of law." By its very terms that provision distinguishes between "intentional misconduct" and a "knowing violation of law" (both examples of subjective bad faith) on the one hand, and "acts . . . not in good faith," on the other. Because the statute exculpates directors only for conduct amounting to gross negligence, the statutory denial of exculpation for "acts . . . not in good faith" must encompass the intermediate category of misconduct captured by the Chancellor's definition of bad faith.

. . .

B. Claims Arising From The Payment Of The NFT Severance Payout To Ovitz

. . .

1. *Was Action By The New Board Required To Terminate Ovitz As The President of Disney?*

The Chancellor determined that although the board as constituted upon Ovitz's termination (the "new board") had the authority to terminate Ovitz, neither that board nor the compensation committee was required to act, because Eisner also had, and properly exercised, that authority. . . . Without such a duty to act, the new board's failure to vote on the termination could not give rise to a breach of the duty of care or the duty to act in good faith.

. . .

2. *In Concluding That Ovitz Could Not Be Terminated For Cause, Did Litvack or Eisner Breach Any Fiduciary Duty?*

It is undisputed that Litvack and Eisner (based on Litvack's advice) both concluded that if Ovitz was to be terminated, it could only be without cause, because no basis existed to terminate Ovitz for cause. . . .

With respect to Eisner, the Chancellor found that faced with a situation where he was unable to work well with Ovitz, who required close and constant supervision, Eisner had three options: 1) keep Ovitz as President and continue trying to make things work; 2) keep Ovitz at Disney, but in a role other than as President; or 3) terminate Ovitz. The first option was unacceptable, and the second would have entitled Ovitz to the NFT, or at the very least would have resulted in a costly lawsuit to determine whether Ovitz was so entitled. After an unsuccessful effort to "trade" Ovitz to Sony, that left only the third option, which was to terminate Ovitz and pay the NFT. The Chancellor found that in choosing this alternative, Eisner had breached no duty and had exercised his business judgment:

> . . . I conclude that Eisner's actions in connection with the termination are, for the most part, consistent with what is expected of a faithful fiduciary. Eisner unexpectedly found himself confronted with a situation that did not have an easy solution. He weighed the alternatives, received advice from counsel and then exercised his business judgment in the manner he thought best for the corporation. Eisner knew all the material information reasonably available when making the decision, he did not neglect an affirmative duty to act (or fail to cause the board to act) and he acted in what he believed were the best interests of the Company, taking into account the cost to the Company of the decision and the potential alternatives. Eisner was not personally interested in the transaction in any way that would make him incapable of exercising business judgment, and I conclude that the plaintiffs have not demonstrated by a preponderance of the evidence that Eisner breached his fiduciary duties or acted in bad faith in connection with Ovitz's termination and receipt of the NFT.

. . .

V. *THE WASTE CLAIM*

The appellants' final claim is that even if the approval of the OEA was protected by the business judgment rule presumptions, the payment of the severance amount to Ovitz constituted waste. This claim is rooted in the doctrine that a plaintiff who fails to rebut the business judgment rule presumptions is not entitled to any remedy unless the transaction constitutes waste. The Court of Chancery rejected the appellants' waste claim, and the appellants claim that in so doing the Court committed error.

To recover on a claim of corporate waste, the plaintiffs must shoulder the burden of proving that the exchange was "so one sided that no business person of ordinary, sound judgment could conclude that the corporation has received adequate consideration." A claim of waste will arise only in the rare, "unconscionable case where directors irrationally squander or give away corporate assets." This onerous standard for waste is a corollary of the proposition that where business judgment presumptions are applicable, the board's decision will be upheld unless it cannot be "attributed to any rational business purpose."

The claim that the payment of the NFT amount to Ovitz, without more, constituted waste is meritless on its face, because at the time the NFT amounts were paid, Disney was contractually obligated to pay them. The payment of a contractually obligated amount cannot constitute waste, unless the contractual obligation is itself wasteful. Accordingly, the proper focus of a waste analysis must be whether the amounts required to be paid in the event of an NFT were wasteful *ex ante*.

Appellants claim that the NFT provisions of the OEA were wasteful because they incentivized Ovitz to perform poorly in order to obtain payment of the NFT provisions. The Chancellor found that the record did not support that contention:

> [T]erminating Ovitz and paying the NFT did not constitute waste because he could not be terminated for cause and because many of the defendants gave credible testimony that the Company would be better off without Ovitz, meaning that would be impossible for me to conclude that the termination and receipt of NFT benefits result in "an exchange that is so one sided that no business person of ordinary, sound judgment could conclude that the corporation has received adequate consideration," or a situation where the defendants have "irrationally squandered or given away corporate assets." In other words, defendants did not commit waste.

That ruling is erroneous, the appellants argue, because the NFT provisions of the OEA were wasteful in their very design. Specifically, the OEA gave Ovitz every incentive to leave the Company before serving out the full term of his contract. The appellants urge that although the OEA may have induced Ovitz to join Disney as President, no contractual safeguards were in place to retain him in that position. In essence, appellants claim that the NFT provisions of the OEA created an irrational incentive for Ovitz to get himself fired.

That claim does not come close to satisfying the high hurdle required to establish waste. The approval of the NFT provisions in the OEA had a rational business purpose: to induce Ovitz to leave CAA, at what would otherwise be a considerable cost to him, in order to join Disney. The Chancellor found that the evidence does not support any notion that the OEA irrationally incentivized Ovitz to get himself fired. . . . Indeed, the Chancellor found that it was "patently unreasonable to assume that

Ovitz intended to perform just poorly enough to be fired quickly, but not so poorly that he could be terminated for cause."

We agree. Because the appellants have failed to show that the approval of the NFT terms of the OEA was not a rational business decision, their waste claim must fail.

VI. *CONCLUSION*

For the reasons stated above, the judgment of the Court of Chancery is affirmed.

NOTES AND QUESTIONS

1.	The court suggests that one rebuts the business judgment rule, inter alia, by showing that the defendants breached their duty if care. Your author has elsewhere argued that that is incorrect:

> Notice how the court puts the cart before the horse. Directors who violate their duty of care do not get the protections of the business judgment rule; indeed, the rule is rebutted by a showing that directors violated their fiduciary duty of "due care." This is exactly backwards. . . . Put another way, the whole point of the business judgment rule is to prevent courts from even asking the question: did the board breach its duty of care?[9]

In an earlier opinion in the Disney litigation, the Delaware Supreme Court took an approach closer to that of your author, in which the court explicitly rejected, as "foreign to the business judgment rule," the plaintiffs' argument that the rule could be rebutted by a showing that the directors failed to exercise "substantive due care."[10] The Court explained that it does "not measure, weigh or quantify directors' judgments. We do not even decide if they are reasonable in this context. Due care in the decision-making context is process due care only." Thus, directors' decisions will be respected by courts unless the directors are interested or lack independence relative to the decision, do not act in good faith, act in a manner that cannot be attributed to a rational business purpose or reach their decision by a grossly negligent process that includes the failure to consider all material facts reasonably available.

2.	Do you agree with the Court that it was rational for the Disney board (a) to have hired Ovitz on such generous terms and (b) to have fired him without cause despite triggering such a mammoth payout? As you consider that question, also consider whether the court is using the word "rational" in this content to mean "reasonable." If so, does that make sense. If not, why not?

3.	Is executive compensation sufficiently different from other business decisions made by the board of directors to justify courts reviewing

---

[9]	Stephen M. Bainbridge, The Business Judgment Rule as Abstention Doctrine, 57 Vand. L. Rev. 83, 94–95 (2004).

[10]	Brehm v. Eisner, 746 A.2d 244, 264 (Del. 2000).

the merits of the board's decision? If so, what should the standard of review be?

4. In *Steiner v. Meyerson*,[11] the Delaware Chancery Court explained that:

> Absent an allegation of fraud or conflict of interest courts will not review the substance of corporate contracts; the waste theory represents a theoretical exception to the statement very rarely encountered in the world of real transactions. There surely are cases of fraud; of unfair self-dealing and, much more rarely negligence. But rarest of all-and indeed, like Nessie, possibly non-existent-would be the case of disinterested business people making non-fraudulent deals (non-negligently) that meet the legal standard of waste!

Nessie made one of her rare appearances in *In re infoUSA*,[12] albeit in a case involving related party transactions rather than compensation as such:

> The list of related-party transactions relating to transportation alone makes for lengthy reading. Between 2001 and 2005, infoUSA paid approximately $8.2 million to Annapuma Corporation, an entity 100% owned by V. Gupta. These expenditures covered the use of private jets, the use of the American Princess yacht, and the use of a personal residence in California, as well as unidentified travel expenses. Vinod Gupta himself incurred much of the travel expenses, and Dolphin alleges that none of the documents provided in response to its § 220 request identified a business purpose for a substantial number of these payments. The log books of the American Princess yacht reveal little regarding the justification for these "business" expenses. Nor did defendants produce minutes or consents reflecting board approval of these substantial transactions as part of their response to Dolphin's § 220 request. Plaintiffs allege that many of these travel expenditures were either personal in nature or provided as gifts by Vinod Gupta to personal or political friends. . . .

> Plaintiffs succeed . . . in alleging a successful claim for waste. The amended consolidated complaint presents a series of related-party transactions and improper benefits allowed to flow to Vinod Gupta from a board that was dominated and controlled by him. Consider, for instance, the skybox at the University of Nebraska-Lincoln Football Stadium, acquired by infoUSA from Annapurna in 2003. The remaining lease on the skybox lasted twenty-one years, for which the company paid $617,000. The company's 2006 proxy statement states that Vinod Gupta originally paid $2 million for the skybox, and the amended consolidated complaint asserts that he received a $1.3 million charitable tax deduction on the purchase. The complaint alleges that the purchase price was based upon a $29,400 per year cost of twenty-eight tickets, and yet the value of

---

[11]   1995 WL 441999, at *5 (Del. Ch. July 19, 1995).
[12]   In re INFOUSA, Inc. Shareholders Litig., 953 A.2d 963 (Del. Ch. 2007).

these tickets was not discounted to a present value. Further, the purchase price did not reflect any amounts paid to Annapurna for use of the skybox in prior years. These allegations, if proven, suggest that a dominated board purchased permanent rights to a skybox that it was already leasing from its CEO, while conveniently forgetting to discount the value of tickets that mature at the same time that a baby born at the time of the transaction would be legally able to buy beer from a stadium vendor. A reasonable person might well consider this a sweetheart deal for Vinod Gupta, but would be hard pressed to find that the consideration was adequate.

Does *infoUSA* suggest that a waste claim can be proven simply by evidence of the extremity of the amounts in question? If so, does that holding square with the business judgment rule precedents discussed in note 1? In that regard, consider *Lewis v. Vogelstein*:[13]

> The judicial standard for determination of corporate waste is well developed. Roughly, a waste entails an exchange of corporate assets for consideration so disproportionately small as to lie beyond the range at which any reasonable person might be willing to trade. Most often the claim is associated with a transfer of corporate assets that serves no corporate purpose; or for which no consideration at all is received. Such a transfer is in effect a gift. If, however, there is any substantial consideration received by the corporation, and if there is a good faith judgment that in the circumstances the transaction is worthwhile, there should be no finding of waste, even if the fact finder would conclude ex post that the transaction was unreasonably risky. Any other rule would deter corporate boards from the optimal rational acceptance of risk . . . . Courts are ill-fitted to attempt to weigh the "adequacy" of consideration under the waste standard or, ex post, to judge appropriate degrees of business risk.

5.   In *Freedman v. Adams*,[14] plaintiff Susan Freedman—a shareholder of XTO Energy Inc. ("XTO")—sued the company and its board of directors over allegedly excessive compensation paid to Bob R. Simpson. As the court explained:

> In the years 2005 through 2007, XTO paid Simpson $97.5 million in non-tax-deductible cash bonus compensation. During the years 2004 through 2007, XTO paid other officers approximately $23.5 million in non-tax-deductible cash bonus compensation. Assuming a corporate tax rate of 35%, the non-tax-deductible bonuses paid to Simpson and the other officers resulted in lost tax benefits of approximately $40 million.

> Generally, under § 162(m), compensation in excess of $1 million paid to the CEO and the other four highest-paid officers of a public company (together with the CEO, the "Covered Officers")

---

[13]   699 A.2d 327, 336 (Del. Ch. 1997).
[14]   2012 WL 1345638 (Del. Ch. Mar. 30, 2012).

is not tax-deductible. But, § 162(m) includes an exception for "[o]ther performance-based compensation." To be eligible for this exception, compensation must be: (1) paid solely on account of the attainment of one or more performance goals determined by a compensation committee comprised solely of two or more outside directors; (2) the material terms of the plan must be disclosed to shareholders and approved by a majority in a separate shareholder vote before the payment of such compensation; and (3) before payment, the compensation committee must certify that the performance goals were satisfied (a "§ 162(m) plan"). Cash bonuses paid to XTO's Covered Officers were not tax-deductible because they were not paid under a § 162(m) plan. When the Complaint was filed, XTO had not proposed a § 162(m) plan to its shareholders.

The Board was aware that the cash bonuses paid to the Covered Officers were not tax-deductible. In fact, XTO's proxy statements for the years 2004 through 2008 (the "contested proxy statements") each included a disclosure substantially similar to the following:

> Section 162(m) of the Internal Revenue Code generally limits the corporate tax deduction for annual compensation paid to certain of our executive officers named in the summary compensation table to $1,000,000, unless the compensation satisfies the requirements for performance-based compensation. Stock options granted under the company's [1998 or 2004] stock incentive plan have generally been entitled to the full tax deductions available because the compensation has qualified as performance-based and, therefore, not applied against the $1,000,000 limit. Base salary and cash bonuses have not been performance-based for purposes of Section 162(m) and, therefore, were not fully deductible by the company. While the compensation committee monitors compensation paid to our named executive officers in light of the provisions of Section 162(m), the committee does not believe that compensation decisions should be constrained necessarily by how much compensation is deductible for federal income tax purposes, and the committee is not limited to paying compensation under plans that are qualified under Section 162(m). During [the year in question], compensation paid to covered named executive officers exceeded the maximum deductible amount.

The company and board claim that their decision is protected by the business judgment rule. Are they correct?

6. What standard of review applies if the CEO is also a controlling shareholder? In *Tornetta v. Musk*,[15] the Delaware Chancery Court provided guidance on how to structure conflict of interest transactions to which a corporation's controlling shareholder is a party, with direct application to

---

[15] 2019 WL 4566943 (Del. Ch. Sept. 20, 2019).

compensation issues. The case involves a shareholder lawsuit challenging an incentive compensation plan granted to Tesla, Inc.'s CEO, Elon Musk. The plan laid out twelve tranches of stock options to be awarded over a ten-year period. In order for Musk to receive each tranche, Tesla had to achieve specified milestones in market capitalization and operating results. According to the Plaintiff, the fair present value f the award was either $2.6 or $3.7 billion, which allegedly dwarfed CEO compensation at tesla's peer companies by orders of magnitude.

The compensation plan was approved by Tesla's board of directors and by its disinterested shareholders. Seventy three percent the disinterested shares represented in person or by proxy at the stockholder meeting during which the plan was approved voted in favor of the plan. They represented 47% of the total number of outstanding disinterested shares.

In his opinion, Vice Chancellor Joseph Slights acknowledged that Delaware courts normally approach boards' executive compensation decisions with a high degree of deference. Critically, however, Musk is not just Tesla's CEO but also its controlling shareholder.[16] A controlling shareholder has been analogized to the proverbial 800-pound gorilla,[17] which gives rise to "an obvious fear that even putatively independent directors may owe or feel a more-than-wholesome allegiance to the interests of the controller, rather than to the corporation and its public stockholders."[18]

In response to that risk, Delaware law imposes a more intrusive standard of review on conflicted controller transactions than on ordinary business decisions. In the latter, the standard of review is the business judgment rule; in the former, however, the burden of proof shifts to the conflicted controller to show that the transaction was fair to the corporation and its minority shareholders. In *Kahn v. Lynch Communications Systems, Inc.*,[19] for example, the Delaware Supreme Court reaffirmed that the "exclusive standard of judicial review in examining the propriety of an interested cash-out merger transaction by a controlling or dominating shareholder is entire fairness." Having said that, however, the *Kahn* court further held that "approval of the transaction by an independent committee of directors or an informed majority of minority shareholders shifts the burden of proof on the issue of fairness from the controlling or dominating shareholder to the challenging shareholder-plaintiff."

The *Kahn* court's description of fairness as the "exclusive" standard of review seemed to preclude invoking the business judgment rule in conflicted controller transactions. In its 2014 decision in *Kahn v. M & F Worldwide Corp.*,[20] however, the Delaware Supreme Court held that "when a controlling

---

[16]   In an earlier decision involving Tesla, Vice Chancellor Slights had determined that Musk was Tesla's controlling shareholder despite owning only 22% of Tesla's voting stock. See In re Tesla Motors, Inc. Stockholder Litig., 2018 WL 1560293 (Del. Ch. Mar. 28, 2018), *appeal refused sub nom.* Musk v. Arkansas Teacher Ret. System, 184 A.3d 1292 (Del. 2018)

[17]   In re Pure Resources, Inc. S'holders Litig., 808 A.2d 421, 436 (Del. Ch. 2002).

[18]   Leo E. Strine, Jr., *The Delaware Way: How We Do Corporate Law and Some of the New Challenges We (and Europe) Face*, 30 Del. J. Corp. L. 673, 678 (2005).

[19]   638 A.2d 1110, 1117 (Del. 1994).

[20]   88 A.3d 635 (Del. 2014).

stockholder merger has, from the time of the controller's first overture, been subject to (i) negotiation and approval by a special committee of independent directors fully empowered to say no, and (ii) approval by an uncoerced, fully informed vote of a majority of the minority investors" the standard of review becomes the business judgment rule.[21]

In *Tornetta*, the Tesla defendants argued that *MFW* was irrelevant to the facts of this case:

> They rely heavily on a "statutory rubric" argument, claiming *MFW*'s dual protections, devised in the context of a squeeze-out merger, mimic the approvals required by 8 Del C. § 251 but have no practical application to transactions where our law does not mandate approval at both the board and stockholder levels. . . . I do agree with Defendants that nothing in *MFW* or its progeny would suggest the Supreme Court intended to extend the holding to other transactions involving controlling stockholders.[22]

Vice Chancellor Slights, however, observed that the risk of coercion is just as present when a conflicted controller enters into a compensation arrangement as when it proposes a freezeout merger:

> Indeed, in the CEO compensation context, the minority knows full well the CEO is staying with the company whether vel non his compensation plan is approved. As our Supreme Court observed in *Tremont II*:

>> [I]n a transaction such as the one considered . . . the controlling shareholder will continue to dominate the company regardless of the outcome of the transaction. The risk is thus created that those who pass upon the propriety of the transaction might perceive that disapproval may result in retaliation by the controlling shareholder.

> These words apply with equal force to the compensation setting.[23]

Accordingly, in order for a conflicted controller transaction to be reviewed under the business judgment rule rather than entire fairness, the transaction must receive both of *MFW*'s dual protections.

On the facts before it, the Vice Chancellor—for purposes of defendants' motion to dismiss—concluded that:

> I have determined on the pleadings that Defendants have satisfied the "majority of the minority" condition but have not

---

[21] As the Supreme Court summarized its holding:

[T]he business judgment standard of review will be applied if and only if: (i) the controller conditions the procession of the transaction on the approval of both a Special Committee and a majority of the minority stockholders; (ii) the Special Committee is independent; (iii) the Special Committee is empowered to freely select its own advisors and to say no definitively; (iv) the Special Committee meets its duty of care in negotiating a fair price; (v) the vote of the minority is informed; and (vi) there is no coercion of the minority.

Id. at 645.

[22] *Tornetta*, 2019 WL 4566943 at *13.

[23] *Id.* at *11–12.

satisfied the "fully functioning, independent special committee" condition. The burden of persuasion shifts to Plaintiff, therefore, to demonstrate the Award is not entirely fair. At this stage, the bar set for Plaintiff is to demonstrate from well-pled facts that it is reasonably conceivable the Award is unfair to Tesla. [H]e has cleared the bar, albeit just barely.[24]

The Vice Chancellor's conclusion that the "majority of the minority" vote requirement was satisfied required him to distinguish then Chancellor (and now Chief Justice) Leo Strine's decision in *In re PNB Holding Co. Shareholders Litigation*.[25] In that case, plaintiff shareholders had challenged a freezeout merger with a controlling shareholder. In that context, Strine held that approval of a conflicted interest transaction by a "majority of the minority" means approval by a majority of the outstanding disinterested shares not just a majority of those present and voting:

> The cleansing effect of ratification depends on the intuition that when most of the affected minority affirmatively approves the transaction, their self-interested decision to approve is sufficient proof of fairness to obviate a judicial examination of that question. I do not believe that the same confidence flows when the transaction simply garners more votes in favor than votes against, or abstentions from, the merger from the minority who actually vote. That position requires an untenable assumption that those who did not return a proxy were members of a "silent affirmative majority of the minority." That is especially so in the merger context when a refusal to return a proxy (if informedly made) is more likely a passive dissent. Why? Because under 8 Del. C. § 251, a vote of a "majority of the outstanding stock of the corporation entitled to vote" is required for merger approval, and a failure to cast a ballot is a de facto no vote. Therefore, giving ratification effect only if a majority of the disinterested shares outstanding were cast in favor of the transaction also coheres with § 251. [FN74]

>   FN74.   I need not, and do not, hold that a qualifying ratification vote always needs to track the percentage approval required for the underlying transaction. One can posit a situation when a particular type of transaction requires, by charter, a 66.67% supermajority vote, and a conflicted stockholder holds 40% of the total vote, with the rest of the votes held by disinterested stockholders. To promote fair treatment, the board makes approval subject to a majority of the minority vote condition. Nothing in this opinion suggests that ratification effect would not be given if an informed majority of the minority of the remaining 60% of the electorate voted in favor of the transaction.[26]

As Vice Chancellor Slights observed, however, DGCL § 251 required that the freezeout merger at issue in *PNB*—like all mergers—be approved

---

[24]   *Id.* at *14.

[25]   2006 WL 2403999 (Del. Ch. 2006).

[26]   *Id.* at *15.

by a majority of the outstanding shares. In contrast, under DGCL § 216(2) ordinary matters only require the affirmative vote of a majority of the shareholders present at the meeting. Accordingly, the court limited *PNB*'s definition of the majority of the minority to cases in which the statute requires approval by a majority of the outstanding shares.

This aspect of the Vice Chancellor's decision is less well supported than the remainder of his analysis. First, neither § 216 nor § 251 expressly applies to conflicted controller transactions. Those statutes speak to the basic vote required to authorize corporate action not to the vote required to insulate a conflict of interest transaction from judicial review for fairness. Second, a close reading of Strine's decision shows that he saw § 251 as strengthening the underlying argument for requiring approval by a majority of the disinterested shares rather than just a majority of the disinterested shares present at the meeting.

Overall, however, Vice Chancellor Slight's opinion is a well-reasoned and persuasive extension of the trend in Delaware law towards judicial deference to corporate actions that benefited from procedural safeguards designed to ensure that the pertinent decision makers are free from coercion by a conflicted controller. It strengthens the argument that *MFW* is not limited to freezeout mergers, but rather now provides a roadmap by which all conflicted controller transactions can receive the protections of the business judgment rule.

Ryan v. Gifford

918 A.2d 341 (Del. Ch. 2007)

On March 18, 2006, The Wall Street Journal sparked controversy throughout the investment community by publishing a one-page article, based on an academic's statistical analysis of option grants, which revealed an arguably questionable compensation practice. Commonly known as backdating, this practice involves a company issuing stock options to an executive on one date while providing fraudulent documentation asserting that the options were actually issued earlier. These options may provide a windfall for executives because the falsely dated stock option grants often coincide with market lows. Such timing reduces the strike prices and inflates the value of stock options, thereby increasing management compensation. This practice allegedly violates any stock option plan that requires strike prices to be no less than the fair market value on the date on which the option is granted by the board. Further, this practice runs afoul of many state and federal common and statutory laws that prohibit dissemination of false and misleading information.

. . .

I.   FACTS

Maxim Integrated Products, Inc. is a technology leader in design, development, and manufacture of linear and mixed-signal integrated circuits used in microprocessor-based electronic equipment. From 1998 to mid-2002 Maxim's board of directors and compensation committee granted stock options for the purchase of millions of shares of Maxim's common stock to John F. Gifford, founder, chairman of the board, and chief executive officer, pursuant to shareholder-approved stock option plans filed with the Securities and Exchange Commission. Under the terms of these plans, Maxim contracted and represented that the exercise price of all stock options granted would be no less than the fair market value of the company's common stock, measured by the publicly traded closing price for Maxim stock on the date of the grant. Additionally, the plan identified the board or a committee designated by the board as administrators of its terms.

[Plaintiff] Ryan is a shareholder of Maxim and . . . filed this derivative action on June 2, 2006, against Gifford; James Bergman, B. Kipling Hagopian, and A.R. Frank Wazzan, members of the board and compensation committee at all relevant times; Eric Karros, member of the board from 2000 to 2002, and M.D. Sampels, member of the board from 2001–2002. Ryan alleges that nine specific grants were backdated between 1998 and 2002, as these grants seem too fortuitously timed to be explained as simple coincidence. All nine grants were dated on unusually low (if not the lowest) trading days of the years in question, or on days immediately before sharp increases in the market price of the company.

. . .

II. CONTENTIONS

Plaintiff contends that . . . Maxim received lower payments upon exercise of the options than would have been received had they not been backdated. Further, Maxim suffers adverse effects from tax and accounting rules. The options priced below the stock's fair market value on the date of the grant allegedly bring the recipient an instant paper gain. At the time, such compensation had to be treated as a cost to the company, thereby reducing reported earnings and resulting in overstated profits. This likely necessitates revision of the company's financial statements and tax reporting. Moreover, Gifford, the recipient of the backdated options, is allegedly unjustly enriched due to receipt of compensation in clear violation of the shareholder-approved plans.

. . .

IV. MOTION TO DISMISS

. . . Plaintiff supports his claim that backdating occurred by pointing to nine option grants over a six-year period where each option was granted during a low point. That is, every challenged option grant occurred during the lowest market price of the month or year in which it was granted. In addition to pointing specifically to highly suspicious timing, plaintiff further supports his allegations with empirical evidence suggesting that backdating occurred. . . . Maxim's average annualized return of 243% on option grants to management was almost ten times higher than the 29% annualized market returns in the same period. This timing, by my judgment and by support of empirical data, seems too fortuitous to be mere coincidence. The appearance of impropriety grows even more when one considers the fact that the board granted options, not at set or designated times, but by a sporadic method.

Plaintiff supports his breach of fiduciary duty claim and his assertion that demand is futile by pointing to the board's decision to ignore limitations set out in the company's stock options plans. The plans do not grant the board discretion to alter the exercise price by falsifying the date on which options were granted. Thus, the alleged facts suggest that the director defendants violated an express provision of two option plans and exceeded the shareholders' grant of express authority.

. . . The business affairs of a corporation are to be managed by or under the direction of its board of directors. In an effort to encourage the full exercise of managerial powers, Delaware law protects the managers of a corporation through the business judgment rule. This rule "is a presumption that in making a business decision the directors of a corporation acted on an informed basis, in good faith and in the honest belief that the action taken was in the best interest of the company."[44] Nevertheless, a showing that the board breached either its fiduciary duty of due care or its fiduciary duty of loyalty in connection with a challenged transaction may rebut this presumption. Such a breach may be shown where the board acts intentionally, in bad faith, or for personal gain.

In *Stone v. Ritter*, the Supreme Court of Delaware held that acts taken in bad faith breach the duty of loyalty.[46] Bad faith, the Court stated, may be shown where "the fiduciary intentionally acts with a purpose other than that of advancing the best interests of the corporation, where the fiduciary acts with the intent to violate applicable positive law, or where the fiduciary intentionally fails to act in the face of known duty to act, demonstrating a conscious disregard for his duties."[47] Additionally, other examples of bad faith might exist. These examples include any action that demonstrates a faithlessness or lack of true devotion to the interests of the corporation and its shareholders.

. . . I am convinced that the intentional violation of a shareholder approved stock option plan, coupled with fraudulent disclosures regarding the directors' purported compliance with that plan, constitute conduct that is disloyal to the corporation and is therefore an act in bad faith. Plaintiffs allege the following conduct: Maxim's directors affirmatively represented to Maxim's shareholders that the exercise price of any option grant would be no less than 100% of the fair value of the shares, measured by the market price of the shares on the date the option

[44]   [Aronson v. Lewis, 473 A.2d 805, 812 (Del.1984).]

[46]   911 A.2d 362, 370 (Del.2006).

[47]   Id. at 369.

is granted. Maxim shareholders, possessing an absolute right to rely on those assurances when determining whether to approve the plans, in fact relied upon those representations and approved the plans. Thereafter, Maxim's directors are alleged to have deliberately attempted to circumvent their duty to price the shares at no less than market value on the option grant dates by surreptitiously changing the dates on which the options were granted. To make matters worse, the directors allegedly failed to disclose this conduct to their shareholders, instead making false representations regarding the option dates in many of their public disclosures.

I am unable to fathom a situation where the deliberate violation of a shareholder approved stock option plan and false disclosures, obviously intended to mislead shareholders into thinking that the directors complied honestly with the shareholder-approved option plan, is anything but an act of bad faith. It certainly cannot be said to amount to faithful and devoted conduct of a loyal fiduciary. Well-pleaded allegations of such conduct are sufficient, in my opinion, to rebut the business judgment rule and to survive a motion to dismiss.[49]

. . .

Finally, defendants contend that plaintiff's claim for unjust enrichment fails because there is no allegation that Gifford exercised any of the alleged backdated options and, therefore, Gifford did not obtain any benefit to which he was not entitled to the detriment of another. This defense is contrary both to the normal concept of remuneration and to common sense.

Unjust enrichment is "the unjust retention of a benefit to the loss of another, or the retention of money or property of another against the fundamental principles of justice or equity and good conscience."[61] A defendant may be liable "even when the defendant retaining the benefit is not a wrongdoer" and "even though he may have received [it] honestly in the first instance."[62]

At this stage, I cannot conclude that there is no reasonably conceivable set of circumstances under which Gifford might be unjustly

---

[49] I pause here to note the procedural posture of this case. This opinion addresses a motion to dismiss. Thus, neither party has had the benefit of any discovery. At this stage, plaintiffs are afforded certain presumptions of truth. Because of these presumptions, plaintiff may survive a motion to dismiss where the complaint relies on empirical data to support claims of: 1) specific instances of backdating; 2) violations of shareholder-approved plans or some other legal obligation; and 3) fraudulent disclosures regarding compliance with that plan. If, however, this case reaches the trial stage, plaintiff may no longer rely on liberal pleading assumptions. Instead, plaintiff must then rely on evidence presented at trial to demonstrate by a preponderance of the evidence that the defendants in fact backdated options, and thus are not afforded the protections of the business judgment rule. Even at that point, directors may still prevail by meeting the hefty burden of proving that the challenged transactions were entirely fair to the corporation and its shareholders. See, e.g., In re Walt Disney Co. Derivative Litig., 907 A.2d 693, 755–58 (Del.Ch.2005).

[61] Schock v. Nash, 732 A.2d 217, 232–33 (Del.1999).

[62] Id.

enriched. Gifford does retain something of value, the alleged backdated options, at the expense of the corporation and shareholders. Further, defendants make no allegations that Gifford is precluded from exercising these options or that the options have expired. Thus, one can imagine a situation where Gifford exercises the options and benefits from the low exercise price. Even if Gifford fails to exercise a single option during the course of this litigation, that fact would not justify dismissal of the unjust enrichment claim. Whether or not the options are exercised, the Court will be able to fashion a remedy. For example, this Court might rely on expert testimony to determine the true value of the option grants or simply rescind them. Either way, Gifford's alleged failure to exercise the options up to this point does not undermine a claim for unjust enrichment. Thus, I deny the motion to dismiss the unjust enrichment claim.

NOTES AND QUESTIONS

1. Is backdating an option necessarily contrary to shareholder interests?

2. A practice closely related to backdating options is spring loading options. In the latter case, the issuer grants stock options to employees concurrently with releasing good news expected to increase the stock price:

> An informative example of springloading is Cyberonics. On June 15, 2004, Cyberonics received news that an advisory panel had recommended that the Food and Drug Administration (FDA) approve Cyberonics's nerve stimulator device for the treatment of depression. Later that day, the Cyberonics board approved stock options with an exercise price of $19.58 (the closing stock price on the previous day) for three executives. The Cyberonics stock price gained with the news of the FDA panel recommendation and closed on June 16 at $34.81. The difference in the exercise price and the stock price gave the CEO an instant "paper profit" of $2.3 million. Stock market analysts alleged that the options allowed the executives to profit from nonpublic information of the FDA panel recommendation before investors had any opportunity to trade, while also avoiding reporting the options as a compensation expense since Cyberonics technically issued the options at market price.[27]

Does spring loading harm shareholders? Would a board decision to issue spring loaded options be protected by the business judgment rule?

3. Would an employee who received stock options without knowing they were backdated or that the firm had not properly accounted for the options be unjustly enriched?

---

[27] William Hughes, Stock Option "Springloading": An Examination of Loaded Justifications and New SEC Disclosure Rules, 33 J. Corp. L. 777, 784 (2008).

4.   Does either the grant or exercise of springloaded options constitute insider trading?

PROBLEMS

1.   To celebrate the fact that Serenity Corporation has been added to the Dow Jones Industrial Average (DJIA), the board of directors of Serenity Corporation adopted a "market bonus plan" under Serenity's CEO and CFO will receive an annual cash bonus based solely on the extent to which the DJIA increases during the prior year. If the DJIA goes up by 10% over a calendar year, for example, the CEO and CFO will get a bonus equal to 10% of their base salary. The plan was designed and proposed by Serenity's compensation committee, which is comprised solely of independent directors. Although the CEO is a member of the board, she recused herself from all board discussions of the bonus plan. A shareholder has sued, alleging that the board has breached its duty of care, acted in bad faith, and committed waste. Evaluate the merits of those claims.

> **FYI**
>
> The DJIA is a price-weighted index of 30 stocks representing a broad basket of major corporations in a wide variety of industries, ranging from consumer finance to manufacturing.

2.   The CEO of Firefly, Inc., recently asked the board of directors to amend his employment agreement to provide for an annual cost-of-living raise pursuant to which the CEO's base salary will increase annually by the percentage increase for the preceding year in the U.S. government's consumer price index. Firefly's compensation committee, which is comprised exclusively of independent members of the board and was advised by independent tax counsel and an independent compensation consultant, carefully considered all information relevant to the request and recommended that the board of directors approve the request, subject to a proviso that the CEO's nonperformance-based compensation should remain under the $1 million limit imposed by Internal Revenue Code § 162(m). After due consideration and acting upon the basis of the committee's recommendation and the information provided by the committee, the board unanimously agreed to the request, subject to the committee's proviso, and the contract was duly amended. A shareholder has sued, alleging that the CEO and the board have each breached their duty of care, acted in bad faith, and committed waste. Evaluate the merits of those claims.

A.   Should the board of directors have conducted its own inquiry into the underlying facts rather than relying on the report of the compensation committee?

B.   What effect would it have on your analysis, if any, if the proviso had not been included in the agreement, such that the CEO's nonperformance-based compensation could eventually exceed the $1 million limit imposed by Internal Revenue Code § 162(m).

C.   What effect would it have on your analysis, if any, if the CEO were a board member and she had participated in the board discussions of the proposal and had voted in favor of the proposal in her capacity as a board member?

D.   What effect would it have on your analysis, if any, if the board had delegated to the committee sole responsibility for making compensation decisions and that the decision therefore had been made by the committee rather than the entire board?

3.   When Simon Reynolds was in the process of being hired as CEO of Tam Industrials, Inc., he negotiated a prospective employment agreement with the board of directors providing that Reynolds "shall be responsible for the general management of the affairs of the company . . .," and that Reynolds "shall report to the Board." The employment agreement runs until the earlier of seven years from the date it is first signed by the parties, Reynolds' 75th birthday, or his termination (1) by reason of death or disability; (2) for cause; or (3) without cause. Under the employment agreement, Reynolds can declare a "Constructive Termination Without Cause" by the company of his employment as a result of, inter alia, "unreasonable interference, in the good-faith judgment of Reynolds, by the Board or a substantial stockholder of the company, in Reynolds' carrying out his duties and responsibilities" under the employment agreement. A Constructive Termination Without Cause takes effect after delivery of notice by Reynolds and the failure by the Board to remedy such interference. In the event of a Termination Without Cause, constructive or otherwise, Reynolds would be entitled to the following:

- Continued payment of his "Base Salary" at the level in effect immediately prior to termination for the remainder of his "Term of Employment," which, as stated, will be 6 ½ years unless Donald dies or turns 75 first. The agreement provided for Reynolds' Base Salary to be $650,000.

- Annual incentive awards for the remainder of the Term of Employment equal to the average of the three most recent annual cash bonuses awarded to Reynolds, or to the annual bonus for the preceding year if he was terminated in the first two years of the agreement.

- Medical benefits for Reynolds and his wife for life, as well as his children until the age of 23.

- Continued participation in all employee benefit plans in which Reynolds is participating on the date of termination until the earlier of the expiration of the Term of Employment or the date on which he receives equivalent benefits from a subsequent employer.

The agreement was signed by the parties. Reynolds joined Tam as CEO. Five years later (at which time Reynolds was 66 years old), Reynolds declared a Constructive Termination Without Cause. The board and Reynolds were unable to reach agreement on a cure for the alleged interference and Reynolds sued to enforce the agreement. The incumbent board members (the New Board) claims that the board members who approved the agreement when Reynolds was hired (the Old Board) breached their duty of care, acted in bad faith, and committed in approving the contract. Accordingly, they argued that the employment agreement was void as against public policy. Evaluate their claims. Also evaluate whether there are any other corporate law claims that might be laid against the contract.

4. Federal Alliance, Inc., is a publicly traded logistics corporation that is deep financial trouble. It is barely able to pay its debts as they come due in the ordinary course of business, has total shareholder equity of less than $10,000, and on June 30 had a current stock price of $0.10 per share. Its creditors are increasingly agitating for the company to enter bankruptcy reorganization proceedings. Zoey Allen is a nationally recognized turnaround expert who has successfully rescued three other logistics and transportation corporations from the brink of bankruptcy and turned each of the three into highly profitable enterprises. One of Federal's largest creditors recommended that Federal hire Allen, calling her "the best in the business and your only hope." On June 1, rumors began circling the stock market that Federal and Allen were negotiating for her to join federal as CEO. A prominent television business analyst called these rumors "the best news to come out of Federal in a decade." By close of trading on June 1, Federal's stock price had risen to $0.50 per share. On June 2, Allen and Federal signed an employment contract. The contract provided that Allen was to receive immediately vesting options to buy 1,000,000 shares of Federal stock with a strike price equal to the price as of the close of trading on the date the contract was executed. Although the contract had been neither orally agreed nor executed in writing until late in the day on June 2, Allen insisted—as a condition of her employment—that the contract be dated June 30. Federal's board of directors was advised by independent legal counsel, independent accountants, and an independent compensation consultant, all of whom advised the board that backdating the contract was "at best unethical and probably illegal." Believing Allen's repeated statements that she would not take the job without the contract being backdated to June 30 and believing that she offered a unique solution, however, a majority of the board voted to approve the contract with a June 30 date. One board member dissented, arguing that "I agree that the choice is between lying and going bankrupt, but I argue for financial bankruptcy rather than moral bankruptcy." When the contract was announced before the opening of trading on June 3 (without revealing the backdating), Federal's stock price jumped to $0.60 per share. Allen immediately exercised her federal stock options, netting a profit of $500,000. When the dissenting board member went public with the fact that the contract had been backdated, the stock price was unaffected. A shareholder has sued, alleging that the Allen and the board have each breached their duty of care, acted in bad faith, and committed waste. Evaluate the merits of those claims.

A. Would your analysis change either if (a) Allen successfully turned Federal around, making it highly profitable and an industry leader or (b) Allen was unable to turn Federal around and it entered bankruptcy a year after hiring her?

D. FEDERAL LAW

1) DISCLOSURE RULES

Federal rules now require extensive disclosures of executive compensation. The bulk of these disclosures are to be made in the issuer's annual proxy statement.

Leigh Johnson et. al., Preparing Proxy Statements Under the SEC's New Rules Regarding Executive and Director Compensation Disclosures
7 U.C. Davis Bus. L.J. 373 (2007)[28]

. . .

III. NEW STANDARDS FOR TABULAR AND NARRATIVE DISCLOSURE OF EXECUTIVE AND DIRECTOR COMPENSATION

A. General

1. Plain English Disclosure

As a starting point, the Rules generally require companies to disclose executive and director compensation and beneficial ownership in plain English. The following standards will help companies incorporate plain English principles: (i) use clear, concise sections, paragraphs and short sentences; (ii) use definite, everyday words and active voice; (iii) avoid multiple negatives, legal jargon, highly technical terminology, glossaries and defined terms; (iv) use descriptive headings and subheadings; (v) use tabular presentation or bullet lists for complex material. Companies should avoid legalistic, overly complex and "boilerplate" disclosures.

2. Officers Covered

The Rules require more extensive tabular presentations of executive compensation and improved narrative disclosure for certain officers. These officers include the principal executive officer, the principal financial officer and the three other most highly compensated executive officers[31] if the individual's total compensation for the last fiscal year

---

[28] Reprinted by permission of the authors and the University of California Davis Business Law Journal.

[31] An "executive officer" includes the registrant's "president, any vice president of the registrant in charge of a principal business unit, division or function (such as sales, administration or finance), any other officer who performs a policy making function or any other person who performs similar policy making functions for the registrant." 17 C.F.R. § 240.3b–7 (2006); 17 C.F.R. § 230.405 (2006). When executive officers of subsidiaries of the registrant

exceeded $100,000 ("Named Executive Officers").[32] Companies also must disclose compensation for up to two additional individuals if they were serving as executive officers at the end of the last completed fiscal year but are no longer executive officers, and if disclosure would be required for them if they still held their former positions. . . .

    3.   Suggestions for Compliance/Examples

   . . .

    b.   Officers Covered

Determining the individuals whose compensation the company must disclose in the proxy statement requires some internal legwork. While the CEO and CFO are readily identifiable, the three other highest-paid executive officers and potential highly paid Non-Executive Employees are harder to determine. Companies will need to calculate the total compensation for each executive officer who could be among the three highest-paid executive officers. These calculations are more complex than those performed in the past because companies now need to quantify all elements of compensation.

   B.   Compensation Discussion and Analysis

    1.   The Rules

Under the Rules, disclosure begins with a new narrative overview, entitled Compensation Discussion and Analysis ("CD&A"). The CD&A is designed to explain the material factors underlying compensation policies and decisions according to data presented in the compensation tables. This discussion includes: (i) an examination of such items as the company's compensation objectives and what a compensation program is designed to reward, (ii) an identification of each element of compensation and (iii) an explanation of why the company chose to pay an element, how the company determined the amount for such element, and how the company's decisions regarding the element fit into the company's overall compensation objectives.[43]

---

perform policy making functions for the registrant they also may be executive officers of the registrant. 17 C.F.R. § 240.3b–7 (2006); 17 C.F.R. § 230.405 (2006).

   [32]   Executive Compensation and Related Party Disclosure, 71 Fed. Reg. at 53,189–53,190. Specific disclosure regarding the principal financial officer, regardless of his level of compensation, is a change from previous requirements. See 17 C.F.R. § 229.402(a)(3) (2006). The $100,000 threshold is not a change from previous requirements; however, this threshold was primarily based on an executive's salary and bonus prior to the adoption of the Rules and now is based on total executive compensation reduced by the sum of the increase in pension values and nonqualified deferred compensation above-market or preferential earnings. See 17 C.F.R. § 229.402(a)(3)(2006); Executive Compensation and Related Party Disclosure, 71 Fed. Reg. at 53,190. This change in calculation may make it harder to identify the Named Executive Officers due to severance payments or other benefits that may make a person a Named Executive Officer even if such executive's salary and bonus would not put the executive in the top five compensated executives.

   [43]   Executive Compensation and Related Party Disclosure, 71 Fed. Reg. at 53,164. These factors provide guidance regarding the CD&A, but the factors are not an exhaustive list. Companies should view this list only as a starting point for disclosure. See Your Upcoming Proxy Disclosures—What You Need to Do Now (CompensationStandards.com webcast Jan. 31, 2006). In support of the new requirement, the SEC notes that certain commentators argue that a

The CD&A discussion covers all forms of compensation paid to Named Executive Officers. Boilerplate disclosure will not suffice.[45] The CD&A must address both in-service and post-termination compensation arrangements. Where appropriate, it also must discuss (among other things) policies regarding long-term, cash and equity compensation, the effect of prior compensation on decisions regarding various elements of compensation, the use of benchmarking, and the role of executive officers in the compensation-decision process. Further, in response to the recent controversies surrounding stock option backdating, companies must address policies related to the timing of option grants and the determination of exercise prices in the CD&A.[48] The Rules consider the CD&A "filed" with the SEC. This makes the CD&A subject to the liability provisions of the Exchange Act and covered by the CEO and CFO certifications required under the Sarbanes-Oxley Act of 2002 ("SOX").

Additionally, the company does not have to disclose target levels with respect to specific quantitative or qualitative performance-related factors involving confidential trade secrets, confidential commercial information, or confidential financial information if such disclosure would result in competitive harm to the company. . . .

2.   Suggestions for Compliance/Examples

When drafting the CD&A, companies may want to review the CD&As of companies who have already developed comprehensive disclosures of compensation practices under the Rules. . . .

At least one commentator has noted companies may have the most difficulty disclosing the reasons why they decided to pay a certain compensation element. . . .

Companies also must focus on preparing disclosures related to the timing of option grants and the determination of the exercise prices of such grants because there is currently increased scrutiny at the SEC and in the investment community at-large with respect to option grant practices. . . . Companies also will need to evaluate their stock option

---

CD&A should provide a "bottom line assessment" of all the compensation elements for senior executives. See Jeffrey N. Gordon, Executive Compensation: What's the Problem, What's the Remedy? The Case for "Compensation Discussion and Analysis," 30 J. Corp. L. 695 (2005). Mr. Gordon also notes that "the CD&A should . . . explain why the compensation committee believes that the compensation is warranted, in light of the demands of the job, the industry, the executive's performance, and other factors deemed relevant." Id. at 677.

[45]   . . . The SEC has complained about the use of boilerplate in Compensation Committee reports in prior years. See Alan L. Beller, Director, Div. of Corp. Fin., Sec. and Exch. Comm'n, Speech by SEC Staff: Remarks at the 58th National Conference of the American Society of Corporate Secretaries (July 10, 2004), http://www.sec.gov/news/speech/spch071004alb.htm. The items required to be discussed in the CD&A under the Rules are designed to force companies to provide original disclosure. See Executive Compensation and Related Party Disclosure, 71 Fed. Reg. at 53,165.

[48]   Executive Compensation and Related Party Disclosure, 71 Fed. Reg. at 53,163–53,164. With respect to the timing of options, companies should disclose (i) policies related to grants made in connection with the release of material, non-public information and (ii) the role of the compensation committee and executives in the oversight of option programs or practices. Id. Similar disclosures are required when a company sets the exercise price for an option based on a date other than the grant date. Id. at 53,164.

grant and reporting practices to determine whether potential disclosure issues exist. In connection with this evaluation, companies may want to review publicly reported stock option grants for officers and directors, ensure that those dates are consistent with the board minutes and review the stock prices around the grant date for potential problems. In order to limit possible issues with future option disclosures, companies may want to take the following actions: (i) grant awards at specified intervals, (ii) grant awards at compensation committee meetings rather than by written consent66 and (iii) reevaluate the advisability of delegating grant authority to certain executive officers.

C.   Compensation Committee Report

The CD&A is designed to disclose company compensation policies and decisions, not the actual deliberations of the compensation committee. Consequently, although the compensation committee certainly should be involved heavily in its preparation, the CD&A is not a report of the compensation committee. In response to concerns from commentators regarding the role of the compensation committee in the executive compensation disclosure process, however, the Rules require a brief Compensation Committee Report similar to the currently required Audit Committee Report. The compensation committee must disclose in its report whether it has reviewed and discussed the CD&A with management, and, based on the review and discussions, whether the committee recommended to the entire board of directors that the company include the CD&A in the company's annual report and proxy statement. The Compensation Committee Report is "furnished" rather than "filed" and must be incorporated by reference in the company's annual report, along with the CD&A. . . .

E.   Summary Compensation Table and Supplemental Table

1.   The Summary Compensation Table

Under the Rules, the Summary Compensation Table continues to serve as the principal vehicle for disclosure of executive compensation and to include the Named Executive Officers' compensation for the last three fiscal years, whether or not actually paid out . . . .

. . . The salary and bonus columns include current and certain deferred compensation . . . . In addition, the compensation cost of stock awards and option awards over the requisite service period must be disclosed . . . . The aggregate increase in the actuarial value to each Named Executive Officer under all defined benefit and actuarial plans (including supplemental plans) accrued during the year and above-market or preferential earnings on nonqualified deferred compensation must be reported . . . . Finally, the "All Other Compensation" and "Other Annual Compensation" columns have been collapsed into one "All Other Compensation" column . . ., which requires disclosure of all compensation not included in the other columns. This includes perquisite disclosure and other personal benefits, amounts paid pursuant to a severance or change in control arrangement and company contributions to defined contribution plans. Footnote disclosure is required for each item of compensation included in the "All Other Compensation" column (other than perquisites) that exceeds $10,000. The Rules also reduce the threshold for perquisite disclosure to $10,000. Significantly, the Rules provide guidance regarding benefits that, in the SEC's view, should be categorized as perquisites or personal benefits. An item is considered a perquisite or personal benefit "if it confers a direct or indirect benefit that has a personal aspect, without regard to whether it may be provided for some business reason or for the convenience of the company, unless it is generally available on a non-discriminatory basis to all employees." On the other hand, if an item is integrally and directly related to the performance of an executive's duties, it is not a perquisite. Applying those guidelines, the SEC cites the following as examples of perquisites and personal benefits: club memberships used for reasons other than business entertainment, personal financial or tax advice, personal use of company vehicles, personal travel financed by the company and housing and other living expenses (including relocation assistance). . . .

    2.   Grants of Plan-Based Awards Table

    A supplemental table, the Grants of Plan-Based Awards Table, follows the Summary Compensation Table . . . provides more disclosure regarding performance-based stock, option and similar awards. Under the Rules, this table requires separate disclosure for each grant made during the current year under both equity and non-equity incentive plans, including estimated future payouts. In addition, stock awards and option awards must be disclosed and valued at the full grant date fair value . . . . In connection with the recent controversies surrounding stock-option backdating practices, the Rules require additional columns to be added to the table if: (i) the option exercise price is less than the closing market price of the underlying security on the date of grant, or (ii) the date on which the company takes action to grant an option is different from the date of grant . . . .

    3.   Narrative Description of the Summary Compensation Table and Supplemental Table

    Companies must provide a narrative description of any additional material factors necessary to an understanding of the information disclosed in the Summary Compensation Table and its supplemental table. This disclosure is designed to put the quantitative tabular disclosures in context. It describes the material terms of employment agreements, option repricings, other material modifications of stock awards, performance factors applicable to performance-based awards and other matters. This detailed disclosure differs from that in the CD&A, which focuses on broad topics regarding the objectives and implementation of executive compensation policies. Like the CD&A, certain confidential trade secrets and confidential or financial information will not have to be disclosed if doing so would result in competitive harm to the company.

    4.   Suggestions for Compliance/Examples

    a.   Summary Compensation Table—Total Compensation Column

. . . Commentators and SEC representatives encourage compensation committees to use tally sheets to obtain a complete picture of total compensation for Named Executive Officers. In light of the Rules, compensation committees should evaluate how cash and equity-based compensation, deferred compensation, retirement plan benefits, perquisites and other compensation paid to Executive Officers are calculated in the tally sheets. Commentators encourage disclosure of the compensation committees' use of a tally sheet in a company's proxy statement, and Institutional Shareholder Services recommends tally sheet disclosure of CEO compensation as well. Further, board members are encouraged to review tally sheets early in the proxy statement preparation process in order to avoid any surprises or embarrassment once they are disclosed, and to enable boards or compensation committees to modify compensation programs where appropriate to do so.

    . . .

    F.   Exercises and Holdings of Previously Awarded Equity

    1.   Outstanding Equity Awards at Fiscal Year-End Table

The next section of compensation disclosure provides investors with an understanding of outstanding equity compensation that remained unexercised or unvested at fiscal year-end through the use of two tables. The Outstanding Equity Awards at Fiscal Year-End Table . . . discloses information regarding outstanding grants of awards under stock option or stock appreciation rights plans. This table also discloses awards granted under restricted stock plans, incentive plans and similar plans, along with the market-based values of such awards as of the company's most recent fiscal-year end. . . .

Summary Compensation Table—2016, 2015, and 2014

The following table, footnotes, and related narrative show information regarding the total compensation of each named executive officer for 2016, 2015, and 2014, except in the case of Mr. Sewell, who was not a named executive officer in 2014.

Name and Principal Position (a)	Year (b)	Salary ($)(c)	Bonus ($)(d)	Stock Awards (1) ($)(e)	Non-Equity Incentive Plan Compensation (2) ($)(f)	All Other Compensation ($)(g)	Total ($)(h)
Tim Cook Chief Executive Officer	2016	3,000,000	—	—	5,370,000	377,719(3)	8,747,719
	2015	2,000,000	—	—	8,000,000	281,327	10,281,327
	2014	1,748,462	—	—	6,700,000	774,176	9,222,638
Luca Maestri Senior Vice President, Chief Financial Officer	2016	1,000,000	—	20,000,083	1,790,000	13,486(4)	22,803,569
	2015	1,000,000	—	20,000,105	4,000,000	337,872	25,337,977
	2014	717,211	—	11,335,043	1,608,255	342,292	14,002,801
Angela Ahrendts Senior Vice President, Retail	2016	1,000,000	—	20,000,083	1,790,000	112,809(5)	22,902,892
	2015	1,000,000	—	20,000,105	4,000,000	779,124	25,779,229
	2014	411,538	500,000	70,001,196	1,648,352	790,038	73,351,124
Eddy Cue Senior Vice President, Internet Software and Services	2016	1,000,000	—	20,000,083	1,790,000	17,461(6)	22,807,544
	2015	1,000,000	—	20,000,105	4,000,000	52,136	25,052,241
	2014	947,596	—	20,000,900	3,437,500	59,743	24,445,739
Dan Riccio Senior Vice President, Hardware Engineering	2016	1,000,000	—	20,000,083	1,790,000	17,461(7)	22,807,544
	2015	1,000,000	—	20,000,105	4,000,000	17,521	25,017,626
	2014	947,596	—	20,000,900	3,437,500	17,239	24,403,235
Bruce Sewell Senior Vice President, General Counsel and Secretary	2016	1,000,000	—	20,000,083	1,790,000	17,461(8)	22,807,544
	2015	1,000,000	—	20,000,105	4,000,000	17,521	25,017,626

Figure 1. Apple Inc. 2017 Proxy Statement

2. Option Exercises and Stock Vested Table

The Option Exercises and Stock Vested Table discloses the amounts received upon exercise of options (or similar awards) or the vesting of stock (or similar awards) during the most recent fiscal year (see Table 4 below). . . .

3. Suggestions for Compliance/Examples

Companies should note that separate line item disclosure is required for each stock option grant in the Outstanding Equity Awards Table, while stock awards must be disclosed in the aggregate. Companies may want to consider additional footnote disclosure in connection with the stock award disclosure, including a description of each grant and the related vesting schedule.

G. Post-Employment Compensation

The final section of executive compensation disclosure under the Rules includes tables and expanded narrative disclosures regarding defined benefit pension plan and non-qualified defined contribution plan compensation. The tables also include enhanced disclosure regarding compensation arrangements triggered upon a termination of service or a change in control. These disclosures are the result of shareholder complaints and SEC concerns that the sizes of many executives' retirement and change of control pay packages may represent a significant portion of executive compensation . . . .

H. Director Compensation

1. The Rules

Under the Rules, a new Director Compensation Table presents information regarding director compensation similar to the information provided in the Summary Compensation Table. However, this table only presents data compiled from the company's last completed fiscal year. Total compensation, fees earned or paid in cash, stock awards, option awards, non-stock incentive plan compensation, change in pension value, nonqualified deferred compensation earnings and all other compensation (such as consulting fees, charitable awards, etc.) must be disclosed for each director. Companies also are required to disclose by footnote to the appropriate column (i) the aggregate numbers of stock awards and option awards outstanding at fiscal year end, (ii) the fair value of each equity award determined . . . at the date of the grant and (iii) information regarding any re-priced or materially modified options, SARS or similar option-like instruments. Narrative disclosure must follow the table and must include any material factors necessary to understand the table, such as a breakdown of the different types of fees.

2. Suggestions for Compliance/Examples

Disclosure items in the Director Compensation Table that are analogous to disclosure items in the Summary Compensation Table will be governed by the Summary Compensation Table instructions regarding those items. Consequently, companies should consider issues raised in connection with the new Summary Compensation Table disclosure requirements when preparing the Director Compensation Table. . . .

Director Compensation—2016

The following table shows information regarding the compensation earned or paid during 2016 to Non-Employee Directors who served on the Board during the year. The compensation paid to Mr. Cook is shown under "Executive Compensation" in the table entitled "Summary Compensation Table—2016, 2015, and 2014" and the related tables. Mr. Cook does not receive any compensation for his service as a member of the Board.

Name	Fees Earned or Paid in Cash ($)	Stock Awards ($) (1)	All Other Compensation ($) (2)	Total ($)
James Bell (3)	100,000	360,375	5,176	465,551
Al Gore	100,000	250,028	2,464	352,492
Bob Iger	125,000	250,028	2,261	377,289
Andrea Jung	130,000	250,028	2,163	382,191
Art Levinson	300,000	250,028	2,351	552,379
Ron Sugar	135,000	250,028	5,494	390,522
Sue Wagner	100,000	250,028	1,647	351,675

(1) In accordance with SEC rules, the amounts shown reflect the aggregate grant date fair value of stock awards granted to Non-Employee Directors during 2016, computed in accordance with Financial Accounting Standards Board Accounting Standards Codification Topic 718 ("FASB ASC 718"). The grant date fair value for RSUs is measured based on the closing fair market value of Apple's common stock on the date of grant. See Note 1—Summary of Significant Accounting Policies found in Part II, Item 8, "Financial Statements and Supplementary Data" in the Notes to Consolidated Financial Statements in the Annual Report.

Each Non-Employee Director received an automatic Annual Director Award of 2,580 RSUs on February 26, 2016, and the grant date fair value for each grant was $250,028. Mr. Bell also received an automatic Initial Director Award of 1,007 RSUs on October 1, 2015, upon joining the Board. The Initial Director Award to Mr. Bell had a grant date fair value of $110,347, resulting in a total grant date fair value of RSUs to Mr. Bell during 2016 of $360,375.

As of September 24, 2016, each Non-Employee Director held 2,580 shares subject to outstanding RSUs. In addition, Mr. Gore had 275,779 shares subject to outstanding and unexercised options, Ms. Jung had 109,590 shares subject to outstanding and unexercised options, and Mr. Levinson had 247,394 shares subject to outstanding and unexercised options.

(2) The amounts shown reflect one or more products received under Apple's Board of Directors equipment program.

(3) Mr. Bell joined the Board on October 1, 2015.

Figure 2. Apple Inc. 2017 Proxy Statement

IV. CONSEQUENCES OF NON-COMPLIANCE

A. "Filed" Status of Compensation Discussion and Analysis

As noted above, the CD&A is considered a part of the proxy statement or any other filing in which it is included and is deemed "filed" with the SEC. Consequently, the CD&A is subject to Regulations 14A or 14C and the liabilities imposed under Section 18 of the Exchange Act. This means that all directors, not just those who are members of the compensation committee, may be liable for false and misleading statements in the CD&A. As a result, all board members need to review the CD&A and discuss it with the compensation committee.

. . .

FYI

Apple's narrative discussion of director compensation explained the varying fees paid directors as follows: "Non-Employee Directors receive an annual cash retainer of $100,000. In 2016, the Chairman of the Board, Dr. Levinson, received an additional cash retainer of $200,000; the Chair of the Audit Committee, Dr. Sugar, received an additional cash retainer of $35,000; the Chair of the Compensation Committee, Ms. Jung, received an additional cash retainer of $30,000; and the Chair of the Nominating Committee, Mr. Iger, received an additional cash retainer of $25,000."

Dodd-Frank § 953

(a) DISCLOSURE OF PAY VERSUS PERFORMANCE.— Section 14 of the Securities Exchange Act of 1934 (15 U.S.C. 78n), as amended by this title, is amended by adding at the end the following:

"(i) DISCLOSURE OF PAY VERSUS PERFORMANCE.— The Commission shall, by rule, require each issuer to disclose in any proxy or consent solicitation material for an annual meeting of the shareholders of the issuer a clear description of any compensation required to be disclosed by the issuer under section 229.402 of title 17, Code of Federal Regulations (or any successor thereto), including information that shows the relationship between executive compensation actually paid and the financial performance of the issuer, taking into account any change in the value of the shares of stock and dividends of the issuer and any distributions.

The disclosure under this subsection may include a graphic representation of the information required to be disclosed.".

(b) ADDITIONAL DISCLOSURE REQUIREMENTS.—

(1) IN GENERAL.—The Commission shall amend section 229.402 of title 17, Code of Federal Regulations, to require each issuer to disclose in any filing of the issuer described in section 229.10(a) of title 17, Code of Federal Regulations (or any successor thereto)—

(A) the median of the annual total compensation of all employees of the issuer, except the chief executive officer (or any equivalent position) of the issuer;

(B) the annual total compensation of the chief executive officer (or any equivalent position) of the issuer; and

(C) the ratio of the amount described in subparagraph (A) to the amount described in subparagraph (B).

(2) TOTAL COMPENSATION.—For purposes of this subsection, the total compensation of an employee of an issuer shall be determined in accordance with section 229.402(c)(2)(x) of title 17, Code of Federal Regulations, as in effect on the day before the date of enactment of this Act.

Regulation S–K Item 402(u)

(1) Disclose.

(i) The median of the annual total compensation of all employees of the registrant, except the PEO of the registrant;

(ii) The annual total compensation of the PEO of the registrant; and

(iii) The ratio of the amount in paragraph (u)(1)(i) of this Item to the amount in paragraph (u)(1)(ii) of this Item. For purposes of the ratio required by this paragraph (u)(1)(iii), the amount in paragraph (u)(1)(i) of this Item shall equal one, or, alternatively, the ratio may be expressed narratively as the multiple that the amount in paragraph (u)(1)(ii) of this Item bears to the amount in paragraph (u)(1)(i) of this Item.

(2)   For purposes of this paragraph (u):

(i)   Total compensation for the median of annual total compensation of all employees of the registrant and the PEO of the registrant shall be determined in accordance with paragraph (c)(2)(x) of this Item. In determining the total compensation, all references to "named executive officer" in this Item and the instructions thereto may be deemed to refer instead, as applicable, to "employee" and, for non-salaried employees, references to "base salary" and "salary" in this Item and the instructions thereto may be deemed to refer instead, as applicable, to "wages plus overtime";

(ii) Annual total compensation means total compensation for the registrant's last completed fiscal year; and

(iii) Registrant means the registrant and its consolidated subsidiaries.

(3)   For purposes of this paragraph (u), employee or employee of the registrant means an individual employed by the registrant or any of its consolidated subsidiaries, whether as a full-time, part-time, seasonal, or temporary worker, as of a date chosen by the registrant within the last three months of the registrant's last completed fiscal year. The definition of employee or employee of the registrant does not include those workers who are employed, and whose compensation is determined, by an unaffiliated third party but who provide services to the registrant or its consolidated subsidiaries as independent contractors or "leased" workers.

(4)   For purposes of this paragraph (u), an employee located in a jurisdiction outside the United States (a "non-U.S. employee") may be exempt from the definition of employee or employee of the registrant under either of the following conditions:

(i)   The employee is employed in a foreign jurisdiction in which the laws or regulations governing data privacy are such that, despite its reasonable efforts to obtain or process the information necessary for compliance with this paragraph (u), the registrant is unable to do so without violating such data privacy laws or regulations. The registrant's reasonable efforts shall include, at a minimum, using or seeking an exemption or other relief under any governing data privacy laws or regulations. If the registrant chooses to exclude any employees using this exemption, it shall list the excluded jurisdictions, identify the specific data privacy law or regulation, explain how complying with this paragraph (u) violates such data privacy law or regulation (including the efforts made by the registrant to use or seek an exemption or other relief under such law or regulation), and provide the approximate number of employees exempted from each jurisdiction based on this exemption. In addition, if a registrant excludes any non-U.S. employees in a particular jurisdiction under this exemption, it must exclude all non-U.S. employees in that jurisdiction. Further, the registrant shall obtain a legal opinion from counsel that opines on the inability of the registrant to obtain or process the information necessary for compliance with this paragraph (u) without violating the jurisdiction's laws or regulations governing data privacy, including the registrant's inability to obtain an exemption or other relief under any governing laws or regulations. The registrant shall file the legal opinion as an exhibit to the filing in which the pay ratio disclosure is included.

(ii) The registrant's non-U.S. employees account for 5% or less of the registrant's total employees. In that circumstance, if the registrant chooses to exclude any non-U.S. employees under this exemption, it must exclude all non-U.S. employees. Additionally, if a registrant's non-U.S. employees exceed 5% of the registrant's total U.S. and non-U.S. employees, it may exclude up to 5% of its total employees who are non-U.S. employees; provided, however, if a registrant excludes any non-U.S. employees in a particular jurisdiction, it must exclude all non-U.S. employees in that jurisdiction. If more than 5% of a registrant's employees are located in any one non-U.S. jurisdiction, the registrant may not exclude any employees in that jurisdiction under this exemption.

(A) In calculating the number of non-U.S. employees that may be excluded under this Item 402(u)(4)(ii) ("de minimis" exemption), a registrant shall count against the total any non-U.S. employee exempted under the data privacy law exemption under Item 402(u)(4)(i) ("data privacy" exemption). A registrant may exclude any non-U.S. employee from a jurisdiction that meets the data privacy exemption, even if the number of excluded employees exceeds 5% of the registrant's total employees. If, however, the number of employees excluded under the data privacy exemption equals or exceeds 5% of the registrant's total employees, the registrant may not use the de minimis exemption. Additionally, if the number of employees excluded under the data privacy exemption is less than 5% of the registrant's total employees, the registrant may use the de minimis exemption to exclude no more than the number of non-U.S. employees that, combined with the data privacy exemption, does not exceed 5% of the registrant's total employees.

(B) If a registrant excludes non-U.S. employees under the de minimis exemption, it must disclose the jurisdiction or jurisdictions from which those employees are being excluded, the approximate number of employees excluded from each jurisdiction under the de minimis exemption, the total number of its U.S. and non-U.S. employees irrespective of any exemption (data privacy or de minimis), and the total number of its U.S. and non-U.S. employees used for its de minimis calculation.

Instruction 1 to Item 402(u)—Disclosing the date chosen for identifying the median employee. A registrant shall disclose the date within the last three months of its last completed fiscal year that it selected pursuant to paragraph (u)(3) of this Item to identify its median employee. If the registrant changes the date it uses to identify the median employee from the prior year, the registrant shall disclose this change and provide a brief explanation about the reason or reasons for the change.

Instruction 2 to Item 402(u)—Identifying the median employee. A registrant is required to identify its median employee only once every three years and calculate total compensation for that employee each year; provided that, during a registrant's last completed fiscal year there has been no change in its employee population or employee compensation arrangements that it reasonably believes would result in a significant change to its pay ratio disclosure. If there have been no changes that the registrant reasonably believes would significantly affect its pay ratio disclosure, the registrant shall disclose that it is using the same median employee in its pay ratio calculation and describe briefly the basis for its reasonable belief. For example, the registrant could disclose that there has been no change in its employee population or employee compensation arrangements that it believes would significantly impact the pay ratio disclosure. If there has been a change in the registrant's employee population or employee compensation arrangements that the registrant reasonably believes would result in a significant change in its pay ratio disclosure, the registrant shall re-identify the median employee for that fiscal year. If it is no longer appropriate for the registrant to use the median employee identified in year one as the median employee in years two or three because of a change in the original median employee's circumstances that the registrant reasonably believes would result in a significant change in its pay ratio disclosure, the registrant may use another employee whose compensation is substantially similar to the original median employee based on the compensation measure used to select the original median employee.

Instruction 3 to Item 402(u)—Updating for the last completed fiscal year. Pay ratio information (i.e., the disclosure called for by paragraph (u)(1) of this Item) with respect to the registrant's last completed fiscal year is not required to be disclosed until the filing of its annual report on Form 10-K for that last completed fiscal year or, if later, the filing of a definitive proxy or information statement relating to its next annual meeting of shareholders (or written consents in lieu of such a meeting) following the end of such fiscal year; provided that, the required pay ratio information must, in any event, be filed as provided in General Instruction G(3) of Form 10-K (17 CFR 249.310) not later than 120 days after the end of such fiscal year.

Instruction 4 to Item 402(u)—Methodology and use of estimates. 1. Registrants may use reasonable estimates both in the methodology used to identify the median employee and in calculating the annual total compensation or any elements of total compensation for employees other than the PEO.

2. In determining the employees from which the median employee is identified, a registrant may use its employee population or statistical sampling and/or other reasonable methods.

3. A registrant may identify the median employee using annual total compensation or any other compensation measure that is consistently applied to all employees included in the calculation, such as information derived from the registrant's tax and/or payroll records. In using a compensation measure other than annual total compensation to identify the median employee, if that measure is recorded on a basis other than the registrant's fiscal year (such as information derived from tax and/or payroll records), the registrant may use the same annual period that is used to derive those amounts. Where a compensation measure other than annual total compensation is used to identify the median employee, the registrant must disclose the compensation measure used.

4. In identifying the median employee, whether using annual total compensation or any other compensation measure that is consistently applied to all employees included in the calculation, the registrant may make cost-of-living adjustments to the compensation of employees in jurisdictions other than the jurisdiction in which the PEO resides so that the compensation is adjusted to the cost of living in the jurisdiction in which the PEO resides. If the registrant uses a cost-of-living adjustment to identify the median employee, and the median employee identified is an employee in a jurisdiction other than the jurisdiction in which the PEO resides, the registrant must use the same cost-of-living adjustment in calculating the median employee's annual total compensation and disclose the median employee's jurisdiction. The registrant also shall briefly describe the cost-of-living adjustments

it used to identify the median employee and briefly describe the cost-of-living adjustments it used to calculate the median employee's annual total compensation, including the measure used as the basis for the cost-of-living adjustment. A registrant electing to present the pay ratio in this manner also shall disclose the median employee's annual total compensation and pay ratio without the cost-of-living adjustment. To calculate this pay ratio, the registrant will need to identify the median employee without using any cost-of-living adjustments.

5.   The registrant shall briefly describe the methodology it used to identify the median employee. It shall also briefly describe any material assumptions, adjustments (including any cost-of-living adjustments), or estimates it used to identify the median employee or to determine total compensation or any elements of total compensation, which shall be consistently applied. The registrant shall clearly identify any estimates used. The required descriptions should be a brief overview; it is not necessary for the registrant to provide technical analyses or formulas. If a registrant changes its methodology or its material assumptions, adjustments, or estimates from those used in its pay ratio disclosure for the prior fiscal year, and if the effects of any such change are significant, the registrant shall briefly describe the change and the reasons for the change. Registrants must also disclose if they changed from using the cost-of-living adjustment to not using that adjustment and if they changed from not using the cost-of-living adjustment to using it.

6.   Registrants may, at their discretion, include personal benefits that aggregate less than $10,000 and compensation under non-discriminatory benefit plans in calculating the annual total compensation of the median employee as long as these items are also included in calculating the PEO's annual total compensation. The registrant shall also explain any difference between the PEO's annual total compensation used in the pay ratio disclosure and the total compensation amounts reflected in the Summary Compensation Table, if material.

Instruction 5 to Item 402(u)—Permitted annualizing adjustments. A registrant may annualize the total compensation for all permanent employees (full-time or part-time) that were employed by the registrant for less than the full fiscal year (such as newly hired employees or permanent employees on an unpaid leave of absence during the period). A registrant may not annualize the total compensation for employees in temporary or seasonal positions. A registrant may not make a full-time equivalent adjustment for any employee.

Instruction 6 to Item 402(u)—PEO compensation not available. A registrant that is relying on Instruction 1 to Item 402(c)(2)(iii) and (iv) in connection with the salary or bonus of the PEO for the last completed fiscal year, shall disclose that the pay ratio required by paragraph (u) of this Item is not calculable until the PEO salary or bonus, as applicable, is determined and shall disclose the date that the PEO's actual total compensation is expected to be determined. The disclosure required by paragraph (u) of this Item shall then be disclosed in the filing under Item 5.02(f) of Form 8-K (17 CFR 249.308) that discloses the PEO's salary or bonus in accordance with Instruction 1 to Item 402(c)(2)(iii) and (iv).

Instruction 7 to Item 402(u)—Transition periods for registrants. 1. Upon becoming subject to the requirements of Section 13(a) or 15(d) of the Exchange Act (15 U.S.C. 78m or 78o(d)), a registrant shall comply with paragraph (u) of this Item with respect to compensation for the first fiscal year following the year in which it became subject to such requirements, but not for any fiscal year commencing before January 1, 2017. The registrant may omit the disclosure required by paragraph (u) of this Item from any filing until the filing of its annual report on Form 10-K (17 CFR 249.310) for such fiscal year or, if later, the filing of a proxy or information statement relating to its next annual meeting of shareholders (or written consents in lieu of such a meeting) following the end of such year; provided that, such disclosure shall, in any event, be filed as provided in General Instruction G(3) of Form 10-K not later than 120 days after the end of such fiscal year.

2. A registrant may omit any employees that became its employees as the result of the business combination or acquisition of a business for the fiscal year in which the transaction becomes effective, but the registrant must disclose the approximate number of employees it is omitting. Those employees shall be included in the total employee count for the triennial calculations of the median employee in the year following the transaction for purposes of evaluating whether a significant change had occurred. The registrant shall identify the acquired business excluded for the fiscal year in which the business combination or acquisition becomes effective.

3. A registrant shall comply with paragraph (u) of this Item with respect to compensation for the first fiscal year commencing on or after the date the registrant ceases to be a smaller reporting company, but not for any fiscal year commencing before January 1, 2017.

Instruction 8 to Item 402(u)—Emerging growth companies. A registrant is not required to comply with paragraph (u) of this Item if it is an emerging growth company as defined in Section 2(a)(19) of the Securities Act (15 U.S.C. 77(b)(a)(19)) or Section 3(a)(80) of the Exchange Act (15 U.S.C. 78c(a)(80)). A registrant shall comply with paragraph (u) of this Item with respect to compensation for the first fiscal year commencing on or after the date the registrant ceases to be an emerging growth company, but not for any fiscal year commencing before January 1, 2017.

Instruction 9 to Item 402(u)—Additional information. Registrants may present additional information, including additional ratios, to supplement the required ratio, but are not required to do so. Any additional information shall be clearly identified, not misleading, and not presented with greater prominence than the required ratio.

Instruction 10 to Item 402(u)—Multiple PEOs during the year. A registrant with more than one non-concurrent PEO serving during its fiscal year may calculate the annual total compensation for its PEO in either of the following manners:

　　1.　　The registrant may calculate the compensation provided to each person who served as PEO during the year for the time he or she served as PEO and combine those figures; or

　　2.　　The registrant may look to the PEO serving in that position on the date it selects to identify the median employee and annualize that PEO's compensation.

Regardless of the alternative selected, the registrant shall disclose which option it chose and how it calculated its PEO's annual total compensation.

Instruction 11 to Item 402(u)—Employees' personally identifiable information. Registrants are not required to, and should not, disclose any personally identifiable information about that employee other than his or her compensation. Registrants may choose to generally identify an employee's position to put the employee's compensation in context, but registrants are not required to provide this information and should not do so if providing the information could identify any specific individual.

Securities and Exchange Commission, Pay Ratio Disclosure

Release No. 9877 (Aug. 5, 2015)

I.　　Background

A.　　Section 953(b) of the Dodd-Frank Act

. . . [W]e are adopting amendments to Item 402 to implement Section 953(b). We refer to this disclosure of the median of the annual total compensation of all employees of the registrant, the annual total compensation of the principal executive officer ("PEO") of the registrant, and the ratio of the two amounts as "pay ratio" disclosure.

Congress did not expressly state the specific objectives or intended benefits of Section 953(b), and the legislative history of the Dodd-Frank Act also does not expressly state the Congressional purpose underlying Section 953(b). . . . [B]ased on our analysis of the statute and comments received, we believe Section 953(b) was intended to provide shareholders with a company-specific metric that can assist in their evaluation of a registrant's executive compensation practices. Accordingly, we have sought to tailor the final rule to meet that purpose while avoiding unnecessary costs.

. . .

Consistent with this understanding of the Congressional purpose of Section 953(b), we believe the final pay ratio rule should be designed to allow shareholders to better understand and assess a particular registrant's compensation practices and pay ratio disclosures rather than to facilitate a comparison of this information from one registrant to another. . . . Consequently, we believe the primary benefit of the pay ratio disclosure is to provide shareholders with a company-specific metric that they can use to evaluate the PEO's compensation within the context of their company.

> **THINK ABOUT IT**
>
> Suppose Congress' purpose in adopting § 953(b) was to generate information that would be used to shame companies who pay ratio is very large. How would that understanding of the provision's purpose have changed the SEC's decisions?

. . .

We also recognize that many commenters raised significant concerns about the costs of providing the required pay ratio disclosure. In implementing the statutory requirements, we have exercised our exemptive authority and provided flexibility in a manner that we expect will reduce costs and burdens for registrants, while preserving what we perceive to be the purpose and intended benefits of the disclosure required by Section 953(b). . . . The final rule, therefore, both maintains the flexibility and accommodations from the proposal (such as permitting the use of statistical sampling and a consistent compensation measure to identify the median employee and reasonable estimates to calculate total compensation) and provides additional flexibility as follows: The final rule takes a flexible approach to the methodology a registrant can use to identify its median employee and calculate the median employee's annual total compensation; provides a de minimis exemption for non-U.S. employees and an exemption for registrants where, despite reasonable efforts to obtain or process the information necessary for compliance with the final rule, they are unable to do so without violating a foreign jurisdiction's laws or regulations governing data privacy; permits cost-of-living adjustments for the compensation of employees in jurisdictions other than the jurisdiction in which the PEO resides so that the compensation is adjusted to the cost of living in the jurisdiction in which the PEO resides; gives registrants the ability to make the median employee determination only once every three years and to choose as a determination date any date within the last three months of a registrant's fiscal year; and provides transition periods for new registrants, registrants engaging in business combinations or acquisitions, and registrants that cease to be smaller reporting companies or emerging growth companies.

. . .

Finally, we recognize the possibility that, based on the specific facts and circumstances of a registrant's work force and corporate operations, the pay ratio disclosure may warrant additional disclosures from a registrant to ensure that, in the registrant's view, the pay ratio disclosure is a meaningful data point for investors when making their say-on-pay votes. While Congress appears to have believed that the pay ratio disclosure would be a useful data point, we recognize that its relative usefulness—taken alone without accompanying disclosures to provide potentially important context—may vary considerably. Rather than prescribe a one-size-fits-all catalogue of additional disclosures that registrants should provide to put the pay ratio disclosure in context, we believe it is the better course to provide registrants the flexibility to provide additional disclosures that they believe will assist investors' understanding of the meaning of pay ratio disclosure when making say-on-pay votes. In this way, we believe we can best fulfill Congress's directive in Section 953(b) while avoiding unnecessary costs and complexities that might result from mandating additional disclosures.

B. Summary of the Proposed Rule

In September 2013, we proposed a new rule to implement Section 953(b) of the Dodd-Frank Act. . . .

The proposed rule would require companies to disclose the median of the annual total compensation of all its employees except the PEO, the annual total compensation of its PEO, and the ratio of the two amounts. The proposed rule would not have specified a single calculation methodology for identifying the median employee. Instead, it would permit registrants to select a methodology for identifying the median employee that was appropriate to the size and structure of their business and the way they compensate employees. Under the proposal, registrants could have chosen to identify the median employee by analyzing their full employee population or by using statistical sampling or another reasonable method. Also, to identify the median, registrants could have used "total compensation," as defined in our existing rules, namely Item 402(c)(2)(x), or any consistently applied compensation measure, such as information derived from tax and/or payroll records. The proposed rule would not prescribe a particular methodology or specific computation parameters.

Once the median employee was identified, the proposed rule would require the registrant to calculate the annual total compensation for that median employee in accordance with the definition of "total compensation" set forth in Item 402(c)(2)(x), which requires companies to provide extensive compensation information for the PEO and other named executive officers. "Total compensation" under Item 402(c)(2)(x) is not ordinarily calculated for all employees. The proposed rule, therefore, would permit registrants to use reasonable estimates in calculating any element of total compensation and in calculating the annual total compensation of the median employee. Also, the proposed rule would define "annual total compensation" to mean total compensation for the last completed fiscal year, which would be consistent with our existing executive compensation disclosure requirements.

WHAT'S THAT?

"Total compensation" under Item 402 includes the sum of salary, bonuses, stock awards, option awards, non-equity incentive plan compensation, changes in pension value and non-qualified deferred compensation earnings, and all other compensation such as perquisites and personal benefits. It also includes the amount of any tax gross-ups, company contributions to defined contribution retirement plans, stock purchase discounts, and life insurance premiums.

Under the proposal, if a registrant used a compensation measure other than annual total compensation to identify the median employee, it would be required to disclose the compensation measure it used. Also, the registrant would be required to briefly describe and consistently apply any methodology it used to identify the median and any material assumptions, adjustments, or estimates used to identify the median employee or determine total compensation or any elements of total compensation for that employee or the PEO, and the registrant would need to clearly identify any amounts it estimated. Finally, registrants would be permitted, but not required, to supplement their disclosure with a narrative discussion or additional ratios if they chose to do so.

Section 953(b) does not define the term "employee." The proposed rule would define that term, for purposes of pay ratio disclosure, to include any individual employed by the registrant or any of its subsidiaries as of the last day of the registrant's last completed fiscal year. The proposed definition would encompass any full-time, part-time, seasonal, or temporary employees of the registrant or any of its subsidiaries, including any non-U.S. employee. Also, a registrant would be permitted, but not required, to annualize the total compensation for a permanent employee who was employed at yearend but did not work for the entire year. In contrast, full-time equivalent adjustments for part-time employees, annualizing adjustments for temporary and seasonal employees, and cost-of-living adjustments for non-U.S. employees would not be permitted.

Also, under the proposal, registrants would be required to provide the proposed pay ratio disclosure in registration statements, proxy and information statements, and annual reports required to include executive compensation information as set forth under Item 402. Registrants, however, would not be required to provide their pay ratio information in reports that did not include Item 402 executive compensation information, such as current and quarterly reports. . . .

D.   Summary of Changes in the Final Rule

The final rule we are adopting generally is consistent with the proposed rule.

1.   Non-U.S. Employee Exemptions and Additional Permitted Disclosure

. . .

The final rule defines the term "employee" to include U.S. employees and employees located in a jurisdiction outside the United States ("non-U.S. employees") of a registrant, as proposed. . . .

To help address concerns about compliance costs, and consistent with the commenters' suggestions, the final rule provides two tailored exemptions from the definition of "employee," which otherwise includes all of a registrant's U.S. and non-U.S. employees in the median employee determination. First, the final rule provides an exemption for circumstances in which foreign data privacy laws or regulations make registrants unable to comply with the final rule. Second, the final rule permits registrants to exempt non-U. S. employees where these employees account for 5% or less of the registrant's total U.S. and non-U.S. employees, with certain limitations.

. . . If a registrant excludes any non-U.S. employees in a particular jurisdiction under this exemption, it must exclude all non-U.S. employees in that jurisdiction, list the excluded jurisdictions, identify the specific data privacy law or regulation, explain how complying with the final rule violates such data privacy law or regulation (including the efforts made by the registrant to use or seek an exemption or other relief under such law or regulation), and provide the approximate number of employees exempted from each jurisdiction based on this exemption. In addition, the registrant must obtain a legal opinion from counsel that opines on the inability of the registrant to obtain or process the information necessary for compliance with the final rule without violating that jurisdiction's data privacy laws or regulations, including the registrant's inability to obtain an exemption or other relief under any governing laws or provisions.

2.   Employees of Consolidated Subsidiaries

We proposed requiring a registrant's pay ratio disclosure to include the employees of any of its subsidiaries (including officers other than the PEO), in addition to its direct employees, in its pay ratio disclosure. Unlike the proposed rule, however, the final rule defines "employee" to include only the employees of the registrant's consolidated subsidiaries. . . .

3.   Employed on Any Date Within Three Months of the Last Completed Fiscal Year

. . . [T]he final rule permits registrants to use any date within three months prior to the last day of their last completed fiscal year to identify the median employee. If in subsequent years the registrant changes the date it uses to identify the median employee, it must disclose this change and provide a brief explanation about the reason or reasons for the change. This provision provides consistency for individual registrants from year to year while also providing registrants with flexibility to choose the determination date. To provide additional transparency about how the pay ratio disclosure has been calculated, the final rule requires registrants to disclose the date used to identify the median employee.

4.   Identifying the Median Employee Once Every Three Years

. . . To help minimize compliance costs, we are revising the rule, as suggested by commenters, to allow registrants to identify the median employee every three years unless there has been a change in its employee population or employee compensation arrangements that the registrant reasonably believes would result in a significant change in the pay ratio disclosure. However, the registrant must still calculate the identified median employee's annual total compensation and use that figure in calculating its pay ratio every year. If there have been no changes that the registrant reasonably believes would significantly affect its pay ratio disclosure, the registrant must disclose that it is using the same median employee in its pay ratio calculation and describe briefly the basis for its reasonable belief. For example, the registrant could disclose that there has been no change in its employee population or employee compensation arrangements that it believes would significantly impact the pay ratio disclosure. If there has been such a change, the registrant must re-identify the median employee for that fiscal year.

Under the final rule's approach, the registrant will identify its median employee for year one and then be permitted to use that employee or one who is similarly compensated (if, for example, the median employee is no longer in the same position or is no longer employed by the registrant) in the following two years for calculating the median employee's annual total compensation and the registrant's pay ratio. The registrant must calculate the median employee's annual total compensation in year one and then recalculate the annual total compensation for that employee in year two and again in year three. If the median employee identified in year one is no longer in the same position or no longer employed by the registrant on the median employee determination date in year two or three, the final rule permits the registrant to replace its median employee with an employee in a similarly compensated position.

. . .

NOTES AND QUESTIONS

1.   In dissenting from the SEC's adoption of the final pay disclosure rule, Commissioner Michael Piwowar made a number of claims:

- "The push for pay ratio disclosure should come as no surprise to anyone familiar with the use of Saul Alinskyan tactics by Big Labor and their political allies." He argued the rule was intended to advance a political goal of limiting CEO pay and increasing worker pay.

- "Today's rulemaking also unfairly targets publicly-traded companies that employ a large number of individuals in states with relatively lower costs of living. The labor market for hiring chief executive officers is markedly different than the market for hiring a non-executive employee of a company. CEO compensation is often set based on the supply and demand for CEOs, while cost of living and local labor market conditions often play bigger factors in setting compensation for other employees."

- "The Commission's economic analysis was deficient because it failed to consider fully whether pay ratio disclosure might increase CEO compensation. Academic studies have found that it is possible that pay ratio disclosure could exacerbate any upward bias in executive pay by providing another benchmark that could be used in certain situations to increase CEO compensation (i.e., for a CEO whose company's pay ratio is lower than its peers' pay ratios)."[29]

Evaluate his complaints.

2.   Must the company identify an actual person who is the median employee?

3.   How would the information provided by the disclosure change if the rule required disclosure of the ratio between the CEO's total compensation and that of the mean employee rather than the median employee?

4.   The median employee's total compensation need only be determined once every three years, but the pay ratio must be disclosed annually. Is there any reason the company might want to calculate the median employee's total compensation annually?

5.   You are company counsel. The CEO asked you to identify situations in which it would be desirable for the company to provide additional disclosures, using supplemental ratios to make the results "look better." The CEO then immediately corrected herself and asked you to identify situations in which additional disclosures would "provide shareholders with a better, more complete, and fuller understanding of the company's compensation practices." Answer her question(s).

6.   What factors should the company consider on selecting the date on which the median employee will be identified? Is it permissible for the company to select a number of dates to perform the calculation and then

---

[29]   Michael S. Piwowar, Dissenting Statement at Open Meeting on Pay Ratio Disclosure (Aug. 5, 2015), https://www.sec.gov/news/statement/dissenting-statement-at-open-meeting-on-pay-ratio-disclosure.html.

disclose only the information from the date from which the most favorable result was obtained?

7.　The leading academic proponents of expanded CEO pay disclosure rules, such as § 953, admit the "main aim" of such rules "is not to enable accurate pricing of the firm's securities," but "to provide some check on arrangements that are too favorable to executives."[30] Is that an appropriate goal of the federal securities laws?

8.　Assuming that § 953(b) was intended, at least in part, to limit or cap CEO pay, will it work? Three leading commentators argue that the answer is no:

> With the SEC only having implemented the relevant rules in 2015 and with companies not needing to make the relevant disclosures until 2018, it is too early to gauge the impact of reform. Still, it seems unlikely pay ratio disclosure will substantially change existing practices. As one commentator opined:
>
>> The idea behind publishing the ratio of executive pay to worker pay seems to be that the disparity will embarrass corporate boards and anger investors into cutting back on executive pay. Sounds good. But I don't see that happening. If there was anger and embarrassment over CEO salaries, those salaries already would be cut. As long as CEOs deliver, what is the incentive to cut their pay?[31]

9.　If you were a shareholder, would you find this information helpful? If so, how?

10.　Microsoft's 2016 annual proxy statement was 77 pages long, of which 26 consisted of required compensation disclosures. How many shareholders do you suspect read that information?

11.　Seven issuers voluntarily jumped the gun and provided pay ratio disclosures in their 2017 annual proxy statements. Reportedly, however, those disclosures were typically deficient:

> The pay ratio disclosure provided by each of these registrants has generally been brief and, in certain cases, perhaps too brief. Only two of these registrants included disclosure that appears to fully comply with the final rule. Four registrants did not disclose the date on which the employee population was determined, and two registrants did not indicate the methodology used to measure compensation and identify the median employee. In addition, one registrant failed to express the relationship between the compensation amounts as a ratio and instead indicated a percentage—which is not expressly permitted by the final rule.[32]

---

[30]　Lucian Bebchuk & Jesse Fried, Pay Without Performance 192 (2004).

[31]　Steven A. Bank et. al., Executive Pay: What Worked?, 42 J. Corp. L. 59, 73 (2016).

[32]　Winston & Strawn, Review of Voluntary CEO Pay Ratio Disclosure Yields Mixed Results (May 30, 2017), http://www.lexology.com/library/detail.aspx?g=09470ce5-e3c3-4afd-a705-92e856083c80.

12.   In September 2017, the SEC issued guidance on how issuers should comply with the rule:

1.   The SEC's guidance around the use of reasonable estimates, assumptions as well as methodologies and statistical sampling centers on the concept of reasonableness. Issuers may make 'reasonable estimates to identify the median employee, including by using statistical sampling and a consistently applied compensation measure (such as payroll or tax records).' In light of the imprecise nature of calculating the pay ratio, the SEC stated that it will not initiate enforcement actions against companies if disclosures that are made or reaffirmed have a reasonable basis and are provided in good faith.

- The SEC's guidance around the use of internal records for calculating the pay ratio similarly provides flexibility to issuers in how they calculate their disclosure.

- Companies may use existing internal records to determine whether they can exclude their non-U.S.-based workforce when that group comprises less than 5% of the total workforce, with certain exclusions.

2.   Companies may use internal tax or payroll records to identify the median employee, "even if those records do not include every element of compensation, such as equity awards widely distributed to employees."

3.   Companies that intend to exclude independent contractors from the pay ratio calculation may use widely recognized tests of who is an employee, such as Internal Revenue Service guidance or other employment law, to determine whether an individual is an employee or independent contractor.[33]

13.   Section 955 of the Dodd-Frank Act amended Exchange Act § 14 by adding new subsection (j), which provides that:

The Commission shall, by rule, require each issuer to disclose in any proxy or consent solicitation material for an annual meeting of the shareholders of the issuer whether any employee or member of the board of directors of the issuer, or any designee of such employee or member, is permitted to purchase financial instruments (including prepaid variable forward contracts, equity swaps, collars, and exchange funds) that are designed to hedge or offset any decrease in the market value of equity securities—

(1)   granted to the employee or member of the board of directors by the issuer as part of the compensation of the employee or member of the board of directors; or

(2)   held, directly or indirectly, by the employee or member of the board of directors.

---

[33]   Abe M. Friedman et al., CamberView Partners Discusses SEC Guidance on New Pay Ratio Rule, The CLS Blue Sky Blog (September 27, 2017).

The goal is to enable "shareholders to better determine whether corporate insiders are permitted by the company to engage in transactions that may lead them to depart from the incentive alignment associated with ownership of shares."[34]

2) THE COMPENSATION COMMITTEE

As the name suggests, the compensation committee reviews and approves (or recommends to the full board) the compensation of senior executives and generally oversees the corporation's compensation policies. Proponents of having a separate compensation committee deal with such matters, rather than the board as a whole, argue that inside directors, even if recused from considering their own compensation, cannot objectively evaluate the compensation of other senior executives in light of the close relationship between one executive's compensation and that of another.

Under NYSE Listed Company Manual § 303A.05, the board of directors of all listed companies must have a compensation committee. The committee must consist solely of independent directors. Listed companies in which a shareholder or group of shareholders acting together own 50 percent or more of the stock are exempt from this requirement.

The NYSE requires that the compensation committee adopt a written charter setting out the committee's purpose, responsibilities, and powers. At a minimum, the charter must grant the compensation committee power to set performance goals for the CEO to meet, evaluate the CEO's performance in light of those goals, and set the CEO's pay. If the board wishes, the compensation committee may simply recommend a pay figure for the CEO, on which all the independent directors would then act. Notice that, in either case, only independent directors are involved in setting the CEO's salary. The committee must also have power to make recommendations to the board of directors with respect to the pay of other executive officers and any incentive or stock-based compensation plans that are subject to board approval. The power to hire, fire, and compensate compensation consultants must be vested in the compensation committee rather than the CEO.

In order to ensure compensation committee independence, the NYSE definition of independent director includes a somewhat curious provision under which someone will not be deemed independent if he "or an immediate family member is, or has been within the last three years, employed as an executive officer of another company where any of the listed company's present executive officers at the same time serves or served on that company's compensation committee." Suppose, for example, that June is a director of Beta Corporation. June is also the

---

[34]   Henry T. C. Hu, Financial Innovation and Governance Mechanisms: The Evolution of Decoupling and Transparency, 70 Bus. Law. 347, 368 (2015).

CFO of Zeus Corporation. Donna is Beta's CLO (aka general counsel), a member of Zeus's board of directors, and a member of Zeus's compensation committee. Under the NYSE rule, because Donna is on Zeus's compensation committee, June cannot be deemed an independent director of Beta. Donna can be deemed an independent director of Zeus, however, because the interlock rule runs in only one direction.

Dodd-Frank § 952 contains a number of provisions relating to compensation committees, including a directive that the SEC direct the self-regulatory organizations (SROs) to adopt listing standards requiring that each member of an issuer's compensation committee be independent.

PROBLEM

In 202X, Delaware corporation Acme International Pharmaceutical, Inc. (Acme) announced plans to spinoff its consumer over-the-counter drugs division to the company's shareholders. The newly formed spun off entity would be called Ajax Consumer Health, Inc. (Ajax), which also would be incorporated in Delaware. The spinoff transaction included a one-time grant of 50,000 Ajax shares to all members of Acme's board of directors.

Acme CEO Jane Jones negotiated a one-time bonus with Acme's compensation committee to reward her for having devised the spinoff plan. The committee agreed to award Jones options to acquire 1,000,000 Ajax common shares. If exercised, Jones' options would result in her owning 15% of Ajax's outstanding common stock.

> **WHAT'S THAT?**
>
> SPIN-OFF, Black's Law Dictionary (11th ed. 2019): A corporate divestiture in which a division of a corporation becomes an independent company and stock of the new company is distributed to the corporation's shareholders.

The compensation committee consisted of three directors: Stephen Smith, Rosemary Clowney, and Norman Baker, the committee's chairperson. Smith and Clowney had been close personal friends with Jones for decades. Both were in the process of negotiating with Jones about lucrative consulting deals to follow the completion of their board service.

The committee did not select its own independent compensation consultant. Rather, the committee was accepted Jones' recommendation to hire Powers Compensation Consultants to advice the committee. The committee did not know that Powers CEO Anne Bowman is Jones' sister-in-law and longtime friend.

Powers' report stated that the transaction was fair to Acme. In footnotes, however, the report acknowledged that Powers had been unable to find a single comparable transaction in which officers and directors of the parent corporation had been granted shares in the spun off entity. The Powers report failed to note that Jones' total direct compensation was 27% higher than the 75th percentile and 51% higher than the median among CEOs in Acme's peer group.

The committee unanimously recommended that the board of directors approve the proposed option plan. At a board meeting at which Jones was present and presided in her capacity as Chairperson of the Board, the board unanimously approved the plan with Jones voting in favor along with her fellow directors.

Evaluate.

3) CLAWBACKS

SEC v. Jenkins
718 F.Supp.2d 1070 (D.Ariz.2010)

. . .

BACKGROUND

During the time relevant to this action, CSK Auto Corporation ("CSK") was a publicly-traded retail company of automotive parts and accessories, operating under three brand names: Checker Auto Parts, Schucks Auto Supply, and Kragen Auto Parts. From January 1997 through August 2007, [Maynard L.] Jenkins was CSK's CEO and the chairman of its board of directors, receiving a base salary, bonuses, and stock option grants.

While Jenkins worked for CSK, the company engaged in a vendor allowance program called "Let's Work Together." The Complaint alleges that, by intentionally failing to properly account for receivables under this program, CSK reported greater pretax income than the company actually earned during fiscal years 2002, 2003, and 2004. Although the SEC does not allege that Jenkins personally was aware of the fraudulent concealment perpetrated by various CSK officers, Jenkins did certify the company's inaccurate financial statements for those years.

Eventually, to correct these overstatements, CSK filed two accounting restatements as required by federal securities laws, which Jenkins also certified. . . . In fact, the SEC has filed both civil complaints and criminal indictments against other CSK officers, alleging that those officers concealed the scheme from Jenkins.

From May 2003 through May 2005, Jenkins received over $2 million in compensation in the form of bonuses and other incentive-based and equity-based compensation. During the same period, Jenkins realized over $2 million from the sale of CSK securities. Jenkins has not reimbursed CSK for any portion of these bonuses, incentive-based compensation, equity-based compensation, or stock sale profits.

The SEC now seeks an order compelling Jenkins to reimburse CSK for this income pursuant to Section 304 of the Sarbanes-Oxley Act of 2002 ("Sarbanes-Oxley" or the "Act"), 15 U.S.C. § 7243 (2006). . . .

DISCUSSION

Section 304 of Sarbanes-Oxley provides:

(a) *Additional compensation prior to noncompliance with Commission financial reporting requirements.* If an issuer is required to prepare an accounting restatement due to the material noncompliance of the issuer, as a result of misconduct, with any financial reporting requirement under the securities laws, the chief executive officer and chief financial officer of the issuer shall reimburse the issuer for—

(1) any bonus or other incentive-based or equity-based compensation received by that person from the issuer during the 12-month period following the first public issuance or filing with the Commission (whichever first occurs) of the financial document embodying such financial reporting requirement; and

(2) any profits realized from the sale of securities of the issuer during that 12-month period.

(b) *Commission exemption authority.* The Commission may exempt any person from the application of subsection (a) of this section, as it deems necessary and appropriate.

15 U.S.C. § 7243.

I.   Section 304 Does Not Require Personal Misconduct.

. . .

"The purpose of statutory construction is to discern the intent of Congress in enacting a particular statute." *United States v. Daas*, 198 F.3d 1167, 1174 (9th Cir.1999). "The starting point for the interpretation of a statute is always its language," and "[a]ny inquiry must cease if the statutory language is unambiguous and the statutory scheme is coherent and consistent." *Alvarado v. Cajun Operating Co.*, 588 F.3d 1261, 1268 (9th Cir.2009) (citation omitted). Applying these steps of statutory interpretation, the Court holds that the text and structure of Section 304 require only the misconduct of the issuer, but do not necessarily require the specific misconduct of the issuer's CEO or CFO. Moreover, Section 304's legislative history supports this textual reading. . . .

A.   The Text of the Statute Requires Misconduct Only by the Issuer.

The relevant statutory phrase specifies that the reimbursement obligation is triggered if an issuer has to prepare an accounting restatement "due to the material noncompliance of the issuer, as a result of misconduct, with any financial reporting requirement under the securities laws." The ordinary, contemporary and common meaning of that language is that the misconduct of the issuer is the misconduct that triggers the reimbursement obligation of the CEO and the CFO. In this case, the issuer is a corporation. In general, a corporation acts through its officers, agents or employees and is liable for the actions of such persons acting within the scope of their agency. Thus, the plain language of the statute indicates that the misconduct of corporate officers, agents or employees acting within the scope of their agency or employment is sufficient misconduct to meet this element of the statute. Before reimbursement can be required, however, the issuer's misconduct must also be sufficiently serious to result in material noncompliance with a financial reporting requirement under the securities laws, and must require the issuer to file an accounting restatement.

. . .

WHAT'S THAT?

FINANCIAL RESTATEMENT, Black's Law Dictionary (10th ed. 2014): A report correcting material errors in a financial statement, esp. to adjust profits and losses after an accounting procedure has been disallowed."

In addition to the plain text of the relevant statutory language, Congress entitled this subsection of Sarbanes-Oxley as "Additional Compensation Prior to Noncompliance with Commission Financial Reporting Requirements." 15 U.S.C. § 7243(a). "Although statutory titles are not part of the legislation, they may be instructive in putting the statute in context." *Singh v. Gonzales*, 499 F.3d 969, 977 (9th Cir.2007). As the title of the subsection makes plain, it was Congress's purpose to recapture the additional compensation paid to a CEO during any period in which the corporate issuer was not in compliance with financial reporting requirements. A CEO need not be personally aware of financial misconduct to have received additional compensation during the period of that misconduct, and to have unfairly benefitted therefrom. When a CEO either sells stock or receives a bonus in the period of financial noncompliance, the CEO may unfairly benefit from a misperception of the financial position of the issuer that results from those misstated financials, even if the CEO was unaware of the misconduct leading to misstated financials. It is not irrational for Congress to require that such additional compensation amounts be repaid to the issuer.

. . .

Further, in ascertaining the purposes to be served by a statute, it is appropriate to look at the larger statutory scheme of which the particular statute is a part. Pursuant to the immediately preceding sections of the Sarbanes-Oxley Act, particularly Section 302, an issuer's CEO and CFO are required to certify each annual or quarterly report of the issuer. In so doing, the CEO and the CFO also certify that they are responsible for the existence, design, and operation of effective internal controls that provide assurances as to the accuracy of the issuer's financial statements. Id. Section 304 provides an incentive for CEOs and CFOs to be rigorous in their creation and certification of internal controls by requiring that they reimburse additional compensation received during periods of corporate non-compliance regardless of whether or not they were aware of the misconduct giving rise to the misstated financials.[2]

. . .

B.   Legislative History Affirms the Court's Textual Reading.

. . .

The House and Senate passed different versions of Sarbanes-Oxley, but only the House's version, which did not become law, included language regarding the CEO or CFO's scienter in the context of disgorgement. . . .

On the other hand, the Senate version of the bill, S. 2673 (the "Senate Bill"), included no similar discussion of scienter. See S. 2673, 107th Cong. § 304 (2002). In contrast to the House Bill, the Senate Bill was passed after additional news of corporate misconduct arose, such as Adelphia's massive restatement to account for previously undisclosed loans, Tyco's former CEO's indictment for tax evasion,

> **FYI**
>
> Although *Jenkins'* reading of the statute is widely accepted, the SEC "has been historically reluctant to utilize § 304." *SEC v. Baker*, 2012 WL 5499497 at *3 (D. Tex. 2012). Moreover, most of the actions the SEC has brought "have involved allegations of improprieties by the CEO or CFO in question." Id.

Worldcom's accounting scheme, and Imclone's CEO's insider trading charges. As it relates to Section 304 of the Act, the language in the Senate Bill ultimately became the version signed into law, without mentioning scienter or requiring misconduct on behalf of the officers in order to trigger reimbursement.

Additionally, the Senate had the opportunity to consider an amendment that would have limited Section 304 to the officers and directors "with knowledge, at the time of the misconduct, of the material noncompliance of the issuer." See Arnold & Porter Legislative History: Sarbanes-Oxley Act of 2002, P.L. 107–204, 116 Stat. 745, History 40-C, 2002 WL 32054475 (July 10, 2002). This amendment arguably would have created a personal misconduct element, but it was tabled.

. . .

---

[2]   To the extent that a CEO is actually aware of misconduct that results in misstated financial statements, the CEO may be responsible for additional civil and criminal penalties. See, e.g., 15 U.S.C. 78u(d), 18 U.S.C. § 1350; 17 C.F.R. § 240.10b–5; id. § 240.13a–14. This additional potential liability in cases in of the CEO's actual awareness of the misconduct, however, provides no support for an argument that Section 304 only permits the reimbursement of additional compensation paid to the CEO in cases of such actual awareness. The statute's plain meaning is to the contrary. In fact, because other securities laws already provide other civil and criminal penalties for a CEO's or CFO's knowing misconduct, interpreting Section 304 as covering situations where CEOs and CFOs were unaware of any misconduct avoids redundancy with existing securities laws.

C.   Delaware's Indemnification Statute Is Irrelevant.

The parties agree that " 'statutory interpretations which would produce absurd results are to be avoided.' " See *Ariz. State Bd. for Charter Schs. v. U.S. Dep't of Educ.*, 464 F.3d 1003, 1008 (9th Cir.2006) (quoting Ma v. Ashcroft, 361 F.3d 553, 558 (9th Cir.2004)). As a preliminary matter, the absurd results canon of statutory interpretation "has no application" where, as here, "a statute is clear" as to what Congress "plainly and intentionally provided." *Peabody Coal Co. v. Navajo Nation*, 75 F.3d 457, 468 (9th Cir.1996) (internal quotations omitted).

Even if congressional intent was unclear, however, Defendant's argument would fail. Defendant contends that the SEC's interpretation of Section 304 would create absurd results because Delaware law, which governs CSK as a Delaware corporation, would allow Jenkins to be indemnified by CSK if Jenkins acted "in good faith" and in a manner that Jenkins "reasonably believed to be in or not opposed to the best interests of the corporation." 8 Del. C. § 145(a). While such a result may disrupt Congress's apparent purpose in having a CEO reimburse the issuer, Defendant cites no authority that a federal statute's interpretation must conform to state statutes. Rather, the Supremacy Clause suggests the analysis cuts the opposite way. See U.S. Const. art. IV, cl. 2. Although, at this point, the Court need not determine the efficacy of Delaware's statutory scheme or the extent to which Delaware's statute conflicts with Section 304, the existence of a state statute does not alter the meaning of the federal statute.

. . .

Dodd-Frank § 954

RECOVERY OF ERRONEOUSLY AWARDED COMPENSATION. The Securities Exchange Act of 1934 is amended by inserting after section 10C, as added by section 952, the following:

"SEC. 10D.   RECOVERY OF ERRONEOUSLY AWARDED COMPENSATION POLICY.

"(a) LISTING STANDARDS.—The Commission shall, by rule, direct the national securities exchanges and national securities associations to prohibit the listing of any security of an issuer that does not comply with the requirements of this section.

"(b) RECOVERY OF FUNDS.—The rules of the Commission under subsection (a) shall require each issuer to develop and implement a policy providing—

"(1) for disclosure of the policy of the issuer on incentive-based compensation that is based on financial information required to be reported under the securities laws; and

"(2) that, in the event that the issuer is required to prepare an accounting restatement due to the material noncompliance of the issuer with any financial reporting requirement under the securities laws, the issuer will recover from any current or former executive officer of the issuer who received incentive-based compensation (including stock options awarded as compensation) during the 3-year period preceding the date on which the issuer is required to prepare an accounting restatement, based on the erroneous data, in excess of what would have been paid to the executive officer under the accounting restatement.".

NOTES AND QUESTIONS

1. How does Dodd-Frank § 954 change the clawback rules under SOX § 304?

2. In July 2015, the SEC issued a proposed rule implementing Dodd-Frank § 954. As of this date, no final action has been taken.

3. Former SEC Commissioner Troy Paredes has argued that:

Section 954 appears to operate as a "no-fault" provision—that is, Section 954 does not require that the restatement triggering the clawback be the result of any misconduct, which of course is to say that an individual may be required to forfeit some of his or her pay even if the executive committed no misdeed. By way of illustration, an executive who has worked diligently and honestly at a company that has robust financial controls and top-notch procedures and systems may nonetheless have to pay back a considerable portion of his or her compensation if the company has to restate because of an accounting error. I can understand why many might find this troubling.[35]

What is the policy justification for recovering compensation from a CEO or CFO who was not personally involved in or at least aware of the misconduct that resulted in the restatement?

4. What might be the unintended consequences of SOX § 304 and Dodd-Frank § 954? Put another way, how should rational corporate executives respond to these provisions when negotiating compensation with their employers?

5. What questions does Dodd-Frank § 954 leave open?

6. Do the provisions of SOX § 304 and Dodd-Frank § 954 unduly intrude into the states' role as primary regulators of corporate governance? Are they consistent with the traditional dividing line between state corporate and federal securities law?

---

[35] Troy Paredes, Remarks at Society of Corporate Secretaries & Governance Professionals, 66th National Conference on "The Shape of Things to Come" (July 13, 2012).

4) SAY ON PAY

Dodd-Frank § 951

SHAREHOLDER VOTE ON EXECUTIVE COMPENSATION DISCLOSURES. The Securities Exchange Act of 1934 (15 U.S.C. 78a et seq.) is amended by inserting after section 14 (15 U.S.C. 78n) the following:

"SEC. 14A.   SHAREHOLDER APPROVAL OF EXECUTIVE COMPENSATION.

"(a) SEPARATE RESOLUTION REQUIRED.—

"(1) IN GENERAL.—Not less frequently than once every 3 years, a proxy or consent or authorization for an annual or other meeting of the shareholders for which the proxy solicitation rules of the Commission require compensation disclosure shall include a separate resolution subject to shareholder vote to approve the compensation of executives, as disclosed pursuant to section 229.402 of title 17, Code of Federal Regulations, or any successor thereto.

"(2) FREQUENCY OF VOTE.—Not less frequently than once every 6 years, a proxy or consent or authorization for an annual or other meeting of the shareholders for which the proxy solicitation rules of the Commission require compensation disclosure shall include a separate resolution subject to shareholder vote to determine whether votes on the resolutions required under paragraph (1) will occur every 1, 2, or 3 years.

"(3) EFFECTIVE DATE.—The proxy or consent or authorization for the first annual or other meeting of the shareholders occurring after the end of the 6-month period beginning on the date of enactment of this section shall include—

"(A) the resolution described in paragraph (1); and

"(B) a separate resolution subject to shareholder vote to determine whether votes on the resolutions required under paragraph (1) will occur every 1, 2, or 3 years.

"(b) SHAREHOLDER APPROVAL OF GOLDEN PARACHUTE COMPENSATION.—

"(1) DISCLOSURE.—In any proxy or consent solicitation material (the solicitation of which is subject to the rules of the Commission pursuant to subsection (a)) for a meeting of the shareholders occurring after the end of the 6-month period beginning on the date of enactment of this section, at which shareholders are asked to approve an acquisition, merger, consolidation, or proposed sale or other disposition of all or substantially all the assets of an issuer, the person making such solicitation shall disclose in the proxy or consent solicitation material, in a clear and simple form in accordance with regulations to be promulgated by the Commission, any agreements or understandings that such person has with any named executive officers of such issuer (or of the acquiring issuer, if such issuer is not the acquiring issuer) concerning any type of compensation (whether present, deferred, or contingent) that is based on or otherwise relates to the acquisition, merger, consolidation, sale, or other disposition of all or substantially all of the assets of the issuer and the aggregate total of all such compensation that may (and the conditions upon which it may) be paid or become payable to or on behalf of such executive officer.

"(2) SHAREHOLDER APPROVAL.—Any proxy or consent or authorization relating to the proxy or consent solicitation material containing the disclosure required by paragraph (1) shall include a separate resolution subject to shareholder vote to approve such agreements or understandings and compensation as disclosed, unless such agreements or understandings have been subject to a shareholder vote under subsection (a).

"(c) RULE OF CONSTRUCTION.—The shareholder vote referred to in subsections (a) and (b) shall not be binding on the issuer or the board of directors of an issuer, and may not be construed—

"(1) as overruling a decision by such issuer or board of directors;

"(2) to create or imply any change to the fiduciary duties of such issuer or board of directors;

"(3) to create or imply any additional fiduciary duties for such issuer or board of directors; or

"(4) to restrict or limit the ability of shareholders to make proposals for inclusion in proxy materials related to executive compensation.

"(d) DISCLOSURE OF VOTES.—Every institutional investment manager subject to section 13(f) shall report at least annually how it voted on any shareholder vote pursuant to subsections (a) and (b), unless such vote is otherwise required to be reported publicly by rule or regulation of the Commission.

"(e) EXEMPTION.—The Commission may, by rule or order, exempt an issuer or class of issuers from the requirement under subsection (a) or (b). In determining whether to make an exemption under this subsection, the Commission shall take into account, among other considerations, whether the requirements under subsections (a) and (b) disproportionately burdens small issuers.".

SEC Exchange Act Rule 14a–21

(a) If a solicitation is made by a registrant, other than an emerging growth company as defined in Rule 12b–2 (§ 240.12b–2), and the solicitation relates to an annual or other meeting of shareholders at which directors will be elected and for which the rules of the Commission require executive compensation disclosure pursuant to Item 402 of Regulation S–K (§ 229.402 of this chapter), the registrant shall, for the first annual or other meeting of shareholders on or after January 21, 2011, or for the first annual or other meeting of shareholders on or after January 21, 2013 if the registrant is a smaller reporting company, and thereafter no later than the annual or other meeting of shareholders held in the third calendar year after the immediately preceding vote under this subsection, include a separate resolution subject to shareholder advisory vote to approve the compensation of its named executive officers, as disclosed pursuant to Item 402 of Regulation S–K.

Instruction to paragraph (A): The registrant's resolution shall indicate that the shareholder advisory vote under this subsection is to approve the compensation of the registrant's named executive officers as disclosed pursuant to Item 402 of Regulation S–K (§ 229.402 of this chapter). The following is a non-exclusive example of a resolution that would satisfy the requirements of this subsection: "RESOLVED, that the compensation paid to the company's named executive officers, as disclosed pursuant to Item 402 of Regulation S–K, including the Compensation Discussion and Analysis, compensation tables and narrative discussion is hereby APPROVED."

(b) If a solicitation is made by a registrant, other than an emerging growth company as defined in Rule 12b–2 (§ 240.12b–2), and the solicitation relates to an annual or other meeting of shareholders at which directors will be elected and for which the rules of the Commission require executive compensation disclosure pursuant to Item 402 of Regulation S–K (§ 229.402 of this chapter}, the registrant shall, for the first annual or other meeting of shareholders on or after January 21, 2011, or for the first annual or other meeting of shareholders on or after January 21, 2013 if the registrant is a smaller reporting company, and thereafter no later than the annual or other meeting of shareholders held in the sixth calendar year after the immediately preceding vote under this subsection, include a separate resolution subject to shareholder advisory vote as to whether the shareholder vote required by paragraph (a) of this section should occur every 1, 2 or 3 years. Registrants required to provide a separate shareholder vote pursuant to § 240.14a–20 of this chapter shall include the separate resolution required by this section for the first annual or other meeting of shareholders after the registrant has repaid all obligations arising from financial assistance provided under the TARP, as defined in section 3(8) of the Emergency Economic Stabilization Act of 2008 (12 U.S.C. 5202(8)), and thereafter no later than the annual or other meeting of shareholders held in the sixth calendar year after the immediately preceding vote under this subsection.

(c)   If a solicitation is made by a registrant, other than an emerging growth company as defined in Rule 12b–2 (§ 240.12b–2), for a meeting of shareholders at which shareholders are asked to approve an acquisition, merger, consolidation or proposed sale or other disposition of all or substantially all the assets of the registrant, the registrant shall include a separate resolution subject to shareholder advisory vote to approve any agreements or understandings and compensation disclosed pursuant to Item 402(t) of Regulation S–K (§ 229.402(t) of this chapter), unless such agreements or understandings have been subject to a shareholder advisory vote under paragraph (a) of this section. Consistent with section 14A(b) of the Exchange Act (15 U.S.C. 78n–1(b)), any agreements or understandings between an acquiring company and the named executive officers of the registrant, where the registrant is not the acquiring company, are not required to be subject to the separate shareholder advisory vote under this paragraph.

Instructions to § 240.14A–21:

1.   Disclosure relating to the compensation of directors required by Item 402(k) (§ 229.402(k) of this chapter) and Item 402(r) of Regulation S–K (§ 229.402(r) of this chapter) is not subject to the shareholder vote required by paragraph (a) of this section. If a registrant includes disclosure pursuant to Item 402(s) of Regulation S–K (§ 229.402(s) of this chapter) about the registrant's compensation policies and practices as they relate to risk management and risk-taking incentives, these policies and practices would not be subject to the shareholder vote required by paragraph (a) of this section. To the extent that risk considerations are a material aspect of the registrant's compensation policies or decisions for named executive officers, the registrant is required to discuss them as part of its Compensation Discussion and Analysis under § 229.402(b) of this chapter, and therefore such disclosure would be considered by shareholders when voting on executive compensation.

2.   If a registrant includes disclosure of golden parachute compensation arrangements pursuant to Item 402(t) (§ 229.402(t) of this chapter) in an annual meeting proxy statement, such disclosure would be subject to the shareholder advisory vote required by paragraph (a) of this section.

3.   Registrants that are smaller reporting companies entitled to provide scaled disclosure in accordance with Item 402(*l*) of Regulation S–K (§ 229.402(*l*) of this chapter) are not required to include a Compensation Discussion and Analysis in their proxy statements in order to comply with this section. For smaller reporting companies, the vote required by paragraph (a) of this section must be to approve the compensation of the named executive officers as disclosed pursuant to Item 402(m) through (q) of Regulation S–K (§ 229.402(m) through (q) of this chapter).

4.   A registrant that has ceased being an emerging growth company shall include the first separate resolution described under § 240.14a–21(a) not later than the end of (i) in the case of a registrant that was an emerging growth company for less than two years after the date of first sale of common equity securities of the registrant pursuant to an effective registration statement under the Securities Act of 1933 (15 U.S.C 77aet seq.), the three-year period beginning on such date; and (ii) in the case of any other registrant, the one-year period beginning on the date the registrant is no longer an emerging growth company.

Laborers' Local v. Intersil

868 F. Supp. 2d 838 (N.D. Cal. 2012)

. . . Intersil is a Delaware corporation, headquartered in Milpitas, California, which designs, develops, manufactures and markets high-performance analog and mixed-signal integrated circuits. Compensia, a citizen of California, is an executive compensation advisory firm that assisted the Intersil Board in connection with the 2010 executive pay. . . . The thirteen individually named defendants are directors and officers of Intersil. Defendant Bell is the CEO, President, and a director of Intersil. His pay was increased by 40.6 percent in 2010. . . .

On March 26, 2011, the Intersil Board recommended shareholder approval of the 2010 executive compensation. The executive compensation plan raised the compensation of the company's named executives by an average of 41.7 percent, pursuant to Intersil's "pay for performance" policy. On May 4, 2011, pursuant to the Dodd-Frank Wall Street Reform and Consumer Protection Act ("Dodd-Frank Act"), a non-binding shareholder vote was held on executive compensation. In that vote, 56 percent of voting Intersil shareholders rejected the Board's 2010 CEO and top executive compensation.

On August 19, 2011, Plaintiff filed this action for breach of fiduciary duty and unjust enrichment on behalf of Intersil by one of its shareholders against several of Intersil's current executives and Board of Directors, alleging that the 2010 executive compensation approved by the Board of Directors was "excessive, irrational, and unreasonable" and that Intersil has been and continues to be severely injured by the executive pay. . . .

. . . The business judgment rule is "a presumption that in making a business decision the directors of a corporation acted on an informed basis, in good faith and in the honest belief that the action taken was in the best interest of the company." Aronson, 473 A.2d at 812. Under the business judgment rule, "directors are entitled to a presumption that they were faithful to their fiduciary duties . . . . [and] the burden is upon the plaintiff in a derivative action to overcome that presumption." *Beam v. Stewart*, 845 A.2d 1040, 1048–49 (Del.2004). . . . A board's decision on executive compensation is "entitled to great deference." *Brehm*, 746 A.2d at 263.

The complaint fails to allege facts showing that Intersil's Board was not adequately informed in making the decision regarding the 2010 executive compensation. . . .

With regards to the honesty and good faith of the Board, Plaintiff points to the shareholder vote to call the directors' decision into question. . . . Plaintiff claims that the negative "say-on-pay" shareholder vote is evidence showing that directors failed to act in the shareholders' best interests and rebuts the presumption that the Board's decision regarding compensation is entitled to business judgment protection.[5]

Section 951 of the Dodd-Frank Act requires public companies to conduct a non-binding shareholder vote on executive compensation at least once every three years. Senator Barney Frank noted that the "say on pay" provision was passed "to empower shareholders." Hearing on Executive Compensation Oversight Before the H. Comm. on Financial Services (Sept. 24, 2010) (statement of Rep. Barney Frank, Chairman, H. Comm. on Financial Services). The shareholder vote is meant to give shareholders "the ability to hold executives accountable, and to

---

[5]   Plaintiff relies heavily on *NECA-IBEW Pension Fund on behalf of Cincinnati Bell, Inc. v. Cox*, 2011 WL 4383368 (S.D. Ohio Sept. 20, 2011), a similar case recently decided in the United States District Court for the Southern District of Ohio applying Ohio state law to interpret the Dodd-Frank Act. The court found that where a majority of shareholders, in a shareholder vote, disapproved of the executive compensation, plaintiff has demonstrated sufficient facts to show that there is reason to doubt that the directors could exercise their independent business judgment over whether to bring suit against themselves for breach of fiduciary duty in awarding the challenged compensation. Id. at *4. However, this case has been called into question by Plumbers Local No. 137 Pension Fund v. Davis, 2012 WL 104776 (D.Or. Jan. 11, 2012). The District Court for the District of Oregon noted that the *Cincinnati Bell* court apparently lacked subject matter jurisdiction and the plaintiff failed to disclose contrary authority in response to the court's specific inquiry. Id. at *5.

A recent case decided by the Georgia Superior Court, *Teamsters Local 237 Additional Security Benefit Fund ("Beazer") v. McCarthy*, No. 2011-cv197841, 2011 WL 4836230 (Superior Court of Fulton County, Ga., 9 Sept. 16, 2011), applied Delaware law in a situation similar to the case at hand. In Beazer, plaintiffs alleged that defendants had breached their duties of loyalty, candor, and good faith by approving "excessive" executive pay and that the results of the shareholder "say on pay" vote rebutted the presumption of the business judgment rule. Id. at *3. . . . The Georgia Superior Court . . . reiterated that the Dodd-Frank Act preserves the preexisting fiduciary duty framework concerning directors' executive compensation decisions and that shareholders' independent business judgment does not rebut the presumption of business judgment. Id. at *11. The court refused to conclude that "an adverse say on pay vote alone suffices to rebut the presumption of business judgment protection applicable to directors' compensation decisions." However, the court did not conclude that such a vote could not be used along with other facts to rebut the business judgment protection. Id. at *12.

disapprove of misguided incentive schemes." 156 Cong. Rec. S5902–01, S5916 (2010) (statement of Sen. Jack Reed). Section 951 expressly states that the shareholder vote is not binding and it "may not be construed . . . to create or imply any change to the fiduciary duties" nor "to create or imply any additional fiduciary duties." 15 U.S.C. § 78n–1(c). While the few courts analyzing section 951 of the Dodd-Frank Act agree that it does not create any new fiduciary duties,[6] no court in California or Delaware has decided whether a negative shareholder vote under the Dodd-Frank Act can be used as evidence to rebut the business judgment rule presumption under Delaware law.

Congress was explicit that the shareholder vote on executive pay is non-binding, but the Act is silent on what consideration courts should give to the shareholder vote. Where resolution of a question of federal law turns on a statute and the intention of Congress, courts first look to the statutory language, and if it is unclear, then to the legislative history. Congress must have intended for the shareholder vote to have some weight if, as discussed above, the goals of section 951 are to empower shareholders and to hold executives accountable. Furthermore, if the shareholder vote approving executive compensation is meant to have no effect whatsoever, it seems unlikely that Congress would have included a specific provision requiring such a vote.

Earlier cases, decided before passage of the Dodd-Frank Act, held that Delaware law allows directors to take good faith actions that they believe will benefit stockholders, "even if they realize that the stockholders do not agree with them." *In re Lear Corp. S'holder Litig.*, 967 A.2d 640, 655 (Del.Ch.2008). In *Lear*, the company's board knew that shareholder approval of the contested decision was unlikely, but there was no shareholder vote that expressly indicated disagreement. The *Lear* court noted that it would be inconsistent with the business judgment rule for a court to "sustain a complaint grounded in the concept that directors act disloyally if they adopt a merger agreement in good faith simply because stockholders might (?), were likely (?), or were almost certain (?) to reject it." *In re Lear*, 967 A.2d at 655. In the case at hand, unlike in *Lear*, no speculation is necessary, because the Intersil Board knew for a fact that a majority of shareholders did not approve the executive compensation. Therefore, reliance on cases such as *Lear*, which were decided before passage of the Dodd-Frank Act and where no shareholder vote took place, is misplaced under these particular facts.

---

[6]   The U.S. District Court in Southern California recently ruled that the Dodd-Frank Act did not create a private right or fiduciary duties. Assad v. Hart, 2012 WL 33220 (S.D.Cal. Jan. 6, 2012); Dennis v. Hart, 2012 WL 33199 (S.D.Cal. Jan. 6, 2012). In both cases, the court held that plaintiff failed to state a claim for breach of fiduciary duty based on defendants' failure to respond to the negative say on pay vote. Assad, 2012 WL 33220, at *4; Dennis, 2012 WL 33199, at *3. However, the court declined to rule on whether a negative vote can rebut the business judgment rule, noting that "[t]o the extent that Plaintiff seeks to use the negative say on pay vote as evidence that the business judgment presumption was rebutted, resolution of the issue depends on California state law." Assad, 2012 WL 33220, at *5; Dennis, 2012 WL 33199, at *4. The court remanded this issue to state courts.

Looking to precedent from other courts that have interpreted the shareholder vote provision of the Dodd-Frank Act, as well as the purpose of the Dodd-Frank Act, this court concludes that a shareholder vote on executive compensation under the Act has substantial evidentiary weight. . . . Ruling only on the particular facts presented in the case before the court, where 56 percent of shareholders disapproved of Intersil's 2010 executive compensation package, the court finds that the shareholder vote alone is not enough to rebut the presumption of the business judgment rule. Additional facts are required for plaintiff to raise a reasonable doubt that the decision was not a valid exercise of business judgment.

. . .

Accordingly, . . . Defendants' motions to dismiss the Complaint for failure to state a claim are GRANTED with leave to amend.

NOTES AND QUESTIONS

1.   What other sorts of evidence would have helped plaintiff make out its claim that the business judgment rule had been rebutted?

2.   As interpreted by *Intersil*, is say on pay consistent with the traditional dividing line between state corporate governance and federal securities law?

3.   Is the *Interstil* court's ruling that a say on pay vote has evidentiary value consistent with the disclaimers Congress made in § 954 regarding the effect of the statute on the fiduciary duties of directors under state law (or, more precisely, the lack thereof)?

4.   Does it matter legally whether the board vote on the executive compensation plan takes place before or after the shareholder say on pay vote? Should it?

5.   According to compensation consulting firm Steven Hall & Partners, in 2016 there were 2,925 say on pay votes. Only 47 companies received a negative shareholder vote (1.6%). Over seventy percent of companies received "for" votes from 90% or more of the voting shares. The average vote across all companies was 90.0% for approval, 8.7% opposed, and 1.3% abstaining. Similar results have obtained in each of the years since say on pay went into effect. In light of these results, is the cost and expense of holding say on pay votes justified?

6.   Is it reasonable to expect say on pay votes to curb compensation practices that induce managers to take on excessive risk?

7.   If you were an issuer CEO, what arguments would you make to shareholders in favor of holding the say on pay vote only every three years?

8.   The United Kingdom was the first country to adopt a say on pay rule, doing so in 2002. "Since that time, there has been a wave of Say on Pay legislation enacted in countries around the world, including the U.S., Australia, Belgium, the Netherlands, and Sweden, with Swiss voters most

recently approving a binding shareholder vote on executive remuneration."[36] Interestingly, the results have been largely similar across countries:

First, when Say on Pay votes are held, shareholders vote to approve the pay levels, pay composition, and pay policies, at almost all companies by very wide margins. Second, third-party voting advisors, such as Institutional Shareholder Services ("ISS"), pay a crucial role in informing institutional investors about executive compensation practices and packages. These advisors' recommendations for, or against, a company's pay plan may also carry significant weight with their institutional clients, and can dramatically impact the outcome of a vote. Third, Say on Pay's strongest effect has been felt at companies that exhibit poor performance with relatively high levels of pay. Fourth, when companies receive low levels of shareholder support in a vote, directors frequently contact their investors to better explain their policies, thereby giving shareholders greater input into pay issues. Fifth, Say on Pay votes appear to have had little long-term impact on executive pay levels, while research on their impact on shareholder value tends to show a small positive impact, although some studies find no, or negative, effects.[37]

5) BAN ON LOANS TO OFFICERS AND DIRECTORS

SOX § 402

(a) PROHIBITION ON PERSONAL LOANS TO EXECUTIVES.—Section 13 of the Securities Exchange Act of 1934 (15 U.S.C. 78m), as amended by this Act, is amended by adding at the end the following:

"(k) PROHIBITION ON PERSONAL LOANS TO EXECUTIVES.—

"(1) IN GENERAL.—It shall be unlawful for any issuer (as defined in section 2 of the Sarbanes-Oxley Act of 2002), directly or indirectly, including through any subsidiary, to extend or maintain credit, to arrange for the extension of credit, or to renew an extension of credit, in the form of a personal loan to or for any director or executive officer (or equivalent thereof) of that issuer. An extension of credit maintained by the issuer on the date of enactment of this subsection shall not be subject to the provisions of this subsection, provided that there is no material modification to any term of any such extension of credit or any renewal of any such extension of credit on or after that date of enactment.

"(2) LIMITATION.—Paragraph (1) does not preclude any home improvement and manufactured home loans (as that

---

[36]   Randall S. Thomas & Christoph Van der Elst, Say on Pay Around the World, 92 Wash. U.L. Rev. 653, 655 (2015).

[37]   Id. at 657.

term is defined in section 5 of the Home Owners' Loan Act (12 U.S.C. 1464)), consumer credit (as defined in section 103 of the Truth in Lending Act (15 U.S.C. 1602)), or any extension of credit under an open end credit plan (as defined in section 103 of the Truth in Lending Act (15 U.S.C. 1602)), or a charge card (as defined in section 127(c)(4)(e) of the Truth in Lending Act (15 U.S.C. 1637(c)(4)(e)), or any extension of credit by a broker or dealer registered under section 15 of this title to an employee of that broker or dealer to buy, trade, or carry securities, that is permitted under rules or regulations of the Board of Governors of the Federal Reserve System pursuant to section 7 of this title (other than an extension of credit that would be used to purchase the stock of that issuer), that is—

"(A) made or provided in the ordinary course of the consumer credit business of such issuer;

"(B) of a type that is generally made available by such issuer to the public; and

"(C) made by such issuer on market terms, or terms that are no more favorable than those offered by the issuer to the general public for such extensions of credit.

"(3) RULE OF CONSTRUCTION FOR CERTAIN LOANS.—Paragraph (1) does not apply to any loan made or maintained by an insured depository institution (as defined in section 3 of the Federal Deposit Insurance Act (12 U.S.C. 1813)), if the loan is subject to the insider lending restrictions of section 22(h) of the Federal Reserve Act (12 U.S.C. 375b).".

Envirokare Tech, Inc. v. Pappas

420 F. Supp. 2d 291 (S.D. N.Y. 2006)

This is an action against plaintiff's former chief executive officer, Steve Pappas, for breach of fiduciary duty and a declaration of the continuing validity of a voting trust containing some of the shares of Envirokare Tech, Inc. ("Envirokare") owned by Pappas. . . .

Facts

The reader may be spared the tale of the company's disenchantment with Pappas and the separation of their relationship. It suffices for present purposes to say that Envirokare now accuses him of gross mismanagement and worse and seeks to recover substantial damages and that Pappas is equally complimentary of the company and seeks substantial damages in his own right.

Envirokare is a Nevada corporation, the by-laws of which provide in relevant part:

"[T]he Corporation shall pay the expenses of officers and directors of the Corporation incurred in defending a civil or criminal action, suit or proceeding, as they are incurred and in advance of the final disposition of such matter, upon receipt of an undertaking in form and substance acceptable to the Board of Directors for the repayment of such advances if it is ultimately determined by a court of competent jurisdiction that the officer or director is not entitled to be indemnified."

By letter dated December 12, 2005, Pappas demanded, through counsel, that the company advance him the costs of defending this action. Enclosed with the letter was an undertaking to repay any such amounts advanced by Envirokare in the event it ultimately was determined that Pappas is not entitled to indemnification. Envirokare's counsel promptly replied that the company would not advance expenses . . . .

Discussion

Sarbanes-Oxley

. . . Envirokare claims that [SOX § 402] forecloses the advancement of expenses to officers and directors by reporting companies because these advances, though authorized by their by-laws and state law are forbidden extensions of credit. . . .

To begin with, Sarbanes-Oxley does not bar all extensions of credit[3] by reporting companies to their officers and directors, only those that take the form of "personal loans." While the statutory language is not especially helpful in discriminating between loans that are "personal" and those that are not, recourse to the context in which the statute was enacted and to common sense remains appropriate.

. . . Envirokare has not called the Court's attention to even a hint that Congress was concerned with stopping the advancement of defense costs to corporate officials pursuant to by-laws and state corporation statutes, and the Court is aware of none. Moreover, Congress, had it intended such a radical step as prohibiting such advances,[7] surely would have made its purpose evident in explicit terms.

This conclusion is reinforced by the absurd consequences that would flow from the adoption of the position taken by Envirokare. As Professor Coffee has pointed out, such an interpretation of the statute "would on its face bar a $2,000 travel advance to a Vice President who is about to fly to London to close a deal for his corporation." It would render it equally unlawful for a corporate officer to take a few dollars from petty cash to buy postage stamps for the purpose of mailing a company's tax return to the Internal Revenue Service.

---

[3]   Pappas does not deny that an advance to pay legal expenses is a loan or extension of credit.

[7]   The statutes of every state and the District of Columbia authorize corporations to indemnify directors for litigation expenses. 2 AMERICAN LAW INSTITUTE, PRINCIPLES OF CORPORATE GOVERNANCE: ANALYSIS AND RECOMMENDATIONS § 7.20, Reporter's Note 1 (1994). Most states, permit advancement of defense costs "upon receipt of an undertaking . . . to repay" if required. 2 DENNIS J. BLOCK, ET AL., THE BUSINESS JUDGMENT RULE 1894 (1998).

. . .

There doubtless will be cases in which distinguishing between forbidden personal loans and permitted advances will present nice questions of law and policy. But the Court is put in mind of *Jacobellis v. Ohio*,[14] where Justice Stewart, faced with the question whether a particular movie constituted hard-core pornography, famously wrote:

> "I shall not attempt further to define the kinds of material I understand to be embraced within that shorthand description; and perhaps I could never succeed in intelligibly doing so. But I know it when I see it, and the motion picture involved in this case is not that."[15]

The Court need not for present purposes define "personal loan," but an advance of defense costs pursuant to state law and corporate by-laws is not within that term. The Sarbanes-Oxley Act does not prohibit such advances.

. . .

NOTES AND QUESTIONS

1.   As the *Pappas* court noted, Congress was concerned with large loans made to executives. Such loans can be used to hide executive compensation. From a tax perspective, salary and dividends are taxable to the recipient, but the proceeds of a loan are not taxable income. From an accounting perspective, loans are corporate assets, so the money in a sense stays on the books, while the company must deduct salary and dividends from assets.

Yet, it is not clear that a flat prohibition—rather than just enhanced disclosure of insider loans—was appropriate. Section 402 directly preempts the interested party transaction provisions of state corporate law, which currently permit the making of loans to directors and officers provided the loans are approved by a majority of the disinterested directors or the shareholders. While that requirement may not have prevented every instance of abuse, preemption of state law ought to be undertaken only when states have clearly failed and the federal alternative is a clear improvement. Neither condition was satisfied here.

Based on her review of pre-SOX studies, Roberta Romano concluded that "executive loans in a large class of cases served their purpose well, [by] aligning the manager's and shareholders' interest."[38] Accordingly, she contended, the "blanket prohibition of executive loans in SOX" was self-evidently a public policy error."[39]

---

[14]   378 U.S. 184, 84 S.Ct. 1676, 12 L.Ed.2d 793 (1964).

[15]   Id. at 197, 84 S.Ct. 1676 (Stewart, J., concurring).

[38]   Roberta Romano, The Sarbanes-Oxley Act and the Making of Quack Corporate Governance, 114 Yale L.J. 1521, 1539 (2005).

[39]   Id.

The provision in the original Senate bill, which was consistent with the conventional federal regulatory approach, required disclosure of executive loans and did not prohibit them. Such an approach would have been far less problematic than the final legislative product from the perspective of shareholder welfare. It would have had the effect of facilitating the termination of loans most unlikely to benefit shareholders, by highlighting their presence to investors who could then place those loans' elimination onto a corporate governance agenda (in the many states where they would otherwise not be involved because shareholder approval of loans is not required). Instead, the legislation is a blunderbuss approach that prohibits all loans, whether or not they are useful in facilitating the shareholders' objective of providing a sought-after incentive effect.[40]

2. In 2013, financial services firm RingsEnd Partners, LLC obtained interpretive guidance from the staff of the SEC's Division of Corporation Finance regarding a proposed equity-based incentive compensation (EBIC) program, which was the first such guidance issued by the SEC:

> Under the EBIC program, participating employees would place shares of stock awarded under a compensation program into a trust, which would use the shares as collateral for a loan from an independent lender. The trust would use the proceeds of the loan to purchase additional shares, and subsequently sell enough shares to pay back the loan and transfer remaining shares to the participating employees. As described in RingsEnd's letter to the staff, the EBIC structure would result in favorable tax treatment for the employees and incentivize them to hold awarded shares for the long term.

> In its March 4, 2013, interpretive guidance letter, the SEC staff confirmed that an issuer that permits its directors and executive officers to participate in the EBIC program would not be deemed thereby to be extending credit or arranging for the extension of credit, for purposes of SOX 402. The staff further confirmed that an issuer would also not be deemed to be extending or arranging for the extension of credit, under SOX 402, if it undertakes certain ministerial or administrative activities so as to enable its directors and executive officers to participate in the EBIC program.[41]

3. An important issue is whether SOX § 402 applies to cashless exercises of stock options. A corporate executive who wishes to exercise stock options must pay the exercise price, which you will recall is normally the market price of the underlying stock when the option was issued. In order to facilitate such transactions without out of pocket costs to the executive, the executive's stock broker may lend the executive the amount necessary to

---

[40] Id. at 1539–40.

[41] Michael G. Oxley, SEC Issues SOX 402 Guidance, Harvard Law School Forum on Corporate Governance and Financial Regulation (April 18, 2013), https://corpgov.law.harvard.edu/2013/04/18/sec-issues-sox-402-guidance/.

exercise the option, delivering payment to the company. Although the executive almost always immediately sells sufficient shares to reimburse the broker, the broker will generally be paid interest on the funds advanced. Do such transactions violate § 402?

E. DIRECTOR COMPENSATION

The most basic way of incentivizing people to do a good job is to pay them for doing so. Oddly, however, it long was against the law for corporations to compensate directors at all.[42] Because boards at that time consisted mainly of people associated with the firm, such as founding entrepreneurs, insiders, or representatives of major shareholders, their stake in the company provided alternative incentives for good performance. As independent directors with no such stake in the company became more common, however, legislatures and courts recognized that compensation now was a necessary incentive and changed the law to allow it. By the mid-1970s, almost all public corporations paid their directors, and the amount of director compensation grew rapidly in the following years.

In re Investors Bancorp, Inc. Stockholder Litig.
177 A.3d 1208 (Del. 2017)

I.

. . . The defendants fall into two groups—ten non-employee director defendants[4] and two executive director defendants.[5] [Investors Bancorp, Inc. ("Investors Bancorp" or the "Company")], the nominal defendant, is a Delaware corporation with its principal place of business in Short Hills, New Jersey. Investors Bancorp is a holding company for Investors Bank, a New Jersey chartered savings bank with corporate headquarters in Short Hills, New Jersey. The Company operates 143 banking branches in New Jersey and New York. . . .

The board sets director compensation based on recommendations of the Compensation and Benefits Committee ("Committee"), composed of seven of the ten non-employee directors. In 2014, the non-employee directors were compensated by (i) a monthly cash retainer; (ii) cash awards for attending board and board committee meetings; and (iii) perquisites and personal benefits. The chairman of each committee received an additional annual retainer. As the Court of Chancery noted, the annual compensation for all non-employee directors ranged from

---

[42] See Charles M. Elson, Director Compensation and the Management-Captured Board—The History of a Symptom and a Cure, 50 SMU L. Rev. 127, 135–48 (1996).

[4] Robert C. Albanese, Dennis M. Bone, Doreen R. Byrnes, Robert M. Cashill, William V. Cosgrove, Brian D. Dittenhafer, Brendan J. Dugan, James J. Garibaldi, Michele N. Siekerka, and James H. Ward III.

[5] Kevin Cummings, the Company's President and CEO, and Domenick A. Cama, the Company's COO and Senior Executive Vice President.

$97,200 to $207,005, with $133,340 as the average amount of compensation per director . . . .

In 2014, Cummings, the Company's President and CEO, received (i) a $1,000,000 base salary; (ii) an Annual Cash Incentive Award of up to 150% of his base salary contingent on certain performance goals; and (iii) perquisites and benefits valued at $278,400, which totaled $2,778,700. Cama, the Company's COO and Senior Executive Vice President, received annual compensation consisting of (i) a $675,000 base salary; (ii) an Annual Cash Incentive Award of up to 120% of his base salary; and (iii) perquisites and benefits valued at $180,794, which totaled $1,665,794.

At the end of 2014, . . . the Committee met to review 2014 director compensation and set compensation for 2015. Gregory Keshishian, a compensation consultant from GK Partners, Inc., presented to the board a study of director compensation for eighteen publicly held peer companies. According to the study, these companies paid their non-employee directors an average of $157,350 in total compensation. The Company's $133,340 average non-employee director compensation in 2014 fell close to the study average. Following the presentation, the Committee recommended to the board that the non-employee director compensation package remain the same for 2015. The only change was to increase the fees paid for attending committee meetings from $1,500 to $2,500.

. . .

Just a few months after setting the 2015 board compensation, in March, 2015, the board proposed the 2015 Employee Incentive Plan [(EIP)]. The EIP was intended to "provide additional incentives for [the Company's] officers, employees and directors to promote [the Company's] growth and performance and to further align their interests with those of [the Company's] stockholders . . . and give [the Company] the flexibility [needed] to continue to attract, motivate and retain highly qualified officers, employees and directors."

The Company reserved 30,881,296 common shares for restricted stock awards, restricted stock units, incentive stock options, and non-qualified stock options for the Company's 1,800 officers, employees, non-employee directors, and service providers. The EIP has limits within each category. Of the total shares, a maximum of 17,646,455 can be issued for stock options or restricted stock awards and 13,234,841 for restricted stock units or performance shares. Those limits are further broken down for employee and non-employee directors:

- A maximum of 4,411,613 shares, in the aggregate (25% of the shares available for stock option awards), may be issued or delivered to any one employee pursuant to the exercise of stock options;

- A maximum of 3,308,710 shares, in the aggregate (25% of the shares available for restricted stock awards and restricted stock units), may be issued or delivered to any one employee as a restricted stock or restricted stock unit grant; and

- The maximum number of shares that may be issued or delivered to all non-employee directors, in the aggregate, pursuant to the exercise of stock options or grants of restricted stock or restricted stock units shall be 30% of all option or restricted stock shares available for awards, "all of which may be granted in any calendar year."

According to the proxy sent to stockholders, "[t]he number, types and terms of awards to be made pursuant to the [EIP] are subject to the discretion of the Committee and have not been determined at this time, and will not be determined until subsequent to stockholder approval." At the Company's June 9, 2015 annual meeting, 96.25% of the voting shares approved the EIP (79.1% of the total shares outstanding).

Three days after stockholders approved the EIP, the Committee held the first of four meetings and eventually approved awards of restricted stock and stock options to all board members. According to the complaint, these awards were not part of the final 2015 compensation package nor discussed in any prior meetings. . . . The Committee met with Cummings, Cama, Keshishian (the compensation consultant), and representatives from Luse Gorman (outside counsel) "to begin the process of determining the allocation of shares."

. . .

The board awarded themselves 7.8 million shares. Non-employee directors each received 250,000 stock options—valued at $780,000—and 100,000 restricted shares—valued at $1,254,000; Cashill and Dittenhafer received 150,000 restricted shares—valued at $1,881,000—due to their years of service. The non-employee director awards totaled $21,594,000 and averaged $2,159,400. Peer companies' non-employee awards averaged $175,817. Cummings received 1,333,333 stock options and 1,000,000 restricted shares, valued at $16,699,999 and alleged to be 1,759% higher than the peer companies' average compensation for executive directors. Cama received 1,066,666 stock options and 600,000 restricted shares, valued at $13,359,998 and alleged to be 2,571% higher than the peer companies' average.

After the Company disclosed the awards, stockholders filed three separate complaints in the Court of Chancery alleging breaches of fiduciary duty by the directors for awarding themselves excessive compensation. . . .

The Court of Chancery dismissed the complaint against the non-employee directors because the EIP contained "meaningful, specific limits on awards to all director beneficiaries" . . . .

II.

Unless restricted by the certificate of incorporation or bylaws, Section 141(h) of Delaware General Corporation Law ("DGCL") authorizes the board "to fix the compensation of directors." Although authorized to do so by statute, when the board fixes its compensation, it is self-interested in the decision because the directors are deciding how much they should reward themselves for board service. If no other factors are involved, the board's decision will "lie outside the business judgment rule's presumptive protection, so that, where properly challenged, the receipt of self-determined benefits is subject to an affirmative showing that the compensation arrangements are fair to the corporation."[34] In other words, the entire fairness standard of review will apply.

... Here, we address the affirmative defense of stockholder ratification of director self-compensation decisions.

A.

Early Supreme Court cases recognized a ratification defense by directors when reviewing their self-compensation decisions. In the 1952 decision *Kerbs v. California Eastern Airways, Inc.*, a stockholder filed suit against the directors attacking a stock option [plan approved by the shareholders].[37]

Addressing the effect of stockholder approval of the stock option plan, our Court held that "ratification cures any voidable defect in the action of the [b]oard. Stockholder ratification of voidable acts of directors is effective for all purposes unless the action of the directors constituted a gift of corporate assets to themselves or was ultra vires, illegal, or fraudulent." ...

The stock option plan approved by the stockholders in *Kerbs* was self-executing, meaning once approved by the stockholders, implementing the awards required no discretion by the directors. The Court addressed a similar dispute in a case decided the following day. In *Gottlieb v. Heyden Chemical Corp.*,[45] the restricted stock option plan granted specific company officers—six of whom were board members—present and future options to purchase fixed amounts of common stock at prices to be set by the board, subject to a price collar. The plan was contingent upon ratification by a majority of the stockholders. In advance of the stockholder meeting, the board disclosed the names of the officers receiving the awards, the number of shares allocated to each, the price per share, and the schedule for future issuances. The stockholders approved the plan.

... [T]he Court noted the effect of stockholder ratification. For the current awards specifically approved by the stockholders:

---

[34]   [Telxon Corp. v. Meyerson, 802 A.2d 257, 257 (Del. 2002).]
[37]   90 A.2d 652.
[45]   90 A.2d 660 (Del. 1960).

Where there is stockholder ratification, ... the burden of proof is shifted to the objector. In such a case the objecting stockholder must convince the court that no person of ordinary sound business judgment would be expected to entertain the view that the consideration furnished by the individual directors is a fair exchange for the options conferred.[49]

But, for the options subject to future awards, the court explained that they were not ratified because the 25,500 shares had not been placed into any contracts prior to approval. The stockholders only approved the allocation of shares "of a certain general pattern," but "nobody [knew] what all of the terms of these future contracts [would] be." The Court concluded that ratification "cannot be taken to have approved specific bargains not yet proposed." . . .

Our Court has not considered ratification of director self-compensation decisions since *Kerbs* and *Gottlieb*. The Court of Chancery has, however, continued to develop this area of the law.

B.

... [I]n *Seinfeld v. Slager*,[70] the court addressed a concern that recognizing ratification for plans approved by stockholders with only general parameters for making compensation awards provided insufficient protection from possible self-dealing. The plan in *Seinfeld* was a broad-based plan applying to directors, officers, and employees [that] contained a single generic limit on awards, with no restrictions on how the awards could be distributed to the different classes of beneficiaries. Rather than essentially approve a blank check, or in the Vice Chancellor's words—give the directors carte blanche—to make awards as the directors saw fit, the court required "some *meaningful* limit imposed by the stockholders on the [b]oard for the plan to . . . receive the blessing of the business judgment rule." Thus, after *Seinfeld*, directors could retain the discretion to make awards after stockholder plan approval, but the plan had to contain meaningful limits on the awards the directors could make to themselves before ratification could be successfully asserted.

III.

A.

As ratification has evolved for stockholder-approved equity incentive plans, the courts have recognized the defense in three situations—when stockholders approved the specific director awards; when the plan was self-executing, meaning the directors had no discretion when making the

---

[49] Gottlieb [v. Heyden Chemical Corp.], 91 A.2d [57] at 58 [(1952)]; see id. ("Where there was stockholder ratification, however, the court will look into the transaction only far enough to see whether the terms are so unequal as to amount to waste, or whether, on the other hand, the question is such a close one as to call for the exercise of what is commonly called 'business judgment.' ").

[70] 2012 WL 2501105, at *11–12.

awards; or when directors exercised discretion and determined the amounts and terms of the awards after stockholder approval. The first two scenarios present no real problems. When stockholders know precisely what they are approving, ratification will generally apply. The rub comes, however, in the third scenario, when directors retain discretion to make awards under the general parameters of equity incentive plans. . . .

We think . . . when it comes to the discretion directors exercise following stockholder approval of an equity incentive plan, ratification cannot be used to foreclose the Court of Chancery from reviewing those further discretionary actions when a breach of fiduciary duty claim has been properly alleged. . . . When stockholders approve the general parameters of an equity compensation plan and allow directors to exercise their "broad legal authority" under the plan, they do so "precisely because they know that authority must be exercised consistently with equitable principles of fiduciary duty."[82] The stockholders have granted the directors the legal authority to make awards. But, the directors' exercise of that authority must be done consistent with their fiduciary duties. Given that the actual awards are self-interested decisions not approved by the stockholders, if the directors acted inequitably when making the awards, their "inequitable action does not become permissible simply because it is legally possible"[83] under the general authority granted by the stockholders.

. . .

B.

The Investors Bancorp EIP is a discretionary plan as described above. It covers about 1,800 officers, employees, non-employee directors, and service providers. Specific to the directors, the plan reserves 30,881,296 shares of common stock for restricted stock awards, restricted stock units, incentive stock options, and non-qualified stock options for the Company's officers, employees, non-employee directors, and service providers. Of those reserved shares and other equity, the non-employee directors were entitled to up to 30% of all option and restricted stock shares, all of which could be granted in any calendar year. [But the number, types, and terms of the awards to be made pursuant to the EIP were subject to the discretion of the Committee and would not be determined until subsequent to stockholder approval.]

. . .

After stockholders approved the EIP, the board eventually approved just under half of the stock options available to the directors and nearly

---

[82]   [Calma on Behalf of Citrix Sys., Inc. v. Templeton, 114 A.3d 563, 584 (Del. Ch. 2015).]

[83]   Schnell v. Chris-Craft Ind., Inc., 285 A.2d 437, 439 (Del. 1971). As noted in Desimone v. Barrows, 924 A.2d 908, 917 (Del. Ch. 2007), "[s]pecifying the precise amount and form of director compensation . . . 'ensure[s] integrity' in the underlying principal-agent relationship between stockholders and directors."

thirty percent of the shares available to the directors as restricted stock awards, based predominately on a five-year going forward vesting period. The plaintiffs argue that the directors breached their fiduciary duties by granting themselves these awards because they were unfair and excessive. According to the plaintiffs, the stockholders were told the EIP would reward future performance, but the Board instead used the EIP awards to reward past efforts for the mutual-to-stock conversion—which the directors had already accounted for in determining their 2015 compensation packages. Also, according to the plaintiffs, the rewards were inordinately higher than peer companies'. As alleged in the complaint, the Board paid each non-employee director more than $2,100,000 in 2015, which "eclips[ed] director pay at every Wall Street firm." This significantly exceeded the Company's non-employee director compensation in 2014, which ranged from $97,200 to $207,005. It also far surpassed the $198,000 median pay at similarly sized companies and the $260,000 median pay at much larger companies. . . .

In addition, according to the complaint, Cama and Cummings' compensation far exceeded their prior compensation and that of peer companies. Cummings' $20,006,957 total compensation in 2015 was seven times more than his 2014 compensation package of $2,778,000. And Cama's $15,318,257 compensation was nine times more than his 2014 compensation package of $1,665,794. Cummings' $16,699,999 award was 3,683% higher than the median award other companies granted their CEOs after mutual-to-stock conversions. And Cama's $13,359,998 award was 5,384% higher than the median other companies granted their second-highest paid executives after the conversions.

. . .

The Investors Bancorp stockholders approved the general parameters of the EIP. The plaintiffs have properly alleged, however, that the directors, when exercising their discretion under the EIP, acted inequitably in granting themselves unfair and excessive awards. Because the stockholders did not ratify the specific awards under the EIP, the affirmative defense of ratification cannot not be used to dismiss the complaint. . . . Thus, the Court of Chancery's decision is reversed, and the case is remanded for further proceedings consistent with this opinion.

NOTES AND QUESTIONS

1.   On remand, how should the Chancery Court determine whether or not the directors' compensation was fair? If you are counsel to the *Investor Bancorp* board would you advise it to settle or go to trial?

2.   After *Investor Bancorp*, what standard of review is applicable to a discretionary plan that contains meaningful limits on non-executive director compensation?

3.   After *Investor Bancorp*, should a plan—whether discretionary or not—include meaningful limits on non-executive director compensation?

4.   Is there any way to guarantee that a planning giving directors discretion as to the amount and form of their compensation will receive the benefit of the business judgment rule?

5.   After *Investor Bancorp*, one of your corporate clients is considering adopting a standalone compensation plan that applies only to its non-executive directors. They ask you to review the pros and cons of doing so.

6.   After *Investor Bancorp*, JP Morgan Chase amended its non-executive director compensation plan to provide that the plan would be in effect until May 31, 2022. The plan authorizes (i) an annual base retainer per director of $350,000 per year, with discretion to increase it by up to $25,000 but not until January 2020; and (ii) additional retainers for special service of $30,000 for the Lead Independent Director, $25,000 for chairing the Audit Committee, the Directors' Risk Policy Committee or the company's bank board, and $15,000 for chairing any other principal standing committee or serving on the bank board, the Audit Committee or the Directors' Risk Policy Committee, with discretion to increase any of these special retainers by $5,000, but also not until January 2020. The plan, as amended, was approved by the shareholders. If challenged, what standard of review likely would be applied? Could you argue that different standards of review should apply to different aspects of the plan? In what ways, if any, does the plan appear to have been structured so as to discourage litigation?

Espinoza v. Zuckerberg

124 A.3d 47 (Del. Ch.2015)

... In this derivative action, a stockholder of Facebook, Inc. challenges the decision of Facebook's board of directors in 2013 to approve compensation for its outside, non-management directors, who comprised six of the eight directors on Facebook's board at the time.... [The two "inside" directors were Chief Executive Officer Mark Zuckerberg and Chief Operating Officer Sheryl K. Sandberg.]

The parties agree that the board's decision to approve the 2013 compensation would be governed by the entire fairness standard of review ... as a self-dealing transaction. After the filing of this lawsuit, however, Mark Zuckerberg, who did not receive the disputed 2013 compensation and who controlled over 61% of the voting power of Facebook's common stock, expressed his approval of the 2013 compensation for the non-management directors in a deposition and an affidavit.... The fundamental issue here is whether Zuckerberg's approvals were in a form sufficient to constitute stockholder ratification....

The controlling stockholder of a Delaware corporation wields significant power .... But a controlling stockholder should not, in my view, be immune from the required formalities that come with such power. Although traditional agency law allows a principal to ratify an agent's conduct through informal assent, this tradition is ill-suited to the context of corporate law ratification, where formal structures govern the collective decision-making of stockholders who coexist as principals. These formalities serve to protect the corporation and all of its stockholders by ... promoting transparency, particularly for non-assenting stockholders. I therefore conclude that stockholders of a Delaware corporation—even a single controlling stockholder—cannot ratify an interested board's decisions without adhering to the corporate formalities specified in the Delaware General Corporation Law for taking stockholder action.

Given this conclusion, the entire fairness standard applies to the board's approval of the 2013 compensation. As such, and given that defendants have not thus far demonstrated that the directors' compensation decisions were entirely fair, their motion for summary judgment is denied. Plaintiff has failed to state a reasonably conceivable claim for waste, however, and thus that claim is dismissed. . . .

I. BACKGROUND

. . .

Nominal Defendant Facebook, Inc. ("Facebook" or the "Company") is a Delaware corporation with headquarters in California. . . . Its Class B common stock has ten votes per share and its Class A common stock has one vote per share. Defendant Mark Zuckerberg is the founder of Facebook. Zuckerberg has served as Facebook's Chief Executive Officer since July 2004 and as the Chairman of Facebook's board of directors since January 2012. Zuckerberg, principally due to his ownership of the super-voting Class B shares, controlled approximately 61.6% of the total voting power of Facebook's common stock as of February 28, 2014. . . .

On August 21, 2013, the Compensation Committee, . . . discussed the compensation of Facebook's non-management directors. The following day, Facebook's board considered the topic at a regular meeting and unanimously approved a proposal . . . to provide non-employee directors with annual RSU grants at a value of $300,000 per year . . . .

On June 6, 2014, plaintiff filed a derivative complaint on behalf of Facebook against the eight members of its board of directors. . . . On August 18, 2014, defendants moved for summary judgment . . . . On the same day, Zuckerberg filed an affidavit in support of the summary judgment motion declaring as follows:

> 10. Regardless of the capacity in which I have considered the issue, my view of the compensation of Facebook's Non-Executive Directors has never changed. I approve of all 2013 equity awards to Facebook's Non-Executive Directors, as well as Facebook's plan for compensation of Non-Executive Directors going forward (pursuant to the Annual Compensation Program). . . .

> 11. Although I was never presented with an opportunity to approve formally the 2013 equity awards to Facebook's Non-Executive Directors or the Annual Compensation Program in

my capacity as a Facebook stockholder, had an opportunity presented itself, I would have done so. If put to a vote, I would vote in favor of the 2013 equity awards to Facebook's Non-Executive Directors, as well as the Annual Compensation Program, and if presented with a stockholder written consent approving them, I would sign it.

. . .

II.   LEGAL ANALYSIS

. . .

B.   Count I: Breach of Fiduciary Duty

Directors are necessarily interested in their compensation, which is a benefit they receive that does not accrue to stockholders generally. Thus, where, as here, directors make decisions about their own compensation, those decisions presumptively will be reviewed as self-dealing transactions under the entire fairness standard rather than under the business judgment rule. A decision dominated by interested directors can gain the protection of the business judgment rule, however, if a fully-informed disinterested majority of stockholders ratifies the transaction. At that point, the doctrinal standard of review becomes one of waste.

Here, defendants contend that the business judgment rule should apply to their approval of the 2013 Compensation on the theory that Zuckerberg, who indisputably holds a majority of the voting power of Facebook's common stock, and who did not receive any of the 2013 Compensation, ratified the 2013 Compensation in his capacity as a Facebook stockholder by virtue of statements he made in his affidavit and his deposition after this action was filed. Plaintiff responds that these acts do not constitute a valid form of stockholder ratification . . . because Zuckerberg did not express assent as a stockholder in a manner permitted by the Delaware General Corporation Law ("DGCL"). . . .

The DGCL provides two methods for stockholders to express assent on a matter concerning the affairs of the corporation: (1) by voting in person or by proxy at a meeting of stockholders, or (2) by written consent. . . .

Before 1937, . . . stockholders of Delaware corporations could express assent only by voting in person or by proxy at a meeting of stockholders. . . .

In 1937, the DGCL was amended to permit stockholders to approve by unanimous written consent any action that was required to be taken, or that could be taken, at an annual or special meeting of stockholders. In 1967, the statute was further amended to remove the unanimity requirement for companies that chose to waive the requirement in their certificate of incorporation. In 1969, non-unanimous consent became the default rule rather than an option requiring an enabling charter provision. Although taken for granted now, non-unanimous written consent troubled the prominent drafter of the 1967 revision of the DGCL, who saw the potential for abuse.[47] Today, under Section 228 of the DGCL, unless the certificate of incorporation restricts the use of written consents, any action that may be taken at any annual or special meeting of stockholders may be taken by majority stockholder consent (or whatever other voting threshold applies for a particular act) "without a meeting, without prior notice and without a vote."

Significantly, although Section 228 permits stockholders to take action by written consent without prior notice, "[p]rompt notice of the taking of the corporate action" by written consent must be provided to the non-consenting stockholders. Thus, Section 228 ensures some level of transparency for non-consenting stockholders. Indeed, this Court has refused to make a written consent effective under Section 228 when the consenting stockholders failed to provide the required prompt notice to the non-consenting stockholders, until the failure to provide notice was remedied.

This Court has recognized more broadly that, "[b]ecause Section 228 permits immediate action without prior notice to minority stockholders, the statute involves great potential for mischief and its requirements must be strictly complied with if any semblance of corporate order is to be maintained."[51] . . . Thus, even if a controlling stockholder manifests a clear intent to ratify a decision outside of a stockholder meeting, the ratification will not be effective unless it complies with the technical requirements of Section 228. . . .

Defendants observe that there "is no case or statute that requires a stockholder vote or written consent for ratification purposes if the approval of a stockholder majority can be expressed another way." Although no case has been identified that explicitly precludes (or permits) the use of informal means to ratify an act in a case like this, it is notable that many Delaware courts that have used stockholder ratification to apply the business judgment rule . . . have done so when the act of ratification occurred at a formal meeting of stockholders. More importantly, references in existing case law to ratification in the context of a stockholder "vote," . . . support the conclusion that adherence to formalities should be required in this context.

One foundational case is *Gantler v. Stephens.*[79] . . . In *Gantler,* the Supreme Court held that the scope of "the shareholder ratification doctrine must be limited . . . to circumstances where a fully informed

---

[47]   *See* Ernest L. Folk, III, Corporation Law Developments—1969, 56 Va. L.Rev. 755, 783 (1970) ("It is apparent that this procedure can be abused where a large block of stock is held in a conveniently small number of hands. It permits the control block to take action in virtual secrecy and then present the minority shareholders with a fait acompli when it fulfills the minimal state statutory obligation of giving them 'prompt' notice of the action taken.").

[51]   Carsanaro v. Bloodhound Techs., Inc., 65 A.3d 618, 641 (Del. Ch. 2013) (internal quotation marks omitted).

[79]   Gantler v. Stephens, 965 A.2d 695 (Del. 2009).

shareholder vote approves director action that does *not* legally require shareholder approval in order to become legally effective."[81] In my view, *Gantler*'s use of the phrase "fully informed shareholder *vote*" in defining the concept of ratification was deliberate and was not intended to mean something less formal than an actual stockholder vote (or an action by written consent in lieu thereof).

Recently, in *Corwin v. KKR,* which confirmed that stockholder approval from a statutorily required vote can be used to invoke the business judgment rule the same way an approval from a voluntary vote can, the Supreme Court again used specific voting language to explain the doctrine of ratification in the corporate context.[83] Specifically, the Supreme Court stated that "the doctrine applies only to fully informed, uncoerced stockholder votes," thereby implicitly excluding less formal methods of stockholder approval.[84]

Another example is 8 Del. C. § 144(a)(2), which prevents the voiding of a director's interested transaction if the "transaction is specifically approved in good faith by vote of the stockholders." In describing that process, this Court stated in *Wheelabrator* that "[a]pproval by fully informed, disinterested shareholders pursuant to § 144(a)(2) invokes the business judgment rule and limits judicial review to issues of gift or waste with the burden of proof upon the party attacking the transaction."[86] Although the statutory language plainly refers to the need for a "vote of the stockholders," *Wheelabrator* simply uses the word approval to indicate this formal requirement, suggesting again that Delaware courts naturally assume that stockholder approval requires adherence to formalities.[87]

Failing to adhere to corporate formalities to effect stockholder ratification ... impinges on the rights of minority stockholders. In traditional agency relationships, a single principal's ratification of an agent's conduct comes at a cost to that principal only. But in the corporate context, the ratification decisions of a controlling stockholder affect the minority stockholders. Although minority stockholders have no power to alter a controlling stockholder's binding decisions absent a fiduciary breach, they are entitled to the benefits of the formalities imposed by the DGCL, including prompt notification under Section 228(e). This requirement promotes transparency and enables minority stockholders

---

[81]   *Gantler*, 965 A.2d at 713.

[83]   [Corwin v. KKR Fin. Holdings LLC, 125 A.3d 304, 312–14 (Del. 2015).]

[84]   *See* id.

[86]   [In re Wheelabrator Techs., Inc. S'holders Litig., 663 A.2d 1194, 1198, (Del. Ch. 1995) (emphasis added) (internal quotation marks omitted).]

[87]   In the analogous context of Section 144(a)(1), which allows for approval of interested transactions by fully informed, disinterested directors, this Court has suggested that such approval must occur at a formal meeting of directors. See Lewis v. Fuqua, 502 A.2d 962, 970 (Del. Ch. 1985) (noting party's concession that 8 Del. C. § 144 did not apply because "the approval did not take place at a formal Board meeting or necessarily after full disclosure of all material facts").

to stay abreast of corporate decision-making and maintain the accountability of boards of directors and controlling stockholders. . . .

It is therefore of no moment that Zuckerberg undisputedly controls Facebook. Although he can outvote all other stockholders and thus has the power to effect any stockholder action he chooses, he still must adhere to corporate formalities (and his fiduciary obligations) when doing so. . . .

D. Count II: Waste of Corporate Assets

Plaintiff asserts in Count II that the 2013 Compensation constituted a waste of corporate assets. . . .

"[W]aste entails an exchange of corporate assets for consideration so disproportionately small as to lie beyond the range at which any reasonable person might be willing to trade."[105] Thus, to state a claim for waste, "a plaintiff must allege particularized facts that lead to a reasonable inference that the director defendants authorized an exchange that is so one sided that no business person of ordinary, sound judgment could conclude that the corporation has received adequate consideration."[106] The test for waste is extreme and rarely satisfied. Consequently, even if a plaintiff successfully raises questions concerning the fairness of director compensation, he does not necessarily succeed in pleading "the rare type of facts from which it is reasonably conceivable" that the compensation awards constituted corporate waste.[108]

In support of the waste claim, plaintiff argues that the average compensation for Facebook's non-employee directors is 43% higher than the average compensation for directors in a specified peer group of companies, despite Facebook's lower-than-average net income and revenue, and stock price movement that plaintiff views as insufficient to justify the compensation awarded. Such allegations are essentially complaints that some portion of defendants' 2013 Compensation was above and beyond what they deserved for their performance. As such, the allegations fall far short of demonstrating that such compensation constitutes a gift or gratuity for which the corporation received no consideration. Under this Court's precedents, allegations that compensation is "excessive or even lavish, as pleaded here, are insufficient as a matter of law to meet the standard required for a claim of waste."[111]

Plaintiff wisely refrains from alleging that the all-star cast on Facebook's board is so lacking in talent or exerts so little effort that Facebook receives nothing in return for compensating its members. Without any such allegations, which presumably could not be made in good faith, the claim that Facebook paid its directors more than it should

---

[105] [Lewis v. Vogelstein, 699 A.2d 327, 335 (Del. Ch. 1997).]

[106] Seinfeld v. Slager, 2012 WL 2501105, at *3 (quoting In re Citigroup Inc. S'holder Deriv. Litig., 964 A.2d 106, 136 (Del. Ch. 2009)) (internal quotation marks omitted).

[108] [Calma on Behalf of Citrix Sys., Inc. v. Templeton, 114 A.3d 563, 591 (Del. Ch. 2015).]

[111] See In re 3COM Corp. S'holders Litig., 1999 WL 1009210, at *5 (Del.Ch. Oct. 25, 1999).

have relative to an alleged peer group of companies fails to state a legally cognizable claim for waste of corporate assets.

NOTES AND QUESTIONS

1.   What are the costs and benefits of after-the-fact notification allowed by DGCL § 228(e), in this case and in general? Does it matter that the corporation in this case was publicly held rather than closely held?

2.   For the year 2013 Zuckerberg's salary was reduced to $1. Suppose instead that his salary, approved by the board, had been substantial (as it had been in 2012). How, if at all, would that have changed the case?

3.   Why did the court not require before-the-fact notification of the planned ratification?

4.   If the case goes to trial, what do you suppose is the likelihood that the plaintiff will prevail? What weight, if any, should be given to Zuckerberg's approval?

5.   If the court had determined that Facebook properly followed the necessary corporate formalities and that the director compensation therefore had been properly approved by the shareholders, would that finding have precluded the court from going on to consider whether the compensation was so excessive as to amount to waste?

6.   Did the compensation paid in *Investor Bancorp* constitute waste?

7.   As we have seen, waste claims indeed are extremely—one might even say notoriously—difficult to prove. In *Zupnick v. Goizueta*,[43] for example, the court explained that:

> To state a cognizable claim for waste . . ., the well-pleaded allegations of the complaint must support the conclusion that "no person of ordinary, sound business judgment would say that the consideration received for the options was a fair exchange for the options granted." *Michelson v. Duncan*, Del.Supr., 407 A.2d 211, 224 (1979). That is "an extreme test, very rarely satisfied by a shareholder plaintiff," because "if under the circumstances any reasonable person might conclude that the deal made sense, then the judicial inquiry ends." *Steiner v. Meyerson*, Del. Ch., C.A. No. 13139, Allen, C. (July 18, 1995), Mem. Op. at 2, 1995 WL 441999.

Why are courts so reluctant to review compensation claims? What recourse does this nearly impossible standard leave shareholders?

NOTE ON DIRECTOR COMPENSATION IN STOCK

In the mid-1990s, prominent corporate governance expert Charles Elson began arguing that the prevailing norm of cash compensation failed adequately to incentivize directors. Indeed, he contended that the combination of growing cash compensation and management's control of the board nomination process acted "to align the interests of the outside directors

---

[43]   698 A.2d 384 (Del. Ch. 1997).

with current management rather than with the shareholders. . . . Directors whose remuneration is unrelated to corporate performance have little personal incentive to challenge their management benefactors."[44]

Whereas other reformers focused on the nomination process, Elson proposed a radical change in the form of director compensation:

> To ensure that directors will examine executive initiatives in the best interest of the business, the outside directors must become substantial shareholders. To facilitate this, directors' fees should be paid primarily in company stock that is restricted as to resale during their term in office. No other form of compensation, which serves to compromise their independence from management, should be permitted. The goal is to create within each director a personally based motivation to actively monitor management in the best interest of corporate productivity and to counteract the oversight-inhibiting environment that management appointment and cash-based/benefit-laden fees create.[45]

In 1996, a NACD blue ribbon panel adopted many of Elson's ideas, recommending the use of stock-based compensation and further opining that directors should personally invest an amount in company stock sufficiently large so as to decouple the director's financial interests from those of management.[46] The core idea rapidly caught on, although few firms went so far as to eliminate all cash compensation and benefits. According to a 2007 report by the Conference Board, 90% of surveyed companies made some form of stock-based compensation to directors, with 38% paying all or part of the basic retainer in stock.[47]

In theory, this change in board compensation practices should align director incentives with the interests of shareholders. Lucian Bebchuk and Jesse Fried, however, claim that the incentives thereby created are minimal:

> Consider, for example, a director who owns 0.005% of the company's shares. And suppose that the director is contemplating whether to approve a compensation arrangement requested by the CEO that would reduce shareholder value by $10 million. Given the director's fraction of total shares, the reduction in the value of the director's holdings that would result from approval of the CEO's request would be only $500. Such a cost, or even one several times larger, is highly unlikely to overcome the various factors exerting pressure on the director to support the CEO's request.[48]

Bebchuk and Fried's critique is unpersuasive for several reasons. First, although Bebchuk and Fried elsewhere invoke the behavioral research on

---

[44]   Charles M. Elson, Director Compensation and the Management-Captured Board—The History of a Symptom and a Cure, 50 SMU L. Rev. 127, 162–64 (1996).

[45]   Id. at 165.

[46]   National Association of Corporate Directors, Report of the NACD Blue Ribbon Commission on Director Professionalism (1996).

[47]   The Conference Board, Directors' Compensation and Board Practices in 2006 6–8 (2007).

[48]   Lucian Bebchuk & Jesse Fried, Pay Without Performance: The Unfulfilled Promise of Executive Compensation 34 (2004).

social and psychological factors in support of various arguments, here they fail to take into account the behavioral research suggesting that most individuals are loss averse. Because directors are loss averse, small losses to a director's stock portfolio will have greater psychological weight than small incentives provided by the CEO, all else being equal. Second, Bebchuk and Fried's hypothetical amount of stock ownership, while perhaps not an uncommon level, fails to take into account the possibility that for many directors the shares they own in the company on whose board they serve will constitute a substantial part of that director's net worth. In other words, what matters is not the percentage a director's holdings represent of the company's float but rather the percentage those holdings represent of the director's personal assets. A director with a portfolio of $1 million, $100,000 of which consists of stock of the company in question, has an incentive to keep the stock price up regardless of whether the company's float is $1 billion or $100 billion.

Jeffrey Gordon identifies a more serious concern with stock-based compensation. He argues that stock-based compensation may create the same sort of perverse incentives for directors that it famously did for the managers of Enron.[49] Importantly, however, much stock-based director compensation takes the form of restricted stock grants rather than stock options. Some economists argue that recipients of restricted stock are less likely to engage in earnings management and other forms of financial fraud than are recipients of stock options.[50] Whether that is true or not, stock options only reward their recipients in the event that the stock price goes up, but holders of restricted stock have the potential for both upside gains and downside losses. Because preventing downside risks from materializing is just as much a part of the monitoring job as promoting potential upside gains, restricted stock seems likely to strike the correct incentive balance.

So what is the answer? Does stock-based compensation in fact provide incentives for independent directors not to shirk? A literature review published in 2000 identified five studies providing empirical support for the proposition that increased director stockownership leads to better decision making by directors.[51] Subsequently, a 2005 study found that banks paying a high percentage of compensation in stock exhibited higher performance and growth than competitors emphasizing cash compensation.[52] As such, despite the criticisms that have been made of the practice, it seems plausible to conclude that the trend towards paying directors in stock has tended to better align independent director incentives with shareholder interests.

To assess your understanding of the material in this chapter, click here to take a quiz.

---

[49] Jeffrey N. Gordon, The Rise of Independent Directors in the United States, 1950–2005: Of Shareholder Value and Stock Market Prices, 59 Stan. L. Rev. 1465, 1488 (2007).

[50] See, e.g., Natasha Burns & Simi Kedia, The Impact of Performance-Based Compensation on Misreporting, 79 J. Fin. Econ. 35 (2006).

[51] R. Franklin Balotti et al., Equity Ownership and the Duty of Care: Convergence, Revolution, or Evolution?, 55 Bus. Law. 661, 672–77 (2000) (summarizing studies).

[52] David A. Becher et al., Incentive Compensation for Bank Directors: The Impact of Deregulation, 78 J. Bus. 1753 (2005).

CHAPTER 7

EXECUTIVE DUTIES

DGCL § 142(a)

Every corporation organized under this chapter shall have such officers with such titles and duties as shall be stated in the bylaws or in a resolution of the board of directors which is not inconsistent with the bylaws. . . . One of the officers shall have the duty to record the proceedings of the meetings of the stockholders and directors in a book to be kept for that purpose. Any number of offices may be held by the same person unless the certificate of incorporation or bylaws otherwise provide.

California Business Corporation Law § 312(a)

A corporation shall have (1) a chairperson of the board, who may be given the title of chair of the board, chairperson of the board, chairman of the board, or chairwoman of the board, or a president or both, (2) a secretary, (3) a chief financial officer, and (4) such other officers with such titles and duties as shall be stated in the bylaws or determined by the board and as may be necessary to enable it to sign instruments and share certificates. . . . Any number of offices may be held by the same person unless the articles or bylaws provide otherwise.

Exchange Act Rule 3b–2

The term *officer* means a president, vice president, secretary, treasury or principal financial officer, comptroller or principal accounting officer, and any person routinely performing corresponding functions with respect to any organization whether incorporated or unincorporated.

Exchange Act Rule 3b–7

The term *executive officer*, when used with reference to a registrant, means its president, any vice president of the registrant in charge of a principal business unit, division or function (such as sales, administration or finance), any other officer who performs a policy making function or any other person who performs similar policy making functions for the registrant. Executive officers of subsidiaries may be deemed executive officers of the registrant if they perform such policy making functions for the registrant.

A. STATE LAW

1) DELEGATION OF CORPORATE POWERS TO OFFICERS

Assume a public corporation incorporated in a Model Business Corporation Act state. The Company's Chief Executive Officer just retired. Who will select the CEO's replacement? In all probability, the board of directors will make that decision. Recall that under MBCA § 8.01(b) all corporate powers are exercised by or under the board's authority—which includes the power to hire and fire. A significant personnel decision, such as the one in question, almost certainly would be made by the board. On the other hand, one would scarcely expect the board of directors of a public corporation to make minor personnel decisions, such as hiring a shop foreman.

Put bluntly, the modern public corporation is just too big for the directors to manage on anything resembling a day-to-day basis. As our discussion of the board's functions explained, moreover, many directors of large corporations are outsiders who have full time jobs elsewhere and therefore can devote relatively little time to the running of the business for which they act as directors. Accordingly, we saw that MBCA § 8.01(b) reflects provides that the "business and affairs of the corporation" shall be "managed by or under the direction of" the board. This formulation is intended to make clear that the board's role is to formulate broad policy and oversee the subordinates who actually conduct the business day-to-day. In addition, the statute provides that corporate powers may be exercised "under the [board's] authority," which allows (but does not require) the board to delegate decision-making authority to corporate officers.[1] In turn, corporate officers may delegate some of their responsibilities to less senior employees, and so forth down the organizational chart.

Suppose a newly appointed CEO wishes to hire an Administrative Assistant. If the CEO signs an employment contract with a prospective assistant, purporting to act on behalf of the corporation, will that contract be binding on the firm? The answer to that question depends on whether the CEO has authority as that term of art is used in agency law. Accordingly, we must (briefly) digress into agency law and the authority of agents.

The agency relationship, in its broadest sense, includes any relationship in which one person (the agent) is authorized to act on behalf of another person (the principal). More specifically, an agency

---

[1] Older corporation statutes required corporations to have specified officers. MBCA (1969) § 50 required a president, one or more vice presidents, a secretary, and a treasurer. Modern statutes allow the corporation to designate in its bylaws such officers as it wishes to have and allow officers to hold multiple offices. See, e.g., MBCA § 8.40. Being an officer, as opposed to a nonofficer employee, has legal significance under state law mainly because the scope of an officer's implied or apparent authority is probably broader than that of a nonofficer employee.

relationship arises when there is a manifestation of consent by the principal that the agent act on the principal's behalf and subject to the principal's control, and the agent consents to so act. The requisite manifestation of consent can be implied from the circumstances, which makes it possible for the parties to have formed a legally effective agency relationship without realizing they had done so. Corporate employees, especially officers, are generally regarded as agents of the corporation.[2]

An agent may have either actual or apparent authority to enter into contracts on behalf of the corporate principal.[3] Likewise, in some settings, the corporation may be estopped from denying the authority of its employees. Determining whether an agent had the requisite authority in any given situation can be challenging. The differences between the various categories of authority are complex and subtle. In addition, many of the categories overlap—it is not at all uncommon for more than one type of authority to be present in a single transaction. Finally, the courts are not always precise when using labels. For example, estoppel and inherent authority are often called apparent authority. For our purposes, however, it is critical for you to understand that the legal consequences of an agent's actions do not depend on the type of authority at hand. For purposes of determining whether or not the corporate principal is bound by the contract vis-à-vis the third party to the transaction, authority is authority and the different types of authority are essentially irrelevant.

Why then does the law distinguish between different categories of authority? It will be helpful to focus for a moment on the two basic types of authority: "actual authority" and "apparent authority." Consider the following hypothetical: Pam owns Whiteacre. Alan is her real estate broker and, indisputably, her agent. Ted is an outsider who claims that Alan entered into a contract on Pam's behalf to sell Whiteacre. Suppose Ted seeks to prove the existence of authority by evidence relating to communications between Pam and Alan, such as a letter from Pam to Allen in which Pam directed Alan to sell Whiteacre. In this instance, Ted is attempting to establish the existence of actual authority. In contrast, suppose Ted seeks to establish authority by evidence relating to communications from Pam to Ted. Suppose Pam sent Ted a letter in which she said that she had ordered Alan to sell Whiteacre. In this case, Ted is trying to establish apparent authority. Importantly, the contract will be no less binding if Ted proves apparent authority rather than actual. The difference between actual and apparent authority thus arises out of the way in which Ted seeks to prove that Alan was authorized to enter into the contract. In other words, the different categories of

---

[2] Restatement (Second) of Agency § 14 C cmt. b.

[3] The Restatement (Second) of Agency also recognized a concept called "inherent agency power," which it defined as "a term used in the Restatement of this subject to indicate the power of an agent which is derived not from authority, apparent authority or estoppel, but solely from the agency relation and exists for the protection of persons harmed by or dealing with a servant or other agent." The Restatement (Third) of Agency has abandoned this concept. See generally Stephen M. Bainbridge, Agency, Partnership, & LLCs (2d ed. 2014).

authority really are ways of classifying the proof the plaintiff must offer to bind the principal to the contract.

Actual authority exists when the agent reasonably believes the principal has consented to a particular course of conduct. Actual authority can be express, as where the principal instructs the agent to "sell Whiteacre on my behalf." In the corporate context, express actual authority is usually vested in officers by a resolution of the board and/or a description of the officer's duties set forth in the bylaws.[4] Actual authority can also be implied, however, if the principal's acts or conduct are such the agent can reasonably infer the requisite consent. An agent has incidental actual authority, for example, to use all means reasonably necessary to carry out a particular result expressly mandated by the principal. A pattern of acquiescence by the board in a course of conduct may also give rise to implied actual authority to enter into similar contracts in the future.

A contract entered into by an agent, purportedly on the principal's behalf, can be binding even if the agent lacks actual authority. Apparent authority exists where words or conduct of the principal lead the third party to reasonably believe that the agent has authority to make the contract. Of particular importance with respect to the authority of corporate officers is the concept of apparent authority implied by custom. Suppose the board of directors instructed the CEO not to hire an assistant. The CEO thus lacked actual authority. The CEO nonetheless signs a prospective assistant to an employment contract that purports to be binding on the corporation. Is it binding? If the assistant (the third party) knew that the corporation had placed the CEO in that position and it was customary for CEOs to have authority to hire assistants, the CEO will have apparent authority by virtue of that custom and the contract will be binding.

Most of the case law on the apparent authority of corporate officers relates to the powers of presidents. Corporate presidents are regarded as general agents of the corporation vested with considerable managerial powers. Accordingly, contracts that are executed by the president on the corporation's behalf and arise out of the ordinary course of business matters are binding on the corporation.[5]

Cases dealing with the authority of subordinate officers are much rarer. As to vice presidents, a number of (mostly older) cases hold they

[4]   Compare Musulin v. Woodtek, Inc., 491 P.2d 1173 (Or.1971) (unless authorized by the bylaws or board resolution, corporate officers lacked authority to execute a promissory note on the corporation's behalf) with King World Prod., Inc. v. Financial News Network, Inc., 660 F.Supp. 1381 (S.D.N.Y.1987) (corporate officer had actual authority to execute a lease based, inter alia, on the job description in his employee contract).

[5]   See, e.g., Evanston Bank v. Conticommodity Servs., Inc., 623 F.Supp. 1014 (N.D.Ill.1985) (president's inherent authority extended only to ordinary matters); Belcher v. Birmingham Trust Nat'l Bank, 348 F.Supp. 61 (N.D.Ala.1968) (president has power to bind corporation in ordinary course of business); Quigley v. W. N. Macqueen & Co., 151 N.E. 487 (Ill.1926) (by virtue of his office, president has power to bind the corporation to contracts made in the ordinary course of business).

have little or no implied or apparent authority to bind the corporation. Accordingly, they have only such authority as is expressly conferred on them in the bylaws or by board resolution.[6] The corporate secretary is assumed to be the custodian of the corporation's books and records. Accordingly, the secretary has actual authority to certify those records. Otherwise, however, the secretary has no authority other than that conferred on him by the bylaws or board resolutions.[7]

An important line of cases limits the implied and apparent authority of corporate officers—of whatever rank—to matters arising in the ordinary course of business. In the leading decision of *Lee v. Jenkins Bros.*, the Second Circuit held:

> The rule most widely cited is that the president only has authority to bind his company by acts arising in the usual and regular course of business but not for contracts of an "extraordinary" nature. . . .

> Apparent authority is essentially a question of fact. It depends not only on the nature of the contract involved, but the officer negotiating it, the corporation's usual manner of conducting business, the size of the corporation and the number of its stockholders, the circumstances that give rise to the contract, the reasonableness of the contract, the amounts involved, and who the contracting third party is, to list a few but not all of the relevant factors. In certain instances a given contract may be so important to the welfare of the corporation that outsiders would naturally suppose that only the board of directors (or even the shareholders) could properly handle it. It is in this light that the "ordinary course of business" rule should be given its content.[8]

As *Lee* suggests, there is no bright line between ordinary and extraordinary acts. It seems reasonable to assume, however, that acts consigned by statute to the board of directors will be deemed

---

[6]   See, e.g., Interstate Nat'l Bank v. Koster, 292 P. 805 (Kan.1930); James F. Monaghan, Inc. v. M. Lowenstein & Sons, 195 N.E. 101 (Mass.1935); Musulin v. Woodtek, 491 P.2d 1173 (Or.1971).

[7]   See, e.g., In re Drive-In Development Corp., 371 F.2d 215 (7th Cir.1966) (corporation estopped to deny validity of board resolutions certified by corporate secretary); Meyer v. Glenmoor Homes, Inc., 54 Cal.Rptr. 786 (Cal.App.1966) (secretary had power to affix corporate seal to documents but no authority re contracts of indebtedness); Blair v. Brownstone Oil & Refining Co., 120 P. 41 (Cal.App.1911) (no authority to execute release); Ideal Foods, Inc. v. Action Leasing Corp., 413 So.2d 416 (Fla.App.1982) (secretary is a ministerial position with no authority to conduct business); Shunga Plaza, Inc. v. American Employers' Ins. Co., 465 P.2d 987 (Kan.1970) (corporate secretary has no power to bind the corporation unless the board has entrusted him with management of the business); Easter Oil Corp. v. Strauss, 52 S.W.2d 336 (Tex.Civ.App.1932) (secretary had no authority to execute promissory note).

[8]   Lee v. Jenkins Bros., 268 F.2d 357, 365–70 (2d Cir.), cert. denied, 361 U.S. 913 (1959). See also In re Mulco Products, Inc., 123 A.2d 95 (Del.Super.Ct.1956); Lucey v. Hero Int'l Corp., 281 N.E.2d 266 (Mass.1972).

extraordinary.[9] Consequently, for example, extraordinary acts doubtless include the various acts specified in MBCA § 8.25(e) that a board of directors may not delegate to a committee.[10] (Of course, once the board has made its decision with respect to an extraordinary matter, implementation of that decision can be delegated to officers.)

In general, when one must decide a particular action is ordinary or extraordinary, the following factors seem especially pertinent: How much of the firm's assets or earnings are involved? Suppose a corporation running an auto parts store has $100,000 in cash available. A decision to spend $500 to buy a cash register would be ordinary, while a decision to spend $50,000 to expand the business into a neighboring location probably would be regarded as extraordinary. How much risk is involved? A decision to buy one cash register is not very risky and would be an ordinary action, while a decision to open a new store might be very risky and therefore extraordinary. A decision to buy inventory on installment where the purchase price is paid off in three months probably would be seen as ordinary. A decision to take out a thirty-year loan probably would be seen as extraordinary. How long will the action have an effect on the corporation? How much would it cost to reverse the decision? A decision to open a new store might be very expensive to reverse, as the corporation might not be able to get out of the lease if things went bad. Such a decision thus would be extraordinary.

As to most matters falling in the gray area between ordinary and extraordinary, a small host of decisions could be cited on either side. There is relatively little consistency of outcome in this area. Courts are divided, for example, as to whether such basic matters as filing a lawsuit[11] or executing a guarantee of another corporation's debts are ordinary or extraordinary.[12] One is tempted to remind the courts that Emerson's famous dictum against a fetish for consistency holds only that a "*foolish* consistency is the hobgoblin of little minds."

---

[9]   See, e.g., Plant v. White River Lumber Co., 76 F.2d 155 (8th Cir.1935) (sale of all or substantially all corporate assets).

[10]   The Model Business Corporation Act provides that the following decisions may not be delegated to a committee of the board, but rather must be made by the board as a whole: (1) Authorize dividends or other distributions, except according to a formula or method, or within limits, prescribed by the board of directors. (2) Approve or propose to shareholders action that the statute requires be approved by shareholders. (3) Fill vacancies on the board of directors or, in general, on any of its committees. (4) Adopt, amend, or repeal bylaws. Model Bus. Corp. Act Ann. § 8.25(e).

[11]   Compare Custer Channel Wing Corp. v. Frazer, 181 F.Supp. 197 (S.D.N.Y.1959) (president had authority to do so) with Lloydona Peters Enter., Inc. v. Dorius, 658 P.2d 1209 (Utah 1983) (no authority to do so); Ney v. Eastern Iowa Tel. Co., 144 N.W. 383 (Iowa 1913) (no authority to do so with respect to the corporation's largest shareholder). See also Youell v. Grimes, 217 F. Supp. 2d 1167, 1177 (D. Kan. 2002) (holding that "officers have the authority to hire counsel on behalf of a corporation without board approval"); Steiner v. Meyerson, 1995 WL 441999, at *10 (Del. Ch. July 19, 1995) ("As Meyerson is Telxon's chief executive officer, he undoubtedly possesses the authority to hire and fire the corporation's legal counsel.").

[12]   Compare Sperti Products, Inc. v. Container Corp. of Am., 481 S.W.2d 43 (Ky.App.1972) (president had authority) with First Nat'l Bank v. Cement Products Co., 227 N.W. 908 (Iowa 1929) (no authority to do so).

How should cases falling between the extremes be resolved? Put bluntly, the authority of corporate officers should be regarded as virtually plenary. Only matters expressly reserved to the board by statute, the articles of incorporation, or the bylaws should be deemed "extraordinary" and, consequently, beyond the scope of senior officers' authority.

One rationale for this position is suggested by simple statutory interpretation. Recall that both the MBCA and Delaware law provide that the business of the corporation "shall be managed by or under the direction of a board of directors." The use of the disjunctive prior to the phrase "under the direction of" suggests that the statute's drafters anticipated that the corporation would be managed by its officers with the board mainly exercising oversight authority. Unless a decision is expressly reserved to the board, the statutory language thus contemplates that a corporation may act through its officers subject to review by the board.

This reading of the statute comports with modern board practice. The de facto role of the board in most large public corporations consists of providing informal advice to senior management (especially the CEO) and episodic oversight. An extensive definition of extraordinary acts thus seems a needless formality.

An alternative justification for the proposed rule rests on the costs the existing rule imposes on third parties. Persons who do business with a corporation do so at some peril of discovering that their transaction will be deemed to implicate an extraordinary act and, accordingly, required express board action. An expansive definition of extraordinary matters increases this risk. Transaction costs thus increase in several respects. An expansive variant of the rule creates uncertainty, obliging third parties to take costly precautions. They may insist, for example, on seeing an express authorization from the board. Uncertainty about the outer perimeters of the rule also encourages opportunism by the corporation. If contracts dealing with extraordinary matters are voidable, the corporation effectively has a put with respect to the transaction. Uncertainty as to the enforceability of a contract gives the board leverage to extract a favorable settlement of the third party's claims.

2) FIDUCIARY DUTIES OF OFFICERS

In *Gantler v. Stephens*,[13] the Delaware Supreme Court held that "officers of Delaware corporations, like directors, owe fiduciary duties of care and loyalty, and that the fiduciary duties of officers are the same as those of directors." Unfortunately, *Gantler* did not resolve the critical question of "whether officers should be liable for simple negligence, like agents generally, or whether some form of more deferential standard of

---

[13]   965 A.2d 695, 708–09 (Del. 2009).

review, such as the business judgment rule, should apply to their decisions."[14] No subsequent Delaware decision has resolved the issue.

Back in 1994, the ALI's Principles of Corporate Governance took a much less equivocal position:

> Although most precedents and statutory provisions deal solely with directors, it is relatively well settled, through judicial precedents and statutory provisions in at least 18 states, that officers will be held to the same duty of care standards as directors. Sound public policy points in the direction of holding officers to the same duty of care and business judgment standards as directors, as does the little case authority that exists on the applicability of the business judgment standard to officers, and the views of most commentators support this position. When it comes to the application of these formulations, of course, full-time officers will generally be expected to be more familiar with the affairs of a corporation than outside directors. Officers will be expected to be more familiar with business affairs under their direct supervision than officers who do not have such responsibility.[15]

Subsequently, courts in several states have likewise concluded that the business judgment rule protects both directors and officer.[16] On the other hand, courts in a few states have held to the contrary.[17]

Stephen M. Bainbridge, The Business Judgment Rule as Abstention Doctrine

57 Vand. L. Rev. 83 (2004)

. . .

An analogy to engineering concepts may be useful. If a mechanical system is likely to fail, and its failure is likely to entail high costs, basic

---

[14]   Amalgamated Bank v. Yahoo! Inc., 132 A.3d 752, 781 (Del. Ch. 2016).

[15]   Principles of Corp. Governance § 4.01 (1994).

[16]   See, e.g., Starsurgical Inc. v. Aperta, LLC, 40 F. Supp. 3d 1069, 1087 (E.D. Wis. 2014) ("The business judgment rule shields corporate officers from liability for decisions made in good faith and creates an evidentiary presumption that an officer or director's decisions are made in good faith."); Fed. Deposit Ins. Corp. v. Loudermilk, 761 S.E.2d 332, 338 (Ga. 2014) (hold that "the business judgment rule applies equally at common law to corporate officers and directors generally"); Selcke v. Bove, 629 N.E.2d 747, 750 (Ill. App. 1994) (holding that "plaintiff's position that the business judgment rule does not apply to corporate officers is unsupported by Illinois law and, notwithstanding the Platt decision, is against the substantial weight of judicial authority from other jurisdictions on the issue"); Sneed v. Webre, 465 S.W.3d 169, 173 (Tex. 2015) ("The business judgment rule in Texas generally protects corporate officers and directors, who owe fiduciary duties to the corporation, from liability for acts that are within the honest exercise of their business judgment and discretion.").

[17]   See, e.g., F.D.I.C. v. Perry, 2012 WL 589569, at *4 (C.D. Cal. 2012) ("In light of the apparent lack of authority and the California legislature's expressed intent not to include corporate officers in codifying common law BJR, this Court holds that BJR does not protect officers' corporate decisions."); Platt v. Richardson, 1989 WL 159584 (M.D. Pa. 1989) (business judgment rule only applies to directors).

engineering theory calls for redundant controls to prevent failure. It would be naïve to assume that markets fully constrain director behavior. Why then is judicial review not an appropriate redundant control? If we assume that corporate law is generally efficient, the losses tolerated by judicial abstention must be outweighed by benefits elsewhere in the system. . . .

A.   Encouraging Risk Taking

In the American Law Institute's Principles of Corporate Governance, a quasi-Restatement of corporate law, the drafters justify the business judgment rule as being necessary to protect "directors and officers from the risks inherent in hindsight reviews of their business decisions" and to avoid "the risk of stifling innovation and venturesome business activity."[157] This claim cannot be a complete explanation of the business judgment rule. Duty of care litigation, after all, probably does far less to stifle innovation and business risk taking than does product liability and securities fraud litigation, but no equivalent of the business judgment rule exists in the latter contexts. Even so, however, encouraging optimal risk taking is part of the story.

As the firm's residual claimants, shareholders do not get a return on their investment until all other claims on the corporation have been satisfied. All else equal, shareholders therefore prefer high return projects. Because risk and return are directly proportional, however, implementing that preference necessarily entails choosing risky projects.

Even though conventional finance theory assumes shareholders are risk averse, rational shareholders still will have a high tolerance for risky corporate projects. First, the basic corporate law principle of limited liability substantially insulates shareholders from the downside risks of corporate activity. The limited liability principle, of course, holds that shareholders of a corporation may not be held personally liable for debts incurred or torts committed by the firm. Because shareholders thus do not put their personal assets at jeopardy, other than the amount initially invested, they effectively externalize some portion of the business' total risk exposure to creditors.

Second, shareholders can largely eliminate firm-specific risk by holding a diversified portfolio. . . . Consequently, according to modern portfolio theory, while investors must be compensated for bearing systematic risk, they need not be compensated for bearing unsystematic risk. Returns on specific investments therefore differ not because the corporations involved have differing levels of firm-specific risk, but rather because firms differ insofar as their sensitivity to systematic risk is concerned. The Capital Asset Pricing Model (CAPM) uses the well-known beta coefficient to measure that relative sensitivity to systematic risk.

---

[157] [American Law Institute, Principles of Corporate Governance: Analysis and Recommendations § 4.01 cmt. d. (1994).] . . .

Given limited liability and diversification, rational shareholders should be indifferent to changes in corporate policies that merely alter exposure to unsystematic risks. Instead, they should focus on (and prefer) policies that portend a higher rate of return by increasing the firm's beta. In contrast, rational corporate managers—and, to a lesser extent, directors—should be risk averse with respect to such policies. Corporate managers typically have substantial firm-specific human capital. Unfortunately for such managers, however, the risks inherent in firm-specific capital investments cannot be reduced by diversification; managers obviously cannot diversify their human capital among a number of different firms. As a result, managers will be averse to risks shareholders are perfectly happy to tolerate.

The diversion of interests as between shareholders and managers will be compounded if managers face the risk of legal liability, on top of economic loss, in the event a risky decision turns out badly. Business decisions rarely involve black-and-white issues; instead, they typically involve prudential judgments among a number of plausible alternatives. Given the vagaries of business, moreover, even carefully made choices among such alternatives may turn out badly.

At this point, the well-known hindsight bias comes into play. Decision makers tend to assign an erroneously high probability of occurrence to a probabilistic event simply because it ended up occurring. If a jury knows that the plaintiff was injured, the jury will be biased in favor of imposing negligence liability even if, viewed ex ante, there was a very low probability that such an injury would occur and taking precautions against such an injury was not cost effective. Even where duty of care cases are tried without a jury, as in Delaware, judges who know with the benefit of hindsight that a business decision turned out badly likewise could be biased towards finding a breach of the duty of care.

Hence, there is a substantial risk that suing shareholders and reviewing judges will be unable to distinguish between competent and negligent management because bad outcomes often will be regarded, ex post, as having been foreseeable and, therefore, preventable ex ante. If liability results from bad outcomes, without regard to the ex ante quality of the decision or the decision-making process, however, managers will be discouraged from taking risks.[188] . . .

---

[188] In Joy v. North, 692 F.2d 880, 885–86 (2d Cir. 1982), Judge Ralph Winter explained:

[C]ourts recognize that after-the-fact litigation is a most imperfect device to evaluate corporate business decisions. The circumstances surrounding a corporate decision are not easily reconstructed in a courtroom years later, since business imperatives often call for quick decisions, inevitably based on less than perfect information. The entrepreneur's function is to encounter risks and to confront uncertainty, and a reasoned decision at the time made may seem a wild hunch viewed years later against a background of perfect knowledge.

. . .

This analysis suggests that rational shareholders would be willing to precommit by contract to refrain from challenging the reasonableness of managerial business decisions. Obviously, however, the practicalities of running a large corporation with fluid stock ownership preclude effecting such a policy by contract.[191] The business judgment rule thus may be seen as providing a default off-the-rack rule that both shareholders and managers would prefer, as Judge Ralph Winter opined in *Joy v. North*:

> Although the rule has suffered under academic criticism, it is not without rational basis. . . . [B]ecause potential profit often corresponds to the potential risk, it is very much in the interest of shareholders that the law not create incentives for overly cautious corporate decisions. . . . Shareholders can reduce the volatility of risk by diversifying their holdings. In the case of the diversified shareholder, the seemingly more risky alternatives may well be the best choice since great losses in some stocks will over time be offset by even greater gains in others. . . . A rule which penalizes the choice of seemingly riskier alternatives thus may not be in the interest of shareholders generally.[192]

Hence, judges should abstain from reviewing the substantive merits of business decisions. When courts review the objective merits of a board decision, as some variants of the standard of review conception allow, they effectively penalize "the choice of seemingly riskier alternatives."

Although Winter's analysis is compelling, it nevertheless is incomplete in several important respects. First, Winter's argument cannot be a complete explanation for the business judgment rule because it assumes that negligence by corporate directors must be a form of unsystematic risk. It must be so, because such negligence could not be diversified away otherwise. If so, however, why is neither fraud nor illegality on the part of such directors also a form of unsystematic risk?

---

[191] The contractual nature of the business judgment rule is implied by Judge Winter's argument that:

> Investors need not buy stock, for investment markets offer an array of opportunities less vulnerable to mistakes in judgment by corporate officers. Nor need investors buy stock in particular corporations. In the exercise of what is genuinely a free choice, the quality of a firm's management is often decisive and information is available from professional advisors. Since shareholders can and do select among investments partly on the basis of management, the business judgment rule merely recognizes a certain voluntariness in undertaking the risk of bad business decisions.

Joy, 692 F.2d at 885.

[192] Id. at 885–86 (footnotes omitted). Or, as Chancellor Allen similarly observed in Gagliardi v. Trifoods Int'l, Inc., 683 A.2d 1049, 1052 (Del. Ch. 1996) (emphasis omitted):

> Shareholders can diversify the risks of their corporate investments. Thus, it is in their economic interest for the corporation to accept in rank order all positive net present value investment projects available to the corporation, starting with the highest risk adjusted rate of return first. Shareholders don't want (or shouldn't rationally want) directors to be risk averse. Shareholders' investment interests, across the full range of their diversifiable equity investments, will be maximized if corporate directors and managers honestly assess risk and reward and accept for the corporation the highest risk adjusted returns available that are above the firm's cost of capital.

Just as a shareholder could protect herself against bad decisions, so could a shareholder protect herself against fraudulent decisions. Yet, the business judgment rule has never protected directors who commit fraud or self-dealing.

Second, the analysis thus far has fudged the distinction between directors and managers. To be sure, some commentators contend that directors have the same incentives for risk aversion as managers. As Chancellor Allen explained in *Gagliardi v. Trifoods International, Inc.*:

> Corporate directors of public companies typically have a very small proportionate ownership interest in their corporations and little or no incentive compensation. Thus, they enjoy (as residual owners) only a very small proportion of any "upside" gains earned by the corporation on risky investment projects. If, however, corporate directors were to be found liable for a corporate loss from a risky project on the ground that the investment was too risky . . ., their liability would be joint and several for the whole loss (with I suppose a right of contribution). Given the scale of operation of modern public corporations, this stupefying disjunction between risk and reward for corporate directors threatens undesirable effects. Given this disjunction, only a very small probability of director liability based on "negligence," "inattention," "waste," etc., could induce a board to avoid authorizing risky investment projects to any extent! Obviously, it is in the shareholders' economic interest to offer sufficient protection to directors from liability for negligence, etc., to allow directors to conclude that, as a practical matter, there is no risk that, if they act in good faith and meet minimal proceduralist standards of attention, they can face liability as a result of a business loss.[195]

Allen likely is correct, but it is doubtful whether outside directors make substantial investments in firm-specific human capital. At the same time, it has become very common for public corporations to require that newly appointed directors purchase substantial blocks of the corporation's shares or compensate directors in the corporation's stock, which practice has been empirically linked to improved corporate performance, probably by aligning director and shareholder interests. Hence, outside directors may not be quite as risk averse as inside directors and other managers. Indeed, to the contrary, the incentives of outside directors may well be somewhat closer to shareholder preferences than to those of managers.

Finally, encouraging risk taking must be deemed an incomplete explanation because it fails to account for many of the rule's applications.

---

[195] 683 A.2d 1049, 1052 (Del. Ch. 1996).

B.   Judges Are Not Business Experts

In *Dodge v. Ford Motor Co.*, the Michigan Supreme Court famously invoked the business judgment rule in refusing to enjoin Henry Ford's plans to expand production. As justification for its decision, the court modestly observed that "The judges are not business experts."[199]

A modern version of this rationale can be constructed by building on the burgeoning insights for legal analysis of cognitive psychology and behavioral economics. . . .

As applied to judicial decision making, the inherent cognitive limitations implied by bounded rationality are reinforced both by the incentive structures familiar from agency cost economics and the well-known institutional constraints on adjudication (such as the necessity in many courts of general jurisdiction to provide speedy trials for criminal defendants). In addition, of course, there is the problem of hindsight bias discussed above. Under such conditions, judges will shirk—i.e., look for ways of deciding cases with minimal effort.

An actor can economize limited cognitive resources in two ways. First, he may adopt institutional governance structures designed to promote more efficient decision making. Second, he may invoke shortcuts; i.e., heuristic problem-solving decision-making processes. Is the business judgment rule an example of the latter tactic? . . .

Business decisions are frequently complex and made under conditions of uncertainty. Accordingly, bounded rationality and information asymmetries counsel judicial abstention from reviewing board decisions. Judges likely have less general business expertise than directors. They also have less information about the specifics of the particular firm in question. . . . Finally, most judges only rarely face business judgment issues. Most judges likely arrive on the bench with little expertise in corporate law and, equally likely, have little incentive to develop substantial institutional expertise in this area after they arrive. Because the legal and business issues are complex, and because judges are as subject as anyone to the cognitive limitations implied by bounded rationality, they have an incentive to duck these cases. In Eric Posner's useful phrase, many judges are "radically incompetent":[214]

> [C]ourts have trouble understanding the simplest of business relationships. This is not surprising. Judges must be generalists, but they usually have narrow backgrounds in a particular field of the law. Moreover, they often owe their positions to political connections, not to merit. Their frequent failure to understand transactions is well-documented. One survey of cases involving consumer credit, for example, showed that the judges did not even understand the concept of present

---

[199]   [170 N.W. 668, 684 (Mich. 1919).]

[214]   Eric A. Posner, A Theory of Contract Law Under Conditions of Radical Judicial Error, 94 Nw. U. L. Rev. 749, 754 (2000).

value. . . . Skepticism about the quality of judicial decisionmaking is reflected in many legal doctrines, including the business judgment rule in corporate law, which restrains courts from second-guessing managers and directors. . . .[215]

Although this line of analysis has considerable traction, it too cannot be a complete explanation for the business judgment rule. In the first instance, business is not the only context in which judges are called upon to review complex issues arising under conditions of uncertainty. . . . Yet, no "medical judgment" or "design judgment" rule precludes judicial review of malpractice or product liability cases. Something else must be going on.

In the second instance, Posner overlooks both the pervasive role Delaware plays in business judgment rule jurisprudence and the unique incentive structure in which Delaware courts function. The rationality of Delaware chancellors is bounded—just like that of everyone else. Like all judges, moreover, Delaware chancellors face significant resource constraints, especially with respect to the time available for decision making. In contrast to judges in other states, however, Delaware chancellors frequently have considerable prior corporate experience as practitioners. Once on the bench, there is a substantial pay-off for Delaware chancellors who continue to master corporate law. Delaware chancellors sit at "the center of the corporate law universe."[222] Unlike other courts, which face corporate cases only episodically, such cases make up a very high percentage of the Delaware chancellors' docket. The frequency with which they face such cases provides a strong incentive for Delaware's chancellors to master both doctrine and the business environment in which the doctrine works. In particular, there is a strong reputational incentive to do so. Sitting without juries in a court of equity, Delaware chancellors put their reputation on the line whenever they make a decision. Because so many major corporations are incorporated in Delaware, chancery court cases are often high profile and the court's decisions therefore are subject to close scrutiny by the media, academics, and practitioners. The reputation of a Delaware chancellor thus depends on his or her ability to decide corporate law disputes quickly and carefully.

For these reasons, the adage that "judges are not business experts" cannot be a complete explanation for the business judgment rule. Yet, many old adages have more than a grain of truth. So too does this one. Justice Jackson famously observed of the Supreme Court: "We are not final because we are infallible, but we are infallible only because we are final."[226] Neither courts nor boards are infallible, but someone must be final. Otherwise, we end up with a never-ending process of appellate

---

[215] Id. at 758 (footnote omitted).

[222] D. Gordon Smith, Chancellor Allen and the Fundamental Question, 21 Seattle U. L. Rev. 577, 578 (1998).

[226] Brown v. Allen, 344 U.S. 443, 540 (1953) (Jackson, J., concurring).

review. The question then is simply who is better suited to be vested with the mantle of infallibility that comes by virtue of being final—directors or judges?

Corporate directors operate within a pervasive web of accountability mechanisms. A very important set of constraints are provided by competition in a number of markets. The capital and product markets, the internal and external employment markets, and the market for corporate control all constrain shirking by directors and managers. Granted, only the most naïve would assume that these markets perfectly constrain director decision making. It would be equally naïve, however, to ignore the lack of comparable market constraints on judicial decision making. Market forces work an imperfect Darwinian selection on corporate decision makers, but no such forces constrain erring judges. As such, rational shareholders will prefer the risk of director error to that of judicial error. Hence, shareholders will want judges to abstain from reviewing board decisions.

> **THINK ABOUT IT**
>
> Does this explanation for the business judgment rule suggest that directors and officers should be protected against liability for breach of the duty of loyalty as well as the duty of care?

. . .

Note the resulting link between this justification of the business judgment rule—i.e., the likelihood of judicial error—and the preceding justification—i.e., encouraging optimal risk taking. In theory, if judicial decision making could flawlessly sort out sound decisions with unfortunate outcomes from poor decisions, and directors were confident that there was no risk of hindsight-based liability, the case for the business judgment rule would be substantially weaker. As long as there is some non-zero probability of erroneous second-guessing by judges, however, the threat of liability will skew director decision making away from optimal risk taking. . . .

C.   Impact on the Board's Internal Dynamics

. . . I have suggested a third rationale for the rule, which is based on the potential implications of judicial review for the internal governance of boards. . . .

Recall that the corporate governance is a superb exemplar of Kenneth Arrow's authority model. Information flows up a branching hierarchy to a central office and binding decisions flow back down. At the apex of that decision-making pyramid is not a single hierarch, however, but a multi-member committee—the board—that usually functions by consensus. . . .

. . . The board of directors is a good example of what Oliver Williamson refers to as a "relational team."[243] Relational teams arise

---

[243] [Oliver E. Williamson, The Economic Institutions of Capitalism 246–47 (1985).]

within organizations when two conditions are satisfied: (1) team members make large investments in firm-specific human capital; and (2) their productivity is costly to measure because of task nonseparability. Members of such a team often develop idiosyncratic working relationships with one another. In fact, one might say that members of a relational team develop not only firm-specific human capital but also team-specific human capital.

Such teams may well make decisions that are superior to those made by individuals acting alone. Individuals are subject to the constraints of bounded rationality and the temptations to shirk or self-deal. Group decision making responds to bounded rationality by creating a system for aggregating the inputs of multiple individuals with differing knowledge, interests, and skills.

Although teams can be a highly effective decision-making mechanism, they are difficult to monitor. . . . Because neither input nor output can be measured effectively, judicial review of board decision making cannot be an effective monitoring mechanism.

The key problem for present purposes . . ., however, is that judicial review could interfere with—or even destroy—the internal team governance structures that regulate board behavior. Research on relational teams shows that they are not only hard to monitor, but that they also are hard to discipline. As they develop team-specific human capital, members of a production team develop idiosyncratic ways of working with one another that generate a form of synergy. Under such circumstances, dismissal becomes a highly undesirable sanction, because no team member can be replaced without disrupting the entire team. Because relational teams often become insular, moreover, even external sanctions falling short of dismissal may have ripple effects throughout the team. Insular workplace teams often fail to deal effectively with outsiders. In particular, relational teams often respond to external monitoring efforts by "circling the wagons" around the intended target of sanctions. Instead of external review, relational teams are best monitored by a combination of mutual motivation, peer pressure, and internal monitoring. As I have explained elsewhere in more detail, however, judicial review might well destroy the interpersonal relationships that foster these forms of internal board governance.[260] Again, shareholders will therefore prefer a rule under which judges abstain from reviewing board decisions.

---

[260] [Stephen M. Bainbridge, Why a Board? Group Decisionmaking in Corporate Governance, 55 Vand. L. Rev. 1, 49–50 (2002).] A related concern is that external review of board decisions could have multiplicative effects throughout the firm as a whole. Because "the efficiency of organization is affected by the degree to which individuals assent to orders, denying the authority of an organization communication is a threat to the interests of all individuals who derive a net advantage from their connection with the organization. . . ." Chester I. Barnard, The Functions of the Executive 169 (2d ed. 1962). By calling into question the legitimacy of the board's authority within the corporation, judicial review could reduce the incentive for subordinates to assent to the board's decisions and thereby undermine the efficient functioning of the entire firm.

This line of analysis justifies several aspects of the business judgment rule unexplained by alternative theories. Under this analysis, for example, the inapplicability of the business judgment rule to fraud or self-dealing is readily explicable. Duty-of-care litigation is typically concerned with collective actions taken by the board of directors as a whole. In taking such actions, we have seen, the board is constrained to exercise reasonable care by a combination of external market forces and internal team governance structures. When an individual director decides to pursue a course of self-dealing, however, he or she usually acts alone and, moreover, betrays his or her fellow directors' trust. It makes sense for courts to be less concerned with damage to internal team governance when the defendant director's misconduct has already harmed that governance structure through betrayal. Instead, by providing a set of external sanctions against self-dealing, the law encourages directors to refrain from such betrayals.

QUESTION

Assuming your author has correctly explained the policy rationales for the business judgment rule in the preceding excerpt, should the business judgment rule apply to officers as well as directors?

B. FEDERAL LAW

1) CERTIFICATIONS

As saw in Chapter 5, the phrase "internal controls" has a long history and somewhat contested meaning in the accounting profession. Unfortunately, Congress compounded the problem by using the phrase in two different sections of the Sarbanes-Oxley Act, which assign very different meanings to it.

Sarbanes-Oxley § 302 requires a reporting company's CEO and CFO to certify, among other things, that the company has "internal controls to

> **FYI**
>
> Part of the SEC's initial reaction to the Enron scandal was an order requiring the CEOs and CFOs of 947 large corporations to file written certifications that their company's latest annual report and any subsequent disclosure documents were free of material misrepresentations or omissions. Congress liked this idea so much that it incorporated it into two separate provisions of Sarbanes-Oxley.

ensure that material information relating to the issuer and its consolidated subsidiaries is made known to such officers by others within those entities." In a June 2003 statement, the SEC explained that internal controls as used in § 302 therefore refers to "disclosure controls and procedures," which the SEC in turn defined "to mean controls and procedures of a company that are designed to ensure that information required to be disclosed by the company in the reports that it files or submits under the Exchange Act is recorded, processed, summarized and reported, within the time periods specified in the Commission's rules and forms." In other words, for purposes of a § 302 certification, the question is whether the company has established appropriate procedures to ensure that the information contained in documents like the 10-K and 10-Q reports is accurate and complete.

In contrast, § 404 refers to "internal control structure and procedures for financial reporting." According to the SEC, the set of internal controls to which § 404 refers is narrower than those dealt with under § 302. In the SECs view, the term *internal controls* as used in § 404 refers to the processes the company uses to ensure that its financial statements comply with GAAP and are free from material misrepresentations and omissions.

Note that, as so defined, §§ 302 and 404 do not preempt the field of internal controls. Recall that COSO defined internal controls as relating to the "effectiveness and efficiency of operations, reliability of financial reporting, and compliance with applicable laws and regulations."[18] Even the broader definition of internal control used for purposes of § 302 is limited to the second category. Both §§ 302 and 404 are confined to internal controls related to accounting and disclosure. The state law oversight duties that grew out of *Caremark* thus remain the controlling law with respect to the first and third COSO categories. Our concern here, however, is with § 302 and related federal provisions.

SOX § 302

(a) REGULATIONS REQUIRED.—The Commission shall, by rule, require, for each company filing periodic reports under section 13(a) or 15(d) of the Securities Exchange Act of 1934 (15 U.S.C. 78m, 78o(d)), that the principal executive officer or officers and the principal financial officer or officers, or persons performing similar functions, certify in each annual or quarterly report filed or submitted under either such section of such Act that—

(1) the signing officer has reviewed the report;

(2) based on the officer's knowledge, the report does not contain any untrue statement of a material fact or omit to state a material fact necessary in order to make the statements made, in light of the circumstances under which such statements were made, not misleading;

(3) based on such officer's knowledge, the financial statements, and other financial information included in the report, fairly present in all material respects the financial condition and results of operations of the issuer as of, and for, the periods presented in the report;

(4) the signing officers—

---

[18] Committee of Sponsoring Organizations of the Treadway Commission, Internal Control—Integrated Framework 9 (1992).

(A) are responsible for establishing and maintaining internal controls;

(B) have designed such internal controls to ensure that material information relating to the issuer and its consolidated subsidiaries is made known to such officers by others within those entities, particularly during the period in which the periodic reports are being prepared;

(C) have evaluated the effectiveness of the issuer's internal controls as of a date within 90 days prior to the report; and

(D) have presented in the report their conclusions about the effectiveness of their internal controls based on their evaluation as of that date;

(5) the signing officers have disclosed to the issuer's auditors and the audit committee of the board of directors (or persons fulfilling the equivalent function)—

(A) all significant deficiencies in the design or operation of internal controls which could adversely affect the issuer's ability to record, process, summarize, and report financial data and have identified for the issuer's auditors any material weaknesses in internal controls; and

(B) any fraud, whether or not material, that involves management or other employees who have a significant role in the issuer's internal controls; and

(6) the signing officers have indicated in the report whether or not there were significant changes in internal controls or in other factors that could significantly affect internal controls subsequent to the date of their evaluation, including any corrective actions with regard to significant deficiencies and material weaknesses.

SOX § 906

(a) IN GENERAL.—Chapter 63 of title 18, United States Code, is amended by inserting after section 1349, as created by this Act, the following:

"§ 1350. Failure of corporate officers to certify financial reports

(a) CERTIFICATION OF PERIODIC FINANCIAL REPORTS.—Each periodic report containing financial statements filed by an issuer with the Securities Exchange Commission pursuant to section 13(a) or 15(d) of the Securities Exchange Act of 1934 (15 U.S.C. 78m(a) or 78o(d)) shall be accompanied by a written statement by the chief executive officer and chief financial officer (or equivalent thereof) of the issuer.

"(b) CONTENT.—The statement required under subsection (a) shall certify that the periodic report containing the financial statements fully complies with the requirements of section 13(a) or 15(d) of the Securities Exchange Act pf 1934 (15 U.S.C. 78m or 78o(d)) and that information contained in the periodic report fairly presents, in all material respects, the financial condition and results of operations of the issuer.

"(c) CRIMINAL PENALTIES.—Whoever—

"(1) certifies any statement as set forth in subsections (a) and (b) of this section knowing that the periodic report accompanying the statement does not comport with all the requirements set forth in this section shall be fined not more than $1,000,000 or imprisoned not more than 10 years, or both; or

"(2) willfully certifies any statement as set forth in subsections (a) and (b) of this section knowing that the periodic report accompanying the statement does not comport with all the requirements set forth in this section shall be fined not more than $5,000,000, or imprisoned not more than 20 years, or both.".

NOTES AND QUESTIONS

1.   What must the CEO and CFO certify under §§ 302 and 906? Does § 302's requirement that they certify that they "designed" the company's internal controls mean that they must have done so personally? If so, should it?

2.   How do the certifications required by §§ 302 and 906 relate to the report management must file pursuant to § 404(a)? Can the CEO and CFO sign the necessary certifications if the § 404 report discloses material weaknesses?

3.   The CEO and CFO need not replicate the internal or external audit as part of the §§ 302 and 906 certification process, but some element of due diligence is necessary. What would you advise them to do before signing the certificates?

4.   Many commentators advise qualifying the § 906 certification by using words such as "to my knowledge" or "based on my knowledge." Why?

5.   What benefits, if any, does the certification requirements provide to investors? To society?

6.   What is the difference between "knowingly" and "willfully" as used in § 906?

7.   There is a critical feature of the certification requirements, which requires the CEO and CFO to do more than just rely on the external auditor's assessment of the firm's internal controls:

Both Section 302 and 906 contain language wherein the officer must certify that the financial statements filed with the SEC "fairly present" the issuer's true financial condition, results of operations, and cash flows. Given its inherently subjective nature, counsel and executives of publicly traded companies immediately sought to clarify what "fairly presents" meant in the certifications. Almost immediately, the SEC specifically rejected suggestions that "fairly present" should mean that the financial statements were GAAP compliant. Thus, even where financial information is presented in conformity with generally accepted accounting principles, it may not necessarily satisfy obligations under the antifraud provisions of the federal securities laws.

Instead, the SEC adopted a broader standard for satisfying the "fairly presents" certification:

> In our view, a 'fair presentation' of an issuer's financial condition, results of operations and cash flows encompasses the selection of appropriate accounting policies, proper application of appropriate accounting policies, disclosure of financial information that is informative and reasonably reflects the underlying transactions and events and the inclusion of any additional disclosure necessary to provide investors with a materially accurate and complete picture of an issuer's financial condition, results of operations and cash flows.

Thus, an officer may certify that financial statements "fairly present" the company's true financial condition and cash flows when the officer has weighed the appropriateness of utilized accounting policies and whether the corporation properly applied those accounting policies. Additionally, an officer must consider whether the disclosure of financial information is informative, whether it reasonably reflects the underlying transactions and events, and whether any additional disclosures are necessary to provide investors with a materially accurate assessment of an issuer's financial picture.[19]

What's the justification for this requirement?

8. Recall that scienter is a key element of many federal antifraud provisions, especially Rule 10b–5. Should an incorrect § 302 or 906 certification constitute evidence that the misrepresentation in question was committed with scienter?

9. Courts have determined that an implied private right of action does not exist under either § 302 or § 906.[20]

---

[19] Erin Massey Everitt, Sarbanes-Oxley's Officer Certification Requirements: Has Increased Accountability Equaled Increased Liability?, 6 DePaul Bus. & Com. L.J. 225, 234–35 (2008).

[20] See, e.g., In re Intelligroup Sec. Litig., 468 F. Supp. 2d 670, 707 (D.N.J. 2006) ("Because neither the text of Section 906 nor the structure of SOX demonstrates Congressional intent to create a private remedy in favor of Plaintiffs, this Court can neither infer a private right of action under this provision . . . .")

2) CODE OF ETHICS

Sarbanes-Oxley § 406 requires companies to disclose whether they have adopted a code of ethics for their senior financial managers and, if not, why not. In order for the company to claim it has adopted the requisite code of ethics, the code must establish standards "reasonably necessary to deter wrongdoing and to promote honest and ethical conduct, including the ethical handling of actual or apparent conflicts of interest between personal and professional relationships." The code must provide for avoidance of conflicts of interest, by identifying an appropriate person to whom the covered officers must disclose any material transaction or relationship that reasonably could give rise to a conflict between the officer's personal interest and business duties. The code must obligate the officers covered to ensure "full, fair, accurate, timely, and understandable disclosure" in reports and documents filed by the company with the SEC. The code must mandate personal and corporate compliance with applicable governmental laws, rules, and regulations. It should provide for prompt internal reporting of code violations to an appropriate person or persons, whom the code should identify. The code should be filed with the SEC as an exhibit to the company's annual report and posted to the company's Web site.

C. SEC RESPONSIBILITIES OF LEGAL COUNSEL

Until Sarbanes-Oxley, lawyers would have rejected the idea that they were gatekeepers. The corporate bar long rejected any notion that it owed anything to anyone other than the managers and boards of directors of its clients. The idea that lawyers might have obligations to shareholders, the investing public, or other capital market participants was abhorrent to the bar. Lawyers were advocates, confidents, and advisors, not auditors.

Yet, in almost every financial scandal, lawyers crop up as facilitators of or even participants in client misconduct. In litigation arising out of the 1980s savings and loan crisis, Judge Stanley Sporkin famously asked:

> Where were these professionals, a number of whom are now asserting their rights under the Fifth Amendment, when these clearly improper transactions were being consummated? Why didn't any of them speak up or disassociate themselves from the transactions? Where also were the outside accountants and attorneys when these transactions were effectuated? What is difficult to understand is that with all the professional talent involved (both accounting and legal), why at least one professional would not have blown the whistle to stop the overreaching that took place in this case.[21]

---

[21]   Lincoln Sav. & Loan Ass'n v. Wall, 743 F. Supp. 901, 920 (D.D.C. 1990).

A decade or so later, the same questions were asked of lawyers who worked for firms like Enron.

There is little doubt that lawyers played an important role in the scandals. Sometimes their negligence allowed management misconduct to go undetected. Sometimes lawyers even acted as facilitators and enablers of management impropriety. According to Enron's internal investigation, for example, there "was an absence of forceful and effective oversight [of the company's disclosures] by . . . in-house counsel, and objective and critical professional advice by outside counsel at Vinson & Elkins,"[22] along with senior management and the auditors. The report expressly criticized Vinson & Elkins, which the investigators argued "should have brought a stronger, more objective and more critical voice to the disclosure process."[23]

An internal investigation at WorldCom likewise faulted, among others, the firm's lawyers as part of a pervasive "breakdown in the . . . the company's corporate-governance structure."[24] An internal investigation criticized WorldCom's general counsel because his legal department was not properly structured "to maximize its effectiveness as a control structure upon which the Board could depend."[25]

It was against this background that, in the floor debate over Sarbanes-Oxley, Senator John Edwards (D-NC) argued that when "executives and/or accountants are breaking the law, you can be sure that part of the problem is that the lawyers who are there and involved are not doing their jobs."[26] Edwards further argued that after "all the . . . corporate misconduct we have seen, it is . . . clear that corporate lawyers should not be left to regulate themselves no more than accountants should be left to regulate themselves."[27] Accordingly, just as the Sarbanes-Oxley Act federalized regulation of the accounting profession, so too did Sarbanes-Oxley bring the corporate lawyer—client relationship into the federal sphere.

The problem is that the nature of the legal market gives lawyers—both in-house and outside counsel—strong incentives to overlook management wrongdoing. As to the former, even if the board of directors formally appoints the in-house general counsel, his tenure normally depends mainly on his relationship with the CEO. As for outside legal counsel, because clients hire attorneys or firms and not the reverse, attorneys must please their clients in order to retain their business, and to attract the business of future clients. This pressure is especially strong

[22] William C. Powers, Jr., et al., Report of Investigation by the Special Investigative Committee of the Board of Directors of Enron Corp. 17 (Feb. 1, 2002).

[23] Id. at 26.

[24] Rebecca Blumenstein & Susan Pulliam, WorldCom Fraud was Widespread, Wall St. J., June 10, 2003, at A3.

[25] Rebecca Blumenstein & Jesse Drucker, MCI's Treasurer, Counsel to Resign After Disclosure, Wall St. J., June 11, 2003, at A3, A12.

[26] 148 Cong. Rec. S6551 (2002).

[27] Id. at S6552.

given the large number of capable firms and attorneys available for hire; law firms are something akin to a fungible good. Consequently, despite an attorney's overarching legal obligations to report misconduct, he might be inclined to intentionally or subconsciously "overlook" marginal conduct. As to both types of attorney, moreover, although their ultimate duty is owed to the corporation itself, their daily responsibilities involve dealing with management and they thus often develop a de facto loyalty to management that trumps their de jure duties. As Senator Edwards explained in the floor debate over the Sarbanes-Oxley:

> We have seen corporate lawyers sometimes forget who their client is. What happens is their day-to-day conduct is with the CEO or the chief financial officer because those are the individuals responsible for hiring them. So as a result, that is with whom they have a relationship. When they go to lunch with their client, the corporation, they are usually going to lunch with the CEO or the chief financial officer. When they get phone calls, they are usually returning calls to the CEO or the chief financial officer.[28]

Accordingly, when the Senate took up the bill that became the Sarbanes-Oxley Act, Senator Edwards proposed a floor amendment, which was subsequently enacted as § 307 of the Act.

SOX § 307

Not later than 180 days after the date of enactment of this Act, the Commission shall issue rules, in the public interest and for the protection of investors, setting forth minimum standards of professional conduct for attorneys appearing and practicing before the Commission in any way in the representation of issuers, including a rule—

> (1) requiring an attorney to report evidence of a material violation of securities law or breach of fiduciary duty or similar violation by the company or any agent thereof, to the chief legal counsel or the chief executive officer of the company (or the equivalent thereof); and

> (2) if the counsel or officer does not appropriately respond to the evidence (adopting, as necessary, appropriate remedial measures or sanctions with respect to the violation), requiring the attorney to report the evidence to the audit committee of the board of directors of the issuer or to another committee of the board of directors comprised solely of directors not employed directly or indirectly by the issuer, or to the board of directors.

Edwards explained that § 307 gave lawyers a very "simple" obligation: "You report the violation. If the violation isn't addressed properly, then

---

[28]   148 Cong. Rec. S6551–52 (2002).

you go to the board."[29] Note the emphasis on reporting to the board.
Section 307 clearly is directed at enhancing the role of the board vis-à-
vis that of management.

In response to § 307, the SEC in January 2003 promulgated attorney
conduct regulations.[30] At the heart of these so-called "Part 205"
regulations is a version of the up-the-ladder reporting requirement
envisioned by Senator Edwards. In promulgating the Part 205
regulations, the SEC postponed action with regard to mandatory noisy
withdrawals. The original proposal obligated an attorney whose internal
complaints did not receive an adequate mitigating response by the issuer
to resign from the corporation and to file a notification with the SEC
explaining the basis for such resignation. This noisy withdrawal rule met
with substantial criticism from the bar. As adopted, Part 205 permits,
but does not require, an attorney to disclose confidential client
information to the SEC under specified conditions, most notably where
necessary to prevent "injury to the financial interest or property of the
issuer or investors."[31]

Unlike the much-debated noisy withdrawal issue, an up-the-ladder
reporting requirement does not require the lawyer to violate client
confidences. The ABA Model Rules make clear that an attorney's client
is the corporate entity, rather than an individual employee or group of
employees.[32] Consequently, discussing client information with anyone
authorized to make decisions within the organization is not a breach of
confidence. The Part 205 Regulations make this point explicit: "By
communicating such information [i.e., about securities violations] to the
issuer's officers or directors, an attorney does not reveal client
confidences or secrets. . . ."[33]

The initial jurisdictional question is whether a lawyer is "appearing
and practicing before the Commission in the representation of an
issuer."[34] Only lawyers doing so are subject to the SEC's ethics standards.
Unfortunately, the definition of "appearing and practicing" is sweeping
but quite vague. As a result, many non-securities lawyers may be
surprised to find that their conduct is covered by the Part 205
regulations.

In particular, the applicable rule provides, in pertinent part, that:

> Appearing and practicing before the Commission: (1)
> Means: . . . Providing advice in respect of the United States
> securities laws or the Commission's rules or regulations
> thereunder regarding any document that the attorney has

---

[29] 148 Cong. Rec. S6552 (2002).

[30] Implementation of Standards of Professional Conduct for Attorneys, Securities Act
Release No. 8185 (Jan. 29, 2003), available at http://www.sec.gov/rules/final/33-8185.htm.

[31] 17 C.F.R. § 205.3(d)(2).

[32] See Model Rules of Prof'l Conduct R. 1.13(a).

[33] 17 C.F.R. § 205.3(b)(1).

[34] 17 C.F.R. § 205.2.

notice will be filed with or submitted to, or incorporated into any document that will be filed with or submitted to, the Commission, including the provision of such advice in the context of preparing, or participating in the preparation of, any such document . . . ."[35]

To be sure, the adopting release states "an attorney's preparation of a document (such as a contract) which he or she never intended or had notice would be submitted to the Commission, or incorporated into a document submitted to the Commission, but which subsequently is submitted to the Commission as an exhibit to or in connection with a filing, does not constitute 'appearing and practicing' before the Commission." Yet, many non-securities lawyers may know that their documents will be so filed and thus will find themselves "appearing and practicing" before the Commission.

The Part 205 regulations facially preempt state rules of professional conduct.[36] As a result, where there is conflict between a state's rules and part 205, the latter prevails, unless the state imposes a more stringent obligation upon its attorneys that is consistent with Part 205. Attorneys who comply with the Regulation's procedures in good faith will be immune from liability for violating state ethics rules that conflict. Because it will not always be self-evident whether counsel is "appearing and practicing" before the SEC, the organized bar thus likely will be compelled to square its rules with those promulgated by the SEC.

As originally proposed, Part 205.3 provided that an attorney "shall act in the best interest of the issuer and its shareholders." As finally adopted, however, the relevant rule provides only that: "An attorney appearing and practicing before the Commission in the representation of an issuer owes his or her professional and ethical duties to the issuer as an organization."[37] The Part 205 Regulations, however, do emphasize that the attorney "represents the issuer as an entity rather than the officers."

Former ABA Model Rule 1.13 acknowledged the potential need for an attorney to report on suspected wrongdoing within the organization, but it also limited the ability of an attorney to do so effectively. The language of the Rule was discretionary rather than prescriptive, allowing an attorney to use his judgment about whether or not to proceed with reporting evidence of misconduct to the board of directors or even to high-level corporate officers. In contrast, Part 205 uses the prescriptive word "shall" to describe an attorney's duty. In pertinent part, the rule provides:

> If an attorney, appearing and practicing before the Commission in the representation of an issuer, becomes aware of evidence of a material violation by the issuer or by any officer,

---

[35]   17 C.F.R. § 205.2(a)(1)(iii).

[36]   17 C.F.R. §§ 205.6(b)–(c).

[37]   17 C.F.R. § 205.3(a).

director, employee, or agent of the issuer, the attorney shall report such evidence to the issuer's chief legal officer (or the equivalent thereof) or to both the issuer's chief legal officer and its chief executive officer (or the equivalents thereof) forthwith.[38]

As a result, an attorney will not have the luxury of using his own judgment about whether or not to report wrongdoing once the statutory level of evidence is triggered. As Senator Edwards anticipated, counsel must report up within the chain of command.

The initial obligation of a lawyer who "becomes aware of evidence of a material violation by the issuer or by any officer, director, employee, or agent of the issuer" is to report such evidence to the issuer's chief legal or executive officer.[39] The lawyer need not cry wolf every time there is the slightest hint of a possible problem, however. Instead, the lawyer's reporting obligation is triggered only by "credible evidence" that would lead a prudent and competent attorney to believe it is "reasonably likely" that a material violation has taken place, is taking place at present, or will occur in the near future. Subject to a slew of exceptions and alternatives, unless the lawyer "reasonably believes that [that officer] has provided an appropriate response within a reasonable time, the attorney shall report the evidence of a material violation to" the audit committee of the board of directors.[40]

An "appropriate response" is defined by Part 205 as a response that leads the attorney to reasonably believe that: (1) There is no material violation; (2) there was a material violation, but the company has taken appropriate remedial measures; or (iii) that the company has retained or directed an attorney to investigate the report and has been advised by such attorney that there is a colorable defense to the alleged violation. The SEC has emphasized that attorneys are free to exercise their own judgment as to whether a response is an appropriate one, so long as their judgment is a reasonable one.

The Part 205 regulations permit a company to establish a so-called "qualified legal compliance committee" (QLCC) composed of at least two or more independent directors, at least one of whom must be a member of the audit committee of the board of directors. The QLCC is tasked with receiving and investigating complaints by in-house or outside counsel of possible material violations. Many companies are using their audit committee as the QLCC, although this has the disadvantage of piling yet another task on the increasingly overworked shoulders of the audit committee.

The advantage of using the QLCC process is that an attorney who makes a report to the QLCC has satisfied his or her reporting obligation

---

[38]   17 C.F.R. § 205.3(b)(1).

[39]   Id.

[40]   17 C.F.R. § 205.3(b)(3).

and, most importantly, is not required to assess the QLCC's response. In addition, a general counsel who receives a report of a material violation can buck the report to the QLCC instead of conducting an individual investigation.

There are a couple of important restrictions on the use of a QLCC. First, the QLCC may only deal with reports that are received after it has been established. In other words, if a report is already working its way up the ladder, it is too late to set up a QLCC to deal with that report. Second, the QLCC cannot just brush the report under the rug. The QLCC must adopt a written policy for how it will handle any report of a possible material violation. The QLCC must be empowered to conduct an investigation, to recommend that the board of directors and/or management take remedial measures and be authorized to notify the SEC if the board of directors and top management fail to implement appropriate remedial measures. Lastly, the QLCC is required to notify the board, CEO, and the general counsel of the results of any investigation and any remedial measures imposed or proposed.

NOTES AND QUESTIONS

1. The roles played by prominent Texas law firm Vinson & Elkins as Enron's principal outside counsel can be separated into three distinct categories: First, the aggressive structuring of the controversial special purpose entity transactions used in Enron's accounting scam. Second, drafting Enron's disclosure documents. Third, conducting an internal investigation of a whistleblower's allegations.[41] The latter category is a rare undertaking and differs significantly from the far more common transactional work now governed by Sarbanes-Oxley and its progeny. Yet, Sarbanes-Oxley § 307 and the Part 205 Regulations seem better designed to deal with the third context than with either of the first two. It is only in the third context, for example, that lawyers deliberately set out to look for evidence of wrongdoing.

In more common transactional settings, § 307 issues may arise in one of three main ways. First, counsel may be aware of aggressive or risky conduct by management, but is unaware of fraud or other illegality. In these cases, the lawyer will not report up-the-ladder, due to lack of knowledge. Second, counsel may have actively participated in—or at least facilitated—actual fraud. In these cases, the lawyer also is unlikely to report up-the-ladder, albeit for the different reason that he now has something to hide. Third, counsel may have grounds for suspicion—but no direct evidence—of fraud or other illegality.

Only in the latter scenario does the up-the-ladder reporting requirement come into play, but it likely is rare. Corporate managers are highly unlikely to seek legal assistance with outright fraud, as opposed to conduct that merely pushes the edge of the envelope. In the post Sarbanes-Oxley § 307

---

[41] See generally Jill E. Fisch & Kenneth M. Rosen, Is There a Role for Lawyers in Preventing Future Enrons?, 48 Vill. L. Rev. 1097 (2003).

environment, managers are even more likely to conceal any hint of impropriety from counsel. In addition, lawyers will very rarely perceive their own situation to fall within the third scenario. As former Delaware Chancellor Allen aptly noted, albeit in a rather different context, "human nature may incline even one acting in subjective good faith to rationalize as right that which is merely personally beneficial."[42] It typically is personally beneficial for lawyers to refrain from antagonizing the corporate managers who hire and fire them. The claim is not that lawyers are pervasively co-opted or immoral. The claim is only that lawyers have both economic incentives and cognitive biases that systematically incline them to stay on the good side of the corporation's managers. Hence, absent the proverbial smoking gun, we can expect lawyers to turn a blind eye to indicia of misconduct by those managers. Section 307 does too little to change those incentives.

2.   The rules draw a distinction between supervisory and subordinate lawyers. A supervisory attorney is one directing or supervising another who is appearing and practicing before the SEC (the definition specifically includes the CLO and law firm partners). Supervisory attorneys must report to the issuer whenever they directly obtain evidence of a material violation or a subordinate has reported evidence of a material violation to them. Subordinate attorney is one who appears or practices before the SEC under the direction or supervision of another attorney. The rule provides an exemption pursuant to which an attorney who appears and practices before the SEC and directly reports to the issuer's CLO is not a subordinate attorney. Subordinates need only report evidence of material violations to their supervising attorney

3.   Some commentators suggested that the SEC should have required that the audit committee and/or the board meet periodically with the general counsel outside the presence of other managers and inside directors. Do you agree?

4.   Some commentators suggested that the SEC require counsel to report possible violations to the board even if the chief legal or executive officer undertook a reasonable response to the violation. Do you agree?

5.   A more radical way of promoting the anti-managerial intent inherent in Sarbanes-Oxley § 307 would be an enhanced due diligence obligation, which would effectively transform securities lawyers into auditors. A legal audit of the firm in connection with major transactions and/or the preparation of significant disclosure documents would increase the likelihood that counsel would become aware of evidence of client misconduct, which could then be reported up the ladder. Indeed, SOX had already moved in this direction by imposing a new obligation for the chief executive officer and chief and financial officer to certify disclosure documents.[43] What are the arguments for and against such a proposal?

---

[42]   City Capital Associates Ltd. Partnership v. Interco Inc., 551 A.2d 787, 796 (Del. Ch. 1988).

[43]   Sarbanes-Oxley § 302.

PROBLEMS

1. Is Sally appearing and practicing before the SEC in any of the following cases?

    A.   Sally, a deputy assistant general counsel for environmental matters, oversees several environmental issues plaguing her company. Every month, she routinely sends her supervisor a status report. While preparing to file a Form 10-Q quarterly report, her superior is asked for a description of an environmental matter for disclosure in the Form 10-Q. The superior offers Sally's report without her knowledge.

    B.   A colleague from the same company's securities compliance unit tells Sally about a pending SEC filing and asks her for a description of the environmental issue she is handling.

    C.   Sally is told the company plans to use her report in the filing and is asked if she thinks it is good enough for the SEC.

2. Jane, a partner at a patent litigation firm, represents Acme, Inc., in a variety of patent matters. Jane is supervising an associate who is preparing a settlement agreement in a lawsuit to which Acme is a party and knows that a copy of that agreement is to be attached to a Form 8-K Acme is preparing to file with the SEC. Jane learns from a personal friend employed by Acme of a preliminary decision by the issuer's CFO not to include certain transactions in the financial statements appearing in the corporation's upcoming Form 10-K. Must Jane report that fact up the ladder?

3. Lorraine Lawyer is a partner of Acme, Inc.'s principal outside law firm and for many years has been Acme's principal contact person at the firm. Lorraine becomes aware of material violations by the issuer. Lorraine reports up the ladder, but the issuer takes no action. Lorraine convenes a press conference and announces to several financial news outlets in attendance that she is parting ways with the issuer. Lorraine also sends a letter to the SEC announcing that she no longer represents the issuer. The letter includes details about the material violations. Has Lorraine acted ethically?

To assess your understanding of the material in this chapter, click here to take a quiz.

CHAPTER 8

INSIDER TRADING

Under current federal law, there are two basic theories under which trading on inside information becomes unlawful. The disclose or abstain rule and the misappropriation theory were created by the courts under Section 10(b) of the Securities Exchange Act of 1934 and Rule 10b–5 thereunder.[1]

Securities Exchange Act § 10

It shall be unlawful for any person, directly or indirectly, by the use of any means or instrumentality of interstate commerce or of the mails, or of any facility of any national securities exchange—

. . .

(b) To use or employ, in connection with the purchase or sale of any security registered on a national securities exchange or any security not so registered, or any securities-based swap agreement—any manipulative or deceptive device or contrivance in contravention of such rules and regulations as the Commission may prescribe as necessary or appropriate in the public interest or for the protection of investors.

Rule 10b–5

It shall be unlawful for any person, directly or indirectly, by the use of any means or instrumentality of interstate commerce, or of the mails or of any facility of any national securities exchange,

(a) To employ any device, scheme, or artifice to defraud,

(b) To make any untrue statement of a material fact or to omit to state a material fact necessary in order to make the statements made, in the light of the circumstances under which they were made, not misleading, or

(c) To engage in any act, practice, or course of business which operates or would operate as a fraud or deceit upon any person,

in connection with the purchase or sale of any security.

---

[1]   Although we now take it for granted that regulating insider trading is a job for the SEC under federal law, it was not always so. Until the 1960s, insider trading was as a matter of state corporate law. Since then, of course, the federal prohibition has largely eclipsed state law in this area. Accordingly, our focus herein will be exclusively on federal law.

Pursuant to its rule-making authority under Exchange Act Section 14(e), the SEC adopted Rule 14e–3 to proscribe insider trading involving information relating to tender offers. Insider trading may also violate other statutes, such as the mail and wire fraud laws, which are beyond the scope of this text. These theories of liability are outside the scope of our focus on corporate governance.

On their face, neither § 10(b) nor Rule 10b–5 expressly prohibit—or even mention—insider trading. For a couple of decades after the Rule was first adopted, moreover, it was used exclusively in face-to-face and control transactions rather than in connection with transactions effected om public secondary trading markets. Instead, like state common law, the initial Rule 10b–5 cases were limited to.[2] Not until 1961 did the SEC finally conclude that insider trading on an impersonal stock exchange violated Rule 10b–5.[3] Only then did the modern federal insider trading prohibition at last begin to take shape.

The modern prohibition thus is a creature of SEC administrative actions and judicial opinions, only loosely tied to the statutory language and its legislative history. U.S. Supreme Court Chief Justice William Rehnquist famously observed that Rule 10b–5 is a judicial oak which has grown from little more than a legislative acorn.[4] Nowhere in Rule 10b–5 jurisprudence is this truer than where the insider trading prohibition is concerned, given the tiny (even nonexistent) legislative acorn on which it rests.

A. DISCLOSE OR ABSTAIN

The modern federal insider trading prohibition began taking shape in the Second Circuit Court of Appeals' famous *Texas Gulf Sulphur* opinion.[5] The Second Circuit held that when an insider has material nonpublic information the insider must either disclose such information before trading or abstain from trading until the information has been disclosed. By that holding the court created what is now known as the "disclose or abstain" rule. The name is something of a misnomer, of course. The court presumably phrased the rule in terms of disclosure because this was an omissions case under Rule 10b–5. In such cases, the defendant must owe a duty of disclosure to some investor for liability to be imposed.[6] As a practical matter, however, disclosure will rarely be an option.

---

[2] See, e.g., Speed v. Transamerica Corp., 99 F.Supp. 808 (D.Del.1951) (omissions in connection with what amounted to tender offer); Kardon v. National Gypsum Co., 73 F.Supp. 798 (E.D.Pa.1947) (sale of control negotiated face to face); In re Ward La France Truck Corp., 13 SEC 373 (1943) (same).

[3] In re Cady, Roberts & Co., 40 SEC 907 (1961).

[4] Blue Chip Stamps v. Manor Drug Stores, 421 U.S. 723, 737 (1975).

[5] SEC v. Texas Gulf Sulphur Co., 401 F.2d 833 (2d Cir.1968), cert. denied, 394 U.S. 976 (1969).

[6] See, e.g., Chiarella v. United States, 445 U.S. 222, 230 (1980) (stating that liability for nondisclosure "is premised upon a duty to disclose arising from a relationship of trust and confidence between parties to a transaction"); see also Dirks v. SEC, 463 U.S. 646, 654 (1983) (stating that there is no general duty to disclose and the duty to disclose must arise from a fiduciary relationship); SEC v. Switzer, 590 F.Supp. 756, 766 (W.D.Okla.1984) (holding that overhearing inadvertently revealed inside information does not create a duty to disclose before trading because for a fiduciary duty to run to a tippee, the inside information must be disclosed for an improper purpose).

In the early 1960s, mining corporation Texas Gulf Sulphur (TGS) was exploring for ore in northern Canada. On November 13, 1963, TGS officers learned that the company might have struck a rich vein of ore in an area near Timmins, Ontario. Over the next several months, the company maintained secrecy, while continuing exploring and buying land in the area.

During the nondisclosure period, various TGS insiders bought TGS stock and options. At the time of the ore strike, they together owned about 1,100 shares of stock and no options. By April 1964, they held 8,200 shares and options to buy 12,300 more. Because of various leaks (perhaps associated with this insider trading—we're not told) and

> **WHAT'S THAT?**
>
> "Information becomes public when disclosed 'to achieve a broad dissemination to the investing public generally and without favoring any special person or group,' or when, although known only by a few persons, their trading on it 'has caused the information to be fully impounded into the price of the particular stock." Moreover, '[t]o constitute non-public information under the act, information must be specific and more private than general rumor.' " *SEC v. Mayhew*, 121 F.3d 44, 50 (2d Cir. 1997) (citations omitted).

rumors (it would have been difficult to keep completely secret the substantial activity in Canada), the price of TGS stock rose steadily. In November, it sold for $17/share. By April 13, it had risen to $31; by the end of the day on April 16 it was $36, and by May 15 it was $58.

On April 12, the company issued a press release (published on Monday, April 13) designed to quell the rumors. Construed narrowly, perhaps it was not false. Yet it seemed designed to create, and probably did create, the false impression that there was no substantial evidence of a valuable ore discovery. On April 15, the company finally disclosed the ore strike, and the news was made public on April 16.

The SEC, seeking an injunction and other remedies, sued the company for issuing a misleading press release and the officers for insider trading.

During the relevant period, TGS had no affirmative duty to disclose the ore strike. As the Second Circuit correctly noted, the timing of disclosure is a matter for the business judgment of corporate managers, subject to any affirmative disclosure requirements imposed by the stock exchanges or the SEC. In this case, moreover, a valuable corporate purpose was served by delaying disclosure: confidentiality prevented competitors from buying up the mineral rights and kept down the price landowners would charge for them. The company therefore had no duty to disclose the discovery, at least up until the time that the land acquisition program was completed.

Given that the corporation had no duty to disclose, and had decided not to disclose the information, the insiders' fiduciary duties to the corporation would preclude them disclosing it for personal gain. In this case, the company's president had specifically instructed insiders in the know to keep the information confidential, but such an instruction was not technically necessary. Agency law precludes a firm's agents from disclosing confidential information that belongs to their corporate principal, as all information relating to the ore strike clearly did.[7]

Disclosure by an insider who wishes to trade thus is only feasible if there is no legitimate corporate purpose for maintaining secrecy. These situations, however, presumably will be relatively rare—it is hard to imagine many business developments that can be disclosed immediately without working some harm to the corporation. In most cases, the disclose or abstain rule really does not provide the insider with a disclosure option: generally, the duty will be one of complete abstention.

The policy foundation on which the Second Circuit erected the disclose or abstain rule was equality of access to information. The court contended that the federal insider trading prohibition was intended to assure that "all investors trading on impersonal exchanges have relatively equal access to material information." Put another way, the majority thought Congress intended "that all members of the investing public should be subject to identical market risks."

The equality of access principle admittedly has some intuitive appeal. The implications of the equal access principle, however, become troubling when we start dealing with attenuated circumstances, especially with respect to market information. Suppose a representative of TGS had approached a landowner in the Timmins area to negotiate purchasing the mineral rights to the land. TGS' agent does not disclose the ore strike, but the landowner turns out to be pretty smart. She knows TGS has been drilling in the area and has heard rumors that it has been buying up a lot of mineral rights. She puts two and two together, reaches the obvious conclusion, and buys some TGS stock. Under a literal reading of *Texas Gulf Sulphur*, has our landowner committed illegal insider trading?

The surprising answer is "probably." The *Texas Gulf Sulphur* court stated that the insider trading prohibition applies to "anyone in possession of material inside information," because § 10(b) was intended to assure that "all investors trading on impersonal exchanges have relatively equal access to material information." The court further stated that the prohibition applies to any persons who have "access, directly or *indirectly*" to confidential information (here is the sticking point) if they know that the information is unavailable to the investing public. The only issue thus perhaps would be a factual one turning on the landowner's state of mind: Did she know she was dealing with confidential information? If so, the equal access policy would seem to justify imposing a duty on her. Query whether the insider trading prohibition should stretch quite that far? Ultimately, the Supreme Court concluded that it should not.

---

[7]   Restatement (Second) of Agency § 395 (1958).

Chiarella v. United States

445 U.S. 222 (1980)

. . .

I

Petitioner is a printer by trade. In 1975 and 1976, he worked as a "markup man" in the New York composing room of Pandick Press, a financial printer. Among documents that petitioner handled were five announcements of corporate takeover bids. When these documents were delivered to the printer, the identities of the acquiring and target corporations were concealed by blank spaces or false names. The true names were sent to the printer on the night of the final printing.

The petitioner, however, was able to deduce the names of the target companies before the final printing from other information contained in the documents. Without disclosing his knowledge, petitioner purchased stock in the target companies and sold the shares immediately after the takeover attempts were made public. By this method, petitioner realized a gain of slightly more than $30,000 in the course of 14 months. . . .

In January 1978, petitioner was indicted on 17 counts of violating § 10(b) of the Securities Exchange Act of 1934 (1934 Act) and SEC Rule 10b–5. After petitioner unsuccessfully moved to dismiss the indictment, he was brought to trial and convicted on all counts.

The Court of Appeals for the Second Circuit affirmed petitioner's conviction. 588 F.2d 1358 (1978). . . .

II

. . .

This case concerns the legal effect of the petitioner's silence. The District Court's charge permitted the jury to convict the petitioner if it found that he willfully failed to inform sellers of target company securities that he knew of a forthcoming takeover bid that would make their shares more valuable. . . .

. . .

The SEC took an important step in the development of § 10(b) when it held that a broker-dealer and his firm violated that section by selling securities on the basis of undisclosed information obtained from a director of the issuer corporation who was also a registered representative of the brokerage firm. In *Cady, Roberts & Co.*, 40 SEC 907 (1961), the Commission decided that a corporate insider must abstain from trading in the shares of his corporation unless he has first disclosed all material inside information known to him. The obligation to disclose or abstain derives from

> "[a]n affirmative duty to disclose material information[, which] has been traditionally imposed on corporate 'insiders,' particular officers, directors, or controlling stockholders. We,

and the courts have consistently held that insiders must disclose material facts which are known to them by virtue of their position but which are not known to persons with whom they deal and which, if known, would affect their investment judgment." *Id.*, at 911.

The Commission emphasized that the duty arose from (i) the existence of a relationship affording access to inside information intended to be available only for a corporate purpose, and (ii) the unfairness of allowing a corporate insider to take advantage of that information by trading without disclosure. *Id.*, at 912, and n. 15.[8]

That the relationship between a corporate insider and the stockholders of his corporation gives rise to a disclosure obligation is not a novel twist of the law. At common law, misrepresentation made for the purpose of inducing reliance upon the false statement is fraudulent. But one who fails to disclose material information prior to the consummation of a transaction commits fraud only when he is under a duty to do so. And the duty to disclose arises when one party has information "that the other [party] is entitled to know because of a fiduciary or other similar relation of trust and confidence between them."[9] In its *Cady, Roberts* decision, the Commission recognized a relationship of trust and confidence between the shareholders of a corporation and those insiders who have obtained confidential information by reason of their position with that corporation. This relationship gives rise to a duty to disclose because of the "necessity of preventing a corporate insider from . . . tak[ing] unfair advantage of the uninformed minority stockholders." *Speed v. Transamerica Corp.*, 99 F.Supp. 808, 829 (D.Del.1951).

. . .

III

In this case, the petitioner was convicted of violating § 10(b) although he was not a corporate insider and he received no confidential information from the target company. Moreover, the "market information" upon which he relied did not concern the earning power or operations of the target company, but only the plans of the acquiring company. Petitioner's use of that information was not a fraud under

---

[8] In *Cady, Roberts*, the broker-dealer was liable under § 10(b) because it received nonpublic information from a corporate insider of the issuer. Since the insider could not use the information, neither could the partners in the brokerage firm with which he was associated. The transaction in *Cady, Roberts* involved sale of stock to persons who previously may not have been shareholders in the corporation. 40 SEC, at 913, and n. 21. The Commission embraced the reasoning of Judge Learned Hand that "the director or officer assumed a fiduciary relation to the buyer by the very sale; for it would be a sorry distinction to allow him to use the advantage of his position to induce the buyer into the position of a beneficiary although he was forbidden to do so once the buyer had become one." Id., at 914, n. 23, quoting Gratz v. Claughton, 187 F.2d 46, 49 (CA2), cert. denied, 341 U.S. 920, 71 S.Ct. 741, 95 L.Ed. 1353 (1951).

[9] Restatement (Second) of Torts § 551(2)(a) (1976). See James & Gray, Misrepresentation—Part II, 37 Md.L.Rev. 488, 523–527 (1978). As regards securities transactions, the American Law Institute recognizes that "silence when there is a duty to . . . speak may be a fraudulent act." ALI, Federal Securities Code § 262(b) (Prop. Off. Draft 1978).

§ 10(b) unless he was subject to an affirmative duty to disclose it before trading. In this case, the jury instructions failed to specify any such duty. In effect, the trial court instructed the jury that petitioner owed a duty to everyone; to all sellers, indeed, to the market as a whole. The jury simply was told to decide whether petitioner used material, nonpublic information at a time when "he knew other people trading in the securities market did not have access to the same information."

The Court of Appeals affirmed the conviction by holding that "*[a]nyone*—corporate insider or not—who regularly receives material nonpublic information may not use that information to trade in securities without incurring an affirmative duty to disclose." 588 F.2d, at 1365 (emphasis in original). Although the court said that its test would include only persons who regularly receive material, nonpublic information, *id.*, at 1366, its rationale for that limitation is unrelated to the existence of a duty to disclose.[14] The Court of Appeals, like the trial court, failed to identify a relationship between petitioner and the sellers that could give rise to a duty. Its decision thus rested solely upon its belief that the federal securities laws have "created a system providing equal access to information necessary for reasoned and intelligent investment decisions." *Id.*, at 1362. The use by anyone of material information not generally available is fraudulent, this theory suggests, because such information gives certain buyers or sellers an unfair advantage over less informed buyers and sellers.

This reasoning suffers from two defects. First not every instance of financial unfairness constitutes fraudulent activity under § 10(b). Second, the element required to make silence fraudulent—a duty to disclose—is absent in this case. No duty could arise from petitioner's relationship with the sellers of the target company's securities, for petitioner had no prior dealings with them. He was not their agent, he was not a fiduciary, he was not a person in whom the sellers had placed their trust and confidence. He was, in fact, a complete stranger who dealt with the sellers only through impersonal market transactions.

---

[14]   The Court of Appeals said that its "regular access to market information" test would create a workable rule embracing "those who occupy . . . strategic places in the market mechanism." 588 F.2d, at 1365. These considerations are insufficient to support a duty to disclose. A duty arises from the relationship between parties, . . . and not merely from one's ability to acquire information because of his position in the market.

The Court of Appeals also suggested that the acquiring corporation itself would not be a "market insider" because a tender offeror creates, rather than receives, information and takes a substantial economic risk that its offer will be unsuccessful. 588 F.2d, at 1366–1367. Again, the Court of Appeals departed from the analysis appropriate to recognition of a duty. The Court of Appeals for the Second Circuit previously held, in a manner consistent with our analysis here, that a tender offeror does not violate § 10(b) when it makes preannouncement purchases precisely because there is no relationship between the offeror and the seller:

"We know of no rule of law . . . that a purchaser of stock, who was not an 'insider' and had no fiduciary relation to a prospective seller, had any obligation to reveal circumstances that might raise a seller's demands and thus abort the sale." General Time Corp. v. Talley Industries, Inc., 403 F.2d 159, 164 (1968), cert. denied, 393 U.S. 1026, 89 S.Ct. 631, 21 L.Ed.2d 570 (1969).

We cannot affirm petitioner's conviction without recognizing a general duty between all participants in market transactions to forgo actions based on material, nonpublic information. Formulation of such a broad duty, which departs radically from the established doctrine that duty arises from a specific relationship between two parties, should not be undertaken absent some explicit evidence of congressional intent.

As we have seen, no such evidence emerges from the language or legislative history of § 10(b). Moreover, neither the Congress nor the Commission ever has adopted a parity-of-information rule. Instead the problems caused by misuse of market information have been addressed by detailed and sophisticated regulation that recognizes when use of market information may not harm operation of the securities markets. For example, the Williams Act limits but does not completely prohibit a tender offeror's purchases of target corporation stock before public announcement of the offer. Congress' careful action in this and other areas[16] contrasts, and is in some tension, with the broad rule of liability we are asked to adopt in this case.

Indeed, the theory upon which the petitioner was convicted is at odds with the Commission's view of § 10(b) as applied to activity that has the same effect on sellers as the petitioner's purchases. "Warehousing" takes place when a corporation gives advance notice of its intention to launch a tender offer to institutional investors who then are able to purchase stock in the target company before the tender offer is made public and the price of shares rises. In this case, as in warehousing, a buyer of securities purchases stock in a target corporation on the basis of market information which is unknown to the seller. In both of these situations, the seller's behavior presumably would be altered if he had the nonpublic information. Significantly, however, the Commission has acted to bar warehousing under its authority to regulate tender offers after recognizing that action under § 10(b) would rest on a "somewhat different theory" than that previously used to regulate insider trading as fraudulent activity.

We see no basis for applying such a new and different theory of liability in this case. . . . Section 10(b) is aptly described as a catchall provision, but what it catches must be fraud. When an allegation of fraud is based upon nondisclosure, there can be no fraud absent a duty to speak. We hold that a duty to disclose under § 10(b) does not arise from the mere possession of nonpublic market information. The contrary

---

[16] Section 11 of the 1934 Act generally forbids a member of a national securities exchange from effecting any transaction on the exchange for its own account. But Congress has specifically exempted specialists from this prohibition—broker-dealers who execute orders for customers trading in a specific corporation's stock, while at the same time buying and selling that corporation's stock on their own behalf. The exception is based upon Congress' recognition that specialists contribute to a fair and orderly marketplace at the same time they exploit the informational advantage that comes from their possession of buy and sell orders. Similar concerns with the functioning of the market prompted Congress to exempt market makers, block positioners, registered odd-lot dealers, bona fide arbitrageurs, and risk arbitrageurs from § 11's general prohibition on member trading.

result is without support in the legislative history of § 10(b) and would be inconsistent with the careful plan that Congress has enacted for regulation of the securities markets.

IV

. . .

The judgment of the Court of Appeals is

Reversed.

NOTES AND QUESTIONS

1.   The theory of liability recognized in *Chiarella* is referred to as the disclose or abstain theory or the classical theory. What must the government prove in order for someone to be held liable under this theory?

2.   In *Dirks v. SEC*,[8] the Supreme Court addressed an important class of actors who are not employees of the corporation but whose relationship with it is sufficiently close to justify treating them as constructive insiders:

> Under certain circumstances, such as where corporate information is revealed legitimately to an underwriter, accountant, lawyer, or consultant working for the corporation, these outsiders may become fiduciaries of the shareholders. The basis for recognizing this fiduciary duty is not simply that such persons acquired nonpublic corporate information, but rather that they have entered into a special confidential relationship in the conduct of the business of the enterprise and are given access to information solely for corporate purposes. . . .
>
> For such a duty to be imposed, however, the corporation must expect the outsider to keep the disclosed nonpublic information confidential, and the relationship at least must imply such a duty.

Id. at 655 n.14.

3.   In order for information to be subject to the disclose or abstain rule, the information must be both material and nonpublic. Give some examples of information that would satisfy those requirements.

4.   Explain the difference between inside and market information. Give examples of each.

NOTE ON TIPPING

In the 1960s and early 1970s, Equity Funding Corporation of America appeared to be a hugely successful financial services conglomerate selling insurance, mutual funds, and other investments to retail customers. In fact, however, since at least 1964, at least 100 Equity Funding senior employees had engaged in one of the massive accounting frauds in U.S. history. Among other things, for example, they set up a computer dedicated exclusively to documenting fictional insurance policies that were then recorded on the

---

[8]   463 U.S. 646 (1983).

company's balance sheet as assets and whose purported premia were recorded on the company's income statement.

Raymond Dirks was a securities analyst who played a critical role in uncovering the massive Equity Funding fraud. Dirks first began investigating Equity Funding after receiving allegations from Ronald Secrist, a former officer of Equity Funding, that the corporation was engaged in widespread fraudulent corporate practices. Dirks passed the results of his investigation to the SEC and the Wall Street Journal, but also discussed his findings with various clients. A number of those clients sold their holdings of Equity Funding securities before any public disclosure of the fraud, thereby avoiding substantial losses. After the fraud was made public and Equity Funding went into receivership, the SEC began an investigation of Dirk's role in exposing the fraud. One might think Dirks deserved a medal (one suspects Mr. Dirks definitely felt that way), but one would be wrong. The SEC censured Dirks for violating the federal insider trading prohibition by repeating the allegations of fraud to his clients.

Under the *Texas Gulf Sulphur* equal access to information standard, tipping of the sort at issue in *Dirks* presented no conceptual problems. The tippee had access to information unavailable to those with whom he traded and, as such, is liable. After *Chiarella*, however, the tipping problem was more complex. Neither Dirks nor any of his customers were agents, officers, or directors of Equity Funding. Likewise, none of them had any other form of special relationship of trust and confidence with those with whom they traded.

In reversing Dirk's censure, the Supreme Court expressly reaffirmed its rejection of the equal access standard and its requirement of a breach of fiduciary duty in order for liability to be imposed. Recognizing that the *Chiarella* standard posed problems for tipping cases, the court held that a tippee's liability is derivative of that of the tipper, "arising from [the tippee's] role as a participant after the fact in the insider's breach of a fiduciary duty."[9] A tippee therefore can be held liable only when the tipper breached a fiduciary duty by disclosing information to the tippee, and the tippee knows or has reason to know of the breach of duty.

On the *Dirks* facts, this formulation precluded imposition of liability. To be sure, Secrist was an employee and, hence, a fiduciary of Equity Funding. But the mere fact that an insider tips nonpublic information is not enough under *Dirks*. What *Dirks* effectively proscribes is not merely a breach of confidentiality by the insider, but rather the breach of a fiduciary duty of loyalty to refrain from profiting on information entrusted to the tipper:

> Absent some personal gain, there has been no breach of duty to stockholders. And absent a breach by the insider [to his stockholders], there is no derivative breach [by the tippee].[10]

9   Dirks v. SEC, 463 U.S. 646, 659 (1983).
10   Id. at 662.

Accordingly, the court held that:

> [T]he initial inquiry is whether there has been a breach of duty by
> the insider. This requires courts to focus on objective criteria, i.e.,
> whether the insider receives a direct or indirect personal benefit
> from the disclosure, such as a pecuniary gain or a reputational
> benefit that will translate into future earnings. There are objective
> facts and circumstances that often justify such an inference. For
> example, there may be a relationship between the insider and the
> recipient that suggests a quid pro quo from the latter, or an
> intention to benefit the particular recipient. The elements of
> fiduciary duty and exploitation of nonpublic information also exist
> when an insider makes a gift of confidential information to a
> trading relative or friend. The tip and trade resemble trading by
> the insider himself followed by a gift of the profits to the recipient.[11]

Secrist tipped off Dirks in order to bring Equity Funding's misconduct to
light, not for any personal gain. Absent the requisite personal benefit,
liability could not be imposed.

Salman v. United States
__ U.S. __, 137 S.Ct. 420 (2016)

Section 10(b) of the Securities Exchange Act of 1934 and the
Securities and Exchange Commission's Rule 10b–5 prohibit undisclosed
trading on inside corporate information by individuals who are under a
duty of trust and confidence that prohibits them from secretly using such
information for their personal advantage.

These persons also may not tip inside information to others for
trading. The tippee acquires the tipper's duty to disclose or abstain from
trading if the tippee knows the information was disclosed in breach of the
tipper's duty, and the tippee may commit securities fraud by trading in
disregard of that knowledge. In *Dirks v. SEC*, 463 U.S. 646, 103 S.Ct.
3255, 77 L.Ed.2d 911 (1983), this Court explained that a tippee's liability
for trading on inside information hinges on whether the tipper breached
a fiduciary duty by disclosing the information. A tipper breaches such a
fiduciary duty, we held, when the tipper discloses the inside information
for a personal benefit. And, we went on to say, a jury can infer a personal
benefit—and thus a breach of the tipper's duty—where the tipper
receives something of value in exchange for the tip or "makes a gift of
confidential information to a trading relative or friend." Id., at 664, 103
S.Ct. 3255.

Petitioner Bassam Salman challenges his convictions for conspiracy
and insider trading. Salman received lucrative trading tips from an
extended family member, who had received the information from
Salman's brother-in-law. Salman then traded on the information. He
argues that he cannot be held liable as a tippee because the tipper (his

---

[11]   Id. at 663–64.

brother-in-law) did not personally receive money or property in exchange for the tips and thus did not personally benefit from them. The Court of Appeals disagreed, holding that *Dirks* allowed the jury to infer that the tipper here breached a duty because he made a " 'gift of confidential information to a trading relative.' " 792 F.3d 1087, 1092 (C.A.9 2015) (quoting [*Dirks v. SEC*, 463 U.S. 646, 664, 103 S.Ct. 3255, 77 L.Ed.2d 911 (1983)]). Because the Court of Appeals properly applied *Dirks*, we affirm the judgment below.

I

Maher Kara was an investment banker in Citigroup's healthcare investment banking group. He dealt with highly confidential information about mergers and acquisitions involving Citigroup's clients. Maher enjoyed a close relationship with his older brother, Mounir Kara (known as Michael). After Maher started at Citigroup, he began discussing aspects of his job with Michael. At first he relied on Michael's chemistry background to help him grasp scientific concepts relevant to his new job.... Michael began to trade on the information Maher shared with him. At first, Maher was unaware of his brother's trading activity, but eventually he began to suspect that it was taking place.

Ultimately, Maher began to assist Michael's trading by sharing inside information with his brother about pending mergers and acquisitions. Maher sometimes used code words to communicate corporate information to his brother. Other times, he shared inside information about deals he was not working on in order to avoid detection. Without his younger brother's knowledge, Michael fed the information to others—including Salman, Michael's friend and Maher's brother-in-law. By the time the authorities caught on, Salman had made over $1.5 million in profits that he split with another relative who executed trades via a brokerage account on Salman's behalf.

Salman was indicted on one count of conspiracy to commit securities fraud ... and four counts of securities fraud. Facing charges of their own, both Maher and Michael pleaded guilty and testified at Salman's trial.

The evidence at trial established that Maher and Michael enjoyed a "very close relationship." Maher "love[d] [his] brother very much," Michael was like "a second father to Maher," and Michael was the best man at Maher's wedding to Salman's sister. Maher testified that he shared inside information with his brother to benefit him and with the expectation that his brother would trade on it. While Maher explained that he disclosed the information in large part to appease Michael (who pestered him incessantly for it), he also testified that he tipped his brother to "help him" and to "fulfil[l] whatever needs he had." ...

... Michael testified that he became friends with Salman when Maher was courting Salman's sister and later began sharing Maher's tips with Salman.... Michael also testified that he told Salman that the information was coming from Maher....

. . . Salman was convicted on all counts. He was sentenced to 36 months of imprisonment, three years of supervised release, and over $730,000 in restitution. . . . Salman appealed to the Ninth Circuit. While his appeal was pending, the Second Circuit issued its opinion in *United States v. Newman*, 773 F.3d 438 (2014), cert. denied, 577 U.S. ___, 136 S.Ct. 242, 193 L.Ed.2d 133 (2015). There, the Second Circuit reversed the convictions of two portfolio managers who traded on inside information. The Newman defendants were "several steps removed from the corporate insiders" and the court found that "there was no evidence that either was aware of the source of the inside information." 773 F.3d, at 443. The court acknowledged that Dirks and Second Circuit case law allow a factfinder to infer a personal benefit to the tipper from a gift of confidential information to a trading relative or friend. But the court concluded that, "[t]o the extent" Dirks permits "such an inference," the inference "is impermissible in the absence of proof of a meaningfully close personal relationship that generates an exchange that is objective, consequential, and represents at least a potential gain of a pecuniary or similarly valuable nature." 773 F.3d, at 452.[1]

Pointing to *Newman*, Salman argued that his conviction should be reversed. While the evidence established that Maher made a gift of trading information to Michael and that Salman knew it, there was no evidence that Maher received anything of "a pecuniary or similarly valuable nature" in exchange—or that Salman knew of any such benefit. The Ninth Circuit disagreed and affirmed Salman's conviction. The court reasoned that . . . Maher's disclosures to Michael were "precisely the gift of confidential information to a trading relative that Dirks envisioned." 792 F.3d, at 1092 (internal quotation marks omitted). To the extent *Newman* went further and required additional gain to the tipper in cases involving gifts of confidential information to family and friends, the Ninth Circuit "decline[d] to follow it." 792 F.3d, at 1093.

A

In this case, Salman contends that an insider's "gift of confidential information to a trading relative or friend," *Dirks*, 463 U.S. at 664, is not enough to establish securities fraud. Instead, Salman argues, a tipper does not personally benefit unless the tipper's goal in disclosing inside information is to obtain money, property, or something of tangible value. . . . Salman urges that defining a gift as a personal benefit renders the insider-trading offense indeterminate and overbroad: indeterminate, because liability may turn on facts such as the closeness of the relationship between tipper and tippee and the tipper's purpose for disclosure; and overbroad, because the Government may avoid having to prove a concrete personal benefit by simply arguing that the tipper meant

---

[1]   The Second Circuit also reversed the Newman defendants' convictions because the Government introduced no evidence that the defendants knew the information they traded on came from insiders or that the insiders received a personal benefit in exchange for the tips. 773 F.3d, at 453–454. This case does not implicate those issues.

to give a gift to the tippee. . . . Finally, Salman contends that gift situations create especially troubling problems for remote tippees—that is, tippees who receive inside information from another tippee, rather than the tipper—who may have no knowledge of the relationship between the original tipper and tippee and thus may not know why the tipper made the disclosure.

The Government disagrees and argues that a gift of confidential information to anyone, not just a "trading relative or friend," is enough to prove securities fraud. . . .

B

We adhere to *Dirks*, which easily resolves the narrow issue presented here.

In *Dirks*, we explained that a tippee is exposed to liability for trading on inside information only if the tippee participates in a breach of the tipper's fiduciary duty. Whether the tipper breached that duty depends "in large part on the purpose of the disclosure" to the tippee. 463 U.S., at 662, 103 S.Ct. 3255. "[T]he test," we explained, "is whether the insider personally will benefit, directly or indirectly, from his disclosure." Ibid. Thus, the disclosure of confidential information without personal benefit is not enough. In determining whether a tipper derived a personal benefit, we instructed courts to "focus on objective criteria, i.e., whether the insider receives a direct or indirect personal benefit from the disclosure, such as a pecuniary gain or a reputational benefit that will translate into future earnings." Id., at 663, 103 S.Ct. 3255. This personal benefit can "often" be inferred "from objective facts and circumstances," we explained, such as "a relationship between the insider and the recipient that suggests a *quid pro quo* from the latter, or an intention to benefit the particular recipient." Id., at 664, 103 S.Ct. 3255. In particular, we held that "[t]he elements of fiduciary duty and exploitation of nonpublic information also exist *when an insider makes a gift of confidential information to a trading relative or friend*." Ibid. (emphasis added). In such cases, "[t]he tip and trade resemble trading by the insider followed by a gift of the profits to the recipient." Ibid. We then applied this gift-giving principle to resolve *Dirks* itself, finding it dispositive that the tippers "received no monetary or personal benefit" from their tips to Dirks, "*nor was their purpose to make a gift of valuable information to Dirks*." Id., at 667, 103 S.Ct. 3255 (emphasis added).

Our discussion of gift giving resolves this case. Maher, the tipper, provided inside information to a close relative, his brother Michael. *Dirks* makes clear that a tipper breaches a fiduciary duty by making a gift of confidential information to "a trading relative," and that rule is sufficient to resolve the case at hand. As Salman's counsel acknowledged at oral argument, Maher would have breached his duty had he personally traded on the information here himself then given the proceeds as a gift to his brother. It is obvious that Maher would personally benefit in that situation. But Maher effectively achieved the same result by disclosing the information to Michael, and allowing him to trade on it. . . . *Dirks* appropriately prohibits that approach, as well. . . . [B]y disclosing confidential information as a gift to his brother with the expectation that he would trade on it, Maher breached his duty of trust and confidence to Citigroup and its clients—a duty Salman acquired, and breached himself, by trading on the information with full knowledge that it had been improperly disclosed.

To the extent the Second Circuit held that the tipper must also receive something of a "pecuniary or similarly valuable nature" in exchange for a gift to family or friends, we agree with the Ninth Circuit that this requirement is inconsistent with *Dirks*.

. . . We reject Salman's argument that *Dirks*'s gift-giving standard is unconstitutionally vague as applied to this case. *Dirks* created a simple and clear "guiding principle" for determining tippee liability, ... At most, Salman shows that in some factual circumstances assessing liability for gift-giving will be difficult. Salman's conduct is in the heartland of Dirks's rule concerning gifts. It remains the case that "[d]etermining whether an insider personally benefits from a particular disclosure, a question of fact, will not always be easy for courts." 463 U.S., at 664, 103 S.Ct. 3255. But there is no need for us to address those difficult cases today, because this case involves "precisely the 'gift of confidential information to a trading relative' that Dirks envisioned." 792 F.3d, at 1092 (quoting 463 U.S., at 664, 103 S.Ct. 3255).

NOTES AND QUESTIONS

1. In a Rule 10b–5 case, what does it mean to say that a person has made a gift of inside information?

2. The test for whether a tipper is liable has three elements. What are they? The test for whether a tippee is liable has also three elements. What are they? Can a tipper be held liable where the tippee is not liable?

3. Tipper provides material nonpublic information to Tippee #1 who tells it to Tippee #2 who trades. Can Tippee #2 be held liable?

4. What if the recipient of the information is not a relative or friend?

Imagine the following: A corporate insider is on a road trip. While passing through a town that he has never been in before and never will be in again, he stops to fill up his car at the gas station. One pump over from him, he sees a young couple with two little children and overhears them discussing their dire financial straits. The corporate insider does not know this couple—they have never met, and they certainly are not related. Nonetheless, he takes pity on the couple, walks over to them, and says:

> You don't know me, but I'm an executive at XYZ Corp. I overheard some of your conversation and I think I can help. I don't have money to give you right now, but as soon as you get home, gather up all of your savings and borrow whatever

money you can and purchase as many shares of XYZ Corp. stock as you possibly can. We're announcing record earnings and a new product line next week—our stock is going to soar. Just don't tell anyone else.

The corporate insider then walks away and never sees or hears from the young couple again. The young couple does as instructed and makes $30,000 the next week.[12]

Would either the insider and/or the couple have liability?

B. MISAPPROPRIATION

In response to the setbacks it suffered in *Chiarella* and *Dirks*, the SEC began advocating a new theory of insider trading liability: the misappropriation theory. Unlike Rule 14e–3 (see below), the SEC did not intend for the misappropriation theory to be limited to tender offer cases (although many misappropriation decisions have in fact involved takeovers). Accordingly, the Commission posited misappropriation as a new theory of liability under Rule 10b–5. Which meant, in turn, that the SEC had to find a way of finessing the fiduciary duty requirement imposed by *Chiarella* and *Dirks*.

The misappropriation theory is commonly (but incorrectly) traced to Chief Justice Burger's *Chiarella* dissent. Burger contended that the way in which the inside trader acquires the nonpublic information on which he trades could itself be a material circumstance that must be disclosed to the market before trading. Accordingly, Burger argued, "a person who has misappropriated nonpublic information has an absolute duty [to the persons with whom he trades] to disclose that information or to refrain from trading."[13] The majority did not address the merits of this theory; instead rejecting it solely on the ground that the theory had not been presented to the jury and thus could not sustain a criminal conviction.

Consequently, the way was left open for the SEC to urge, and the lower courts to adopt, the misappropriation theory as an alternative basis of insider trading liability. The Second Circuit swiftly moved to take advantage of that opportunity. In *United States v. Newman*,[14] employees of an investment bank misappropriated confidential information concerning proposed mergers involving clients of the firm. As was true of Vincent Chiarella, the Newman defendants' employer worked for prospective acquiring companies, while the trading took place in target company securities. As such, the Newman defendants owed no fiduciary duties to the investors with whom they traded. Moreover, neither the investment bank nor its clients traded in the target companies' shares contemporaneously with the defendants.

---

[12] Matthew J. Wilkins, You Don't Need Love . . . but It Helps: Insider Trading Law After *Salman*, 106 Ky. L.J. 433, 446 (2018).

[13] Chiarella v. United States, 445 U.S. 222, 240 (1980) (Burger, C.J., dissenting).

[14] 664 F.2d 12 (2d Cir.1981).

Unlike Chief Justice Burger's *Chiarella* dissent, the Second Circuit did not assert that the Newman defendants owed any duty of disclosure to the investors with whom they traded or had defrauded. Instead, the court held that by misappropriating confidential information for personal gain, the defendants had defrauded their employer and its clients, and this fraud sufficed to impose insider trading liability on the defendants with whom they traded.[15]

United States v. O'Hagan
521 U.S. 642 (1997)

This case concerns the interpretation and enforcement of § 10(b) and § 14(e) of the Securities Exchange Act of 1934, and rules made by the Securities and Exchange Commission pursuant to these provisions, Rule 10b–5 and Rule 14e–3(a). Two prime questions are presented. . . . (1) Is a person who trades in securities for personal profit, using confidential information misappropriated in breach of a fiduciary duty to the source of the information, guilty of violating § 10(b) and Rule 10b–5? (2) Did the Commission exceed its rulemaking authority by adopting Rule 14e–3(a), which proscribes trading on undisclosed information in the tender offer setting, even in the absence of a duty to disclose? Our answer to the first question is yes, and to the second question, viewed in the context of this case, no.

I

Respondent James Herman O'Hagan was a partner in the law firm of Dorsey & Whitney in Minneapolis, Minnesota. In July 1988, Grand Metropolitan PLC (Grand Met), a company based in London, England, retained Dorsey & Whitney as local counsel to represent Grand Met regarding a potential tender offer for the common stock of the Pillsbury Company, headquartered in Minneapolis. Both Grand Met and Dorsey & Whitney took precautions to protect the confidentiality of Grand Met's tender offer plans. . . . [O]n October 4, 1988, Grand Met publicly announced its tender offer for Pillsbury stock.

On August 18, 1988, while Dorsey & Whitney was still representing Grand Met, O'Hagan began purchasing call options for Pillsbury stock. Each option gave him the right to purchase 100 shares of Pillsbury stock by a specified date in September 1988. . . . By the end of September, he owned 2,500 unexpired Pillsbury options, apparently more than any other individual investor. O'Hagan also purchased, in September 1988, some 5,000 shares of Pillsbury common stock, at a price just under $39 per share. When Grand Met announced its tender offer in October, the price of Pillsbury stock rose to nearly $60 per share. O'Hagan then sold

---

[15]   See U.S. v. Newman, 664 F.2d 12, 17 (2d Cir.1981); see also United States v. Carpenter, 791 F.2d 1024 (2d Cir.1986), aff'd on other grounds, 484 U.S. 19 (1987); SEC v. Materia, 745 F.2d 197 (2d Cir.1984), cert. denied, 471 U.S. 1053 (1985).

his Pillsbury call options and common stock, making a profit of more than $4.3 million.

The Securities and Exchange Commission (SEC or Commission) initiated an investigation into O'Hagan's transactions, culminating in a 57-count indictment. The indictment alleged that O'Hagan defrauded his law firm and its client, Grand Met, by using for his own trading purposes material, nonpublic information regarding Grand Met's planned tender offer. According to the indictment, O'Hagan used the profits he gained through this trading to conceal his previous embezzlement and conversion of unrelated client trust funds.[2] ... O'Hagan was charged with 20 counts of mail fraud; 17 counts of securities fraud, in violation of § 10(b) of the Securities Exchange Act of 1934 (Exchange Act), and SEC Rule 10b–5; 17 counts of fraudulent trading in connection with a tender offer, in violation of § 14(e) of the Exchange Act, and SEC Rule 14e–3(a); and 3 counts of violating federal money laundering statutes. A jury convicted O'Hagan on all 57 counts, and he was sentenced to a 41-month term of imprisonment.

A divided panel of the Court of Appeals for the Eighth Circuit reversed all of O'Hagan's convictions. Liability under § 10(b) and Rule 10b–5, the Eighth Circuit held, may not be grounded on the "misappropriation theory" of securities fraud on which the prosecution relied. The Court of Appeals also held that Rule 14e–3(a)—which prohibits trading while in possession of material, nonpublic information relating to a tender offer—exceeds the SEC's § 14(e) rulemaking authority because the rule contains no breach of fiduciary duty requirement. The Eighth Circuit further concluded that O'Hagan's mail fraud and money laundering convictions rested on violations of the securities laws, and therefore could not stand once the securities fraud convictions were reversed. ...

Decisions of the Courts of Appeals are in conflict on the propriety of the misappropriation theory under § 10(b) and Rule 10b–5, and on the legitimacy of Rule 14e–3(a) under § 14(e). We granted certiorari, and now reverse the Eighth Circuit's judgment.

II

. . .

A

. . .

Under the "traditional" or "classical theory" of insider trading liability, § 10(b) and Rule 10b–5 are violated when a corporate insider trades in the securities of his corporation on the basis of material, nonpublic information. Trading on such information qualifies as a

---

[2]   O'Hagan was convicted of theft in state court, sentenced to 30 months' imprisonment, and fined. . . . . . . The Supreme Court of Minnesota disbarred O'Hagan from the practice of law. . . . . . .

"deceptive device" under § 10(b), we have affirmed, because "a relationship of trust and confidence [exists] between the shareholders of a corporation and those insiders who have obtained confidential information by reason of their position with that corporation." *Chiarella v. United States*, 445 U.S. 222, 228 (1980). That relationship, we recognized, "gives rise to a duty to disclose [or to abstain from trading] because of the 'necessity of preventing a corporate insider from . . . taking unfair advantage of . . . uninformed . . . stockholders.' " Id., at 228–229 (citation omitted). The classical theory applies not only to officers, directors, and other permanent insiders of a corporation, but also to attorneys, accountants, consultants, and others who temporarily become fiduciaries of a corporation. See *Dirks v. SEC*, 463 U.S. 646, 655, n. 14 (1983).

The "misappropriation theory" holds that a person commits fraud "in connection with" a securities transaction, and thereby violates § 10(b) and Rule 10b–5, when he misappropriates confidential information for securities trading purposes, in breach of a duty owed to the source of the information. Under this theory, a fiduciary's undisclosed, self-serving use of a principal's information to purchase or sell securities, in breach of a duty of loyalty and confidentiality, defrauds the principal of the exclusive use of that information. In lieu of premising liability on a fiduciary relationship between company insider and purchaser or seller of the company's stock, the misappropriation theory premises liability on a fiduciary-turned-trader's deception of those who entrusted him with access to confidential information.

The two theories are complementary, each addressing efforts to capitalize on nonpublic information through the purchase or sale of securities. The classical theory targets a corporate insider's breach of duty to shareholders with whom the insider transacts; the misappropriation theory outlaws trading on the basis of nonpublic information by a corporate "outsider" in breach of a duty owed not to a trading party, but to the source of the information. The misappropriation theory is thus designed to "protect the integrity of the securities markets against abuses by 'outsiders' to a corporation who have access to confidential information that will affect the corporation's security price when revealed, but who owe no fiduciary or other duty to that corporation's shareholders." [Brief for United States 14.]

In this case, the indictment alleged that O'Hagan, in breach of a duty of trust and confidence he owed to his law firm, Dorsey & Whitney, and to its client, Grand Met, traded on the basis of nonpublic information regarding Grand Met's planned tender offer for Pillsbury common stock.

This conduct, the Government charged, constituted a fraudulent device in connection with the purchase and sale of securities.[5]

B

We agree with the Government that misappropriation, as just defined, satisfies § 10(b)'s requirement that chargeable conduct involve a "deceptive device or contrivance" used "in connection with" the purchase or sale of securities. We observe, first, that misappropriators, as the Government describes them, deal in deception. A fiduciary who "[pretends] loyalty to the principal while secretly converting the principal's information for personal gain," Brief for United States 17, "dupes" or defrauds the principal.

> **THINK ABOUT IT**
>
> Why couldn't the Government have prosecuted O'Hagan as a "constructive insider" of Pillsbury per *Dirks* footnote 14?

. . . Deception through nondisclosure is central to the theory of liability for which the Government seeks recognition. As counsel for the Government stated in explanation of the theory at oral argument: "To satisfy the common law rule that a trustee may not use the property that [has] been entrusted [to] him, there would have to be consent. To satisfy the requirement of the Securities Act that there be no deception, there would only have to be disclosure."[6]

The misappropriation theory advanced by the Government is consistent with *Santa Fe Industries, Inc. v. Green*, 430 U.S. 462 (1977), a decision underscoring that § 10(b) is not an all-purpose breach of fiduciary duty ban; rather, it trains on conduct involving manipulation or deception. . . . In contrast to the Government's allegations in this case, in *Santa Fe Industries*, all pertinent facts were disclosed by the persons charged with violating § 10(b) and Rule 10b–5 . . .; therefore, there was no deception through nondisclosure to which liability under those provisions could attach. . . . Similarly, full disclosure forecloses liability under the misappropriation theory: Because the deception essential to the misappropriation theory involves feigning fidelity to the source of information, if the fiduciary discloses to the source that he plans to trade on the nonpublic information, there is no "deceptive device" and thus no § 10(b) violation—although the fiduciary-turned-trader may remain liable under state law for breach of a duty of loyalty.[7]

---

[5]   The Government could not have prosecuted O'Hagan under the classical theory, for O'Hagan was not an "insider" of Pillsbury, the corporation in whose stock he traded.

[6]   Under the misappropriation theory urged in this case, the disclosure obligation runs to the source of the information, here, Dorsey & Whitney and Grand Met. Chief Justice Burger, dissenting in *Chiarella*, advanced a broader reading of § 10(b) and Rule 10b–5; the disclosure obligation, as he envisioned it, ran to those with whom the misappropriator trades. . . . The Government does not propose that we adopt a misappropriation theory of that breadth.

[7]   Where, however, a person trading on the basis of material, nonpublic information owes a duty of loyalty and confidentiality to two entities or persons—for example, a law firm and its

We turn next to the § 10(b) requirement that the misappropriator's deceptive use of information be "in connection with the purchase or sale of [a] security." This element is satisfied because the fiduciary's fraud is consummated, not when the fiduciary gains the confidential information, but when, without disclosure to his principal, he uses the information to purchase or sell securities. The securities transaction and the breach of duty thus coincide. This is so even though the person or entity defrauded is not the other party to the trade, but is, instead, the source of the nonpublic information. . . . A misappropriator who trades on the basis of material, nonpublic information, in short, gains his advantageous market position through deception; he deceives the source of the information and simultaneously harms members of the investing public. . . .

The misappropriation theory comports with § 10(b)'s language, which requires deception "in connection with the purchase or sale of any security," not deception of an identifiable purchaser or seller. The theory is also well-tuned to an animating purpose of the Exchange Act: to insure honest securities markets and thereby promote investor confidence. . . . Although informational disparity is inevitable in the securities markets, investors likely would hesitate to venture their capital in a market where trading based on misappropriated nonpublic information is unchecked by law. An investor's informational disadvantage vis-a-vis a misappropriator with material, nonpublic information stems from contrivance, not luck; it is a disadvantage that cannot be overcome with research or skill. . . .

In sum, considering the inhibiting impact on market participation of trading on misappropriated information, and the congressional purposes underlying § 10(b), it makes scant sense to hold a lawyer like O'Hagan a § 10(b) violator if he works for a law firm representing the target of a tender offer, but not if he works for a law firm representing the bidder. The text of the statute requires no such result.[9] The misappropriation at issue here was properly made the subject of a § 10(b) charge because it meets the statutory requirement that there be "deceptive" conduct "in connection with" securities transactions. . . .

III

We consider next the ground on which the Court of Appeals reversed O'Hagan's convictions for fraudulent trading in connection with a tender

---

client—but makes disclosure to only one, the trader may still be liable under the misappropriation theory.

[9]   As noted earlier, however, the textual requirement of deception precludes § 10(b) liability when a person trading on the basis of nonpublic information has disclosed his trading plans to, or obtained authorization from, the principal—even though such conduct may affect the securities markets in the same manner as the conduct reached by the misappropriation theory. . . . [O]nce a disloyal agent discloses his imminent breach of duty, his principal may seek appropriate equitable relief under state law. Furthermore, in the context of a tender offer, the principal who authorizes an agent's trading on confidential information may, in the Commission's view, incur liability for an Exchange Act violation under Rule 14e–3(a).

offer, in violation of § 14(e) of the Exchange Act and SEC Rule 14e–3(a). A sole question is before us as to these convictions: Did the Commission, as the Court of Appeals held, exceed its rulemaking authority under § 14(e) when it adopted Rule 14e–3(a) without requiring a showing that the trading at issue entailed a breach of fiduciary duty? We hold that the Commission, in this regard and to the extent relevant to this case, did not exceed its authority.

The governing statutory provision, § 14(e) of the Exchange Act, reads in relevant part:

> "It shall be unlawful for any person . . . to engage in any fraudulent, deceptive, or manipulative acts or practices, in connection with any tender offer. . . . The [SEC] shall, for the purposes of this subsection, by rules and regulations define, and prescribe means reasonably designed to prevent, such acts and practices as are fraudulent, deceptive, or manipulative."

. . .

Relying on § 14(e)'s rulemaking authorization, the Commission, in 1980, promulgated Rule 14e–3(a). That measure provides:

> "(a) If any person has taken a substantial step or steps to commence, or has commenced, a tender offer (the 'offering person'), it shall constitute a fraudulent, deceptive or manipulative act or practice within the meaning of section 14(e) of the [Exchange] Act for any other person who is in possession of material information relating to such tender offer which information he knows or has reason to know is nonpublic and which he knows or has reason to know has been acquired directly or indirectly from:
>
> "(1) The offering person,
>
> "(2) The issuer of the securities sought or to be sought by such tender offer, or
>
> "(3) Any officer, director, partner or employee or any other person acting on behalf of the offering person or such issuer,
>
> "to purchase or sell or cause to be purchased or sold any of such securities or any securities convertible into or exchangeable for any such securities or any option or right to obtain or to dispose of any of the foregoing securities, unless within a reasonable time prior to any purchase or sale such information and its source are publicly disclosed by press release or otherwise."

. . .

In the Eighth Circuit's view, because Rule 14e–3(a) applies whether or not the trading in question breaches a fiduciary duty, the regulation exceeds the SEC's § 14(e) rulemaking authority. . . .

We need not resolve in this case whether the Commission's authority under § 14(e) to "define . . . such acts and practices as are fraudulent" is broader than the Commission's fraud-defining authority under § 10(b), [as the Government contended,] for we agree with the United States that Rule 14e–3(a), as applied to cases of this genre, qualifies under § 14(e) as a "means reasonably designed to prevent" fraudulent trading on material, nonpublic information in the tender offer context.[17] A prophylactic measure, because its mission is to prevent, typically encompasses more than the core activity prohibited. . . .

. . . [I]t is a fair assumption that trading on the basis of material, nonpublic information will often involve a breach of a duty of confidentiality to the bidder or target company or their representatives. The SEC, cognizant of the proof problem that could enable sophisticated traders to escape responsibility, placed in Rule 14e–3(a) a "disclose or abstain from trading" command that does not require specific proof of a breach of fiduciary duty. That prescription, we are satisfied, applied to this case, is a "means reasonably designed to prevent" fraudulent trading on material, nonpublic information in the tender offer context. . . .

NOTES AND QUESTIONS

1.   According to the Court, liability under § 10(b) could not have been imposed if O'Hagan had disclosed "to the source of the information" that he planned to trade on the nonpublic information. Recall that O'Hagan was a partner in the Dorsey & Whitney law partnership. To whom should O'Hagan have made the requisite disclosure?

2.   Suppose O'Hagan had informed both Dorsey & Whitney and Grand Met of his intentions to buy Pillsbury stock and both firms had approved. What result?

3.   Suppose O'Hagan had informed both Dorsey & Whitney and Grand Met of his intentions to buy Pillsbury stock for his own benefit, at least one of them had objected, but O'Hagan bought anyway. What result?

4.   The court's opinion argues that:

The misappropriation theory advanced by the Government is consistent with *Santa Fe Industries, Inc. v. Green*, 430 U.S. 462 (1977), a decision underscoring that § 10(b) is not an all purpose breach of fiduciary duty ban; rather, it trains on conduct involving manipulation or deception. . . . In contrast to the Government's allegations in this case, in *Santa Fe Industries*, all pertinent facts were disclosed by the persons charged with violating § 10(b) and Rule 10b–5 . . .; therefore, there was no deception through nondisclosure to which liability under those provisions could attach. . . .

---

[17]   We leave for another day, when the issue requires decision, the legitimacy of Rule 14e–3(a) as applied to "warehousing," which the Government describes as "the practice by which bidders leak advance information of a tender offer to allies and encourage them to purchase the target company's stock before the bid is announced." . . .

The court thus glided past what is in fact a serious federalism issue. The modern insider trading prohibition is a creature of SEC administrative actions and judicial opinions, only loosely tied to the statutory language and its legislative history. U.S. Supreme Court Chief Justice William Rehnquist famously observed that Rule 10b–5 is "a judicial oak which has grown from little more than a legislative acorn."[16] Nowhere in Rule 10b–5 jurisprudence is this truer than where the insider trading prohibition is concerned, given the tiny (arguably nonexistent) legislative acorn on which it rests. As a former SEC solicitor once admitted, the "[m]odern development of the law of insider trading is a classic example of common law in the federal courts."[17]

In *Santa Fe Industries, Inc. v. Green*,[18] the Supreme Court held that Rule 10b–5 is concerned with disclosure and fraud, not with fiduciary duties.[19] The court did so in large measure out of a concern that the contrary decision would result in federalizing much of state corporate law and thereby overriding well-established state policies of corporate regulation. While its holding is not squarely on point, the rationale of *Santa Fe* seems directly

---

[16]   Blue Chip Stamps v. Manor Drug Stores, 421 U.S. 723, 737 (1975).

[17]   Paul Gonson & David E. Butler, In Wake of "Dirks," Courts Debate Definition of "Insider," Legal Times, Apr. 2, 1984, at 16, col. 1.

[18]   430 U.S. 462 (1977).

[19]   In *Santa Fe*, the plaintiffs were minority shareholders of a Santa Fe subsidiary who were dissatisfied with the consideration they were paid for their stock in a short-form merger Santa Fe had effected with the subsidiary. Although plaintiffs had state law remedies, such as the statutory appraisal proceeding, they opted to sue under Rule 10b–5. Plaintiffs claimed that the merger violated Rule 10b–5 because it was effected without prior notice to the minority shareholders and was done without any legitimate business purpose. They also claimed that their shares had been undervalued. Both claims raised, quite directly, the question of what conduct is covered by the rule. The Supreme Court held that plaintiffs had not stated a cause of action under Rule 10b–5.

Drawing on the plain text and legislative history of the rule, the court concluded that a 10b–5 cause of action arises only out of deception or manipulation. Deception requires a misrepresentation or omission. Because the plaintiffs received full disclosure, there was no misrepresentation or omission. In addition, neither of plaintiffs' claims went to disclosure violations; rather, both went to the substance of the transaction. Plaintiffs were not claiming that Santa Fe lied to them, but that the transaction was unfair. In other words, they were claiming that a breach of fiduciary duty gives rise to a cause of action under 10b–5. The Supreme Court held that a mere breach of duty will not give rise to liability under 10b–5.

Manipulation is conduct intended to mislead investors by artificially affecting market activity. In other words, defendant must engage in conduct that creates artificial changes in the price of a security or volume of trading in a security. Again, Santa Fe was mainly being charged with a breach of the state law fiduciary duties a majority shareholder owes to minority shareholders. Nothing Santa Fe did constituted unlawful manipulation.

In addition to its textual arguments, the Supreme Court also relied on policy considerations grounded in federalism. The court clearly was concerned that allowing plaintiffs to go forward in this case would federalize much of state corporate law, in many cases overriding well-established state policies of corporate regulation. In the court's view, if the Santa Fe plaintiffs were allowed to sue, every breach of fiduciary duty case would give rise to a federal claim under Rule 10b–5. The court refused to give the Rule 10b–5 such an expansive reach, instead holding that it did not reach "transactions which constitute no more than internal corporate mismanagement." Id. at 479. Santa Fe was a critical holding in Rule 10b–5's evolution, putting the substantive fairness of a transaction outside the rule's scope. The rule henceforth was limited to disclosure violations. Santa Fe also implied a second—and potentially even more significant—constraint on the rule in suggesting that misconduct covered by state corporate law should be left to state law. For a more detailed treatment of the relationship between Santa Fe and the Supreme Court's insider trading jurisprudence, see Stephen M. Bainbridge, Incorporating State Law Fiduciary Duties into the Federal Insider Trading Prohibition, 52 Wash & Lee L. Rev. 1189, 1258–61 (1995).

applicable to the insider trading prohibition. The court held, for example, that Rule 10b–5 did not reach claims "in which the essence of the complaint is that shareholders were treated unfairly by a fiduciary."[20] This is of course the very essence of the complaint made in insider trading cases. The court also held that extension of Rule 10b–5 to breaches of fiduciary duty was unjustified in light of the state law remedies available to plaintiffs. As we have seen, insider trading plaintiffs likewise have state law remedies available to them. Granted, those remedies vary from state to state and are likely to prove unavailing in many cases, but the same was true of the state law appraisal remedy at issue in *Santa Fe*. Finally, the court expressed reluctance "to federalize the substantial portion of the law of corporations that deals with transactions in securities, particularly where established state policies of corporate regulation would be overridden,"[21] which is precisely what the federal insider trading prohibition did. Given that *Santa Fe* requires that all other corporate fiduciary duties be left to state law, why should insider trading be singled out for special treatment?

Dirks and *Chiarella* simply ignored the doctrinal tension between their fiduciary duty-based regime and Santa Fe. In *O'Hagan*, Justice Ginsburg's majority opinion sought to solve the problem by describing *Santa Fe* as "underscoring that § 10(b) is not an all-purpose breach of fiduciary duty ban; rather it trains on conduct involving manipulation or deception."[22] Accordingly, she held that federal law focuses on the failure to disclose that one is about to inside trade. She thus explained that a "fiduciary who '[pretends] loyalty to the principal while secretly converting the principal's information for personal gain' . . . 'dupes' or defrauds the principal."[23]

Justice Ginsburg's approach fails to solve the problem. Granted, insider trading involves deception in the sense that the defendant by definition failed to disclose nonpublic information before trading. Persons subject to the disclose or abstain theory, however, often are also subject to a state law-based fiduciary duty of confidentiality, which precludes them from disclosing the information. As to them, the insider trading prohibition collapses into a requirement to abstain from trading on material nonpublic information. As such, it really is their failure to abstain from trading, rather than their nondisclosure, which is the basis for imposing liability. A former SEC Commissioner more or less admitted as much: "Unlike much securities regulation, the insider trading rules probably do not result in more information coming into the market: The 'abstain or disclose' rule for those entrusted with confidential information usually is observed by abstention."[24] Yet, *Santa Fe* clearly precludes the creation of such duties. The conceptual

---

[20]　Id. at 477.

[21]　Id. at 479.

[22]　U.S. v. O'Hagan, 521 U.S. 642, 655 (1997).

[23]　Id. at 653–54.

[24]　Charles C. Cox & Kevin S. Fogarty, Bases of Insider Trading Law, 49 Ohio St. L.J. 353 (1988).

conflict between the Supreme Court's current insider trading jurisprudence and its more general Rule 10b–5 precedents remains unresolved.[25]

All of which leads to a basic question: Why is insider trading a matter for federal securities law instead of state corporate law fiduciary duties?

SEC v. Yun

327 F.3d 1263 (11th Cir. 2003)

. . .

I.

A.

Donna Yun is married to David Yun, the president of Scholastic Book Fairs, Inc., a subsidiary of Scholastic Corporation ("Scholastic"), a publisher and distributor of children's books whose stock is quoted on the NASDAQ National Market System and whose option contracts are traded on the Chicago Board Options Exchange. On January 27, 1997, David attended a senior management retreat at which Scholastic's chief financial officer revealed that the company would post a loss for the current quarter, and that before the quarter ended, the company would make a public announcement revising its earnings forecast downward. He cautioned the assembled executives not to sell any of their Scholastic holdings until after the announcement, which would likely result in a decline in the market price of Scholastic shares, and warned them to keep the matter confidential. Approximately two weeks later, on February 13, Scholastic's chief financial officer informed David that the negative earnings announcement would be made on February 20.

Over the weekend of February 15–16, David and Donna discussed a statement of assets that he had provided her in connection with their negotiation of a post-nuptial division of assets. David explained to Donna that he had assigned a $55 value to his Scholastic options listed on the asset statement, even though Scholastic's stock was then trading at $65 per share, because he believed that the price of the shares would drop following Scholastic's February 20 earnings announcement. He also told her not to disclose this information to anyone else, and she agreed to keep the information confidential.

The following Tuesday, February 18, Donna went to her place of work—a real estate office located in a nearby housing development. The office was a small sales trailer, approximately eleven by thirteen feet, that Donna shared with other real estate agents, including Jerry Burch. During the late morning or early afternoon, Donna telephoned Sam Weiss—the attorney assisting her in negotiating the post-nuptial division of assets—from her office to discuss David's statement of assets.

---

[25]   See generally Stephen M. Bainbridge, Incorporating State Law Fiduciary Duties into the Federal Insider Trading Prohibition, 52 Wash. & Lee L. Rev. 1189 (1995); Larry E. Ribstein, Federalism and Insider Trading, 6 Sup. Ct Econ. Rev. 123 (1998).

While she was speaking to Weiss, Burch entered the office to gather materials for a real estate client. Standing three to four feet from Donna, Burch heard her tell Weiss what David had said about Scholastic's impending earnings announcement and that David expected the price of the company's shares to fall. As he testified at trial, Burch did not learn enough from what he overheard to feel "comfortable" trading in Scholastic's stock.

That evening, Donna and Burch attended a real estate awards banquet at the Isleworth Country Club. Donna, Burch, and another agent, Maryann Hartmann, carpooled to the reception. All three stayed at the reception for three hours and left together.

The next morning Burch called his broker and requested authority to purchase put options in Scholastic.[6] When the broker advised Burch that he knew of no new information indicating the price of Scholastic stock would decline, Burch stated that based on information he had obtained at a cocktail party, he nonetheless wanted to purchase the put options. The broker warned Burch of the risks of trading in options, and cautioned him about insider trading prohibitions. Despite these warnings, between the afternoon of February 19 and midday on February 20, Burch purchased $19,750 in Scholastic put options, which was equal to two-thirds of his total income for the previous year and nearly half the value of his entire investment portfolio.

> **THINK ABOUT IT**
>
> At trial, it was proven that Donna tipped more information to Burch about the forthcoming losses by Scholastic. Suppose, however, that Burch's only information had come from overhearing Donna's telephone call with Sam Weiss. Would that change the result?

After the stock market closed on February 20, Scholastic announced that its earnings would be well below the analysts' expectations. When the market opened the next day, the price of Scholastic shares had dropped approximately 40 percent to $36 per share. Burch then sold his Scholastic puts, realizing a profit of $269,000—a 1,300 percent return on his investment. Within hours, the SEC commenced an investigation of Burch's trades to determine whether insider trading had occurred. The investigation culminated in the present lawsuit. In a one-count complaint, the SEC alleged that Donna and Burch had violated section 10(b) of the Exchange Act and Rule 10b–5,[9] and sought both legal and equitable relief.

B.

. . .

This is a tipper-tippee case. The SEC prosecuted it under the "misappropriation theory" of insider trading liability. Its complaint

---

[6]   A put option is an option contract that gives the holder of the option the right to sell a certain quantity of an underlying security to the writer of the option, at a specified price up to a specified date. The value of a put increases as the price of the stock decreases.

alleged that Donna was an outsider who had a fiduciary relationship with David, and that she breached that duty when she divulged to Burch confidential information, which David had given her, "for her direct and/or indirect benefit because of her business relationship and friendship with . . . Burch." . . .

[Donna and Burch were convicted at trial of violating Exchange Act § 10(b) and Rule 10b–5. They appealed.]

II.

A.

> **THINK ABOUT IT**
>
> David clearly is a classic insider of—and thus owed a fiduciary duty to—Scholastic. Why isn't that duty enough for Donna and Burch to have liability?

. . . [To] prevail in an insider trading case, the SEC must establish that the misappropriator breached a duty of loyalty and confidentiality owed to the source of the confidential information. Certain business relationships, such as attorney-client or employer-employee, clearly provide the requisite duty of loyalty and confidentiality. On the other hand, it is unsettled whether non-business relationships, such as husband and wife, provide the duty of loyalty and confidentiality necessary to satisfy the misappropriation theory. The leading case on when a duty of loyalty and confidentiality exists in the context of family members—the case relied on by the parties and the district court for the elements of a confidential relationship—is *United States v. Chestman*, 947 F.2d 551 (2d Cir.1991) (en banc).

In a divided en banc decision, the Second Circuit held that marriage alone does not create a relationship of loyalty and confidentiality. Either an "express agreement of confidentiality" or the "functional equivalent" of a "fiduciary relationship" must exist between the spouses for a court to find a confidential relationship for purposes of § 10(b) and Rule 10b–5 liability. Since the spouses had not entered into a confidentiality agreement, the court turned its focus to determining what constitutes a fiduciary relationship or its functional equivalent. "At the heart of the fiduciary relationship," the court declared, "lies reliance, and de facto control and dominance." Id. at 568 (citations and internal quotation marks omitted). Having so concluded, the court explained that the functional equivalent of a fiduciary relationship "must share these qualities." Id. at 569. Applying the requisite qualities of reliance, control, and dominance to the husband and wife relationship at hand, the Chestman majority held that no fiduciary relationship or its functional equivalent existed. The spouses' sharing and maintaining of "generic confidences" in the past was insufficient to establish the functional equivalent of a fiduciary relationship. Id. at 571. Accordingly, the court decided that the defendants were not subject to sanctions for insider trading violations.

A lengthy dissent by Judge Winter, joined by four judges, took issue with the narrowness in which the majority would find a relationship of loyalty and confidentiality amongst family members, pointing out that under the majority's approach, the disclosure of sensitive corporate information essentially could be "avoided only by family members extracting formal, express promises of confidentiality." Id. at 580. Such an approach, in the view of the dissent, was "unrealistic in that it expects family members to behave like strangers toward each other." Id. Moreover, the normal reluctance to recognize obligations based on family relationships—the concern that intra-family litigation would exacerbate strained relationships and weaken the sense of mutual obligation underlying family relationships—was inapplicable in insider trading cases because the suits are brought by the government. See id. at 580. Given the circumstances of the case, the dissent concluded that a confidential relationship existed between the husband and wife which gave rise to a duty of loyalty and confidentiality on his part not to disclose the sensitive information.[21]

We are inclined to accept the dissent's view that the *Chestman* decision too narrowly defined the circumstances in which a duty of loyalty and confidentiality is created between husband and wife. We think that the majority, by insisting on either an express agreement of confidentiality or a strictly defined fiduciary-like relationship, ignored the many instances in which a spouse has a reasonable expectation of confidentiality. In our view, a spouse who trades in breach of a reasonable and legitimate expectation of confidentiality held by the other spouse sufficiently subjects the former to insider trading liability. If the SEC can prove that the husband and wife had a history or practice of sharing business confidences, and those confidences generally were maintained by the spouse receiving the information, then in most instances the conveying spouse would have a reasonable expectation of confidentiality such that the breach of the expectation would suffice to yield insider trading liability. Of course, a breach of an agreement to maintain business confidences would also suffice.

. . .

We conclude that the SEC provided sufficient evidence both that an agreement of confidentiality and a history or pattern of sharing and keeping of business confidences existed between David and Donna Yun such that David could have reasonably expected Donna to keep confidential what he told her about Scholastic's pending announcement. First, the SEC presented evidence that Donna explicitly accepted the duty to keep in confidence the business information she received. She

---

[21] In the context of family-controlled businesses, the dissent noted, "it is inevitable that from time to time normal familial interactions will lead to the revelation of confidential corporate matters to various family members[, and] the very nature of familial relationships may cause the disclosure of corporate matters to avoid misunderstandings among family members or suggestions that a family member is unworthy of trust." Chestman, 947 F.2d at 579.

testified that she considered the information confidential because, "David always told me, anything that he talks to me in regards to the company is confidential and can't go past he or I." That she fully understood and agreed to the understanding of confidentiality is further manifested by the fact that she declined to disclose any information about David's company to her attorney until she had "absolute certainty that there was confidentiality with everything [she] was sharing with him." Second, both David and Donna testified that David repeatedly shared confidential information about Scholastic with Donna, including information regarding its sales goals. This certainly qualified as a history or pattern of sharing business confidences. Overall, the SEC presented evidence upon which a jury could find that a duty of loyalty and confidentiality existed between David and Donna Yun; the SEC therefore established the first element of a "misappropriation theory" claim.

B.

Having reached this conclusion, we turn to the question of whether the evidence was sufficient to show that Donna breached her duty to David. According to the allegations of the complaint, the answer to this question depends on whether Donna deliberately communicated the confidential information to Burch "for her direct and/or indirect benefit because of her business relationship and friendship with . . . Burch." The SEC contends . . . that it did not have to prove that Donna divulged the information for her own benefit; all it had to show was that Donna acted with "severe recklessness." According to the SEC, the "intent to benefit" element only applies in cases brought under the classical theory of liability; the element has no application in cases brought under the misappropriation theory of liability. In other words, whether Donna expected to benefit from the disclosure of the confidential information is irrelevant.

. . . After considering the policies underpinning the insider trading rules, we are led to the conclusion that the SEC must prove that a misappropriator expected to benefit from the tip.

. . .

FYI

"The parties do not dispute that *Dirks'* personal-benefit analysis applies in both classical and misappropriation cases, so we will proceed on the assumption that it does." *Salman v. United States*, 137 S.Ct. 420, 425 n.2 (2016).

Having concluded that the SEC must prove that Donna expected to benefit from disclosing the confidential information to Burch . . . we now consider whether the SEC provided sufficient evidence for a jury reasonably to find such an expectation. Viewing the facts in the light most favorable to the SEC, we conclude that the SEC did so.[38]

---

[38] Determining whether a tipper expected to benefit personally from a particular disclosure is a question of fact. See *Dirks*, 463 U.S. at 664, 103 S.Ct. at 3266. We, therefore, can

The showing needed to prove an intent to benefit is not extensive. . . .

In this case, the SEC presented evidence that the two appellants were "friendly," worked together for several years, and split commissions on various real estate transactions over the years. This evidence is sufficient for a jury reasonably to conclude that Donna expected to benefit from her tip to Burch by maintaining a good relationship between a friend and frequent partner in real estate deals. Accordingly, the SEC has sufficiently established the second element of a misappropriation theory claim—a breach of a duty of loyalty and confidentiality. . . .

NOTES AND QUESTIONS

1.   Is the *Yun* court's analysis of the personal benefit issue consistent with the Supreme Court's decision in *Salman*?

2.   The insider trading at issue in *Yun* court took place before SEC Rule 10b5–2 went into effect. The Rule provides "a nonexclusive list of three situations in which a person has a duty of trust or confidence for purposes of the 'misappropriation' theory. . . ."[26]

(1) Whenever a person agrees to maintain information in confidence;

(2) Whenever the person communicating the material nonpublic information and the person to whom it is communicated have a history, pattern, or practice of sharing confidences, such that the recipient of the information knows or reasonably should know that the person communicating the material nonpublic information expects that the recipient will maintain its confidentiality; or

(3) Whenever a person receives or obtains material nonpublic information from his or her spouse, parent, child, or sibling; provided, however, that the person receiving or obtaining the information may demonstrate that no duty of trust or confidence existed with respect to the information, by establishing that he or she neither knew nor reasonably should have known that the person who was the source of the information expected that the person would keep the information confidential, because of the parties' history, pattern, or practice of sharing and maintaining confidences, and because there was no agreement or understanding to maintain the confidentiality of the information.

On the facts of *Yun*, would Rule 10b5–2 result in the imposition of liability because Donna received the information from her spouse who, in turn, had received it from his employer?

3.   An example of a case turning on the court's determination that the disclosure did not impose any fiduciary duties on the recipient of the inside

---

reverse only if the jury's findings were clearly erroneous. See, e.g., Commodity Futures Trading Comm'n v. R.J. Fitzgerald & Co., 310 F.3d 1321, 1331 (11th Cir.2002).

[26]   Exchange Act Rel. No. 43,154 (Aug. 15, 2000).

information is *Walton v. Morgan Stanley & Co.*[27] There, the defendant investment banking firm, representing one of its own corporate clients, investigated another corporation that was a possible target of a takeover bid by its client. In the course of negotiations, the investment banking firm was given, on a confidential basis, unpublished material information. Subsequently, after the proposed takeover was abandoned, the firm was charged with relying on the information when it traded in the target corporation's stock. For purposes of the decision, it was assumed that the firm knew the information was confidential, but that it had been received in arm's length negotiations. In the absence of any fiduciary relationship, the Court of Appeals found no basis for imposing tippee liability on the investment firm. Would the outcome of that case change under Rule 10b5–2?

4. Should companies adopt policies prohibiting employees from discussing any aspect of the company's business with family members and friends? Would such a policy be enforceable or practical? Is it reasonable to expect spouses, for example, not to share information about their work?

NOTE ON PENALTIES

The SEC has no authority to prosecute criminal actions against inside traders, but it is authorized by Exchange Act § 21(d)(1) to ask the Justice Department to initiate a criminal prosecution.[28] In addition, the Justice Department may bring such a prosecution on its own initiative. Under § 32(a) of the Act, a willful violation of Rule 10b–5 or 14e–3 is a felony that can be punished by a $5 million fine ($25 million in the case of corporations) and up to 20 years in jail.[29] Since the mid-1980s insider trading scandals, criminal prosecutions have become fairly common in this area.

The SEC long has had the authority to pursue various civil penalties in insider trading cases. Under Exchange Act § 21(d), the SEC may seek a permanent or temporary injunction whenever "it shall appear to the Commission that any person is engaged or is about to engage in any acts or practices constituting a violation" of the Act or any rules promulgated thereunder.[30] Courts have made it quite easy for the SEC to obtain injunctions under § 21(d). The SEC must make a "proper showing," but that merely requires the SEC to demonstrate that a violation of the securities laws occurred and there is a reasonable likelihood of future violations.[31] At

---

[27] 623 F.2d 796 (C.A.2 1980).

[28] 15 U.S.C. § 78(d)(1) ("The Commission may transmit such evidence as may be available concerning . . . a violation of any provision of this chapter or the rules or regulations thereunder to the Attorney General, who may, in his discretion, institute the necessary criminal proceedings under this chapter.").

[29] 15 U.S.C. § 78ff(a). "The 'willfulness' requirement of § 32(a) of the Exchange Act does not require the Government to prove specific intent to violate the act. . . . The Government must, however, prove an intent to commit the act which constitutes a violation of that section of the statute under which the defendant is charged." U.S. v. Koenig, 388 F. Supp. 670, 711 (S.D.N.Y. 1974).

[30] 15 U.S.C. § 78(d)(1).

[31] See SEC v. Commonwealth Chem. Sec., Inc., 574 F.2d 90, 99–100 (2d Cir.1978) ("Our recent decisions have emphasized, perhaps more than older ones, the need for the SEC to go beyond the mere facts of past violations and demonstrate a realistic likelihood of recurrence.");

least in the Second Circuit, the SEC is not required to meet traditional requirements for equitable relief, such as irreparable harm, which is significant because so much insider trading litigation takes place in the federal courts in New York, which are within the Second Circuit.[32]

Once the court's equity jurisdiction "has been properly invoked by the showing of a securities law violation, the court possesses the necessary power to fashion an appropriate remedy."[33] Thus, in addition to or in place of injunctive relief, the SEC may seek disgorgement of profits, correction of misleading statements, disclosure of material information, or other special remedies.[34] In the insider trading context, disgorgement of profits to the government is the most commonly used enforcement tool.

> The primary purpose of disgorgement orders is to deter violations of the securities laws by depriving violators of their ill-gotten gains. "The effective enforcement of the federal securities laws requires that the SEC be able to make violations unprofitable. The deterrent effect of an SEC enforcement action would be greatly undermined if securities law violators were not required to disgorge illicit profits."[35]

Consistent with the principle that disgorgement is intended to deter insider trading, courts have held that tippers can be forced to disgorge an amount equivalent to their tippee's profits.[36]

During the 1980s, Congress significantly expanded the civil sanctions available to the SEC for use against inside traders. The Insider Trading Sanctions Act of 1984 (ITSA) created a civil monetary penalty of up to three times the profit gained or loss avoided by a person who violates rules 10b–5 or 14e–3 "by purchasing or selling a security while in the possession of material non-public information." An action to impose such a penalty may be brought in addition to or in lieu of any other actions that the SEC or Justice

---

SEC v. Lund, 570 F. Supp. 1397, 1404 (C.D.Cal.1983) (court denied an injunction on the grounds that the defendant's action was "an isolated occurrence" and that his "profession [was] not likely to lead him into future violations"). In addition to the likelihood of future violations, courts weighing an SEC request to enjoin the defendant have also considered such factors as "the degree of scienter involved, the sincerity of defendant's assurances against future violations, the isolated or recurrent nature of the infraction, [and the] defendant's recognition of the wrongful nature of his conduct. . . ." SEC v. Universal Major Industries, 546 F.2d 1044, 1048 (2d Cir. 1976).

[32]   See SEC v. Management Dynamics, Inc., 515 F.2d 801 (2d Cir.1975); SEC v. Manor Nursing Centers, Inc., 458 F.2d 1082 (2d Cir.1972). See also SEC v. Chapman, 826 F. Supp.2d 847, 857 (D.Md.2011) ("The SEC need not prove irreparable injury or inadequacy of other remedies. . . . Instead, the Court must issue an injunction if the SEC 'demonstrates a reasonable and substantial likelihood that the defendant, if not enjoined, will violate securities laws in the future.' ").

[33]   SEC v. Manor Nursing Centers, 458 F.2d 1082, 1103 (2d Cir.1972).

[34]   See 15 U.S.C. § 78(d)(5) ("In any action or proceeding brought or instituted by the Commission under any provision of the securities laws, the Commission may seek, and any Federal court may grant, any equitable relief that may be appropriate or necessary for the benefit of investors.").

[35]   SEC v. Fischbach Corp., 133 F.3d 170, 175 (2d Cir.1997) (citations omitted).

[36]   See SEC v. Clark, 915 F.2d 439, 454 (9th Cir.1990) ("It is well settled that a tipper can be required to disgorge his tippees' profits. . . . Such a rule is a necessary deterrent to evasion of Rule 10b–5 liability by either: (1) enriching a friend or relative; or (2) tipping others with the expectation of reciprocity.").

Department is entitled to bring. Because the SEC thus may seek both disgorgement and treble damages, an inside trader faces potential civil liability of up to four times the profit gained.

In the Insider Trading and Securities Fraud Act of 1988 (ITSFEA), Congress made a number of further changes designed to augment the enforcement resources and penalties available to the SEC. Among other things, it authorized the SEC to pay a bounty to informers of up to 10 percent of any penalty collected by the SEC. The treble money fine was extended to controlling persons, so as to provide brokerage houses, for example, with greater incentives to monitor the activities of their employees.

PROBLEMS

1.   You are on the subway in New York when you overhear two people you do not know talking about an upcoming merger, news not yet public. They seem to know their stuff. If you buy stock based on this information, and profit when the information turns out true, have you violated the federal insider trading rules?

2.   Henry Lee learned about acquisition negotiations between Acme Materials and Metro while living with his girlfriend, an associate at a prominent New York law firm retained by Acme Materials. Lee was present while the attorney, working in their apartment, reviewed deal documents and discussed the transaction on the phone with colleagues. Lee used this information to secretly begin acquiring Metro shares.

   A.   Is Lee liable for breaching the disclose or abstain theory of insider trading liability?

   B.   Is Lee liable for breaching the misappropriation theory of insider trading liability?

   C.   Several days after Lee began buying Metro shares, Lee's girlfriend directly told him that she was working on an acquisition of Metro, but cautioned him that he could not use the information for any purpose. Lee agreed not to misuse the information. Unbeknownst to his girlfriend and despite their agreement, Lee continued acquiring Metro shares. Is Lee's girlfriend guilty of tipping inside information? Is Lee liable for misappropriation of inside information?

3.   LeBron James knows that when he becomes a free agent on July 1, 20XX, he intends to sign with the New York Knicks. Would it be illegal insider trading if between today and July 1, James started buying stock in publicly-traded Madison Square Garden, Inc., which owns the Knicks, knowing that Madison Square Garden's stock would likely surge on the news of his signing?

4.   Charles Cutthroat, CEO of a major public company, has become highly stressed as a result of the pressure of merger negotiations and begins seeing Paula Psychic, a psychiatrist, for therapy. In the course of their sessions, Charles discloses confidential information about the merger. Unbeknownst to Charles, Paula buys stock of Charles' company on the basis

of that information and in a short time sells that stock at a profit. Has Charles made a gift to Paula in violation of SEC Rule 10b–5? What if:

    A.   Charles warned Paula not to trade on information that he might reveal in therapy sessions?

    B.   Charles warned Paula not to trade but he realizes that she had disregarded his warning and he has done nothing about it?

    C.   Charles is aware that Paula has been trading on information that he has revealed and is also aware that Paula is grateful and treats him better than other patients by making it easy to reschedule appointments and by not charging him for sessions that he has missed without notice?

C. COMPLIANCE PROGRAMS

1) CORPORATE LEVEL PROGRAMS

"A significant purpose of the Exchange Act was to eliminate the idea that use of inside information for personal advantage was a normal emolument of corporate office."[37] As a matter of good corporate practice, all publicly held corporations should adopt policies designed to prevent illegal trading by insiders—especially § 16 officers. Such policies protect the insiders by providing guidance as to when trading is least likely to result in liability. Given the severe penalties for inside trading, and the inevitable temptation to profit from access to inside information, such policies are

> **WHAT'S THAT?**
>
> Rule 16a–1(f) defines the term officer as the president, principal financial officer, principal accounting officer, any vice-president of the issuer in charge of a principal business unit, division or function (such as sales, administration or finance), any other officer who performs a policy-making function, or any other person who performs similar policy-making functions for the issuer.

necessary to, in a sense, protect insiders from themselves. Even more important, however, such policies also protect the issuer itself from potential controlling person liability. Not surprisingly, perhaps, most public corporations have adopted such policies.[38]

There are two potential sources of control person liability in this context. First, Securities Exchange Act § 20(a) provides that any "person who, directly or indirectly, controls any person liable under any provision of this chapter or of any rule or regulation thereunder shall also be liable jointly and severally with and to the same extent as such controlled

---

[37] Dirks v. SEC, 463 U.S. 646, 653 n.10 (1983).

[38] See, e.g., Marc I. Steinberg & John Fletcher, Compliance Programs for Insider Trading, 47 SMU L. Rev. 1783, 1828 (1994); see also Alan J. Berkeley, Form of Summary Memorandum and Sample Corporate Policy on Insider Trading, ALI-ABA Course of Study on Securities Law for Nonsecurities Lawyers, SF43 ALI-ABA 457, 464 (2001) (stating that "companies are increasingly adopting and implementing insider trading compliance programs").

person to any person to whom such controlled person is liable . . ., unless the controlling person acted in good faith and did not directly or indirectly induce the act or acts constituting the violation or cause of action." The good faith defense available under Securities Exchange Act § 20(a) "provides an incentive [for issuers] to implement procedures to preserve confidential information and to deter insider trading."[39]

Second, the 1988 adoption of ITSFEA created a separate basis for control person liability in Securities Exchange Act § 21A. As subsequently amended, § 21A(a)(1)(3) provides that:

> The amount of the penalty which may be imposed on any person who, at the time of the violation, directly or indirectly controlled the person who committed such violation, shall be determined by the court in light of the facts and circumstances, but shall not exceed the greater of $1,000,000, or three times the amount of the profit gained or loss avoided as a result of such controlled person's violation. If such controlled person's violation was a violation by communication, the profit gained or loss avoided as a result of the violation shall, for purposes of this paragraph only, be deemed to be limited to the profit gained or loss avoided by the person or persons to whom the controlled person directed such communication.

Section 21A(b)(1), however, further provides that:

> No controlling person shall be subject to a penalty under subsection (a)(1)(B) unless the Commission establishes that—

> > (A) such controlling person knew or recklessly disregarded the fact that such controlled person was likely to engage in the act or acts constituting the violation and failed to take appropriate steps to prevent such act or acts before they occurred; or

> > (B) such controlling person knowingly or recklessly failed to establish, maintain, or enforce any policy or procedure required under section 78o(f)–[1] of this title or section 80b–4a of this title and such failure substantially contributed to or permitted the occurrence of the act or acts constituting the violation.

Because adoption and effective implementation of a reasonable compliance program makes it significantly more difficult for the SEC to show that the issuer acted recklessly and/or failed to take appropriate steps with respect to potential illegal trading by its insiders, Accordingly, good corporate practice mandates creation and rigorous enforcement of effective corporate compliance programs intended to prevent insider trading by officers and other employees of the issuer.

---

[39]   Steinberg & Fletcher, supra, at 1786.

Another consideration is that evidence of insider transactions is highly relevant to private securities litigation. Public corporations, especially in technology sectors, have become highly vulnerable to such litigation. A technology corporation that fails to meet its quarterly earnings projection will experience a drop in its stock price when that news is announced, and often will be sued shortly thereafter for fraud under Rule 10b–5.

In 1995, Congress adopted the Private Securities Litigation Reform Act (PSLRA) to curtail what Congress believed was a widespread problem of merit-less strike suits. Of particular relevance to insider trading compliance programs, one of the PSLRA's provisions established a new (and arguably higher) pleading standard with respect to the scienter element of Rule 10b–5, requiring that a complaint detail facts giving rise to a "strong inference" of scienter.

Post-PSLRA, plaintiffs' securities lawyers began routinely seeking to satisfy the scienter pleading standard by alleging that insiders sold shares in suspicious amounts and/or at suspicious times.[40] Insider sales supposedly provide inferential evidence that senior management knew that earnings forecasts would not be met and sold to avoid the price drop that follows from announcements of lower than expected earnings. Evidence that transactions took place during a trading window established by a corporate insider trading compliance program will help rebut claims that the insider transactions establish the existence of scienter.[41]

Insider trading compliance programs commonly have two components. First, corporate policies commonly limit trading by insiders to specified time periods. Second, at least as to directors and executive officers, corporate insider trading compliance programs commonly require preapproval of proposed transactions by a specified compliance officer. As a matter of good corporate practice, an issuer's insider trading compliance program commonly will apply to any and all transactions in any of the issuer's securities, including not just common stock, but also preferred stock, convertible debentures, options, warrants, and any derivatives.

As a matter of good corporate practice, an insider trading compliance program should create prophylactic rules governing the timing of insider transactions. Recall that under *Texas Gulf Sulphur*, an insider who possesses material nonpublic information may not trade until such information has been widely disseminated. While the *Texas Gulf Sulphur*

---

[40] In addition, insider selling activity can be used as evidence that the nonpublic information in question was material. See Basic Inc. v. Levinson, 485 U.S. 224, 240 n.18 (1988) (stating that "trading and profit making by insiders can serve as an indication of materiality").

[41] Finally, the board of directors may have a state law fiduciary duty to ensure that the corporation has adopted an insider trading compliance program. See, e.g., In re Caremark Int'l Inc. Deriv. Litig., 698 A.2d 959 (Del. Ch. 1996) (suggesting in dicta that directors of a health care corporation had a duty to adopt programs ensuring corporate compliance with relevant state and federal regulations).

standard works well for the sort of dramatic, one-time event news at issue there, it works less well for the more mundane sorts of nonpublic information to which insiders routinely have access. An issuer always has undisclosed information about numerous different aspects of its business. By the time all of that information has been disseminated publicly, moreover, new undisclosed information doubtless will have been developed. In response to this concern, firms should develop policies limiting the periods within which insiders may trade.

Prophylactic trading restrictions of this sort typically are tied to the company's periodic disclosure process. Per SEC regulations, public corporations must send an annual report to the shareholders and also file with the SEC a Form 10-Q after each of the first three quarters of their fiscal year and a Form 10-K after year's end. Because of the substantial and wide-ranging disclosures required in these reports, which are publicly available, there is a relatively low probability that an insider who trades during the time immediately following their dissemination will be deemed to have traded on material nonpublic information. As *Texas Gulf Sulphur* suggests, however, the insider may not trade the moment the report goes in the mail. Instead, the insider must wait until the market has had time to digest the report.

Corporate insider trading compliance policies typically create a "trading window" during which insiders are affirmatively permitted to trade. The window commonly opens a day or two after filing of the periodic report and closes a specified number of days later (commonly 10 to 30). The premise underlying the delay between the release of operating results and the opening of the trading window a day or two later is that it takes time for information to be absorbed by the marketplace. As we have seen, providing the market with such an opportunity is effectively mandated by *Texas Gulf Sulphur*.

A corporate compliance program establishing a trading window, of course, may not trump the federal securities laws. Because corporations generally do not have an affirmative duty to disclose information simply because it is material, there will be many instances where insiders have access to material information that is not yet ripe for disclosure. An insider who possesses material information that has not been disclosed must refrain from trading at all times—whether or not a trading window is open. As a matter of good corporate practice, public corporations should prohibit trading during an otherwise open trading window whenever insiders have access to undisclosed material nonpublic information even though the company has timely released its financial operating results in a periodic disclosure statement. This is referred to as "closing the window" or as a "blackout period." The window can be closed either through a general announcement that trading should not occur or by declining to preclear specific proposed transactions.

A trading window is appropriately closed during the period prior to the announcement of a proposed merger or acquisition or the announcement of a significant joint venture or other strategic partnering relationship. Because the insider trading prohibition requires the insider to either disclose the information or abstain from trading, and because the insider has no right to disclose confidential corporate information, the insider is effectively obliged to comply with a company-imposed closure and refrain from trading during the period the issuer chooses to keep the information confidential.

A trading window approach contemplates a limited period in which insiders are permitted to trade, while prohibiting them from trading outside that period. In contrast, some corporations adopt so-called "blackout periods" during which insiders are prohibited from trading. A corporation might, for example, adopt a policy prohibiting insiders from trading during the period immediately prior to dissemination of a quarterly or annual report. Outside the blackout period, insiders are presumptively free to trade, although transactions by officers and directors should be precleared on a case-by-case basis as described below.

An effective blackout policy obviously must preclude insiders from trading stock they hold directly. In order to ensure compliance, however, it should also apply to stock held indirectly, such as stock held in a 401(k) plan or other employee benefit program.

Many commentators argue that, as a matter of good corporate practice, the issuer should require preclearance of trading by corporate directors and officers even during an otherwise open trading window. Non-officer employees are typically exempted from the preclearance requirement. In my opinion, the greater access of corporate directors and officers to material nonpublic information mandates the adoption of such policies as a matter of good corporate practice.

Corporate compliance programs directed at insider trading by directors and officers in fact customarily include a requirement for preclearance of their transactions by a specified corporate official. Typically, the compliance officer will be a very senior corporate officer, such as the general counsel, corporate secretary, or chief financial officer. A director or officer wishing to trade in the company's securities should notify the compliance officer one or more business days before the proposed transaction is to be effected. In a trading window-based program, the compliance officer may disapprove the proposed transaction even though the trading window is open.

Clearly, the compliance officer should not approve a transaction when the insider seeking approval is known to possess material nonpublic information. As a matter of sound corporate practice, moreover, it would be appropriate for the compliance officer to disapprove a proposed transaction where there is material nonpublic information presently unknown to the insider requesting approval but to which that insider might have access. Indeed, because insider trading compliance programs have such a substantial prophylactic component, it would be appropriate for the compliance officer to disapprove a transaction even where the insider in question does not have authorized access to the material nonpublic information in question. Disapproval of a proposed transaction under such circumstances is appropriate because (1) it prevents subsequent litigation of the question "what did the insider know and when did he/she know it?" and (2) insiders without authorized access to nonpublic information nevertheless often come into possession of such information inadvertently or surreptitiously.

The compliance officer should conduct periodic cross-checks of available materials, which may include Forms 3, 4 and 5, Form 144, officers and directors questionnaires, and reports received from the Company's stock administrator and transfer agent, to detect unauthorized trades.

Sound compliance programs should include insulation walls so that only persons with need for material nonpublic information have access to such information. Such walls were formerly known in colloquial legal speech as "Chinese walls." As a California appellate judge aptly noted, however:

> "Chinese Wall" is [a] piece of legal flotsam that should be emphatically abandoned. The term has an ethnic focus that many would consider a subtle form of linguistic discrimination. Certainly, the continued use of the term would be insensitive to the ethnic identity of the many persons of Chinese descent. . . .
>
> Aside from this discriminatory flavor, the term "Chinese Wall" is being used to describe a barrier of silence and secrecy. . . . [But] "Chinese Wall" is not even an architecturally accurate metaphor for the barrier to communication created to preserve confidentiality. Such a barrier functions as a hermetic seal to prevent two-way communication between two groups. The Great Wall of China, on the other hand, was only a one-way barrier. It was built to keep outsiders out—not to keep insiders in.[42]

In law firms, terms such as "ethical wall" or "ethical screen" are emerging as alternatives. In the present context, however, the term "insulation wall" seems superior. First, it does not connote the professional responsibility aspects associated with the ethical wall terminology. Second, it provides a more exact "architecturally accurate metaphor" than does ethical wall.

Key features of such a wall would include organizational and physical separation of persons with access to information especially likely to be abused from persons who do not need such access. Prohibitions against and penalties for discussing confidential matters with unauthorized personnel or in locations where such discussions could be overheard are also an important part of the insulation wall. Likewise,

---

[42] Peat, Marwick, Mitchell & Co. v. Superior Court, 245 Cal. Rptr. (App. 1988) (Low, P.J., concurring).

procedures for preventing unapproved personnel from accessing confidential information and files, delinking approved personnel compensation from trading profits, and regular training of personnel on their legal and commercial responsibilities.

Having a compliance program in place, of course, does not ensure that compliance will actually take place. Indeed, abuse of just such a policy was one of the most unsavory features of the infamous Enron scandal. As Enron was going down the tubes, rank-and-file Enron employees were prevented from selling Enron stock held in their 401(k) plans during a lengthy blackout period imposed while the plan changed administrators. At the same time, however, top Enron executives were selling large amounts of stock they owned directly. Section 306 of the Sarbanes-Oxley Act was adopted in direct response to this part of the Enron saga.

SOX § 306(a)

PROHIBITION OF INSIDER TRADING DURING PENSION FUND BLACKOUT PERIODS.—

(1) IN GENERAL.—Except to the extent otherwise provided by rule of the Commission pursuant to paragraph (3), it shall be unlawful for any director or executive officer of an issuer of any equity security (other than an exempted security), directly or indirectly, to purchase, sell, or otherwise acquire or transfer any equity security of the issuer (other than an exempted security) during any blackout period with respect to such equity security if such director or officer acquires such equity security in connection with his or her service or employment as a director or executive officer.

(2) REMEDY.—

(A) IN GENERAL.—Any profit realized by a director or executive officer referred to in paragraph (1) from any purchase, sale, or other acquisition or transfer in violation of this subsection shall inure to and be recoverable by the issuer, irrespective of any intention on the part of such director or executive officer in entering into the transaction.

(B) ACTIONS TO RECOVER PROFITS.—An action to recover profits in accordance with this subsection may be instituted at law or in equity in any court of competent jurisdiction by the issuer, or by the owner of any security of the issuer in the name and in behalf of the issuer if the issuer fails or refuses to bring such action within 60 days after the date of request, or fails diligently to prosecute the action thereafter, except that no such suit shall be brought more than 2 years after the date on which such profit was realized.

(3) RULEMAKING AUTHORIZED.—The Commission shall, in consultation with the Secretary of Labor, issue rules to clarify the application of this subsection and to prevent evasion thereof.

Such rules shall provide for the application of the requirements of paragraph (1) with respect to entities treated as a single employer with respect to an issuer under section 414(b), (c), (m), or (o) of the Internal Revenue Code of 1986 to the extent necessary to clarify the application of such requirements and to prevent evasion thereof. Such rules may also provide for appropriate exceptions from the requirements of this sub-section, including exceptions for purchases pursuant to an automatic dividend reinvestment program or purchases or sales made pursuant to an advance election.

(4) BLACKOUT PERIOD.—For purposes of this subsection, the term "blackout period", with respect to the equity securities of any issuer—

(A) means any period of more than 3 consecutive business days during which the ability of not fewer than 50 percent of the participants or beneficiaries under all individual account plans maintained by the issuer to purchase, sell, or otherwise acquire or transfer an interest in any equity of such issuer held in such an individual account plan is temporarily suspended by the issuer or by a fiduciary of the plan; and

(B) does not include, under regulations which shall be prescribed by the Commission—

(i) a regularly scheduled period in which the participants and beneficiaries may not purchase, sell, or otherwise acquire or transfer an interest in any equity of such issuer, if such period is—

(I) incorporated into the individual account plan; and

(II) timely disclosed to employees before becoming participants under the individual account plan or as a subsequent amendment to the plan; or

(ii) any suspension described in subparagraph (A) that is imposed solely in connection with persons becoming participants or beneficiaries, or ceasing to be participants or beneficiaries, in an individual account plan by reason of a corporate merger, acquisition, divestiture, or similar transaction involving the plan or plan sponsor.

(5) INDIVIDUAL ACCOUNT PLAN.—For purposes of this subsection, the term "individual account plan" has the meaning provided in section 3(34) of the Employee Retirement Income Security Act of 1974 (29 U.S.C. 1002(34), except that such term shall not include a one-participant retirement plan (within the meaning of section 101(i)(8)(B) of such Act (29 U.S.C. 1021(i)(8)(B))).

(6) NOTICE TO DIRECTORS, EXECUTIVE OFFICERS, AND THE COMMISSION.—In any case in which a director or executive officer is subject to the requirements of this subsection in connection with a blackout period (as defined in paragraph (4)) with respect to any equity securities, the issuer of such equity securities shall timely notify such director or officer and the Securities and Exchange Commission of such blackout period.

As the SEC explained:

> Section 306(a) . . . makes it unlawful for any director or executive officer of an issuer of any equity security, directly or indirectly, to purchase, sell or otherwise acquire or transfer any equity security of the issuer during any pension plan blackout period with respect to such equity security, if the director or executive officer acquired the equity security in connection with his or her service or employment as a director or executive officer. Section 306(a) also requires an issuer to timely notify its directors and executive officers and the Commission of a blackout period that could affect them. . . .
>
> Section 306(a) equalizes the treatment of corporate executives and rank-and-file employees with respect to their ability to engage in transactions involving issuer equity securities during a pension plan blackout period if the securities have been acquired in connection with their service to, or employment with, the issuer. When a director or executive officer engages in a transaction involving issuer equity securities at a time when participants or beneficiaries in the issuer's pension plans cannot engage in similar transactions through their plan accounts, the director or executive officer obtains an unfair advantage that the statute seeks to ameliorate. Section 306(a) restricts the ability of directors and executive officers to trade in such securities until a pension plan blackout period has ended and the ability to trade through the pension plan has been restored to plan participants and beneficiaries. This should align the interests of directors and executive officers more closely with those of the rank-and-file employees who engage in transactions involving issuer equity securities through an issuer's pension plans.[43]

In exercising its rulemaking authority under § 306, the SEC exempted a number of transactions from the restrictions, most notably including transactions effected by a director or officer pursuant to a Rule 10b5–1 plan.

---

[43]   In Re Insider Trades During Pension Fund Blackout Periods, Release No. 25909 (Jan. 22, 2003).

2) Individual Rule 10b5–1 Plans

In 2000, the SEC adopted Rule 10b5–1, which states that Rule 10b–5's prohibition of insider trading is violated whenever someone trades "on the basis of" material nonpublic information. There are three affirmative defenses available under Rule 10b5–1, under each of which:

> [A] person's purchase or sale is not "on the basis of" material nonpublic information if the person making the purchase or sale demonstrates that:
>
> (A) Before becoming aware of the information, the person had:
>
> (1) Entered into a binding contract to purchase or sell the security,
>
> (2) Instructed another person to purchase or sell the security for the instructing person's account, or
>
> (3) Adopted a written plan for trading securities. . . .[44]

These affirmative defenses are available only if the contract, instruction, or plan meets the following conditions:

> (1) Specified the amount of securities to be purchased or sold and the price at which and the date on which the securities were to be purchased or sold;
>
> (2) Included a written formula or algorithm, or computer program, for determining the amount of securities to be purchased or sold and the price at which and the date on which the securities were to be purchased or sold; or
>
> (3) Did not permit the person to exercise any subsequent influence over how, when, or whether to effect purchases or sales; provided, in addition, that any other person who, pursuant to the contract, instruction, or plan, did exercise such influence must not have been aware of the material nonpublic information when doing so. . . .[45]

The purchase or sale must be made pursuant to the plan, which includes a requirement that the plan not have been changed so as to permit the transaction. Finally, the plan must have been established "in good faith and not as part of a plan or scheme to evade the prohibitions of this section."[46]

There has long been concern executives abuse Rule 10b5–1 by establishing or amending trading plans while in possession of material nonpublic information on the basis of which they proceeded to trade while using the plan for cover:

---

[44]   17 C.F.R. § 240.10b5–1(c)(1)(i).

[45]   Id. at § 240.10b5–1(c)(1)(i)(B).

[46]   Id. at § 240.10b5–1(c)(1)(ii).

In one high-profile example, the SEC filed a civil complaint on June 4, 2009, against the former CEO of Countrywide Financial, Angelo Mozilo, and other former Countrywide executives,

> **FOR MORE INFORMATION**
>
> For a sample 10b5–1 plan provided by the SEC, see https://www.sec.gov/ Archives/edgar/data/878927/000 119312510207408/dex993.htm

alleging that they used Rule 10b5–1 plans to trade illegally on inside information (to the tune of nearly $140 million, in Mr. Mozilo's case). Although all of these sales occurred through Rule 10b5–1 plans, the SEC alleges—citing internal correspondence such as an e-mail stating that the company was "flying blind"— that Mr. Mozilo had material nonpublic information about Countrywide's deteriorating mortgage business when he instituted his trading plans. The SEC also took particular note of the fact that he implemented no fewer than four separate plans during a three-month period, and that sales under the plans began soon after their adoption.[47]

Securities attorney Manuel Rivera suggests the following best practices so as to minimize the risk that a corporation's insiders will abuse their Rule 10b5–1 plan:

> Getting the board involved and pre-clearing plans, amendments, and terminations. The Council of Institutional Investors recommended that public company boards of directors be explicitly responsible for oversight of Rule 10b5–1 plans. The board, or an appropriate board committee such as the nominating and corporate governance committee or compensation committee, could be vested with responsibility for overseeing Rule 10b5–1 plans for corporate insiders. Board oversight could increase vigilance concerning inappropriate practices and encourage best practices in the adoption, amendment, or termination of Rule 10b5–1 plans. In addition, new Rule 10b5–1 plans, plan amendments and plan terminations should be pre-cleared by a designated internal compliance officer.

> Permitting plan adoption or modification only at designated times. To avoid suspicions of actions while in possession of material non-public information, Rule 10b5–1 plans should be adopted and modified only at times when the corporate insider can buy or sell securities under the company's insider-trading policy, such as during an open trading window or soon after an

---

[47]   David Lamarre, Keeping Current: Securities, 19-DEC Bus. L. Today 20, 20 (2009). See also M. Todd Henderson et. al., Offensive Disclosure: How Voluntary Disclosure Can Increase Returns from Insider Trading, 103 Geo. L.J. 1275 (2015) (showing that Rule 10b5–1 plans "can create legal cover for opportunistic insider trading").

earnings announcement (when material non-public information will be communicated to the public).

Creating a template for plans entered into by company insiders. The company should select one broker to handle all Rule 10b5–1 plans of company insiders and require that company insiders establish and administer their plans through this broker. The designated broker should not handle other securities transactions for the company insider, to avoid undue influence over the broker. In addition, the company should obtain the broker's standard form of Rule 10b5–1 plan and amend the form in order to codify standard terms that are consistent with the company's policy decisions concerning these plans. For example, the standard plan of a broker may provide for a waiting period of two weeks between adoption of a plan and execution of a trade, but if, as discussed below, the company determines to require a longer gap period, the broker's form would be customized to provide this. In addition, if warranted, the company may require all insiders to adopt Rule 10b5–1 plans. For example, if the company makes restricted stock unit awards to insiders, the company could require the insiders to adopt plans providing that upon delivery of stock upon satisfaction of vesting conditions, a sufficient number of the vested shares will be sold to satisfy the associated tax withholding obligation. Some proxy advisory firms, such as ISS, believe that corporate executives should be prohibited from trading company stock outside of a Rule 10b5–1 plan.

Implementing a waiting period before the initial trade. Because a short period between adoption or adoption of a Rule 10b5–1 plan and the first trade execution under the plan may signal that an insider possessed material non-public information at the time his decision concerning adoption or amendment of the plan occurred, it is advisable to implement a meaningful waiting period before initial trading activity can occur. A common period used for this purpose is thirty days, and some companies require longer periods.

Adopt disclosure best practices. Although the SEC does not require current disclosure of the adoption of Rule 10b5–1 plans on Form 8-K, some companies make voluntary disclosures of corporate insider plans. Since trades by directors and executive officers must be reported on Form 4 and require a Form 144 filing, making the market aware of the existence of these plans and their terms upon adoption may reduce the perception of unplanned insider selling. Disclosure best practices espoused by ISS include a requirement that the adoption, amendment, or termination of a Rule 10b5–1 plan be disclosed on an accelerated basis—within two business days—by filing a Form 8-K, and requiring Form 4 reports concerning trade executions to mention that the transactions were pursuant to a Rule 10b5–1 plan.

Discourage overlapping plans, frequent plan modifications, and terminations. Corporate policies should discourage company insiders from adopting multiple Rule 10b5–1 plans with overlapping execution terms, since this can be viewed as an attempt to use timing to take advantage of material non-public information. Generally, plans should have a term of at least a year, since short-term plans are more likely to be scrutinized as having been motivated by inside knowledge. Similarly, modification of existing plans should occur only when the insider does not possess material non-public information, otherwise the purpose of the plan would be defeated. In addition, if corporate insiders terminate plans, this could be interpreted as an abusive practice in that it may raise questions about whether the plan was adopted in good faith. Companies should consider adopting policies that discourage insiders from amending or terminating Rule 10b5–1 plans. One recommendation is that companies require board approval to amend or terminate a plan, such approval to be granted only under extraordinary circumstances. In addition, some companies bar corporate insiders from adopting new Rule 10b5–1 plans for six months or a year after a plan termination, to deter insiders from adopting plans or terminating them other than in good faith.[48]

In April 2017, the CorporateCounsel.net blog reported on the results of a survey of corporate Rule 10b5–1 practices:[49]

1. Does your company require insiders to sell shares only pursuant to a Rule 10b5–1 trading plan

- Yes, insiders are required to use Rule 10b5–1 plans in order to sell shares—4%

- No, but they are strongly encouraged—44%

- No, and they are not explicitly encouraged—52%

- Not sure, it hasn't come up—0%

2. Does your company review and approve each insider's Rule 10b5–1 trading plan?

- Yes, it is subject to prior review and approval by the company pursuant to the insider trading policy—78%

---

[48] Manuel G. Rivera, *Staying Ahead of the Curve in Complying With Current and Anticipated Securities Regulations*, 2013 WL 2136544 at *13–15.

[49] Reprinted by permission.

- Yes, but only the template plan is reviewed and not the actual trading schedule—13%
- No, but we have a broker that we require to be used and have reviewed that brokers template—7%
- No, and there is no requirement to go through a specific broker—2%

3.   Does your company allow sales of shares through Rule 10b5–1 trading plans during blackout periods?

- Yes—82%
- No—13%
- Not sure, it hasn't come up—4%

4.   Does your company require a waiting period between execution of Rule 10b5–1 trading plans and time of first sale?

- Yes, it is a two week waiting period or less—11%
- Yes, it is a one month waiting period (or close to it)—33%
- Yes, it is a two month waiting period (or close to it)—4%
- Yes, it is a waiting period until the next open window—28%
- No—15%
- Not sure, it hasn't come up—9%

5.   Does your company allow insiders to voluntarily terminate a Rule 10b5–1 plan?

- Yes—86%
- No, only terminations dictated by the trading plan are allowed—14%

6.   Does your company make public disclosure of the insiders' Rule 10b5–1 trading plans?

- Yes, but only for directors and/or one or more officers—20%
- Yes, for all directors and employees—2%
- No—78%

7.   If your company makes public disclosure, how does it do it?

- Form 8-K—42%
- Press release—0%
- Website posting—0%
- Combination of above—0%
- Other—58%

QUESTIONS

1. What happens if an insider who has set up a Rule 10b5–1 plan makes a trade that is not permitted under the plan?

2. Should an insider be permitted to adopt or amend a Rule 10b5–1 plan during an open trading window?

3. Should the issuer's company insider trading policy permit insiders with a Rule 10b5–1 plan to adopt or amend the plan during a trading blackout?

4. Should the issuer's company insider trading policy require insiders to adopt a Rule 10b5–1 plan?

5. Should a Rule 10b5–1 plan allow the adopting insider to vary the number of shares acquired in transactions effected under the plan?

D. REGULATION FD

The SEC long has been concerned that selective disclosure to analysts undermines public confidence in the integrity of the stock markets:

> [M]any issuers are disclosing important nonpublic information, such as advance warnings of earnings results, to securities analysts or selected institutional investors or both, before making full disclosure of the same information to the general public. Where this has happened, those who were privy to the information beforehand were able to make a profit or avoid a loss at the expense of those kept in the dark.
>
> We believe that the practice of selective disclosure leads to a loss of investor confidence in the integrity of our capital markets. Investors who see a security's price change dramatically and only later are given access to the information responsible for that move rightly question whether they are on a level playing field with market insiders.[50]

Unfortunately for the SEC, the *Dirks* tipping regime was an inadequate constraint on the selective disclosure practice because, inter alia, it can be difficult to prove that the tipper received a personal benefit in connection with a disclosure.

Recall that *Dirks v. SEC*[51] held that not at tips by corporate insiders are illegal. Instead, tipping is illegal, inter alia, only if the tipper receives a personal benefit in exchange for making the tip. Where representatives of an issuer were authorized to disclose information to selected analysts

---

[50] Selective Disclosure and Insider Trading, Exchange Act Rel. No. 43,154 (Aug. 15, 2000). On the relationship between investment analysis and insider trading, see Daniel R. Fischel, Insider Trading and Investment Analysts: An Economic Analysis of Dirks v. SEC, 13 Hofstra L. Rev. 127 (1984); Donald C. Langevoort, Investment Analysts and the Law of Insider Trading, 76 Va. L. Rev. 1023 (1990).

[51] 463 U.S. 646 (1983).

or investors and did so for the issuer's benefit, rather than personal gain, this essential element is absent.[52] Because the tipper committed no breach, the tipper faced no liability and the tippee was free to trade on the basis of the information or tip the information to someone else with impunity. Only where the SEC could show some sort of mixed motive on the tipper's part, as where the tipper was motivated by personal gain as well as pursuing corporate advantage would liability be appropriate.[53]

In 2000, the SEC adopted Regulation FD (commonly known as Reg FD) to create a non-insider trading-based mechanism for restricting selective disclosure.[54] If someone acting on behalf of a public corporation discloses material nonpublic information to securities market professionals or "holders of the issuer's securities who may well trade on the basis of the information," the issuer must also disclose that information to the public.[55]

The rule does not define what constitutes "material information," instead incorporating the standard securities law definition of materiality. In adopting Reg FD, however, the SEC specifically pointed to certain areas especially likely to be deemed material: (1) earnings announcements; (2) merger and acquisition negotiations; (3) new products or discoveries; (4) a change in control or top management; (5) a change in the issuer's outside auditors; (6) major events affecting the issuer's securities, such as a default on debt securities or a stock split; and (7) the company entering bankruptcy or a receivership.

Where the issuer intentionally discloses such information in a covered communication, it must simultaneously disclose the information in a manner designed to convey it to the general public.[56] Hence, for

---

[52]   Stephen J. Choi, A Framework for the Regulation of Securities Market Intermediaries, 1 Berkeley Bus. L.J. 45, 56–57 (2004) (explaining that the absence of a personal benefit to the tipper "corporate officers the ability to pass inside information freely to analysts"); Clay Richards, Selective Disclosure: "A Fencing Match Conducted on a Tightrope" and Regulation FD—The SEC's Latest Attempt to "Electrify the Tightrope," 70 Miss. L.J. 417, 425 (2000) (noting that Dirks was widely believed to have insulated corporate officers and analysts from liability because the "personal benefit" test was not satisfied in selective disclosure cases); Scott Russell, Note, Regulation Fair Disclosure: The Death of the Efficient Capital Market Hypothesis and the Birth of Herd Behavior, 82 B.U. L. Rev. 527, 531 (2002) (explaining that "corporations have engaged in selective disclosure under the apparent protection of . . . Dirks v. SEC").

[53]   SEC v. Phillip J. Stevens, SEC Litig. Rel. No. 12,813, 1991 WL 296537 at *1 (Mar. 19, 1991) (stating that the tip was illegal because it "was seen by [defendant] Stevens as having direct, tangible benefit to his status as a corporate manager").

[54]   17 C.F.R. § 243.100–.103. See Donald C. Langevoort, Insider Trading: Regulation, Enforcement, and Prevention § 12.12 at 12–37 (2012) (explaining that Reg FD "is not an insider trading rule, but rather a contingent affirmative disclosure obligation designed to force companies either to publicize information or keep it completely confidential"); see generally Marc I. Steinberg, Insider Trading, Selective Disclosure, and Prompt Disclosure: A Comparative Analysis, 22 U. Penn. J. Int'l Econ. L. 635 (2001).

[55]   17 C.F.R. § 243.100(b)(1). Specifically, Reg FD applies to issuers that have a class of securities registered with the SEC pursuant to § 12 of the Exchange Act or is subjected to the SEC periodic disclosure regime under § 15(d) of the Act. 17 C.F.R. § 240.101(b). Mutual funds, foreign governments, and foreign private issuers are explicitly excluded from coverage by Reg FD. Id.

[56]   Id. at § 243.100(a)(1). According to Reg FD, "[a] selective disclosure of material nonpublic information is 'intentional' when the person making the disclosure either knows, or

example, if the issuer holds a briefing for selected analysts, it must simultaneously announce the same information by filing a Form 8-K with the SEC or "through another method (or combination of methods) of disclosure that is reasonably designed to provide broad, non-exclusionary distribution of the information to the public."[57]

As a general matter, acceptable methods of public disclosure for purposes of Regulation FD will include press releases distributed through a widely circulated news or wire service, or announcements made through press conferences or conference calls that interested members of the public may attend or listen to either in person, by telephonic transmission, or by other electronic transmission (including use of the Internet). The public must be given adequate notice of the conference or call and the means for accessing it.[58]

The SEC suggested that issuers consider following a three-step model "for making a planned disclosure of material information, such as a scheduled earnings release":[59]

- First, issue a press release, distributed through regular channels, containing the information;

- Second, provide adequate notice, by a press release and/or website posting, of a scheduled conference call to discuss the announced results, giving investors both the time and date of the conference call, and instructions on how to access the call; and

- Third, hold the conference call in an open manner, permitting investors to listen in either by telephonic means or through Internet webcasting.

Where the disclosure was not intentional, as where a corporate officer let something slip in casual conversation with an analyst, the issuer must make public disclosure "promptly" after a senior officer learns of the disclosure. " 'Promptly' means as soon as reasonably practicable (but in no event after the later of 24 hours or the commencement of the next day's trading on the New York Stock Exchange) after a senior official of the issuer (or, in the case of a closed-end investment company, a senior official of the issuer's investment adviser) learns that there has been a non-intentional disclosure by the issuer or person acting on behalf of the issuer of information that the senior official knows, or is reckless in not knowing, is both material and nonpublic."[60] In turn, senior official "means any director, executive officer

---

is reckless in not knowing, that the information he or she is communicating is both material and nonpublic." Id. at § 243.101(a).

[57]   Id. at § 243.101(e).

[58]   Selective Disclosure and Insider Trading, Exchange Act Rel. No. 43,154 (Aug. 15, 2000).

[59]   Id.

[60]   17 C.F.R. § 243.101(d).

..., investor relations or public relations officer, or other person with similar functions."[61]

The communications that trigger a Reg FD disclosure obligation are those made to a person outside the issuer who falls into one (or more) of four categories. First, a broker or dealer, or a person associated with a broker or dealer. Second, an investment adviser, an institutional investment manager, or someone associated with either such person. Third, an investment company, a hedge fund, or a person affiliated with either such fund. Finally, "a holder of the issuer's securities, but only under circumstances in which it is reasonably foreseeable that the person will purchase or sell the issuer's securities on the basis of the information."[62]

The purpose of limiting Reg FD to such communications is to permit the issuer to make ordinary business conversations with stakeholders such as clients, consultants, journalists, regulators, and the like who are unlikely to use the disclosed information for trading purposes. Towards that end, the Regulation explicitly exempts three commercially important categories of business communications. First, disclosures to "a person who owes a duty of trust or confidence to the issuer (such as an attorney, investment banker, or accountant)" are exempt.[63] Second, communications to any person who expressly agrees to keep the disclosed information confidential are exempt. Finally, the Regulation exempts a broad range of communications commonly made in connection with a registered offering of securities.

Where an issuer fails to comply with its Reg FD disclosure obligations, the SEC typically seeks limited relief in the form of a cease and desist order. The Regulation specifically provides that a failure to comply is not of itself a violation of Rule 10b–5.[64] It likewise provides that a failure to comply does not adversely affect the issuer's ability to use S–2 or S–8 short form registration statements.[65]

It took the SEC almost a decade to decide that corporations could use the internet to disclose information. Not until 2008 did the SEC conclude that posting information to the company's website was even potentially a sufficient way of complying with Reg FD. Whether such disclosure suffices is determined on a case-by-case basis, considering factors such as "(1) whether the company website was 'a recognized channel of distribution;' (2) whether the website posting made the information available to the general marketplace; and (3) whether there

---

[61]   Id. at § 243.101(f). "Executive officer" is defined in Rule 3b–7 under the Exchange Act of 1934 as the issuer's "president, any vice president of the registrant in charge of a principal business unit, division or function (such as sales, administration or finance), any other officer who performs a policy making function or any other person who performs similar policy making functions for the registrant." 17 C.F.R. 240.3b–7.

[62]   17 C.F.R. § 243.100(b)(1).

[63]   Id. at § 243.100(b)(2)(i).

[64]   Id. at § 243.102.

[65]   Id. at § 243.103.

was a reasonable waiting period for investors and the market to react to the posted information."[66]

When it came to social media, however, the SEC moved a bit faster. As the WSJ reported on April 2, 2013:

> In a ruling that portends changes to how companies communicate with investors, the Securities and Exchange Commission said Tuesday that postings on sites such as Facebook and Twitter are just as good as news releases and company websites as long as the companies have told investors which outlets they intend to use.
>
> The move was sparked by an investigation into a July Facebook posting from Netflix Inc. Chief Executive Reed Hastings, who boasted on the social-media site that the streaming-video company had exceeded one billion hours in a month for the first time, sending the firm's shares higher. The SEC opened the investigation in December to determine if the post had violated rules that bar companies from selectively disclosing information. . . .
>
> In its Tuesday ruling, the agency said social-media sites would also suffice—in some circumstances. It blessed sites as long as companies make clear to investors they plan to use them. It also suggested a corporate executive's personal Facebook page wasn't as likely as a company's social-media page to be a channel through which companies would be allowed to make important announcements. . . .
>
> Joseph Grundfest, a former member of the commission who now teaches at Stanford Law School, said the SEC is bowing to reality in blessing social media. Twitter, where users can post comments of 140 characters or less, says more than 200 million people world-wide use the service at least twice a month. Facebook says it has more than one billion users. "As a practical matter, Reed Hastings' personal Web page probably informed more people more quickly of the information than" a formal SEC filing, said Mr. Grundfest, who published a paper in January urging the SEC not to pursue an enforcement action against Mr. Hastings. "You don't have 200,000 people a day checking Netflix filings on" the SEC's electronic-document site.[67]

The SEC announcement explained that:

> The SEC's report of investigation confirms that Regulation FD applies to social media and other emerging means of

---

[66]   See Jill Fisch, Regulation FD: An Alternative Approach to Addressing Information Asymmetry, in Research Handbook on Insider Trading 112, 127 (Stephen M. Bainbridge ed. 2012).

[67]   Jessica Holzer & Greg Bensinger, SEC Embraces Social Media, Wall St. J., April 2, 2013, at A1.

communication used by public companies the same way it
applies to company websites. The SEC issued guidance in 2008
clarifying that websites can serve as an effective means for
disseminating information to investors if they've been made
aware that's where to look for it. Today's report clarifies that
company communications made through social media channels
could constitute selective disclosures and, therefore, require
careful Regulation FD analysis. . . .

Regulation FD requires companies to distribute material
information in a manner reasonably designed to get that
information out to the general public broadly and non-
exclusively. It is intended to ensure that all investors have the
ability to gain access to material information at the same time.[68]

Corporate law professor Usha Rodrigues observed that:

This move seems easy and right. . . . There seems to be no
stopping social media.

Next question: how broadly will companies authorize social
media disclosure? Dealbook's Michael J. de la Merced observes
that "the new move may reduce spontaneity because companies
may limit their communications to official corporate accounts
and file the information with the agency at the same time."[69]

Corporate commentator Broc Romanek opined that:

Even though the SEC's press release touts the new report
as a greenlight for companies—the press release's title is "SEC
Says Social Media OK for Company Announcements if Investors
are Alerted"—I'm dubious that companies and their advisors
will see it that way. For starters, the new guidance comes from
an Enforcement report (here's an explanation of what a Section
21(a) report is)—perhaps not the best vehicle to encourage new
practices. [Not surprisingly, many mass media reporters were
fooled by the SEC's title and report that the SEC has "new"
disclosure rules.]

And it doesn't get into the nitty gritty like IM's new
guidance does. Given the slow adoption rate of social media by
IR, finance and governance professionals—compared to the rest
of the world—I'm not convinced this will be enough to get folks
moving. . . .[70]

---

[68]   Press Release, SEC Says Social Media OK for Company Announcements if Investors
are Alerted (Apr. 2, 2013), http://www.sec.gov/news/press/2013/2013-51.htm.

[69]   Usha Rodrigues, From the "Inevitable File," The Conglomerate (Apr. 3, 2013), http://
www.theconglomerate.org/2013/04/from-the-inevitable-file.html.

[70]   Broc Romanek, Social Media: SEC Issues Reg FD Guidance (In Form of Enforcement
Report), The CorporateCounsel.net (Apr. 3, 2013), http://www.thecorporatecounsel.net/Blog/
2013/04/tech.html.

Problems and Questions

1.   Susie Lamont is an independent director of Solar Power Inc. Acme's board of directors has authorized Lamont to act as the board's primary contact person with activist investors, such as hedge funds. In a recent private meeting with the top manager of a hedge fund that owns approximately 3% of Acme's common stock, Lamont disclosed that was unlikely to receive a much-anticipated loan guarantee from the U.S. Department of Energy. When Solar Power broadly disclosed this material information in a press release the next morning, its stock price dropped 6 percent. Did Lamont violate Regulation FD? Does it matter whether or not the hedge fund traded on the information prior to the issuance of the press release? Does it matter whether the hedge fund agreed to keep the information confidential or not? (If the hedge fund did so and then traded anyway, did the hedge fund commit illegal insider trading?)

2.   Harold Drum is the CEO and Chairman of the Board of Drum Industries, Inc., a public corporation subject to Regulation FD. Drum Industries maintains a Twitter account that is routinely used to provide investors with earnings guidance and similar updates. In addition, however, Drum maintains a personal Twitter account. Drum's personal Twitter account has never previously been used to announce earnings or other investor information. Yesterday, Drum tweeted: "Drum Industries shatters previous record with $3.27 earnings per share for the first quarter." Has Drum violated Regulation FD?

3.   Can an issuer disclose material nonpublic information to its employees (who may also be shareholders) without making public disclosure of the information?

4.   During a nonpublic meeting with analysts, an issuer's CEO provides material nonpublic information on a subject she had not planned to cover. Although the CEO had not planned to disclose this information when she entered the meeting, after hearing the direction of the discussion, she decided to provide it, knowing that the information was material and nonpublic. Would this be considered an intentional disclosure that violated Regulation FD because no simultaneous public disclosure was made?

E. Concluding Exercise

You are the newly hired general counsel for Acme Corporation. Acme's CEO has given you a copy of the company's current insider trading policy and asked you to review it. Acme's CEO informs you that she wants the policy to clearly prohibit any illegal insider trading, while at the same time allowing company employees maximum freedom to make legal trades.

Sample Insider Trading Policy

An employee, officer, or director of Acme Corporation (the "Company") who possesses material, non-public information (which is described below) about the Company may not trade in securities of the Company. This policy also prohibits an employee, officer, or director from trading in the securities of any other public corporation with which the Company has a business relationship, including but not limited to customers and suppliers (collectively, "business partners"), if the employee, officer, or director has material non-public information relating to our business partner. Employees, officers, and directors must not pass on to others inside information about the Company or recommend the purchase or sale of securities while in possession of material non-public information (even if the information itself is not disclosed). This policy applies whether or not the employee, officer, or director who gives the tip derives any personal benefit in doing so.

Information is material if a reasonable investor would consider it important in making a decision to buy, sell, or retain stock. Both positive and negative information may be material.

It does not matter whether the inside information was obtained in the course of employment or service as a director, or by any other incidental means. Employees, officers, and directors are responsible for ensuring compliance with this policy by their family and personal household members. It also does not matter if there is an independent, justifiable reason for a purchase or sale; if the employee, officer, or director has material, non-public information, the policy applies.

All trades in the Company's securities are prohibited when the Company's trading window is closed ("blackout periods"), except trades pursuant to a qualified 10b5–1 plan authorized by the General Counsel. These blackout periods commence 14 days prior to the end of each of the Company's four fiscal quarters and end two full business days after the Company's quarterly or annual results have been released to the public.

It is also the policy of the Company that, if the Company makes a public announcement of material information (including earnings releases), employees, officers, and directors may not engage in any transactions in the Company's securities until at least two full business days after the information has been released.

Compliance with this insider trading policy is a condition of continued employment with the Company. Any employee, officer, or director who violates the Company's insider trading policy will also be subject to disciplinary action imposed by the Company, which may include dismissal for cause.

QUESTIONS

1.   Are there any terms used in the policy that should be defined therein?

2.   Are there any transactions that could potentially involve the use of inside information that are not covered by the policy?

    A.   Are there any transactions that appear to be covered by the policy but are should be exempted because they pose a low risk of insider trading?

3.   Is the policy provision on blackout periods complete?

4.   Should the policy require preclearance of trades and, if so, by whom and under what circumstances?

5.   Does the policy prohibit an employee's family members from trading in the company's stock? If not, should it?

6.   To what extent, if any, should the policy apply to independent contractors?

7.   Is the company policy on disclosure of information to others overly broad? Put another way, can you identify situations in which a covered person could legitimately disclose information to another that appear to be prohibited by the policy?

F. SECTION 16

Section 16 of the Exchange Act imposes three substantive obligations on specified corporate insiders:

1.   Disclosure: Pursuant to § 16(a), insiders of an issuer must report transactions in the issuer's equity securities to the SEC.

2.   Ban on short swing profits: In addition to the complicated insider trading rules under § 10(b), Congress also provided a much simpler prophylactic rule under § 16(b). In brief, § 16(b) provides that any profits an insider of an issuer earns on purchases and sales of the issuer's equity securities that occur within six months of each other must be forfeited to the issuer. As with all prophylactic rules, § 16(b) is both over-and under-inclusive. It captures many trades unaffected by the use of inside information, while missing many trades flagrantly based on nonpublic information.

3.   Ban on short sales: Section 16(c) prohibits insiders of an issuer from short selling the issuer's equity securities.

As a prohibition of insider trading, § 16(b) is far more limited in scope than the regime developed by the courts under Rule 10b–5. The chief limitation is that it applies only to directors, officers, and holders of ten percent or more of a registered company's equity securities. Besides the resulting smaller class of prospective defendants, moreover, there are several other important limitations on § 16(b)'s scope relative to Rule 10b–5. Section 16(b), for example, applies only to insider transactions in their own company's stock. There is no tipping liability, no misappropriation liability, and no constructive insider doctrine. Second, § 16(b) applies only to firms that must register under the Exchange Act. Finally, it applies only to equity securities, such as stocks and convertible debt.

Exchange Act § 16

(a) *Disclosures required.*

(1) *Directors, officers, and principal stockholders required to file.* Every person who is directly or indirectly the beneficial owner of more than 10 percent of any class of any equity security (other than an exempted security) which is registered pursuant to section 78*l* of this title, or who is a director or an officer of the issuer of such security, shall file the statements required by this subsection with the Commission.

(2) *Time of filing.* The statements required by this subsection shall be filed—

(A) at the time of the registration of such security on a national securities exchange or by the effective date of a registration statement filed pursuant to section 78*l*(g) of this title;

(B) within 10 days after he or she becomes such beneficial owner, director, or officer, or within such shorter time as the Commission may establish by rule;

(C) if there has been a change in such ownership, or if such person shall have purchased or sold a security-based swap agreement involving such equity security, before the end of the second business day following the day on which the subject transaction has been executed, or at such other time as the Commission shall establish, by rule, in any case in which the Commission determines that such 2-day period is not feasible.

(3) *Contents of statements.* A statement filed—

(A) under subparagraph (A) or (B) of paragraph (2) shall contain a statement of the amount of all equity securities of such issuer of which the filing person is the beneficial owner; and

(B) under subparagraph (C) of such paragraph shall indicate ownership by the filing person at the date of filing, any such changes in such ownership, and such purchases and sales of the security-based swap agreements or security-based swaps as have occurred since the most recent such filing under such subparagraph.

(4) *Electronic filing and availability.* Beginning not later than 1 year after July 30, 2002—

(A) a statement filed under subparagraph (C) of paragraph (2) shall be filed electronically;

(B) the Commission shall provide each such statement on a publicly accessible Internet site not later than the end of the business day following that filing; and

(C) the issuer (if the issuer maintains a corporate website) shall provide that statement on that corporate website, not later than the end of the business day following that filing.

(b) *Profits from purchase and sale of security within six months.* For the purpose of preventing the unfair use of information which may have been obtained by such beneficial owner, director, or officer by reason of his relationship to the issuer, any profit realized by him from any purchase and sale, or any sale and purchase, of any equity security of such issuer (other than an exempted security) or a security-based swap agreement involving any such equity security within any period of less than six months, unless such security or security-based swap agreement was acquired in good faith in connection with a debt previously contracted, shall inure to and be recoverable by the issuer, irrespective of any intention on the part of such beneficial owner, director, or officer in entering into such transaction of holding the security or security-based swap agreement purchased or of not repurchasing the security or security-based swap agreement sold for a period exceeding six months. Suit to recover such profit may be instituted at law or in equity in any court of competent jurisdiction by the issuer, or by the owner of any security of the issuer in the name and in behalf of the issuer if the issuer shall fail or refuse to bring such suit within sixty days after request or shall fail diligently to prosecute the same thereafter; but no such suit shall be brought more than two years after the date such profit was realized. This subsection shall not be construed to cover any transaction where such beneficial owner was not such both at the time of the purchase and sale, or the sale and purchase, of the security or security-based swap agreement or a security-based swap involved, or any transaction or transactions which the Commission by rules and regulations may exempt as not comprehended within the purpose of this subsection.

. . .

1) PERSONS SUBJECT TO § 16

Covered Issuers. Section 16 applies only to insiders of issuers who have one or more classes of equity securities registered with the SEC under the Exchange Act. Under Exchange Act § 12(a), an issuer must register any class of equity securities listed for trading on a national stock exchange. In addition, § 12(g) requires that an issuer register its equity securities if it has more than $10 million in assets and a class of equity securities held of record by at least 2,000 persons or 500 persons who are not accredited investors.

Covered Persons. Unlike Rule 10b–5, § 16 applies only to officers, directors, or shareholders who own more than 10% of the company's stock. Unlike the status of a director, the other two categories present certain complexities. As such, we must ask both who is a shareholder and who is an officer?

Shareholders. Determining whether a shareholder is subject to § 16 requires us to ask three questions. First, is the holder the beneficial owner of the shares? Second, how do we determine the appropriate numerator and denominator to calculate the holder's percentage interest? Third, does § 16 apply only to individuals or can the holdings of certain groups of shareholders be aggregated to meet the 10% threshold?

The first question arises because Section 16 explicitly applies only to beneficial owners of equity securities. As such, Congress obviously contemplated that record holders such as depository institutions and brokers holding stock for clients would not be subject to the statute. Prior to 1991, however, working out the precise parameters of beneficial ownership was left to the courts because neither the statute nor any SEC rule defined it. In that year, however, the SEC adopted Rule 16a–1(a), which defines the term beneficial owner for purposes of § 16 to "mean any person who is deemed a beneficial owner pursuant to section 13(d) of the Act and the rules thereunder." In turn, Rule 13d–3 provides that:

> [A] beneficial owner of a security includes any person who, directly or indirectly, through any contract, arrangement, understanding, relationship, or otherwise has or shares: (1) Voting power which includes the power to vote, or to direct the voting of, such security; and/or, (2) Investment power which includes the power to dispose, or to direct the disposition of, such security.

In addition, subsection (d) of the Rule further provides that:

> A person shall be deemed to be the beneficial owner of a security . . . if that person has the right to acquire beneficial ownership of such security, . . . including but not limited to any right to acquire: (A) Through the exercise of any option, warrant or right; (B) through the conversion of a security; (C) pursuant to the power to revoke a trust, discretionary account, or similar arrangement; or (D) pursuant to the automatic termination of a trust, discretionary account or similar arrangement; provided, however, any person who acquires a security or power specified in paragraphs (d)(1)(i)(A), (B) or (C), of this section, with the purpose or effect of changing or influencing the control of the issuer, or in connection with or as a participant in any transaction having such purpose or effect, immediately upon such acquisition shall be deemed to be the beneficial owner of the securities which may be acquired through the exercise or conversion of such security or power.

The Rule exempts persons who hold securities solely because they are a broker who acts as record owner of shares beneficially owned by their customers, pledgees of securities, or underwriters.

Some examples may be helpful:

- A stockbroker's customer beneficially owns securities held by a broker in street name.

- An insider is presumed to have beneficial ownership of shares held of record by the insider's spouse, minor children, and other relatives living in the insider's home, although the insider may disclaim ownership of such shares when filing a Form 4.

- "Smith is a director of a registered company and has recently become president of a non-profit foundation which is operated exclusively for charitable purposes and is qualified under Section 501(c)(3) of the Internal Revenue Code. The foundation owns approximately 3 percent of the outstanding common stock of the registered company." If Smith's position at the foundation gives him "voting power, investment power, or other indications of control with respect to the securities held by the foundation," he can be deemed the beneficial owner of the shares held by the foundation.[71]

- "An insider is the trustee of an irrevocable trust. Neither the insider nor any member of his or her family in the beneficiary of the trust." According to the SEC, a "trustee of an irrevocable trust or a trust revocable at the discretion of another person, who has no interest in the income or corpus of the trust, is not the beneficial owner of any securities held in the trust," even if the trustee "has the power to manage the assets of the trusts, including the power to make acquisitions and dispositions and to vote the securities held by the trusts."[72]

- In contrast to the prior example, a trustee who has an interest in the income or corpus of the trust generally will be deemed the beneficial owner of shares held by the trust.

- Where "an insider, as settlor, establishes a trust with the settlor as the sole beneficiary and in whose administration the settlor has a voice," the insider will continue to be deemed the beneficial owner of such shares.

Returning our attention to Rule 16a–1, even if someone would be deemed a beneficial owner of equity securities pursuant to Rule 13d–3,

---

[71] Interpretive Release on Rules Applicable to Insider Reporting and Trading, 23 SEC Docket 856 (1981).

[72] Id.

Rule 16(a)(1) exempts from Section 16's coverage a number of financial institutions unlikely to have control over the issuer:

[T]he following institutions or persons shall not be deemed the beneficial owner of securities of such class held for the benefit of third parties or in customer or fiduciary accounts in the ordinary course of business (or in the case of an employee benefit plan specified in paragraph (a)(1)(vi) of this section, of securities of such class allocated to plan participants where participants have voting power) as long as such shares are acquired by such institutions or persons without the purpose or effect of changing or influencing control of the issuer or engaging in any arrangement subject to Rule 13d–3(b) (§ 240.13d–3(b)):

(i)   A broker or dealer registered under section 15 of the Act (15 U.S.C. 78*o*);

(ii)   A bank as defined in section 3(a)(6) of the Act (15 U.S.C. 78c);

(iii)   An insurance company as defined in section 3(a)(19) of the Act (15 U.S.C. 78c);

(iv)   An investment company registered under section 8 of the Investment Company Act of 1940 (15 U.S.C. 80a–8);

(v)   Any person registered as an investment adviser under Section 203 of the Investment Advisers Act of 1940 (15 U.S.C. 80b–3) or under the laws of any state;

(vi)   An employee benefit plan as defined in Section 3(3) of the Employee Retirement Income Security Act of 1974, as amended, 29 U.S.C. 1001 et seq. ("ERISA") that is subject to the provisions of ERISA, or any such plan that is not subject to ERISA that is maintained primarily for the benefit of the employees of a state or local government or instrumentality, or an endowment fund;

(vii) A parent holding company or control person, provided the aggregate amount held directly by the parent or control person, and directly and indirectly by their subsidiaries or affiliates that are not persons specified in § 240.16a–1(a)(1)(i) through (x), does not exceed one percent of the securities of the subject class;

(viii) A savings association as defined in Section 3(b) of the Federal Deposit Insurance Act (12 U.S.C. 1813);

(ix)   A church plan that is excluded from the definition of an investment company under section 3(c)(14) of the Investment Company Act of 1940 (15 U.S.C. 80a–30);

(x)   A non-U.S. institution that is the functional equivalent of any of the institutions listed in paragraphs (a)(1)(i) through (ix) of this section, so long as the non-U.S. institution is subject to a regulatory scheme that is substantially comparable to the regulatory scheme applicable to the equivalent U.S. institution and the non-U.S. institution is eligible to file a Schedule 13G pursuant to § 240.13d–1(b)(1)(ii)(J); and

(xi) A group, provided that all the members are persons specified in § 240.16a–1 (a)(1)(i) through (x).

Now that we have defined the class of persons potentially deemed beneficial owners of equity securities, we must turn to determining what percentage of the relevant class of equity securities they hold. As for the numerator, Rule 13d–3 provides that "all securities of the same class beneficially owned by a person, regardless of the form which such beneficial ownership takes, shall be aggregated in calculating the number of shares beneficially owned by such person." The denominator normally will be number of shares of the class outstanding. Where the individual in question is deemed a beneficial owner by virtue of subsection (d), however, that subsection provides that "[a]ny securities not outstanding which are subject to such options, warrants, rights or conversion privileges shall be deemed to be outstanding for the purpose of computing the percentage of outstanding securities of the class owned by such person but shall not be deemed to be outstanding for the purpose of computing the percentage of the class by any other person."

We come finally to the question of whether the holdings of a group of shareholders acting together can be aggregated so that they are collectively subject to Section 16's requirements. Recall that Rule 16a–1(a) defines the term beneficial owner for purposes of § 16 to "mean any person who is deemed a beneficial owner pursuant to section 13(d) of the Act and the rules thereunder." In turn, Exchange Act § 13(d)(3) provides that when two or more persons act as a group for the purpose of acquiring, holding or disposing of shares of the issuer they will collectively be deemed a "person" under the statute. Accordingly, such a group must file a Schedule 13D report with the SEC if the members' aggregate holdings exceed the 5% threshold.

Generally speaking, some kind of agreement is necessary before it can be said that a group exists. Not only must there be an agreement, but the agreement must go to certain types of conduct. The relevant statutory provision, Exchange Act § 13(d)(3) identifies "acquiring, holding, or disposing" of stock as the requisite purposes. Shortly after the Williams Act was adopted, the question arose whether two or more persons acting together for the purpose of voting shares, as when they cooperate in conducting a proxy contest, form a group for purposes of this provision. The courts split on that question. The SEC subsequently adopted Rule 13d–5(b)(1), which expanded the statutory list of purposes to include voting. Consequently, a group is formed when two or more shareholders agree to act together for the purposes of voting their shares, even if they do not intend to buy any additional shares. The rule's adoption seems to have resolved the controversy, even if the SEC's authority to effectively amend the statute remains somewhat obscure.

Proving the existence of the requisite agreement is a complex and potentially difficult question of fact. On the one hand, "Section 13(d) allows individuals broad freedom to discuss the possibilities of future agreements without filing under securities laws." On the other hand, an agreement to act in concert need not be formal or written. The existence of such an agreement may be proven by circumstantial evidence.

In *Segen ex rel. KFx Inc. v. Westcliff Capital Management, LLC*,[73] the defendants were part of two § 13(d) groups that both collectively owned more than 10% of the issuer's stock. The court explained that:

> [E]ach individual member of the [groups], even though considered a member of their respective "groups" for the purposes of aggregation to determine ownership percentage vis-à-vis the ten percent insider threshold, is only liable for its own short-swing profits resulting from its own trades. See SEC Release No. 34–28869, 56 Fed.Reg. at 7245 ("[O]nly those securities in which a member of a group has a direct or indirect pecuniary interest would be . . . subject to short-swing profit recovery. Thus, while securities holdings of group members may subject the group members to section 16, if the group member does not have or share a pecuniary interest in securities held by other group members, the transactions of the other group members do not create section 16 obligations for that member.").

In other words, while the holdings of members of a § 13(d) group can be aggregated for purposes of determining whether each member of the group is a 10% shareholder, the individual group members generally will have liability only for short swing profits made by trading their own shares.

Officers. Determining whether one is an officer can be tricky. Exchange Act Rule 3b–2 defines an officer as a "president, vice president, secretary, treasury or principal financial officer, comptroller or principal accounting officer, and any person routinely performing corresponding functions. . . ." The latter catchall phrase is the potential trouble spot. Should the statutory term "officer" be construed narrowly so that objective factors, especially one's title, determine whether one was subject to § 16(b)? Or should the term be interpreted more broadly, so as to take into account subjective considerations such as the nature of one's functions and/or whether one's role gave one access to inside information?

An early decision, *Colby v. Klune*,[74] expressed doubt as to whether the SEC had authority to adopt Rule 3b–2. Instead, the court adopted a formulation that looked to subjective considerations, which defined an officer as "a corporate employee performing important executive duties

[73]   299 F.Supp.2d 262 (S.D.N.Y. 2004).
[74]   178 F.2d 872 (2d Cir. 1949).

of such character that he would be likely, in discharging those duties, to obtain confidential information that would aid him if he engaged in personal market transactions." The Ninth Circuit later concurred with the view that title alone is not dispositive, but focused on access to information as the relevant consideration, holding that § 16(b) "is not based simply upon a person's title within his corporation; rather, liability follows from the existence of a relationship with the corporation that makes it more probable than not that the individual has access to inside information."[75]

The SEC ultimately intervened in the debate by adopting Rule 16a–1(f), under which either one's title or one's function could result in officer status:

> The term "officer" shall mean an issuer's president, principal financial officer, principal accounting officer (or, if there is no such accounting officer, the controller), any vice president of the issuer in charge of a principal business unit, division or function (such as sales, administration or finance), any other officer who performs a policy making function, or any other person who performs similar policy making functions for the issuer. Officers of the issuer's parent(s) or subsidiaries shall be deemed officers of the issuer if they perform such policy making functions for the issuer. In addition, when the issuer is a limited partnership, officers or employees of the general partner(s) who perform policy making functions for the limited partnership are deemed officers of the limited partnership.

Someone who holds one of the listed titles is likely to be deemed an officer, whether or not he has access to inside information, subject to a "very limited exception applicable only where the title is essentially honorary or ceremonial."[76] An executive with policymaking functions that give the executive access to inside information, however, will be deemed an officer even if the executive lacks one of the formal titles usually associated with that position.

Insider Insiders. In *Blau v. Lehman*,[77] Lehman Brothers held a substantial (albeit less than 10%) number of shares in Tide Water Associated Oil Company. At that time, Lehman Brothers was a partnership engaged in investment banking, securities brokerage, and trading for its own account. Tide Water was a reporting company and, as such, its officers, directors, and 10% shareholders were subject to § 16.

---

[75] Merrill Lynch, Pierce, Fenner & Smith, Inc. v. Livingston, 566 F.2d 1119 (9th Cir.1978).

[76] National Medical Enterprises, Inc. v. Small, 680 F.2d 83 (9th Cir.1982). Conversely, the mere fact that one's position is described in, say, the corporate bylaws as that of an officer does not suffice to make one an officer for this purpose. See Lockheed Aircraft Corp. v. Campbell, 110 F.Supp. 282 (S.D.Cal.1953) (holding that assistant treasurer and assistant secretary were not officers for § 16(b) purposes even though their positions were described in the bylaws as those of officers).

[77] 368 U.S. 403 (1962).

Joseph A. Thomas was a Lehman Brothers partner and served as a Tide Water director. Plaintiff Blau, a Tide Water shareholder, claimed "Lehman Brothers 'deputed . . . Thomas, to represent its interests as a director on the Tide Water Board of Directors.' " Accordingly, Blau argued, Lehman Brothers could be held liable under § 16(b) as though the entity—i.e., Lehman Brothers—were a director.

The Supreme Court agreed that, in principle, that so-called "deputization" could result in one being indirectly treated as an insider:

> No doubt Lehman Brothers, though a partnership, could for purposes of § 16 be a "director" of Tide Water and function through a deputy, since § 3(a)(9) of the Act provides that "person" means . . . partnership' and § 3(a)(7) that " 'director' means any direct or of a corporation or any person performing similar functions with respect to any organization, whether incorporated or unincorporated." Consequently, Lehman Brothers would be a "director" of Tide Water, if as petitioner's complaint charged Lehman actually functioned as a director through Thomas, who had been deputized by Lehman to perform a director's duties not for himself but for Lehman.[78]

On the facts before it, however, the Supreme Court concluded that there had been no such deputization and, accordingly, "Thomas, not Lehman Brothers as an entity, . . . was the director of Tide Water."[79]

Later cases have identified a number of factors to be considered in determining whether an entity has become a director by deputization, including:

—The director took part in the decision to trade the issuer's securities. . . .

—The director succeeded another employee of the deputing entity as a director of the issuer.

—The director joined the issuer's board, thinking it would be in the interests of the deputing entity.

—The management of both the issuer and the deputing entity believed the director to be a deputy.

—The director admitted in writing that he was representing the interests of the deputing entity.

—The deputing entity's board consented to the director serving as a director of the issuer.

—The deputing entity had deputies on boards of other corporations.

—The director had a duty to report to the deputing entity.

---

[78] Id. at 409–410 (footnotes omitted).
[79] Id. at 410.

—The deputing entity owned a controlling block of the issuer's stock.

—A majority of the issuer's directors were officers of the deputing entity.

Other factors that tend to indicate that a person is not a deputy include:

—The director never discussed operating details of the issuer with the deputing entity.

—The director disclaimed any interest in the deputing entity's profit.

—The issuer, not the deputing entity, initiated the invitation to join the issuer's board.

—The issuer initially invited the director to join its board before the deputing entity began purchasing the issuer's stock.

—The director turned down an offer to become a director after the deputing entity already owned a sizable block of the issuer's stock.

—No other representative of the deputing entity was ever mentioned for the directorship if the director declined to be elected.

—The director's professional experience was the prime motivation for choosing him.

—The director was not protecting any affairs of the deputing entity or seeking to promote any policies for that entity.[80]

2) COVERED SECURITIES

All three of Section 16's substantive provisions apply only to equity securities. In turn, Exchange Act § 3(a)(11) defines "equity security" as "any stock or similar security; or any security future on any such security; or any security convertible, with or without consideration, into such a security, or carrying any warrant or right to subscribe to or purchase such a security; or any such warrant or right." In addition, Rule 3a11–1 includes limited partnership interests, interests in a joint venture, voting trust certificates, and options as equity securities. Accordingly, equity security broadly encompasses corporate stock—whether common or preferred—and equivalent ownership interests in some other forms of limited liability entities, as well as instruments convertible into or derived from them.

In contrast, none of § 16's substantive provisions apply to exempt securities. Exchange Act § 3(a)(12) defines exempted securities to include

---

[80]   Arnold S. Jacobs, An Analysis of Section 16 of the Exchange Act of 1934, 32 N.Y.L. Sch. L. Rev. 209, 283–85 (1987) (footnotes omitted).

a wide range of instruments, such as U.S. government notes and bonds, state and local government bonds, some types of investment fund securities, specified pension plans, and some securities issued by churches. Many of these instruments, of course, would not fall within the definition of an equity security in any event. In addition, § 3(a)(12) authorizes the SEC to exempt such other securities as it deems appropriate "in the public interest and for the protection of investors." In exercising that power, the SEC, has specifically exempted from § 16 asset-backed securities and those issued by foreign private issuers.

3)   REPORTING OBLIGATION

Section 16(a) requires insiders to report their holdings in the issuer's equity securities within 10 days after they first become subject to Section 16. Thereafter, an insider must report any transactions in the issuer's equity securities within two business days of their occurrence. The report must be filed electronically with the SEC. In addition, the report must be posted to the issuer's corporate website.

4)   BAN ON SHORT-SWING PROFITS

Under § 16(b), any profits earned on purchases and sales within a six month period must be disgorged to the issuer. Shareholders of the issuer may sue insiders derivatively and a shareholder's lawyer can get a contingent fee out of any recovery or settlement:

To enforce this strict liability rule on insider trading, Congress chose to rely solely on the issuers of stock and their security holders. Unlike most of the federal securities laws, § 16(b) does not confer enforcement authority on the Securities and Exchange Commission. It is, rather, the security holders of an issuer who have the ultimate authority to sue for enforcement of § 16(b). If the issuer declines to bring a § 16(b) action within 60 days of a demand by a security holder, or fails to prosecute the action "diligently," then the security holder may "institut[e]" an action to recover insider short-swing profits for the issuer.[81]

In *Gollust v. Mendell*,[82] the Supreme Court defined the class of issuer shareholders with standing to sue under Section 16(b) quite liberally. Noting that the "only textual restrictions on the standing of a party to bring suit under § 16(b) are that the plaintiff must be the 'owner of [a] security' of the 'issuer' at the time the suit is 'instituted,'" the court stressed that "Congress intended to grant enforcement standing of considerable breadth."[83] Interestingly, while liability is limited to short swing profits earned on transactions in equity securities, the standing provision of § 16(b) is not limited to holders of such securities. Instead, while "plaintiffs seeking to sue under the statute must own a 'security,'

---

[81]   Gollust v. Mendell, 501 U.S. 115, 122 (1991) (citations omitted).

[82]   501 U.S. 115 (1991).

[83]   Id. at 122–23.

§ 16(b) places no significant restriction on the type of security adequate to confer standing."[84] Accordingly, not just shareholders of the issuer have standing, but so do the holders of the issuer's bonds, debentures, warrants, and other securities. Only a "note, draft, bill of exchange, or banker's acceptance which has a maturity at the time of issuance of not exceeding nine months" is excluded.

In contrast to standard corporate derivative lawsuits, where the representative plaintiff must satisfy a contemporaneous ownership standard, there is no such requirement under § 16. "In fact, the terms of the statute do not even require that the security owner have had an interest in the issuer at the time of the defendant's short-swing trading, and the courts to have addressed this issue have held that a subsequent purchaser of the issuer's securities has standing to sue for prior short-swing trading."[85] Although the statute does not expressly require that the plaintiff retain ownership of a security of the issuer until final judgment is rendered, the Court in *Gollust* held that "Congress understood and intended that, throughout the period of his participation, a plaintiff authorized to sue insiders on behalf of an issuer would have some continuing financial interest in the outcome of the litigation, both for the sake of furthering the statute's remedial purposes by ensuring that enforcing parties maintain the incentive to litigate vigorously, and to avoid the serious constitutional question that would arise from a plaintiff's loss of all financial interest in the outcome of the litigation he had begun."[86]

In order to have standing, a plaintiff must own a security issued by the same company that issued the equity securities traded by the insider. Accordingly, holders of securities issued by a parent or subsidiary of the issuer lack standing.

Matching Transactions. Although there must be both a sale and a purchase within six months of each other in order to trigger § 16(b), it applies whether the sale follows the purchase or vice versa. Accordingly, shares are fungible for § 16(b) purposes. The trader thus need not earn his or her gains from buying and selling specific shares of stock. Instead, if the trader unloads 10 shares of stock and buys back 10 different shares of stock in the same company at a cheaper price, he or she is liable.

Examples: (1) Susan is chief financial officer of Acme, Inc. She buys 1,000 Acme shares at $8 on February 1. She sells 1,000 shares at $10 on May 1. Because the sale and purchase took place within six months, § 16(b) is triggered. She has earned a $2 profit per share and therefore must disgorge $2,000 to Acme.

(2) Sam is senior vice president of Ajax, Inc. He has owned 10,000 shares for many years. On June 1 he sells 1,000 shares at $10. On

---

[84] Id. at 123.
[85] Id.
[86] Id. at 126.

September 15, he buys 1,000 shares at $8. He also must disgorge $2,000 to Ajax ($2 per share times 1000 shares).

Courts interpret the statute to maximize the amount the company recovers. They do not use any of the standard accounting tools (e.g., FIFO: first in, first out). Much less do they let shareholders identify specific shares of stock; for example, courts will not allow the defendant to argue that "in November I sold the share I bought in January, not the share I bought in October." Instead, they match the lowest priced purchases and the highest priced sales. Again, an example will be helpful:

Shania is president of Acme, Inc. Her transactions were as follows:

- March 1: bought 100 shares at $10
- April 1: sold 70 shares at $12
- May 1: bought 50 shares on May 1 at $9
- May 15: sold 25 shares at $13
- December 31: sold 35 shares at $20

The December 31 sale cannot be matched with either the March 1 or May 1 purchase, because they are more than six months apart. The other transactions are all matchable. A court will match them in the way that maximizes Acme's recovery:

- Match the 25 shares sold on May 15 with 25 of the shares bought on May 1, because they have the largest price differential. With a $4 profit per share ($13 minus $9) times 25 shares, Shania owes Acme $100.

- Next match 25 of the shares sold on April 1 with the remaining 25 shares purchased on May 1 for a profit of $75 ($3 per share ($12 minus $9) times 25 shares).

- Now match the remaining 45 shares sold on April 1 with 45 of the shares bought on March 1 for a profit of $90 ($2 per share ($12 minus $10) times 45 shares).

- Shania therefore owes Acme a total of $265.

Different Matching Rules for Shareholders. Section 16(b) treats officers and directors on the one hand and shareholders on the other hand differently, by providing that:

> This subsection shall not be construed to cover any transaction where such beneficial owner was not such both at the time of the purchase and sale, or the sale and purchase, of the security . . . involved . . . .

A shareholder thus has § 16(b) liability only if she owned more than 10 percent of the company's shares both at the time of the purchase and of the sale. In contrast, although pursuant to Rule 16a–2, you cannot match a transaction by an officer or director made prior to his or her appointment as an officer or director to one made after he or she is appointed, you can match transactions that occur after he or she ceases to be an officer or director with those made while he or she still held office.

The Supreme Court first took up this distinction in *Reliance Electric Co. v. Emerson Electric Co.*[87] Emerson bought 13.2 percent of Dodge Manufacturing Co. stock in a hostile tender offer. To avoid being taken over by Emerson, Dodge agreed to merge with Reliance. Emerson gave up the fight and decided to sell its Dodge shares. In an attempt to minimize any potential § 16(b) liability, Emerson first sold Dodge shares representing 3.24 percent of the outstanding common stock. It then sold the remainder, which represented 9.96 percent of the outstanding. When Reliance sued under § 16(b), the Supreme Court held that shareholders are subject to the statute only if they own more than 10 percent of the stock immediately before the sale. Emerson therefore had no liability with respect to its sale of the final 9.96 percent. *Reliance* is a good example of how form prevails over substance in § 16(b)—even though Emerson's two sales were part of a related series of transactions effected pursuant to a single plan, which plausibly could have been deemed a step transaction, the court treated the second sale as having independent legal significance.

Notice that Emerson did not raise, and the Supreme Court thus did not address, the significance of the fact that Emerson had not been a 10 percent shareholder at the time it made its initial tender offer. Instead, that issue came up in *Foremost-McKesson, Inc. v. Provident Securities Co.*,[88] in which the Supreme Court held that a purchase by which a shareholder crosses the 10% threshold cannot be matched with subsequent sales for § 16(b) purposes. Again, an example may be helpful.

Selena is not an officer or director of Ajax, Inc. At all relevant times, Ajax has 1,000 shares outstanding. Selena's transactions are as follows:

- January 1: buys 50 shares at $10
- February 1: buys 55 shares at $10
- April 1: buys 50 shares at $10.
- May 1: sells 60 shares at $15
- May 2: sells 55 shares at $20

Liability equals $250 (50 shares times ($15–$10)). The January 1 purchase cannot be matched with either sale, because on January 1 Selena was not yet a 10 percent shareholder. The February 1 purchase cannot be matched with either sale because it is the transaction by which Selena became a (more than) 10 percent shareholder. Only the April 1 purchase is potentially matchable, because only at the time of that purchase did Selena own more than 10 percent of Ajax's stock. As to the

---

[87]   404 U.S. 418 (1972).

[88]   423 U.S. 232 (1976).

sales, only the May 1 sale can be matched with the April 1 purchase. On May 2, Selena owned less than 10 percent of Ajax's stock.

Form Versus Substance. Form usually triumphs over substance in § 16(b) cases. There are some exceptions, however, the most notable of which is the unconventional transaction doctrine. The Exchange Act defines "sale" very broadly: it includes every disposition of a security for value. For purposes of § 16(b), however, certain transactions are not deemed sales; namely, so-called unconventional transactions.

The leading case in this area is *Kern County Land Co. v. Occidental Petroleum Corp.*[89] In 1967, Occidental launched a tender offer for 500,000 shares of Kern County Land Co. (Old Kern). The offer later was extended and the number of shares being sought was increased. When the offer closed in June, Occidental owned more than 10% of Old Kern's stock. To avoid being taken over by Occidental, Old Kern negotiated a defensive merger with Tenneco. Under the merger agreement, Old Kern stock would be exchanged for Tenneco stock. In order to avoid becoming a minority shareholder in Tenneco, Occidental sold to a Tenneco subsidiary an option to purchase the Tenneco shares Occidental would acquire in the merger, which could not be exercised until the § 16(b) six-month period had elapsed. Tenneco and Old Kern merged during the six-month period following Occidental's tender offer. Somewhat later, more than 6 months after the tender offer, Occidental sold Tenneco stock pursuant to the option.

The successor corporation to Old Kern (New Kern) sued under § 16(b). It offered two theories. First, the merger and resulting exchange of Old Kern for Tenneco stock constituted a sale, which had occurred less than six months after the purchase effected by the tender offer. Second, the tender offer constituted a purchase and that the grant of the option (rather than the exercise of the option) constituted a sale. Because the option was granted less than six months after the tender offer, New Kern argued that Occidental was liable for any profit earned on the shares covered by the option. The Supreme Court rejected both of New Kern's arguments, holding that Occidental had no § 16(b) liability. Both the merger and the grant of the option were unconventional transactions and, as such, were not deemed a sale for § 16(b) purposes.

Courts consider three factors in deciding whether a transaction is conventional or unconventional: (1) whether the transaction is volitional; (2) whether the transaction is one over which the beneficial owner has any influence; and (3) whether the beneficial owner had access to confidential information about the transaction or the issuer. In the case at bar, Occidental was a hostile bidder with no access to confidential information about Old Kern or Tenneco. In addition, as to the merger, the exchange was involuntary—because the other shareholders had

---

[89]   411 U.S. 582 (1973).

approved the merger, Occidental had no option but to exchange its shares.

Although *Kern* still stands for the proposition that substance sometimes triumphs over form even in § 16(b), it no longer states the rule for options. Instead, the SEC treats the acquisition of an option as the purchase (or sale) of the underlying stock. Thus, the purchase of an option to buy stock (a call) could be matched either with a sale of the underlying stock or with the purchase of an option to sell the stock (a put). For example, suppose an investor bought call options on 10 shares for $1 each, exercisable at $50 per share. If he exercised the options and sold the stock for $60 a share, he would have § 16(b) liability of $60×10−(10×$1 + 10×$50) = $90. A purchase of stock could similarly be matched with the purchase of a put.

PROBLEMS

Quietude, Inc. (a reporting company, has at all relevant times had 100 million shares of common stock outstanding, which is its sole equity security. What § 16(b) liability do the following individuals have, if any?

1.   As of January 1, Quietude CEO Dave Malcolm owned 20,000,000 shares of Quietude common stock, which he had owned for over a year. On January 1, Malcolm executed a non-exempt sale of all 20,000,000 shares @ $50 per share. On May 1, Malcolm executed a non-exempt purchase of 5,000,000 shares @ $10 per share. On May 2, Malcolm executed a non-exempt purchase of 11,000,000 shares @ $10 per share.

2.   On February 1, Anabella Serra—who was neither a director nor officer of Quietude—purchased 5.7 million shares of Quietude stock @ $8 per share. On February 15, Serra purchased 5.4 million shares @ $8 per share. On March 2, Serra sold 2 million shares @ $9 per share. On March 3, Serra bought 4 million shares @ $8 per share.

3.   As of June 1, Quietude CFO Amy Washburne owned 100,000 shares of Quietude common stock, which she had owned for over a year. On June 2, Washburne executed a non-exempt sale of 10,000 shares @ $10 per share. On August 2, Washburne executed a non-exempt purchase of 20,000 shares @ $7 per share.

4.   On June 2, Quietude Vice President of Engineering Carli Frye purchased 10,000 Quietude shares @ $10 per share. On August 15, Frye resigned from Quietude effective immediately. On September 12, Frye sold all 10,000 shares @ $12 per share.

5.   On July 1, Quietude Vice President for Research Simon Peters purchased 500 Quietude shares @ $13 per share. On August 1, Tam bought 1,000 shares @ $10 per share. On September 1, Tam bought 500 shares @ $14 per share. On October 1, Tam sold 1,800 shares @ $20 per share.

(a) SECTION 16(b) AND EXECUTIVE COMPENSATION

Section 16 and the rules thereunder contain a number of exemptions from short-swing profit liability.[90] The most important of these is Rule 16b–3, which broadly exempts from the definition of "purchase" any transaction, other than a discretionary transaction, in which an officer or director of the issuer acquires an equity security of the issuer from the issuer. Although the Rule is not limited to compensatory transactions, it has important implications for the structure and operation of executive compensation plans that involve grants of stock or stock options.

Rule 16b–3. Transactions between an issuer and its officers or directors.

(a) General. A transaction between the issuer (including an employee benefit plan sponsored by the issuer) and an officer or director of the issuer that involves issuer equity securities shall be exempt from section 16(b) of the Act if the transaction satisfies the applicable conditions set forth in this section.

(b) Definitions—

(1) A Discretionary Transaction shall mean a transaction pursuant to an employee benefit plan that:

(i) Is at the volition of a plan participant;

(ii) Is not made in connection with the participant's death, disability, retirement or termination of employment;

(iii) Is not required to be made available to a plan participant pursuant to a provision of the Internal Revenue Code; and

(iv) Results in either an intra-plan transfer involving an issuer equity securities fund, or a cash distribution funded by a volitional disposition of an issuer equity security.

(2) An Excess Benefit Plan shall mean an employee benefit plan that is operated in conjunction with a Qualified

---

[90] The statute itself contains two exemptions. Section 16(d) exempts market making activities from subsections (b) and (c) of the statute. Section 16(e) exempts arbitrage transactions made in compliance with the SEC rules governing such transactions. In addition, the SEC has carved out numerous exemptions by rule.

Rule 16b–5 exempts from § 16(b) an acquisition or disposition of an issuer's equity securities by a bona fide gift, pursuant to a will, or under the laws of descent and distribution. Any such transactions, however, are reportable under Section 16(a).

Rule 16b–7 exempts from Section 16(b) transactions effected pursuant to a merger, consolidation, reclassification, and similar transactions that do not result in a significant change in the issuer's business or assets. In order to qualify for the exemption, the insider must surrender a security in exchange for the acquired security. In addition, the security surrendered must have been issued by a company that, before the transactions, owned 85% or more of the equity securities of all other companies party to the merger or consolidation, or 85% or more of the combined assets of all of the companies undergoing merger or consolidation. In other words, the entities involved must have at least 85% cross-ownership.

Plan, and provides only the benefits or contributions that would be provided under a Qualified Plan but for any benefit or contribution limitations set forth in the Internal Revenue Code of 1986, or any successor provisions thereof.

(3)(i)   A Non-Employee Director shall mean a director who:

(A) Is not currently an officer (as defined in § 240.16a–1(f)) of the issuer or a parent or subsidiary of the issuer, or otherwise currently employed by the issuer or a parent or subsidiary of the issuer;

(B) Does not receive compensation, either directly or indirectly, from the issuer or a parent or subsidiary of the issuer, for services rendered as a consultant or in any capacity other than as a director, except for an amount that does not exceed the dollar amount for which disclosure would be required pursuant to § 229.404(a) of this chapter; and

(C) Does not possess an interest in any other transaction for which disclosure would be required pursuant to § 229.404(a) of this chapter.

(ii) Notwithstanding paragraph (b)(3)(i) of this section, a Non-Employee Director of a closed-end investment company shall mean a director who is not an "interested person" of the issuer, as that term is defined in Section 2(a)(19) of the Investment Company Act of 1940.

(4) A Qualified Plan shall mean an employee benefit plan that satisfies the coverage and participation requirements of sections 410 and 401(a)(26) of the Internal Revenue Code of 1986, or any successor provisions thereof.

(5) A Stock Purchase Plan shall mean an employee benefit plan that satisfies the coverage and participation requirements of sections 423(b)(3) and 423(b)(5), or section 410, of the Internal Revenue Code of 1986, or any successor provisions thereof.

(c) Tax-conditioned plans. Any transaction (other than a Discretionary Transaction) pursuant to a Qualified Plan, an Excess Benefit Plan, or a Stock Purchase Plan shall be exempt without condition.

(d) Acquisitions from the issuer. Any transaction, other than a Discretionary Transaction, involving an acquisition from the issuer (including without limitation a grant or award), whether or not intended for a compensatory or other particular purpose, shall be exempt if:

(1)   The transaction is approved by the board of directors of the issuer, or a committee of the board of directors that is composed solely of two or more Non-Employee Directors;

(2)   The transaction is approved or ratified, in compliance with section 14 of the Act, by either: the affirmative votes of the holders of a majority of the securities of the issuer present, or represented, and entitled to vote at a meeting duly held in accordance with the applicable laws of the state or other jurisdiction in which the issuer is incorporated; or the written consent of the holders of a majority of the securities of the issuer entitled to vote; provided that such ratification occurs no later than the date of the next annual meeting of shareholders; or

(3)   The issuer equity securities so acquired are held by the officer or director for a period of six months following the date of such acquisition, provided that this condition shall be satisfied with respect to a derivative security if at least six months elapse from the date of acquisition of the derivative security to the date of disposition of the derivative security (other than upon exercise or conversion) or its underlying equity security.[3]

(e)   Dispositions to the issuer. Any transaction, other than a Discretionary Transaction, involving the disposition to the issuer of issuer equity securities, whether or not intended for a compensatory or other particular purpose, shall be exempt, provided that the terms of such disposition are approved in advance in the manner prescribed by either paragraph (d)(1) or paragraph (d)(2) of this section.

(f)   Discretionary Transactions. A Discretionary Transaction shall be exempt only if effected pursuant to an election made at least six months following the date of the most recent election, with respect to any plan of the issuer, that effected a Discretionary Transaction that was:

(1)   An acquisition, if the transaction to be exempted would be a disposition; or

(2)   A disposition, if the transaction to be exempted would be an acquisition.

---

[3]   The approval conditions of paragraphs (d)(1), (d)(2) and (e) of this section require the approval of each specific transaction, and are not satisfied by approval of a plan in its entirety except for the approval of a plan pursuant to which the terms and conditions of each transaction are fixed in advance, such as a formula plan. Where the terms of a subsequent transaction (such as the exercise price of an option, or the provision of an exercise or tax withholding right) are provided for in a transaction as initially approved pursuant to paragraphs (d)(1), (d)(2) or (e), such subsequent transaction shall not require further specific approval.

Securities and Exchange Commission, Ownership Reports and Trading By Officers, Directors and Principal Security Holders

Exchange Act Release No. 52,202 (Aug. 3, 2005)

Rule 16b–3 exempts from Section 16(b) certain transactions between issuers of securities and their officers and directors. In its *Levy v. Sterling* opinion, the Third Circuit construed Rule 16b–3(d), which applies to "grants, awards, or other acquisitions," to limit this exemption to transactions that have some compensation-related aspect. Specifically, since "grants" and "awards" are compensation-related, the Third Circuit reasoned that "other acquisitions" also must be compensation-related in order to be exempted by Rule 16b–3(d). This construction of Rule 16b–3(d) is not in accord with our clearly expressed intent in adopting the rule.

The current version of Rule 16b–3 was adopted in 1996, and implemented substantial revisions designed to simplify the conditions that must be satisfied for the exemption to apply. In contrast to prior versions of Rule 16b–3, which had exempted only employee benefit plan transactions, the 1996 revisions broadened the Rule 16b–3 exemption and extended it to other transactions between issuers and their officers and directors. . . .

Rule 16b–3(a) provides that "A transaction between the issuer (including an employee benefit plan sponsored by the issuer) and an officer or director of the issuer that involves issuer equity securities shall be exempt from section 16(b) of the Act if the transaction satisfies the applicable conditions set forth in this section." As this makes clear, the only limitations on the exemption for transactions between the issuer and its officer or director are the objective conditions set forth in later subsections of the rule, each of which applies to a different category of transactions.

As adopted in 1996, Rule 16b–3(d), entitled "Grants, awards and other acquisitions from the issuer," exempted from Section 16(b) liability "Any transaction involving a grant, award or other acquisition from the issuer (other than a Discretionary Transaction)"[29] if any one of three alternative conditions is satisfied. These conditions require:

- Approval of the transaction by the issuer's board of directors, or board committee composed solely of two or more Non-Employee Directors;

---

[29] "Discretionary Transaction" is defined in Rule 16b–3(b)(1). Generally, a Discretionary Transaction is an employee benefit plan transaction that is at the volition of a plan participant and results in either an intra-plan transfer involving an issuer equity securities fund, or a cash distribution funded by a volitional disposition of an issuer equity security. However, the definition excludes such transactions that are made in connection with the participant's death, disability, retirement or termination of employment, or are required to be made available to a plan participant pursuant to a provision of the Internal Revenue Code. A Discretionary Transaction is exempted by Rule 16b–3 only if it satisfies the conditions of Rule 16b–3(f).

- Approval or ratification of the transaction, in compliance with Exchange Act Section 14, by the issuer's shareholders; or

- The officer or director to hold the acquired securities for a period of six months following the date of acquisition.[32]

Consistent with the terms of Rule 16b–3 and statements in the 1996 Adopting Release and 1995 Proposing Release regarding the meaning of the rule, the Commission staff has interpreted the Rule 16b–3(d) exemption to include a number of transactions outside of the compensatory context, such as:

- The acquisition of acquiror equity securities (including derivative securities) by acquiror officers and directors through the conversion of target equity securities in connection with a corporate merger; and

- An officer's or director's indirect pecuniary interest in transactions between the issuer and certain other persons or entities.

The application of Rule 16b–3(d) to such transactions also has been recognized in Section 16(b) litigation. In its 2002 opinion in *Gryl v. Shire Pharmaceuticals Group PLC*,[36] the U.S. Court of Appeals for the Second Circuit construed Rule 16b–3(d) to exempt acquiror directors' acquisition of acquiror options upon conversion of their target options in a corporate merger. Although the securities acquired in *Gryl* were options, the Second Circuit's holding in no way relied upon a compensatory purpose. Instead, *Gryl* construed Rule 16b–3(d)(1) to require only that the transaction involve an acquisition of issuer equity securities from the issuer, the acquirer be a director or officer of the issuer at the time of the transaction, and the transaction be approved in advance by the issuer's board of directors.[37]

. . .

Rule 16b–3(d), as adopted, exempts any transaction, other than a Discretionary Transaction, involving an acquisition by an officer or director from the issuer (including without limitation a grant or award), whether or not intended for a compensatory or other particular purpose,

---

[32]   Rule 16b–3(d)(2). With respect to shareholder, board and Non-Employee Director committee approval, Rule 16b–3(d) requires approval in advance of the transaction. Shareholder approval must be by either: the affirmative votes of the holders of a majority of the securities of the issuer present, or represented, and entitled to vote at a meeting duly held in accordance with the applicable laws of the state or other jurisdiction in which the issuer is incorporated; or the written consent of the holders of the majority of the securities of the issuer entitled to vote. Shareholder ratification, consistent with the same procedural conditions, may confer the exemption only if such ratification occurs no later than the date of the next annual meeting of shareholders following the transaction.

[36]   298 F.3d 136 (2d Cir. 2002).

[37]   Id. at 141. Rule 16b–3(d)(1) also permits approval by "a committee of the board of directors that is composed solely of two or more Non-Employee Directors." *Gryl* noted that "[t]hat aspect of the Board Approval exemption is not at issue in this appeal." Id. at n. 2.

if any one of the Rule's three alternative conditions is satisfied. Rule 16b–3(e), as adopted, exempts any transaction, other than a Discretionary Transaction, involving the disposition by an officer or director to the issuer of issuer equity securities, whether or not intended for a compensatory or other particular purpose, provided that the terms of such disposition are approved in advance in the manner prescribed by either Rule 16b–3(d)(1) or Rule 16b–3(d)(2).

NOTES AND QUESTIONS

1.   Does Rule 16b–3 exempt issuer equity securities transactions between the issuer and persons who are subject to Section 16 who are more than 10 percent beneficial owners but are not officers or directors?

2.   Could the six-month holding period of Rule 16b–3(d)(3) be used to exempt an officer's or director's purchase of the issuer's stock in an underwritten public offering?

3.   Are the dispositions of issuer securities that take place in cashless exercises through a broker eligible for exemption pursuant to Rule 16b–3(e)?

5)   BAN ON SHORT SALES

Subsection 16(c)(1) prohibits insiders from selling the issuer's stock short. In a short sale, the investor sells stock that he does not currently own for delivery at a subsequent date agreed upon with the buyer. The investor hopes that the price of the stock will have fallen by the delivery date, so as to make a profit. Suppose John sold short 100 shares at a price of $10 for delivery in 60 days. When the 60 days expires, John must transfer 100 shares to the buyer and will receive $1,000 in return. Because John did not own the shares at the time he entered into the transaction, he will have to go out and buy them on the market. If the stock price has fallen, say to $9 per share, John can buy the 100 shares for $900 and will have earned a $100 profit (the difference between the $1,000 he received from the buyer and the $900 it cost him to buy the shares for delivery). If the stock price has risen, say to $11 per share, however, John will have to pay $1,100 buy the 100 shares for delivery to the buyer and will therefore lose $100.

An insider who knows that bad news is forthcoming may be tempted to sell the issuer's stock short to profit on the anticipated drop in the issuer's stock price expected to occur when the bad news is made public. Indeed, the insider may even be tempted to generate bad news, so as to create short selling opportunities. Section 16(c)(1) is

WHAT'S THAT?

HEDGING CONTRACT, Black's Law Dictionary (10th ed. 2014): A contract of purchase or sale that amounts to insurance against changing prices by which a dealer contracts to buy or sell for future delivery the same amount of a commodity as he or she is buying or selling in the present market."

intended to eliminate that temptation by banning insiders from selling their issuer's shares short.

Section 16(c)(2) prohibits a related practice known as "short sales against the box." These are hedging transactions, in which "an owner of stock resorts to a short sale in order to avoid the risk of future price fluctuations. He owns sufficient securities to make delivery, but chooses to make a short sale involving the borrowing of shares for delivery, rather than to sell and make delivery of the shares which he owns."

To assess your understanding of the material in this chapter, click here to take a quiz.

PART IV

SHAREHOLDERS

CHAPTER 9

VOTING AND PROXIES

Our focus throughout this book has been how corporate governance seeks to reduce the agency costs associated with the separation of ownership and control in the public corporation. Traditionally, shareholders played a very minor role in that process. To be sure, egregious misconduct by officers or directors can be challenged via lawsuits alleging breach of fiduciary duty. Absent fairly egregious behavior, however, courts are loath to interfere with decisions by boards and managers:

> A complaint which alleges merely that some course of action other than that pursued by the Board of Directors would have been more advantageous gives rise to no cognizable cause of action. Courts have more than enough to do in adjudicating legal rights and devising remedies for wrongs. The directors' room rather than the courtroom is the appropriate forum for thrashing out purely business questions which will have an impact on profits, market prices, competitive situations, or tax advantages. As stated by Cardozo, J., . . . the substitution of someone else's business judgment for that of the directors "is no business for any court to follow."[1]

Shareholders dissatisfied with firm performance were thus largely left with the option of voting the incumbent directors out of office and replacing them with new board members presumably better able to run the company effectively.

Until the 1990s, however, this sort of shareholder electoral activism was rare. We will explore the reasons why that was the case and why shareholder activism has become somewhat more common in the chapters that follow. In this Chapter, we begin with an overview of the mechanics by which shareholders exercise their voting rights.

A. STATE LAW

1) HOLDING STOCK IN STREET NAME

Shares of corporate stock originally were represented by physical stock certificates. When a corporation sold shares to an investor, the company recorded the investor's name in its stock ledger—a list of stockholders, their contact information, and how many shares they owned—and then issued a certificate representing those shares to the investor. The investor was now said to be a "stockholder of record." When

---

[1]   Kamin v. Am. Exp. Co., 383 N.Y.S.2d 807, 810–11 (N.Y. Sup. Ct. 1976), aff'd sub nom. Kamin v. Am. Express Co., 387 N.Y.S.2d 993 (N.Y. App. Div. 1st Dept. 1976).

the investor sold the shares, he signed the certificate over to the purchaser, who then submitted it to the company. The company thereupon recorded the sale on its ledger and issued to a new certificate to the new owner.

This process worked well when corporations were small and shares changed hands rarely. Once public corporations began having their shares traded on stock markets, however, the system proved far too cumbersome. As a result, most shares of publicly held corporations today are held in what is called street name:

> The vast majority of publicly traded shares in the United States are registered on the companies' books not in the name of beneficial owners—i.e., those investors who paid for, and have the right to vote and dispose of, the shares—but rather in the name of "Cede & Co.," the name used by The Depository Trust Company ("DTC").

> Shares registered in this manner are commonly referred to as being held in "street name." . . . DTC holds the shares on behalf of banks and brokers, which in turn hold on behalf of their clients (who are the underlying beneficial owners or other intermediaries).[2]

Delaware Vice Chancellor Travis Laster has explained that:

> The history of how we arrived at this ownership structure is important and informative.[4]

> Prior to 1970, negotiation was the most common method used to transfer stock in the United States. The owner would endorse the physical certificate to the name of the assignee on the back of the certificate. This endorsement instruct [ed] the corporation, upon notification, [about] the change in ownership of the shares on its corporate books. If the parties used the services of a broker, the seller would transfer the certificate to his brokerage firm. The brokerage firm representing the customer buying the security would receive the physical

[2]   Crown EMAK Partners, LLC v. Kurz, 992 A.2d 377, 381–82 (Del. 2010).

[4]   A variety of sources provide consistent accounts of the origins of the depository system. See, e.g., Securities and Exchange Commission, Study Of Unsafe And Unsound Practices Of Brokers And Dealers, H.R. Doc. No. 92–231, 92d Cong., 2d Sess. 9–10 (1971) [hereinafter SEC Study]; Uniform Commercial Code, Prefatory Note to Article 8 (revised 1994) [hereinafter Prefatory Note]; Street Name at 10–6 n.5; Teresa Carnell & James J. Hanks, Jr., Shareholder Voting and Proxy Solicitation: The Fundamentals, Maryland Bar Journal 23, 26 (Jan./Feb. 2004); David C. Donald, Heart of Darkness: The Problem at the Core of the U.S. Proxy System and Its Solution, 6 Va. L. & Bus. Rev. 41, 45, 50–61 (2011); Marcel Kahan & Edward Rock, The Hanging Chads of Corporate Voting, 96 Geo. L.J. 1227, 1237–38 & nn.45–50, 1273–74 (2008); Emily I. Osiecki, Alabama By-Products Corp. v. Cede & Co.: Shareholder Protection Through Strict Statutory Construction, 22 Del. J. Corp. L. 221, 223–28 (1997); Suellen M. Wolfe, Escheat and the Challenge of Apportionment: A Bright Line Test To Slice A Shadow, 27 Ariz. St. L.J. 173, 178–88 (1995); Businesses & Subsidiaries—The Depository Trust Company (DTC), http://www.dtcc.com/about/businesses-and-subsidiaries/dtc.aspx (last visited June 5, 2015).

certificate and transfer it to the buyer as the new record owner of the security. Occasionally, the new owner might request that the physical certificate remain at the street address of the brokerage firm to facilitate the transfer of the certificate in a subsequent sale.

Transfer of securities in the traditional certificate-based system was a complicated, labor-intensive process. Each time securities were traded, the physical certificates had to be delivered from the seller to the buyer, and in the case of registered securities the certificates had to be surrendered to the issuer or its transfer agent for registration of transfer.

By the late 1960s, increased trading rendered the certificate system obsolete. The paperwork burden reached "crisis proportions."

Stock certificates and related documents were piled "halfway to the ceiling" in some offices; clerical personnel were working overtime, six and seven days a week, with some firms using a second or even a third shift to process each day's transaction. Hours of trading on the exchange and over the counter were curtailed to give back offices additional time after the closing bell. Deliveries to customers and similar activities dropped seriously behind, and the number of errors in brokers' records, as well as the time to trace and correct these errors, exacerbated the crisis.

"The difficulty that brokers and dealers experienced in keeping their records due to the volume of transactions and their thin capitalization caused many brokerage firms to declare bankruptcy and many investors to realize losses." Id. at 182.

Congress responded by passing the Securities Investor Protection Act of 1970, which directed the SEC to study the practices leading to the growing crisis in securities transfer. The SEC recommended discontinuing the physical movement of certificates and adopting a depository system. Congress then passed the Securities Acts Amendments of 1975, which directed the SEC to "use its authority under this chapter to end the physical movement of securities certificates in connection with the settlement among brokers and dealers of transactions in securities consummated by means of the mails or any means or instrumentalities of interstate commerce." In a resulting report, the SEC found that "registering securities in other than the name of the beneficial owner" was essential to establishing "a national system for the prompt and accurate clearance and settlement of securities transactions."

Thus was born the federal policy of immobilizing share certificates through a depository system. "Congress called for a more efficient process for comparison, clearing, and settlement in a national market system, and for the end of the physical movement of securities certificates in connection with the settlement of transactions among brokers and dealers." To comply, "[b]rokerages and banks created [depositories] to allow them to deposit certificates centrally (so-called 'jumbo certificates,' often representing tens or hundreds of thousands of shares) and leave them at rest."

In 1973, just after the paperwork crisis and with the federal writing on the wall, the members of the New York Stock Exchange created DTC to serve as a depository and clearing agency. Originally there were three regional depositories in addition to DTC: the Midwest Securities Depository Trust Company, which held through its nominee, Kray & Co.; the Pacific Securities Depository Trust Company, which held through its nominee, Pacific & Co; and the Philadelphia Depository Trust Company, which held through its nominee, Philadep & Co. "[I]n the 1990's DTC . . . assumed the activities of the [other] depositories." Today DTC is the world's largest securities depository and the only domestic depository. "DTC is owned by its 'participants,' which are the member organizations of the various national stock exchanges (e.g., State Street Bank, Merrill Lynch, Goldman Sachs & Co.)."

DTC has been estimated to hold "about three-quarters of [the] shares in publicly traded companies." "The shares of each company held by DTC are typically represented by only one or more 'immobilized' jumbo stock certificates held in DTC's vaults." "The immobilized jumbo certificates are the direct result of Section 17A(e) of the Exchange Act, in which Congress instructed the SEC to 'use its authority . . . to end the physical movement of securities certificates. . . .' "

The depository system is what enables public trading of securities to take place. In 2014, the NYSE reported average daily volume of approximately 1 billion shares and approximately 4 million separate trades. The failure of the certificate-based system to keep up with much lower trading volumes in the 1960s demonstrates that it cannot meet current demand. Without immobilization and DTC, "implementing a system to settle securities within five business days (T+5), much less today's norm of T+3 or the current goals of T+1 or T+0, would simply be impossible." Trading at current levels is only possible because of share immobilization and DTC.

Because of the federal policy of share immobilization, it is now Cede—not the ultimate beneficial owner and not the DTC-participant banks and brokers—that appears on the stock ledger of a Delaware corporation. Cede is typically the largest holder on the stock ledger of most publicly traded Delaware corporations. To preserve the pre-immobilization status quo—at least at the federal level—the SEC provided that for purposes of federal law, the custodial banks and brokers remain the record holders. Depositories are defined as "clearing agencies." The term "record holder" is defined as "any broker, dealer, voting trustee, bank, association or other entity that exercises fiduciary powers which holds securities of record in nominee name or otherwise or as a participant in a clearing agency registered pursuant to section 17A of the Act." The term "entity that exercises fiduciary powers" is similarly defined as "any entity that holds securities in nominee name or otherwise on behalf of a beneficial owner but does not include a clearing agency registered pursuant to section 17A of the Act or a broker or a dealer." Federal law thus looks through DTC when determining a corporation's record holders. For example, when determining whether an issuer has 500 or more record holders of a class of its equity securities such that it must register under 15 U.S.C. § 78l(g), DTC does not count as a single holder of record. Each DTC participant member counts as a holder of record.

The federal regulations also ensure that a corporation can easily find out the identities of the banks and brokers who hold shares through DTC. Federal regulations require that DTC "furnish a securities position listing promptly to each issuer whose securities are held in the name of the clearing agency or its nominee." The participant listing is known colloquially as the "Cede breakdown," and it identifies for a particular date the custodial banks and brokers that hold shares in fungible bulk as of that date along with the number of shares held. A Delaware corporation can obtain a Cede breakdown with ease. In 1981, this court noted that a Cede breakdown could be obtained in a matter of minutes. A Cede breakdown can now be obtained through DTC's website or by calling the DTC "Proxy Services Hotline." Issuers use the Cede breakdown to understand their stockholder profile, and proxy solicitors use it when advising clients. . . .

A publicly traded corporation cannot avoid going through DTC. Federal law requires that when submitting a matter for a stockholder vote, an issuer must send a broker search card at least twenty business days prior to the record date to any "broker, dealer, voting trustee, bank, association, or other entity that exercises fiduciary powers in nominee name" that the company "knows" is holding shares for beneficial owners. Rule

14a–13 provides that "[i]f the registrant's list of security holders indicates that some of its securities are registered in the name of a clearing agency registered pursuant to Section 17A of the Act (e.g., 'Cede & Co.,' nominee for Depository Trust Company), the registrant shall make appropriate inquiry of the clearing agency and thereafter of the participants in such clearing agency." An issuer cannot look only at its own records and treat Cede as a single, monolithic owner.[3]

2) STOCKHOLDER MEETINGS

Shareholders normally vote only at properly noticed and called shareholder meetings.[4] All statutes require that there be at least one shareholder meeting a year (called, logically enough, the annual meeting of shareholders). In addition, all statutes have some provision for so-called special meetings—i.e., meetings held between annual meetings to consider some extraordinary matter that cannot wait. Who is entitled to call a special meeting varies from state to state. Almost all state corporation laws allow the board to call a special meeting. MBCA § 7.02(a)(1) empowers the board of directors and any other person authorized by the articles or bylaws to call a special meeting. MBCA § 7.02(a)(2) empowers the holders of at least 10% of the voting shares to call a special meeting. The articles may specify a lower or higher percentage, but not to exceed, 25% of the voting power. In contrast, per DGCL § 211(d) special meetings may be called only by the board of directors and any other person authorized by the articles or bylaws.

DGCL § 222 requires that notice must be given no less than 10 days or more than 60 days before the meeting. The notice must in writing and specify: (1) the place the meeting will be held;[5] (2) the date and hour of the meeting, (3) the means of remote communications, if any; and (4) for special shareholder meetings, the purposes for which the meeting is called. MBCA § 7.05 is substantially similar.

WHAT'S THAT?

PROXY, Black's Law Dictionary (10th ed. 2014): "Someone who is authorized to act as a substitute for another; esp., in corporate law, a person who is authorized to vote another's stock shares."

Whether it is an annual or special meeting, most shareholders will not show up. Large corporations with thousands of shareholders frequently hold their shareholder meetings in

---

[3] In re Appraisal of Dell Inc., CV 9322-VCL, 2015 WL 4313206, at *4–7 (Del. Ch. July 13, 2015), as revised (July 30, 2015).

[4] A majority of states allow shareholders to act without a meeting by unanimous written consent. See, e.g., MBCA § 7.04. A substantial minority, including Delaware, permit shareholders to act by written consent even if the shareholders are not unanimous. See, e.g., DGCL § 228.

[5] DGCL § 211(a)(1) provides that, by default, the shareholder meeting should be held in the place provided in bylaws, but if no such place is specified, the meeting shall be held in the location determined by the board of directors.

small halls or even just a very large conference room. Most shareholders vote by proxy, which is the corporate law equivalent of absentee voting. Since the 1930s, proxy voting has been extensively regulated by the federal securities laws. Hence, many of the mechanics of shareholder voting are governed by federal rather than state law. Generally speaking, state law governs substantive aspects of shareholder voting, such as how many votes a shareholder gets, when they get to vote, and the types of questions on which they get to vote. Federal law governs the procedures by which shareholders vote and the disclosures to which shareholders are entitled.

Whether shareholders will vote in person or by proxy, statutory notice and quorum requirements must be satisfied if their action is to be valid. MBCA § 7.05(a), for example, requires no less than 10 but no more than 60 days' notice for both annual and special meetings. Under MBCA § 7.05(b), notice of an annual meeting need not state the purposes for which the meeting is called, although the federal proxy rules mandate such notice. Under MBCA § 7.05(c), by contrast, only those matters specified in the notice may be taken up at a special meeting. As discussed below, however, special optional notice rules have developed to deal with the problem of so-called "empty voting."

The Model Act's default quorum is a majority of the shares entitled to vote, although the articles of incorporation can specify either a higher or lower figure.[6] Although there is some case law to the contrary, the Model Act effectively precludes a shareholder from "breaking the quorum" by leaving the meeting. If a shareholder's stock is represented at the meeting in person or by proxy for any reason, that shareholder's stock is deemed to be present for quorum purposes for the remainder of the meeting.[7]

3) VOTING RIGHTS

Virtually all state corporate codes adopt one vote per common share as the default rule, but allow corporations to depart from the norm by adopting appropriate provisions in their organic documents. Firms have devised at least three variants on the traditional model, each of which in some way repackages the bundle of rights associated with common stock: non-voting stock, dual class stock in which each class has different voting rights, and common stock having only voting rights. All of the major stock exchanges, however, have adopted listing standards severely restricting the use of such variants and they therefore long were quite rare. In recent years, however, a few prominent firms—especially in the tech industry—

---

[6]   MBCA § 7.25(a). Delaware law is similar, except it forbids the articles from setting a quorum of less than one-third the shares entitled to vote. DGCL § 216.

[7]   See MBCA § 7.25(b); but see, e.g., Levisa Oil Corp. v. Quigley, 234 S.E.2d 257 (Va.1977) (shareholder may break quorum by departing meeting); see also Textron, Inc. v. American Woolen Co., 122 F.Supp. 305 (D.Mass.1954) (shareholder present before a quorum is established may depart and, if so, may not be counted towards a quorum).

have used dual class structures so as to ensure that their founder retain control after the corporation goes public.

Subject to the special rules governing election of directors and group voting, which are discussed in subsequent sections, MBCA § 7.25(c) provides that "action on a matter . . . is approved if the votes cast . . . favoring the action exceed the votes cast opposing the action." In contrast, DGCL § 216 states that "the affirmative vote of the majority of shares present in person or represented by proxy at the meeting and entitled to vote on the subject matter shall be the act of the stockholders." The distinction between the two formulations is subtle but significant. Suppose there are 1000 shares entitled to vote, 800 of which are represented at the meeting either in person or by proxy, and which are voted as follows:

In Favor	399
Opposed	398
Abstain	3

Under the MBCA, the motion carries, as more shares were voted in favor of the motion than against it. Under the Delaware statute, however, a majority of the shares present at the meeting—401—must be voted in favor of the motion for it to carry, and this motion therefore fails. In effect, Delaware treats abstentions as no votes, while the MBCA ignores them.

The articles of incorporation may require a higher vote than the default statutory minimum, either across the board or on specified issues. State corporation laws also typically provide that certain extraordinary actions require approval by a higher vote. MBCA § 10.03 requires, for example, that amendments to the articles of incorporation be approved by a majority of the shares entitled to vote. Again, suppose there are 1000 shares entitled to vote, 800 of which are represented at the meeting either in person or by proxy. In order for the amendment to be adopted, 501 shares must be voted in favor. The same vote is required for approval of a merger (per § 11.04) or sale of all or substantially all the corporation's assets (per § 12.02). Delaware law is similar.

4) ELECTION OF DIRECTORS

One of the curiosities of the corporate electoral system is that it traditionally did not provide for a straight up or down—for or against—vote for directors. Instead, shareholders typically are given three options: vote for all of the nominees for director, withhold support for all of them, and withhold support from specified directors.

Withholding support from a director candidate is not the same as a vote against that candidate. Delaware General Corporation Law § 216(3) provides: "Directors shall be elected by a plurality of the votes of the shares present in person or represented by proxy at the meeting and entitled to vote on the election of directors." The Comments to Model Business Corporation Act § 7.28(a), which also uses a "plurality" standard, explain that: "A 'plurality' means that the individuals with the largest number of votes are elected as directors up to the maximum number of directors to be chosen at the election." Say the firm had 10 vacancies to be filled and there were exactly ten candidates. Hence, an unpopular director would be reelected even if holders of a majority of the shares withheld their votes from him.

In 2006, however, Delaware amended the statutory provisions on director election to accommodate majority voting. Section 141(b) of the Delaware General Corporation Law was amended by adding the following sentences: "A resignation [of a director] is effective when the resignation is delivered unless the resignation specifies a later effective date or an effective date determined upon the happening of an event or events. A resignation which is conditioned upon the director failing to receive a specified vote for reelection as a director may provide that it is irrevocable." This amendment was designed to validate bylaws that had been voluntarily adopted by a number of companies, most notably Pfizer, pursuant to which directors who received a majority of withhold "votes" are required to submit their resignation to the board.[8]

Section 216 was amended at the same time by adding the following sentence: "A bylaw amendment adopted by stockholders which specifies the votes that shall be necessary for the election of directors shall not be further amended or repealed by the board of directors." This amendment validates bylaw provisions requiring that a director receive a majority vote in order to be elected. Under such provisions, it is now possible to vote "against" a director. The MBCA has adopted a similar provision authorizing use of a majority vote rule on an opt-in basis. As of late 2006, more than 250 companies—including 31% of Fortune 500 firms—had adopted some form of majority voting bylaw.[9]

---

[8]   One question presented by these so-called Pfizer or plurality-plus policies is whether the board retains authority to turn down the resignation of a director who fails to get the requisite majority vote. In City of Westland Police & Fire Retirement System v. Axcelis Technologies, Inc., 1 A.3d 281 (Del. 2010), the Delaware Supreme Court confirmed that the board has substantial discretion to do just that. Axcelis Technologies had a seven-member board staggered into three classes. In 2008, all three of the incumbent directors up for reelection failed to receive a majority of the votes cast. Pursuant to the company's plurality-plus policy, all three submitted their resignations. The board rejected all three resignations. A shareholder initiated a § 220 request to inspect the relevant books and records of the company preparatory to filing a derivative suit challenging the board's decision. In order to prevent shareholders from conducting fishing expeditions, Delaware courts will grant such inspection requests only where there is a credible basis from which to infer that some wrongdoing may have occurred. In acknowledging that § 220 requests sometimes can be meritorious in this context, the Court observed that "the question arises whether the directors, as fiduciaries, made a disinterested, informed business judgment that the best interests of the corporation require the continued service of these directors, or whether the Board had some different, ulterior motivation." It thus seems fair to infer that the business judgment rule will be the standard by which courts evaluate board decisions under such policies.

[9]   William J. Sjostrom, Jr. & Young Sang Kim, Majority Voting for the Election of Directors, 40 Conn. L. Rev. 459 (2007).

Critics of majority voting schemes contend that failed elections can have a destabilizing effect on the corporation. Selecting and vetting a director candidate is a long and expensive process, which has become even more complicated by the new stock exchange listing standards defining director independence. Suppose, however, that the shareholders voted out the only qualified financial expert sitting on the audit committee. The corporation immediately would be in violation of its obligations under those standards.

Critics also complain that qualified individuals would be deterred from service. The enhanced liability and increased workload imposed by Sarbanes-Oxley and related regulatory and legal developments has made it much harder for firms to recruit qualified outside directors. The risk of being singled out by shareholders for a no vote presumably will make board service even less attractive, especially in light of the concern board members demonstrate for their reputations.

Classified (a.k.a. Staggered) Boards. Typically, the entire board of directors is elected annually, whether by standard or cumulative voting, to a one-year term.[10] Alternatively, however, the articles of incorporation or bylaws may provide for a classified or staggered board of directors.[11] In this model, the board is divided into two or three classes. In a board with two classes of directors, the members serve two-year terms so that only half the board is up for election in any given year. In a board with three classes, directors serve three year terms and only a third of the board is up for election annually.

Classified boards have significant change of control implications and are often used as a defense against proxy contests and corporate takeovers. Under a staggered board with three classes, for example, the shareholders must wait two annual meeting cycles before they can replace a majority of the board. In order for the classified board to actually delay a change of control, of course, the classification scheme must be protected from the possibility that the shareholders will remove the directors without cause or pack the board with new appointments. Classified board provisions in articles of incorporation therefore typically are coupled with additional terms reserving to the board the sole right to determine the number of directors and to fill any vacancies. If permitted by state law, drafters of a classified board scheme also limit or abolish the right of shareholders to call a special shareholders meeting or to remove directors without cause.

Cumulative Voting. Under the standard voting rules, a majority shareholder can elect the entire board of directors. This is why prospective buyers place a higher value on control blocks vis-à-vis shares

---

[10]   Under MBCA § 8.05(b), the directors' term in office technically expires at the next annual shareholders' meeting following their election. Under DGCL § 141(b), a director's term continues until his successor is elected.

[11]   See, e.g., DGCL § 141(d). Curiously, MBCA § 8.06 permits staggered boards only if there are nine or more directors.

owned by noncontrolling shareholders. Cumulative voting provides an alternative mechanism for electing the board of directors that can assure board representation for the minority. An example will be helpful.

Assume ABC Corporation has 3 shareholders: A, who owns 250 shares; B, who owns 300 shares; C, who owns 650.[12] The bylaws specify a four-member board of directors. Under standard voting procedures, directors are elected by a plurality of the votes cast at the meeting on a one share-one vote basis. Suppose, for example, that each of A, B and C are supporting four different candidates for director. The following will result:

> **FYI**
>
> You can think of director balloting as voting for a slate: Each share entitles its owner to cast one vote towards determining which slate will be elected. Alternatively, you can think of each director position as a seat that can be filled by only one person. Each share entitles its owner to cast one vote towards determining the occupant of that seat.

A-1: 250 for	B-1: 300 for	C-1: 650 for; elected
A-2: 250 for	B-2: 300 for	C-2: 650 for; elected
A-3: 250 for	B-3: 300 for	C-3: 650 for; elected
A-4: 250 for	B-4: 300 for	C-4: 650 for; elected

Consequently, C elects the entire board of directors. This is of vital importance, because directors make most corporate decisions. In this example, the board will be composed entirely of people nominated by C.

In cumulative voting, by contrast, the number of votes each shareholder may cast is determined by multiplying the number of shares owned by the number of director positions up for election. Each shareholder then may concentrate his votes by casting all of his votes for one candidate (or distributing his votes among two or more candidates).[13] The directors receiving the highest number of votes will be elected. In this example, A has 1000 votes available to be cast; B has 1200 votes; and C has 2600 votes. A and B each nominate themselves and cast all of their votes for themselves on their respective ballots. A receives 1000 votes. B receives 1200 votes. C nominates herself and her friends C–1, C–2, and C–3. But C cannot cast her votes so as to elect all four of her nominees. C might, for example, cast 1100 votes for herself and 1000 votes for C–1. Both C and C–1 will be elected. Unfortunately for C, however, she has only 500 votes left to divide between C–2 and C–3. Accordingly, they cannot be elected.

---

[12] The example is taken from Michael P. Dooley, Fundamentals of Corporation Law 376 (1995).

[13] See, e.g., MBCA § 7.28(c).

The following formula is used to determine the number of shares a shareholder needs to own to elect a specific number of directors under cumulative voting:

$$X = \frac{[(DN \times TN)]}{N+1} + 1$$

Where N is the total number of directors to be elected; DN is the number of directors a shareholder wishes to elect; TN is the total number of voting shares outstanding; and X is the number of shares needed to elect the desired number of directors. If you solve this equation for directors DN = 4; you will find that C needs 961 shares in order to elect all 4 directors. Notice that even if B and C cumulated their votes together, they could not prevent A from electing at least one director. If you work out all the permutations, you will find that in this hypothetical A can elect one director, B can elect one, and C can elect two. Unless all three agree, no combination of shareholders can elect all four directors.

An alternative formula may be used to calculate the number of directors a shareholder can elect by cumulating her votes:

$$N = \frac{(X-1)*(D+1)}{S}$$

Where N is the number of directors that can be elected; X is the number of shares the shareholder owns; D is the total number of directors to be elected, and S is the total number of outstanding shares.

Cumulative voting was very much in vogue in the late 1800s. A number of states adopted mandatory cumulative voting as part of their state constitutions. Others did the same by statute. During the last few decades, however, cumulative voting in public corporations has increasingly fallen out of favor. Opponents of cumulative voting argue it produces an adversarial board and results in critical decisions being made in private meetings held by the majority faction before the formal board meeting. Today, most states—including Delaware and MBCA jurisdictions—allow cumulative voting on an opt-in basis. In other words, standard voting is the default rule in these states but the corporation may provide for cumulative voting in its articles of incorporation. In all states, of course, cumulative voting is limited to the election of directors—shareholders are not allowed to cumulate votes as to other types of shareholder decisions.

QUESTIONS

1.   Jessica owns 1,000 of Acme Corporation's 10,000 outstanding shares of common stock. There are ten directors to be elected at the next annual shareholder meeting. What is the maximum number of directors, if any, Jessica may elect at the next annual meeting assuming she properly cumulates her shares and gets no votes from other shareholders?

2.   In most states, cumulative voting is an opt-in rule; in other words, a corporation will only use cumulative voting if its articles of incorporation specifically so provide. In some states, however, cumulative voting is the default rule on an opt-out basis. In other words, cumulative voting applies unless a corporation's articles of incorporation provide for straight voting. In some, most notably California, only public corporations can opt out of cumulative voting. Which rule makes the most policy sense?

5) REMOVAL OF DIRECTORS AND FILLING BOARD VACANCIES

DGCL § 141(k)

Any director or the entire board of directors may be removed, with or without cause, by the holders of a majority of the shares then entitled to vote at an election of directors, except as follows:

(1) Unless the certificate of incorporation otherwise provides, in the case of a corporation whose board is classified as provided in subsection (d) of this section, stockholders may effect such removal only for cause; or

(2) In the case of a corporation having cumulative voting, if less than the entire board is to be removed, no director may be removed without cause if the votes cast against such director's removal would be sufficient to elect such director if then cumulatively voted at an election of the entire board of directors, or, if there be classes of directors, at an election of the class of directors of which such director is a part.

Whenever the holders of any class or series are entitled to elect 1 or more directors by the certificate of incorporation, this subsection shall apply, in respect to the removal without cause of a director or directors so elected, to the vote of the holders of the outstanding shares of that class or series and not to the vote of the outstanding shares as a whole.

DGCL § 223

(a) Unless otherwise provided in the certificate of incorporation or bylaws:

(1) Vacancies and newly created directorships resulting from any increase in the authorized number of directors elected by all of the stockholders having the right to vote as a single class may be filled by a majority of the directors then in office, although less than a quorum, or by a sole remaining director;

(2) Whenever the holders of any class or classes of stock or series thereof are entitled to elect 1 or more directors by the certificate of incorporation, vacancies and newly created directorships of such class or classes or series may be filled by a majority of the directors elected by such class or classes or series thereof then in office, or by a sole remaining director so elected.

If at any time, by reason of death or resignation or other cause, a corporation should have no directors in office, then any officer or any stockholder or an executor, administrator, trustee or guardian of a stockholder, or other fiduciary entrusted with like responsibility for the person or estate of a stockholder, may call a special meeting of stockholders in accordance with the certificate of incorporation or the bylaws, or may apply to the Court of Chancery for a decree summarily ordering an election as provided in § 211 or § 215 of this title.

(b) In the case of a corporation the directors of which are divided into classes, any directors chosen under subsection (a) of this section shall hold office until the next election of the class for which such directors shall have been chosen, and until their successors shall be elected and qualified.

(c) If, at the time of filling any vacancy or any newly created directorship, the directors then in office shall constitute less than a majority of the whole board (as constituted immediately prior to any such increase), the Court of Chancery may, upon application of any stockholder or stockholders holding at least 10 percent of the voting stock at the time outstanding having the right to vote for such directors, summarily order an election to be held to fill any such vacancies or newly created directorships, or to replace the directors chosen by the directors then in office as aforesaid, which election shall be governed by § 211 or § 215 of this title as far as applicable.

(d) Unless otherwise provided in the certificate of incorporation or bylaws, when 1 or more directors shall resign from the board, effective at a future date, a majority of the directors then in office, including those who have so resigned, shall have power to fill such vacancy or vacancies, the vote thereon to take effect when such resignation or resignations shall become effective, and each director so chosen shall hold office as provided in this section in the filling of other vacancies.

DGCL § 225(c)

If 1 or more directors has been convicted of a felony in connection with the duties of such director or directors to the corporation, or if there has been a prior judgment on the merits by a court of competent jurisdiction that 1 or more directors has committed a breach of the duty of loyalty in connection with the duties of such director or directors to that corporation, then, upon application by the corporation, or derivatively in the right of the corporation by any stockholder, in a subsequent action brought for such purpose, the Court of Chancery may remove from office such director or directors if the Court determines that the director or directors did not act in good faith in performing the acts resulting in the prior conviction or judgment and judicial removal is necessary to avoid irreparable harm to the corporation. In connection with such removal, the Court may make such orders as are necessary to effect such removal. In any such application, service of copies of the application upon the registered agent of the corporation shall be deemed to be service upon the corporation and upon the director or directors whose removal is sought; and the registered agent shall forward immediately a copy of the application to the corporation and to such director or directors, in a postpaid, sealed, registered letter addressed to such corporation and such director or directors at their post office addresses last known to the registered agent or furnished to the registered agent by the applicant. The Court may make such order respecting further or other notice of such application as it deems proper under the circumstances.

MBCA § 8.08

(a) The shareholders may remove one or more directors with or without cause unless the articles of incorporation provide that directors may be removed only for cause.

(b) If a director is elected by a voting group of shareholders, only the shareholders of that voting group may participate in the vote to remove that director.

(c) A director may be removed if the number of votes cast to remove exceeds the number of votes cast not to remove the director, except to the extent the articles of incorporation or bylaws require a greater number; provided that if cumulative voting is authorized, a director may not be removed if, in the case of a meeting, the number of votes sufficient to elect the director under cumulative voting is voted against removal and, if action is taken by less than unanimous written consent, voting shareholders entitled to the number of votes sufficient to elect the director under cumulative voting do not consent to the removal.

(d)   A director may be removed by the shareholders only at a meeting called for the purpose of removing the director and the meeting notice must state that removal of the director is a purpose of the meeting.

MBCA § 8.10

(a)   Unless the articles of incorporation provide otherwise, if a vacancy occurs of a board of directors, including a vacancy resulting from an increase in the number of directors:

(1)   the shareholders may fill the vacancy;

(2)   the board of directors may fill the vacancy; or

(3)   if the directors remaining in office constitute fewer than a quorum of the board, they may fill the vacancy by the affirmative vote of a majority of all the directors remaining in office.

(b)   If the vacant office was held by a director elected by a voting group of shareholders, only the holders of shares of that voting group are entitled to vote to fill the vacancy if it is filled by the shareholders, and only the directors elected by that voting group are entitled to fill the vacancy if it is filled by the directors.

(c)   A vacancy that will occur at a specific later date (by reason of a resignation effective at a later date under section 8.07(b) or otherwise) may be filled before the vacancy occurs but the new director may not take office until the vacancy occurs.

Auer v. Dressel

118 N.E.2d 590 (N.Y.1954)

This . . . proceeding was brought by class A stockholders of appellant R. Hoe & Co., Inc., for an order in the nature of mandamus to compel the president of Hoe to comply with a positive duty imposed on him by the corporation's by-laws. Section 2 of article I of those by-laws says that 'It shall be the duty of President to call a special meeting whenever requested in writing so to do, by stockholders owning a majority of the capital stock entitled to vote at such meeting'. On October 16, 1953, petitioners submitted to the president written requests for a special meeting of class A stockholders, which writings were signed in the names of the holders of record of slightly more than 55% of the class A stock. The president failed to call the meeting and, after waiting a week, the petitioners brought the present proceeding. . . . There was no discretion in this corporate officer as to whether or not to call a meeting when a demand therefor was put before him by owners of the required number of shares. The important right of stockholders to have such meetings called will be of little practical value if corporate management can ignore the requests, force the stockholders to commence legal proceedings, and then, by purely formal denials, put the stockholders to lengthy and expensive litigation, to establish facts as to stockholdings which are peculiarly within the knowledge of the corporate officers. . . .

The petition was opposed on the . . . ground that none of the four purposes for which petitioners wished the meeting called was a proper one for such a class A stockholders' meeting. Those four stated purposes were these: (A) to vote, upon a resolution indorsing the administration of petitioner Joseph L. Auer, who had been removed as president by the directors, and demanding that he be reinstated as such president; (B) voting upon a proposal to amend the charter and by-laws to provide that vacancies on the board of directors, arising from the removal of a director by stockholders or by resignation of a director against whom charges have been preferred, may be filled, for the unexpired term, by the stockholders only of the class theretofore represented by the director so removed or so resigned; (C) voting upon a proposal that the stockholders hear certain charges preferred, in the requests, against four of the directors, determine whether the conduct of such directors or any of them was inimical to the corporation and, if so, to vote upon their removal and vote for the election of their successors; and (D) voting upon a proposal to amend the by-laws so as to provide that half of the total number of directors in office and, in any event, not less than one third of the whole authorized number of directors constitute a quorum of the directors.

The Hoe certificate of incorporation provides for eleven directors, of whom the class A stockholders, more than a majority of whom join in this petition, elect nine and the common stockholders elect two. The obvious purpose of the meeting here sought to be called (aside from the indorsement and reinstatement of former president Auer) is to hear charges against four of the class A directors, to remove them if the charges be proven, to amend the by-laws so that the successor directors be elected by the class A stockholders, and further to amend the by-laws so that an effective quorum of directors will be made up of no fewer than half of the directors in office and no fewer than one third of the whole authorized number of directors. No reason appears why the class A stockholders should not be allowed to vote on any or all of those proposals.

The stockholders, by expressing their approval of Mr. Auer's conduct as president and their demand that he be put back in that office, will not be able, directly, to effect that change in officers, but there is nothing invalid in their so expressing themselves and thus putting on notice the directors who will stand for election at the annual meeting. As to purpose

(B), that is, amending the charter and by-laws to authorize the stockholders to fill vacancies as to class A directors who have been removed on charges or who have resigned, it seems to be settled law that the stockholders who are empowered to elect directors have the inherent power to remove them for cause . . . . Of course, . . . there must be the service of specific charges, adequate notice and full opportunity of meeting the accusations, but there is no present showing of any lack of any of those in this instance. Since these particular stockholders have the right to elect nine directors and to remove them on proven charges, it is not inappropriate that they should use their further power to amend the by-laws to elect the successors of such directors as shall be removed after hearing, or who shall resign pending hearing. Quite pertinent at this point is *Rogers v. Hill,* 289 U.S. 582, 589, 53 S.Ct. 731, 734, 77 L.Ed. 1385, which made light of an argument that stockholders, by giving power to the directors to make by-laws, had lost their own power to make them . . . . Such a change in the by-laws, dealing with class A directors only, has no effect on the voting rights of the common stockholders, which rights have to do with the selection of the remaining two directors only. True, the certificate of incorporation authorizes the board of directors to remove any director on charges, but we do not consider that provision as an abdication by the stockholders of their own traditional, inherent power to remove their own directors. Rather, it provides an additional method. Were that not so, the stockholders might find themselves without effective remedy in a case where a majority of the directors were accused of wrongdoing and, obviously, would be unwilling to remove themselves from office.

. . .

There is urged upon us the impracticability and unfairness of constituting the numerous stockholders a tribunal to hear charges made by themselves, and the incongruity of letting the stockholders hear and pass on those charges by proxy. Such questions are really not before us at all on this appeal. The charges here are not, on their face, frivolous or inconsequential, and all that we are holding as to the charges is that a meeting may be held to deal with them. . . .

Campbell v. Loew's, Inc.

134 A.2d 852 (Del. Ch. 1957)

This is the decision on plaintiff's request for a preliminary injunction to restrain the holding of a stockholders' meeting or alternatively to prevent the meeting from considering certain matters or to prevent the voting of certain proxies. Certain other relief is also requested.

. . . Two factions have been fighting for control of Loew's. One faction is headed by Joseph Tomlinson (hereafter 'Tomlinson faction') while the other is headed by the President of Loew's, Joseph Vogel (hereafter 'Vogel faction'). At the annual meeting of stockholders last February a compromise was reached by which each nominated six directors and they in turn nominated a thirteenth or neutral director. But the battle had only begun. Passing by much of the controversy, we come to the July 17–18 period of this year when two of the six Vogel directors and the thirteenth or neutral director resigned. A quorum is seven.

On the 19th of July the Tomlinson faction asked that a directors' meeting be called for July 30 to consider, inter alia, the problem of filling director vacancies. On the eve of this meeting one of the Tomlinson directors resigned. This left five Tomlinson directors and four Vogel directors in office. Only the five Tomlinson directors attended the July 30 meeting. They purported to fill two of the director vacancies and to take other action. This Court has now ruled that for want of a quorum the two directors were not validly elected and the subsequent action taken at that meeting was invalid.

On July 29, the day before the noticed directors' meeting, Vogel, as president, sent out a notice calling a stockholders' meeting for September 12 for the following purposes:

1.   to fill director vacancies.

2.   to amend the by-laws to increase the number of the board from 13 to 19; to increase the quorum from 7 to 10 and to elect six additional directors.

3.   to remove Stanley Meyer and Joseph Tomlinson as directors and to fill such vacancies.

. . .

Plaintiff contends that the president had no authority in fact to call a special meeting of stockholders to act upon policy matters which have not been defined by the board of directors. [The court rejected this argument.]

. . .

Plaintiff next argues that the shareholders of a Delaware corporation have no power to remove directors from office even for cause and thus the call for that purpose is invalid.

. . . I believe that the stockholders have the power to remove a director for cause. This power must be implied when we consider that otherwise a director who is guilty of the worst sort of violation of his duty could nevertheless remain on the board. It is hardly to be believed that a director who is disclosing the corporation's trade secrets to a competitor would be immune from removal by the stockholders. Other examples, such as embezzlement of corporate funds, etc., come readily to mind.

. . .

I therefore conclude that as a matter of Delaware corporation law the stockholders do have the power to remove directors for cause. I need not and do not decide whether the stockholders can by appropriate charter or by-law provision deprive themselves of this right.

... [I]t is certainly true that when the shareholders attempt to remove a director for cause, "* * * there must be the service of specific charges, adequate notice and full opportunity of meeting the accusation * * *". See *Auer v. Dressel* [306 N.Y. 427, 118 N.E.2d 593], above. While it involved an invalid attempt by directors to remove a fellow director for cause, nevertheless, this same general standard was recognized in *Bruch v. National Guarantee Credit Corp.* [13 Del.Ch. 180, 116 A. 741], above. The Chancellor said that the power of removal could not 'be exercised in an arbitrary manner. The accused director would be entitled to be heard in his own defense'.

    . . .

Matters for stockholder consideration need not be conducted with the same formality as judicial proceedings. The proxy statement [sent out in conjunction with the call for the special meeting] specifically recites that the two directors are sought to be removed for the reasons stated in the president's accompanying letter. Both directors involved received copies of the letter. Under the circumstances I think it must be said that the two directors involved were served with notice of the charges against them. It is true, as plaintiff says, that the notice and the proxy statement failed to contain a specific statement of charges. But as indicated, I believe the accompanying letter was sufficient compliance with the notice requirement.

... I do not believe the material sent out had to advise the stockholders that the accused must be afforded an opportunity to defend the charges before the stockholders voted. Such an opportunity had to be afforded as a matter of law and the failure to so advise them did not affect the necessity for compliance with the law. Thus, no prejudice is shown.

I next consider plaintiff's contention that the charges against the two directors do not constitute 'cause' as a matter of law. It would take too much space to narrate in detail the contents on the president's letter. I must therefore give my summary of its charges. First of all, it charges that the two directors (Tomlinson and Meyer) failed to cooperate with Vogel in his announced program for rebuilding the company; that their purpose has been to put themselves in control; that they made baseless accusations against him and other management personnel and attempted to divert him from his normal duties as president by bombarding him with correspondence containing unfounded charges and other similar acts; that they moved into the company's building, accompanied by lawyers and accountants, and immediately proceeded upon a planned scheme of harassment. They called for many records, some going back twenty years, and were rude to the personnel.

Tomlinson sent daily letters to the directors making serious charges directly and by means of innuendos and misinterpretations.

Are the foregoing charges, if proved, legally sufficient to justify the ouster of the two directors by the stockholders? I am satisfied that a charge that the directors desired to take over control of the corporation is not a reason for their ouster. Standing alone, it is a perfectly legitimate objective which is a part of the very fabric of corporate existence. Nor is a charge of lack of cooperation a legally sufficient basis for removal for cause.

The next charge is that these directors, in effect, engaged in a calculated plan of harassment to the detriment of the corporation. Certainly a director may examine books, ask questions, etc., in the discharge of his duty, but a point can be reached when his actions exceed the call of duty and become deliberately obstructive. In such a situation, if his actions constitute a real burden on the corporation then the stockholders are entitled to relief. The charges in this area made by the Vogel letter are legally sufficient to justify the stockholders in voting to remove such directors. In so concluding I of course express no opinion as to the truth of the charges.

I therefore conclude that the charge of 'a planned scheme of harassment' as detailed in the letter constitutes a justifiable legal basis for removing a director.

I next consider whether the directors sought to be removed have been given a reasonable opportunity to be heard by the stockholders on the charges made.

. . .

There seems to be an absence of cases detailing the appropriate procedure for submitting a question of director removal for cause for stockholder consideration. I am satisfied, however, that to the extent the matter is to be voted upon by the use of proxies, such proxies may be solicited only after the accused directors are afforded an opportunity to present their case to the stockholders. This means, in my opinion, that an opportunity must be provided such directors to present their defense to the stockholders by a statement which must accompany or precede the initial solicitation of proxies seeking authority to vote for the removal of such director for cause. If not provided then such proxies may not be voted for removal. And the corporation has a duty to see that this opportunity is given the directors at its expense. Admittedly, no such opportunity was given the two directors involved. Indeed, the corporation admittedly refused to supply them with a stockholders' list.

To require anything less than the foregoing is to deprive the stockholders of the opportunity to consider the case made by both sides before voting and would make a mockery of the requirement that a director sought to be removed for cause is entitled to an opportunity to be heard before the stockholders vote. . . .

NOTES AND QUESTIONS

1.   In *Rohe v. Reliance Training Network, Inc.,*[14] the court held that:

[DGCL §] 141(k) makes clear that the directors of RTN may be removed with or without cause by a majority of the shares of the company. Section 141(k) provides no limitation on the right of stockholders to remove a member of a non-classified board. Like the right to elect directors, Delaware law considers the right to remove directors to be a fundamental element of stockholder authority.

As a result, . . . the stockholders' right to remove directors could not be impaired by either the certificate or the bylaws.[15]

2.   Also in *Rohe,* the court observed that, "by negative implication [from § 141(k)], directors do not have the authority to remove other directors.[16] Likewise, in *Ross Systems Corp. v. Ross,*[17] the court stated that "[t]he only persons empowered to remove a director are the corporation's shareholders." In contrast, a few state corporation law statutes authorize the board to remove one of its members for cause.[18]

If a board thought one or more of its members should be removed, what can the board do, if anything, to effect that result?

PROBLEMS

1.   The board of directors wishes to remove Dave Director from the board. They have no valid reason for doing so. May they do so anyway?

2.   Same facts as #1, except that Dave's fellow directors do not wish to remove him. Could the corporation's shareholders remove Dave over the objections of Dave's fellow directors, even if they give no reason for doing so?

3.   Dan Director has a pattern of misfeasance. He is tardy or absent from many board meetings. He is rarely prepared for those meetings he does attend. He contributes little to discussions. He has made numerous errors in a variety of contexts. Dan's fellow directors are fed up. They wish to remove him. Can they?

4.   Same facts as # 3, except that Dan's fellow directors do not wish to remove him. Could the corporation's shareholders remove Dan over the objections of Dan's fellow directors?

5.   Same facts as #3. Could a court order Dan's removal at the request of either the board or the shareholders?

6.   Doris Director has committed several malfeasances. She padded expense accounts. She was a silent partner in a business acquired by the

---

[14]   2000 WL 1038190 (Del. Ch.).

[15]   Id. at *11.

[16]   Id. at *11 n.30.

[17]   1993 WL 49778 at *17 (Del. Ch.).

[18]   See, e.g., Mass. Gen. L., tit. XXII, chap. 156B, § 51(c) (any director, and any officer elected by the stockholders, may be removed from his office for cause by vote of a majority of the directors then in office).

corporation, which fact was not disclosed prior to the sale. Could a court order Doris' removal at the request of either the board or the shareholders?

6) DIRECTOR RESIGNATION

DGCL § 141(b) provides that:

Each director shall hold office until such director's successor is elected and qualified or until such director's earlier resignation or removal. Any director may resign at any time upon notice given in writing or by electronic transmission to the corporation. A resignation is effective when the resignation is delivered unless the resignation specifies a later effective date or an effective date determined upon the happening of an event or events.

The American Bar Association's authoritative Corporate Director's Guidebook recommends that:

If, after a thorough discussion, a director disagrees with any significant action the board is taking, the director should consider abstaining or voting against the proposal. The director should also consider requesting that the abstention or dissent be recorded in the meeting's minutes. Except in unusual circumstances, taking such a position should not cause a director to consider resigning. Resignations should be considered if a director believes that management is not dealing with the directors, the shareholders, or the public in good faith or that the information being disclosed by the corporation is inadequate, incomplete, or incorrect and the director is unable to convince the board to take action. Directors may also consider resigning when they feel their point of view is being disregarded entirely. Public corporations are required to disclose director resignations in an SEC filing, and this disclosure, like others, should be done in consultation with legal advisors.[19]

An earlier edition of the Guidebook stated that:

If, after a thorough discussion, a director disagrees with any significant action proposed to be taken by the board, the director may vote against the proposal and request that the dissent be recorded in the meeting's minutes. Except in unusual circumstances, taking such a position should not cause a director to consider resigning. However, if a director believes that information being disclosed by the corporation is inadequate, incomplete or incorrect, or that management is not dealing with the directors, the shareholders or the public in good faith, the director should first encourage that corrective action be taken. If that request is not satisfied or the problem

---

[19]   The Corporate Laws Committee, ABA Section of Business Law, Corporate Director's Guidebook—Sixth Edition, 66 Bus. Law. 975, 1011–12 (2011).

continues, the director should encourage the board to replace management and, if such a change does not occur, the director should resign.[20]

In *Shocking Technologies, Inc. v. Michael*,[21] the court held that:

> First, fair debate may be an important aspect of board performance. A board majority may not muzzle a minority board member simply because it does not like what she may be saying. Second, criticism of the conduct of a board majority does not necessarily equate with criticism of the corporation and its mission. The majority may be managing the business and affairs of the corporation, but a dissident board member has significant freedom to challenge the majority's decisions and to share her concerns with other shareholders. On the other hand, internal disagreement will not generally allow a dissident to release confidential corporate information.

In *Wechsler v. Squadron, Ellenoff, Plesent & Sheinfeld, LLP*,[22] the court held that:

> Can a director of a public corporation who believes that the company is engaged in ongoing securities fraud "blow the whistle" by disclosing to the SEC information protected by the company's attorney-client privilege, where the company's Board has not waived the privilege? As a matter of public policy, the Court holds that the answer is yes, although the company could sue the whistle-blowing director for breach of fiduciary duty if such disclosure were not in the company's best interest.

PROBLEMS

1.   Donna Director joined the board of directors of Liberty Starters Corporation, a Delaware corporation, in October 20XX.[23] Liberty had been formed a year earlier to manufacture 48-volt automotive starter motors, which had come into demand for use in luxury hybrid automobiles. The company had hired employees, raised capital, rented a production facility, and leased equipment. But the company had not yet begun production. Donna became aware that the production delay was being caused by the incompetence of the factory manager and personal clashes between the chairman of the board and the chief executive officer. She also learned that one of the disagreements between the chairman and CEO arose out of the latter's refusal to fire the factory manager. Donna raised the issue at several successive meetings of the board of directors, but the other directors dismissed her concerns as overwrought and premature.

---

[20]   The Corporate Laws Committee, ABA Section of Business Law, Corporate Director's Guidebook—Third Edition, 56 Bus. Law. 1571, 1589 (2001).

[21]   2012 WL 4482838 (De. Ch. 2012).

[22]   994 F. Supp. 202, 204 (S.D.N.Y. 1998).

[23]   This problem is loosely based on Barnes v. Andrews, 298 F. 614 (S.D.N.Y. 1924).

    A.   Continue raising the issue at board meetings until a majority of the directors agree to take action.

    B.   Inform the company's principal shareholders.

    C.   Inform the company's principal creditors.

    D.   Resign from the board of directors.

    E.   Resign from the board of directors and publicly criticize the company's board and management.

What should Donna do?

    2.   The board of directors of Reinsurance Capital, Inc., a public corporation listed on NASDAQ, consists of Charles Pritchard, William Pritchard, and Deborah Director.[24] Deborah discovers that Charles and William were misappropriating funds from the company. The company's periodic disclosure filings fraudulently fail to disclose their misconduct. Charles and William reject her demands that they return the funds to the company. Deborah is considering a number of possible actions:

    A.   Notify NASDAQ and the SEC of the misappropriation and fraudulent filings.

    B.   Resign from the board of directors.

    C.   Resign from the board of directors and publicly criticize Charles and William.

    D.   Resign from the board of directors and notifying NASDAQ and the SEC of the misappropriation and fraudulent filings.

What should Deborah do?

B. FEDERAL PROXY REGULATION

1) ORIGINS

Most shareholders attend neither the corporation's annual meeting nor any special meetings. Instead, they are represented—and vote—by proxy. Shareholders send in a card (called a proxy card) on which they have marked their vote. The card authorizes a proxy agent to vote the shareholder's stock as directed on the card. The proxy card may specify how the shares are to be voted or may simply give the proxy agent discretion to decide how the shares are to be voted. (Confusingly, older materials sometimes refer to both the proxy card and the proxy agent as a proxy without explanatory qualification.)

In 1934, when the federal Securities Exchange Act was first adopted, state corporate law was largely silent on the issue of corporate communications with shareholders. Typical state statutes required only that the corporation send shareholders notice of a shareholders meeting, stating where and when the meeting would be held. Under most state

---

    [24]   This problem is loosely based on Francis v. United Jersey Bank, 432 A.2d 814 (N.J. 1981).

FOR MORE INFORMATION

For an excellent overview of the history of the federal securities laws, see Joel Seligman, The Transformation of Wall Street: A History of the Securities and Exchange Commission and Modern Corporate Finance (2003).

laws, the notice merely was required to briefly identify the issues to be voted on—and some states did not even require that minimal disclosure in connection with annual meetings. (In most states, the corporation statute still does not require much more than this minimal notice.)

By 1934, however, we had already seen the development of large public corporations having thousands of shareholders and using the proxy system of voting. Congressional hearings on the Exchange Act presented numerous allegations that incumbent managers used the corporate shareholder list and corporate funds to solicit proxies in connection with a shareholder meeting. Obviously, because the incumbents were the ones asking for proxies, the proxy cards and soliciting materials were designed to encourage shareholders to vote as the incumbents desired. The proxy system thus allegedly helped incumbent directors and managers to perpetuate themselves in office.

Congress ultimately settled on disclosure as the principal vehicle by which the proxy system was to be regulated at the federal level. Incumbent corporate managers and directors were not to solicit proxies from shareholders without giving the shareholders enough information on which to make an informed voting decision. Comparable disclosures were to be required from insurgents soliciting proxies in opposition to the incumbents, as well.

After several legislative false starts, however, the Congress ultimately dumped the job of creating a disclosure-based proxy regime in the SEC's lap. As adopted, Exchange Act § 14(a) provides:

> It shall be unlawful for any person, by use of the mails or by any means or instrumentality of interstate commerce or of any facility of a national securities exchange or otherwise, in contravention of such rules and regulations as the Commission may prescribe as necessary or appropriate in the public interest or for the protection of investors, to solicit or to permit the use of his name to solicit any proxy or consent or authorization in respect of any security (other than an exempted security) registered pursuant to Section 12 of this title.

Notice that § 14(a) is not self-executing. It proscribed nothing until the SEC adopted implementing rules and regulations. Pursuant to this broad grant of authority, the SEC has created a complex regulatory scheme governing the manner in which proxies are solicited and, therefore, the manner in which shareholder decisions are made.

2) THE REGULATORY FRAMEWORK

Per Exchange Act § 14(a), federal proxy regulation extends only to corporations registered with the SEC under § 12 of that Act, which means that virtually all public corporations are picked up by this requirement, while most close corporations are exempt. Because § 14(a) simply states that it shall be unlawful to solicit proxies in contravention of such rules as the SEC may proscribe, however, the rest of the regulatory framework is provided not by statute but entirely by SEC rules.

Given the wording of Exchange Act § 14(a), the definition of "solicit" is the linchpin of the entire regulatory structure. The standard judicial definition of "solicit" includes not only "direct requests to furnish, revoke or withhold proxies, but also . . . communications which may indirectly accomplish such a result or constitute a step in a chain of communications designed ultimately to accomplish such a result."[25] The basic question is whether a communication is reasonably calculated to influence a shareholder's vote. If so, subject to the exceptions discussed below, it is a proxy solicitation.

The proxy rules include a number of exceptions to the definition of solicitation, which are designed to encourage communication between shareholders. Among the more important exemptions of general application are:

- Rule 14a–1(*l*)(2)(iv) exempts public statements of how the shareholder intends to vote and its reasons for doing so.

- Rule 14a–2(b)(1), subject to numerous exceptions, exempts persons who do not seek "the power to act as proxy for a security holder" and do not furnish or solicit "a form of revocation, abstention, consent or authorization." Consequently, for example, a newspaper editorial advising a vote against incumbent managers is now definitively exempted.[26] Note that the Rule thus addresses—although hardly eliminates—the obvious First Amendment concerns implicated by regulating speech in connection with shareholder voting.

- Rule 14a–2(b)(2) preserves the long-standing exemption for solicitations of 10 or fewer persons.

[25] Long Island Lighting Co. v. Barbash, 779 F.2d 793, 796 (2d Cir.1985). In LILCO, an environmentalist group ran newspaper and radio ads critical of the defendant electrical utility's management. The utility managers alleged that the group was acting in conjunction with an insurgent shareholder conducting a proxy contest. The incumbent managers sued the environmentalists, alleging that their ads constituted a proxy solicitation. Over a strong dissent by Judge Ralph Winter (a former professor of corporate law at Yale), the court declined to reach the obvious First Amendment issues posed by the case. Instead, having adopted the definition of a solicitation quoted in the text, the court remanded for a determination of whether the defendants had solicited proxies under that definition.

[26] Note that all of the exemptions under Rule 14a–2(b) are limited in that they do not exempt the communication from Rule 14a–9's prohibition of fraudulent and misleading proxy solicitations.

- Rule 14a–2(b)(3) exempts the furnishing of proxy voting advice by someone with whom the shareholder has a business relationship. (A number of firms now provide such voting advice to institutional investors.)

Under SEC Rule 14a–3, the incumbent board of directors' first step in soliciting proxies must be the distribution to shareholders of the firm's annual report.[27] The annual report contains detailed financial statements and a discussion by management of the firm's business. It is intended to give shareholders up-to-date information about what the firm is doing and to give shareholders a basis on which to assess how well management is performing.

Once the annual report is in the shareholders' hands, the proxy solicitation process can begin. The solicitor's goal is to get the shareholder to sign and date a proxy card, voting his shares in the manner the solicitor desires. (The figure below is a sample paper proxy card provided by the SEC.)

Along with the proxy card, the SEC requires that the solicitor provide solicited shareholders with a proxy statement containing mandated disclosures relating to the matters to be acted upon. The cover page of the proxy statement typically includes the state law-required notice of where and when the meeting is to be held, and will also state what issues are to be decided at the meeting. A proxy statement relating to an annual meeting, at which directors are being elected, will typically open with biographical information about the candidates. The proxy statement will also include disclosures about board of director committees, board and executive compensation, relationships between the firm and its directors and senior officers, and a description of any other matters to come before the shareholders.

Per Rule 14a–6, a preliminary proxy card and statement must be filed with the SEC at least 10 calendar days before proxies are first solicited. Filing of preliminary materials is not required, however, with respect to an uncontested annual meeting at which only basic matters such as election of directors and appointment of an independent auditor are to be decided. In either case, definitive copies of the proxy card, proxy statement, and any other soliciting materials (such as letters to shareholders) must be filed with the SEC no later than the day they are first used.

In a proxy contest, a key factor will be the dissident's ability to communicate directly with the shareholders. Towards that end, the dissident will want access to the corporation's list of shareholders. SEC Rule 14a–7, however, does not require the incumbent board to provide a copy of the shareholder list to the dissident. The incumbents are given

---

[27] The annual report may be sent to the shareholders before proxies are solicited or may be sent in the same package as the proxy solicitation materials. The main point is that the annual report must be in the shareholder's hands when they make voting decisions.

an alternative: they can provide the shareholder list to the dissident or they can require that the dissident provide its proxy materials to the corporation, which is obligated to promptly mail those materials to the shareholders (at the dissident's expense). The incumbents usually prefer the latter route, as it gives them greater control over the process by which proxies are solicited. Commonly, however, dissidents are able to circumvent this restriction by seeking access to the shareholder list under state law.

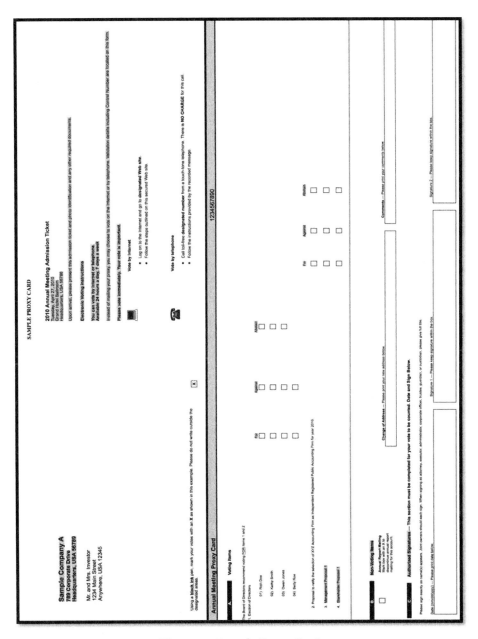

Figure 3. Sample Proxy Card

Securities and Exchange Commission, Concept Release on the U.S. Proxy System

Release No. 3052 (July 14, 2010)

Issuers, securities intermediaries, and shareholders often retain third parties to perform a number of proxy-related functions, including forwarding proxy materials, collecting voting instructions, voting shares, soliciting proxies, tabulating proxies, and analyzing proxy issues.

1.   Transfer Agents

Issuers are required to maintain a record of security holders for state law purposes and often hire a transfer agent to maintain that record. Transfer agents, as agents of the issuer, are obliged to confirm to a vote tabulator (if the transfer agent does not itself perform the tabulation function) matters such as the amount of shares outstanding, as well as the identity and holdings of registered owners entitled to vote. Transfer agents are required to register with the Commission, which inspects and currently regulates some of their functions.

2.   Proxy Service Providers

To facilitate the proxy material distribution and voting process for beneficial owners, securities intermediaries typically retain a proxy service provider to perform a number of processing functions, including forwarding the proxy materials by mail or electronically and collecting voting instructions.[57] To enable the proxy service provider to perform these functions, the securities intermediary gives the service provider an electronic data feed of a list of beneficial owners and the number of shares held by each beneficial owner on the record date. The proxy service

---

[57]   A single proxy service provider, Broadridge Financial Services, Inc. ("Broadridge"), states that it currently handles over 98% of the U.S. market for such proxy vote processing services. [Ed.: In Crown EMAK Partners, LLC v. Kurz, 992 A.2d 377, 381–82 (Del. 2010), the Delaware Supreme Court explained that:

For many years, banks and brokers maintained their own proxy departments to handle the back-office administrative processes of distributing proxy materials and tabulating voting instructions from their clients. Today, however, the overwhelming majority have eliminated their proxy departments and subcontracted these processes out to [Broadridge Financial Services, Inc. ("Broadridge")]. . . .

To make these arrangements work, Broadridge's bank and broker clients formally transfer to Broadridge the proxy authority they receive from DTC (via the [DTC] Omnibus Proxy) via written powers of attorney. On behalf of the brokers and banks, Broadridge delivers directly to each beneficial owner a proxy statement and, importantly, a voting instruction form (referred to as a "VIF") rather than a proxy card. Beneficial owners do not receive proxy cards because they are not vested with the right to vote shares or to grant proxy authority-those rights belong only to the legal owners (or their designees). Beneficial owners merely have the right to instruct how their shares are to be voted by Broadridge (attorney-in-fact of the DTC participants), which they accomplish by returning a VIF.

DTC is generally regarded as the entity having the power under Delaware law to vote the shares that it holds on deposit for the banks and brokers who are members of DTC. Through the DTC omnibus proxy, DTC transfers its voting authority to those member banks and brokers. The banks and brokers then transfer the voting authority to Broadridge, which votes the shares held at DTC by each bank and broker in proportion to the aggregate voting instructions received from the ultimate beneficial owners.]

provider, on behalf of the intermediary, then requests the appropriate number of proxy material sets from the issuer for delivery to the beneficial owners. Upon receipt of the packages, the proxy service provider, on behalf of the intermediary, mails either the proxy materials with a VIF, or a Notice of Internet Availability of Proxy Materials, to beneficial owners. Although we do not directly regulate such proxy service providers, our regulations governing the proxy process-related obligations of securities intermediaries apply to the way in which proxy service providers perform their services because they act as agents for, and on behalf of, those intermediaries and typically vote proxies on behalf of those intermediaries pursuant to a power of attorney.

3.   Proxy Solicitors

Issuers sometimes hire third-party proxy solicitors to identify beneficial owners holding large amounts of the issuers' securities and to telephone shareholders to encourage them to vote their proxies consistent with the recommendations of management. This often occurs when there is a contested election of directors, and issuer's management and other persons are competing for proxy authority to vote securities in the election (commonly referred to as a "proxy contest"). In addition, an issuer may hire a proxy solicitor in uncontested situations when voting returns are expected to be insufficient to meet state quorum requirements or when an important matter is being considered. Issuers and other soliciting persons are required to disclose the use of such services and estimated costs for such services in their proxy statements.

4.   Vote Tabulators

Under many state statutes, an issuer must appoint a vote tabulator (sometimes called "inspectors of elections" or "proxy tabulators") to collect and tabulate the proxy votes as well as votes submitted by shareholders in person at a meeting. We understand that often the issuer's transfer agent will act as the vote tabulator because most major transfer agents have the infrastructure to communicate with registered holders, proxy service providers, and securities intermediaries, while also being able to reconcile the identity of voters that are registered owners and the number of votes to the issuer's records. However, sometimes the issuer will hire an independent third party to perform this function, often to certify important votes. The vote tabulator is ultimately responsible for determining that the correct number of votes has been submitted by each registered owner.[61] In addition, proxies submitted by securities intermediaries that are not registered owners, but have been granted direct voting rights through DTC's omnibus proxy, are reconciled with DTC's securities position listing. Although the Commission does regulate

---

[61]   . . . [T]ransfer agents, who already possess the list of record owners, often tabulate the vote, so they possess the necessary information to make this determination. It is our understanding that, when the vote tabulator is an entity other than the transfer agent, the issuer or its transfer agent typically will provide the vote tabulator with the list of record owners to enable the vote tabulator to make this determination.

transfer agents (which often serve as vote tabulators) in their roles as transfer agents, the Commission does not currently regulate vote tabulators or the function of tabulating proxies by transfer agents.

5. Proxy Advisory Firms

Institutional investors typically own securities positions in a large number of issuers. Therefore, they are presented annually with the opportunity to vote on many matters and often must exercise fiduciary responsibility in voting. Some institutional investors may retain an investment adviser to manage their investments, and may also delegate proxy voting authority to that adviser. To assist them in their voting decisions, investment advisers (or institutional investors if they retain voting authority) frequently hire proxy advisory firms to provide analysis and voting recommendations on matters appearing on the proxy. In some cases, proxy advisory firms are given authority to execute proxies or voting instructions on behalf of their client. Some proxy advisory firms also provide consulting services to issuers on corporate governance or executive compensation matters, such as helping to develop an executive compensation proposal to be submitted for shareholder approval. Some proxy advisory firms may also qualitatively rate or score issuers, based on judgments about the issuer's governance structure, policies, and practices. . . . Some, but not all, proxy advisory firms operating in our markets are currently registered with us as investment advisers.

3) THE IMPLIED PRIVATE RIGHT OF ACTION

There are many ways to violate the proxy rules, because there are so many technical rules that must be complied with, but the likeliest source of liability is an illegal proxy solicitation. It is illegal to solicit proxies until the solicitor has delivered a proxy statement to the shareholders. It also is illegal to solicit proxies using materials that have not been filed with the SEC. Finally, it is illegal to solicit proxies using false or misleading soliciting materials. In examining these issues, we focus on several questions: (1) Does a cause of action exist for violations of the proxy rules and, if so, who has standing to bring such an action? (2) What must the plaintiff show in order to prevail in such a cause of action? (3) What remedies are available to injured parties?

No matter how closely one scrutinizes Securities Exchange Act § 14(a), one will not find anything relating to a private party cause of action under the statute or rules. In *J. I. Case Co. v. Borak*,[28] however, the Supreme Court implied a private right of action from the statute. Case proposed to merge with American Tractor Co. Borak owned around 2000 shares of Case stock and sought to enjoin the merger on the grounds, inter alia, that the company's proxy materials were false and misleading. Borak claimed that the merger was approved by a small margin and would not have been approved but for the false and

---

[28]   377 U.S. 426 (1964).

misleading statements. Case argued that Borak had no standing to sue, as the federal proxy rules provided no private party cause of action.

Despite the lack of any statutory authorization for a private party cause of action, Justice Clark's opinion for the Court found that such an action in fact existed. To be sure, Justice Clark purported to find a statutory basis for the cause of action in Exchange Act § 27. Noting that § 27 gives district courts jurisdiction over "all suits in equity and actions at law brought to enforce any liability or duty" under the Act, Justice Clark contended that "[t]he power to enforce implies the power to make effective the right of recovery afforded by the Act. And the power to make the right of recovery effective implies the power to utilize any of the procedures or actions normally available to the litigant. . . ." The trouble with that argument is that Section 27 speaks of liabilities imposed by the Act, but nothing in § 14(a) or the rules thereunder creates such liabilities vis-à-vis shareholders.

Borak is better understood as an exercise of judicial fiat. A private right of action exists not because Congress intended it, but because a majority of the Supreme Court said so. The general legitimacy of implied private rights of action is beyond our purview, however.[29] Instead, we are concerned solely with Justice Clark's policy justification for this particular cause of action.

Justice Clark was quite above-board as to his motivation—he wanted to deter fraud and other proxy violations. According to Justice Clark, private enforcement provides "a necessary supplement" to SEC efforts. He implied that shareholders are in a better position than the SEC to detect proxy violations—they have fewer proxy statements to review and presumably are better informed about the company. Again, however, the argument is spurious. Most shareholders do not carefully review proxy materials. Instead, they are rationally apathetic. They lack both the desire and the incentive to closely monitor the firm. Justice Clark doubtless knew that individual shareholders were unlikely to emerge as champions of corporate truth and justice. Instead, it seems probable that he was trying to provide incentives for the plaintiffs' bar to become more active in proxy litigation.

This inference is supported by Clark's characterization of the implied private right of action as being both direct and derivative in nature. Strikingly, he did so over Borak's strong argument that the suit was only direct in nature. At the time *Borak* was decided, the modern federal class action procedure had not yet been adopted. If proxy actions were allowed to proceed only directly, and plaintiffs' lawyers were limited to representing individual shareholders, the contingent fees generated by proxy litigation would be insufficient to attract quality lawyers. (The situation would be even worse in cases like *Borak*, where plaintiff sought

---

[29] See Reschini v. First Fed. Sav. & Loan Ass'n of Ind., 46 F.3d 246, 255 (3d Cir.1995) (*Borak* "is still good law as a construction of the 1934 Act and Rule 14a–9. However, it is not clear that *Borak*, if it arose for the first time today, would be decided the same way.").

only equitable relief.) Because the implied cause of action had a derivative element, however, a plaintiffs' lawyer could effectively sue on behalf of all shareholders, by nominally suing in the corporation's name, generating larger damage claims and bigger contingent fees.[30]

The Supreme Court's emphasis on promoting private attorneys general became even more pronounced in its next major proxy decision, *Mills v. Electric Auto-Lite Co.*[31] Mergenthaler Linotype Company owned over 50% of Auto-Lite's stock. About one-third of Mergenthaler's voting stock, in turn, was owned by American Manufacturing Co. American had voting control of Mergenthaler and through it Auto-Lite. Auto-Lite and Mergenthaler agreed to merge. The merger agreement required approval by two-thirds of Auto-Lite's outstanding shares, which therefore required affirmative votes from at least some of the minority shareholders. Plaintiffs alleged that the proxy materials used to solicit those votes were false and misleading and sued to enjoin the shareholder vote.

In the portion of its opinion dealing with remedies, the Supreme Court created a strong incentive for members of the plaintiffs' bar to act as private attorneys general. The Court opined that shareholder-plaintiffs "who have established a violation of the securities laws by their corporation and its officials, should be reimbursed by the corporation or its survivor for the costs of establishing the violation." Note carefully that plaintiffs' counsel was entitled to attorney's fees simply for finding a violation—there was no requirement that the plaintiff ultimately prevail in the sense of recovering damages. Indeed, in *Mills*, the shareholders ultimately recovered nothing, but the plaintiffs' attorneys' fees were still paid by the corporation. *Mills* thus created a powerful economic incentive for lawyers to sue even in cases where it was clear that no injury had been caused by the violation.

The sweeping mandate in *Mills* to plaintiff's attorneys to go forth and uncover proxy rule violations was somewhat pared back by later Supreme Court decisions.[32] Today, the case law requires that the plaintiff's cause of action must create either a common fund from recovered damages or some substantial nonmonetary benefit in order for fees to be awarded.[33] Because injunctive relief likely satisfies the "substantial benefit" standard, however, there is still an incentive to sue

---

[30]   *Borak* held that proxy suits can be brought either directly or derivatively. With the development of the modern class action, the characterization of proxy litigation as derivative became less important. For example, even though state law will govern some aspects of a proxy suit brought derivatively (such as whether demand is required), this is not the showstopper that requirement can be for fiduciary litigation because the proxy suit can also be brought directly. On the other hand, the characterization of proxy litigation does allow management standing to sue insurgents at corporate expense.

[31]   396 U.S. 375 (1970).

[32]   See, e.g., Alyeska Pipeline Service Co. v. Wilderness Society, 421 U.S. 240 (1975) (holding that absent statutory authorization, courts should not award attorney's fees to a plaintiff simply because plaintiff he served as a private attorney general).

[33]   See, e.g., Goldberger v. Integrated Resources, Inc., 209 F.3d 43 (2d Cir.2000); Amalgamated Clothing and Textile Workers Union v. Wal-Mart Stores, Inc., 54 F.3d 69 (2d Cir.1995); Smillie v. Park Chemical Co., 710 F.2d 271 (6th Cir.1983).

even where it seems unlikely that monetary damages ultimately will be forthcoming.

When proxy litigation is grounded on an allegation of fraud, four key elements must be considered: (1) the materiality of the alleged misrepresentation or omission; (2) causation; (3) reliance; and (4) the defendant's state of mind.

Recall that in *Mills v. Electric Auto-Lite Co.*,[34] the plaintiffs were shareholders of Auto-Lite, which was controlled by Mergenthaler Linotype Company, which in turn was controlled by American Manufacturing Co. Plaintiffs alleged that the proxy materials used in connection with the shareholder vote on a proposed merger between Auto-Lite and Mergenthaler were false and misleading because they failed to disclose that all of Auto-Lite's directors were Mergenthaler nominees.

Under *Mills*, a statement or omission is material when "it might have been considered important by a reasonable shareholder who was in the process of deciding how to vote." In other words, the statement or omission must have "a significant propensity to affect the voting process." Today, it is still the case that materiality is an essential element of the cause of action, but the definition of materiality has changed. In the *TSC Industries* case, the Supreme Court adopted a uniform standard of materiality under the securities laws: whether "there is a substantial likelihood that a reasonable shareholder would consider it important in deciding how to vote."[35]

Would the *Mills* omission be material under today's standard? On the one hand, the proxy statement did inform shareholders that Mergenthaler owned over 50% of Auto-Lite and that the boards of both companies had approved the merger. Arguably, reasonable shareholders should have been able to figure out for themselves that all of Auto-Lite's directors were elected by Mergenthaler. On the other hand, facts tending to show that the merger was approved by a board subject to a conflict of interest likely would be considered important by a reasonable shareholder. If the proxy statement had highlighted the fact that all of Auto-Lite's directors were Mergenthaler nominees, the conflict of interest would have been flagged, and the shareholders might have assessed the merger more carefully. (Note that in assessing materiality of disclosures, courts ignore the fact that most shareholders are rationally apathetic.)

In *Virginia Bankshares, Inc. v. Sandberg*,[36] the Supreme Court further refined the materiality standard by addressing its application to statements of belief or opinion. First American Bancshares (FABI) owned 100 percent of Virginia Bankshares (VBI). In turn, VBI owned 85 percent of First American Bank of Virginia (Bank). VBI merged Bank into itself,

---

[34]   396 U.S. 375 (1970).

[35]   TSC Indus., Inc. v. Northway, Inc., 426 U.S. 438, 449 (1976).

[36]   501 U.S. 1083 (1991).

and paid Bank shareholders $42 per share. Under Virginia law (the applicable standard), the merger required a two-thirds vote. Because VBI owned 85 percent of the voting stock, a proxy solicitation was unnecessary to effect the transaction. Nevertheless, VBI solicited proxies from the other shareholders. In pertinent part, the proxy statement opined: "The Plan of Merger has been approved by the Board of Directors because it provides an opportunity for the Bank's public shareholders to achieve a high value for their shares." Plaintiff Sandberg (a minority shareholder) claimed that the shares were worth $60, that the directors knew $42 was a low price, and that the directors nevertheless went along with a low-priced merger because they hoped not to lose their seats on the board. Justice Souter's majority opinion concluded that the statement was material, but only after an astonishingly tortuous analysis. Justice Scalia's concurring opinion summed up the resulting rule of law far more succinctly:

> As I understand the Court's opinion, the statement "In the opinion of the Directors, this is a high value for the shares" would produce liability if in fact it was not a high value and the directors knew that. It would not produce liability if in fact it was not a high value but the directors honestly believed otherwise. The statement "The Directors voted to accept the proposal because they believe it offers a high value" would not produce liability if in fact the directors' genuine motive was quite different—except that it would produce liability if the proposal in fact did not offer a high value and the Directors knew that.

Justice Scalia went on to caution, however:

> [N]ot every sentence that has the word "opinion" in it, or that refers to motivation for directors' actions, leads us into this psychic thicket. Sometimes such a sentence actually represents facts as facts rather than opinions—and in that event no more need be done than apply the normal rules for § 14(a) liability. I think that is the situation here. In my view, the statement at issue in this case is most fairly read as affirming *separately* both the fact of the Directors' opinion *and* the accuracy of the facts upon which the opinion was assertedly based.

According to the prevailing view, reliance is not an essential element of the plaintiff's cause of action under the proxy rules.[37] In contrast, the law is well-settled that a proxy litigation plaintiff seeking monetary damages must show that the violation caused an injury to the shareholders—but it is a funny kind of causation. In *Mills*, the Supreme Court held that a plaintiff proves causation by showing that the proxy solicitation itself (as opposed to the defect) was an "essential link" in the

---

[37] See, e.g., Cowin v. Bresler, 741 F.2d 410 (D.C.Cir.1984).

accomplishment of the transaction.[38] Note that under this standard almost any violation "causes" an injury. In most transactions requiring shareholder approval, the proxy solicitation will be an essential link in accomplishing the transaction, because the solicitation was necessary to obtain the requisite shareholder vote.

In both *Virginia Bankshares* and *TSC Industries*, the Supreme Court declined to decide whether the defendant must have acted with scienter or merely negligently in order to be held liable for fraud in a § 14(a) action. As to issuer liability, and that of officers and directors, courts generally hold that negligence suffices.[39] As to collateral participants, such as accountants who certify financial statements contained in a proxy statement (as is done when a merger is to be voted on), at least one court has held that plaintiff must prove scienter.[40]

Probably the most common remedy in proxy litigation is some form of prospective relief, such as an ex ante injunction against the shareholder vote. The court typically forbids the company from going forward with the shareholder meeting until the party soliciting proxies provides a new proxy statement, correcting whatever violation has been identified, and resolicits the proxies. Retrospective monetary relief, however, is available in appropriate cases. Damages must be shown, which means that plaintiff must establish a monetary injury. Because the violation itself is not an injury, plaintiff must show some sort of actual loss or harm resulting from the violation.

The most drastic option, at least from the firm's perspective, is a setting aside of the transaction. In *Mills*, for example, the merger could be undone and the two firms restored to their prior position as separate entities. This option is chosen very rarely. Courts tend to look at mergers

---

[38] Mills v. Electric Auto-Lite Co., 396 U.S. 375, 385 (1970). In *Mills*, the Supreme Court left open the question of "whether causation could be shown where the management controls a sufficient number of shares to approve the transaction without any votes from the minority." In *Virginia Bankshares*, the Supreme Court concluded that the requisite causation could not be shown in that situation. Virginia Bankshares, Inc. v. Sandberg, 501 U.S. 1083 (1991). Plaintiff advanced two explanations for VBI's decision to solicit proxies, both of which plaintiff argued supported a finding of causation. First, plaintiff argued that FABI wanted minority shareholder approval for reasons of goodwill, an explanation the court deemed too speculative to provide the requisite causation. Second, and far more significantly, plaintiff argued that VBI sought shareholder ratification to insulate the transaction from challenge under state law fiduciary duty rules. On the facts at bar, the Court also rejected this argument. Under Virginia law, VBI would be immunized from breach of fiduciary duty claims only if the transaction was approved by a majority of the minority shareholders after full disclosure. If VBI lied in the proxy material, there could be no valid approval. Absent valid approval, VBI gets no protection from the shareholder vote, and the proxy solicitation could not have been an essential step in the merger. Absent that showing, plaintiff cannot prove causation.

If VBI had been honest, there might have been ratification and the proxy might have been an essential step, but because there would not have been a misleading statement, the plaintiff would still lose. Cf. Howing Co. v. Nationwide Corp., 972 F.2d 700 (6th Cir.1992) (upon remand by the Supreme Court for reconsideration in light of Virginia Bankshares, holding that loss of a state law appraisal remedy in a freeze-out merger satisfies the causation requirement).

[39] See, e.g., Wilson v. Great American Indus., Inc., 855 F.2d 987 (2d Cir.1988); Gerstle v. Gamble-Skogmo, 478 F.2d 1281 (2d Cir.1973); see also Shidler v. All American Life & Fin. Corp., 775 F.2d 917 (8th Cir.1985) (rejecting an argument that strict liability was the standard).

[40] Adams v. Standard Knitting Mills, 623 F.2d 422 (6th Cir.1980).

and similar transactions the way a cook looks at an omelet: once the eggs have been scrambled, you can't put them back in the shells. When a merger takes place, all sorts of commingling takes place. Employees are fired or transferred, assets (such as bank accounts) are mixed up and reallocated, operating procedures are changed, and the like. The courts are very aware of this commingling process and therefore will set aside a merger only where it is possible to do so without harming the overall value of the firms and no other remedy can make the injured parties whole.

4) USING THE PROXY RULES TO AFFECT CORPORATE GOVERNANCE

Gaines v. Haughton
645 F.2d 761 (9th Cir.1981)

Ora E. Gaines, the plaintiff-appellant herein, appeals from an order of dismissal and summary judgment for defendants (Lockheed Aircraft Corporation and a number of former and present directors and officers of Lockheed) in a shareholder lawsuit alleging both derivative claims of breach of fiduciary duty/waste of corporate assets and class action claims of federal securities violations. . . .

FACTS

From as early as 1961 to as late as 1975, Lockheed engaged in the practice of hiring "consultants" and "foreign sales agents" and paying them large fees and commissions in connection with foreign sales of Lockheed aircraft and equipment. Approximately $30–38 million was paid directly to foreign governments and officials during this period.[1] Shortly after the existence of these clandestine, "off the books" questionable payments was revealed by Securities and Exchange Commission (SEC) and United States Senate proceedings in July-August 1975, Gaines an individual Lockheed shareholder commenced his lawsuit in the United States District Court for the Central District of California. . . .

. . . The class action counts based on federal securities law allege that defendants-appellees (hereinafter "appellees") violated the filing and proxy requirements of §§ 13(a) and 14(a) of the Securities Exchange Act of 1934, as amended ("the 1934 Act"), by (1) failing to disclose the existence and details of the questionable foreign payments to the shareholders in proxy solicitation materials each year from 1961–74, and (2) by filing materially false and misleading annual and other periodic financial reports on behalf of Lockheed.

---

[1]   There are no allegations that Lockheed made improper payments to domestic officials or that any federal criminal laws were violated by the foreign payments. . . . The Foreign Corrupt Practices Act of 1977 was signed into law after the conclusion of the scenario herein.

. . .

Apart from the commencement of Gaines' lawsuit, the revelation of Lockheed's foreign payments in July-August 1975 precipitated several other events. . . . On April 13, 1976, and in response to an SEC complaint, Lockheed entered into a consent decree and permanent injunction which enjoined future improper payments, improper accounting methods, and other forms of concealment; required amendment of prior SEC filings; provided for an internal corporate investigation and report procedures to be conducted under SEC supervision; and ordered other remedial actions. On June 23, 1978, Lockheed agreed to a consent order of the Federal Trade Commission containing even more sweeping prohibitions than those contained in the SEC permanent injunction. . . .

THE DISTRICT COURT DECISION

. . .

The District Court also dismissed Gaines' federal securities claims pursuant to Fed.R.Civ.P. 12(b)(6) for failure to state a claim upon which relief can be granted. Because Gaines . . . had not alleged any direct relationship between the proxy materials distributed and the improper foreign payments, Judge Whelan dismissed Gaines' § 14(a) claim for lack of "casual connection" between the alleged violation and the alleged injury. . . .

DISCUSSION

. . .

. . . The Dismissal of the § 14(a) Claim

. . .

Section 14(a) of the 1934 Act provides:

> It shall be unlawful for any person, by the use of the mails or by any means or instrumentality of interstate commerce or of any facility of a national securities exchange or otherwise, in contravention of such rules and regulations as the Commission may prescribe as necessary or appropriate in the public interest or for the protection of investors, to solicit or to permit the use of his name to solicit any proxy or consent or authorization in respect to any security (other than an exempted security) registered pursuant to section 78l of this title.

[SEC Rule 14a–9] provides:

> (a) No solicitation subject to this regulation shall be made by means of any proxy statement, form of proxy, notice of meeting or other communication, written or oral, containing any statement which, at the time and in the light of the circumstances under which it is made, is false or misleading with respect to any material fact, or which omits to state any material fact necessary in order to make the statements therein

not false or misleading or necessary to correct any statement in any earlier communication with respect to the solicitation of a proxy for the same meeting or subject matter which has become false or misleading.

(b) The fact that a proxy statement, form of proxy or other soliciting material has been filed with or examined by the Commission shall not be deemed a finding by the Commission that such material is accurate or complete or not false or misleading, or that the Commission has passed upon the merits of or approved any statement contained therein or any matter to be acted upon by security holders. No representation contrary to the foregoing shall be made.

Note: The following are some examples of what, depending upon particular facts and circumstances, may be misleading within the meaning of this section.

(a) Predictions as to specific future market values.

(b) Material which directly or indirectly impugns character, integrity or personal reputation, or directly or indirectly makes charges concerning improper, illegal or immoral conduct or associations, without factual foundation.

(c) Failure to so identify a proxy statement, form of proxy and other soliciting material as to clearly distinguish it from the soliciting material of any other person or persons soliciting for the same meeting or subject matter.

(d) Claims made prior to a meeting regarding the results of a solicitation.

"The purpose of s 14(a) is to prevent management or others from obtaining authorization for corporate action by means of deceptive or inadequate disclosure in proxy solicitation." *J.I. Case Co. v. Borak*, 377 U.S. 426, 431, 84 S.Ct. 1555, 1559, 12 L.Ed.2d 423 (1964). The Supreme Court has recognized an implied private cause of action under that section in favor of stockholders and investors who have been injured as a result of false or misleading proxy solicitations. Id. at 430–31, 84 S.Ct. at 1558–59.

. . .

. . . Transactional Causation and Materiality

Gaines' § 14(a) claim is ultimately premised on appellees' failure to disclose "corrupt and improper foreign payments" and related corporate misconduct to the Lockheed shareholders in the proxy solicitation materials for director elections each year from 1961 to 1975. . . .

The precise roles of "materiality," "causation-in-fact," and "proximate cause" in federal securities litigation are often unclear.

Granted that causation is sometimes presumed when the alleged nondisclosure concealed "material" information, see [*Mills v. Electric Auto-Lite Co.*, 396 U.S. 375, 385 (1970)] ("Where there has been a finding of materiality, a shareholder has made a sufficient showing of causal relationship between the violation and the injury for which he seeks redress if, as here, he proves that the proxy solicitation itself, rather than the particular defect in the solicitation materials, was an essential link in the accomplishment of the (corporate) transaction."), this rationale— the equation of causation to materiality—is logically limited to situations in which shareholder approval was sought (and fraudulently secured) for a transaction requiring such approval, typically so-called "fundamental corporate changes."

In *Mills*, for instance, the Supreme Court made clear that § 14(a) was intended to ensure that proxies would be solicited with " 'explanation to the stockholder of the real nature of the questions *for which authority to cast his vote is sought*,' " 396 U.S. at 381, 90 S.Ct. at 620 (emphasis added), quoting H.R.Rep.No.1383, 73d Cong., 2d Sess., 14 (1934); S.Rep.No.792, 73d Cong., 2d Sess., 12 (1934). The purpose of § 14(a) was clearly to prohibit management from deceptively securing stockholder approval for transactions requiring such approval. See 396 U.S. at 384– 85, 90 S.Ct. at 621–22.

Thus, for damages claims relating to the directors' failure to disclose misconduct and/or mismanagement (other than self-dealing or fraud against the corporation), there is no "causal nexus" or "transactional causation," without regard to the issue of materiality, so long as the underlying transaction did not require shareholder approval. The directors' failure to disclose the questionable foreign payments (or other alleged misconduct) is not the legal cause of the pecuniary loss to the corporation, if any. As Judge Henley stated for the Eighth Circuit in *Abbey v. Control Data Corp.*, 603 F.2d 724 (8th Cir. 1979), cert. denied, 444 U.S. 1017, 100 S.Ct. 670, 62 L.Ed.2d 647 (1980)]:

> Any injury to CDC shareholders from the corporation's illegal foreign payments stems directly from the corporate waste and mismanagement involved in authorizing those payments and not from allegedly misleading proxy solicitations dealing with unrelated corporate business matters. Consequently, we determine that Abbey's § 14(a) claim is . . . at best marginally related to the federal policies underlying that section.

603 F.2d at 732.

In *In re Tenneco Securities Litigation*, 449 F.Supp. 528 (S.D.Tex.1978), the district court employed similar reasoning in dismissing a § 14(a) claim predicated on the nondisclosure of questionable foreign payments:

> The harm to the plaintiffs must have resulted from the corporate transaction they authorized as a result of the false or

misleading proxy solicitation. This "transactional causation" is an essential element of a § 14(a) action. . . .

In the instant case, the only "corporate transaction" authorized by the shareholders was the election of directors. The § 14(a) violation alleged by the plaintiffs is the failure of the director-candidates to include in their proxy solicitation that they had made the allegedly illegal payments. . . .

In order to recover damages under § 14(a) the proxy violation must have caused the economic harm alleged. The economic loss alleged here is the amount of corporate funds allegedly expended for the payments. . . . Such acts of corporate waste and breach of fiduciary duty form the bases of state claims and do not state a claim under the federal securities laws.

Id. at 531 (citations omitted). . . .

For equitable and declaratory relief claims relating to the election of directors, alleged to have been facilitated by the nondisclosure of the underlying misconduct, the causation approach presents problems; as the Second Circuit noted in [*Weisberg v. Coastal States Gas Corp.*, 609 F.2d 650 (2d Cir. 1979), cert. denied, 445 U.S. 951, 100 S.Ct. 1600 (1980)]:

In [§ 14(a) suits for damages predicated on the directors' subsequent failure to disclose corporate misconduct to the shareholders in proxy solicitations], the plaintiff sought damages because of allegedly improper payments, which did not require shareholder approval. The causal link between the proxy solicitation for the election of directors and the injury complained of the improper payments was attenuated at best. In the instant case, however, the challenged "transaction" is the election of the directors, and we have no doubt that the "proxy solicitation itself . . . was an essential link in the accomplishment" of that transaction, within the meaning of *Mills*.

609 F.2d at 654.

We agree with the *Weisberg* court that when the plaintiff-shareholder attacks only the election itself, instead of seeking money damages or other relief for the underlying misconduct, the proper analysis shifts from causation to materiality. We draw a sharp distinction, however, between allegations of director misconduct involving breach of trust or self-dealing the nondisclosure of which is presumptively material and allegations of simple breach of fiduciary duty/waste of corporate assets the nondisclosure of which is never material for § 14(a) purposes. . . .

. . . The distinction between "mere" bribes and bribes coupled with kickbacks to the directors makes a great deal of sense, indeed, is fundamental to a meaningful concept of materiality under § 14(a) and the preservation of state corporate law.

Many corporate actions taken by directors in the interest of the corporation might offend and engender controversy among some stockholders. Investors share the same diversity of social and political views that characterizes the polity as a whole. The tenor of a company's labor relations policies, economic decisions to relocate or close established industrial plants, commercial dealings with foreign countries which are disdained in certain circles, decisions to develop (or not to develop) particular natural resources or forms of energy technology, and the promulgation of corporate personnel policies that reject (or embrace) the principle of affirmative action, are just a few examples of business judgments, soundly entrusted to the broad discretion of the directors, which may nonetheless cause shareholder dissent and provoke claims of "wasteful," "unethical," or even "immoral" business dealings. Should corporate directors have a duty under § 14(a) to disclose all such corporate decisions in proxy solicitations for their re-election? We decline to extend the duty of disclosure under s 14(a) to these situations. While we neither condone nor condemn these and similar types of corporate conduct (including the now-illegal practice of questionable foreign payments), we believe that aggrieved shareholders have sufficient recourse to state law claims against the responsible directors and, if all else fails, can sell or trade their stock in the offending corporation in favor of an enterprise more compatible with their own personal goals and values.

Absent credible allegations of self-dealing by the directors or dishonesty or deceit which inures to the direct, personal benefit of the directors a fact that demonstrates a betrayal of trust to the corporation and shareholders and the director's essential unfitness for corporate stewardship we hold that director misconduct of the type traditionally regulated by state corporate law need not be disclosed in proxy solicitations for director elections. This type of mismanagement, unadorned by self-dealing, is simply not material or otherwise within the ambit of the federal securities laws. A contrary holding would place an unwarranted premium on the form rather than the substance of a shareholder's complaint and, moreover, would represent a move toward the federalization of corporate law that the Supreme Court has repeatedly and emphatically rejected.

CASE IN POINT

In *Amalgamated Clothing & Textile Workers Union, AFL-CIO v. J. P. Stevens & Co.,* 475 F. Supp. 328 (S.D.N.Y. 1979), vacated sub nom. *Amalgamated Clothing & Textile Workers Union v. J. P. Stevens & Co.,* 638 F.2d 7 (2d Cir. 1980), plaintiffs alleged that Stevens' board of directors violated the proxy rules by failing to disclose an alleged corporate policy to "thwart," "resist," and "abuse" federal labor laws. The court dismissed the suit on grounds that a rule effectively requiring the board "to accuse itself of antisocial or illegal policies" would be a "silly, unworkable rule."

Accordingly, we affirm the dismissal of Gaines' equitable § 14(a) claim relating to the election of Lockheed directors because the character of the alleged nondisclosures was immaterial as a matter of law.

NOTES AND QUESTIONS

1.   Does *Gaines* leave any room for a later court to hold that "director misconduct of the type traditionally regulated by state corporate law" is material under some circumstances?

2.   In *Roeder v. Alpha Indus., Inc.,*[41] Alpha senior management allegedly paid bribes to an employee of Rayethon Company in order to obtain subcontractor work on a government contract. Unlike the plaintiff in *Gaines*, the *Roeder* plaintiff alleged that the company's failure to disclose the allegations violated Securities Exchange Act Rule 10b–5. The court held that:

> Information about bribery is relevant to important questions about the competency of management. Management's willingness to engage in practices that probably or obviously are illegal, and its decision to put the corporation at risk by so doing, may be critically important factors to investors. Investors may prefer to steer away from an enterprise that circumvents fair competitive bidding and opens itself to accusations of misconduct. Furthermore, regardless of financial motives, investors may not want to associate themselves with such an enterprise.

> Defendants assert that they should not be required to accuse themselves "of antisocial or illegal policies." In a sense, they are right: information does not become material simply because some may regard it as antisocial or illegal. But otherwise material information does not become any less material because someone may be indicted if it is discovered by the authorities. The securities laws do not operate under the assumption that material information need not be disclosed if management has reason to suppress it. Investors may want to know about illegal activity for the same reason management will be reluctant to reveal it: it threatens to damage the corporation severely. Excepting from the disclosure rules information management has reason to hide would eviscerate the protection for investors embodied in the securities laws.[42]

But while the information was material, the company had no affirmative duty to disclose it: "Roeder claims that a corporation has an affirmative duty to disclose all material information even if there is no insider trading, no statute or regulation requiring disclosure, and no inaccurate, incomplete, or misleading prior disclosures. The prevailing view, however, is that there is no such affirmative duty of disclosure."[43]

---

[41]   814 F.2d 22 (1st Cir. 1987).

[42]   Id. at 25.

[43]   Id. at 27.

Can you reconcile *Gaines* and *Roeder?*

3.   In *Greenhouse v. MCG Capital Corp.*,[44] in which plaintiff claimed that the firm's CEO had misrepresented his college career, the court rejected plaintiff's argument that management's integrity is always material:

> In support of their integrity argument, Appellants present the case of *Gebhardt v. ConAgra Foods, Inc.*, 335 F.3d 824 (8th Cir.2003). But in *Gebhardt*, unlike here, there plainly was a misrepresented fact that was actually material: management violated generally accepted accounting principles and significantly overstated their earnings. Id. at 830 ("The keystone of plaintiffs' materiality   argument   is   their   allegation   that   UAP's misrepresentations caused ConAgra to appear to be earning more than it was."). If ConAgra's leaders knowingly misrepresented their earnings, of course one byproduct might be that investors would reasonably question the integrity of the company's management; like here, the "integrity concerns" in *Gebhardt* are merely derivative of the misrepresentation that was the basis for the suit. The key difference, however, is that the fact misrepresented in *Gebhardt*—the company's earnings—might plausibly alter the total mix of information to a reasonable investor; here, Mitchell's failure to complete his fourth year in college could not.

> Likewise, Appellants cite *Zell v. Intercaptial Income Sec., Inc.,* 675 F.2d 1041 (9th Cir.1982), for the same proposition. But again, *Zell* dealt with a fact of an indisputably different quantum: the defendant's proxy statement failed to disclose "a score of lawsuits charging violations of state and federal securities laws." Id. at 1043. That both misrepresentations call management's integrity into question follows almost necessarily from the fact that they are lies; it does not, however, aid in the determination of whether Mitchell's lie was about a material fact.

> Finally, Appellants cite a 40-year old SEC case for the proposition that integrity is "always a material factor." *In the Matter of Franchard Corp.*, 42 SEC 163, Release No. 33–4710, 1964 WL 67454 (SEC July 31, 1964). In addition to the fact that it predates the Supreme Court's pronouncement in *Basic* and other key cases on materiality, Appellants fail to note that this statement is, yet again, ancillary to concerns growing from actual material facts that were not disclosed (and thus were at issue) in the case. Reading the full context out of which Appellants pluck their quote that integrity "is always a material factor," one learns that the underlying fact at issue was that the company's registration statements continually failed to disclose transfers of large sums from the company to the controlling stockholder and chief executive officer, which he used in his own ventures. This, in turn, created a likelihood of shift in control and caused clear conflicts of interest with the company and its shareholders.

---

[44]   392 F.3d 650 (4th Cir. 2004).

In short, in each of these "integrity" cases, and unlike this case, a real, live, material fact was at issue. Appellants seem to have chosen these cases because the courts appear to have noted, offhandedly, that management's integrity is important and necessarily implicated with such revelations. Of course, to some extent, "management's integrity" will always be implicated in any falsehoods. But . . . not all lies are actionable; the securities laws are only concerned with lies about material facts. Reading the law otherwise, as Appellants would have us do, simply reads materiality out of the statute. Under their theory, almost any misrepresentation by a CEO—including, perhaps, one about his or her marital fidelity, political persuasion, or golf handicap—that might cause investors to question management's integrity could, as such, serve as a basis for a securities-fraud class action. The law simply does not permit such a result.[45]

Is *Greenhouse* consistent with *Roeder*?

PROBLEM

Mega Bank Holding Co., Inc., a large and diversified financial services corporation providing, among other things, investment banking services, recently announced that it had reached a settlement with the U.S. Department of Justice and several other federal agencies of criminal and civil claims. The Department of Justice claimed that Mega had committed securities fraud and violated certain banking regulations in connection with Mega's "packaging, marketing, sale, and issuance of residential mortgage-backed securities (RMBS)." In the settlement, Mega admitted having committed the alleged violations and further admitted that "in certain instances, loans that did not comply with underwriting guidelines were included in the RMBS sold and marketed to investors, but Mega did not disclose this to those investors." Mega paid $1.7 billion to settle those claims.

Mega is a Delaware corporation. Its common stock is listed for trading on the NYSE. Its common stock and several classes of debt securities are registered with the SEC under § 12 of the Exchange Act. Mega is therefore a reporting company and at all relevant times was current in its reporting obligations.

Shareholders brought a number of derivative and class actions suits against Mega and its directors, which were combined for trial before Judge Helen Watkins of the U.S. District Court for the Southern District of New York. Among the many claims in the lawsuit is an allegation that the directors of Mega should be liable for violating Securities Exchange Act § 14(a) and SEC Rule 14a–9 thereunder because Mega's proxy statements for the last two years were "materially false and misleading because they falsely stated that the Company's Board of Directors maintained adequate and effective risk oversight over management and failed to disclose to the

---

[45] Id. at 659–60.

Company's shareholders material deficiencies in the Board's oversight of management and internal controls."

1. If it were true that Mega's board of directors failed to maintain "adequate and effective risk oversight over management," would Mega's shareholders have a state law claim against the directors? What would plaintiffs need to prove in order to prevail on such a claim, if any?

2. Mega's directors have moved to dismissed the § 14(a) cause of action for failure to state a claim, citing the *Gaines* decision. How should Judge Watkins rule?

3. Would your answer to Question 2 change if the directors' fees paid to Mega's board members varied with Mega's stock price, so that higher profits and a resulting higher stock price meant the directors received higher compensation?

5) THE OUTER LIMITS OF THE SEC'S AUTHORITY UNDER SECTION 14(a)

The relationship between the SEC, the stock exchanges, and corporate governance came to a head in the 1980s debate over dual class stock. As a defense against hostile takeovers, a number of companies in the mid-1980s adopted a charter amendment creating two classes of common stock. The Class A shares are simply the preexisting common stock, having one vote per share. The newly created Class B shares, distributed to the shareholders as a stock dividend, have most of the attributes of regular common stock, but possess an abnormally large number of votes (usually ten) per share. Class B shares typically are not transferable, but may be converted into Class A shares for sale. Normal shareholder turnover thus concentrates the superior voting shares in the hands of long-term investors, especially incumbent managers, giving them voting control without the investment of any additional funds. Rule 19c–4 was intended to prevent such transactions, as well as other transactions creating multiple classes of stock with disparate voting rights.

Business Roundtable v. SEC
905 F.2d 406 (D.C. Cir. 1990)

In 1984 General Motors announced a plan to issue a second class of common stock with one-half vote per share. The proposal collided with a longstanding rule of the New York Stock Exchange that required listed companies to provide one vote per share of common stock. The NYSE balked at enforcement, and after two years filed a proposal with the Securities and Exchange Commission to relax its own rule. The SEC did not approve the rule change but responded with one of its own. On July 7, 1988, it adopted Rule 19c–4, barring national securities exchanges and national securities associations, together known as self-regulatory organizations (SROs), from listing stock of a corporation that takes any corporate action "with the effect of nullifying, restricting or disparately reducing the per share voting rights of [existing common stockholders]." Voting Rights Listing Standards; Disenfranchisement Rule, 53 Fed.Reg. 26,376, 26,394 (1988) ("Final Rule"), codified at 17 CFR § 240.19c–4 (1990). The rule prohibits such "disenfranchisement" even where approved by a shareholder vote conducted on one share/one vote principles. Because the rule directly controls the substantive allocation of powers among classes of shareholders, we find it in excess of the Commission's authority under § 19 of the Securities Exchange Act of 1934, as amended (the "Exchange Act"). Neither the wisdom of the requirement, nor of its being imposed at the federal level, is here in question.[46]

. . .

Two components of § 19 give the Commission authority over the rules of self-regulatory organizations. First, § 19(b) requires them to file with the Commission any proposed change in their rules. The Commission is to approve the change if it finds it "consistent with the requirements of [the Exchange Act] and the rules and regulations thereunder applicable" to the self-regulatory organization. § 19(b)(2), 15 U.S.C. § 78s(b)(2). This provision is not directly at issue here, but, as we shall see, both the procedure and the terms guiding Commission approval are important in understanding the scope of the authority the Commission has sought to exercise. That is found in § 19(c), which allows the Commission on its own initiative to amend the rules of a self-regulatory organization as it

> deems necessary or appropriate [1] to insure the fair administration of the self-regulatory organization, [2] to conform its rules to requirements of [the Exchange Act] and the rules and regulations thereunder applicable to such organization, or [3] *otherwise in furtherance of the purposes of [the Exchange Act]*.

§ 19(c), 15 U.S.C. § 78s(c) (emphasis and enumeration added). As no one suggests that either of the first two purposes justifies Rule 19c–4, the issue before us is the scope of the third, catch-all provision.

---

[46] As a technical matter, Rule 19c–4 added a new rule to the listing standards of each national securities exchange making available transaction reports under Exchange Act Rule 11Aa3–1 and each national securities association registered under Exchange Act section 15A. Registered exchanges and securities associations are collectively referred to as self-regulatory organizations (SROs).

The new listing standards created by rule 19c–4 prohibited a covered exchange from listing or continuing to list the equity securities of an issuer that took one of the prohibited actions. It likewise prohibited a covered securities association from authorizing the equity securities of such an issuer for quotation and/or transaction reporting on an automated quotation system. The Intermountain and Spokane Stock Exchanges were the only national securities exchanges excluded from coverage. The National Association of Securities Dealers (NASD) was the only securities association affected by the rule, just as the NASDAQ system was the only affected automated quotation system. Finally, only those issuers registered with the SEC pursuant to Exchange Act section 12, 15 U.S.C. § 78l (1988), were covered by the rule.

. . .

What then are the "purposes" of the Exchange Act? The Commission supports Rule 19c–4 as advancing the purposes of a variety of sections, but we first take its strongest—§ 14's grant of power to regulate the proxy process. The Commission finds a purpose "to ensure fair shareholder suffrage." Indeed, it points to the House Report's declarations that "[f]air corporate suffrage is an important right," H.R.Rep. No. 1383, 73d Cong., 2d Sess. 13 (1934) ("1934 House Report"), and that "use of the exchanges should involve a corresponding duty of according to shareholders fair suffrage," *id.* at 14. . . .

But unless the legislative purpose is defined by reference to the *means* Congress selected, it can be framed at *any* level of generality—to improve the operation of capital markets, for instance. In fact, although § 14(a) broadly bars use of the mails (and other means) "to solicit . . . any proxy" in contravention of Commission rules and regulations, it is not seriously disputed that Congress's central concern was with disclosure. See *J.I. Case Co. v. Borak,* 377 U.S. 426, 431, 84 S.Ct. 1555, 1559, 12 L.Ed.2d 423 (1964) ("The purpose of § 14(a) is to prevent management or others from obtaining authorization for corporate action by means of deceptive or inadequate disclosure in proxy solicitation."); see also *Santa Fe Industries, Inc. v. Green,* 430 U.S. 462, 477–78, 97 S.Ct. 1292, 1302–04, 51 L.Ed.2d 480 (1977) (emphasizing Exchange Act's philosophy of full disclosure and dismissing the fairness of the terms of the transaction as "at most a tangential concern of the statute" once full and fair disclosure has occurred).

While the House Report indeed speaks of fair corporate suffrage, it also plainly identifies Congress's target—the solicitation of proxies by well informed insiders "without fairly informing the stockholders of the purposes for which the proxies are to be used." 1934 House Report at 14. The Senate Report contains no vague language about "corporate suffrage," but rather explains the purpose of the proxy protections as ensuring that stockholders have "adequate knowledge" about the "financial condition of the corporation . . . [and] the major questions of policy, which are decided at stockholders' meetings." S.Rep. No. 792, 73d Cong., 2d Sess. 12 (1934) ("1934 Senate Report"). Finally, both reports agree on the power that the proxy sections gave the Commission—"power to control the conditions under which proxies may be solicited." 1934 House Report at 14. See also 1934 Senate Report at 12 (similar language).

That proxy regulation bears almost exclusively on disclosure stems as a matter of necessity from the nature of proxies. Proxy solicitations are, after all, only *communications* with potential absentee voters. The goal of federal proxy regulation was to improve those communications and thereby to enable proxy voters to control the corporation as effectively as they might have by attending a shareholder meeting.

We do not mean to be taken as saying that disclosure is necessarily the sole subject of § 14. For example, the Commission's Rule 14a–4(b)(2) requires a proxy to provide some mechanism for a security holder to withhold authority to vote for each nominee individually. It thus bars a kind of electoral tying arrangement, and may be supportable as a control over management's power to set the voting agenda, or, slightly more broadly, voting procedures. But while Rule 14a–4(b)(2) may lie in a murky area between substance and procedure, Rule 19c–4 much more directly interferes with the substance of what the shareholders may enact. It prohibits certain reallocations of voting power and certain capital structures, even if approved by a shareholder vote subject to full disclosure and the most exacting procedural rules.

. . . In 1934 Congress acted on the premise that shareholder voting could work, so long as investors secured enough information and, perhaps, the benefit of other procedural protections. It did not seek to regulate the stockholders' choices. If the Commission believes that premise misguided, it must turn to Congress.

With its step beyond control of voting procedure and into the distribution of voting power, the Commission would assume an authority that the Exchange Act's proponents disclaimed any intent to grant. Noting that opponents expressed alarm that the bill would give the Commission "power to interfere in the management of corporations," the Senate Committee on Banking and Currency said it had "no such intention" and that the bill "furnish[ed] no justification for such an interpretation." 1934 Senate Report at 10.

There are, of course, shadings within the notion of "management." With the present rule the Commission does not tell any corporation where to locate its next plant. But neither does state corporate law; it regulates the distribution of powers among the various players in the process of corporate governance, and the Commission's present leap beyond disclosure is just that sort of regulation. The potpourri of listing standards previously submitted to the Commission under § 19(b), see note 4 above, suggests the sweep of its current claim. These govern requirements for independent directors, independent audit committees, shareholder quorums, shareholder approval for certain major corporate transactions, and other major issues traditionally governed by state law. If Rule 19c–4 is closely enough related to the proxy regulation purpose of § 14, then all these issues appear equally subject to the Commission's discretionary control.

Surprisingly, the Commission does not concede a lack of jurisdiction over such issues. When questioned at oral argument as to what state corporation rules are not related to "fair corporate suffrage," SEC counsel conceded only that further intrusions into state corporate governance "would present more difficult situations." . . . If Rule 19c–4 were validated on such broad grounds, the Commission would be able to establish a federal corporate law by using access to national capital markets as its enforcement mechanism. This would resolve a longstanding controversy over the wisdom of such a move in the face of disclaimers from Congress and with no substantive restraints on the power. It would, moreover, overturn or at least impinge severely on the tradition of state regulation of corporate law. As the Supreme Court has said, "[c]orporations are creatures of state law, and investors commit their funds to corporate directors on the understanding that, except where federal law *expressly* requires certain responsibilities of directors with respect to stockholders, state law will govern the internal affairs of the corporation." *Sante Fe Industries,* 430 U.S. at 479, 97 S.Ct. at 1304 (emphasis in original, quoting *Cort v. Ash,* 422 U.S. 66, 84, 95 S.Ct. 2080, 2090–91, 45 L.Ed.2d 26 (1975)). At least one Commissioner shared this view, stating "[s]ection 19(c) does not provide the Commission *carte blanche* to adopt federal corporate governance standards through the back door by mandating uniform listing standards." Final Rule, 53 Fed.Reg. at 26,395/1 (Grundfest, Comm'r, concurring). . . . We read the Act as reflecting a clear congressional determination not to make any such broad delegation of power to the Commission.

If the Commission's one share/one vote rule is to survive, then, some kind of firebreak is needed to separate it from corporate governance as a whole. But the Commission's sole suggestion of such a firebreak is a reference to "the unique historical background of the NYSE's one share, one vote rule." Brief for Respondent at 21 n. 24. It is true that in the Senate hearings leading to enactment of the Exchange Act there were a few favorable references to that rule. But these few references are culled from 9500 pages of testimony in the Senate hearings. No legislator directly discussed the NYSE's rule and no references were made to it in any of the Committee Reports. The most these references show is that legislators were aware of the rule and that it was an important part of the background. Even if we imputed the statements to a member of Congress, none comes near to saying, "The purposes of this act, although they generally will not involve the Commission in corporate governance, do include preservation of the one share/one vote principle." And even then we doubt that such a statement in the legislative history could support a special and anomalous exception to the Act's otherwise intelligible conceptual line excluding the Commission from corporate governance.

. . .

The petition for review is granted and Rule 19c–4 is vacated.

NOTES AND QUESTIONS

1. Does *Business Roundtable* stand for the proposition that federal law must be limited to disclosure and related procedures? Suppose, for example, that Congress passed a statute authorizing the SEC to adopt Rule 19c–4. Would such a statute be valid?

2. In an omitted portion of the *Business Roundtable* opinion, the Court stated that:

> The Commission has on occasion ... given hints that eventuated in the exchanges' proposing a change, a practice viewed by one observer as "regulation by raised eyebrow." See Donald E. Schwartz, Federalism and Corporate Governance, 45 Ohio St.L.J. 545, 571 (1984).

Shortly after the principal decision came down, the SEC cocked its eyebrow at the SROs and all of them voluntarily—or so it was claimed—adopted versions of Rule 19c–4. The SEC then approved those rules under Exchange Act § 19(b). Your author has argued that this use of the SEC's regulatory authority is dubious, at best.

Newly confirmed SEC Commissioner Robert J. Jackson, Jr., gave his inaugural speech at Berkeley on February 15, 2018. In it, he criticized—in an admittedly nuanced way—the growing phenomenon of dual class stock. As he explained, most U.S. public corporations have a single class of common stock in which all shares have one vote per share. In recent years, however, some companies—especially in the tech sector—have gone public with a so-called dual class capital structure, which typically has two classes of common stock. One class will have the traditional one vote per share, but the other will have multiple votes—usually 10— per share. The former shares are the ones sold to the public in the IPO, while insiders hold the super-voting shares. Facebook is a paradigmatic example: Mark Zuckerberg's super-voting shares represent only 16% of the company's equity but give him 60% of the total voting power.

Commissioner Jackson acknowledged that there has been a longstanding debate over dual class stock and, moreover, that such capital structures can sometimes be justified:

> On one hand, you have visionary founders who want to retain control while gaining access to our public markets. On the other, you have a structure that undermines accountability: management can outvote ordinary investors on virtually anything.

> There is reason to think that, at least for a defined period of time early in a company's life, dual-class can be beneficial. The structure can allow entrepreneurs to build for the long term—and even transform entire industries—without being subject to short-term pressure. When many managers are at the mercy of daily stock-market pressure, dual-class can help America's most innovative companies create the sustainable long-term value we need to grow our economy.

But Commissioner Jackson argues that permanent dual class capital structures, in which the insiders' super-voting stock can be inherited by their children is problematic. It contributes to wealth inequality and creates a virtual hereditary corporate aristocracy:

So perpetual dual-class ownership—forever shares—don't just ask investors to trust a visionary founder. It asks them to trust that founder's kids. And their kids' kids. And their grandkid's kids. (Some of whom may, or may not, be visionaries.) It raises the prospect that control over our public companies, and ultimately of Main Street's retirement savings, will be forever held by a small, elite group of corporate insiders—who will pass that power down to their heirs.

Commissioner Jackson raises a legitimate concern, but it's also a concern over which his agency has no legitimate authority.

Back in the 1990s, the SEC tried to regulate dual class stock via the back door. Using its power under Securities Exchange Act of 1934 § 19(c), which authorizes the Commission to adopt, repeal, or modify stock exchange listing standards,[47] the Commission adopted Rule 19c–4, which created new listing standards essentially banning dual class stock. In *Business Roundtable v. SEC*,[48] however, the D.C. Circuit struck down Rule 19c–4 as being beyond the scope of the SEC's authority. The Court held that the Commission has no authority to regulate generally corporate governance and that the Commission's authority to regulate proxies did not create an exception to that rule with respect to shareholder voting rights. Instead, the SEC's authority over shareholder voting is limited to disclosure and process; the SEC has no authority over the substance of shareholder voting, including the number of votes shares can possess. The substance of shareholder voting thus is solely and exclusively a matter for state corporate law.[49]

After Rule 19c–4 was struck down, the stock exchanges—purportedly voluntarily—adopted new listing standards governing the use of dual class stock. Those standards permitted listing of stock of a company that had a dual class capital structure in place when they conducted their IPO, but did not allow existing public companies to recapitalize to create a dual class structure.[50]

The stock exchange listing standards make sense. Although insiders are fiduciaries charged with protecting the shareholders' interests, dual class stock gives them voting control and thus eliminates both proxy contests and hostile takeovers as a potential accountability constraint on them. The insiders' temptation to therefore act in their own self-interest is obvious.

While the insiders' conflict of interest may justify some restrictions on some disparate voting rights plans, it hardly

---

[47] I'm using the term "stock exchange" here broadly to include NASDAQ.

[48] Bus. Roundtable v. SEC, 905 F.2d 406 (D.C. 1990).

[49] See Stephen M. Bainbridge, Comments to the Securities and Exchange Commission on No. 4-537: The Scope of the SEC's Authority Over Shareholder Voting Rights (May 7, 2007).

[50] Stephen M. Bainbridge, Revisiting the One-Share/One-Vote Controversy: The Exchanges' Uniform Voting Rights Policy, 22 Sec. Reg. L.J. 175 (1994).

justifies a sweeping prohibition of dual class stock. First, not all such plans involve a conflict of interest. Dual class IPOs are the clearest case. Public investors who don't want lesser voting rights stock simply won't buy it. Those who are willing to purchase it presumably will be compensated by a lower per share price than full voting rights stock would command and/or by a higher dividend rate. In any event, assuming full disclosure, they become shareholders knowing that they will have lower voting rights than the insiders and having accepted as adequate whatever trade-off is offered by the firm in recompense. In effect, management's conflict of interest is thus constrained by a form of market review.

It is for this reason that Commissioner Jackson's argument is unpersuasive. Yes, perpetual dual class capital structures ask investors to trust both the insiders and their kids. By buying the lesser voting rights shares in a dual class IPO, however, investors are effectively stating that they do trust the insiders and their kids. Or, at least, that they accept the tradeoff between the price they're paying for the shares and the reduction in accountability.

Even if that were not the case, however, how would Commissioner Jackson propose to regulate perpetual dual class stock? He quite properly expresses concern about the recent actions by FTSE Russell, S&P Dow, and MSCI to exclude dual class stock companies from their market indices:

> [M]iddle class investors often own stock in American public companies through an index. . . . If we ban all dual-class companies from our major indices, Main Street investors may lose out on the chance to be a part of the growth of our most innovative companies. The next Google or the next Facebook will deliver spectacular returns, but average Americans will, quite literally, not be invested in their growth.

Conversely, Commissioner Jackson nowhere proposes formal SEC action, presumably recognizing the Commission's lack of authority in this area.

Instead, the Commissioner wants the stock exchanges to "consider proposed listing standards addressing the use of perpetual dual-class stock." As we have seen, the stock exchanges previously intervened in this area when Rule 19c–4 was struck down. In doing so, however, they were not really acting voluntarily. Instead, knuckled under to what the late securities law professor Donald Schwartz colorfully referred to as the SEC's "raised eyebrow" power.[51] The stock exchanges routinely need SEC approval and cooperation as a basic part of their business operations. They need to keep the cop on their beat happy. If that cop informally tells them to jump, they jump. Accordingly, as the D.C. Circuit noted in *Business Roundtable,* "[t]he Commission has

---

[51]   See Donald E. Schwartz, Federalism and Corporate Governance, 45 Ohio St. L.J. 545, 571 (1984).

on occasion ... given hints that eventuated in the exchanges' proposing a change, a practice viewed by one observer as 'regulation by raised eyebrow.' "[52]

The SEC's use of its raised eyebrow power following its loss in *Business Roundtable* was a troubling abuse of regulatory power:

> Rather than obeying the law applicable to it, the Commission chose to end-run *Business Roundtable* by pressuring the exchanges to adopt "voluntary" listing standards modeled on Rule 19c–4. In doing so, the SEC also did an end-run around both Congress and the Supreme Court to create uniform, national corporate governance standards. As *Business Roundtable* confirmed, the SEC lacked authority to directly regulate dual class stock. Suspecting that the front door was locked, the Commission tried using Rule 19c–4 to sneak federal regulation through the back door. *In Business Roundtable*, however, the court squarely barred the Commission from doing indirectly what it could not do directly. Finding the back door to be locked as well, the SEC therefore sneaked through the cellar window. In doing so, it ran roughshod over the clear Congressional intent that the SEC was not to regulate corporate governance generally or the substance of shareholder voting rights in particular.[53]

The SEC was wrong to use its raised eyebrow power back in 1994. It would be equally wrong to do so now.

To assess your understanding of the material in this chapter, click here to take a quiz.

---

[52] *Business Roundtable*, 905 F.2d at 410 n.5 (citing Professor Schwartz's article). As Professor Scott explains:

> The marketplaces have complex and multilayered relationships with the SEC. Even in areas where the SEC has no direct authority, like the promulgation of corporate governance rules, it is risky for a marketplace to resist strong SEC suggestions. The marketplaces usually have several issues pending for the SEC at any one time, including a variety of listing proposals, trading rule changes, and disciplinary matters. While there is no overt "linking" of issues by the SEC, a marketplace is not likely to take a strong position in opposition to the SEC's "raised eyebrow," particularly when the SEC is exerting similar pressure on all the marketplaces.

Helen S. Scott, The SEC, the Audit Committee Rules, and the Marketplaces: Corporate Governance and the Future, 79 Wash. U. L.Q. 549, 555 (2001).

[53] Bainbridge, supra note 50, at 9 n.28.

CHAPTER 10

SHAREHOLDER ACTIVISM

What is shareholder activism?

The term "shareholder activism" describes a wide range of activities undertaken by the shareholders of public corporations that are designed to bring about some form of corporate change. Shareholder activism can relate to a range of issues, including corporate governance (e.g., non-classified boards, board diversity, proxy access, etc.), corporate investments, executive compensation, corporate oversight, corporate citizenship (e.g., environmental, social, political issues, etc.), and various other corporate issues.[1]

Shareholder activism traditionally was the province mainly of corporate social responsibility advocates and so-called shareholder gadflies:

The motivations of shareholder activists may vary widely based on the type of shareholder. Some shareholder activists appear to act out of a genuine desire to change corporate policies, typically related to social, environmental, or political causes. . . . Other shareholders, in particular corporate gadflies, may be motivated by a host of other factors, including personal vendettas, personal gain, 'thrills,' or other agendas. For example, one of the most famous corporate gadflies, Evelyn Davis, reportedly earned approximately $600,000 per year selling her annual newsletter to corporate executives who, in turn, hoped that she would not submit shareholder proposals or otherwise disrupt their annual meetings.[2]

Around 1990, however, that began to change as some investors—especially major institutional investors—began taking on a more active role in corporate governance. Unlike earlier activists, their agenda had a much clearer focus on share value and the return on their investment. In this Chapter, we discuss the various categories of institutions and the reasons why at least some of them have chosen to become more active. In the chapters that follow, we will look in more detail at the tools by which these investors engage companies, but the following chart offers a preview of that discussion:

---

[1]   Cynthia M. Krus, Corporate Secretary's Answer Book Q 6:40 (2018).

[2]   Id.

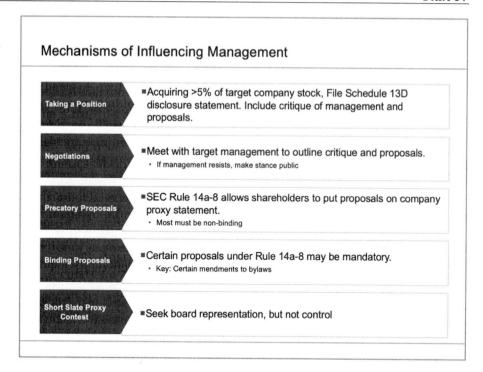

A. THE RISE OF INSTITUTIONAL INVESTOR ACTIVISM

Since the early 1990s, various governance activists and academics have argued that institutional investor corporate governance activism is becoming an important constraint on the principal-agent problem. Institutional investors, they argue, approach corporate governance quite differently than individual investors. Because institutions typically own larger blocks than individuals and have an incentive to develop specialized expertise in making and monitoring investments, the former should play a far more active role in corporate governance than retail investors. The institutions' greater access to firm information, coupled with their concentrated voting power, should enable them to more actively monitor the firm's performance and to make changes in the board's composition when performance lagged. As a result, concentrated ownership in the hands of institutional investors might lead to a reduction in shirking and, hence, a reduction in agency costs.

A comprehensive survey conducted at the end of the 1990s, however, found relatively little evidence that shareholder activism mattered.[3] Even the most active institutional investors spent only trifling amounts on corporate governance activism. Institutions devoted little effort to

---

[3]   Bernard S. Black, Shareholder Activism and Corporate Governance in the United States, in The New Palgrave Dictionary of Economics and the Law 459 (1998). Due to a resurgence of direct individual investment in the stock market, motivated at least in part by the day trading phenomenon and technology stock bubble, the trend towards institutional domination stagnated. Large blocks held by a single investor remained rare. Few U.S. corporations had any institutional shareholders who owned more than 5–10% of their stock.

monitoring management; to the contrary, they typically disclaimed the ability or desire to decide company-specific policy questions. They rarely conducted proxy solicitations or put forward shareholder proposals. They did not seek to elect representatives to boards of directors. They rarely coordinated their activities. Most importantly, empirical studies of U.S. institutional investor activism found "no strong evidence of a correlation between firm performance and percentage of shares owned by institutions."[4]

Ten years later, institutional investor activism remained rare. An important study by Stephen Choi and Jill Fisch published in 2008, for example, found that much public pension fund activism took the form of securities fraud litigation rather than corporate governance activities.[5] With some notable exceptions, most funds did not engage in such core governance activities as nominating directors or making shareholder proposals. Choi and Fisch concluded that their "findings offer reasons to be skeptical of the so-called promise of institutional activism."[6]

Why? Cost-benefit analysis suggests that activism is not a game worth playing for most institutional investors. On the cost side of the equation, monitoring expenses loom especially large. Because it is impossible to predict ex ante which corporations would benefit from activist attention, activist institutions must constantly monitor all of their portfolio firms. Because corporate disclosures rarely give one a full picture of the corporation's prospects, moreover, an activist cannot simply be content perusing disclosure documents for signs of trouble. Instead, costly direct monitoring mechanisms must be established. With many institutional investors holding portfolios of shares in hundreds or even thousands of corporations, the aggregate cost of such mechanisms would be very substantial. The high churn rate at many funds further compounds the problem as the make up of the portfolio rapidly changes, requiring constant creation of new monitoring mechanisms to deal with new holdings.

Monitoring costs are just the price of entry for activist institutions, however. Once they identify a problem firm, steps must be taken to address the problem. In some cases, it may suffice for the activist institution to propose some change in the rules of the game, but less tractable problems will necessitate more extreme remedial measures, such as removal of the incumbent board of directors.

In public corporations with dispersed ownership of the sort under debate here, such measures necessarily require the support of other shareholders, which makes a shareholder insurrection against inefficient but entrenched managers a costly and difficult undertaking. Putting together a winning coalition will require, among other things, ready

---

[4]   Id. at 462.
[5]   Stephen J. Choi & Jill E. Fisch, On Beyond CalPERS: Survey Evidence on the Developing Role of Public Pension Funds in Corporate Governance, 61 Vand. L. Rev. 315 (2008).
[6]   Id. at 318.

mechanisms for communicating with other investors. Unfortunately, SEC rules on proxy solicitations, stock ownership disclosure, and controlling shareholder liabilities have long impeded communication and collective action. Even though the 1992 SEC rule amendments somewhat lowered the barriers to collective action, important impediments remain.

Putting a precise dollar amount on the costs to an institutional investor—or group thereof—of waging an activist campaign obviously is difficult. It will depend on such factors as the form the activism takes, the size of the target, the extent to which target management resists, and so on. One effort to estimate the costs incurred by an activist who goes so far as to conduct a proxy contest, however, found that the average campaign cost $10.5 million, which represented 12% of the mean activist stake.[7] The cost of an activist campaign thus was significant both in absolute terms and, in particular, relative to the activist's mean return on its investment.

Turning to the benefits side of the equation, the returns to activism likely are low. Because many companies must be monitored, and because careful monitoring of an individual firm is expensive, institutional activism is likely to focus on crisis management. In many crises, however, institutional activism is unlikely to be availing. In some cases, intervention will come too late. In others, the problem may prove intractable, as where technological changes undercut the firm's competitive position.

Even where gains might arise from activism, only a portion of the gains would accrue to the activist institutions. Suppose that the troubled company has 110 outstanding shares, currently trading at $10 per share, of which the potential activist institution owns ten. The institution correctly believes that the firm's shares would rise in value to $20 if the firm's problems were solved. If the institution is able to effect a change in corporate policy, its ten shares will produce a $100 paper gain when the stock price rises to reflect the company's new value. All the other shareholders, however, will also automatically receive a pro rata share of the gains. As a result, the activist institution confers a gratuitous $1,000 benefit on the other shareholders.

Put another way, the gains resulting from institutional activism are a species of public goods. They are costly to produce, but because other shareholders cannot be excluded from taking a pro rata share, they are subject to non-rivalrous consumption. As with any other public good, the temptation arises for shareholders to free ride on the efforts of those who produce the good.

Given that activism will only rarely produce gains, and that when such gains occur they will be dispensed upon both the active and the passive, it seemed to little sense for cost-conscious money managers to

---

[7]   Nickolay M. Gantchev, The Costs of Shareholder Activism: Evidence from a Sequential Decision Model 4 (April 2010).

incur the expense entailed in shareholder activism. Instead, they will remain passive in hopes of free riding on someone else's activism. As in other free riding situations, because everyone is subject to and likely to yield to this temptation, the probability is that the good in question—here shareholder activism—will be under-produced.

In recent years, however, the landscape has shifted rather dramatically. The first decade of the new millennium saw repeated efforts by corporate governance activists to extend the shareholder franchise and otherwise empower shareholders to take an active governance role. In response, the major stock exchanges adopted new listing standards expanding the voting rights of investors. Likewise, the Delaware General Corporation Law and the Model Business Corporation Act were amended to allow corporations to require a majority vote—rather than the traditional plurality—to elect directors.

In 2008, the activists' efforts gained renewed impetus with the election of Barack Obama as President of the United States, the expansion of Democratic majorities in both houses of Congress, and the installation of a Democratic majority at the Securities and Exchange Commission. Echoing such constituencies as unions and state and local government pension plans, Washington Democrats blamed the financial crisis of 2007 in large part on corporate governance failures. Accordingly, much of their response took the form of new shareholder entitlements, such as say on pay and expanded ability to use shareholder proposals under Rule 14a–8 to effect changes in corporate election procedures. At the state level, Delaware General Corporation Law § 113 codified a Delaware Supreme Court decision recognizing a right for shareholders to unilaterally adopt bylaws governing the process by which corporate decisions are made, specifically including those requiring reimbursement of expenses of certain proxy contestants. Section 112 of the DGCL was adopted to authorize bylaws allowing shareholder access to the company's proxy materials to nominate directors.

In addition to the activists' political gains at both the federal and state levels, "changes in managerial compensation, shareholder concentration and activism, and board composition, outlook, and ideology," arguably have played even greater roles in empowering activist shareholders.[8] An important change is that significant amounts of new capital

> **WHAT'S THAT?**
>
> POISON PILL, Black's Law Dictionary (10th ed. 2014). A rights plan (a.k.a. a poison pill) is defined as: "Something in a company's financial or legal structure that is intended to make it difficult for another company or for a group of shareholders to take control of it; esp., a corporation's defense against an unwanted takeover bid whereby shareholders are granted the right to acquire equity or debt securities at a favorable price to increase the bidder's acquisition costs."

---

8   Edward B. Rock, Adapting to the New Shareholder-Centric Reality, 161 U. Penn. L. Rev. 1907, 1910 (2013).

have flowed into activist funds, especially hedge funds, giving them greater "financial firepower."[9] Another important factor is that many firms have disarmed, abandoning poison pill and classified board defenses.

As a result, activists have had increasing success in influencing corporate management through proxy contests and other interventions. Today, even the largest and most successful companies are no longer immune to shareholder activism.

B. INSTITUTIONAL INVESTORS AND THEIR PROPENSITY TO ACTIVISM

Until late in the 20th Century, institutional investors consisted mainly of banks, insurance companies, and mutual funds. None of these have incentives to be activists; to the contrary, all of them have strong disincentives. Put bluntly, even if activism made sense from a cost-benefit perspective, corporate managers are well-positioned to buy off these funds. Bank trust departments are an important class of institutional investors, for example, but are unlikely to emerge as activists because their parent banks often have or anticipate commercial lending relationships with the firms they will purportedly monitor. Similarly, insurers "as purveyors of insurance products, pension plans, and other financial services to corporations, have reason to mute their corporate governance activities and be bought off."[10]

Mutual fund families whose business includes managing private pension funds for corporations are subject to the same concern. A 2010 study examined the relationship between how mutual funds voted on shareholder proposals relating to executive compensation and pension-management business relationships between the funds' families and the targeted firms. The authors concluded that such ties influence fund managers to vote with corporate managers rather than shareholder activists at both client and non-client portfolio companies.[11] Voting with management at non-client firms presumably is motivated by a desire to attract new business and send signals of loyalty to existing clients.

Despite these limitations that historically constrained activism by traditional institutional investors, they have become an increasingly important complement to activism by hedge funds and other activists. First, institutions now hold a much higher percentage of the U.S. stock market than do retail investors. Fifty years ago, retail investors owned a majority of U.S. stocks. In contrast, today "retail investors directly own

---

[9]   Stephen F. Arcano, Activist Shareholders in the US: A Changing Landscape, The Harvard Law School Forum on Corporate Governance and Financial Regulation (June 28, 2013).

[10]   Mark J. Roe, Strong Managers, Weak Owners: The Political Roots of American Corporate Finance 62 (1994).

[11]   Rasha Ashraf et al., Do Pension-Related Business Ties Influence Mutual Fund Proxy Voting? Evidence from Shareholder Proposals on Executive Compensation (November 23, 2010), http://ssrn.com/abstract=1351966.

approximately 25 percent of publicly-traded equities and approximately 15 percent of publicly-traded debt, while institutional investors own approximately 75 percent and 85 percent, respectively."[12] Second, institutional investors vote at a much higher rate than individual investors.[13] Taken together, these developments mean that institutions wield far greater power than retail investors ever did. Finally, although traditional institutions still rarely initiate shareholder action, they are increasingly willing to piggy back on activist campaigns by hedge funds.[14]

While activist investors frame and seek to force governance/performance changes, they are successful only if they can attract broad support from institutional investors capable of assessing alternative strategies presented to them, even if they will not formulate the strategies themselves. In effect, activists must make their case to sophisticated but not proactive governance rights holders. Such a reactive role is a more plausible model for institutional investor engagement, reflecting both their expertise and incentives.[15]

In contrast to the more stolid types of institutions, union and state and local pension funds have been quite active with respect to corporate governance issues. Some commentators argue, however, that these are precisely the institutions most likely to use their position to self-deal or to otherwise reap private benefits not shared with other investors. With respect to union and public pension fund sponsorship of Rule 14a–8 proposals, for example, Roberta Romano observes that:

> It is quite probable that private benefits accrue to some investors from sponsoring at least some shareholder proposals. The disparity in identity of sponsors—the predominance of public and union funds, which, in contrast to private sector funds, are not in competition for investor dollars—is strongly suggestive of their presence. Examples of potential benefits which would be disproportionately of interest to proposal sponsors are progress on labor rights desired by union fund managers and enhanced political reputations for public pension fund managers, as well as advancements in personal employment.... Because such career concerns—enhancement of political reputations or subsequent employment opportunities—do not provide a commensurate benefit to

12   So-Yeon Lee, Why the "Accredited Investor" Standard Fails the Average Investor, 31 Rev. Banking & Fin. L. 987, 997 (2012)

13   See Jill E. Fisch, Standing Voting Instructions: Empowering the Excluded Retail Investor, 102 Minn. L. Rev. 11, 60 n.6 (2017) (reporting that "retail investors vote only 29% of their shares, while institutional investors vote 90%").

14   Sharon Hannes, Super Hedge Fund, 40 Del. J. Corp. L. 163, 205 (2015) ("Institutional investors who are the shareholders of a corporation that is targeted by a hedge fund activism campaign can vote for the activist in a proxy fight or otherwise voice their support for its campaign; they can also directly finance activist hedge funds.").

15   Ronald J. Gilson & Jeffrey N. Gordon, The Agency Costs of Agency Capitalism: Activist Investors and the Revaluation of Governance Rights, 113 Colum. L. Rev. 863, 897 (2013).

private fund managers, we do not find them engaging in investor activism.[16]

None of this is to deny, of course, that union and state and local pension funds also often have interests that converge with those of investors generally.[17]

Indeed, some commentators argue that pension funds are taking the lead in an important emerging area of concern:

> [P]ension funds are engaging in "risk-related activism"—the exercise of shareholder governance rights to motivate firms to effectively monitor, manage, and disclose risk, including nonfinancial environmental, social, and governance (ESG) risks. The term "ESG" is now widely used by institutional investors and investment professionals to refer not only to sustainability measures or to environmental, social, or governance practices specifically, but to all nonfinancial fundamentals that can impact firms' financial performance, such as corporate governance, labor and employment standards, human resource management, and environmental practices.[18]

Finally, we come to hedge funds. Marcel Kahan and Edward Rock explain that:

> [A]ctivist hedge funds have emerged as critical new players in both corporate governance and corporate control. Hedge funds have created headaches for CEOs and corporate boards by pushing for changes in management and changes in business strategy, including opposing acquisitions favored by management both as shareholders of the acquirer and as shareholders of the target, and by making unsolicited bids. . . . In many of these instances, hedge funds have been able to win outright or at least to wrest substantial concessions from the management of the companies they target.[19]

---

[16] Roberta Romano, Less Is More: Making Shareholder Activism A Valued Mechanism of Corporate Governance, 18 Yale J. Reg. 174, 231–32 (2001).

[17] See Stewart J. Schwab & Randall S. Thomas, Realigning Corporate Governance: Shareholder Activism by Labor Unions, 96 Mich. L. Rev. 1020, 1079–80 (1998).

[18] Virginia Harper Ho, Risk-Related Activism: The Business Case for Monitoring Nonfinancial Risk, 41 J. Corp. L. 647, 650–51 (2016).

[19] Marcel Kahan & Edward Rock, Embattled CEOs, 88 Tex. L. Rev. 987, 998 (2010).

Brian R. Cheffins & John Armour, The Past, Present, and Future of Shareholder Activism by Hedge Funds

37 J. Corp. L. 51 (2011)[20]

Shareholder activism has been described as "the exercise and enforcement of rights by minority shareholders with the objective of enhancing shareholder value over the long term." While defining shareholder activism by reference to the use of shareholder rights to enhance shareholder value delineates the basic parameters of this corporate governance tactic, the formulation is too general in nature to distinguish hedge fund interventions from those carried out by mainstream institutional investors such as mutual funds and public pension funds. . . .

> Mutual fund and public-pension fund activism, if it occurs, tends to be incidental and ex post: when fund management notes that portfolio companies are underperforming, or that their governance regime is deficient, they will sometimes be active (footnote omitted). In contrast, hedge fund activism is strategic and ex ante: hedge fund managers first determine whether a company would benefit from activism, then take a position and become active.

Employing the adjectives "defensive" and "offensive" provides a convenient way to distinguish the sort of activism in which mainstream institutional shareholders engage from the sort for which hedge funds—private investment vehicles that do not necessarily hedge their positions but have historically taken advantage of exclusions and regulatory "safe harbors" to operate largely outside statutory rules on investment companies and investment advisers—have achieved notoriety. Defensive shareholder activism occurs when an investor with a pre-existing stake in a company becomes dissatisfied with corporate performance or corporate governance and reacts by lobbying for changes, whether "behind the scenes" or with a public challenge to management (e.g. proposing the election of directors the dissident supports). A shareholder acting in this sort of ex post fashion will not own enough shares to guarantee victory in a contest for boardroom control or to dictate corporate policy but potentially can use their stake as a departure point in garnering support for the changes they advocate. To the extent pension funds and mutual funds engage in shareholder activism, it will most often be of this reactive ex post sort, as they work "defensively" to protect the value of existing investments.

The key feature that makes activism "defensive" is that the shareholder or shareholders taking the initiative will have held a sizeable stake before stepping forward. This "initial endowment" is not a

---

[20]   Reprinted by permission of Brian R. Cheffins, John Armour, and the Journal of Corporation Law.

feature of offensive shareholder activism. What happens instead is that an investor lacking a meaningful stake in a company builds up one "offensively" on the presumption that the company is not currently maximizing shareholder returns and with the intention of agitating for change to unlock shareholder value should this be necessary. The investor crucially will plan ex ante to press for a fresh approach if management does not take the initiative. As the quote from Kahan and Rock indicates, this is precisely the sort of activism for which hedge funds have gained notoriety.

The adjective "offensive" potentially connotes an aggressive posture towards incumbent management. This form of activism does not necessarily imply, however, shareholder/executive antagonism. While hedge fund activists have gained notoriety for their confrontational approach, they often aim for a collegial, if firm, "hands on" approach with incumbent management. As Warren Lichtenstein, the founder of Steel Partners II, a prominent activist hedge fund, said in 2004, "The best situation is where we find a cheap stock with great management and a great business, and we can sit back and make money." Correspondingly, Lichtenstein found when Steel Partners II bought shares, "Many times managements are happy there's a long-term, supportive investor."

Lichtenstein's reference to the desirable properties of a "cheap stock" reveals an overlap in investment philosophies between activist hedge funds and the prototypical "value investor" who seeks through diligent analysis of corporate fundamentals to purchase shares trading at a bargain price, the proverbial dollar for 50 cents. Hedge funds that engage in offensive shareholder activism typically rely on the "value approach" when identifying targets, forming as such a subset of hedge funds that invests in equities in a manner akin to classic, value-oriented investors. Managers of activist hedge funds correspondingly tend not to be experts in quantitative theories of finance—a typical attribute of a hedge fund manager—but are often former investment bankers or research analysts used to working hard to understand balance sheets and income statements. Activist hedge funds in turn often justify their investment strategy on the basis the companies they buy stakes in are undervalued, and the targets themselves, despite usually having sound operating cash flows and returns on assets, typically have a low share price relative to book value and low dividend payout ratios.

If an activist hedge fund identifies and invests in an "undervalued" company and the share price subsequently increases due to a belated reaction by the market rather than due to any prompting by the hedge fund, this will be relatively "easy money" for the hedge fund. The situation will be the same if management, on its own initiative, makes changes that serve to increase shareholder returns. Under such circumstances activist hedge funds who buy sizeable stakes in target companies merely need to wait to sell when the time is right and thus will be doing little more than engaging in conventional "stock picking."

The readiness to take a hands-on role to shake things up is the crucial additional dimension to hedge fund activism. Activist hedge funds, rather than merely adopting the passive approach that characterizes value investing and waiting for the market to self-correct—which may well never happen if a company's shares do not get noticed and instead drift lower—are prepared to take the initiative and accelerate matters by lobbying for changes calculated to boost shareholder returns. As a private equity fund manager said in 2007 of various prominent hedge fund activists, "I'd like to thank my friends Carl Icahn, Nelson Peltz, Jana Partners . . . for teeing up deals because . . . many times [activist targets] are being driven into some form of auction." Hence, despite Warren Lichtenstein characterizing Steel Partners II as a potentially "supportive investor," activist hedge funds do not give management a full-scale "vote of confidence" when they invest in companies.

Table 3. **Hedge Fund Categories**

Category	Description
Arbitrage	Focuses on perceived price disparities between linked products, such as buying an issuer's convertible bonds while simultaneously selling short the issuer's common stock.
Equity	Comparable to a traditional mutual fund in that takes long positions in a portfolio of common stocks expected to show unusual growth. A variant specializes in short selling stocks expected to decline in price.
Event Driven	Tries to take advantage of temporary mispricing or arbitrage opportunities the arise in connection with major corporate transactions such as mergers, bankruptcies, and restructurings. Most activist funds fall into this category.
Macro	Invests in indexes and derivatives that move in parallel with macroeconomic factors. It can involve currency trading or interest rate arbitrage transactions.

NOTE ON THE ACTIVIST GAME PLAN

Delaware Chief Justice Leo Strine observes that activist hedge funds do "not originally invest in companies they like and only become active when they become dissatisfied with the corporation's management or business plan. Rather, activist hedge funds identify companies and take an equity position in them only when they have identified a way to change the corporation's operations in a manner that the hedge fund believes will cause its stock price to rise."[21]

Cheffins and Armour explain that:

> Hedge fund activists, when they opt to be proactive, will typically begin by sounding out management with a telephone call, letter, or e-mail pressing the incumbent board to make changes designed to increase shareholder value. Hedge funds often lobby for finance-oriented changes, such as having a target company squeeze value from the balance sheet by spinning off underperforming non-core assets and by using share buy-backs or a sizeable one-off dividend to distribute "excess" cash to shareholders. More radically, a hedge fund activist may advocate an outright sale of the target, either as a going concern or through divestiture of key operations. Hedge funds also sometimes lobby in favor of increased operational efficiency and reputedly began putting more emphasis on strategic changes when the tighter credit markets associated with the 2008 financial crisis made it more difficult for target companies to engage in financial engineering.
>
> If a quiet approach fails to yield the desired results, an activist hedge fund can step up the pressure, perhaps by criticizing management in public or by threatening a lawsuit against the company's directors. A particularly forceful strategy is to threaten what Gilson and Schwartz term a "transfer by vote," this being the securing of managerial control by winning a proxy contest intended to determine who serves on the board. Activist investors say that because of the high costs involved they avoid proxy battles if possible. Moreover, the preference of hedge fund managers to avoid hands-on involvement in the running of target companies implies that securing board control will typically not be a high priority. Nevertheless, Alon Brav, Wei Jiang, Frank Partnoy, and Randall Thomas report in a widely cited study that in 13% of hedge fund activism incidents they uncovered through searches of filings under federal securities law the hedge fund was involved in a proxy contest to replace incumbent directors. A likely explanation for many of the proxy battles that do occur is that hedge funds use contests for board seats to signal to potential future targets that they are prepared to invest heavily in pursuing an activist campaign should this be required.[22]

Although hedge funds are reluctant to engage in proxy contests seeking board control, they are much more willing to engage in so-called short slate contests:

> Hedge funds have shaken up the U.S. corporate governance scene since the early 2000s by pushing for changes at targeted

---

[21] Leo E. Strine, Jr., Who Bleeds When the Wolves Bite?: A Flesh-and-Blood Perspective on Hedge Fund Activism and Our Strange Corporate Governance System, 126 Yale L.J. 1870, 1892 (2017).

[22] Brian R. Cheffins & John Armour, The Past, Present, and Future of Shareholder Activism by Hedge Funds, 37 J. Corp. L. 51 (2011).

companies such as sales, restructurings, higher dividend payments, and changes to corporate management. Hedge funds frequently take substantial positions in targeted companies' stock, between 5% and 10%, and then begin lobbying for change. Their activism "is backed up—implicitly or explicitly—by the threat of a proxy contest for corporate control." Fos and Tsoutsoura find that hedge fund activism has caused an increase in the number of proxy contests.

In another paper, Fos reports data on the number of control contests versus short slate contests: during the period 1994–2012, there were 199 control contests, but 708 contests involved short-slate contests to some extent. He notes that in the same years, hedge funds sponsored 602 contested proxy contests of all sorts (control contests, short-slate contests, and issue contests), or approximately 57% of all such fights. The hedge funds' sponsorship of proxy contests greatly increased in the latter part of this time period (2003–2012) so that they sponsored 70% of total proxy fights during that interval. Fos suggests that hedge funds prefer non-control contests, such as running a short slate of candidates, because they seek to change the management of a firm, not to manage the firm themselves.[23]

Hedge fund activists also tend to prefer short slate contests as opposed to full slate contests because proxy advisory services are more likely to support the former, as are passive non-activist institutional investors such as pension and mutual funds. In addition, a full slate proxy contest that succeeds in replacing at least a majority of the board may trigger change of control provisions in bond indentures, takeover defenses, and severance packages for executives.

In most cases, the dissident slate is nominated on the platform of an identified strategic or structural change for the issuer—a financial restructuring, cost-cutting, or a proposed sale of the company. By electing the dissident slate, shareholders are, in effect, voting their support for the activist's platform. Although the empirical analysis of this activism has, to date, been limited, early studies suggest that such activism may increase firm value. Moreover, improving corporate governance through proxy contests is far less costly than a hostile takeover, making it potentially viable at large public companies.[24]

---

[23]   Randall S. Thomas & Patrick C. Tricker, Shareholder Voting in Proxy Contests for Corporate Control, Uncontested Director Elections and Management Proposals: A Review of the Empirical Literature, 70 Okla. L. Rev. 9, 38–39 (2017).

[24]   Jill E. Fisch, The Overstated Promise of Corporate Governance, 77 U. Chi. L. Rev. 923, 935 (2010).

QUESTIONS

1.   How might hedge fund activist shareholder campaigns benefit other shareholders, including individuals rather than just other institutional investors?

2.   How might hedge fund activist shareholder campaigns harm other shareholders, including individuals rather than just other institutional investors?

3.   Should activist investors owe fiduciary duties to their fellow shareholders, which would require the activists to ensure that they do not harm the interests of their fellow shareholders?

4.   Hedge fund investors rarely own more than 10% of a company's stock and frequently own much smaller sums. Accordingly, to the extent their activism raises the stock price, most of those gains are captured by other investors. Why would hedge funds be willing to share the fruits of their activism with other investors in this manner? Can you imagine ways in which hedge funds might capture private gains from their activism that are not shared with other investors?

5.   Former Delaware Chief Justice Leo Strine observes that:

> The term "hedge fund activism" is an odd one. Hedge funds were originally associated more with the tempering, the "hedging," of risk. And that remains true. Many, if not indeed most, hedge funds are involved in trading strategies that do not involve the subject of this Feature. Many of them still focus on strategies combining leverage, "long" equity investments, and "short" downside-protecting hedges that gave hedge funds their name. But . . . I focus on the more oxymoronic part of the industry, which rather than primarily acting to hedge risk, takes an aggressive investment interest in the stock (and other securities and more exotic interests tied to the value of that stock) of a public company and seeks to make returns by influencing the corporation to change its capital structure or business plan. The funds that do this make up a minority of the overall hedge fund industry, but they have an outsized role in the debate about corporate governance because they have had an important effect on the manner in which public companies operate.[25]

As Chief Justice Strine notes, the more traditional types of hedge funds use a number of investing strategies, which differ significantly from the techniques used by activist funds:

> Some specialize in securities of distressed firms, while others make directional bets on the movement of currency exchange or interest rates. Still others pursue convertible arbitrage, going long in a convertible bond and shorting the underlying common stock. Many follow market momentum, moving in groups in and out of

---

[25]   Leo E. Strine, Jr., Who Bleeds When the Wolves Bite?: A Flesh-and-Blood Perspective on Hedge Fund Activism and Our Strange Corporate Governance System, 126 Yale L.J. 1870, 1885–86 (2017).

asset classes worldwide. Recently, some have taken up risky lending, funding leveraged buyouts and firms in bankruptcy reorganization, and trading in junk bonds and credit derivatives. The tie that binds the hedge funds together, despite the variety of investment styles, is their promise to deliver above-market returns, a task that becomes harder and harder as more funds pursue the same strategies.

One subset of hedge funds invests in domestic equities in the classic, value investor mode. The activist funds tend to come from this value-directed group. They maintain concentrated portfolios and often avoid the hedged or multi-strategy approaches followed by other funds, with their managers tending to be former investment bankers or research analysts rather than quantitative experts.[26]

NOTE ON WOLF PACK ACTIVISM

A Yale Law Journal comment explained that:

Wolf pack activism has surged in the past three years. A wolf pack is composed of a group of activist investors working in unison to gain control of corporate boards. These activist investors collectively buy stock in a public company and then leverage their aggregate stake to influence corporate decision-making. Wolf packs allow activist investors to pool their informational and financial resources, thereby greatly reducing the cost of seizing corporate control.... The rise of wolf packs may permanently shift the balance of power between corporate boards and control-seeking shareholders.

. . .

Economists believe that wolf packs tend to form when a single lead investor acquires a substantial stake in a target company. After the lead company makes its purchase, it often encourages other activist investors to purchase stocks in the target company. The activist investor makes these tips in the hopes of securing a broader coalition of votes for its proxy fight. The lead activist's large purchase may also independently spur purchases from other activist investors. These investors may catch wind of upcoming activist activity and buy stocks in an attempt to profit from the lead activist's success. In short, there is both empirical and anecdotal evidence of coordination among activist investors.[27]

---

[26]   William W. Bratton, Hedge Funds and Governance Targets, 95 Geo. L.J. 1375, 1382–83 (2007).

[27]   Carmen X.W. Lu, Unpacking Wolf Packs, 125 Yale L.J. 773, 773–776 (2016). Chief Justice Strine notes that there often is "suspicion that the alpha wolf has been organizing the hunt with the other wolves." Leo E. Strine, Jr., Who Bleeds When the Wolves Bite?: A Flesh-and-Blood Perspective on Hedge Fund Activism and Our Strange Corporate Governance System, 126 Yale L.J. 1870, 1896–97 (2017).

A leading securities regulation treatise explains some of the legal consequences under Exchange Act §§ 13 and 16 of forming a wolf pack:

> With respect to reporting based on beneficial ownership, . . . the section 16 reporting rules parallel the rules applicable to section 13(d) of the Williams Act. . . . It is clear that the Commission intended to create parallel definitions of beneficial ownership under sections 16 and 13(d). Section 13(d)'s beneficial ownership definition, which for the most part is carried over to section 16, is used only for determining one's status as a ten percent beneficial holder.
>
> . . . Under section 13(d), a group of persons acting together will count as one person for the purpose of computing the ownership threshold. The same group concept applies to section 16(a). In order to establish ten percent beneficial ownership as a group, plaintiff must establish an agreement to acquire, hold, or dispose of the company's stock. . . .
>
> The agreement that is a precondition to finding a group need not be in writing. Nor is it necessary that the agreement be one to gain or exert control; it is sufficient that the agreement include the acquisition of securities. It is not necessary that the agreement be unconditional nor subject to specific terms. . . . Once the existence of a group to acquire the shares is established, section 16(b) liability does not depend on a showing that the group acted in concert when selling their shares.[28]

PROBLEMS

1.   Celestial Capital Group, Harmony Hedge Fund, and Bookman Investment Fund are all hedge funds. Celestial, Harmony, and Bookman have entered into a contract pursuant to which Bookman will acquire 4.9% of the outstanding common stock of Target Corp. At present, none of the three funds own any Target stock. The contract also specifies that all three funds will cooperate with one another, share information about their efforts, support each other in both public and private, and not sell any Target shares without prior approval from the other two funds. Over the following six weeks, Bookman acquired the specified 4.9% of Target's common stock. On February 3, Bookman acquired an additional 1% of Bookman's shares. When Bookman files its Schedule 13D ten days later, must it include Celestial and Harmony as members of its 13D group even though they have not yet acquired any shares? If not, must Bookman's agreement with Celestial and Harmony be disclosed in the Schedule and, if so, how?

2.   Ultimately, Celestial, Harmony, and Bookman acquired a substantial amount of Target common stock. They held extensive negotiations with Target's board, which resulted in Target adopting a number of new corporate governance arrangements, replaced several board members with persons recommended by the hedge funds, and increased the

---

[28]   Thomas Lee Hazen. Treatise on the Law of Securities Regulation § 13.4 (2017).

company's quarterly dividend by 50%. Target's stock price rose in response to these changes and the hedge funds sold at a substantial profit. The following is a list of all their stock transactions.

FUND	DATE	ACTION	# OF SHARES	PRICE
BOOKMAN	February 1	Buy	4,900,000	$40
BOOKMAN	February 3	Buy	1,000,000	$39
CELESTIAL	February 14	Buy	4,500,000	$41
HARMONY	February 15	Buy	4,500,000	$40
BOOKMAN	February 15	Buy	5,750,000	$40
CELESTIAL	April 5	Sell	4,500,000	$50
HARMONY	April 5	Sell	4,500,000	$50
BOOKMAN	April 6	Sell	11,750,000	$50

Target has 100 million shares of common stock outstanding. What liability under § 16(b) do Celestial, Harmony, and Bookman have, if any?

3.   How would your answer change if the order of transactions were as follows:

FUND	DATE	ACTION	# OF SHARES	PRICE
BOOKMAN	February 1	Buy	4,900,000	$40
BOOKMAN	February 3	Buy	1,000,000	$39
CELESTIAL	February 14	Buy	4,500,000	$41
HARMONY	February 15	Buy	4,500,000	$40
BOOKMAN	February 15	Buy	5,750,000	$40
BOOKMAN	April 3	Sell	11,750,000	$50
CELESTIAL	April 5	Sell	4,500,000	$50
HARMONY	April 5	Sell	4,500,000	$50

NOTE ON MANAGING ACTIVIST SHAREHOLDERS

Corporate Governance expert Holly Gregory offers the following pointers for managers dealing with potential shareholder activists (and, of course, to the lawyers who advise such managers):

> Understanding key shareholders' interests and developing relationships with long-term shareholders can help position the company to address calls by activist investors for short-term actions that may impair long-term value. However, boards also should view the input they receive from activist investors as valuable, because it could help identify potential areas of vulnerability. Moreover, establishing an open and positive dialogue with activist investors, and engaging with them in meaningful

discussions, can assist boards in avoiding a public shareholder activist campaign in the future. This requires:

- Identifying the company's key shareholders and the issues about which they care the most.

- Objectively assessing strategy and performance from the perspective of an activist investor, including proactively identifying areas in which the company may be subject to activism.

- Monitoring corporate governance benchmarks and trends in shareholder activism to keep abreast of "hot topic" issues.

- Comparing the company's corporate governance practices to evolving best practice.

- Attending to potential vulnerabilities in board composition. Activist investors scrutinize the tenure, age, demographics, and experience of each director. They will target directors whose expertise is arguably outdated, who have poor track records as officers or directors of other companies, or who have served on the board for long tenures. They will also look for gaps in the expertise needed by the board given the current dynamic business environment, and for a lack of gender or ethnic diversity. . . .

- Addressing potential vulnerabilities in CEO compensation, including disparity with respect to peer companies and other named executive officers. Activist investors could claim that this signals a culture in which too much deference is given to the CEO and there is a lack of team emphasis in the compensation of management.

- Reviewing structural defenses with the assistance of seasoned proxy fight and corporate governance counsel. Many companies have not reviewed their charter and bylaws recently, and in a proxy contest the language of many bylaw provisions can take on a different meaning. Boards should be aware that proxy advisory firm ISS recently announced that it will generally oppose management proposals to ratify a company's existing charter or bylaw provisions, unless the provisions align with best practice.

- Effectively communicating long-term plans with respect to strategy and performance pressures, defending past performance, and addressing calls for an exploration of strategic alternatives.

- Preparing a response plan for engaging with activist investors to ensure that the board and management convey a measured and unified position.[29]

Proxy advisor Institutional Shareholder Services (ISS) argues that engagement is beneficial for both the company and its investors:

> Institutional investors are more receptive and likely to support Management's positions when the company has been in contact with them periodically over the course of the year. Although shareholder engagement may not always garner immediate results, it has the potential to lead to mutual agreements on various matters over time.
>
> Being in regular contact benefits both parties by facilitating a better understanding of the company (for shareholders) as well as the views and policies of its institutional shareholders (for issuers). If the only time your company reaches out to shareholders is when something bad is happening or about to happen, you can expect them to be wary to engage with and support you.[30]

Although most specialists in this area agree that there is no one size fits all model for shareholder engagement, ISS' recommendations are generally accepted as a useful starting point for developing a program tailored to the company's own needs:

> [W]hen engaging with shareholders on topics of strategy, performance, or boardroom independence, it is generally best to have Management, particularly the CEO, whose intimate knowledge of strategic issues and familiarity with day-to-day operations, meet with shareholders.
>
> Conversely, on issues regarding executive compensation, shareholder rights and other corporate governance matters, specific Board members, such as the Lead Director, Chairman (if "independent"), or Chairs of certain committees, would be best positioned to engage with shareholders.[31]

C. CONCERNS ABOUT EMPTY VOTING

The regulatory regime governing shareholder voting has been premised on the idea that managers, proxy dissidents, and the rest of the shareholders all share the same economic interest in the firm. Increasingly, however, it is possible that activist shareholders may have very different interests than the company's other shareholders.

---

[29] Holly J. Gregory, Looking Ahead: Key Trends in Corporate Governance, Practical L., Dec. 2018/Jan. 2019, at 34, 39.

[30] Tarun Mehta, Shareholder Engagement: Maximizing the Shareholder Relationship (2013).

[31] Id.

Securities and Exchange Commission, Concept Release on the U.S. Proxy System
Release No. 3052 (July 14, 2010)

... [T]his release primarily focuses on whether the U.S. proxy system operates with the accuracy, reliability, transparency, accountability, and integrity that shareholders and issuers should rightfully expect. These expectations are shaped in part by the Commission's proxy solicitation, disclosure and other rules, the rules of the national securities exchanges, as well as by the substantive rights granted under state corporate law and the charter and bylaw provisions of individual corporations.

At their core, these expectations are based on the foundational understanding that, absent contractual or legal provisions to the contrary, a "shareholder" possesses both voting rights and an economic interest in the company.

The ability to separate a share's voting rights from the economic stake through, for instance, what has been dubbed "empty voting" and "decoupling" challenges this foundational understanding. The term "empty voting" has been defined to refer to the circumstance in which a shareholder's voting rights substantially exceed the shareholder's economic interest in the company.[310] In this circumstance, the exercise of the right to vote is viewed as "empty" because the votes have been emptied of a commensurate economic interest in the shares (and, at the extreme, may even be associated with a negative economic interest in the sense of benefiting from a decline in the share price). Here, the bundle of rights and obligations customarily associated with share ownership has been "decoupled." Empty voting is an example of decoupling and can occur in a variety of ways, some of which we describe briefly below.

Such decoupling raises potential practical and theoretical considerations for voting of shares. For example, an empty voter with a negative economic interest in the company may prefer that the company's share price fall rather than increase. Such a person's voting motivation contradicts the widely-held assumption that equity securities are voted based on an interest in increasing shareholder value and in a way to protect shareholders' interests or enhance the value of the investment in the securities. That assumption—a core premise of state statutes requiring shareholder votes to elect directors and approve certain corporate decisions—may be undermined by the possibility that persons

---

[310] For the purposes of this release, empty voting does not include dual class or similar share structures in which the corporate charter prescribes disproportionate allocation of voting and economic rights, albeit in a fully disclosed fashion. Likewise, for purposes of this release empty voting does not encompass the situation in which the individuals within an institutional investor who determine that investor's voting decisions act independently of the person or persons making economic investment decisions in regard to the security being voted. Unlike the dual class situation, this latter situation could involve undisclosed decoupling of voting decisions from economic considerations.

with voting power may have little or no economic interest or, even worse, have a negative economic interest in the shares they vote. It is a source of some concern that elections of directors and other important corporate actions, such as business combinations, might be decided by persons who could have the incentive to elect unqualified directors or block actions that are in the interests of the shareholders as a whole. Significant decoupling of voting rights from economic interest could potentially undermine investor confidence in the public capital markets.

On the other hand, empty voting may not always be contrary to the interests of shareholders. One article argues, for instance, that informed investors could potentially improve electoral outcomes through empty voting by taking long economic positions, acquiring disproportionate voting power from less informed shareholders,[313] and casting votes that are more informed and thus more likely to contribute to shareholder value.

As discussed below, regardless of whether empty voting is deemed to be "good" or "bad," there is a strong argument for ensuring that there is transparency about the use of empty voting. If a voter acquires shares with a view to influencing or controlling the outcome of a vote but takes steps to reduce the risk of economic loss or even achieve a negative economic interest, disclosure of the empty voter's status and intentions could be important information to other shareholders.[315]

The Commission needs to further evaluate empty voting and related techniques in order to properly review the reliability, accuracy, transparency, accountability, and integrity of the current proxy system and the challenges that may be posed by empty voting and related techniques. Therefore, we are seeking information on the myriad ways in which decoupling can occur, and its nature, extent, and effects on shareholder voting and the proxy process. We understand that responses explicitly intended to address aspects of empty voting have already started to occur at the state corporate law and individual corporation level.[317]

A variety of techniques can be used to accomplish empty voting. One technique is to hold shares but to hedge the economic interest in those

---

[313] Notably, the nature of the decoupling in these circumstances is qualitatively different than that in which a person holding the right to vote has no economic interest, or a negative economic interest, in the issuer. Rather, such an investor has a positive economic interest, and while there is decoupling insofar as that investor holds voting rights that derive from shares owned by a different investor, that investor has voting interests that are aligned with the economic interest of investors generally.

[315] Item 6 of Schedule 13D requires disclosure of contracts, arrangements, understandings, or relationships with respect to the securities covered by the Schedule, but the filing of Schedule 13D is triggered only when a person owns greater than 5% of a Section 12-registered equity security, as such ownership is calculated according to the pertinent rules.

[317] For example, Delaware has amended its General Corporation Law to allow corporations to adopt measures to respond to certain record date capture strategies. Some corporations have adopted bylaws that, under certain circumstances, require shareholders submitting a proposal to disclose how they have hedged the economic interests associated with their share positions.

shares. A shareholder could hedge that economic interest in a wide variety of ways, including by buying either exchange-traded or OTC put options. In a recent Commission enforcement action, a registered investment adviser agreed to settle charges that it had violated Section 13(d) of the Exchange Act in furtherance of a strategy of "essentially buying votes." The investment adviser purchased shares of a prospective acquirer "for the exclusive purpose of voting the shares in a merger and influencing the outcome of the vote" on a proposed acquisition of a company in which the investment adviser owned a large block of stock. At the same time, the investment adviser entered into swap transactions with the banks from which it purchased the acquirer's shares, so that it "was able to acquire the voting rights to nearly ten percent of [the acquirer]'s stock without having any economic risk and no real economic stake in the company, [and] was able to do this without making a significant financial outlay."

While the practice of empty voting was not asserted as a substantive violation in the enforcement action, the matter illustrates how hedging techniques can be used to obtain voting power without having economic exposure on the securities being voted. The use of hedging by insiders also can result in empty voting. Executives entering into "collars" transactions, for instance, retain full voting rights despite having hedged a portion of their economic interest.[321]

Empty voting can also be accomplished by the use of credit derivatives (rather than through the use of put options and other equity derivatives), a process dubbed "hybrid decoupling." For example, instead of using put options to hedge its economic interest in shares, a shareholder may enter into credit default swap transactions with a derivatives dealer. If a company experiences poor economic performance, the likelihood of the company defaulting on its debt increases, and so the shareholder's credit default swap holdings will likely rise in value.

Finally, hedging-based strategies need not even involve holding either the debt or equity of the company in which the shareholder is voting, or derivatives linked to such debt or equity. A shareholder may, for instance, be able to hedge its exposure to a company's shares through purchasing assets correlated in some fashion to the company's share price. In the case of an acquisition, for example, a shareholder in the potential acquirer which also holds a larger equity interest in the target company, may arguably be characterized as being an empty voter with a negative economic interest in the acquirer. That is, the more the acquirer overpays for the target, the more net profit the investor would achieve.

---

[321] In a "collar" transaction, the investor sells a call option at one strike price and purchases a put option at a lower strike price. For little or no cost, the investor thereby limits the potential for appreciation or depreciation to the range—the "collar"—defined by the two strike prices. Academic research indicates that CEOs, directors, and senior executives have used this strategy to hedge their economic interest in the firm's stock.

Other correlated assets that may be used in empty voting strategies may include, for example, shares of a competitor or a supplier.[323]

There are a variety of situations in which empty voting may arise without any hedging at all. For example, active trading between a voting record date and the actual voting date may result in many voters having voting rights different from their economic stakes. An investor who sells shares after the voting record date retains the right to vote the shares without having any economic interest in them. Another example of empty voting without hedging is the voting of employees' unallocated shares in an employee stock ownership plan ("ESOP"). In an ESOP, while employees only have a contingent economic interest in the unallocated shares, the shares have full voting rights and are voted by a trustee, who either exercises discretion in voting or votes in proportion to vested ESOP shares. Effectively, either the trustee or the employees may become empty voters.

One important non-hedging based technique that appears to have been used outside the United States is borrowing shares in the stock lending market. Under standard stock lending arrangements, the borrower of the shares has the voting rights associated with the shares borrowed, but relatively little or no economic interest in the shares. Thus, simply by paying a fee to borrow the shares, the borrower can "buy" votes associated with the shares without having any corresponding economic interest. And the size of the fee could be reduced by borrowing the shares immediately before the record date, and returning the shares immediately afterwards. Within the U.S. this sort of practice appears to be limited by Regulation T, under which securities loans by institutional investors through their broker-dealers are restricted to distinct "permitted purposes" under the Federal Reserve Board's Regulation T, such as execution of a short sale.[327]

---

[323] And just as "equity decoupling" and "hybrid decoupling" could sometimes incentivize some shareholders to use their voting rights against the best interests of the company and other shareholders, some believe that a pattern that has been termed "debt decoupling"—the unbundling of the economic rights, contractual control rights, and other rights normally associated with debt—may sometimes raise incentive issues as to some debtholders. These debtholders, dubbed "empty creditors," may sometimes even have the incentive to use the control rights the debtholders have in their loan agreements or bond indentures to try to cause a company to go into bankruptcy.

[327] . . . This regulation limits the purposes for which broker-dealers who do not transact with customers from the general public may lend shares. Regulation T's "purpose test" generally provides that borrowers may only borrow securities for short selling, covering delivery fails, and similar purposes. Essentially, Regulation T requires broker-dealers to make a good faith effort to ascertain the borrower's purpose and cannot lend shares for voting purposes because that is not a permitted purpose under Regulation T. The standard securities lending agreement in the U.S. generally will contain a representation and warranty that the borrower, and any person to whom the borrower relends the borrowed securities, are only borrowing consistent with the "purpose test" (unless the borrowed securities are "exempted securities").

NOTES AND QUESTIONS

1.   Why is empty voting a concern?

2.   Under what state corporate law principles, if any, is empty voting regulated?

3.   Should hedge funds be required to disclose their holdings if those holdings could result in empty voting?

4.   In 2009, the Delaware legislature amended DGCL § 213(a) to address empty voting concerns:

> In order that the corporation may determine the stockholders entitled to notice of any meeting of stockholders or any adjournment thereof, the board of directors may fix a record date, which record date shall not precede the date upon which the resolution fixing the record date is adopted by the board of directors, and which record date shall not be more than 60 nor less than 10 days before the date of such meeting. If the board of directors so fixes a date, such date shall also be the record date for determining the stockholders entitled to vote at such meeting unless the board of directors determines, at the time it fixes such record date, that a later date on or before the date of the meeting shall be the date for making such determination. . . .

How does § 213(a) reduce concerns about empty voting?

To assess your understanding of the material in this chapter, click here to take a quiz.

CHAPTER 11

SHAREHOLDER ACTIVISM VIA PROXY CONTEST

The proxy contest is an important tool for shareholder activists. It is, however, a costly tool and one fraught with obstacles.

A. TYPES OF PROXY CONTESTS

Proxy contests come in three basic forms. An issue contest usually occurs when a dissident shareholder objects to some proposal put forward by the incumbent board of directors and solicits proxies in opposition to the proposal. Occasionally, however, an issue contest may be initiated by a dissident putting forward a proposal to which management objects. Historically, issue contests were rare, but "starting in the 1980s, an increasing number of proxy contests concerned issues other than director elections. For example, issue contests have involved charter amendments, merger agreements, acquisitions of other companies, liquidation plans, stock repurchases, reincorporations into other states, recapitalization plans, shareholder resolutions, and executive compensation schemes."[1]

Traditionally, most proxy contests were control contests; i.e., proxy contests in which a challenger puts forward a slate of directors as an alternative to the slate proposed by the incumbent board of directors. The dissident seeks to persuade the shareholders to elect the dissident's candidates to at least a majority of the available board positions.

In recent years, however, so-called short slate proxy contests have become much more common. In short slate contests, the dissident puts forward a slate that, if elected, would comprise less than a majority of the board. The dissident's goal is not to obtain control of the target corporation, but rather to obtain a position of influence. As such, short slate contests have become a favored tool of activist investors, especially hedge funds, who prefer "prefer non-control contests . . . because they seek to change the management of a firm, not to manage the firm themselves."[2] Short slate contests are also advantageous for activists because proxy advisory services are more likely to recommend support for a short slate contest than a control contest, because a successful short slate contest is seen as being able to induce needed changes in management and/or policy without being as disruptive as a total change

---

[1]   Lucian Arye Bebchuk, A Framework for Analyzing Legal Policy Towards Proxy Contests, 78 Cal. L. Rev. 1073, 1126–27 (1990).

[2]   Randall S. Thomas & Patrick C. Tricker, Shareholder Voting in Proxy Contests for Corporate Control, Uncontested Director Elections and Management Proposals: A Review of the Empirical Literature, 70 Okla. L. Rev. 9, 38–39 (2017).

of control. Finally, electing a short slate of directors nominated by the dissident is less likely to trigger change of control provisions in corporate contracts.

B. HISTORIC DISINCENTIVES TO ACTIVISM VIA PROXY CONTESTS

Law and economics scholar Henry Manne famously described proxy contests as "the most expensive, the most uncertain, and the least used of the various techniques" for acquiring corporate control.[3] Until the last few years, no one questioned his assessment. Insurgents contemplating a proxy battle face a host of legal and economic disincentives. Various state statutes permit corporations to adopt measures—so-called shark repellents—making it more difficult for an insurgent to gain control of the board of directors via a proxy contest. Among the more important of these are classified boards, the elimination of cumulative voting, and dual class stock plans. Other impediments include management's informational advantages and investor perceptions that proxy insurgents are not serious contenders for control. The two most common obstacles for a would-be insurgent, however, are the rules governing reimbursement of expenses and shareholder apathy.

This section reviews the principal costs that discourage proxy contests. Despite the resulting disincentives, in recent years proxy contests have become somewhat more common as a new set of countervailing incentives favoring proxy contests have emerged. We examine these changes in the next section.

1) REIMBURSEMENT OF EXPENSES

William L. Cary, Federalism and Corporate Law: Reflections Upon Delaware
83 Yale LJ 663 (1974)[4]

One area in which Delaware seems aligned with management involves proxy contests and take-overs. The courts apparently allow reimbursement of incumbent directors for reasonable expenses in defending their positions in a policy dispute.[65] By contrast, the law of New York still remains unsettled, although it may be moving in the direction of Delaware. At least three members of the New York Court of Appeals felt that the burden should be on the recipients to prove the

---

[3]   Henry G. Manne, Mergers and the Market for Corporate Control, 73 J. Pol. Econ. 110, 114 (1965).

[4]   Reprinted by permission of the Yale Law Journal.

[65]   See, e.g., Steinberg v. Adams, 90 F. Supp. 604, 607 (S.D.N.Y. 1950); Campbell v. Loew's, Inc., 36 Del. Ch. 563, 134 A.2d 852, 864 (Ch. 1957).

propriety and reasonableness of the items to be reimbursed.[67] Although the difference may not be great, the Delaware decisions indicate a clearer penchant in favor of management.

Rosenfeld v. Fairchild Engine & Airplane Corp.
309 N.Y. 168, 128 N.E.2d 291 (1955)

In a stockholder's derivative action brought by plaintiff, an attorney, who owns 25 out of the company's over 2,300,000 shares, seeks to compel the return of $261,522, paid out of the corporate treasury to reimburse both sides in a proxy contest for their expenses. The Appellate Division, . . . has unanimously affirmed a judgment of an Official Referee, . . . dismissing plaintiff's complaint on the merits, and we agree. . . .

Of the amount in controversy $106,000 was spent out of corporate funds by the old board of directors while still in office in defense of their position in said contest; $28,000 was paid to the old board by the new board after the change of management following the proxy contest, to compensate the former directors for such of the remaining expenses of their unsuccessful defense as the new board found was fair and reasonable; payment of $127,000, representing reimbursement of expenses to members of the prevailing group, was expressly ratified by a 16 to 1 majority vote of the stockholders.

. . . The Appellate Division found that the difference between plaintiff's group and the old board "went deep into the policies of the company", and that among these Ward's contract was one of the "main points of contention."

By way of contrast with the findings here, in *Lawyers' Advertising Co. v. Consolidated Ry., Lighting & Refrigerating Co.,* 187 N.Y. 395, . . . which was an action to recover for the cost of publishing newspaper notices not authorized by the board of directors, it was expressly found that the proxy contest there involved was "by one faction in its contest with another for the control of the corporation . . . a contest for the perpetuation of their offices and control." We there said by way of *dicta* that under *such* circumstances the publication of certain notices on behalf of the management faction was not a corporate expenditure which the directors had the power to authorize.

Other jurisdictions and our own lower courts have held that management may look to the corporate treasury for the reasonable expenses of soliciting proxies to defend its position in a bona fide policy contest. . . .

It should be noted that plaintiff does not argue that the aforementioned sums were fraudulently extracted from the corporation;

---

[67] See Rosenfeld v. Fairchild Engine & Airplane Corp., 309 N.Y. 168, 128 N.E.2d 291, 297 (1955) (Van Voorhis, J., dissenting). For evidence that New York is moving toward the Delaware approach, see Begleiter v. Moreland, 33 Misc. 2d 118, 119, 225 N.Y.S.2d 577, 579–80 (Sup. Ct. 1961).

indeed, his counsel conceded that "the charges were fair and reasonable," but denied "they were legal charges which may be reimbursed for." . . .

If directors of a corporation may not in good faith incur reasonable and proper expenses in soliciting proxies in these days of giant corporations with vast numbers of stockholders, the corporate business might be seriously interfered with because of stockholder indifference and the difficulty of procuring a quorum, where there is no contest. In the event of a proxy contest, if the directors may not freely answer the challenges of outside groups and in good faith defend their actions with respect to corporate policy for the information of the stockholders, they and the corporation may be at the mercy of persons seeking to wrest control for their own purposes, so long as such persons have ample funds to conduct a proxy contest. The test is clear. When the directors act in good faith in a contest over policy, they have the right to incur reasonable and proper expenses for solicitation of proxies and in defense of their corporate policies, and are not obliged to sit idly by. . . .

It is also our view that the members of the so-called new group could be reimbursed by the corporation for their expenditures in this contest by affirmative vote of the stockholders. . . .

The rule then which we adopt is simply this: In a contest over policy, as compared to a purely personal power contest, corporate directors have the right to make reasonable and proper expenditures, subject to the scrutiny of the courts when duly challenged, from the corporate treasury for the purpose of persuading the stockholders of the correctness of their position and soliciting their support for policies which the directors believe, in all good faith, are in the best interests of the corporation. The stockholders, moreover, have the right to reimburse successful contestants for the reasonable and bona fide expenses incurred by them in any such policy contest, subject to like court scrutiny. That is not to say, however, that corporate directors can, under any circumstances, disport themselves in a proxy contest with the corporation's moneys to an unlimited extent. Where it is established that such moneys have been spent for personal power, individual gain or private advantage, and not in the belief that such expenditures are in the best interests of the stockholders and the corporation, or where the fairness and reasonableness of the amounts allegedly expended are duly and successfully challenged, the courts will not hesitate to disallow them.

The judgment of the Appellate Division should be affirmed, without costs.

■ VAN VOORHIS, JUDGE (dissenting).

. . .

No resolution was passed by the stockholders approving payment to the management group. It has been recognized that not all of the $133,966 in obligations paid or incurred by the management group was designed merely for information of stockholders. This outlay included payment for all of the activities of a strenuous campaign to persuade and cajole in a hard-fought contest for control of this corporation. It included, for example, expenses for entertainment, chartered airplanes and limousines, public relations counsel and proxy solicitors. However legitimate such measures may be on behalf of stockholders themselves in such a controversy, most of them do not pertain to a corporate function but are part of the familiar apparatus of aggressive factions in corporate contests. . . .

The Appellate Division acknowledged in the instant case that "It is obvious that the management group here incurred a substantial amount of needless expense which was charged to the corporation," but this conclusion should have led to a direction that those defendants who were incumbent directors should be required to come forward with an explanation of their expenditures under the familiar rule that where it has been established that directors have expended corporate money for their own purposes, the burden of going forward with evidence of the propriety and reasonableness of specific items rests upon the directors. . . .

The second ground assigned by the Appellate Division for dismissing the complaint against incumbent directors is stockholder ratification of reimbursement to the insurgent group. Whatever effect or lack of it this resolution had upon expenditures by the insurgent group, clearly the stockholders who voted to pay the insurgents entertained no intention of reimbursing the management group for their expenditures. . . . Upon the contrary, they were removing the incumbents from control mainly for the reason that they were charged with having mulcted the corporation by a long-term salary and pension contract to one of their number, J. Carlton Ward, Jr. . . .

What expenses of the incumbent group should be allowed and what should be disallowed should be remitted to the trial court to ascertain, after taking evidence, in accordance with the rule that the incumbent directors were required to assume the burden of going forward in the first instance with evidence explaining and justifying their expenditures. Only such as were reasonably related to informing the stockholders fully and fairly concerning the corporate affairs should be allowed. The concession by plaintiff that such expenditures as were made were reasonable in amount does not decide this question. By way of illustration, the costs of entertainment for stockholders may have been, and it is stipulated that they were, at the going rates for providing similar entertainment. That does not signify that entertaining stockholders is reasonably related to the purposes of the corporation. . . .

Regarding the $127,556 paid by the new management to the insurgent group for their campaign expenditures, the question immediately arises whether that was for a corporate purpose. The Appellate Division has recognized that upon no theory could such expenditures be reimbursed except by approval of the stockholders and, as has been said, it is the insurgents' expenditures alone to which the stockholders' resolution of ratification was addressed. If *unanimous* stockholder approval had been obtained and no rights of creditors or of the public intervened, it would make no practical difference whether the purpose were *ultra vires*—i.e., not a corporate purpose.... Upon the other hand, an act which is *ultra vires* cannot be ratified merely by a majority of the stockholders of a corporation.

The ... cases which are cited consist of *Hall v. Trans-Lux Daylight Picture Screen Corp.*, 20 Del.Ch. 78, 171 A. 226, ... and the Federal cases applying Delaware law, *Hand v. Missouri-Kansas Pipe Line Co., D.C.*, 54 F.Supp. 649, and *Steinberg v. Adams*, [90 F.Supp. 604]....

The case most frequently cited and principally relied upon from among these Delaware decisions is *Hall v. Trans-Lux Daylight Picture Screen Corp.*, supra. There the English case was followed of *Peel v. London & North Western Ry. Co.*, [1 Ch. 5 (1907)], which distinguished between expenses merely for the purpose of maintaining control, and contests over policy questions of the corporation. In the *Hall* case the issues concerned a proposed merger, and a proposed sale of stock of a subsidiary corporation. These were held to be policy questions, and payment of the management campaign expenses was upheld.

In our view, the impracticability of such a distinction is illustrated by the statement in the *Hall* case, ... that "It is impossible in many cases of intracorporate contests over directors, to sever questions of policy from those of persons." This circumstance is stressed in Judge Rifkind's opinion in the *Steinberg* case ...:

"The simple fact, of course, is that generally policy and personnel do not exist in separate compartments. A change in personnel is sometimes indispensable to a change of policy. A new board may be the symbol of the shift in policy as well as the means of obtaining it."

That may be all very well, but the upshot of this reasoning is that inasmuch as it is generally impossible to distinguish whether "policy" or "personnel" is the dominant factor, any averments must be accepted at their face value that questions of policy are dominant. Nowhere do these opinions mention that the converse is equally true and more pervasive, that neither the "ins" nor the "outs" ever say that they have no program to offer to the shareholders, but just want to acquire or to retain control, as the case may be. In common experience, this distinction is unreal....

The main question of "policy" in the instant corporate election, as is stated in the opinions below and frankly admitted, concerns the long-term contract with pension rights of a former officer and director, Mr. J. Carlton Ward, Jr. The insurgents' chief claim of benefit to the corporation from their victory consists in the termination of that agreement, resulting in an alleged actuarial saving of $350,000 to $825,000 to the corporation, and the reduction of other salaries and rent by more than $300,000 per year. The insurgents had contended in the proxy contest that these payments should be substantially reduced so that members of the incumbent group would not continue to profit personally at the expense of the corporation. If these charges were true, which appear to have been believed by a majority of the shareholders, then the disbursements by the management group in the proxy contest fall under the condemnation of the English and the Delaware rule.

These circumstances are mentioned primarily to illustrate how impossible it is to distinguish between "policy" and "personnel," as Judge Rifkind expressed it, but they also indicate that personal factors are deeply rooted in this contest. That is certainly true insofar as the former management group is concerned. It would be hard to find a case to which the careful reservation made by the English Judge in the *Peel* case, supra, was more directly applicable.

NOTES AND QUESTIONS

1.   Under *Rosenfeld v. Fairchild Engine & Airplane Corp.*, a shareholder may properly challenge an incumbent board of directors' decision to expend corporate funds "for the purpose of persuading the stockholders of the correctness of their position and soliciting their support" on all of the following grounds, *except*:

A.   The directors were engaged in a purely personal power contest with an insurgent.

B.   The directors were not acting in good faith.

C.   The directors did not believe that the expenditures were in the best interests of the stockholders and the corporation.

D.   The amount of funds expended was unreasonably high.

E.   All of the above are grounds on which a shareholder may properly challenge expenses incurred by the board.

2.   True or False: Under *Rosenfeld*, a dissident shareholder who conducts and loses a proxy contest may have his or her expenses reimbursed out of the corporate treasury if the corporation's board of directors consents.

3.   What policy justification is there for the rules limiting reimbursement of dissident shareholder proxy context expenses?

4.   In order to find an inefficiently managed firm, a potential insurgent group will need to investigate many firms. Under *Rosenfeld*, it may be compensated for the cost of a proxy fight if it wins. Yet it will not be compensated either for the cost of investigating firms that it discovers are properly managed, or for the cost of proxy fights it loses. How does this affect the incentive to renovate inefficiently managed firms?

5.   If insurgent groups are reimbursed only when they win, should incumbents be reimbursed when they lose?

NOTES AND QUESTIONS ON CA, INC. V. AFSCME EMPLOYEES PENSION PLAN AND DGCL § 113

In *AFSCME,* which is excerpted in Chapter 12, AFSCME's pension fund used SEC Rule 14a–8 to propose an amendment to CA's bylaws pursuant to which a shareholder who successfully conducted a short slate proxy contest would be entitled to reimbursement of its reasonable expenses. CA objected to inclusion of the proposal in the proxy statement and asked the SEC for a no-action letter supporting exclusion.[5]

Before answering CA's request, the SEC invoked Delaware's new constitutional provision allowing the SEC to certify questions of law to the Delaware Supreme Court. The SEC certified two questions: (1) Was AFSCME's proposal a proper subject for shareholder action under Delaware law and (2) would the proposal, if adopted, cause CA to violate any Delaware law?

The Delaware Supreme Court held that the proposal is a proper subject of shareholder action. The Supreme Court declined to "articulate with doctrinal exactitude a bright line" that would divide those bylaws that shareholders may permissibly adopt from those that go too far in infringing upon the directors' right to manage the corporation. Bylaws that relate to the process for electing directors, however, go to "a subject in which shareholders of Delaware corporations have a legitimate and protected interest." Accordingly, the AFSCME proposal was a proper subject for stockholder action.

On the other hand, the court also noted that, if adopted, the proposal would cause CA to violate Delaware law in some cases. The proposal could require the board to reimburse a successful short slate proxy contestant even if a proper application of fiduciary principles would preclude the board from doing so. As examples of such cases, the Court pointed to a proxy contest undertaken for "personal or petty concerns, or to promote interests that do not further, or are adverse to, those of the corporation." In order not to violate the board's fiduciary duties under Delaware law, the proposal therefore would have to include a fiduciary out pursuant to which the board may refuse to reimburse an insurgent when doing so would violate the board's fiduciary duties.

In response to *CA*, the Delaware legislature adopted DGCL § 113, which expressly authorizes proxy expense reimbursement bylaws:

(a) The bylaws may provide for the reimbursement by the corporation of expenses incurred by a stockholder in soliciting proxies in connection with an election of directors, subject to such procedures or conditions as the bylaws may prescribe, including:

(1) Conditioning eligibility for reimbursement upon the number or proportion of persons nominated by the stockholder

5   CA, Inc. v. AFSCME Employees Pension Plan, 953 A.2d 227 (Del. 2008). Under SEC Rule 14a–8, shareholders meeting specified eligibility requirements may a proposal and accompanying supporting statement not exceeding 500 words in length for inclusion in the company's proxy statement and on the company's proxy card. An included proposal must then be brought up at the shareholder meeting for a vote.

seeking reimbursement or whether such stockholder previously sought reimbursement for similar expenses;

(2)   Limitations on the amount of reimbursement based upon the proportion of votes cast in favor of 1 or more of the persons nominated by the stockholder seeking reimbursement, or upon the amount spent by the corporation in soliciting proxies in connection with the election;

(3)   Limitations concerning elections of directors by cumulative voting pursuant to § 214 of this title; or

(4)   Any other lawful condition.

(b)   No bylaw so adopted shall apply to elections for which any record date precedes its adoption.

1.   What sort of conditions does § 113 allow the bylaw to put on reimbursement? What sort of conditions would incumbent managers likely prefer? What sort of conditions would shareholders likely prefer?

2.   Although § 113 mostly codifies the *CA* decision, the statute does not expressly require a fiduciary out. Whether courts will follow the *CA* decision and continue to require that a bylaw include a fiduciary out in order to be valid remains uncertain. A precedent for doing so is provided by the Delaware Supreme Court's treatment of Delaware's force-the-vote statute. In *Smith v. Van Gorkom*,[6] the Delaware Supreme Court held that directors could not submit a merger to shareholders without making a recommendation that it be approved. The Delaware legislature later overturned that result by adopting DGCL § 251(c), which provides: "The terms of the agreement may require that the agreement be submitted to the stockholders whether or not the board of directors determines at any time subsequent to declaring its advisability that the agreement is no longer advisable and recommends that the stockholders reject it." In *Omnicare, Inc. v. NCS Healthcare, Inc.*,[7] the court held that § 251 did not trump the fiduciary duties of directors. "Taking action that is otherwise legally possible, however, does not ipso facto comport with the fiduciary responsibilities of directors in all circumstances. . . . Section 251 provisions . . . are 'presumptively valid in the abstract.' Such provisions in a merger agreement may not, however, 'validly define or limit the directors' fiduciary duties under Delaware law or prevent the [NCS] directors from carrying out their fiduciary duties under Delaware law."[8] If so, however, what is the point of § 251? In any case, *Omnicare* thus stands as a clear precedent for a judicial mandate that § 113 bylaws include a fiduciary out despite the statute's silence on the point.

2) SHAREHOLDER APATHY AND RELATED PROBLEMS

The insurgent's problems are said to be compounded by the other shareholders' rational apathy. As the theory goes, a rational shareholder

---

[6]   488 A.2d 858 (Del.1985).

[7]   818 A.2d 914 (Del.2003).

[8]   Id. at 937–38.

will expend the effort to make an informed decision only if the expected benefits of doing so outweigh its costs. Given the length and complexity of proxy statements, especially in a proxy contest where the shareholder is receiving multiple communications from the contending parties, the opportunity cost entailed in reading the proxy statements before voting is quite high and very apparent. Shareholders also probably do not expect to discover grounds for opposing management from the proxy statements. Finally, most shareholders' holdings are too small to have any significant effect on the vote's outcome. Accordingly, shareholders can be expected to assign a relatively low value to the expected benefits of careful consideration. Shareholders are thus rationally apathetic. For the average shareholder, the necessary investment of time and effort in making informed voting decisions simply is not worthwhile.[9]

Instead of carefully considering the contending parties' arguments, retail shareholders typically adopt the so-called Wall Street Rule: it's easier to switch than fight. To the extent the shareholders are satisfied, they will vote for management. Disgruntled shareholders, in contrast, will have long since sold out. As a result, shareholders are likely to vote for management even where that is not the decision an informed shareholder would reach. The insurgent thus risks laying out considerable funds for no return on that investment.

3) THE CHANGING PROXY CONTEST LANDSCAPE

Starting in the 1990s, various factors combined to make hostile tender offers a much less attractive, and proxy contests a much more attractive, acquisition technique than they had been up to that point. Perhaps the most important factors in the proxy contest's resurgence were two supreme court decisions. *Paramount Communications, Inc. v. Time Inc.*,[10] by the Delaware Supreme Court, significantly weakened the standards by which target takeover defenses are measured. Under Delaware law, incumbent directors must show that the hostile offer poses a threat to corporate policy and that their response was reasonable in relation to the threat.[11] *Time* both recognized a much broader class of cognizable threats and weakened the proportionality requirement. As a result, effective management takeover defenses should pass muster more easily. Not only does this trend make hostile tender offers more difficult, it also encourages bidders to conduct a proxy contest before making a tender offer. If elected, the bidder's nominees often can lower the target's defenses and thereby permit the tender offer to go forward.

---

[9]   Frank H. Easterbrook and Daniel R. Fischel, Voting in Corporate Law, 26 J. L. & Econ. 395, 402 (1983); Martin Lipton, Corporate Governance in the Age of Finance Corporatism, 136 U. Penn. L. Rev. 1, 66–67 (1987). The problem is compounded by the likelihood that a substantial number of shareholders will attempt to freeride on the efforts of the few informed shareholders.

[10]   571 A.2d 1140 (Del.1989).

[11]   See Unocal Corp. v. Mesa Petroleum Co., 493 A.2d 946 (Del.1985).

In *CTS Corp. v. Dynamics Corp.*,[12] the U.S. Supreme Court for the first time upheld a state takeover law against constitutional challenge. Since *CTS*, state takeover laws have routinely withstood constitutional scrutiny. By erecting new barriers to hostile tender offerors, they make tender offers less attractive. Because most permit the target's board of directors to waive their application to a particular bid, they also encourage pre-offer proxy contests.

Proxy contests probably will never become commonplace. They remain expensive and risky. Yet, they are an essential part of both the market for corporate influence and that for corporate control. As to the former, activist campaigns—especially the use of short slate contests by hedge funds to elect board representatives—are an essential threat in the activist playbook. As to the latter, so long as outsiders want to buy companies whose incumbent directors and officers want to remain independent, proxy contests will be part of the buyer's toolkit.

4) PROXY ADVISORY FIRMS

A major factor in the increasing importance of proxy contests has been the rise of proxy advisory services.

Securities and Exchange Commission, Concept Release on the U.S. Proxy System
Release No. 3052 (July 14, 2010)

. . .

1. The Role and Legal Status of Proxy Advisory Firms

Over the last twenty-five years, institutional investors, including investment advisers, pension plans, employee benefit plans, bank trust departments and funds, have substantially increased their use of proxy advisory firms, reflecting the tremendous growth in institutional investment as well as the fact that, in many cases, institutional investors have fiduciary obligations to vote the shares they hold on behalf of their beneficiaries. Institutional investors typically own securities positions in a large number of issuers.

Every year, at shareholders' meetings, these investors face decisions on how to vote their shares on a significant number of matters, ranging from the election of directors and the approval of stock option plans to shareholder proposals submitted under Exchange Act Rule 14a–8, which often raise significant policy questions and corporate governance issues. At special meetings of shareholders, investors also face voting decisions when a merger or acquisition or a sale of all or substantially all of the assets of the company is presented to them for approval.

---

[12]   481 U.S. 69 (1987).

In order to assist them in exercising their voting rights on matters presented to shareholders, institutional investors may retain proxy advisory firms to perform a variety of functions, including the following:

- Analyzing and making voting recommendations on the matters presented for shareholder vote and included in the issuers' proxy statements;

- Executing votes on the institutional investors' proxies or VIFs in accordance with the investors' instructions, which may include voting the shares in accordance with a customized proxy voting policy resulting from consultation between the institutional investor and the proxy advisory firm, the proxy advisory firm's proxy voting policies, or the institution's own voting policy;

- Assisting with the administrative tasks associated with voting and keeping track of the large number of voting decisions;

- Providing research and identifying potential risk factors related to corporate governance; and

- Helping mitigate conflict of interest concerns raised when the institutional investor is casting votes in a matter in which its interest may differ from the interest of its clients.

Firms that are in the business of supplying these services to clients for compensation—in particular, analysis of and recommendations for voting on matters presented for a shareholder vote—are widely known as proxy advisory firms. Institutional clients compensate proxy advisory firms on a fee basis for providing such services, and proxy advisory firms typically represent that their analysis and recommendations are prepared with a view toward maximizing long-term share value or the investment goals of the institutional client.

Issuers may also be consumers of the services provided by some proxy advisory firms. Some proxy advisory firms provide consulting services to issuers on corporate governance or executive compensation matters, such as assistance in developing proposals to be submitted for shareholder approval. Some proxy advisory firms also qualitatively rate or score issuers' corporate governance structures, policies, and practices, and provide consulting services to corporate clients seeking to improve their corporate governance ratings. As a result, some proxy advisory firms provide vote recommendations to institutional investors on matters for which they also provided consulting services to the issuer. Some proxy advisory firms disclose these dual client relationships; others also have opted to attempt to address the conflict through the creation of "fire walls" between the investor and corporate lines of business.

Depending on their activities, proxy advisory firms may be subject to the federal securities laws in at least two notable respects. First, because of the breadth of the definition of "solicitation,"[243] proxy advisory firms may be subject to our proxy rules because they provide recommendations that are reasonably calculated to result in the procurement, withholding, or revocation of a proxy. As a general matter, the furnishing of proxy voting advice constitutes a "solicitation" subject to the information and filing requirements in the proxy rules. In 1979, however, we adopted Exchange Act Rule 14a–2(b)(3)245 to exempt the furnishing of proxy voting advice by any advisor to any other person with whom the advisor has a business relationship from the informational and filing requirements of the federal proxy rules, provided certain conditions are met. Specifically, the advisor:

- Must render financial advice in the ordinary course of its business;

- Must disclose to the person any significant relationship it has with the issuer or any of its affiliates, or with a shareholder proponent of the matter on which advice is given, in addition to any material interest of the advisor in the matter to which the advice relates;

- May not receive any special commission or remuneration for furnishing the proxy voting advice from anyone other than the recipients of the advice; and

- May not furnish proxy voting advice on behalf of any person soliciting proxies.

Even if exempt from the informational and filing requirements of the federal proxy rules, the furnishing of proxy voting advice remains subject to the prohibition on false and misleading statements in Rule 14a–9.

Second, when proxy advisory firms provide certain services, they meet the definition of investment adviser under the Advisers Act and thus are subject to regulation under that Act. A person is an "investment adviser" if the person, for compensation, engages in the business of providing advice to others as to the value of securities, whether to invest in, purchase, or sell securities, or issues reports or analyses concerning securities. As described above, proxy advisory firms receive compensation for providing voting recommendations and analysis on matters submitted for a vote at shareholder meetings. These matters may include shareholder proposals, elections for boards of directors, or corporate actions such as mergers. We understand that typically proxy advisory firms represent that they provide their clients with advice designed to enable institutional clients to maximize the value of their investments. In other words, proxy advisory firms provide analyses of shareholder proposals, director candidacies or corporate actions and

---

[243] Exchange Act Rule 14a–1(*l*)(iii) [17 CFR 240.14a–1(*l*)(iii)] defines the solicitation of proxies to include "[t]he furnishing of a form of proxy or other communication to security holders under circumstances reasonably calculated to result in the procurement, withholding or revocation of a proxy."

provide advice concerning particular votes in a manner that is intended to assist their institutional clients in achieving their investment goals with respect to the voting securities they hold. In that way, proxy advisory firms meet the definition of investment adviser because they, for compensation, engage in the business of issuing reports or analyses concerning securities and providing advice to others as to the value of securities.

The Supreme Court has construed Section 206 of the Advisers Act as establishing a federal fiduciary standard governing the conduct of investment advisers. The Court stated that "[t]he Advisers Act of 1940 reflects a congressional recognition of the delicate fiduciary nature of an investment advisory relationship as well as a congressional intent to eliminate, or at least to expose, all conflicts of interest which might incline an investment adviser—consciously or unconsciously—to render advice which was not disinterested." As investment advisers, proxy advisory firms owe fiduciary duties to their advisory clients.

In addition, Section 206 of the Advisers Act, the antifraud provision, applies to any person that meets the definition of investment adviser, regardless of whether that person is registered with the Commission. Section 206(1) of the Advisers Act prohibits an investment adviser from "employ[ing] any device, scheme, or artifice to defraud any client or prospective client." Section 206(2) prohibits an investment adviser from engaging in "any transaction, practice or course of business which operates as a fraud or deceit on any client or prospective client." As we stated recently, the Commission has authority under Section 206(4) of the Advisers Act to adopt rules "reasonably designed to prevent, such acts, practices, and courses of business as are fraudulent, deceptive or manipulative." Congress gave the Commission this authority to, among other things, address the "question as to the scope of the fraudulent and deceptive activities which are prohibited [by Section 206]," and thereby permit the Commission to adopt rules that may prohibit acts that are not themselves fraudulent.

Proxy advisory firms also may have to register with the Commission as investment advisers. Whether a particular investment adviser is required to register with the Commission depends on several factors. Investment advisers are generally prohibited from registering with the Commission if they have less than $25 million in assets under management. Congress established this threshold in 1996 to bifurcate regulatory responsibility between the Commission and the states. The Commission retains authority to exempt advisers from the prohibition on registration if the prohibition would be "unfair, a burden on interstate commerce, or otherwise inconsistent with the purposes" of the prohibition.

Proxy advisory firms are unlikely to have sufficient assets under management to register with the Commission because they typically do not manage client assets. Proxy advisory firms may nonetheless be eligible to register because they qualify for one of the exemptions from the registration prohibition under Rule 203A–2 under the Advisers Act. In particular, some proxy advisory firms may be able to rely on the exemption for "pension consultants" if they have pension plan clients with an aggregate minimum value of $50 million.

Proxy advisory firms that are registered as investment advisers with the Commission are subject to a number of additional regulatory requirements that provide important protections to the firm's clients. For example, registered investment advisers have to make certain disclosures on their Form ADV.[264] Among other things, these disclosures include information about arrangements that the adviser has that involve certain conflicts of interest with its advisory client. In addition, proxy advisory firms that are registered investment advisers are required to adopt, implement, and annually review an internal compliance program consisting of written policies and procedures that are reasonably designed to prevent the adviser or its supervised persons from violating the Advisers Act. Every registered proxy advisory firm that is registered as an investment adviser also must designate a chief compliance officer to oversee its compliance program. This compliance officer must be knowledgeable about the Advisers Act and have authority to develop and enforce appropriate compliance policies and procedures for the adviser. A proxy advisory firm that is registered as an investment adviser also is required to establish, maintain, and enforce policies and procedures reasonably designed to prevent the misuse of material non-public information. Proxy advisory firms that are registered as investment advisers also are required to create and preserve certain records that our examiners review when performing an inspection of an adviser.

2. Concerns About the Role of Proxy Advisory Firms

The use of proxy advisory firms by institutional investors raises a number of potential issues. For example, to the extent that conflicts of interest on the part of proxy advisory firms are insufficiently disclosed and managed, shareholders could be misled and informed shareholder voting could be impaired. To the extent that proxy advisory firms develop, disseminate, and implement their voting recommendations without adequate accountability for informational accuracy in the development and application of voting standards, informed shareholder voting may be likewise impaired. Furthermore, some have argued that proxy advisory firms are controlling or significantly influencing shareholder voting without appropriate oversight, and without having an

---

[264] See Advisers Act Rule 203–1 [17 CFR 275.203–1]. Form ADV consists of two parts. The information provided by advisers in Part I of that form provides the Commission with census-like information on investment adviser registrants and is critical to the examination program in assessing risk and planning examinations. It also requires investment advisers to report disciplinary events of the adviser and its employees. See Advisers Act Rule 204–1 [17 CFR 275.204–1].

actual economic stake in the issuer.[270] In evaluating any potential regulatory response to such issues, we are interested in learning commentators' views regarding appropriate means of addressing these issues, including the application of the proxy solicitation rules and Advisers Act registration provisions to proxy advisory firms. We are also interested in learning commentators' views as to whether these issues are affected—and if so, how—by the fact that there is one dominant proxy advisory firm in the marketplace, Institutional Shareholder Services ("ISS"),[271] whose long-standing position, according to the Government Accountability Office, "has been cited by industry analysts as a barrier to competition."

. . . Below we outline the two principal areas of concern about the proxy advisory industry that have come to our attention.

a.   Conflicts of Interest

Perhaps the most frequently raised concern about the proxy advisory industry relates to conflicts of interest. The Government Accountability Office has issued two reports since 2004 examining conflicts of interest in proxy voting by institutional investors. The GAO Report issued in 2007 addressed, among other things, conflicts of interest that may exist for proxy advisory firms, institutional investors' use of the firms' services and the firms' potential influence on proxy vote outcomes, as well as the steps that the Commission has taken to oversee these firms. The GAO Report noted that the most commonly cited conflict of interest for proxy advisory firms is when they provide both proxy voting recommendations to investment advisers and other institutional investors and consulting services to corporations seeking assistance with proposals to be presented to shareholders or with improving their corporate governance ratings.

In particular, this conflict of interest arises if a proxy advisory firm provides voting recommendations on matters put to a shareholder vote while also offering consulting services to the issuer or a proponent of a shareholder proposal on the very same matter. The issuer in this situation may purchase consulting services from the proxy advisory firm in an effort to garner the firm's support for the issuer when the voting recommendations are made. Similarly, a proponent may engage the proxy advisory firm for advice on voting recommendations in an effort to garner the firm's support for its shareholder proposals. The GAO Report also noted that the firm might recommend a vote in favor of a client's shareholder proposal in order to keep the client's business.

---

[270] . . . It has been suggested, for example, that some issuers have adopted corporate governance practices simply to meet a proxy advisory firm's standards, even though they may not see the value of doing so. . . .

[271] . . . As of June 2007, ISS's client base included an estimate of 1,700 institutional investors, more than the other four major firms combined. Id. ISS was acquired by RiskMetrics in January 2007, which in turn was acquired on June 1, 2010 by MSCI, Inc. . . .

A conflict also arises when a proxy advisory firm provides corporate governance ratings on issuers to institutional clients, while also offering consulting services to corporate clients so that those issuers can improve their corporate governance ranking. The GAO Report also described the potential for conflicts of interest when owners or executives of the proxy advisory firm have significant ownership interests in, or serve on the board of directors of, issuers with matters being put to a shareholder vote on which the proxy advisory firm is offering vote recommendations. In such cases, institutional investors told the GAO that some proxy advisory firms would not offer vote recommendations to avoid the appearance of a conflict of interest.

It is our understanding that at least one proxy advisory firm provides a generic disclosure of such conflicts of interest by stating that the proxy advisory firm "may" have a consulting relationship with the issuer, without affirmatively stating whether the proxy advisory firm has or had a relationship with a specific issuer or the nature of any such relationship. Some have argued that this type of general disclosure is insufficient, even if the proxy advisory firm has confidentiality walls between its corporate consulting and proxy research departments.

b.   Lack of Accuracy and Transparency in Formulating Voting Recommendations

Some commentators have expressed the concern that voting recommendations by proxy advisory firms may be made based on materially inaccurate or incomplete data, or that the analysis provided to an institutional client may be materially inaccurate or incomplete. To the extent that a voting recommendation is based on flawed data or analysis, issuers have expressed a desire for a process to correct the mistake. We understand, however, that proxy advisory firms may be unwilling, as a matter of policy, to accept any attempted communication from the issuer or to reconsider recommendations in light of such communications. Even if a proxy advisory firm entertains comment from the issuer and amends its recommendation, votes may have already been cast based on the prior recommendation. Accordingly, some issuers have expressed a desire to be involved in reviewing a draft of the proxy advisory firm's report, if only for the limited purpose of ensuring that the voting recommendations are based on accurate issuer data. Some proxy advisory firms have claimed that they are willing to discuss matters with issuers, but that some issuers are unwilling to enter into such discussions.

There also is a concern that proxy advisory firms may base their recommendation on one-size-fits-all governance approach. As a result, a policy that would benefit some issuers, but that is less suitable for other issuers, might not receive a positive recommendation, making it less likely to be approved by shareholders.

Rule 14a–2(b)(3)'s exemption of proxy advisory firms does not mandate that a firm relying on the exemption have specific procedures in place to ensure that its research or analysis is materially accurate or complete prior to recommending a vote.* While voting advice by firms relying on the Rule 14a–2(b)(3) exemption remains subject to the antifraud provisions of the proxy rules contained in Rule 14a–9—and those antifraud provisions should deter the rendering of voting advice that is misleading or inaccurate—it is our understanding that certain participants in the proxy process believe that additional oversight mechanisms could improve the likelihood that voting recommendations are based on materially accurate and complete information. In addition, as a fiduciary, the proxy advisory firm has a duty of care requiring it to make a reasonable investigation to determine that it is not basing its recommendations on materially inaccurate or incomplete information.

NOTES AND QUESTIONS

1. The proxy advisory market in the U.S. is effectively a duopoly. ISS has about 61% of the market, while Glass Lewis has a market share of 36%. Why might the lack of competition be a concern?

2. In arguing that institutional investors have incentives to be rationally apathetic, we emphasized the costs entailed in monitoring and responding to problems at portfolio companies. How do proxy advisory firms reduce those costs?

3. The rise of proxy advisory firms was a response to regulatory pressure not market forces, as is their continued importance. Why might that be cause for concern?

4. In August 2019, the SEC issued administrative guidance to proxy advisory services about their responsibilities under the proxy rules.[13] The SEC took the position that proxy advice falls within the definition of a solicitation of proxies. If that meant that ISS and Glass Lewis would have to file with the SEC a public copy of the advice they give clients, it would have destroyed the firms' business model, which relies on being able to provide that information privately to fee-paying clients. The SEC, however, concluded that such advice would be exempt from the filing requirements by

---

* [Ed. Rule 14a–2(b)(3) provides that the rules requiring that someone who solicits proxies provide a proxy statement and file it with the SEC prior to use do not apply to:

The furnishing of proxy voting advice by any person (the "advisor") to any other person with whom the advisor has a business relationship, if:

(i) The advisor renders financial advice in the ordinary course of his business;

(ii) The advisor discloses to the recipient of the advice any significant relationship with the registrant or any of its affiliates, or a security holder proponent of the matter on which advice is given, as well as any material interests of the advisor in such matter;

(iii) The advisor receives no special commission or remuneration for furnishing the proxy voting advice from any person other than a recipient of the advice and other persons who receive similar advice under this subsection; and

(iv) The proxy voting advice is not furnished on behalf of any person soliciting proxies or on behalf of a participant in an election subject to the provisions of § 240.14a–12(c) . . . .]

[13] Commission Interpretation and Guidance Regarding the Applicability of the Proxy Rules, Exchange Act Rel. No. 86,721 (Aug. 21, 2019).

virtue of Rules 14a–2(b)(1)[14] and 14a–2(b)(3). Such advice would, however, be subject to Rule 14a–9's anti-fraud provision. The SEC advised that ISS and Glass Lewis consider three areas of disclosure to avoid potential liability thereunder:

- an explanation of the methodology used to formulate its voting advice on a particular matter (including any material deviations from the provider's publicly-announced guidelines, policies, or standard methodologies for analyzing such matters) where the omission of such information would render the voting advice materially false or misleading;

- to the extent that the proxy voting advice is based on information other than the registrant's public disclosures, such as third-party information sources, disclosure about these information sources and the extent to which the information from these sources differs from the public disclosures provided by the registrant if such differences are material and the failure to disclose the differences would render the voting advice false or misleading; and

- disclosure about material conflicts of interest that arise in connection with providing the proxy voting advice in reasonably sufficient detail so that the client can assess the relevance of those conflicts.

In October 2019, ISS filed a lawsuit against the SEC claiming that the SEC lacked authority under the Exchange Act to issue such guidance and that, in any case, the guidance amounted to a new substantive rule that should have been formally adopted in compliance with the requirements of the Administrative Procedure Act.

In November 2019, the SEC proposed amendments to its rules governing proxy solicitations intended to codify its August 2019 guidance.[15] The proposal would amend Rules 14a–2(b)(1) and 14a–3(b)(2) to provide that proxy advisory services relying on those exemptions to the public filing and proxy statement delivery requirements would have to disclose material conflicts of interest in their proxy voting advice. The services must provide issuers an opportunity to review and provide feedback on proxy voting advice before it is issued. Finally, issuers may request that proxy voting advice businesses include in their voting advice a hyperlink or analogous electronic medium directing the recipient of the advice to a written statement that sets forth the registrant's or soliciting person's views on the proxy voting advice.

---

[14]   Rule 14a–2(b)(1) provides that the rules requiring that someone who solicits proxies provide a proxy statement and file it with the SEC prior to use do not apply to:

> Any solicitation by or on behalf of any person who does not, at any time during such solicitation, seek directly or indirectly, either on its own or another's behalf, the power to act as proxy for a security holder and does not furnish or otherwise request, or act on behalf of a person who furnishes or requests, a form of revocation, abstention, consent or authorization. . . .

[15]   Amendments to Exemptions from the Proxy Rules for Proxy Voting Advice, Exchange Act Rel. No. 87,457 (Nov. 5, 2019).

The proposal also would amend Rule 14a–9 to include examples of situations in which the failure to disclose certain information in the proxy voting advice could be considered misleading within the meaning of the rule.

> For example, if a proxy voting advice business were to recommend against the election of a director who serves on the registrant's audit committee on the basis that the director is not independent under the proxy voting advice business's independence standard for audit committee members, and the standard applied by the proxy voting advice business is more limiting than the Commission's rules, it may be necessary for the proxy voting advice business to make clear that the business's recommendation is based on its own different independence standard, rather than the Commission's standard, in order for such recommendation to be not misleading.

> Similarly, a concern could arise if a proxy voting advice business recommends that clients vote against a say-on-pay proposal of a smaller reporting company ("SRC") that provides scaled executive compensation disclosure in compliance with Commission rules for SRCs, rather than the expanded disclosure required of larger registrants. To the extent that such a proxy voting advice business does not make clear to its clients that it is making a negative voting recommendation based on its own disclosure criteria, notwithstanding that the registrant has complied with the compensation disclosure standards established by the Commission, the proxy voting advice business's clients may misunderstand the basis for the proxy voting advice business's recommendation.

In light of that rulemaking proposal the ISS's lawsuit over the guidance was stayed pending promulgation of the SEC's final rules. As this book went to print, the SEC had not taken final action on the proposal.

5.   In August 2019, the SEC also provided advice to investment advisers whose clients have empowered them to execute proxies on behalf of the clients.[16]

> When making voting determinations on behalf of clients, many investment advisers retain proxy advisory firms to perform a variety of functions and services. Some of these are administrative, such as providing the investment adviser with an electronic platform that enables the adviser to manage voting mechanics more efficiently. Other services provided by proxy advisory firms relate to the substance of voting, such as: providing research and analysis regarding the matters subject to a vote; promulgating general voting guidelines that investment advisers can adopt; and making voting recommendations to investment advisers on specific matters subject to a vote. We understand that these voting recommendations may be based on a proxy advisory firm's own

---

[16] Commission Guidance Regarding Proxy Voting Responsibilities of Investment Advisers, Investment Advisers Act Rel. No 5,325 (Aug. 21, 2019).

voting guidelines or on custom voting guidelines that the investment adviser has created. We understand further that custom guidelines, where they are used, may be more or less detailed, depending on the level of instruction an investment adviser has provided to a proxy advisory firm. Contracting with proxy advisory firms to provide these types of functions and services can reduce burdens for investment advisers (and potentially reduce costs for their clients) as compared to conducting them in-house.

The SEC made clear that while outsourcing these functions was appropriate, the investment adviser's fiduciary duties to its clients and its obligations under the Investment Adviser Act of 1940 impose certain obligations on the adviser. Those obligations require the adviser to consider, for example, whether uniform voting policies are in the best interests of its clients or whether it should have policies tailored to each client's specific needs and circumstances. In addition, "certain types of matters may necessitate that the adviser conduct a more detailed analysis than what may be entailed by application of its general voting guidelines, to consider factors particular to the issuer or the voting matter under consideration. Such matters might include, but are not limited to, corporate events (mergers and acquisition transactions, dissolutions, conversions, or consolidations) or contested elections for directors." In general, the new guidance should lead advisers to make much more individualized voting decisions and to exercise considerably greater due diligence in its relationship with proxy advisory services, all of which will significantly reduce the benefits outsourcing to those services was intended to generate.

C. DEFENSES AGAINST PROXY CONTESTS

Brandon R. Harper, The Dupont Proxy Battle: Successful Defense Measures Against Shareholder Activism
41 Del. J. Corp. L. 117 (2016)[17]

E.I. du Pont de Nemours and Company's ("DuPont") proxy contest victory against activist hedge fund manager Nelson Peltz of Trian Partners provides a blueprint for defending against a common shareholder activism tactic, the proxy battle. . . .

. . .

During the most recent financial downturn, DuPont appointed Ellen Kullman as CEO. In order to guide DuPont through the recession, she employed a plan to restructure the company, which saved DuPont about $225 million by 2010. Since her start as CEO in 2009, not only was Kullman able to weather the storm of the recession, but she was able to

---

[17] Reprinted by permission of Brandon R. Harper and the Delaware Journal of Corporation Law.

increase shareholder value by about $30 per share. Kullman's philosophy for DuPont's success was consistent with what historically benefitted the company: innovation. In 2010, Kullman's focus on innovation caused the company to release a historically significant 1,786 new products. . . . Under Kullman's leadership, the stock price rose 20% in 2011, which marked the largest increase in value the company had ever seen in a one-year period.

Ellen Kullman's focus for DuPont, as evidenced by her attention to innovation as a vehicle for increased growth and improved shareholder value, has always been on the long-term. . . .

Beginning in early 2013, Nelson Peltz of Trian Partners owned roughly 3% of DuPont after purchasing $1.6 billion worth of shares in the company. . . . Peltz began to propose "white paper" restructuring plans, recommending that DuPont be broken into smaller business segments. . . . The division of companies would mean one company comprised of agriculture and nutrition businesses ("GrowthCo"), a separate company for its specialty-chemical products, such as Tyvek and Kevlar ("CylcicalCo/CashCo"), and a third company for Performance Chemicals. Trian's goal was to see DuPont create one public company focused on its faster-growing businesses and another that generated cash flow.

. . . Peltz's letter [to Dupont's board of directors] explained . . . that he and the DuPont Board "discussed adding a Trian representative and an industry-insider to the Board" but the "idea has been summarily rejected." . . .

Peltz nominated himself and three other individuals for seats on DuPont's 12-person Board of directors. . . .

Two prominent proxy service providers came forward to show their support for Peltz in the DuPont proxy battle. ISS and Glass Lewis believed in Nelson Peltz's "Initiatives," and agreed that Trian should have a presence on the DuPont Board. . . .

DuPont's management, led by CEO Ellen Kullman, successfully blocked Peltz and Trian from gaining Board control by winning the May proxy battle. Peltz pushed to gain four seats on DuPont's Board of directors, but lost, and shareholders elected all 12 of the company's nominees. . . . DuPont successfully defeated Peltz by being proactive and addressing its own deficiencies amid Trian's public scrutiny of them. The three ways in which DuPont defended against Peltz and won the proxy battle were (1) the preemptive spinoff of the Performance Chemicals business; (2) the appointment of two new Board members; and (3) total transparency with shareholders on all ongoing DuPont activities and business.

Primary in Peltz's criticism of DuPont's diminished value was the company's overly complex business model. One of his "initiatives" was to break up the multi-faceted structure into three separate businesses, including Performance Chemicals, but DuPont had already announced to spinoff its Performance Chemicals segment (Chemours) in October 2013. . . . The decision to spin off Chemours proved to be the first, and biggest, step in the right direction because it worked to convince shareholders to keep their faith in DuPont's management. That faith was necessary to win shareholder votes. . . . It was the foundation of DuPont's defense against Trian's activist campaign that instilled trust in the shareholders, showing them that management was active, and taking the necessary steps to improve the company's value.

. . . By bringing in two experienced and capable directors to sit as new Board members, DuPont effectively proved to shareholders that it was again making the necessary changes to better position the company for increased value, but also garnered support from within the Board against Trian. DuPont was able to bring in individuals who shared management's current vision for the future success of the company, and in doing so, brought the members of the Board "on the same page," presenting a unified front against Trian.

Further, DuPont maintained shareholder transparency by using media tools like a campaign website, advertisements, tailored proxy materials, and correspondence from the CEO to shareholders directly. DuPont management also tactfully refuted any illegitimate claims made by Peltz regarding the company's performance.

. . . Trian's white papers still had their intended effect. Trian exposed DuPont's deficiencies and criticized its management's ineptitude, and while not winning the proxy battle, Trian could be well on its way to winning the proverbial war. The immediate concentrated goal of winning the proxy contest was met, but that victory arguably came at the expense of the CEO's standing at DuPont. On October 5, 2015, Kullman announced that she would step down as CEO, effective on October 16, 2015. . . .

NOTES AND QUESTIONS

1. Companies frequently enter into settlement agreements with activists far before shareholder meetings and nomination deadlines. What incentives induce companies to enter into such settlements?

2. DuPont succeeded mainly by preempting Peltz, increasing shareholder value, and engaging with other shareholders. These approaches are now standard parts of the defense playbook.

> Martin Lipton . . . advises the target to create a team of two to five officers, a lawyer, investment banker, proxy-soliciting firm and a public-relations firm to deal with the activist. The team should continuously engage in meetings and become familiar with the types of activism usually employed by the hedge fund. Among other things, Lipton advises the target's board and the team to oversee shareholder relations, review its capital return policy and "[p]roactively address reasons for any shortfall versus peer

company benchmarks; anticipate key questions and challenges from analysts and activists, and be prepared with answers."[18]

In addition, however, there are numerous structural defenses companies can adopt in response to shareholder activism:

Classified (Staggered) Boards—A classified board is one in which directors are divided into separate classes (normally three) with each class elected to different, overlapping terms. In any given year, only one-third of the board seats are available. As a result, an opponent will need more than one election to take control of the board. This may act to deter proxy fights, and it gives management time to respond to threats to its control. . . .

Event Risk Contracts—These are contractual devices that create special rights for bondholders or preferred shareholders if a change in control takes place. An event risk contract is similar to a flip-in shareholder rights plan, but rather than punishing an outsider attempting to take control, it punishes the common shareholders who voted the managers out. In the event of a change in control, new stock is issued to preferred shareholders, or bondholders are allowed to sell at a premium, supposedly in order to protect their rights under a new regime. These restrictions act as disincentives to shareholder voting, since the value of common shares will decrease when the new rights are triggered.

Poison Pills—Although shareholder rights plans were initially developed to oppose unsolicited tender offers, they can be an effective means of interfering with the shareholder franchise as well. A rights plan limits the number of shares that a single party "can accumulate before launching a proxy contest." The most common trigger is now 20%, but "some plans go as low as 10%." Rights plans can also stop a dissident from forming coalitions with other shareholders if collectively they would own a greater percentage of voting stock than the trigger level. . . .

Advance Notice Requirements—Advance notice provisions serve to eliminate the element of surprise employed by challengers, giving management advance notice of challengers' plans. . . .

Elimination of Shareholders' Ability to Call a Special Meeting—Many state corporation statutes allow shareholders to call a special meeting, unless that right is limited in the company's bylaws. Other states, such as Delaware, do not allow shareholders to call such a meeting unless the right is specified in the bylaws. The ability to call a special meeting is advantageous to shareholders, since it allows them to change a company's control without having to wait for its annual meeting. . . .

Elimination of Shareholders' Ability to Take Action by Written Consent—Closely related to the right to call a special meeting is

---

[18] Scott E. Prince, Trimming the Hedges: Why the Adoption of Wachtell, Lipton, Rosen and Katz's Anti-Golden Leash Bylaw Is Ill-Advised, 9 Ohio St. Entrep. Bus. L.J. 145, 169 (2014).

the right to act through consents. Shareholder consents are very powerful tools for an insurgent because action is taken against incumbent directors immediately upon delivery of the consents; there is no need for a meeting. Since action can be taken at any time, management will not be able to respond to the threat until it is too late. Most state corporation laws limit this right by requiring unanimity to take action through a consent. Delaware and a number of other states allow non-unanimous consent solicitations. Many statutes, however, allow the corporation to opt out of the consent practice through an amendment or through a restriction in the certificate. . . .

Supermajority Voting Requirements—Supermajority voting was originally formulated as an antitakeover device. By requiring a greater percentage of stockholders to approve a proposed action, stockholders are given more power to defeat actions adverse to their interests. Supermajority provisions can be used in combination with other defenses such as the staggered board to entrench management. . . .

Dilution of Ownership Through an Employee Stock Ownership Plan ("ESOP")—An ESOP places shares of the company under the employees' control. This is an effective tactic to oppose a proxy fight since employees, concerned with job preservation, are usually fearful of control changes. Additionally, "[m]anagement generally acts as a trustee of the firm's pension fund and of the firm's ownership plan, and hence it can significantly influence how the firm's shares held by the . . . stock ownership plan are voted."

Manipulation of the Size of the Board—Under the laws of almost every state, the directors have the power to fix the size of the board and to appoint new directors to fill vacancies, unless the bylaws or charter declares otherwise. Directors can manipulate the size of the board to defend against a proxy fight. In a "musical chairs" defense, corporations can eliminate seats occupied by opponents or reduce the size of the board to foil a cumulative voting system. Managers can also increase the size of the board and appoint allies to those seats in order to maintain a majority.

Moving the Date of the Election—When faced with a proxy fight, boards have frequently attempted to use their power to set the record date and election date to harass, delay or otherwise impede their opponents. In one case, a board moved the date of an election forward in order to deny its opponents time to gather enough proxies to win the election. When faced with a potential election defeat, boards also may cancel or otherwise delay the election.

Continuing Director Provisions—These rules guarantee that only current directors of the firm or their handpicked successors can perform certain acts. This is one of the strongest possible defenses because even if the proxy fight succeeds, the new managers will be left with a hollow victory as they will be limited in their available actions.[19]

We will consider the legality of these defenses in the sections that follow.

1)   BASIC LEGAL STANDARD

Blasius Indus., Inc. v. Atlas Corp.
564 A.2d 651 (Del. Ch. 1988)

Blasius Acquires a 9% Stake in Atlas. Blasius ... began to accumulate Atlas shares for the first time in July, 1987. On October 29, it filed a Schedule 13D with the Securities Exchange Commission disclosing that, with affiliates, it then owed 9.1% of Atlas' common stock. It stated in that filing that it intended to encourage management of Atlas to consider a restructuring of the Company or other transaction to enhance shareholder values. It also disclosed that Blasius was exploring the feasibility of obtaining control of Atlas, including instituting a tender offer or seeking "appropriate" representation on the Atlas board of directors.

Blasius has recently come under the control of two individuals, Michael Lubin and Warren Delano, who after experience in the commercial banking industry, had, for a short time, run a venture capital operation for a small investment banking firm. ... Since then, they have made several attempts to effect leveraged buyouts, but without success.

In May, 1987, ... Lubin and Delano caused Blasius to raise $60 million through the sale of junk bonds. A portion of these funds were used to acquire a 9% position in Atlas. According to its public filings with the SEC, Blasius' debt service obligations arising out of the sale of the junk bonds are such that it is unable to service those obligations from its income from operations.

The prospect of Messrs. Lubin and Delano involving themselves in Atlas' affairs, was not a development welcomed by Atlas' management. Atlas had a new CEO, defendant Weaver, who had, over the course of the past year or so, overseen a business restructuring of a sort. Atlas had sold three of its five divisions. It had just announced (September 1, 1987) that it would close its once important domestic uranium operation. The goal was to focus the Company on its gold mining business. By October, 1987, the structural changes to do this had been largely accomplished. Mr. Weaver was perhaps thinking that the restructuring that had occurred should be given a chance to produce benefit before another restructuring (such as Blasius had alluded to in its Schedule 13D filing) was attempted, when he wrote in his diary on October 30, 1987:

---

[19]   Morgan N. Neuwirth, Shareholder Franchise-No Compromise: Why the Delaware Courts Must Proscribe All Managerial Interference with Corporate Voting, 145 U. Pa. L. Rev. 423, 438–43 (1996).

13D by Delano & Lubin came in today. Had long conversation w/MAH & Mark Golden [of Goldman, Sachs] on issue. All agree we must dilute these people down by the acquisition of another Co. w/stock, or merger or something else.

The Blasius Proposal of a Leverage Recapitalization or Sale. Immediately after filing its 13D on October 29, Blasius' representatives sought a meeting with the Atlas management. Atlas dragged its feet. A meeting was arranged for December 2, 1987 following the regular meeting of the Atlas board. Attending that meeting were Messrs. Lubin and Delano for Blasius, and, for Atlas, Messrs. Weaver, Devaney (Atlas' CFO), Masinter (legal counsel and director) and Czajkowski (a representative of Atlas' investment banker, Goldman Sachs).

At that meeting, Messrs. Lubin and Delano suggested that Atlas engage in a leveraged restructuring and distribute cash to shareholders. In such a transaction, which is by this date a commonplace form of transaction, a corporation typically raises cash by sale of assets and significant borrowings and makes a large one time cash distribution to shareholders. The shareholders are typically left with cash and an equity interest in a smaller, more highly leveraged enterprise. . . .

Immediately following the meeting, the Atlas representatives expressed among themselves an initial reaction that the proposal was infeasible. . . .

The Delivery of Blasius' Consent Statement. On December 30, 1987, Blasius caused Cede & Co. (the registered owner of its Atlas stock) to deliver to Atlas a signed written consent (1) adopting a precatory resolution recommending that the board develop and implement a restructuring proposal, (2) amending the Atlas bylaws to, among other things, expand the size of the board from seven to fifteen members-the maximum number under Atlas' charter, and (3) electing eight named persons to fill the new directorships. Blasius also filed suit that day in this court seeking a declaration that certain bylaws adopted by the board on September 1, 1987 acted as an unlawful restraint on the shareholders' right, created by Section 228 of our corporation statute, to act through consent without undergoing a meeting.

The reaction was immediate. Mr. Weaver conferred with Mr. Masinter, the Company's outside counsel and a director, who viewed the consent as an attempt to take control of the Company. . . . A telephone meeting was held the next day. At that meeting, the board voted to amend the bylaws to increase the size of the board from seven to nine and appointed John M. Devaney and Harry J. Winters, Jr. to fill those newly created positions. Atlas' Certificate of Incorporation creates staggered terms for directors; the terms to which Messrs. Devaney and Winters were appointed would expire in 1988 and 1990, respectively.

The Motivation of the Incumbent Board in Expanding the Board and Appointing New Members. In increasing the size of Atlas' board by two and filling the newly created positions, the members of the board realized that they were thereby precluding the holders of a majority of the Company's shares from placing a majority of new directors on the board through Blasius' consent solicitation, should they want to do so. Indeed the evidence establishes that that was the principal motivation in so acting.

The conclusion that, in creating two new board positions on December 31 and electing Messrs. Devaney and Winters to fill those positions the board was principally motivated to prevent or delay the shareholders from possibly placing a majority of new members on the board, is critical to my analysis of the central issue posed by the first filed of the two pending cases. If the board in fact was not so motivated, but rather had taken action completely independently of the consent solicitation, which merely had an incidental impact upon the possible effectuation of any action authorized by the shareholders, it is very unlikely that such action would be subject to judicial nullification. The board, as a general matter, is under no fiduciary obligation to suspend its active management of the firm while the consent solicitation process goes forward.

There is testimony in the record to support the proposition that, in acting on December 31, the board was principally motivated simply to implement a plan to expand the Atlas board that preexisted the September, 1987 emergence of Blasius as an active shareholder. I have no doubt that the addition of Mr. Winters, an expert in mining economics, and Mr. Devaney, a financial expert employed by the Company, strengthened the Atlas board and, should anyone ever have reason to review the wisdom of those choices, they would be found to be sensible and prudent. I cannot conclude, however, that the strengthening of the board by the addition of these men was the principal motive for the December 31 action. . . .

The January 6 Rejection of the Blasius Proposal. On January 6, the board convened for its scheduled meeting. At that time, it heard a full report from its financial advisor concerning the feasibility of the Blasius restructuring proposal. The Goldman Sachs presentation included a summary of five year cumulative cash flows measured against a base case and the Blasius proposal, an analysis of Atlas' debt repayment capacity under the Blasius proposal, and pro forma income and cash flow statements for a base case and the Blasius proposal, assuming prices of $375, $475 and $575 per ounce of gold.

After completing that presentation, Goldman Sachs concluded with its view that if Atlas implemented the Blasius restructuring proposal (i) a severe drain on operating cash flow would result, (ii) Atlas would be unable to service its long-term debt and could end up in bankruptcy, (iii) the common stock of Atlas would have little or no value, and (iv) since Atlas would be unable to generate sufficient cash to service its debt, the debentures contemplated to be issued in the proposed restructuring could have a value of only 20% to 30% of their face amount. Goldman Sachs also said that it knew of no financial restructuring that had been undertaken by a company where the company had no chance of repaying its debt, which, in its judgment, would be Atlas' situation if it implemented the Blasius restructuring proposal. Finally, Goldman Sachs noted that if Atlas made a meaningful commercial discovery of gold after implementation of the Blasius restructuring proposal, Atlas would not have the resources to develop the discovery.

The board then voted to reject the Blasius proposal. Blasius was informed of that action. The next day, Blasius caused a second, modified consent to be delivered to Atlas. A contest then ensued between the Company and Blasius for the votes of Atlas' shareholders. . . .

One of the principal thrusts of plaintiffs' argument is that, in acting to appoint two additional persons of their own selection, including an officer of the Company, to the board, defendants were motivated not by any view that Atlas' interest (or those of its shareholders) required that action, but rather they were motivated improperly, by selfish concern to maintain their collective control over the Company. That is, plaintiffs say that the evidence shows there was no policy dispute or issue that really motivated this action, but that asserted policy differences were pretexts for entrenchment for selfish reasons. If this were found to be factually true, one would not need to inquire further. The action taken would constitute a breach of duty. *Schnell v. Chris Craft Industries*, Del.Supr., 285 A.2d 437 (1971); *Guiricich v. Emtrol Corp.*, Del.Supr., 449 A.2d 232 (1982). . . .

On balance, I cannot conclude that the board was acting out of a self-interested motive in any important respect on December 31. I conclude rather that the board saw the "threat" of the Blasius recapitalization proposal as posing vital policy differences between itself and Blasius. It acted, I conclude, in a good faith effort to protect its incumbency, not selfishly, but in order to thwart implementation of the recapitalization that it feared, reasonably, would cause great injury to the Company.

> **CASE IN POINT**
>
> *Schnell v. Chris-Craft Indus., Inc.*, 285 A.2d 437 (Del. 1971).
>
> Shortly before a shareholder meeting at which a dissident group planned to conduct a proxy contest, the board moved the date of the meeting from January 11 to December 8. This left the shareholder group insufficient time to conduct a successful conduct. The court granted the group an injunction postponing the meeting because "management has attempted to utilize the corporate machinery and the Delaware Law for the purpose of perpetuating itself in office; and, to that end, for the purpose of obstructing the legitimate efforts of dissident stockholders in the exercise of their rights to undertake a proxy contest against management."

The real question the case presents, to my mind, is whether, in these circumstances, the board, even if it *is* acting with subjective good faith (which will typically, if not always, be a contestable or debatable judicial conclusion), may validly act for the principal purpose of preventing the shareholders from electing a majority of new directors. . . .

1. *Why the deferential business judgment rule does not apply to board acts taken for the primary purpose of interfering with a stockholder's vote, even if taken advisedly and in good faith.*

A. *The question of legitimacy.*

The shareholder franchise is the ideological underpinning upon which the legitimacy of directorial power rests. Generally, shareholders have only two protections against perceived inadequate business performance. They may sell their stock (which, if done in sufficient numbers, may so affect security prices as to create an incentive for altered managerial performance), or they may vote to replace incumbent board members.

It has, for a long time, been conventional to dismiss the stockholder vote as a vestige or ritual of little practical importance. It may be that we are now witnessing the emergence of new institutional voices and arrangements that will make the stockholder vote a less predictable affair than it has been. Be that as it may, however, whether the vote is seen functionally as an unimportant formalism, or as an important tool of discipline, it is clear that it is critical to the theory that legitimates the exercise of power by some (directors and officers) over vast aggregations of property that they do not own. Thus, when viewed from a broad, institutional perspective, it can be seen that matters involving the integrity of the shareholder voting process involve consideration not present in any other context in which directors exercise delegated power.

B. *Questions of this type raise issues of the allocation of authority as between the board and the shareholders.*

The distinctive nature of the shareholder franchise context also appears when the matter is viewed from a less generalized, doctrinal point of view. From this point of view, as well, it appears that the ordinary considerations to which the business judgment rule originally responded are simply not present in the shareholder voting context. That is, a decision by the board to act for the primary purpose of preventing the effectiveness of a shareholder vote inevitably involves the question who, as between the principal and the agent, has authority with respect to a matter of internal corporate governance. That, of course, is true in a very specific way in this case which deals with the question who should constitute the board of directors of the corporation, but it will be true in every instance in which an incumbent board seeks to thwart a shareholder majority. A board's decision to act to prevent the shareholders from creating a majority of new board positions and filling them does not involve the exercise of *the corporation's power* over its property, or with respect to *its* rights or obligations; rather, it involves allocation, between shareholders as a class and the board, of effective power with respect to governance of the corporation. . . .

2.   *What rule does apply: per se invalidity of corporate acts intended primarily to thwart effective exercise of the franchise or is there an intermediate standard?*

Plaintiff argues for a rule of *per se* invalidity once a plaintiff has established that a board has acted for the primary purpose of thwarting the exercise of a shareholder vote. . . . A *per se* rule that would strike down, in equity, any board action taken for the primary purpose of interfering with the effectiveness of a corporate vote would have the advantage of relative clarity and predictability. It also has the advantage of most vigorously enforcing the concept of corporate democracy. The disadvantage it brings along is, of course, the disadvantage a *per se* rule always has: it may sweep too broadly.

In . . . recent cases dealing with shareholder votes, this court struck down board acts done for the primary purpose of impeding the exercise of stockholder voting power. In doing so, a *per se* rule was not applied. Rather, it was said that, in such a case, the board bears the heavy burden of demonstrating a compelling justification for such action.

In *Aprahamian v. HBO & Company,* Del.Ch., 531 A.2d 1204 (1987), the incumbent board had moved the date of the annual meeting on the eve of that meeting when it learned that a dissident stockholder group had or appeared to have in hand proxies representing a majority of the outstanding shares. The court restrained that action and compelled the meeting to occur as noticed, even though the board stated that it had good business reasons to move the meeting date forward, and that that action was recommended by a special committee. The court concluded as follows:

> The corporate election process, if it is to have any validity, must be conducted with scrupulous fairness and without any advantage being conferred or denied to any candidate or slate of candidates. In the interests of corporate democracy, those in charge of the election machinery of a corporation must be held to the highest standards of providing for and conducting corporate elections. The business judgment rule therefore does not confer any presumption of propriety on the acts of directors in postponing the annual meeting. Quite to the contrary. When the election machinery appears, at least facially, to have been manipulated those in charge of the election have the burden of persuasion to justify their actions.

Aprahamian, 531 A.2d at 1206–07.

3.   *Defendants have demonstrated no sufficient justification for the action of December 31 which was intended to prevent an unaffiliated*

majority of shareholders from effectively exercising their right to elect eight new directors.

The board was not faced with a coercive action taken by a powerful shareholder against the interests of a distinct shareholder constituency (such as a public minority). It was presented with a consent solicitation by a 9% shareholder. Moreover, here it had time (and understood that it had time) to inform the shareholders of its views on the merits of the proposal subject to stockholder vote. The only justification that can, in such a situation, be offered for the action taken is that the board knows better than do the shareholders what is in the corporation's best interest. While that premise is no doubt true for any number of matters, it is irrelevant (except insofar as the shareholders wish to be guided by the board's recommendation) when the question is who should comprise the board of directors. The theory of our corporation law confers power upon directors as the agents of the shareholders; it does not create Platonic masters. It may be that the Blasius restructuring proposal was or is unrealistic and would lead to injury to the corporation and its shareholders if pursued. Having heard the evidence, I am inclined to think it was not a sound proposal. The board certainly viewed it that way, and that view, held in good faith, entitled the board to take certain steps to evade the risk it perceived. It could, for example, expend corporate funds to inform shareholders and seek to bring them to a similar point of view. But there is a vast difference between expending corporate funds to inform the electorate and exercising power for the primary purpose of foreclosing effective shareholder action. A majority of the shareholders, who were not dominated in any respect, could view the matter differently than did the board. If they do, or did, they are entitled to employ the mechanisms provided by the corporation law and the Atlas certificate of incorporation to advance that view. They are also entitled, in my opinion, to restrain their agents, the board, from acting for the principal purpose of thwarting that action.

. . .

NOTES AND QUESTIONS

1. What legal standard is established by *Blasius*? When does it apply rather than, say, the business judgment rule?

2. Is *Blasius* a workable legal standard?

3. In a footnote, the *Blasius* court explained that:

Delaware courts have long exercised a most sensitive and protective regard for the free and effective exercise of voting rights. This concern suffuses our law, manifesting itself in various settings. . . .

A similar concern, for credible corporate democracy, underlies those cases that strike down board action that sets or moves an annual meeting date upon a finding that such action was intended to thwart a shareholder group from effectively mounting an election campaign. The cases invalidating stock issued for the primary purpose of diluting the voting power of a control block also reflect the law's concern that a credible form of corporate democracy be maintained.

> Similarly, a concern for corporate democracy is reflected (1) in our statutory requirement of annual meetings (8 Del.C. § 211), and in the cases that aggressively and summarily enforce that right, and (2) in our consent statute (8 Del. C. § 228) and the interpretation it has been accorded.

In light of those comments, consider whether the *Blasius* decision calls into question some or all of the defenses against shareholder activism discussed in the preceding section.

4.   In *Coalition to Advocate Public Utility Responsibility, Inc. v. Engels*,[20] the directors of Northern States Power Company (referred to by the court as N.S.P.) tried to manipulate the corporation's bylaws to prevent an insurgent director candidate—one Alpha Smaby[21]—from being elected:

> 4)   N.S.P. has historically elected Directors each year for a one-year term. In February of 1973, there were 14 Directors. At the Board of Directors' meeting of February 28, 1973, the Board of Directors considered in detail a proposed draft proxy soliciting statement which contemplated the continuation of the 14 member Board. These draft materials made direct and substantial reference to Alpha Smaby and urged the shareholders to reject her candidacy. . . .

> 6)   Subsequent to the February meeting, the exact date is not known at this time, it was decided by the Directors of N.S.P. to reduce the number of Directors from 14 to 12 and to classify the Directors in groups of four for election to staggered terms of one, two and three years. Without the changes, just over 7% of the vote would be sufficient to elect one Director under the cumulative voting provision, but after the changes about 20% of the vote would be required. There was good reason to believe that Alpha Smaby might control up to 9% of the voting shares. Although the above changes were not formally approved by the Board of Directors until a special meeting was called on March 27, 1973, the proposed

---

[20]   364 F. Supp. 1202 (D. Minn. 1973)

[21]   According to Wikipedia:

Alpha Sunde Smaby (February 11, 1910–July 18, 1991) was an American politician and teacher.

Born in Sacred Heart, Minnesota, Smaby graduated from University of Minnesota and Winona State University. She then taught school and then worked for Cargill, Inc. Smaby served in the Minnesota House of Representatives from 1965 until 1969 and was a Democrat. During the 1968 United States Presidential campaign, Smaby was a delegate to the Democratic Party Convention and supported United States Senator Eugene McCarthy. Smaby died of cancer in Saint Paul, Minnesota.

Alpha Sunde Smaby, https://en.wikipedia.org/w/index.php?title=Alpha_Sunde_Smaby (last visited July 25, 2017).

changes were submitted to the SEC approximately one week prior to the Board's formal approval.

7) N.S.P. candidly admits that such changes were not proposed because of long-term business considerations but that the changes were specifically aimed at the candidacy of Alpha Smaby. It is clear to the Court that the changes were instigated in an attempt to make her effort to win a seat on the Board more difficult and, in fact, were done to frustrate her efforts.

. . .

Plaintiffs concede that the actions of the defendants do not violate any state statutory law but argue that the manipulation of the corporate machinery by insiders for the sole purpose of frustrating the candidacy of a minority shareholder . . . is a breach of the insiders' fiduciary duty to the minority shareholders. Plaintiffs rely heavily on . . . Delaware cases which basically stand for the proposition that actions by insiders, although otherwise lawful, may be enjoined if they act to injure the rights of minority shareholders. In [*Schnell v. Chris-Craft Industries*, 285 A.2d 437 (Del.Supr.1971),] the Delaware Supreme Court held that management's efforts to use the corporate machinery and Delaware law for the purpose of perpetrating itself in office and obstructing legitimate efforts of the dissident stockholders in the exercise of their rights to undertake a proxy contest against management was impermissible. The insiders had advanced the date of the stockholders' meeting in an effort to frustrate the efforts of minority shareholders who desired to wage a proxy contest. The actions of the insiders were enjoined despite the fact that they were in compliance with the company by-laws and applicable Delaware law. The basis for these opinions rests on the fiduciary duty imposed on Directors and Officers of a corporation to deal fairly and justly with the corporation and all of its shareholders including minority shareholders. The Officers and Directors of N.S.P. are in a fiduciary relationship with the minority shareholders and as such owe them a duty to deal with them fairly and in good faith.

In the instant case, the actions of the insiders, if not unfair, were certainly questionable in light of their fiduciary obligation to the plaintiff shareholders. Not only did the defendants change the rules in the middle of the game, but they refused to disclose the existence of the changes when approached by the plaintiffs. Both of these actions served to frustrate the plaintiff shareholders' legitimate efforts to run for the Board of Directors and may well be a breach of fiduciary duty. . . .

Both of the changes made by the N.S.P. board were permitted by statute. So why did the court invalidate them? Would the *Blasius* court have reached the same result?

Suppose that one month after the 1973 annual shareholder meeting the N.S.P. board amended the company's bylaws to effect a reduction in the number of directors and to classify the board effective with the 1974 annual shareholder meeting. Would the court enjoin those changes? Would the *Blasius* court enjoin those changes?

5.   In *Portnoy v. Cryo-Cell Int'l, Inc.*,[22] the incumbent directors feared losing a proxy contest and took a variety of steps intended to ensure their victory. One of those steps involved a deal pursuant to which a large shareholder—one Andrew Filipowski—agreed to support the incumbent board provided that the board would include the shareholder on its slate of candidates and—if successful in winning the proxy contest—would increase the number of board members from six to seven and appoint a crony of the shareholder to fill the resulting vacancy. Then Vice Chancellor Leo Strine explained that:

> As defined by Vice Chancellor Hartnett in his important decision in *Schreiber v. Carney*, "[v]ote-buying . . . is simply a voting agreement supported by consideration personal to the stockholder, whereby the stockholder divorces his discretionary voting power and votes as directed by the offeror." . . .
>
> To say that the law of corporations has struggled with how to address the subject of so-called "vote buying" is no insult to judges or corporate law scholars, the question of what inducements and agreements may legitimately be forged to cement a voting coalition is doubtless as old as the concept of a polity itself. For these very real-world reasons, *Schreiber* refused to say that any sort of arrangement involving the exchange of consideration in connection with a stockholder's agreement to vote a particular way was forbidden vote buying. Indeed, distinguished scholars have anguished (the adjective I take away from their work) over how to deal with such arrangements, with most concluding that flat-out prohibitions are neither workable nor of utility to diversified stockholders. . . .
>
> To deal with these complexities, *Schreiber* declined to find that vote buying was, in the first instance, per se improper. Rather, *Schreiber* articulated a two-pronged analysis. In the first instance, if the plaintiff can show that the "object or purpose [of the vote buying was] to defraud or in some way disenfranchise the other stockholders," the arrangement would be "illegal per se." Putting this in terms that I think are truer to the way our corporate law works, what I take from this is that if the plaintiff proved that the arrangement under challenge was improperly motivated, then the arrangement would be set aside in equity, irrespective of its technical compliance with the DGCL.[157] That is, in keeping with the traditional vigilance this court has displayed in ensuring the fairness of the corporate election process, and in particular the process by which directors are elected, purposely inequitable

---

[22]   940 A.2d 43 (Del. Ch. 2008).

[157]   See Schnell v. Chris-Craft Indus., Inc., 285 A.2d 437, 439 (Del.1971) (holding that "inequitable action does not become permissible simply because it is legally possible") . . . .

conduct in the accumulation of voting power will not be tolerated. Even when a vote buying arrangement cannot be found, in the first instance, to be motivated by a fraudulent, disenfranchising, or otherwise inequitable intent, *Schreiber* concluded that "because vote-buying is so easily susceptible of abuse it must be viewed as a voidable transaction subject to a test for intrinsic fairness."

Subjecting an agreement to add a potential insurgent to a management slate to the *Schreiber* intrinsic fairness test would, in my view, be an inadvisable and counterproductive precedent. If one takes a judicial standard of review seriously, as the members of this court do, the decision to subject all such arrangements to the entire fairness standard could result in creating litigable factual issues about a large number of useful compromises that result in the addition of fresh blood to management slates, new candidates who will tend to represent actual owners of equity and might therefore be more independent of management and more useful representatives of the interests of stockholders generally. . . .

. . . If the only arrangement at issue is a promise to add a potential insurgent to the management slate in exchange for the insurgent's voting support, then the arrangement is subject to stockholder policing in an obvious, but nonetheless, potent form. That policing occurs at the ballot box itself.

Here, to be specific, the Cryo-Cell stockholders went to the polls knowing that Filipowski had been added to the Management Slate. Those stockholders also knew that Filipowski had contracted to vote the Filipowski Group's shares for the Management Slate. Although it was not publicly disclosed that Filipowski's agreement to vote for the Management Slate had been conditioned on his addition to that Slate, and that the incumbents had added Filipowski to the Management Slate in exchange for his support, that inference was, I think, unmistakable to any rational stockholder. . . .

In expressing concerns about over-breadth in this area, this decision echoes concerns voiced by the Supreme Court and this court about the difficulty of applying the compelling justification test articulated in *Blasius* in a manner that works sensible results.[162] But like those decisions, this decision is rooted in the premise that the *Schnell* doctrine, authorizing this court to set aside conduct that is inequitably motivated and that unfairly tilts the electoral playing field, is itself a potent tool of equity.

Why shouldn't *Blasius* apply to vote buying? If *Blasius* had been applied, what compelling justification—if any—could the incumbent board have put forward to justify the deal with Filipowski?

Strine's opinion in *Portnoy* can be seen as part of a larger trend in Delaware corporate law towards judicial deference to informed, non-coerced

---

[162] See, e.g., Williams v. Geier, 671 A.2d 1368, 1376 (Del.1996) ("*Blasius*' burden of demonstrating a 'compelling justification' is quite onerous, and is therefore applied rarely.") . . . .

shareholder votes. The leading example of that trend is *Corwin v. KKR Financial Holdings LLC*,[23] in which the Delaware Supreme Court held that the business judgment rule was the proper standard of review for a merger between a target corporation and a minority shareholder that was approved by a fully informed, non-coerced vote of the disinterested shareholders. "When the real parties in interest—the disinterested equity owners—can easily protect themselves at the ballot box by simply voting no, the utility of a litigation-intrusive standard of review promises more costs to stockholders in the form of litigation rents and inhibitions on risk taking than it promises in terms of benefits to them." Put another way, *Corwin* posits that informed, disinterested, non-coerced shareholders—rather than plaintiffs' lawyers or courts—should have the last word on the merits of a transaction.

6.   Given the apparent ability of courts to use the *Schnell* doctrine to police incumbent interference with the shareholder franchise, is the *Blasius* standard really necessary?

7.   Some courts have suggested that *Blasius* should be limited to proxy contests involving director elections:

> *Blasius* anticipates a defensive measure in response to a threat to corporate control. Beyond this, its application has been largely limited to disputes over the election of directors. Accordingly, "courts will apply the exacting *Blasius* standard sparingly, and only in circumstances in which self-interested or faithless fiduciaries act to deprive stockholders of a full and fair opportunity to participate in the matter." Of particular significance here, "the reasoning of *Blasius* is far less powerful when the matter up for consideration has little or no bearing on whether the directors will continue in office."[24]

Is there a good reason for not applying *Blasius* to issue contests?

2) ACTIVIST PILLS

Poison pills—a.k.a. shareholder rights plans—were developed as a defense for target companies faced with a hostile takeover bid. As noted above, however, they can also be used as a defense against proxy contests.

Rights are corporate securities that give the holder of the right the option of purchasing shares. Because issuance of rights does not require shareholder approval, a rights-based pill may be adopted by the board of directors without any shareholder action. When adopted as part of a poison pill plan, the rights initially attach to the corporation's outstanding common stock, cannot be traded separately from the common stock, and are priced so that exercise of the option would be economically irrational. The rights become exercisable, and separate from the common stock, upon a so-called distribution event, which is typically defined as the acquisition of, or announcement of an intent to

---

[23]   125 A.3d 304 (Del. 2015).

[24]   In re Bear Stearns Litig., 870 N.Y.S.2d 709, 733 (N.Y. Sup. 2008) (citations and footnote omitted).

acquire, some specified percentage of the issuer's stock by a prospective acquirer. (Twenty percent is a commonly used trigger level.) Although the rights are now exercisable and will remain so for the remainder of their specified life (typically ten years), they remain out of the money.

The pill's flip-over feature typically is triggered if, following the acquisition of a specified percentage of the target's common stock, the target is subsequently merged into the acquirer or one of its affiliates. In such an event, the holder of each right becomes entitled to purchase common stock of the acquiring company, typically at half-price, thereby impairing the acquirer's capital structure and drastically diluting the interest of the acquirer's other stockholders. In other words, once triggered, the flip-over pill gives target shareholders the option to purchase acquiring company shares at a steep discount to market. As with the older style preferred stock pills, this causes dilution for the bidder's pre-existing shareholders and may have undesirable balance sheet effects.

The pill's flip-in element is typically triggered by the actual acquisition of some specified percentage of the issuer's common stock. (Again, twenty percent is a commonly used trigger.) If triggered, the flip-in pill entitles the holder of each right—except, and this is key, the acquirer and its affiliates or associates—to buy shares of the target issuer's common stock or other securities at half price. In other words, the value of the stock received when the right is exercised is equal to two times the exercise price of the right. The flip-in plan's deterrent effect thus comes from the dilution caused in the target shares held by the acquirer.

Third Point LLC v. Ruprecht

2014 WL 1922029 (Del. Ch. May 2, 2014)

This action arises from a corporation's alleged misuse of a stockholder rights plan. In response to an apparent threat posed by increasing hedge fund activity in its stock, the corporation adopted a rights plan that would be triggered at a lower percentage of ownership for those stockholders who file a Schedule 13D with the U.S. Securities and Exchange Commission ("SEC") than those stockholders who file a Schedule 13G. . . .

I. BACKGROUND

A. The Parties

Plaintiff Third Point LLC ("Third Point") is the investment manager for a series of investment funds that, collectively, manage approximately $14.5 billion in assets. Daniel Loeb is Third Point's CEO. The firm, which often seeks to cause changes in the business policies or capital structure of the companies it invests in, can be characterized fairly as an activist hedge fund. Currently, Third Point is Nominal Defendant's, Sotheby's, largest stockholder, beneficially owning approximately 9.6% of Sotheby's common stock.

Defendant William F. Ruprecht is the Chairman of the Board of Directors, President, and CEO of Sotheby's. . . . Ruprecht is the only Sotheby's employee currently serving as a director of the Company.

. . .

B. Facts

Sotheby's is led by an unstaggered board consisting of twelve directors. Ruprecht is the lone management representative on the Board, and ten of the eleven other directors are "independent" within the meaning of the NYSE listing standards. Together, the directors own approximately 0.87% of the Company's outstanding shares. . . .

On May 15, 2013, . . . Third Point disclosed that it had acquired 500,000 shares of Sotheby's stock. On June 11, 2013, Morrow & Company ("Morrow"), the Company's proxy solicitor, notified Jennifer Park, Sotheby's Investor Relations director, that Trian Fund Management, L.P. ("Trian"), an activist hedge fund with ties to Nelson Peltz, had acquired 250,000 shares in the Company. Park, in turn, notified Ruprecht, William Sheridan, the Company's CFO at the time, and Gilbert Klemann, the Company's General Counsel, of the development and stated that "[Trian's] usual MO is to buy 4.9% and then call us and make a lot of noise." . . .

On July 19, 2013, Ruprecht informed the Board that "there is an increasing probability that we are going to be subject to an imminent activist effort to shift our management agenda." . . .

On August 1, 2013, Matthew Cohen of Third Point emailed Park to inform her that Third Point owned over 500,000 shares in the Company and to ask for a meeting with Ruprecht "as part of [Third Point's] efforts to better understand the company and strategic plans." Park promptly arranged a date and time for a meeting. . . .

On August 6, 2013, the Board held a regularly scheduled meeting at which Goldman and Wachtell were invited to provide "an update on shareholder activism, a vulnerability assessment, [and] a discussion of the key roles of directors and preparation considerations." . . . Regarding activism in general, the Board was informed that stockholder activism levels were "high," at least in part because of activists' prior successes in waging proxy contests. The presentation also contained a slide titled "Activist Investor Tactics Typically Follow a Familiar Pattern." According to the presentation, this pattern usually consists of activists building a stake in an entity, individually or by teaming up with other institutional or activist stockholders to form a "wolf pack," applying pressure on the entity, including threatening to agitate against a board's preferred strategic alternatives, and finally taking action against the board by threatening "withhold the vote" campaigns, demanding board seats, launching a short-slate proxy contest, or making aggressive use of derivatives.

. . . Goldman and Wachtell reported that Third Point had, among other things, bid for a company in which it had invested. The Board's financial and legal advisors also discussed with them Third Point's previous successes in negotiating a transaction with entities it had invested in that arguably allowed it to obtain a benefit that was not available to the entity's other stockholders. An example was the repurchase by Yahoo! of 40 million of its shares from Third Point. . . .

[On] August 26, Third Point filed its initial Schedule 13D, disclosing it had acquired a 5.7% stake in the Company. According to the filing, Third Point intended to "engage in a dialogue with members of the Board or management," and also might pursue discussions with other stockholders or "knowledgeable industry or market observers (including art market participants)." Third Point stated that these discussions "may relate to potential changes of strategy and leadership at" Sotheby's. . . . Third Point also reserved the right to purchase additional Sotheby's shares and to pursue "[a]n extraordinary corporate transaction, such as a merger, reorganization or liquidation, involving the issuer or any of its subsidiaries."

. . .

On October 2, 2013, Third Point filed an amended Schedule 13D revealing that the fund had increased its stake in Sotheby's to 6.35 million shares, or approximately 9.4% of the Company. Attached to the Schedule 13D was a letter from Loeb to Ruprecht. In the letter, Loeb raised several concerns about Sotheby's, including "the Company's chronically weak operating margins and deteriorating competitive position relative to Christie's," "Management's lack of alignment with shareholders," Ruprecht's "generous package of cash, pay, perquisites, and other compensation," "a sleepy board and overpaid executive team," and "lack of expense discipline."

Loeb's "prescription for repairing Sotheby's" consisted of the Company bringing in "the right technicians," such as Loeb himself, several new directors recruited by Loeb, and "a designee from another large shareholder." According to the letter, "[o]nce installed, these new directors would determine what other steps are necessary to ensure that the Company benefits from the rigor and direction that comes with having an 'owners perspective' in the boardroom." In addition, Loeb emphasized the need to replace Ruprecht as CEO. In that regard, his letter stated that Third Point already had identified potential CEO candidates, both internal and external to the Company, and had already commenced informal discussions with the external candidates.

Loeb apparently made several of the accusations in his letter without actual knowledge of their veracity. In addition, the record supports an inference that Loeb included the letter with the Schedule 13D as part of an "all out assault" meant to destabilize the Company. In contemporaneous emails, Loeb described his letter as both part of a "holy jihad" intended to "make sure all the Sotheby's infidels are made aware that there is only one true God," and part of a "Special Operation on Sotheby's," which was intended to "shock and awe" the Company and "undermine the credibility" of Ruprecht. . . .

On October 3, 2013, the Board held a special meeting, which included Goldman and Wachtell, to discuss Third Point's updated Schedule 13D and Loeb's letter. After leading the Board through a point-by-point discussion of Loeb's letter, Ruprecht "noted discussions that he and the Company's management had had with advisors from [Wachtell] and [Goldman] regarding possible responses to the letter from Mr. Loeb, including the possible adoption of a Shareholder Rights Plan (the 'Rights Plan')."

Andrew Brownstein of Wachtell reviewed the proposed Rights Plan with the Board. . . . After Brownstein's review, "the Board engaged in an extensive discussion of the features of the proposed Rights Plan" and "whether the recent accumulations of stock and related items posed a threat to the Company to which adoption of a Rights Plan was an appropriate response." At Ruprecht's suggestion, the Rights Plan topic was tabled and slated to be addressed at the previously scheduled Board meeting to be held the following day.

On October 4, the Board held its regularly scheduled meeting. The first item of business was another "Activist Investor Update." After continuing the discussion from the previous day, the Board unanimously approved the adoption of the Rights Plan. . . . At the October 4 meeting, the Board did not make any explicit findings regarding the existence of a threat. The Company's press release announcing the adoption of the plan, however, stated that the Rights Plan was "intended to protect Sotheby's and its shareholders from efforts to obtain control that are inconsistent with the best interests of the Company and its shareholders."

. . .

By its own terms, the Rights Plan expires in one year unless it is approved by a stockholder vote. Nothing in the Rights Plan, however, appears to prohibit the Board from re-adopting it in whole or in part after it expires. In addition, the Rights Plan contains a "qualifying offer" exception, in which the Rights Plan will not apply to an "any-and-all" shares offer for the Company that cashes out all Sotheby's stockholders and gives them at least 100 days to consider the offer.

Of greater relevance to the current litigation, however, is the Rights Plan's two-tiered structure. Under the Rights Plan's definition of "Acquiring Person," those who report their ownership in the Company pursuant to Schedule 13G may acquire up to a 20% interest in Sotheby's. A person is eligible to file a Schedule 13G only if, among other things, they have "not acquired the securities with any purpose, or with the effect of, changing or influencing the control of the issuer, or in connection with or as a participant in any transaction having that purpose or effect" and they own less than 20% of the issuer's securities. All other stockholders, including those who report their ownership pursuant to Schedule 13D, such as Third Point . . ., are limited to a 10% stake in the Company before triggering the Rights Plan or "poison pill."

. . .

II. ANALYSIS

. . . As a threshold issue, . . . I must determine the proper legal standard under which to analyze the conduct of Sotheby's Board.

1. The legal standard

a. *Unocal* provides the proper legal framework for this dispute

Nearly thirty years ago, in the seminal case *Moran v. Household International, Inc.*,[8] the Supreme Court validated the concept of a rights plan. In reaching that conclusion, the Supreme Court's analysis was guided by, and in accordance with, the teachings of its then-recent decision in *Unocal Corp. v. Mesa Petroleum Co.*[9] Since *Moran*, both this Court and the Supreme Court have used *Unocal* exclusively as the lens through which the validity of a contested rights plan is analyzed. . . .

b. It is possible, but unlikely, that *Blasius* nevertheless may be implicated within the *Unocal* framework in this case

. . . In *MM Cos. v. Liquid Audio, Inc.*,[12] the Supreme Court reemphasized that "the *Blasius* and *Unocal* standards of enhanced judicial review ('tests') are not mutually exclusive." The Court held that the "compelling justification" standard set out in *Blasius* could be applied within the *Unocal* framework, but only where " 'the primary purpose of the board's action is to interfere with or impede exercise of the shareholder franchise and the shareholders are not given a full and fair opportunity to vote' effectively." The Court noted specifically, however, that because of its strict criteria, the "compelling justification" standard announced in Blasius "is rarely applied either independently or within the Unocal standard of review."

In that regard, Plaintiffs have not cited to any case in which this Court or the Supreme Court has invoked *Blasius* to examine a rights plan. There are any number of possible explanations for this dearth of authority, including, but not limited to, that: (1) no Delaware court has ever found that a board of directors adopted a rights plan for the "primary purpose" of interfering with or impeding the exercise of the stockholder

---

[8]   500 A.2d 1346, 1347 (Del.1985).

[9]   493 A.2d 946, 949 (Del.1985).

[12]   813 A.2d 1118 (Del.2003).

franchise;[17] (2) while rights plans can interfere with the franchise, they do not do so in the manner that *Blasius* was concerned with so long as a proxy contest remains a viable option;[18] or (3) to the extent a stockholder rights plan does adversely affect the franchise, that circumstance is adequately dealt with under the *Unocal* standard such that application of *Blasius* has proven unnecessary. Therefore, although *Blasius* might have some theoretical application to the facts of this case, it appears that, based on the relevant precedent, or more precisely, the lack thereof, *Unocal* provides the appropriate framework.

c.   The *Unocal* standard

The well-known *Unocal* standard consists of two prongs. The first is "a reasonableness test, which is satisfied by a demonstration that the board of directors had reasonable grounds for believing that a danger to corporate policy and effectiveness existed." In other words, a board must articulate a legally cognizable threat. This first prong "is essentially a process-based review."[20] "Directors satisfy the first part of the *Unocal* test by demonstrating good faith and reasonable investigation."[21] A good process standing alone, however, is not sufficient if it does not lead to the finding of an objectively reasonable threat. "[N]o matter how exemplary the board's process, or how independent the board, or how reasonable its investigation, to meet their burden under the first prong of *Unocal* defendants must actually articulate some legitimate threat to corporate policy and effectiveness."[22]

The second prong of *Unocal* is a "proportionality test, which is satisfied by a demonstration that the board of directors' defensive response was reasonable in relation to the threat posed." Proportionality review itself consists of two parts. First, the Court must consider whether

---

[17]   See Yucaipa Am. Alliance Fund II, L.P. v. Riggio, 1 A.3d 310, 331 (Del. Ch.2010) aff'd, 15 A.3d 218 (Del.2011) ("because the [ ]board did not act 'for the primary purpose of thwarting the exercise of a shareholder vote,' *Blasius* does not apply by its own terms."); Stahl v. Apple Bancorp, Inc. 1990 WL 114222, at *7 (Del. Ch.1990) ("Moreover the approach taken in *Blasius* . . . is appropriate when board action appears directed primarily towards interfering with the fair exercise of the franchise (e.g., moving a meeting date; adopting a bylaw regulating shareholder voting, etc.). The stock rights plan may or may not have that effect, but it does not represent action taken for the primary purpose of interfering with the exercise of the shareholders' right to elect directors.").

[18]   See *Yucaipa*, 1 A.3d at 335 ("Although the Supreme Court and this court recognize that poison pills and certain other defenses affect the ability of stockholders to run proxy contests on an unfettered basis and that those effects should be closely examined when conducting a *Unocal* review, the Supreme Court and this court have also recognized that pills such as those in Moran do not disenfranchise any stockholder in the sense of preventing them from freely voting and do not prevent a stockholder from soliciting revocable proxies.") (citation omitted); *Stahl*, 1990 WL 114222, at *8 ("The thrust of the Supreme Court's reasoning in *Moran* was simply that the restrictions imposed by the stock rights plan on a proxy contest were immaterial to conducting a proxy fight effectively. In adopting the stock rights plan here, it has not been shown that the board could not have reasonably concluded similarly. If it did the restrictions here at issue should be valid, as were those in *Moran*").

[20]   Air Prods. & Chems., Inc. v. Airgas, Inc., 16 A.3d 48, 92 (Del. Ch.2011).

[21]   Paramount Commc'ns, Inc. v. Time, Inc., 571 A.2d 1140, 1152 (Del.1990); see also *Unocal*, 493 A.2d at 955.

[22]   Air Prods. & Chems., Inc. v. Airgas, Inc., 16 A.3d at 92.

a board's defensive actions were "draconian, by being either preclusive or coercive."[24] Next, if the board's response to the threat was not draconian, the Court then must decide whether its actions fell "within a range of reasonable responses to the threat" posed. The defendant board bears the burden of proving the reasonableness of its actions under *Unocal*.

. . .

Plaintiffs here make no serious argument that the Sotheby's Board will be unlikely to meet its burden of demonstrating that it conducted a good faith and reasonable investigation into the threat posed by Third Point. The Board undeniably is comprised of a majority of independent directors. In addition, it is undisputed that the Board retained competent outside financial and legal advisors, which it appears to have utilized and relied on frequently. "The presence of a majority of outside directors, coupled with a showing of reliance on advice by legal and financial advisors, 'constitute[s] a prima facie showing of good faith and reasonable investigation.' "[26]

Having determined that the Board probably can demonstrate on a full record that it conducted the requisite investigation, the next relevant inquiry is whether the Board determined that Third Point presented an objectively reasonable and legally cognizable threat to Sotheby's. While the Board has asserted that, at all relevant times, Third Point has presented a multitude of threats to the Company, for purposes of the October 2013 adoption, I need focus only on one: "creeping control." At the time the Board elected to adopt the Rights Plan in October 2013, it had several hedge funds accumulating its stock simultaneously, and at least as to Third Point, the accumulation was occurring on a relatively rapid basis. The Board also was informed by its advisors that it was not uncommon for activist hedge funds to form a group or "wolfpack," for the purpose of jointly acquiring large blocks of a target company's stock. Based on these facts . . . there is sufficient support for the Board's assertion that its good faith investigation led it to determine that Third Point posed a legally cognizable threat, and I consider that threat objectively reasonable. Thus, Plaintiffs have not demonstrated a reasonable probability of success with respect to the first prong of the Unocal analysis for the October 2013 adoption of the Rights Plan.

. . .

For the reasons stated previously, the role of *Blasius* in the stockholder rights plan context is not entirely clear. Nevertheless, I address Plaintiffs' argument regarding the Board's intent in adopting the Rights Plan because, at a minimum, the use of the *Unocal* standard is intended to "smoke out" impermissible pre-textual justifications for defensive actions.

---

[24]   Unitrin, Inc. v. Am. Gen. Corp., 651 A.2d 1361, 1367 (Del.1995).

[26]   Selectica, Inc. v. Versata Enters., Inc., 2010 WL 703062, at *12 (Del. Ch. Feb. 26, 2010) (quoting Polk v. Good, 507 A.2d 531, 537 (Del.1986)).

On this truncated record, there is sufficient evidence to support a reasonable inference that the Company has been concerned with the prospect of a proxy fight with an activist stockholder since the Summer of 2013. But the facts here do not support the conclusion that Plaintiffs have a reasonable probability of demonstrating that the Board adopted the Rights Plan in October 2013 for the primary purpose of interfering with the franchise of any stockholder, including Third Point, several months later. As stated previously, the Company was facing a rapid increase in hedge fund ownership in its stock that at least one Sotheby's insider believed was "collusive." Based on the advice of its outside legal and financial advisors, it appears, at least at this stage of the proceedings, that the Company believed certain hedge funds were attempting to gain effective control of the Company without paying a premium, and that it was objectively reasonable for the Company to perceive that threat. Because it is reasonably likely that the Board will be able to show that they were motivated to adopt the Rights Plan in response to this control threat and that "any effect of electoral rights was an incident to that end," Plaintiffs have not shown that it is reasonably probable that Plaintiffs will be able to establish that interference with the franchise was a major, let alone primary, purpose behind the Board's decision.

There are additional factors that, on the present record, also weigh against the argument that Plaintiffs have a reasonable probability of demonstrating that the Board's primary motivation was impeding the voting rights of any Sotheby's stockholder. First, the record is nearly devoid of facts that would support an inference of entrenchment on the part of the Board. The Board is not staggered, turns over at an above-average rate, and is dominated by outside, independent directors. Moreover, with the possible exception of Ruprecht, there has been no showing that serving on the Sotheby's Board is material, financially or otherwise, to any director such that they have a disabling personal incentive to quash a proxy contest. Although potentially there are reasons beyond entrenchment that would drive an independent, well-advised board to act for the primary purpose of impeding the stockholder franchise, the fact that no discernable entrenchment motive exists here weighs against a finding that the Board acted with such a "primary purpose."

. . .

Finally, the apparent effect of the Rights Plan itself also weighs against a conclusion that there is a reasonable probability that Plaintiffs can show it was adopted for the primary purpose of interfering with the stockholder franchise. As stated by Chief Justice Strine, then writing as Vice Chancellor in *Mercier v. Inter-Tel*:

> In prior decisions, this court has decided that because board action influencing the election process did not have the effect of precluding or coercing stockholder choice, that action was not

taken for the primary purpose of disenfranchising stockholders. Because non-preclusive, non-coercive action did not have the primary purpose of disenfranchisement, the *Blasius* standard did not apply and thus no compelling justification for the board's action had to be shown. That is, the lack of disenfranchising effect provided that the trigger for the test was not pulled.[29]

In this case, Plaintiffs have not shown a reasonable likelihood that they will be able to demonstrate that the Rights Plan is either coercive or preclusive. This Rights Plan does not contain any features that would outright force a stockholder to vote in favor of the Board or allow the Board to induce votes in its favor through more subtle means. Said differently, the Rights Plan does not impose any consequences on stockholders for voting their shares as they wish. Thus, the Rights Plan is not "coercive." Nor is the Rights Plan here preclusive. It is undisputed that Third Point's proxy contest with the Board is eminently winnable by either side. Therefore, even with a 10% cap on the number of shares it can acquire, there is no credible argument that Third Point's success in the pending proxy contest is "realistically unattainable." Because the Rights Plan at issue here is not coercive or preclusive, the effect of the Rights Plan is another consideration that weighs against finding that Plaintiffs have a reasonable probability of showing that the Rights Plan was adopted for the primary purpose of interfering with the stockholder franchise.

In sum, on the record before me I cannot conclude that Plaintiffs have a reasonable probability of being able to establish that the Board acted with the necessary "primary purpose" to invoke *Blasius*' compelling justification standard. Accordingly, I turn to the issue of whether the adoption of the Rights Plan in October 2013 satisfies the second prong of the *Unocal* standard.

. . .

For the reasons stated supra, the Rights Plan at issue here is neither preclusive nor coercive. Because it is not draconian, proportionality review turns on whether the Rights Plan adopted by the Board falls within the "range of reasonableness." "The reasonableness of a board's response is evaluated in the context of the specific threat identified—the 'specific nature of the threat [ ] 'sets the parameters for the range of permissible defensive tactics' at any given time.' "[32] When evaluating whether a defensive measure falls within the range of reasonableness, the role of the Court is to decide "whether the directors made a reasonable decision, not a perfect decision."[33] Courts applying enhanced scrutiny under Unocal should "not substitute their business judgment for

---

[29]   [Mercier v. Inter-Tel (Del.), Inc., 929 A.2d 786, 818 (Del. Ch.2007).]

[32]   Air Prods. & Chems., Inc. v. Airgas, Inc., 16 A.3d 48, 122 (Del. Ch.2011).

[33]   Paramount Commc'ns Inc. v. QVC Network Inc., 637 A.2d 34, 45 (Del.1994).

that of the directors" and if, on balance, "a board selected one of several reasonable alternatives, a court should not second-guess that choice."[34]

In this case there is a reasonable probability that the Board will be able to show that in October 2013 it was faced with the legally cognizable and objectively reasonable threat that Third Point, alone or with others, could acquire a controlling interest in the Company without paying Sotheby's other stockholders a premium. Thus, the relevant inquiry is whether the adoption of the Rights Plan was a reasonable and proportionate response to that threat of creeping control.

I consider it reasonably probable that the Board will be able to meet its burden to demonstrate that the adoption of the Rights Plan in October 2013 was a proportionate response to the control threat posed by Third Point. Plaintiffs here have not litigated the issue of or whether a 10% rights plan comports with Delaware law. Because the entire Board, collectively, owns less than 1% of Sotheby's stock, a 10% threshold allows activist investors to achieve a substantial ownership position in the Company. This is supported further by the fact that at its current ownership level just below 10%, Third Point is the Company's largest single stockholder. When the Rights Plan was adopted there also was the objectively reasonable possibility that Third Point was working in connection with one or more other hedge funds in an attempt to create a control block within the Company's stockholder base. A trigger level much higher than 10% could make it easier for a relatively small group of activist investors to achieve control, without paying a premium, through conscious parallelism.[35] . . .

The gravamen of Plaintiffs' argument that the Rights Plan is disproportionate pertains mostly to its two-tier structure which permits "passive" investors to buy 20% of the Company shares while "activist" stockholders cannot purchase more than 10%. As an initial matter, I note that while the Rights Plan is "discriminatory" in that sense, it also arguably is a "closer fit" to addressing the Company's needs to prevent an activist or activists from gaining control than a "garden variety" rights plan that would restrict the ownership levels for every stockholder, even those with no interest in obtaining control or asserting influence. In any event, the importance of the "discriminatory" nature of the challenged Rights Plan appears to be overstated in the circumstances of this case. Because I already have determined that the Board is likely to be able to show that the Rights Plan's 10% trigger for activist stockholders is reasonable and proportionate, the reason the discriminatory nature of the Rights Plan would be most likely to be found unreasonable or disproportionate is that it allows Schedule 13G filers, who may be more

---

[34] Id.

[35] Yucaipa Am. Alliance Fund II, L.P. v. Riggio, 1 A.3d 310, 360 n.254 (Del. Ch.2010) aff'd, 15 A.3d 218 (Del.2011). While it may be the case that Sotheby's could have achieved the same goal with a trigger level higher than 10%, Delaware law mandates a reasonable response, not a perfectly tailored solution.

inclined to vote with the Company's management, to acquire up to 20% of the Company's shares, and not because a 10% cap on activist stockholders is, itself, unreasonable or disproportionate.

In this case, Third Point is the Company's largest stockholder meaning that there are no Schedule 13G filers who own more than 10% of Sotheby's stock. Thus, while the question of whether Schedule 13G filers should be permitted under a rights plan to buy a larger interest in a company than activist stockholders is important in a general sense, I am not persuaded it can or should serve as a basis to enjoin the Sotheby's annual meeting when, as a practical matter, it is a complete non-issue in terms of the current composition of Sotheby's stockholders.

. . .

III. CONCLUSION

For the foregoing reasons, Plaintiffs' motions for a preliminary injunction are denied.

NOTES AND QUESTIONS

1. Do you agree with the court's conclusion that *Unocal* rather than *Blasius* was the correct standard of review?

2. What is the threat to corporate policy and effectiveness that justified the pill in *Third Point*?

3. At what point would a triggering point be low enough so as to make success in a proxy contest "realistically unattainable"?

4. In March 2014, Third Point requested that the Sotheby's board waive the 10% trigger, which would allow Third Point to buy up to 20% of Sotheby's common stock. Sotheby's board of directors rejected that request. The minutes of the relevant board meeting stated:

> Mr. McClymont updated the Board on a conversation that he had had with Mr. Loeb regarding [the waiver] letter. The directors discussed among themselves and with their advisors the Board's rationale for putting the Rights Plan in place in October 2013: the Board's determination that the rapid accumulation of shares by Marcato and Third Point constituted a threat to the Company's corporate policy and effectiveness and might be evidence of an attempt to achieve a change in effective control of the Company without having to pay any premium to shareholders. The directors then considered whether the same rationale still applied in determining how to respond to Third Point's request. With its advisors, the Board considered the basis for the Rights Plan in the context of Third Point's letter and discussed at length whether Third Point and other activist investors continued to pose a threat to corporate policy and effectiveness and a risk of creeping control. The Board reviewed the interactions over the past eight months between Sotheby's, on the one hand, and Third Point and Mr. Loeb, on the other, including the risk that Third Point could obtain

"negative control" or effectively a controlling influence without paying a premium with respect to certain matters if it achieved a 20% stake. . . . The Board considered Mr. Brownstein's advice and ultimately concluded that nothing had changed that would warrant a change in the Rights Plan, including the exemption requested by Third Point.

The court explained that prior Delaware precedents held negative control could pose a threat for *Unocal* purposes "in which a person or entity obtains an explicit veto right through contract or through a level of share ownership or board representation at a level that does not amount to majority control, but nevertheless is sufficient to block certain actions that may require, for example, a supermajority vote." Did Third Point have explicit negative control? If not, did it have effective negative control? In either case, would a waiver of the 10% threshold give Third Point's negative control and, if so, would that constitute a threat under *Unocal*? Suppose for example that Sotheby's decided to hire a new CEO. Could Third Point exercise negative control over that decision? Are there facts over and above the amount of stock Third Point owned that would be relevant to that question?

     5.   *Kallick v. Sandridge Energy, Inc.*,[25] involved what is known as a poison put (a.k.a. a proxy put). Sandridge had issued notes whose indenture provided that the election of a new board majority not approved by the incumbent board would constitute a Change of Control. Note that approving a dissident slate would not preclude the incumbent board from also seeking reelection or from conducting a proxy contest to do so. The indentures further provided that, in the event of a Change of Control, Sandridge was required to repurchase the notes.

     In November 2012, TPG-Axon—a hedge fund that owned 7% of Sandridge's outstanding common stock—sent the incumbent board of directors pointing out the significant decline in Sandridge's stock price (from a high of $68 in 2008 to $6 at the time of the letter) and urging various changes by the board:

> TPG complained of a series of strategic missteps, including an erroneous focus on natural gas at the expense of oil; lax spending and financial discipline; and "appalling" corporate governance. In the latter category, TPG noted that Sandridge's chairman and CEO, Tom Ward, has been paid more than $150 million over the last five years, and that he appeared to have engaged in self-dealing on behalf of himself and his family. TPG demanded that Sandridge's bylaws be amended to declassify the board, that the board be reconfigured to include stockholder representatives, that Ward be replaced as CEO, and that the board look into strategic alternatives to maximize the value of its assets, including an asset sale.

Sandridge's board rejected TPG's proposals. In response, TPG began a consent solicitation designed to remove the incumbent board and replace it with new directors (the solicitation also sought to eliminate the company's

---

[25]   68 A.3d 242 (Del. Ch. 2013).

classified board structure). The incumbent board refused to approve the proposed slate, however, and took the position that electing the proposed new board would trigger the poison put and the holders of the notes would be entitled to put $4.3 billion worth of notes back to the company. The court concluded that *Unocal* was the appropriate standard of review. Using that standard, how should the court rule on the validity of the put provisions?

A. Would it matter if the record contained considerable evidence that Sandridge's board of directors had insisted on including the poison put in the notes and that its creditors had simply acquiesced in that request?

B. Conversely, would it matter if the record contained considerable evidence that Sandridge's creditors had insisted on including the poison put in the notes and that Sandridge's management had argued strenuously against doing so but had eventually agreed so as to obtain badly needed funding?

C. Why would a creditor insist on a poison put in a debt agreement?

3) ADVANCE NOTICE BYLAWS

JANA Master Fund, Ltd. v. CNET Networks, Inc.
954 A.2d 335 (Del. Ch. 2008)

I.   FACTUAL AND PROCEDURAL BACKGROUND

Plaintiff JANA Master Fund, Ltd. ("JANA"), an investment fund, owns with its affiliates approximately eleven percent of the outstanding common stock of defendant CNET Networks, Inc. ("CNET"). CNET, a Delaware corporation, is an interactive media company whose ventures include news.com, MP3.com, GameSpot, ZDNet, and Urban Baby. CNET has a staggered, eight-member board, and two of the current directors are up for reelection this year. Motivated by what it perceives to be poor financial performance on the part of CNET stock, JANA seeks to replace the two current directors, expand the size of the board from eight to thirteen, and nominate five individuals to fill the newly created positions. Such actions, if successful, will result in a new majority in control of the board of CNET.

On December 26, 2007, JANA wrote to CNET to advise the current board of its intention to solicit proxies from the other CNET shareholders in favor of its nominees and proposals . . . . CNET took the position that . . . JANA's proposed proxy solicitation violated provisions of the company's bylaws. Specifically, CNET's letter cited JANA's "fail[ure] to comply with the provisions of the Company's bylaws which require a stockholder seeking to nominate candidates for director election or seeking to transact other corporate business at an annual meeting to beneficially own $1,000 of the Company's common stock for at least one year."

. . .

II. BYLAWS

. . . CNET argues that the so-called "Notice Bylaw" of Article II, Section 3 governs both shareholder nominations for directors and other shareholder proposals. This provision provides, in part:

> Any stockholder of the Corporation that has been the beneficial owner of at least $1,000 of securities entitled to vote at an annual meeting for at least one year may seek to transact other corporate business at the annual meeting, provided that such business is set forth in a written notice and mailed by certified mail to the Secretary of the Corporation and received no later than 120 calendar days in advance of the date of the Corporation's proxy statement released to security-holders in connection with the previous year's annual meeting of security holders (or, if no annual meeting was held in the previous year or the date of the annual meeting has been changed by more than 30 calendar days from the date contemplated at the time of the previous year's proxy statement, a reasonable time before the solicitation is made). Notwithstanding the foregoing, such notice must also comply with any applicable federal securities laws establishing the circumstances under which the Corporation is required to include the proposal in its proxy statement or form of proxy.

Thus, the language indicates that a shareholder must have owned stock in CNET for a full year before it "may seek to transact other corporate business" under this provision.

JANA contends that this provision does not or cannot apply to its nominations and proposals. First, JANA argues, this bylaw only applies to nominations and proposals made under Rule 14a–8 of the federal securities laws; i.e., this bylaw only governs nominations and proposals a shareholder wishes to have included on management's form of proxy. Because JANA intends to independently finance its own proxy materials, it claims this bylaw is inapplicable. Second, JANA suggests that if this bylaw can be read to apply, it is invalid under Delaware law because it is an unreasonable restriction on shareholder franchise.

CNET takes the opposite position, arguing that the bylaw is both applicable and valid. First, CNET cites the plain language of the provision, which it says contains nothing that limits the scope of the bylaw's requirements to proposals and nominations under Rule 14a–8. Second, CNET argues that this bylaw is valid because it was adopted by the shareholders of the corporation and reasonably serves a valid corporate purpose.[7]

---

[7] The bylaw was adopted by CNET before the company's IPO, when there were apparently very few shareholders, all but one of whom were management.

III. STANDARD OF REVIEW

... To the extent there is any ambiguity in interpreting bylaws, "doubt is resolved in favor of the stockholders' electoral rights."[16]

IV. ANALYSIS

The language of the Notice Bylaw leads to only one reasonable conclusion: the bylaw applies solely to proposals and nominations that are intended to be included in the company's proxy materials pursuant to Rule 14a–8. One may parse the bylaw as follows: (1) notice of CNET's annual meeting will be provided to stockholders sometime between ten and sixty days before the meeting is held;[17] (2) any stockholder who has owned $1,000 of stock for at least a year before the meeting may seek to transact other corporate business at the meeting;[18] (3) to do so, that stockholder must send the CNET secretary notice of what business he/she plans to conduct a certain number of days before CNET needs to send out its proxy materials;[19] and, finally, (4) in addition, such notice must also comply with the federal securities laws governing shareholder proposals a corporation must include in its own proxy materials.[20] There are three related reasons I conclude this bylaw can be read only to apply to proposals under Rule 14a–8. First, the notion that a stockholder "may seek to transact other corporate business" does not make sense outside the context of Rule 14a–8. Second, it is reasonable to conclude this bylaw applies only to proposals shareholders want included on management's proxy materials because the bylaw sets the deadline for notice specifically in advance of the release of management's proxy form. Third, and most

---

[16]   Openwave Sys. Inc. v. Harbinger Capital Partners Master Fund I, Ltd., 924 A.2d 228, 239 (Del.Ch.2007); see also Centaur Partners, IV v. Nat'l Intergroup, Inc., 582 A.2d 923, 927 (Del.1990) ("There exists in Delaware 'a general policy against disenfranchisement.' ") (quoting Blasius Indus. v. Atlas Corp., 564 A.2d 651, 669 (Del.Ch.1988)); Harrah's Entm't, Inc. v. JCC Holding Co., 802 A.2d 294, 310 (Del.Ch.2002) ("When a corporate charter is alleged to contain a restriction on the fundamental electoral rights of stockholders under default provisions of law ... it has been said that the restriction must be 'clear and unambiguous' to be enforceable. The policy basis for this rule of construction rests in the 'belief that the shareholder franchise is the ideological underpinning upon which the legitimacy of directorial power rests.' " (footnotes omitted, quoting Centaur Partners, 582 A.2d at 927)).

[17]   See Amended and Restated Bylaws of CNET Networks, Inc., Art. II, § 3 ("Written or printed notice of the annual meeting, stating the place, day and hour thereof, shall be given to each stockholder entitled to vote thereat, in the manner stated in Article VII, Section 1, at such address as appears on the books of the Corporation or to any electronic mail address provided to the Corporation by a stockholder, not less than ten days nor more than sixty days before the date of the meeting.").

[18]   See id. ("Any stockholder of the Corporation that has been the beneficial owner of at least $1,000 of securities entitled to vote at an annual meeting for at least one year may seek to transact other corporate business at the annual meeting").

[19]   See id. ("provided that such business is set forth in a written notice and mailed by certified mail to the Secretary of the Corporation and received no later than 120 calendar days in advance of the date of the Corporation's proxy statement released to security-holders in connection with the previous year's annual meeting of security holders or, if no annual meeting was held in the previous year or the date of the annual meeting has been changed by more than 30 calendar days from the date contemplated at the time of the previous year's proxy statement, a reasonable time before the solicitation is made").

[20]   See id. ("Notwithstanding the foregoing, such notice must also comply with any applicable federal securities laws establishing the circumstances under which the Corporation is required to include the proposal in its proxy statement or form of proxy.").

importantly, the explicit language of the final sentence makes clear that the scope of the bylaw is limited to proposals and nominations a shareholder wishes to have included on management's form of proxy.

> A.   Shareholders "may seek" to bring proposals under
>   Rule 14a–8; outside that rule, shareholders
>   simply "may bring" such proposals.

. . .

In sum, Rule 14a–8 is a compromise that allows for the presentation of some shareholder proposals without the cost of soliciting proxies, but what a shareholder may do under Rule 14a–8 is far different than what a shareholder may do on his or her own. Notably, the other rules promulgated under the authority of section 14 of the 1934 Exchange Act do not give management the power to stop shareholders from presenting proposals and nominations.

It is in this sense, then, that one understands the use of the phrase "any stockholder of the corporation . . . may seek to transact other corporate business at the annual meeting." To the extent a shareholder wishes to submit a proposal that will be reported in management's proxy, the shareholder may seek inclusion. To the extent a shareholder wishes to put a proposal before his or her fellow shareholders in the form of an independently financed proxy solicitation, however, the federal securities laws do not require the shareholder to seek management's approval.

The language itself is key here, particularly the predicate of the sentence: "may seek to transact . . . business." The business of an annual meeting is the election and voting process. Thus, the bylaw says that a qualified shareholder may seek to transact an election-in other words, may seek to put an issue or nominations up for an election. The phrase "may seek" suggests that the shareholder must ask for permission or approval to make such a proposal. A shareholder essentially requests the inclusion of a proposal in management's proxy materials under Rule 14a–8; outside that rule, however, a shareholder simply makes a proposal. Thus, the "may seek to transact" language of the bylaw envisions use of Rule 14a–8. Because JANA intends to finance its own proxy solicitation, such language indicates that the bylaw does not apply to JANA's proposals.

> B.   The bylaw establishes a deadline that would permit the
>   corporation to include approved proposals in its form of proxy.

The second indication that the Notice Bylaw does not apply to JANA's independently funded proxy solicitation is that the bylaw establishes its deadline for notice by reference to the date on which the CNET will mail its own proxy materials. Specifically, a shareholder seeking to make a proposal under the bylaw is required to inform the CNET corporate secretary via written notice "received no later than 120 calendar days in advance of the state of the Corporation's proxy statement" or, if there was no annual meeting the previous year or if this year's meeting date has changed significantly from the previous year, "a reasonable time before the solicitation is made."

In other words, this bylaw requires a shareholder bringing a proposal to give advance notice, but ties the deadline for that notice explicitly to the release of CNET's proxy materials. The most reasonable explanation for so requiring is that the bylaw is designed to allow management time to include the shareholder proposal in its own proxy materials. . . .

CNET's contention that this bylaw merely acts as an advance notice bylaw is undercut by this Court's previous encounters with advance notice bylaws. An advance notice bylaw is one that requires stockholders wishing to make nominations or proposals at a corporation's annual meeting to give notice of their intention in advance of so doing.[46] This Court has upheld such bylaws in the past, but has warned that "when advance notice bylaws unduly restrict the stockholder franchise or are applied inequitably, they will be struck down."[48] This Court cannot find a single example of a permissible advance notice bylaw that has set the notice required by reference to the release of the company's proxy statement.[49] Although not dispositive, this suggests that the CNET Notice Bylaw is designed to govern shareholder proposals under Rule 14a–8 rather than to operate as an advance notice bylaw. CNET is correct that it has no other advance notice provision and that if the Notice Bylaw is interpreted to apply only to 14a–8 proposals, then "any of CNET's thousands of stockholders are free to raise for the first time and present any proposals they desire at the Annual Meeting." Although this may sound daunting, it is the default rule in Delaware.[51]

---

[46] See, e.g., Openwave Sys. Inc. v. Harbinger Capital Partners Master Fund I, Ltd., 924 A.2d 228, 238–39 (Del.Ch.2007) (defining advance notice bylaws as "provisions that require stockholders to provide the corporation with prior notice of their intent to nominate directors along with information about their nominees"); Accipiter Life Sciences Fund, L.P. v. Helfer, 905 A.2d 115, 125 (Del.Ch.2006).

[48] Openwave, 924 A.2d at 239.

[49] See Openwave, 924 A.2d 228 (upholding bylaws that require advance notice be given "not less than 20 days nor more than 90 days prior to the first anniversary of the preceding year's annual meeting"); Accipiter, 905 A.2d 115 (upholding bylaws that require notice be given within ten days from the public announcement of the annual meeting date); Harbinger Capital Partners Master Fund I, Ltd. v. Nw. Corp., C.A. No. 1937-N, 2006 WL 572823 (Del.Ch. Feb. 23, 2006) (denying motion to expedite in case challenging advance notice bylaw that required plaintiff "to identify its slate of proposed board candidates three months in advance of the meeting"); Mentor Graphics Corp. v. Quickturn Design Sys., Inc., 728 A.2d 25, 42 (Del.Ch.1998) (discussing, but not ruling on the validity of, an advance notice bylaw requiring notice be given 90–100 days before a meeting), aff'd sub nomine Quickturn Design Sys., Inc. v. Shapiro, 721 A.2d 1281 (Del.1998); see also In re Unitrin, Inc. S'holders Litig., C.A. No. 13656, 1994 WL 698483 (Del.Ch. Oct. 13, 1994) (implicitly upholding an advance notice bylaw requiring notice be given 60 days in advance of meeting), rev'd on other grounds sub nomine Unitrin, Inc. v. Am. Gen'l Corp., 651 A.2d 1361 (Del.1995).

[51] See 8 Del. C. § 222(a) (requiring advance notice of business in special meetings but not in annual meetings).

C. The reference to Rule 14a–8 in the final
sentence of the bylaw defines its scope.

Most persuasively, the final sentence of the Notice Bylaw establishes that the bylaw applies only to proposals that shareholders seek to have included on the company's proxy materials. That sentence provides, "Notwithstanding the foregoing, such notice must also comply with any applicable federal securities laws establishing the circumstances under which the Corporation is required to include the proposal in its proxy statement or form of proxy." The "applicable federal securities laws" that establish "the circumstances under which the Corporation is required to include" shareholder proposals in its proxy materials clearly refer to Rule 14a–8. Such reference reminds shareholders seeking to make proposals under the bylaw that Rule 14a–8 sets requirements in addition to those laid out in the bylaw itself.

The specific language used in the final sentence of the bylaw mandates my conclusion that the bylaw only applies to Rule 14a–8 proposals. By using the phrase "such notice," the sentence refers back to the notice described in the preceding sentence that a shareholder must give (i.e., the notice given to the CNET corporate secretary in advance of the release of the corporation's proxy materials). The sentence goes on to say that, despite any earlier indication to the contrary, such notice must comply fully with Rule 14a–8. The bylaw incorporates all of the requirements of Rule 14a–8, a rule promulgated by the SEC to give certain—but not all—shareholders limited access to the corporate proxy materials. There is no reason for CNET to have grafted Rule 14a–8's burdensome requirements onto its Notice Bylaw if that bylaw applied outside the context of 14a–8 proposals.

The "rule of construction in favor of franchise rights"[56] buttresses this conclusion. Delaware courts have long recognized that the "right of shareholders to participate in the voting process includes the right to nominate an opposing slate."[57] As I have concluded above, the Notice Bylaw clearly purports to incorporate all of Rule 14a–8's requirements. Those substantial requirements find themselves part of Rule 14a–8 because that rule is a compromise: shareholders have access to management's proxy materials, but only if they meet the rule's significant procedural prerequisites. The SEC was justified in imposing such taxing requirements because corporate proxy machinery needed to be protected from abuse by self-serving shareholders. The rule's requirements do not burden those shareholders who seek to fund their own proxy solicitation. Because Rule 14a–8 imposes restrictions and requirements on the nomination process, and because the "rule of

---

[56]   See 8 Del. C. § 222(a) (requiring advance notice of business in special meetings but not in annual meetings).

[57]   Linton v. Everett, C.A. No. 15219, 1997 WL 441189, at *9 (Del.Ch. July 31, 1997); see also Hubbard v. Hollywood Park Realty Enters., Inc., C.A. No. 11779, 1991 WL 3151, at *5 (Del.Ch. Jan. 14, 1991).

construction in favor of franchise rights" instructs me to interpret bylaw provisions "in the manner most favorable to the free exercise of traditional electoral rights,"[61] I conclude that CNET's Notice Bylaw does not apply to shareholder proposals and nominations brought outside rule 14a–8.[62]

. . .

Because JANA does not request CNET to include its proposals or nominations in the corporate proxy materials, JANA need not comply with the Notice Bylaw's requirements. Because I have concluded that the bylaw does not apply to JANA in this circumstance, I will not consider its hypothetical validity were it to apply as CNET contended.

NOTES AND QUESTIONS

1. Why are the Delaware courts suspicious of advance notice bylaws?

2. If CNET intended for its advance notice bylaw to be limited to Rule 14a–8 proposals, why did the company bother adopting such a bylaw in light of the notice requirement in the Rule?

3. In *Levitt Corp. v. Office Depot, Inc.*,[26] the company's advance notice bylaw stated that:

> At an annual meeting of the stockholders, only such business shall be conducted as shall have been properly brought before the meeting. To be properly brought before an annual meeting, business must be (i) specified in the notice of the meeting (or any supplement thereto) given by or at the direction of the Board of Directors, (ii) otherwise properly brought before the meeting by or at the direction of the Board of Directors or (iii) otherwise properly brought before the meeting by a stockholder of the corporation who was a stockholder of record at the time of giving of notice provided for in this Section, who is entitled to vote at the meeting and who complied with the notice procedures set forth in this Section. For business to be properly brought before an annual meeting by a stockholder, the stockholder must have given timely notice thereof in writing to the Secretary. . . .

> To be timely, a stockholder's notice shall be received at the company's principal office . . ., not less than 120 calendar days before the date of Company's proxy statement released to shareholders in connection with the previous year's annual meeting. . . .

> Such stockholder's notice shall set forth as to each matter the stockholder proposes to bring before the annual meeting (i) a brief description of the business desired to be brought before the meeting and the reasons for conducting such business at the meeting and any material interest in such business of such stockholder and the

---

[61] *Harrah's Entm't*, 802 A.2d at 312.

[26] 2008 WL 1724244 (Del. Ch. Apr. 14, 2008).

beneficial owner, if any, on whose behalf the proposal is made; and (ii) as to the stockholder giving the notice and the beneficial owner, if any, on whose behalf the proposal is made (A) the name and address of such stockholder . . ., (B) the class and number of shares of the corporation which are owned of record and beneficially . . ., and (iii) in the event that such business includes a proposal to amend either the Articles of Incorporation or the Bylaws of the corporation, the language of the proposed amendment.

A dissident shareholder contended that advance notice of a shareholder nomination for the board was not required because electing directors was an item of business "specified in the notice of the meeting (or any supplement thereto) given by or at the direction of the Board of Directors." The court agreed:

> [T]he Notice stated that an item of business for the Annual Meeting is to "elect twelve (12) members of the Board of Directors." Office Depot has argued that the Notice brought before the Annual Meeting only the narrow business of voting for or against its slate of directors. Such a reading does not find support in the text of the Notice, which broadly refers to "elec[ting] . . . members of the Board of Directors." Instead, the Notice establishes that the business of electing directors, unrestricted by any limiting qualification, has been properly brought before the Annual Meeting.
>
> The remaining question is whether the business of electing directors includes the nomination of directors. Of course, nominating candidates and voting for preferred candidates are separate steps. Levitt has recognized as much. Notwithstanding this difference, nomination is a critical part of the election process-in the absence of other nominations, the stockholder constituency has no electoral choice as between candidates; instead, the shareholders are left with only an "up or down" vote on the company sponsored candidates. Despite the role of nominations in giving substance to elections, i.e., providing shareholders with a selection of candidates, neither . . . the Delaware General Corporation Law nor any provision of Office Depot's Bylaws discusses or imposes limitations on the nomination process. Perhaps the best explanation for this silence is that the concept of nominations is included within the broader category of elections. Typically, the election process is understood as spanning from nomination to voting to vote tabulation to announcement and certification of the results. Given that the Notice speaks generally of "elect[ing] . . . Directors," an item of business that contemplates putting forth individuals for stockholder consideration, the Court can discern no persuasive reason why the business of electing directors should not include the subsidiary business of nominating directors for election, especially where no guidance on the nomination process is found in Office Depot's Bylaws or in the Delaware General Corporation Law.

Do you agree?

4.   Walmart's notice to its shareholders of the 2017 shareholder meeting included the following item of business: "To elect as directors the 11 nominees identified in this proxy statement . . . ." If Walmart had an advance notice bylaw identical to Office Depot's bylaw, would a Walmart shareholder have to provide advance notice of a shareholder nomination?

5.   Acme's board of directors adopted an advance notice bylaw 63 days before the scheduled date of the company's next annual meeting. The bylaw required that a shareholder submit notice of a nomination 70 days before scheduled date of the annual meeting. A shareholder who wished to make a nomination at the next annual meeting asks whether the bylaw could be subject to legal challenge. What result?

To assess your understanding of the material in this chapter, click here to take a quiz.

CHAPTER 12

SHAREHOLDER ACTIVISM VIA PROPOSALS

As the Delaware Chancery Court has explained:

At the heart of the corporate form lies the fundamental principle of separation of ownership and management. Directors must keep generally informed of corporate affairs so as to fulfill their "affirmative duty to protect [the shareholders'] interests and to proceed with a critical eye in assessing information." Managers, of course, have the far more onerous task of operating the company each day. Shareholders, however, are generally passive and may exercise their rights usually once a year by voting at the corporation's annual meeting.

Yet, even with only this single task, most shareholders are rationally apathetic, the prevailing wisdom explains. Individual investors have too little "skin in the game" to rationally devote the time and energy necessary to keep themselves aware of the details of the corporation's performance or to campaign for corporate change. Furthermore, with ownership diffused among so many holders, there exists a problem of collective action. Although the rise of institutional investment may have significantly narrowed the "gulf between management and ownership . . . because there may now be perhaps as few as ten or twelve such holders contributing a decisive voice to a particular issue," the simple fact remains that most shareholders have better things to do than attend a company's annual meeting. Nevertheless, these shareholders-be they individual or institutional—may vote via proxy.

As a result, the real action in corporate elections is in the proxy solicitation process, and that process is heavily regulated by both state and federal law. More importantly, the solicitation process is extraordinarily expensive. The traditional proxy contest "involve[s] a fight between management and insurgent shareholders over the control of the corporation in the annual election of directors." Generally, although management is reimbursed for its proxy expenses from the corporate coffers, insurgent shareholders finance their own bid and can hope for reimbursement only if that bid is successful. Such a rule undoubtedly proves intimidating and likely discourages many shareholders from attempting to wage a proxy contest.

To attempt to give shareholders a greater ability to bring proposals without the cost associated with a fully waged proxy contest, the Securities Exchange Commission in 1942 adopted Rule 14a–8. The current version of Rule 14a–8 describes the circumstances under which management must include a shareholder proposal in its own proxy materials. Permitting a shareholder access to the company's proxy greatly reduces the cost that would otherwise be associated with a proxy fight, but the SEC gave and the SEC hath taken away. Rule 14a–8 may allow a shareholder access to management's proxy, but such access comes at a price. First, to be eligible to even submit a proposal for inclusion, a shareholder must own a certain amount of equity and have been a holder for a year.34 Second, a shareholder can submit only one proposal per year and the text of the proposal cannot exceed 500 words. Third, and most importantly, management may exclude a shareholder proposal for any of thirteen reasons enumerated in the Rule. Thus, although Rule 14a–8 does open the doors to management's proxy materials, management retains significant power as a gatekeeper.[1]

A. RULE 14a–8

Absent Rule 14–8, there would be no vehicle for shareholders to put proposals on the firm's proxy statement. Shareholders' only practicable alternative would be to conduct a proxy contest in favor of whatever proposal they wished to put forward. The chief advantage of the shareholder proposal rule, from the perspective of the proponent, thus is that it is cheap. The proponent need not pay any of the printing and mailing costs, all of which must be paid by the corporation, or otherwise comply with the expensive panoply of regulatory requirements.

Shareholder proposals traditionally were used mainly by social activists. Prior to the end of apartheid in South Africa, for example, many proposals favored divestment from South Africa. The rule is still widely used by social activists, but the rule also is increasingly being used by institutional investors to press matters more closely related to corporate governance. For example, proposals in recent years have included such topics as repealing takeover defenses, confidential proxy voting, regulating executive compensation, and the like.

Not all shareholder proposals must be included in the proxy statement. Rule 14a–8 lays out various eligibility requirements, which a shareholder must satisfy in order to be eligible to use the rule. The rule also lays out various procedural hurdles the shareholder must clear. Finally, the Rule identifies a number of substantive bases for excluding a proposal.

---

[1]   Jana Master Fund, Ltd. v. CNET Networks, Inc., 954 A.2d 335, 340–41 (Del. Ch. 2008).

Rule 14a–8

This section addresses when a company must include a shareholder's proposal in its proxy statement and identify the proposal in its form of proxy when the company holds an annual or special meeting of shareholders. In summary, in order to have your shareholder proposal included on a company's proxy card, and included along with any supporting statement in its proxy statement, you must be eligible and follow certain procedures. Under a few specific circumstances, the company is permitted to exclude your proposal, but only after submitting its reasons to the Commission. We structured this section in a question-and-answer format so that it is easier to understand. The references to "you" are to a shareholder seeking to submit the proposal.

(a) Question 1: What is a proposal? A shareholder proposal is your recommendation or requirement that the company and/or its board of directors take action, which you intend to present at a meeting of the company's shareholders. Your proposal should state as clearly as possible the course of action that you believe the company should follow. If your proposal is placed on the company's proxy card, the company must also provide in the form of proxy means for shareholders to specify by boxes a choice between approval or disapproval, or abstention. Unless otherwise indicated, the word "proposal" as used in this section refers both to your proposal, and to your corresponding statement in support of your proposal (if any).

(b) Question 2: Who is eligible to submit a proposal, and how do I demonstrate to the company that I am eligible?

(1) In order to be eligible to submit a proposal, you must have continuously held at least $2,000 in market value, or 1%, of the company's securities entitled to be voted on the proposal at the meeting for at least one year by the date you submit the proposal. You must continue to hold those securities through the date of the meeting.

(2) If you are the registered holder of your securities, which means that your name appears in the company's records as a shareholder, the company can verify your eligibility on its own, although you will still have to provide the company with a written statement that you intend to continue to hold the securities through the date of the meeting of shareholders. However, if like many shareholders you are not a registered holder, the company likely does not know that you are a shareholder, or how many shares you own. In this case, at the time you submit your proposal, you must prove your eligibility to the company in one of two ways:

(i) The first way is to submit to the company a written statement from the "record" holder of your securities (usually a broker or bank) verifying that, at the time you submitted your proposal, you continuously held the securities for at least one year. You must also include your own written statement that you intend to continue to hold the securities through the date of the meeting of shareholders; or

(ii)   The second way to prove ownership applies only if you have filed a Schedule 13D (§ 240.13d–101), Schedule 13G (§ 240.13d–102), Form 3 (§ 249.103 of this chapter), Form 4 (§ 249.104 of this chapter) and/or Form 5 (§ 249.105 of this chapter), or amendments to those documents or updated forms, reflecting your ownership of the shares as of or before the date on which the one-year eligibility period begins. If you have filed one of these documents with the SEC, you may demonstrate your eligibility by submitting to the company:

(A)   A copy of the schedule and/or form, and any subsequent amendments reporting a change in your ownership level;

(B)   Your written statement that you continuously held the required number of shares for the one-year period as of the date of the statement; and

(C)   Your written statement that you intend to continue ownership of the shares through the date of the company's annual or special meeting.

(c)   Question 3: How many proposals may I submit? Each shareholder may submit no more than one proposal to a company for a particular shareholders' meeting.

(d)   Question 4: How long can my proposal be? The proposal, including any accompanying supporting statement, may not exceed 500 words.

(e)   Question 5: What is the deadline for submitting a proposal?

(1)   If you are submitting your proposal for the company's annual meeting, you can in most cases find the deadline in last year's proxy statement. However, if the company did not hold an annual meeting last year, or has changed the date of its meeting for this year more than 30 days from last year's meeting, you can usually find the deadline in one of the company's quarterly reports on Form 10-Q (§ 249.308a of this chapter), or in shareholder reports of investment companies under § 270.30d–1 of this chapter of the Investment Company Act of 1940. In order to avoid controversy, shareholders should submit their proposals by means, including electronic means, that permit them to prove the date of delivery.

(2)   The deadline is calculated in the following manner if the proposal is submitted for a regularly scheduled annual meeting. The proposal must be received at the company's principal executive offices not less than 120 calendar days before the date of the company's proxy statement released to shareholders in connection with the previous year's annual meeting. However, if the company did not hold an annual meeting the previous year, or if the date of this year's annual meeting has been changed by more than 30 days from the date of the previous year's meeting, then the deadline is a reasonable time before the company begins to print and send its proxy materials.

(3)   If you are submitting your proposal for a meeting of shareholders other than a regularly scheduled annual meeting, the deadline is a reasonable time before the company begins to print and send its proxy materials.

(f)   Question 6: What if I fail to follow one of the eligibility or procedural requirements explained in answers to Questions 1 through 4 of this section?

(1)   The company may exclude your proposal, but only after it has notified you of the problem, and you have failed adequately to correct it. Within 14 calendar days of receiving your proposal, the company must notify you in writing of any procedural or eligibility deficiencies, as well as of the time frame for your response. Your response must be postmarked, or transmitted electronically, no later than 14 days from the date you received the company's notification. A company need not provide you such notice of a deficiency if the deficiency cannot be remedied, such as if you fail to submit a proposal by the company's properly determined deadline. If the company intends to exclude the proposal, it will later have to make a submission under § 240.14a–8 and provide you with a copy under Question 10 below, § 240.14a–8(j).

(2)   If you fail in your promise to hold the required number of securities through the date of the meeting of shareholders, then the company will be permitted to exclude all of your proposals from its proxy materials for any meeting held in the following two calendar years.

(g)   Question 7: Who has the burden of persuading the Commission or its staff that my proposal can be excluded? Except as otherwise noted, the burden is on the company to demonstrate that it is entitled to exclude a proposal.

(h)   Question 8: Must I appear personally at the shareholders' meeting to present the proposal?

(1)   Either you, or your representative who is qualified under state law to present the proposal on your behalf, must attend the meeting to present the proposal. Whether you

attend the meeting yourself or send a qualified representative to the meeting in your place, you should make sure that you, or your representative, follow the proper state law procedures for attending the meeting and/or presenting your proposal.

(2) If the company holds its shareholder meeting in whole or in part via electronic media, and the company permits you or your representative to present your proposal via such media, then you may appear through electronic media rather than traveling to the meeting to appear in person.

(3) If you or your qualified representative fail to appear and present the proposal, without good cause, the company will be permitted to exclude all of your proposals from its proxy materials for any meetings held in the following two calendar years.

(i) Question 9: If I have complied with the procedural requirements, on what other bases may a company rely to exclude my proposal?

(1) Improper under state law: If the proposal is not a proper subject for action by shareholders under the laws of the jurisdiction of the company's organization;

Note to paragraph (i)(1): Depending on the subject matter, some proposals are not considered proper under state law if they would be binding on the company if approved by shareholders. In our experience, most proposals that are cast as recommendations or requests that the board of directors take specified action are proper under state law. Accordingly, we will assume that a proposal drafted as a recommendation or suggestion is proper unless the company demonstrates otherwise.

(2) Violation of law: If the proposal would, if implemented, cause the company to violate any state, federal, or foreign law to which it is subject;

Note to paragraph (i)(2): We will not apply this basis for exclusion to permit exclusion of a proposal on grounds that it would violate foreign law if compliance with the foreign law would result in a violation of any state or federal law.

(3) Violation of proxy rules: If the proposal or supporting statement is contrary to any of the Commission's proxy rules, including § 240.14a–9, which prohibits materially false or misleading statements in proxy soliciting materials;

(4) Personal grievance; special interest: If the proposal relates to the redress of a personal claim or grievance against the company or any other person, or if it is designed to result in a benefit to you, or to further a personal interest, which is not shared by the other shareholders at large;

(5) Relevance: If the proposal relates to operations which account for less than 5 percent of the company's total assets at

the end of its most recent fiscal year, and for less than 5 percent of its net earnings and gross sales for its most recent fiscal year, and is not otherwise significantly related to the company's business;

(6)   Absence of power/authority: If the company would lack the power or authority to implement the proposal;

(7)   Management functions: If the proposal deals with a matter relating to the company's ordinary business operations;

(8)   Director elections: If the proposal:

(i)   Would disqualify a nominee who is standing for election;

(ii)   Would remove a director from office before his or her term expired;

(iii) Questions the competence, business judgment, or character of one or more nominees or directors;

(iv) Seeks to include a specific individual in the company's proxy materials for election to the board of directors; or

(v)   Otherwise could affect the outcome of the upcoming election of directors.

(9)   Conflicts with company's proposal: If the proposal directly conflicts with one of the company's own proposals to be submitted to shareholders at the same meeting;

Note to paragraph (i)(9): A company's submission to the Commission under this section should specify the points of conflict with the company's proposal.

(10) Substantially implemented: If the company has already substantially implemented the proposal;

Note to paragraph (i)(10): A company may exclude a shareholder proposal that would provide an advisory vote or seek future advisory votes to approve the compensation of executives as disclosed pursuant to Item 402 of Regulation S–K (§ 229.402 of this chapter) or any successor to Item 402 (a "say-on-pay vote") or that relates to the frequency of say-on-pay votes, provided that in the most recent shareholder vote required by § 240.14a–21(b) of this chapter a single year (i.e., one, two, or three years) received approval of a majority of votes cast on the matter and the company has adopted a policy on the frequency of say-on-pay votes that is consistent with the choice of the majority of votes cast in the most recent shareholder vote required by § 240.14a–21(b) of this chapter.

(11) Duplication: If the proposal substantially duplicates another proposal previously submitted to the company by another proponent that will be included in the company's proxy materials for the same meeting;

(12) Resubmissions: If the proposal deals with substantially the same subject matter as another proposal or proposals that has or have been previously included in the company's proxy materials within the preceding 5 calendar years, a company may exclude it from its proxy materials for any meeting held within 3 calendar years of the last time it was included if the proposal received:

(i)   Less than 3% of the vote if proposed once within the preceding 5 calendar years;

(ii) Less than 6% of the vote on its last submission to shareholders if proposed twice previously within the preceding 5 calendar years; or

(iii) Less than 10% of the vote on its last submission to shareholders if proposed three times or more previously within the preceding 5 calendar years; and

(13) Specific amount of dividends: If the proposal relates to specific amounts of cash or stock dividends.

(j)   Question 10: What procedures must the company follow if it intends to exclude my proposal?

(1)   If the company intends to exclude a proposal from its proxy materials, it must file its reasons with the Commission no later than 80 calendar days before it files its definitive proxy statement and form of proxy with the Commission. The company must simultaneously provide you with a copy of its submission. The Commission staff may permit the company to make its submission later than 80 days before the company files its definitive proxy statement and form of proxy, if the company demonstrates good cause for missing the deadline.

(2)   The company must file six paper copies of the following:

(i)   The proposal;

(ii) An explanation of why the company believes that it may exclude the proposal, which should, if possible, refer to the most recent applicable authority, such as prior Division letters issued under the rule; and

(iii) A supporting opinion of counsel when such reasons are based on matters of state or foreign law.

(k)   Question 11: May I submit my own statement to the Commission responding to the company's arguments?

Yes, you may submit a response, but it is not required. You should try to submit any response to us, with a copy to the company, as soon as possible after the company makes its submission. This way, the Commission staff will have time to consider fully your submission before it issues its response. You should submit six paper copies of your response.

(*l*) Question 12: If the company includes my shareholder proposal in its proxy materials, what information about me must it include along with the proposal itself?

(1) The company's proxy statement must include your name and address, as well as the number of the company's voting securities that you hold. However, instead of providing that information, the company may instead include a statement that it will provide the information to shareholders promptly upon receiving an oral or written request.

(2) The company is not responsible for the contents of your proposal or supporting statement.

(m) Question 13: What can I do if the company includes in its proxy statement reasons why it believes shareholders should not vote in favor of my proposal, and I disagree with some of its statements?

(1) The company may elect to include in its proxy statement reasons why it believes shareholders should vote against your proposal. The company is allowed to make arguments reflecting its own point of view, just as you may express your own point of view in your proposal's supporting statement.

(2) However, if you believe that the company's opposition to your proposal contains materially false or misleading statements that may violate our anti-fraud rule, § 240.14a–9, you should promptly send to the Commission staff and the company a letter explaining the reasons for your view, along with a copy of the company's statements opposing your proposal. To the extent possible, your letter should include specific factual information demonstrating the inaccuracy of the company's claims. Time permitting, you may wish to try to work out your differences with the company by yourself before contacting the Commission staff.

(3) We require the company to send you a copy of its statements opposing your proposal before it sends its proxy materials, so that you may bring to our attention any materially false or misleading statements, under the following timeframes:

(i) If our no-action response requires that you make revisions to your proposal or supporting statement as a condition to requiring the company to include it in its proxy materials, then the company must provide you with a copy of its opposition statements no later than 5 calendar days after the company receives a copy of your revised proposal; or

(ii) In all other cases, the company must provide you with a copy of its opposition statements no later than 30 calendar days before its files definitive copies of its proxy statement and form of proxy under § 240.14a–6.

1) SEC REVIEW

The SEC referees the shareholder proposal process, albeit sometimes reluctantly. If the subject corporation's management believes the proposal can be excluded from the proxy statement, management must notify the SEC that the firm intends to exclude the proposal. A copy of the notice must also be sent to the proponent.[2] Management's notice must be accompanied by an opinion of counsel if any of the stated grounds entail legal issues, such as when management claims the proposal is improper under state corporate law. Although the rule does not require the proponent to reply, the SEC staff will consider any arguments the proponent may wish to make in support of the resolution's eligibility for inclusion in management's proxy statement.

If the SEC staff agrees that the proposal can be excluded, it traditionally issued a so-called no action letter, which states that the staff will not recommend that the Commission bring an enforcement proceeding against the issuer if the proposal is excluded. In 2019, however, the SEC announced that going forward would respond orally to most no-action requests, reserving written responses to cases in which the staff's views would provide broadly applicable guidance to other issuers. In either case, if the staff determines that the proposal should be included in management's proxy statement, the staff notifies the issuer that the SEC may bring an enforcement action if the proposal is excluded. The SEC staff can also take an intermediate position; in effect, it says to the proponent: "As your proposal or your supporting statement are presently drafted, they can be excluded under Rule 14a–8. However, if you revise them as follows, we believe that management must include the proposal." Whichever side loses at the staff level can ask the Commissioners to review the staff's decision. After review by the Commissioners, the losing party can seek judicial review by the United States Circuit Court of Appeals for the District of Columbia. These reviews are very rare. If management is the losing party, it typically acquiesces in the staff's decision. If the shareholder proponent loses, he typically seeks injunctive relief in federal district court.

In September 2019, the SEC announced some modifications to these longstanding procedures:

> The staff will continue to actively monitor correspondence and provide informal guidance to companies and proponents as appropriate. In cases where a company seeks to exclude a

---

[2]   Rule 14a–8(j). Under Rule 14a–8(f)(1), if the alleged defect is potentially remediable, the company must reply within 14 calendar days after receiving the proposal. If the proponent can remedy the alleged deficiency, it must do so within 14 calendar days. This process is separate from the procedure under which management notifies the SEC of its intent to exclude the proposal.

proposal, the staff will inform the proponent and the company of its position, which may be that the staff concurs, disagrees or declines to state a view, with respect to the company's asserted basis for exclusion. Starting with the 2019–2020 shareholder proposal season, however, the staff may respond orally instead of in writing to some no-action requests. The staff intends to issue a response letter where it believes doing so would provide value, such as more broadly applicable guidance about complying with Rule 14a–8. . . .

If the staff declines to state a view on any particular request, the interested parties should not interpret that position as indicating that the proposal must be included. In such circumstances, the staff is not taking a position on the merits of the arguments made, and the company may have a valid legal basis to exclude the proposal under Rule 14a–8. And, as has always been the case, the parties may seek formal, binding adjudication on the merits of the issue in court.[3]

QUESTION

Although the proxy solicitation process itself is quite expensive, the marginal direct cost to the company of any one proposal in its proxy materials is small. Why then do corporate officials waste time and money fighting these proposals?

2) ELIGIBILITY

Under Rule 14a–8(b)(1), a shareholder-proponent must have owned at least 1% or $2,000 (whichever is less) of the issuer's voting securities for at least one year prior to the date on which the proposal is submitted. What happens if the individual shareholder cannot satisfy these requirements? (1) Suppose three shareholders want to jointly support a proposal: A, who has owned $800 in stock for 2 years; B, who has owned $900 in stock for 18 months; and C, who has owned $500 in stock for 13 months. (2) D and E want to sponsor a separate proposal. D has owned $1200 in stock for two years; E has owned $1200 in stock for two months.

The SEC permits aggregation of shareholdings for purposes of meeting the dollar limit but not the time limit. In case 1 above, A, B, and C satisfy the eligibility standard because they jointly own more than $2000 in stock and have all held stock for more than one year. In case 2, however, D and E would not meet the eligibility test. Although they collectively satisfy the $2,000 requirement, they cannot satisfy the time period requirement because E has held stock for less than a year. In order for their proposal to be included, they would have to find a third shareholder who has held at least $800 in stock for at least one year.

---

[3]   SEC, Announcement Regarding Rule 14a–8 No-Action Requests (Sept. 6, 2019).

3) PROCEDURAL ISSUES

Number of Submissions. Per Rule 14a–8(c), the proponent may only submit one proposal per corporation per year. There is no limit to the number of companies to which a proponent can submit proposals in a given year, however. As long as the proponent meets the eligibility requirements for each firm, an activist thus may press the same proposal at multiple firms.

Prior Submissions. The proponent may continue to submit the same proposal to the same firm year after year in the hopes that it will eventually be adopted by the shareholders, provided the proposal annually receives a specified level of support. A resubmitted proposal (or a substantially similar one) must be included if it was submitted: (i) once during the preceding five years and received 3% or more of the vote; (ii) twice in the preceding five years and received 6% or more of the vote the last time it was submitted; or (iii) 3 or more times in the preceding five years and received 10% or more of the vote the last time it was submitted.[4]

Attendance. Although the proxy system generally is designed to facilitate participation by shareholders who choose not to attend the shareholders' meeting, the shareholder proposal rule requires the proponent to present the proposal in person at the meeting. If the proponent fails to show up, Rule 14a 8(h) bars the proponent from using the rule at that company for the following two years.

Timing. The proposal must be submitted to the corporation at least 120 days before the date on which proxy materials were mailed for the previous year's annual shareholder's meeting.[5] For example, if the firm mailed its proxy materials on May 1, 2010, one counts back 120 days from May 1 to determine when a proposal must be submitted to be included in the 2011 proxy statement, which works out to January 2, 2011. The SEC is surprisingly strict in enforcing this requirement.

Length. Under Rule 14a–8(d), a proposal and any accompanying supporting statement may not exceed 500 words in length. (There is no length restriction on rebuttal statements by management.) In the past, a shareholder who wished to make a more expansive case for his proposal thus was required to conduct a full-fledged proxy solicitation, with all the expense and regulatory burden associated therewith.

---

[4]   Rule 14a–8(i)(12).

[5]   Rule 14–8(e).

B. PROPOSALS AS AN ACTIVISM TOOL

Paul Rose, Shareholder Proposals in the Market for Corporate Influence
66 Fla. L. Rev. 2179 (2014)[6]

The results [of studies of shareholder proposals] are mixed, but several trends emerge. First, in early studies—particularly those reviewing proxy seasons in the mid-1990s and earlier—shareholder proposals were found to have little or no effect on either stock price or firm value. As noted above, institutional investors began to engage in corporate governance matters in the mid-1980s, and, like the individual investors before them, apparently had little impact. Single proposals by individual "gadfly" investors were—and generally still are—unlikely to have much impact on the stock price, corporate governance mechanisms, or corporate performance, because they were unlikely to receive significant support from other shareholders and therefore more likely to be ignored by management. Shareholders as a group lacked cohesive views on appropriate governance structures, and information costs were too high to allow most institutional investors to make an effort to determine what those structures should be. As a result, most shareholders were (and many remain today) rationally apathetic with respect to corporate governance matters. It was only when managers failed spectacularly that most shareholders were willing to vote against management.

. . .

There are, to be sure, a large number of investors—particularly retail investors—who do not actively vote their shares. If brokers held these shares, the brokers historically had the discretion to vote on behalf of the beneficial shareholders for "routine" corporate governance matters, except in cases in which the shareholders instructed the brokers how they wanted their shares voted. For reasons of convenience, or in some cases perhaps because of conflicts of interest, brokers have traditionally voted with management. As a result, broker discretionary voting has been seen as a bulwark against shareholder proposal activism and is therefore a target of those seeking to expand shareholder rights. As shareholder activists have pushed for modifications to the national exchanges' voting policies over the years, the NYSE has enacted several changes to its broker discretionary voting rules. These changes include the elimination of broker discretionary voting on the following: equity compensation plans, in 2003; uncontested director elections, in 2010; and, in 2012, a number of other corporate governance matters such as "proposals to de-stagger the board of directors, majority voting in the election of directors, eliminating supermajority voting requirements,

---

[6]   Reprinted by permission of Paul Rose and the Florida Law Review.

providing for the use of consents, providing rights to call a special meeting, and certain types of anti-takeover provision overrides."[120]

The effect of these changes to the exchange rules is a clear win for supporters of shareholder primacy; more pragmatically, the changes particularly benefit the corporate governance and proxy advisory industry, which influences the voting of many institutional investors. Work by Professors Stephen Choi, Jill Fisch, and Marcel Kahan indicates that most institutional investors use proxy advisors as data compilers rather than following their advice blindly, although there is a small percentage of investors who give proxy advisors the power to vote the investors' shares according to the proxy advisors' criteria. It follows then, that (at least prior to 2013) there is on one hand a large group of investors who likely either do not pay attention to shareholder proposals or outsource their corporate governance voting to brokers and who arguably tend to vote with management. On the other hand, there is a small group of shareholders who outsource their corporate governance voting to proxy advisors but tend to take positions against management on corporate governance matters. There is also a substantial group of shareholders between these two poles that are "persuadable" shareholder voters. As explained by Professors Ronald J. Gilson and Jeffrey N. Gordon, most shareholders—particularly many large, institutional investors such as mutual funds—are rationally reticent to support governance changes. Some institutional investors and governance entrepreneurs such as activist hedge funds and proxy advisors seek to persuade these reticent investors of the case for change:

---

[120] Memorandum from NYSE Regulation to All NYSE and NYSE Amex Equities Members and Member Orgs. (Jan. 25, 2012), available at http://www.nyse.com/nysenotices/nyse/information-memos/detail?memo_id=12-4. Sullivan & Cromwell notes the irony of the rule changes outlined in the memorandum:

> Because retail shareholders often do not provide instructions to vote their shares, the NYSE interpretive change removes a significant number of "for" votes from the voting pool. In 2012, this did not have a significant impact on the support for these proposals measured as a percentage of votes cast—virtually all shares that were voted continued to be in favor of these proposals. It did, however, have a significant impact on the support for these proposals measured as a percentage of total shares outstanding, which is the measurement that generally applies as a state law matter in the case of a charter amendment. Many companies have a requirement in their charter that certain amendments must be approved by the affirmative vote of a supermajority (often two-thirds or 80%) of shares outstanding. For these companies, it was significantly more likely in 2012 that a management proposal for a charter amendment that is seen by shareholders as a governance enhancement will nevertheless fail to receive the vote necessary to effect the charter amendment.

> For example, in 2012 the average level of shareholder support for management proposals to eliminate supermajority voting provisions (which the company was proposing, in many cases, in response to a successful shareholder proposal in an earlier year) was 70% of shares outstanding, compared to 84% in 2011, with the difference being attributable almost entirely to fewer shares being voted. In 2012, these management proposals to eliminate supermajority voting failed at eight companies, double the number from 2011.

2012 Proxy Season Review, Sullivan & Cromwell LLP 11–12 (July 9, 2012), http://www.sullcrom.com/siteFiles/Publications/2012_Proxy_Season_Review-7-20-2012.pdf.

Such actors would develop the skills to identify strategic and governance shortfalls with significant valuation consequences, to acquire a position in a company with governance-related underperformance, and then to present reticent institutions with their value proposition . . . . Once the issue is framed and presented, the undervaluation of governance rights is reduced: The institutions will vote (or indicate willingness to vote) in favor of the specialized actors' perspective if the issue is framed in a compelling way.

Similar to political voting, a large central group of voters is not irrevocably and ideologically committed to one side or the other. They will cast their votes opportunistically for whichever side presents the most compelling arguments or simply offers a change from past policies. And, like attitudes towards political issues, shareholders show rapid shifts in support for various shareholder proposals. [Today], shareholders increasingly value their governance rights and their support for numerous shareholder rights issues is strengthening.

The reasons for these shifts are not entirely endogenous, however. Indeed, the increasing interest in proxy voting in particular is the intended result of regulatory changes that have encouraged institutional investors to take a more active role in corporate governance, including a rule under the Investment Advisers Act that requires investment advisers such as mutual funds to vote proxies in the best interests of the fund shareholders, and the Department of Labor's similar imposition of fiduciary duties on pension fund managers. The SEC has pursued several other initiatives to promote more active shareholder engagement in corporate governance, including a loosening of rules governing proxy communications among shareholders and rules requiring the disclosure of proxy voting by investment companies. The whittling down of broker discretionary voting has likely had a significant effect on support for corporate governance proposals.

. . .

In 2003, there was a 56% jump in the number of corporate governance proposals, from 273 proposals in 2002 to 427 in 2003.[129] Many of the proposals were offered in reaction to corporate scandals and were dropped because of regulatory changes. As a general matter, corporate governance proposals tend to be "trendy": many become relatively popular quickly, but just as quickly fade away. However, while governance trends come and go, 2003 marked a significant shift in the use of shareholder proposals as a tool of corporate governance. Undoubtedly, the jump in proposals in 2003 is largely attributable to heightened attention on governance issues after there were numerous indictments and civil charges filed in 2002 and 2003 against executives, accountants, and bankers from Adelphia Communications, Arthur Andersen, Charter Communications, Credit Suisse, Dynegy, Enron, HealthSouth, Merrill Lynch, Qwest Communications, Rite Aid, Tyco

International, and WorldCom, among others; it is also clearly attributable to the passage of the Sarbanes-Oxley Act in July 2002.

Looking beyond the initial jump, over the eleven years from 2003–2013 . . ., shareholder proposals decreased gradually from 2003–2008, rose again in 2009, and again experienced a decline from 2009–2011. The period from 2011–2013 appears relatively steady. The decline in proposals from 2008–2013 has several main drivers. First, as discussed in detail below, some proposals are quite successful, and so there are simply fewer companies that are targeted by governance activists in subsequent years. Trendy proposals often fail and may not be brought up again. Finally, shareholders and managers are increasingly engaging in behind-the-scenes negotiations; again, this is likely due to the success of both shareholder governance initiatives as well as event-driven hedge funds, each of which may increase managerial willingness to engage with shareholders.

. . . The following proposals have appeared at least twenty times each year in which they have been submitted, and they tend to receive significant support—20% or more-from the outstanding shares of the companies at which they are submitted. These include proposals to:

- Repeal a classified board of directors;
- Appoint an independent chairman or separate the board chairman and CEO positions;
- Require a majority vote to elect directors;
- Create a cumulative voting system;
- Redeem poison pills;
- Eliminate or reduce supermajority voting requirement provisions in the charter;
- Provide shareholders with the right to act by written consent; and
- Provide shareholders with the right to call a special meeting.

NOTES AND QUESTIONS

1.   Why would institutional investors prefer using shareholder proposals to proxy contests as a tool for activism?

2.   How might Regulation FD affect management's ability to negotiate with an activist who has put forward a proposal?

3.   Given that there are certain types of proposals that come up routinely, should the board of directors establish policies on those issues in advance of receiving a shareholder proposal?

C. MANAGEMENT RESISTANCE TO PROPOSALS: GROUNDS FOR EXCLUDING A PROPOSAL

A proposal that fails to meet any of the eligibility requirements of the Rule may be excluded from the company's proxy statement. In addition, Rule 14a–8(i) contains 13 substantive grounds on which proposals also may be excluded from the company's proxy statement. As noted above, of course, management will typically seek a no-action letter from the SEC before excluding the proposal.

1) PROPER SUBJECT OF SHAREHOLDER ACTION: HEREIN OF USING RULE 14a–8 TO ADOPT OR AMEND BYLAWS

Most shareholder proposals are phrased as recommendations. The use of precatory language follows from Rule 14a–8(i)(1), which provides that a shareholder proposal must be a proper subject of action for security holders under the law of the state of incorporation. Recall that under state law, all corporate powers shall be exercised by or under the authority of the board. Consequently, state corporate law commits most powers of initiation to the board of directors—the shareholders may not initiate corporate actions, they may only approve or disapprove of corporate actions placed before them for a vote. The SEC's explanatory note to Rule 14a–8(i)(1) recognizes this aspect of state law by explaining that mandatory proposals may be improper. The note goes on, however, to explain the SEC's belief that a shareholder proposal is proper if phrased as a request or recommendation to the board.

If a precatory proposal passes, the board is not obligated to implement it. Indeed, a board decision not to do so should be protected by the business judgment rule. On the other hand, the risk of adverse publicity and poor shareholder relations may encourage a board to implement an approved precatory proposal even where the board opposes the proposal on the merits.

Shareholder amendments to the bylaws may constitute an exception to the general rule that proposals cannot mandate board action. The validity of such proposals is considered in the next case.

CA, Inc. v. AFSCME Employees Pension Plan

953 A.2d 227 (Del. 2008)

This proceeding arises from a certification by the United States Securities and Exchange Commission (the "SEC"), to this Court, of two questions of law pursuant to Article IV, Section 11(8) of the Delaware Constitution[1] and Supreme Court Rule 41. . . .

---

[1]   Article IV, Section 11(8) was amended in 2007 to authorize this Court to hear and determine questions of law certified to it by (in addition to the tribunals already specified therein) the United States Securities and Exchange Commission. 76 Del. Laws 2007, ch. 37 § 1, effective May 3, 2007. This certification request is the first submitted by the SEC to this Court.

I. *FACTS*

CA is a Delaware corporation whose board of directors consists of twelve persons, all of whom sit for reelection each year. . . .

AFSCME, a CA stockholder, is associated with the American Federation of State, County and Municipal Employees. On March 13, 2008, AFSCME submitted a proposed stockholder bylaw (the "Bylaw" or "proposed Bylaw") for inclusion in the Company's proxy materials for its 2008 annual meeting of stockholders. The Bylaw, if adopted by CA stockholders, would amend the Company's bylaws to provide as follows:

> RESOLVED, that pursuant to section 109 of the Delaware General Corporation Law and Article IX of the bylaws of CA, Inc., stockholders of CA hereby amend the bylaws to add the following Section 14 to Article II:

> The board of directors shall cause the corporation to reimburse a stockholder or group of stockholders (together, the "Nominator") for reasonable expenses ("Expenses") incurred in connection with nominating one or more candidates in a contested election of directors to the corporation's board of directors, including, without limitation, printing, mailing, legal, solicitation, travel, advertising and public relations expenses, so long as (a) the election of fewer than 50% of the directors to be elected is contested in the election, (b) one or more candidates nominated by the Nominator are elected to the corporation's board of directors, (c) stockholders are not permitted to cumulate their votes for directors, and (d) the election occurred, and the Expenses were incurred, after this bylaw's adoption. The amount paid to a Nominator under this bylaw in respect of a contested election shall not exceed the amount expended by the corporation in connection with such election.

CA's current bylaws and Certificate of Incorporation have no provision that specifically addresses the reimbursement of proxy expenses. . . .

It is undisputed that the decision whether to reimburse election expenses is presently vested in the discretion of CA's board of directors, subject to their fiduciary duties and applicable Delaware law.

On April 18, 2008, CA notified the SEC's Division of Corporation Finance (the "Division") of its intention to exclude the proposed Bylaw from its 2008 proxy materials. The Company requested from the Division a "no-action letter" stating that the Division would not recommend any enforcement action to the SEC if CA excluded the AFSCME proposal.[2]
. . .

---

[2] Under Sections (i)(1) and (i)(2) of SEC Rule 14a–8, a company may exclude a stockholder proposal from its proxy statement if the proposal "is not a proper subject for action by the shareholders under the laws of the jurisdiction of the company's organization," or where

III. *THE FIRST QUESTION*

A. *Preliminary Comments*

The first question [certified to us by the SEC] is whether the Bylaw is a proper subject for shareholder action, more precisely, whether the Bylaw may be proposed and enacted by shareholders without the concurrence of the Company's board of directors. Before proceeding further, we make some preliminary comments in an effort to delineate a framework within which to begin our analysis.

First, the DGCL empowers both the board of directors and the shareholders of a Delaware corporation to adopt, amend or repeal the corporation's bylaws. 8 Del. C. § 109(a) relevantly provides that:

> After a corporation has received any payment for any of its stock, the power to adopt, amend or repeal bylaws shall be in the stockholders entitled to vote . . .; provided, however, any corporation may, in its certificate of incorporation, confer the power to adopt, amend or repeal bylaws upon the directors. . . . The fact that such power has been so conferred upon the directors . . . shall not divest the stockholders . . . of the power, nor limit their power to adopt, amend or repeal bylaws.

Pursuant to Section 109(a), CA's Certificate of Incorporation confers the power to adopt, amend or repeal the bylaws upon the Company's board of directors. . . .

Second, the vesting of that concurrent power in both the board and the shareholders raises the issue of whether the stockholders' power is coextensive with that of the board, and vice versa. As a purely theoretical matter that is possible, and were that the case, then the first certified question would be easily answered. That is, under such a regime any proposal to adopt, amend or repeal a bylaw would be a proper subject for either shareholder or board action, without distinction. But the DGCL has not allocated to the board and the shareholders the identical, coextensive power to adopt, amend and repeal the bylaws. Therefore, how that power is allocated between those two decision-making bodies requires an analysis that is more complex.

Moving from the theoretical to this case, by its terms Section 109(a) vests in the shareholders a power to adopt, amend or repeal bylaws that is legally sacrosanct, i.e., the power cannot be non-consensually eliminated or limited by anyone other than the legislature itself. If viewed in isolation, Section 109(a) could be read to make the board's and the shareholders' power to adopt, amend or repeal bylaws identical and coextensive, but Section 109(a) does not exist in a vacuum. It must be read together with 8 Del. C. § 141(a), which pertinently provides that:

> The business and affairs of every corporation organized under this chapter shall be managed by or under the direction of a board of directors,

---

the proposal, if implemented, "would cause the company to violate any state law to which it is subject." See 17 C.F.R. § 240.14a–8.

except as may be otherwise provided in this chapter or in its certificate of incorporation.

No such broad management power is statutorily allocated to the shareholders. Indeed, it is well established that stockholders of a corporation subject to the DGCL may not directly manage the business and affairs of the corporation, at least without specific authorization in either the statute or the certificate of incorporation. Therefore, the shareholders' statutory power to adopt, amend or repeal bylaws is not coextensive with the board's concurrent power and is limited by the board's management prerogatives under Section 141(a). . . .

B. *Analysis*

1.

. . .

Implicit in CA's argument is the premise that *any* bylaw that in *any* respect might be viewed as limiting or restricting the power of the board of directors automatically falls outside the scope of permissible bylaws. That simply cannot be. That reasoning, taken to its logical extreme, would result in eliminating altogether the shareholders' statutory right to adopt, amend or repeal bylaws. Bylaws, by their very nature, set down rules and procedures that bind a corporation's board and its shareholders. In that sense, most, if not all, bylaws could be said to limit the otherwise unlimited discretionary power of the board. Yet Section 109(a) carves out an area of shareholder power to adopt, amend or repeal bylaws that is expressly inviolate. Therefore, to argue that the Bylaw at issue here limits the board's power to manage the business and affairs of the Company only begins, but cannot end, the analysis needed to decide whether the Bylaw is a proper subject for shareholder action. The question left unanswered is what is the scope of shareholder action that Section 109(b) permits yet does not improperly intrude upon the directors' power to manage corporation's business and affairs under Section 141(a). . . .

2.

It is well-established Delaware law that a proper function of bylaws is not to mandate how the board should decide specific substantive business decisions, but rather, to define the process and procedures by which those decisions are made. As the Court of Chancery has noted:

Traditionally, the bylaws have been the corporate instrument used to set forth the rules by which the corporate board conducts its business. To this end, the DGCL is replete with specific provisions authorizing the bylaws to establish the procedures through which board and committee action is taken. . . . [T]here is a general consensus that bylaws that regulate the process by which the board acts are statutorily authorized.

. . .

. . . Sections 109 and 141, taken in totality, ... make clear that bylaws may pervasively and strictly regulate the process by which boards act, subject to the constraints of equity.

Examples of the procedural, process-oriented nature of bylaws are found in both the DGCL and the case law. For example, 8 Del. C. § 141(b) authorizes bylaws that fix the number of directors on the board, the number of directors required for a quorum (with certain limitations), and the vote requirements for board action. 8 Del. C. § 141(f) authorizes bylaws that preclude board action without a meeting. And, almost three decades ago this Court upheld a shareholder-enacted bylaw requiring unanimous board attendance and board approval for any board action, and unanimous ratification of any committee action.[18] Such purely procedural bylaws do not improperly encroach upon the board's managerial authority under Section 141(a). . . .

Although CA concedes that "restrictive procedural bylaws (such as those requiring the presence of all directors and unanimous board consent to take action) are acceptable," it points out that even facially procedural bylaws can unduly intrude upon board authority. The Bylaw being proposed here is unduly intrusive, CA claims, because, by mandating reimbursement of a stockholder's proxy expenses, it limits the board's broad discretionary authority to decide whether to grant reimbursement at all. CA further claims that because (in defined circumstances) the Bylaw mandates the expenditure of corporate funds, its subject matter is necessarily substantive, not process-oriented, and, therefore falls outside the scope of what Section 109(b) permits.[19]

Because the Bylaw is couched as a command to reimburse ("The board of directors shall cause the corporation to reimburse a stockholder"), it lends itself to CA's criticism. But the Bylaw's wording, although relevant, is not dispositive of whether or not it is process-related. The Bylaw could easily have been worded differently, to emphasize its process, as distinguished from its mandatory payment, component. By saying this we do not mean to suggest that this Bylaw's reimbursement component can be ignored. What we do suggest is that a bylaw that requires the expenditure of corporate funds does not, for that reason alone, become automatically deprived of its process-related character. A hypothetical example illustrates the point. Suppose that the

---

[18]   Frantz Mfg. Co. v. EAC Indus., 501 A.2d 401 (Del.1985). See also Hollinger, 844 A.2d at 1079–80 (shareholder-enacted bylaw abolishing a board committee created by board resolution does not impermissibly interfere with the board's authority under Section 141(a)).

[19]   CA actually conflates two separate arguments that, although facially similar, are analytically distinct. The first argument is that the Bylaw impermissibly intrudes upon board authority because it mandates the expenditure of corporate funds. The second is that the Bylaw impermissibly leaves no role for board discretion and would require reimbursement of the costs of a subset of CA's stockholders, even in circumstances where the board's fiduciary duties would counsel otherwise. Analytically, the first argument is relevant to the issue of whether the Bylaw is a proper subject for unilateral stockholder action, whereas the second argument more properly goes to the separate question of whether the Bylaw, if enacted, would violate Delaware law.

directors of a corporation live in different states and at a considerable distance from the corporation's headquarters. Suppose also that the shareholders enact a bylaw that requires all meetings of directors to take place in person at the corporation's headquarters. Such a bylaw would be clearly process-related, yet it cannot be supposed that the shareholders would lack the power to adopt the bylaw because it would require the corporation to expend its funds to reimburse the directors' travel expenses. Whether or not a bylaw is process-related must necessarily be determined in light of its context and purpose.

The context of the Bylaw at issue here is the process for electing directors—a subject in which shareholders of Delaware corporations have a legitimate and protected interest. The purpose of the Bylaw is to promote the integrity of that electoral process by facilitating the nomination of director candidates by stockholders or groups of stockholders. Generally, and under the current framework for electing directors in contested elections, only board-sponsored nominees for election are reimbursed for their election expenses. Dissident candidates are not, unless they succeed in replacing at least a majority of the entire board. The Bylaw would encourage the nomination of non-management board candidates by promising reimbursement of the nominating stockholders' proxy expenses if one or more of its candidates are elected. In that the shareholders also have a legitimate interest, because the Bylaw would facilitate the exercise of their right to participate in selecting the contestants. . . .

The shareholders of a Delaware corporation have the right "to participate in selecting the contestants" for election to the board. The shareholders are entitled to facilitate the exercise of that right by proposing a bylaw that would encourage candidates other than board-sponsored nominees to stand for election. The Bylaw would accomplish that by committing the corporation to reimburse the election expenses of shareholders whose candidates are successfully elected. That the implementation of that proposal would require the expenditure of corporate funds will not, in and of itself, make such a bylaw an improper subject matter for shareholder action. Accordingly, we answer the first question certified to us in the affirmative.

That, however, concludes only part of the analysis. The DGCL also requires that the Bylaw be "not inconsistent with law."[23] Accordingly, we turn to the second certified question, which is whether the proposed Bylaw, if adopted, would cause CA to violate any Delaware law to which it is subject.

IV. *THE SECOND QUESTION*

In answering the first question, we have already determined that the Bylaw does not facially violate any provision of the DGCL or of CA's

---

[23]   8 Del. C. § 109(b).

Certificate of Incorporation. The question thus becomes whether the Bylaw would violate any common law rule or precept. . . .

This Court has previously invalidated contracts that would require a board to act or not act in such a fashion that would limit the exercise of their fiduciary duties. In *Paramount Communications, Inc. v. QVC Network, Inc.*,[27] we invalidated a "no shop" provision of a merger agreement with a favored bidder (Viacom) that prevented the directors of the target company (Paramount) from communicating with a competing bidder (QVC) the terms of its competing bid in an effort to obtain the highest available value for shareholders. We held that:

> The No-Shop Provision could not validly define or limit the fiduciary duties of the Paramount directors. To the extent that a contract, or a provision thereof, purports to require a board to act or not act in such a fashion as to limit the exercise of fiduciary duties, it is invalid and unenforceable. [. . .] [T]he Paramount directors could not contract away their fiduciary obligations. Since the No-Shop Provision was invalid, Viacom never had any vested contract rights in the provision.

. . . [*QVC* involved a binding contractual arrangement] that the board of directors had voluntarily imposed upon themselves. This case involves a binding bylaw that the shareholders seek to impose involuntarily on the directors in the specific area of election expense reimbursement. Although this case is distinguishable in that respect, the distinction is one without a difference. The reason is that the internal governance contract—which here takes the form of a bylaw—is one that would also prevent the directors from exercising their full managerial power in circumstances where their fiduciary duties would otherwise require them to deny reimbursement to a dissident slate. That this limitation would be imposed by a majority vote of the shareholders rather than by the directors themselves, does not, in our view, legally matter.[32]

. . . AFSCME argues that it is unfair to claim that the Bylaw prevents the CA board from discharging its fiduciary duty where the effect of the Bylaw is to relieve the board entirely of those duties in this specific area.

That response, in our view, is more semantical than substantive. No matter how artfully it may be phrased, the argument concedes the very proposition that renders the Bylaw, as written, invalid: the Bylaw mandates reimbursement of election expenses in circumstances that a proper application of fiduciary principles could preclude. That such circumstances could arise is not far fetched. . . .[34]

---

[27]   637 A.2d 34 (Del.1994).

[32]   Only if the Bylaw provision were enacted as an amendment to CA's Certificate of Incorporation would that distinction be dispositive. See8 Del. C. § 102(b)(1) and § 242.

[34]   Such a circumstance could arise, for example, if a shareholder group affiliated with a competitor of the company were to cause the election of a minority slate of candidates committed

It is in this respect that the proposed Bylaw, as written, would violate Delaware law if enacted by CA's shareholders. As presently drafted, the Bylaw would afford CA's directors full discretion to determine what *amount* of reimbursement is appropriate, because the directors would be obligated to grant only the "reasonable" expenses of a successful short slate. Unfortunately, that does not go far enough, because the Bylaw contains no language or provision that would reserve to CA's directors their full power to exercise their fiduciary duty to decide whether or not it would be appropriate, in a specific case, to award reimbursement at all.

In arriving at this conclusion, we express no view on whether the Bylaw as currently drafted, would create a better governance scheme from a policy standpoint. We decide only what is, and is not, legally permitted under the DGCL. That statute, as currently drafted, is the expression of policy as decreed by the Delaware legislature. Those who believe that CA's shareholders should be permitted to make the proposed Bylaw as drafted part of CA's governance scheme, have two alternatives. They may seek to amend the Certificate of Incorporation to include the substance of the Bylaw; *or* they may seek recourse from the Delaware General Assembly.

Accordingly, we answer the second question certified to us in the affirmative.

NOTES AND QUESTIONS

1. In *CA,* the Court declined "to articulate with doctrinal exactitude a bright line that divides those bylaws that shareholders may unilaterally adopt under Section 109(b) from those which they may not under Section 141(a)," explaining in a footnote that they were deciding only the validity of the specific bylaw in question:

> We do not attempt to delineate the location of that bright line in this Opinion. What we do hold is case specific; that is, wherever may be the location of the bright line that separates the shareholders' bylaw-making power under Section 109 from the directors' exclusive managerial authority under Section 141(a), the proposed Bylaw at issue here does not invade the territory demarcated by Section 141(a).

2. At the end of its opinion, the court suggests that the shareholders might "seek to amend the Certificate of Incorporation to include the substance of the Bylaw." Under DGCL § 242(b) (1), however, the Board must propose amendments to the Certificate before a shareholder vote may be taken. What do you suppose is the likelihood that the Board of CA, Inc., would agree to propose the amendment, so that the shareholders could vote on it?

---

to using their director positions to obtain, and then communicate, valuable proprietary strategic or product information to the competitor.

3.   Suppose the shareholders of Ajax, Inc., adopted a reimbursement bylaw with the requisite fiduciary out.[7] Sometime later a shareholder successfully conducted a short slate proxy contest. The shareholder sought reimbursement under the bylaw. The board concluded that reimbursement would be inconsistent with its fiduciary duties. The shareholder sues. Should the court apply the business judgment rule or some more exacting standard of review to the issue?

4.   In *AFSCME v. AIG,* 462 F.3d 121 (2nd Cir. 2006), AFSCME proposed the following amendment to AIG's bylaws:

> The Corporation shall include in its proxy materials for a meeting of stockholders the name, together with the Disclosure and Statement (both defined below), of any person nominated for election to the Board of Directors by a stockholder or group thereof that satisfies the requirements of this section 6.10 (the "Nominator"), and allow stockholders to vote with respect to such nominee on the Corporation's proxy card. Each Nominator may nominate one candidate for election at a meeting.

> To be eligible to make a nomination, a Nominator must:

> (a)   have beneficially owned 3% or more of the Corporation's outstanding common stock (the "Required Shares") for at least one year;

> (b)   provide written notice received by the Corporation's Secretary within the time period specified in section 1.11 of the Bylaws containing (i) with respect to the nominee, (A) the information required by Items 7(a), (b) and (c) of SEC Schedule 14A (such information is referred to herein as the "Disclosure") and (B) such nominee's consent to being named in the proxy statement and to serving as a director if elected; and (ii) with respect to the Nominator, proof of ownership of the Required Shares; and

> (c)   execute an undertaking that it agrees (i) to assume all liability of any violation of law or regulation arising out of the Nominator's communications with stockholders, including the Disclosure (ii) to the extent it uses soliciting material other than the Corporation's proxy materials, comply with all laws and regulations relating thereto.

> The Nominator shall have the option to furnish a statement, not to exceed 500 words, in support of the nominee's candidacy (the "Statement"), at the time the Disclosure is submitted to the Corporation's Secretary. The Board of Directors shall adopt a procedure for timely resolving disputes over whether notice of a

---

[7]   A fiduciary out is a provision contained in the articles of incorporation, the bylaws, or a contract that allows the board of directors to decline to carry out the specified task if the board concludes that doing so would violate its fiduciary duties. In the present case, the term refers to a provision in the bylaw that, as the Supreme Court mandated, "would reserve to CA's directors their full power to exercise their fiduciary duty to decide whether or not it would be appropriate, in a specific case, to award reimbursement at all."

nomination was timely given and whether the Disclosure and Statement comply with this section 6.10 and SEC Rules.

Would this bylaw be a proper subject of shareholder action under Delaware law? Should the bylaw include a fiduciary out in order to pass muster?

5.   Is the process/substance distinction consistent with the language of Section 109(b), which provides in pertinent part that "bylaws may contain any provision, not inconsistent with law or with the certificate of incorporation, relating to the business of the corporation, the conduct of its affairs, and its rights or powers or the rights or powers of its stockholders, directors, officers or employees"?

6.   In *Boilermakers Local 154 Ret. Fund v. Chevron Corp.*,[8] shareholders of Chevron sued the board of directors for having adopted a so-called forum selection bylaw providing that litigation relating to Chevron's internal affairs should be conducted in Delaware, the state where Chevron is incorporated. The court explained that:

> As a matter of easy linguistics, the forum selection bylaws address the "rights" of the stockholders, because they regulate where stockholders can exercise their right to bring certain internal affairs claims against the corporation and its directors and officers. They also plainly relate to the conduct of the corporation by channeling internal affairs cases into the courts of the state of incorporation, providing for the opportunity to have internal affairs cases resolved authoritatively by our Supreme Court if any party wishes to take an appeal. . . .
>
> Perhaps recognizing the weakness of any argument that the forum selection bylaws fall outside the plain language of 8 Del. C. § 109(b), the plaintiffs try to argue that judicial gloss put on the language of the statute renders the bylaws facially invalid. The plaintiffs contend that the bylaws . . . attempt to regulate an "external" matter, as opposed to, an "internal" matter of corporate governance. The plaintiffs attempt to support this argument with a claim that traditionally there have only been three appropriate subject matters of bylaws: stockholder meetings, the board of directors and its committees, and officerships.
>
> But even if one assumes that judicial statements could limit the plain statutory words in the way the plaintiffs claim (which is dubious), the judicial decisions do not aid the plaintiffs. The plaintiffs take a cramped view of the proper subject matter of bylaws. The bylaws of Delaware corporations have a "procedural, process-oriented nature."[74] It is doubtless true that our courts have said that bylaws typically do not contain substantive mandates, but direct how the corporation, the board, and its stockholders may take certain actions. 8 Del. C. § 109(b) has long been understood to allow the corporation to set "self-imposed rules and regulations

---

[8]   73 A.3d 934 (Del. Ch. 2013).

[74]   CA, Inc. v. AFSCME Emps. Pension Plan, 953 A.2d 227, 236–37 (Del.2008).

[that are] deemed expedient for its convenient functioning."[76] The forum selection bylaws here fit this description. They are process-oriented, because they regulate *where* stockholders may file suit, not *whether* the stockholder may file suit or the kind of remedy that the stockholder may obtain on behalf of herself or the corporation. The bylaws also clearly address cases of the kind that address "the business of the corporation, the conduct of its affairs, and . . . the rights or powers of its stockholders, directors, officers or employees," because they govern where internal affairs cases governed by state corporate law may be heard. These are the kind of claims most central to the relationship between those who manage the corporation and the corporation's stockholders.

By contrast, the bylaws would be regulating external matters if the board adopted a bylaw that purported to bind a plaintiff, even a stockholder plaintiff, who sought to bring a tort claim against the company based on a personal injury she suffered that occurred on the company's premises or a contract claim based on a commercial contract with the corporation. The reason why those kinds of bylaws would be beyond the statutory language of 8 Del. C. § 109(b) is obvious: the bylaws would not deal with the rights and powers of the plaintiff-stockholder *as a stockholder.* . . .

Nor is it novel for bylaws to regulate how stockholders may exercise their rights as stockholders. For example, an advance notice bylaw "requires stockholders wishing to make nominations or proposals at a corporation's annual meeting to give notice of their intention in advance of so doing."[79] Like such bylaws, which help organize what could otherwise be a chaotic stockholder meeting, the forum selection bylaws are designed to bring order to what the boards of Chevron and FedEx say they perceive to be a chaotic filing of duplicative and inefficient derivative and corporate suits against the directors and the corporations.

The plaintiffs' argument, then, reduces to the claim that the bylaws do not speak to a "traditional" subject matter, and should be ruled invalid for that reason alone. For starters, the factual premise of this argument is not convincing. . . . But in any case, the Supreme Court long ago rejected the position that board action should be invalidated or enjoined simply because it involves a novel use of statutory authority. In *Moran v. Household International* in 1985, . . . the court reiterated that "our corporate law is not static. It must grow and develop in response to, indeed in anticipation of, evolving concepts and needs. Merely because the General Corporation Law is silent as to a specific matter does not mean that it is prohibited."[84]

---

[76]   Gow v. Consol. Coppermines Corp., 165 A. 136, 140 (Del.Ch.1933).

[79]   JANA Master Fund, Ltd. v. CNET Networks, Inc., 954 A.2d 335, 344 (Del.Ch.2008) (citation omitted), aff'd, 947 A.2d 1120 (Del.2008) (Table).

[84]   [Ed.: Moran v. Household Int'l, Inc., 500 A.2d 1346, 1351 (Del.1985) (quoting Unocal Corp. v. Mesa Petroleum Co., 493 A.2d 946, 957 (Del.1985)).]

In an omitted portion of the opinion, the court explains that "neither the wisdom of the Chevron [board] in adopting the forum selection bylaws to address the prevalence of multiforum litigation, [n]or in proceeding by way of a bylaw, rather than proposing an amendment to the certificate of incorporation, are proper matters for this court to address." Are forum selection provisions wise? And, if so, is it wise to adopt them in the bylaws rather than the articles of incorporation?

7. The exclusive forum bylaw of First Citizen Bancshares, Inc., provided that:

> Unless the corporation consents in writing to the selection of an alternative forum, the United States District Court for the Eastern District of North Carolina or, if such court lacks jurisdiction, any North Carolina state court that has jurisdiction, shall, to the fullest extent permitted by law, be the sole and exclusive forum for (1) any derivative action or proceeding brought on behalf of the corporation, (2) any action asserting a claim of breach of a fiduciary duty owed by any director, officer or other employee of the corporation to the corporation or the corporation's shareholders, (3) any action asserting a claim arising pursuant to any provision of the General Corporation Law of the State of Delaware, and (4) any action asserting a claim governed by the internal affairs doctrine. Any person or entity purchasing or otherwise acquiring or holding any interest in shares of capital stock of the Corporation shall be deemed to have notice of and consented to the provisions of this Section 8.

The provision is somewhat unusual in that it specifies a court outside of Delaware as the exclusive forum, but the bylaw was nevertheless upheld as valid by the Delaware Chancery Court.[9]

The firm's general counsel has proposed adding the following sentence to the bylaw, which is to be inserted prior to the last sentence of the current version:

> If any action the subject matter of which is within the scope of this Section is filed in a court other than a court located within the State of Delaware (a "Foreign Action") in the name of any stockholder, such stockholder shall be deemed to have consented to: (x) the personal jurisdiction of the state and federal courts located within the State of Delaware in connection with any action brought in any such court to enforce this Section (an "Enforcement Action"), and (y) having service of process made upon such stockholder in any such Enforcement Action by service upon such

---

[9]   See City of Providence v. First Citizens BancShares, Inc., 99 A.3d 229, 235 (Del. Ch. 2014) (holding that "the fact that the Board selected the federal and state courts of North Carolina—the second most obviously reasonable forum given that FC North is headquartered and has most of its operations there—rather than those of Delaware as the exclusive forums for intra-corporate disputes does not, in my view, call into question the facial validity of the Forum Selection Bylaw").

stockholder's counsel in the Foreign Action as agent for such stockholder.

What is the function and purpose of that provision?

8. In 2015, the Delaware legislature amended the DGCL by adding new section 115, which effectively codified the *Boilermakers* decision. At the same time, the legislature also amended DGCL § 109(b) to ban so-called fee shifting bylaws:

> In May 2014, the Delaware Supreme Court held in *ATP Tour, Inc. v. Deutscher Tennis Bund* that "the board of a Delaware non-stock corporation may lawfully adopt a bylaw that shifts all litigation expenses to a plaintiff in intra-corporate litigation who does not obtain a judgment on the merits that substantially achieves, in substance and amount, the full remedy sought." Concern that this ruling would lead to the adoption of fee-shifting bylaws in stock corporations prompted a quick legislative response.

> Within one year of the *ATP* decision, the Corporation Law Council of the Delaware State Bar Association proposed legislation to "limit *ATP* to its facts" and prevent the boards of Delaware stock corporations from adopting fee-shifting bylaws. In an explanatory memo, the Council expressed concern that such bylaws would deter stockholders from enforcing otherwise meritorious claims. . . .

> The legislation the Council proposed was signed into law on June 24, 2015, and became effective on August 1, 2015. It amended . . . Section 109(b) to provide that "bylaws may not contain any provision that would impose liability on a stockholder for the attorneys' fees or expenses of the corporation or any other party in connection with an internal corporate claim . . . ."[10]

2) NOT OTHERWISE SIGNIFICANT

Lovenheim v. Iroquois Brands Ltd.
618 F.Supp. 554 (D.D.C. 1985)

I. BACKGROUND

Plaintiff Peter C. Lovenheim, owner of two hundred shares of common stock in Iroquois Brands, Ltd. (hereinafter "Iroquois/Delaware"), seeks to bar Iroquois/Delaware from excluding from the proxy materials being sent to all shareholders in preparation for an upcoming shareholder meeting information concerning a proposed resolution he intends to offer at the meeting. Mr. Lovenheim's proposed resolution relates to the procedure used to force-feed geese for production of pâté de foie gras in France,[2] a type of pâté imported by Iroquois/Delaware.

---

[10] Solak v. Sarowitz, 2016 WL 7468070, at *2 (Del. Ch. Dec. 27, 2016).

[2] Pâté de foie gras is made from the liver of geese. According to Mr. Lovenheim's affidavit, force-feeding is frequently used in order to expand the liver and thereby produce a larger

Specifically, his resolution calls upon the Directors of Iroquois/Delaware to:

> form a committee to study the methods by which its French supplier produces pâté de foie gras, and report to the shareholders its findings and opinions, based on expert consultation, on whether this production method causes undue distress, pain or suffering to the animals involved and, if so, whether further distribution of this product should be discontinued until a more humane production method is developed.

Mr. Lovenheim's right to compel Iroquois/Delaware to insert information concerning his proposal in the proxy materials turns on the applicability of § 14(a) of the Securities Exchange Act of 1934 . . . ("the Exchange Act"), and the shareholder proposal rule promulgated by the Securities and Exchange Commission ("SEC"), Rule 14a–8. . . .

Iroquois/Delaware has refused to allow information concerning Mr. Lovenheim's proposal to be included in proxy materials being sent in connection with the next annual shareholders meeting. In doing so, Iroquois/Delaware relies on an exception to the general requirement of Rule 14a–8, Rule 14a–8([i])(5). That exception provides that an issuer of securities "may omit a proposal and any statement in support thereof" from its proxy statement and form of proxy:

> if the proposal relates to operations which account for less than 5 percent of the issuer's total assets at the end of its most recent fiscal year, and for less than 5 percent of its net earnings and gross sales for its most recent fiscal year, and is not otherwise significantly related to the issuer's business. . . .

---

quantity of pâté. Mr. Lovenheim's affidavit also contains a description of the force-feeding process:

> Force-feeding usually begins when the geese are four months old. On some farms where feeding is mechanized, the bird's body and wings are placed in a metal brace and its neck is stretched. Through a funnel inserted 10–12 inches down the throat of the goose, a machine pumps up to 400 grams of corn-based mash into its stomach. An elastic band around the goose's throat prevents regurgitation. When feeding is manual, a handler uses a funnel and stick to force the mash down.

Affidavit of Peter C. Lovenheim at para. 7. Plaintiff contends that such force-feeding is a form of cruelty to animals. Id.

Plaintiff has offered no evidence that force-feeding is used by Iroquois/Delaware's supplier in producing the pâté imported by Iroquois/Delaware. However his proposal calls upon the committee he seeks to create to investigate this question.

II. LIKELIHOOD OF PLAINTIFF
PREVAILING ON MERITS

. . .

C. Applicability of Rule 14a–8([i])(5) Exception

. . . [T]he likelihood of plaintiff's prevailing in this litigation turns primarily on the applicability to plaintiff's proposal of the exception to the shareholder proposal rule contained in Rule 14a–8([i])(5).

Iroquois/Delaware's reliance on the argument that this exception applies is based on the following information contained in the affidavit of its president: Iroquois/Delaware has annual revenues of $141 million with $6 million in annual profits and $78 million in assets. In contrast, its pâté de foie gras sales were just $79,000 last year, representing a net loss on pâté sales of $3,121. Iroquois/Delaware has only $34,000 in assets related to pâté. Thus none of the company's net earnings and less than .05 percent of its assets are implicated by plaintiff's proposal. These levels are obviously far below the five percent threshold set forth in the first portion of the exception claimed by Iroquois/Delaware.

Plaintiff does not contest that his proposed resolution relates to a matter of little economic significance to Iroquois/Delaware. Nevertheless he contends that the Rule 14a–8([i])(5) exception is not applicable as it cannot be said that his proposal "is not otherwise significantly related to the issuer's business" as is required by the final portion of that exception. In other words, plaintiff's argument that Rule 14a–8 does not permit omission of his proposal rests on the assertion that the rule and statute on which it is based do not permit omission merely because a proposal is not economically significant where a proposal has "ethical or social significance."[3] . . .

The Court would note that the applicability of the Rule 14a–8([i])(5) exception to Mr. Lovenheim's proposal represents a close question given the lack of clarity in the exception itself. In effect, plaintiff relies on the word "otherwise," suggesting that it indicates the drafters of the rule intended that other noneconomic tests of significance be used. Iroquois/Delaware relies on the fact that the rule examines other significance in relation to the issuer's business. Because of the apparent ambiguity of the rule, the Court considers the history of the shareholder

---

[3] The assertion that the proposal is significant in an ethical and social sense relies on plaintiff's argument that "the very availability of a market for products that may be obtained through the inhumane force-feeding of geese cannot help but contribute to the continuation of such treatment." Plaintiff's brief characterizes the humane treatment of animals as among the foundations of western culture and cites in support of this view the Seven Laws of Noah, an animal protection statute enacted by the Massachusetts Bay Colony in 1641, numerous federal statutes enacted since 1877, and animal protection laws existing in all fifty states and the District of Columbia. An additional indication of the significance of plaintiff's proposal is the support of such leading organizations in the field of animal care as the American Society for the Prevention of Cruelty to Animals and The Humane Society of the United States for measures aimed at discontinuing use of force-feeding.

proposal rule in determining the proper interpretation of the most recent version of that rule.

Prior to 1983, paragraph 14a–8([i])(5) excluded proposals "not significantly related to the issuer's business" but did not contain an objective economic significance test such as the five percent of sales, assets, and earnings specified in the first part of the current version. Although a series of SEC decisions through 1976 allowing issuers to exclude proposals challenging compliance with the Arab economic boycott of Israel allowed exclusion if the issuer did less than one percent of their business with Arab countries or Israel, the Commission stated later in 1976 that it did "not believe that subparagraph ([i])(5) should be hinged solely on the economic relativity of a proposal." Securities Exchange Act Release No. 12,999, 41 Fed. Reg. 52,994, 52,997 (1976). Thus the Commission required inclusion "in many situations in which the related business comprised less than one percent" of the company's revenues, profits or assets "where the proposal has raised policy questions important enough to be considered 'significantly related' to the issuer's business."

As indicated above, the 1983 revision adopted the five percent test of economic significance in an effort to create a more objective standard. Nevertheless, in adopting this standard, the Commission stated that proposals will be includable notwithstanding their "failure to reach the specified economic thresholds if a significant relationship to the issuer's business is demonstrated on the face of the resolution or supporting statement." Securities Exchange Act Release No. 19,135, 47 Fed. Reg. 47,420, 47,428 (1982). Thus it seems clear based on the history of the rule that "the meaning of 'significantly related' is not limited to economic significance." . . .

. . . The Court therefore holds that in light of the ethical and social significance of plaintiff's proposal and the fact that it implicates significant levels of sales, plaintiff has shown a likelihood of prevailing on the merits with regard to the issue of whether his proposal is "otherwise significantly related" to Iroquois/Delaware's business.[3]

NOTES AND QUESTIONS

1. Why did Lovenheim merely ask Iroquois Brands' board to form a study committee? Put another way, why didn't Lovenheim offer a proposal prohibiting the company from selling pâté?

2. Think about your favorite social or political cause. Suppose you wanted to get a shareholder proposal relating on that cause on a corporate proxy statement. Assume that the proposal would not meet the 5 percent economic significance test of Rule 14a–8(i)(5). On what basis would you show

---

[3] The result would, of course, be different if plaintiff's proposal was ethically significant in the abstract but had no meaningful relationship to the business of Iroquois/Delaware as Iroquois/Delaware was not engaged in the business of importing pâté de foie gras.

that the proposal has sufficient ethical or social significance to justify its inclusion in the proxy statement under Lovenheim?

3.   Although Iroquois Brands contended that Lovenheim's proposal might cause investors to conclude that the company was involved in cruelty to animals, the court dismissed that concern as "largely speculative." Was the court correct in giving such short shrift to this possibility?

4.   Courts have not always applied the 5% standards as precisely as they should. In *New York City Employees' Retirement System v. Dole Food Co., Inc.,* 795 F.Supp. 95 (S.D.N.Y.1992), for example, the New York City employees' pension fund petitioned Dole to include a proposal recommending that Dole form a committee to study the impact of various national health care reform proposals would have on Dole.

The district court ordered Dole to include the proposal in the proxy statement. In rejecting Dole's arguments under Rule 14a–8(i)(5), the court held that health care reform had economic significance because health insurance and care imposed large financial costs on Dole. Specifically, the court opined: "It is substantially likely that Dole's health insurance outlays constitute more than five percent of its income." The opinion does not set out any evidence as to Dole's health insurance expenses. Query whether courts ought to simply assume away a critical element of the standard. In any event, the court also misconstrued Rule 14a–8(i)(5). The rule does not speak of expenses that represent more than 5 percent of income. The Rule talks about operations—lines of business—that represent 5 percent of the company's total business, measured in various ways, none of which include expenditures. Despite the court's flawed reasoning, however, the result is probably right. Employee health benefits (or the decision not to provide such benefits) are a matter of considerable economic significance. Federal changes to the health insurance system doubtless would have had a major economic impact on employers. Accordingly, the proposal arguably had economic significance even though it did not satisfy any of the 5% thresholds.

PROBLEM

Sustainvest Asset Management LLC submitted the following proposal to Dunkin' Brands Group, Inc., the parent company of Dunkin' Donuts:

> Whereas, Dunkin Brands Corporate Social Responsibility (CSR) states the company is "committed to showing constant improvement in the area of corporate social responsibility. This involves continuous improvement in four areas that govern CSR strategy: Our Guests, Our Planet, Our People and Our Neighborhoods" yet a large part of revenue was derived from the sale of "K-Cup" pods brand product packaging which is not recyclable nor compostable and new studies suggest plastic packaging that reaches the ocean is toxic to marine animals and potentially to humans.

> Whereas, it was announced in July 2016 that more than 300 million Dunkin' K-Cup pods were sold in the first year since being made available at retail outlets nationwide.

Whereas, the #7 plastic used in Dunkin Brand K-Cups is a mix of plastics which is what makes it a problem for recycling.

Whereas, K-Cups have been confirmed to be BPA-free and made of "safe" plastic, but some studies show that even this type of material can have harmful effects when heated. When you come into contact with these plastic chemicals, they can act like estrogen in your body, negatively effecting hormones. The plastics can find their way into landfills to be incinerated or into the world's oceans where plastics concentrate and transfer toxic chemicals such as polychlorinated biphenyls and dioxins into the marine food web and potentially to human diets.

Whereas, officials in the city of Hamburg, the second-largest city in Germany are now banning the use of K-Cups from all government buildings due to "causing unnecessary resource consumption and waste generation and often contain polluting aluminum. . .We in Hamburg thought that these shouldn't be bought with taxpayers' money."

Whereas, recent financial data shows that Americans have decreased the amount of K-Cup's usage. Manufacturers of these cups, Keurig Green Mountain Inc. and JM Smucker, saw a decrease in pod sales during the fourth quarter of 2015, which could suggest future declines. With Dunkin Brands sharing 50 percent of the profits earned through the sale of K-cups with its franchisees this could not only pose an environmental threat but also a threat to the bottom line.

Whereas, several recyclable or compostable alternative pods have been brought to the market which could be considered by Dunkin Brands.

RESOLVED: Shareowners of Dunkin Brands request the Board to issue a report at reasonable cost, omitting confidential information, by October 1, 2018 assessing the environmental impacts of continuing to use K-Cup Pods brand packaging.

Supporting Statement: Proponents believe the report should include an assessment of the reputational, financial, and operational risks associated with continuing to use K-Cup packaging and, to the extent possible, goals and a timeline to either phase out this type of packaging or find an environmentally friendly alternative.[11]

In seeking to exclude the proposal, the company argued that:

The Company reported total revenues of approximately $828.9 million and net income of approximately $195.6 million for the fiscal year ended December 31, 2016 and total assets of approximately $3.2 billion as of December 31, 2016. The Company generates most of its revenue relating the sale of K-Cup pods in the

---

[11]   SEC No-Action Letter, Dunkin' Brands Group, Inc., 2018 WL 388146, at *10–11 (Feb. 22, 2018).

form of licensing fees, which are included in "Other Revenues" on the Company's income statement, and the remainder from royalties attributed to the sale of K-Cup pods in Dunkin' Donuts franchised restaurants, which are included in "Franchise fees and royalty income." Combined, these licensing and royalty revenues relating to K-Cup pod sales accounted for less than five percent of the Company's gross sales in fiscal 2016. Similarly, the Company confirms to the Staff that its net earnings related to the K-Cup pods licensing and royalty revenue represented less than five percent of the Company's net earnings for fiscal 2016 and its assets relating to K-Cup pods accounted for less than five percent of the Company's total assets as of December 31, 2016. The Company expects that these percentages will similarly be below five percent for fiscal 2017.[12]

Can the proposal be excluded under Rule 14a–8(i)(5)?

3) ORDINARY BUSINESS

Rule 14a–8(i)(7) allows the issuer to exclude so-called ordinary business matters. The question here is whether a proposal is an ordinary matter for the board or an extraordinary matter on which shareholder input is appropriate. The answer hinges on whether the proposal involves significant policy questions. As for deciding whether a policy question is significant, most courts assume that *Lovenheim*-style ethical or social significance suffices.

The SEC's policy on enforcing Rule 14a–8(i)(7) with respect to shareholder proposals concerned mainly with social—rather than economic—issues has fluctuated over the years. The SEC long handled such proposals on a case-by-case basis. In 1992, however, it departed from that practice and adopted a bright-line position that for the first time effectively excluded an entire category of social issue proposals. Cracker Barrel Old Country Stores attempted to exclude a shareholder proposal calling on the board of directors to include sexual orientation in its anti-discrimination policy. In a no action letter issued by the SEC's Division of Corporation Finance, the Commission took the position that all employment-related shareholder proposals raising social policy issues could be excluded under the "ordinary business" exclusion.

Subsequent litigation developed two issues. First, if a shareholder proponent sued a company whose management relied on *Cracker Barrel* to justify excluding an employment-related proposal from the proxy statement, should the reviewing court defer to the SEC's position? In *Amalgamated Clothing and Textile Workers Union v. Wal-Mart Stores, Inc.*,[13] a federal district court held that deference was not required and, moreover, that proposals relating to a company's affirmative action

---

[12] Id. at *3.
[13] 821 F.Supp.2d 877 (S.D.N.Y.1993).

policies were not per se excludible as ordinary business under Rule 14a–8(i)(7).

Second, was the SEC's *Cracker Barrel* position valid? In other words, could the SEC properly apply the *Cracker Barrel* interpretation in internal agency processes, such as when issuing a no action letter? In *New York City Employees' Retirement System v. SEC*, the district court ruled that the SEC's *Cracker Barrel* position was itself invalid because the SEC had failed to comply with federal administrative procedures in promulgating the position. The Second Circuit reversed, thereby allowing the SEC to apply *Cracker Barrel* internally, but in doing so concurred with the trial court's view that *Cracker Barrel* was not binding on courts.[14]

In 1998, the SEC adopted amendments to Rule 14a–8 that, among other things, reversed its *Cracker Barrel* position.[15] In promulgating this change, the SEC emphasized that employment discrimination was a consistent topic of public debate, thereby highlighting the on-going importance of *Lovenheim*-style social and ethical considerations. Indeed, the SEC explicitly noted its belief that the Rule 14a–8(i)(7) exception did not justify excluding proposals that raise significant social policy issues.

Reversal of the *Cracker Barrel* position returned the SEC to its prior case-by-case approach. Specific management decisions relating to employment, such as hiring, promotion, and termination of employees, as well as other business decisions, such as product lines and quality, remain excludable. The SEC does not want shareholders to "micromanage" the company. Proposals broadly relating to such matters but focusing on significant social policy issues, such as affirmative action and other employment discrimination matters, generally are not excludable.[16]

Trinity Wall St. v. Wal-Mart Stores, Inc.

792 F.3d 323 (3d Cir. 2015)

I. INTRODUCTION

. . .

Appellant Wal-Mart Stores, Inc., the world's largest retailer, and one of its shareholders, Appellee Trinity Wall Street—an Episcopal parish headquartered in New York City that owns Wal-Mart stock—are locked in a heated dispute. It stems from Wal-Mart's rejection of Trinity's

---

[14] New York City Employees' Retirement Sys. v. SEC, 45 F.3d 7 (2d Cir.1995).

[15] Amendments To Rules On Shareholder Proposals, Exchange Act Release No. 40018 (May 21, 1998).

[16] See, e.g., New York City Employees' Retirement Sys. v. Dole Food Co., 795 F.Supp. 95 (S.D.N.Y.1992), in which the proponent offered a proposal requesting Dole to study the potential impact on the company of various pending national health care reform proposals. Dole relied on Rule 14an8(i)(7) to exclude the proposal, among other provisions. The court rejected Dole's argument. Although employee benefits generally are an ordinary business matter, "a significant strategic decision" as to employee benefits fell outside the scope of ordinary business matters.

request to include its shareholder proposal in Wal-Mart's proxy materials for shareholder consideration.

Trinity's proposal, while linked to Wal-Mart's sale of high-capacity firearms (guns that can accept more than ten rounds of ammunition) at about one-third of its 3,000 stores, is nonetheless broad. It asks Wal-Mart's Board of Directors to develop and implement standards for management to use in deciding whether to sell a product that (1) "especially endangers public safety"; (2) "has the substantial potential to impair the reputation of Wal-Mart"; and/or (3) "would reasonably be considered by many offensive to the family and community values integral to the Company's promotion of its brand." Standing in Trinity's way, among other things, is a rule of the Securities and Exchange Commission ("SEC" or "Commission"), known as the "ordinary business" exclusion ("Rule 14a–8(i)(7)"). As its name suggests, the rule lets a company omit a shareholder proposal from its proxy materials if the proposal relates to its ordinary business operations.

Wal-Mart obtained what is known as a "no-action letter" from the staff of the SEC's Division of Corporate Finance (the "Corp. Fin. staff" or "staff"), thus signaling that there would be no recommendation of an enforcement action against the company if it omitted the proposal from its proxy materials. Trinity thereafter filed suit in federal court, seeking to enjoin Wal-Mart's exclusion of the proposal. The . . . District Court . . . handed the church a victory on the merits some seven months later by holding that, because the proposal concerned the company's Board (rather than its management) and focused principally on governance (rather than how Wal-Mart decides what to sell), it was outside Wal-Mart's ordinary business operations. Wal-Mart appeals, seeking a ruling that it could exclude Trinity's proposal from its 2015 proxy materials and did not err in excluding the proposal from its 2014 proxy materials.

Stripped to its essence, Trinity's proposal—although styled as promoting improved governance—goes to the heart of Wal-Mart's business: what it sells on its shelves. For the reasons that follow, we hold that it is excludable under Rule 14a–8(i)(7) and reverse the ruling of the District Court.

II. FACTS & PROCEDURAL HISTORY

. . .

A.   Trinity Objects to Wal-Mart's Sale of Assault Rifles.

. . . Trinity [is] one of the wealthiest religious institutions in the United States, with a balance sheet of over $800 million in assets and real estate valued at approximately $3 billion. Its strong financial footing, according to Trinity, empowers it to "pursue a mission of good works beyond the reach of other religious institutions." Part of that mission is to reduce violence in society.

Alarmed by the spate of mass murders in America, in particular the shooting at Sandy Hook Elementary School in December 2012, Trinity resolved to use its investment portfolio to address the ease of access to rifles equipped with high-capacity magazines (the weapon of choice of the Sandy Hook shooter and other mass murderers). Its principal focus was Wal-Mart.

During its review of Wal-Mart's merchandising practices, Trinity discovered what it perceived as a major inconsistency. Despite the retailer's stated mission to "make a difference on the big issues that matter to us all," it continued in some states to sell the Bushmaster AR-15 (a model of assault rifle). Trinity also perceived Wal-Mart as taking an unprincipled approach in deciding which products to sell. For example, despite its position on the AR-15, Wal-Mart does not sell adult-rated movie titles (i.e., those rated NC-17) or similarly rated video or computer games. Nor does it sell to children under 17 " 'R' rated movies or 'Mature' rated video games." Wal-Mart also doesn't sell "music bearing a 'Parental Advisory Label' " because of concerns about the music containing "strong language or depictions of violence, sex, or substance abuse." And apparently due to safety concerns, it has stopped selling (1) handguns in the United States; (2) high-capacity magazines separate from a gun; and (3) guns through its website. Trinity attributes these perceived inconsistencies to the "lack of written policies and Board oversight concerning its approach to products that could have momentous consequences for both society and corporate reputation and brand value[.]"

B.   Trinity's Shareholder Proposal.

Trinity pressed Wal-Mart to explain its continued sale of the Bushmaster AR-15. Wal-Mart's response was as follows:

> There are many viewpoints on this topic and many in our country remain engaged in the conversations about the sale and regulation of certain firearms. In areas of the country where we sell firearms, we have a long standing commitment to do so safely and responsibly. Over the years, we've been very purposeful about finding the right balance between serving hunters and sportsmen and ensuring that we sell firearms responsibly. Wal-Mart's merchandising decisions are based on customer demand and we recognize that most hunters and sportsmen use firearms responsibly and wish to continue to do so. . . .
>
> While there are some like you, Rev. Cooper, who ask us to stop selling firearms, there are many customers who ask us to continue to sell these products in our stores.

Unmoved, Trinity drafted a shareholder proposal aimed at filling the governance gap it perceived. The proposal, which is the subject of this appeal, provides:

Resolved:

Stockholders request that the Board amend the Compensation, Nominating and Governance Committee charter . . . as follows:

"27. Providing oversight concerning [and the public reporting of] the formulation and implementation of . . . policies and standards that determine whether or not the Company should sell a product that:

1)   especially endangers public safety and well-being;

2)   has the substantial potential to impair the reputation of the Company; and/or

3)   would reasonably be considered by many offensive to the family and community values integral to the Company's promotion of its brand."

The narrative part of the proposal makes clear it is intended to cover Wal-Mart's sale of certain firearms. It provides that the oversight and reporting is intended to cover policies and standards that would be applicable to determining whether or not the company should sell guns equipped with magazines holding more than ten rounds of ammunition ("high capacity magazines") and to balancing the benefits of selling such guns against the risks that these sales pose to the public and to the Company's reputation and brand value.

C.   Wal-Mart Seeks a No-Action Letter from the SEC.[4]

On January 30, 2014, Wal-Mart notified Trinity and the Corp. Fin. staff of its belief that it could exclude the proposal from its 2014 proxy materials under Rule 14a–8(i)(7). Trinity predictably disagreed, stating that its proposal didn't "meddl[e] in ordinary course decision-making" but focused on "big picture oversight and supervision that is the responsibility of the Board." In support of that assertion, Trinity offered three reasons why its proposal was not excludable:

1.   [it] addresses corporate governance through Board oversight of important merchandising policies and is substantially removed from particularized decision-making in the ordinary course of business;

2.   [it] concerns the Company's standards for avoiding community harm while fostering public safety and corporate ethics and does not relate exclusively to any individual product; and

---

[4]   In the words of the SEC, a "no-action letter is one in which an authorized staff official indicates that the staff will not recommend any enforcement action to the Commission if the proposed transaction described in the incoming correspondence is consummated." Procedures Utilized by the Division of Corporate Finance for Rendering Informal Advice, Release No. 6,253, 1980 WL 25632, at *1 n. 2 (Oct. 28, 1980).

3.   [it] raises substantial issues of public policy, namely a concern for the safety and welfare of the communities served by the Company's stores.

Trinity also touted the proposal as: not dictating "the specifics of how that Board oversight will operate or how best to report publicly on the policies being followed by the Company and their implementation," not seeking to "determine what products should or should not be sold by the Company," allowing policy development "not by shareholders, but by management, using its knowledge and discretion," and addressing "the ethical responsibility of the Company to take account of public safety and well-being, and the related risks of damage to the Company's reputation and brand."

On March 20, 2014, the Commission's Corp. Fin. staff issued a "no-action" letter siding with Wal-Mart . . . because "[p]roposals concerning the sale of particular products and services are generally excludable under [the rule]." Wal-Mart Stores, Inc., SEC No-Action Letter, 2014 WL 409085, at *1 (Mar. 20, 2014). . . .

Because no-action letters are not binding—they reflect only informal views of the staff and are not decisions on the merits—Trinity's proposal still had life.

D.   Trinity Takes its Fight to Federal Court: Round One.

On April 1, 2014, and just 17 days before Wal-Mart's proxy materials were due at the printer, Trinity filed a declaratory judgment action against Wal-Mart in the District of Delaware. It sought a declaration that "Wal-Mart's decision to omit the proposal from [its] 2014 Proxy Materials violates Section 14(a) of the 1934 Act and Rule 14a–8." . . .

E.   Round Two.

. . . The District Court . . . concluded that, although the proposal "could (and almost certainly would) shape what products are sold by Wal-Mart," it is "best viewed as dealing with matters that are not related to Wal-Mart's ordinary business operations." Thus Rule 14(a)–8 could not block its inclusion in Wal-Mart's proxy materials. The Court fastened its holding to the view that the proposal wasn't a directive to management but to the Board to "oversee the development and effectuation of a Wal-Mart policy." In this way, "[a]ny direct impact of adoption of Trinity's proposal would be felt at the Board level; it would then be for [it] to determine what, if any, policy should be formulated and implemented." Stated differently, the day-to-day responsibility for implementing whatever policies the Board develops was outside the scope of the proposal.

In the alternative, the Court held that even if the proposal does tread on the core of Wal-Mart's business—the products it sells—it "nonetheless 'focuses on sufficiently significant social policy issues' " that "transcend[ ] the day-to-day business matters" of the company, making the proposal "appropriate for a shareholder vote." Among the policy issues the District

Court noted are "the social and community effects of sales of high capacity firearms at the world's largest retailer and the impact this could have on Wal-Mart's reputation, particularly if such a product sold at Wal-Mart is misused and people are injured or killed as a result."

III. REGULATORY BACKGROUND

. . .

The SEC's "proxy rules are concerned with assuring full disclosure to investors of matters likely to be considered at shareholder meetings." [3 Thomas Lee Hazen, Treatise on the Law of Securities Regulation § 10.2[1] (6th ed. 2009).] To that end, the SEC adopted . . . Rule 14a–8 "to catalyze what many hoped would be a functional 'corporate democracy.' " Alan R. Palmiter, The Shareholder Proposal Rule: A Failed Experiment in Merit Regulation, 45 Ala. L.Rev. 879, 879 (1994). The rule mandates subsidized shareholder access to a company's proxy materials, requiring "reporting companies . . . to print and mail with management's proxy statement, and to place on management's proxy ballot, any 'proper' proposal submitted by a qualifying shareholder." Id. at 886 . . . . The idea was to provide shareholders a way to "bring before their fellow stockholders matters of [shareholder concern]" that are "proper subjects for stockholders' action under the laws of the state under which [the Company] was organized," 1982 Proposing Release, 1982 WL 600869, at *3, and to "have proxies with respect to such proposals solicited at little or no expense to the security holder," id. at *2.

. . .

The ordinary business exclusion has been called the "most perplexing" of all the 14a–8 bars. See Daniel E. Lazaroff, Promoting Corporate Democracy and Social Responsibility: The Need to Reform the Federal Proxy Rules on Shareholder Proposals, 50 Rutgers L.Rev. 33, 94 (1997). This stems from the opaque term "ordinary business," which is neither self-defining nor consistent in its meaning across different corporate contexts. Neither the courts nor Congress have offered a corrective. . . .

[In 1976 the SEC issued guidance explaining that] the exclusion should be "interpreted somewhat more flexibly than in the past" and reaffirmed that the term "ordinary business operations" has been wrongly interpreted to "include certain matters which have significant policy, economic or other implications inherent in them. For instance, a proposal that a utility company not construct a nuclear power plant has in the past been [wrongly] considered" to be excludable. [Adoption of Amendments Relating to Proposals by Security Holders, Release No. 12, 999, 1976 WL 160347 (Nov. 22, 1976) ("1976 Adopting Release").] Therefore, "proposals of that nature, as well as others that have major implications, will in the future be considered beyond the realm of an issuer's ordinary business operations." Id.

. . .

IV. ANALYSIS

. . .

A. Trinity's Proposal Relates to Wal-Mart's Ordinary Business Operations.

We employ a two-part analysis to determine whether Trinity's proposal "deals with a matter relating to the company's ordinary business operations [.]"Under the first step, we discern the "subject matter" of the proposal. See 1983 Adopting Release, 1983 WL 33272, at *7. Under the second, we ask whether that subject matter relates to Wal-Mart's ordinary business operations. If the answer to the second question is yes, Wal-Mart must still convince us that Trinity's proposal does not raise a significant policy issue that transcends the nuts and bolts of the retailer's business.

1.   What is the subject matter of Trinity's proposal?

Beginning with the first step, we are mindful of the Commission's consistent nod to substance over form and its distaste for clever drafting. [It] matters little how a shareholder styles its proposal; the emphasis should always be on its substance. . . . Thus, even though Trinity's proposal asks for the development of a specific merchandising policy—and not a review, report or examination—we still ask whether the subject matter of the action it calls for is a matter of ordinary business.

Applying that principle, we part ways with the District Court. We perceive it put undue weight on the distinction between a directive to management and a request for Board action. In the District Court's view, if the proposal had directed management to arrange its product assortment in a certain way, it would have been excludable. But because it merely asked the "Board [to] oversee the development and effectuation of a Wal-Mart policy," it was not. Trinity, 75 F.Supp.3d at 630 . . . . The concern with this line of reasoning is that [in 1976] the SEC . . . rejected the proposed bright line whereby shareholder proposals involving "matters that would be handled by management personnel without referral to the board . . . generally would be excludable," but those involving "matters that would require action by the board would not be." 1976 Proposing Release, 1976 WL 160410, at *8. Thus, though the District Court's rationale and holding are not implausible, we do not adopt them.

Distancing itself from the District Court's formal approach, Trinity argues that the subject matter of its proposal is the improvement of "corporate governance over strategic matters of community responsibility, reputation for good corporate citizenship, and brand reputation, none of which can be considered ordinary business," and the focus is on the "shortcomings in Wal-Mart's corporate governance and oversight over policy matters." We cannot agree. As the National Association of Manufacturers points out, Trinity's contention, like the District Court's analysis, relies "on how [the proposal] is framed and to whom, rather than [its] substance." Brief of amicus curiae Nat'l Assoc. of Mfrs. 15. Contrary to what Trinity would have us believe, the immediate consequence of the adoption of a proposal—here the improvement of corporate governance through the formulation and implementation of a merchandising policy—is not its subject matter. If it were, then, analogizing to the review context, the subject matter of a review would be the review itself rather than the information sought by it. For example, under Trinity's position, the subject matter of a proposal that calls for a report on how a restaurant chain's menu promotes sound dietary habits would be corporate governance as opposed to important matters involving the promotion of public health. . . . The subject matter of the proposal is instead its ultimate consequence—here a potential change in the way Wal-Mart decides which products to sell. . . .

. . . For us, the subject matter of Trinity's proposal is how Wal-Mart approaches merchandising decisions involving products that (1) especially endanger public-safety and well-being, (2) have the potential to impair the reputation of the Company, and/or (3) would reasonably be considered by many offensive to the family and community values integral to the company's promotion of the brand. A contrary holding— that the proposal's subject matter is "improved corporate governance"— would allow drafters to evade Rule 14a–8(i)(7)'s reach by styling their proposals as requesting board oversight or review. We decline to go in that direction.

2.   Does Wal-Mart's approach to whether it sells particular products relate to its ordinary business operations?

Reaching the second step of the analysis, we ask whether the subject matter of Trinity's proposal relates to day-to-day matters of Wal-Mart's business. Wal-Mart says the answer is yes because, even though the proposal doesn't demand any specific changes to the make-up of its product offerings . . . it "seeks to have a [B]oard committee address policies that could (and almost certainly would) shape what products are sold by Wal-Mart." Reply Br. 9 . . . . That is, Trinity's proposal is just a sidestep from "a shareholder referendum on how [Wal-Mart] selects its inventory." Brief of amicus curiae the Nat'l Assoc. of Mfrs. at 11. And thus its subject matter strikes at the core of Wal-Mart's business.

We agree. A retailer's approach to its product offerings is the bread and butter of its business. As amicus the National Association of Manufacturers notes, "Product selection is a complicated task influenced by economic trends, data analytics, demographics, customer preferences, supply chain flexibility, shipping costs and lead-times, and a host of other factors best left to companies' management and boards of directors." Id. at 12 . . . . Though a retailer's merchandising approach is not beyond shareholder comprehension, the particulars of that approach involve operational judgments that are ordinary-course matters.

Moreover, that the proposal doesn't direct management to stop selling a particular product or prescribe a matrix to follow is, we think, a straw man. A proposal need only relate to a company's ordinary business to be excludable. It need not dictate any particular outcome. To make the point even clearer, suppose that Trinity's proposal had merely asked Wal-Mart's Board to reconsider whether to continue selling a given product. Though the request doesn't dictate a particular outcome, we have no doubt it would be excludable . . ., as the action sought relates to Wal-Mart's ordinary business operations. This is so even though it doesn't suggest any changes. The same is true here. In short, so long as the subject matter of the proposal relates—that is, bears on—a company's ordinary business operations, the proposal is excludable unless some other exception to the exclusion applies.

B.   Trinity's Proposal Does Not Focus on a Significant Policy Issue that Transcends Wal-Mart's Day-to-Day Business Operations.

As discussed above, there is a significant social policy exception to the default rule of excludability for proposals that relate to a company's ordinary business operations. . . .

The difficulty in this case is divining the line between proposals that focus on sufficiently significant social policy issues that transcend a company's ordinary business (not excludable) from those that don't (excludable). . . .

We think the inquiry is again best split into two steps. The first is whether the proposal focuses on a significant policy (be it social or, as noted below, corporate). If it doesn't, the proposal fails to fit within the social-policy exception to Rule 14a–8(i)(7)'s exclusion. If it does, we reach the second step and ask whether the significant policy issue transcends the company's ordinary business operations.

1.   Does Trinity's proposal raise a significant social policy issue?

We first turn to whether Trinity's proposal focuses on a "sufficiently significant" policy issue like "significant [employment] discrimination." 1998 Adopting Release, 1998 WL 254809, at *4. . . . [It] is hard to counter that Trinity's proposal doesn't touch the bases of what are significant concerns in our society and corporations in that society. Thus we deem that its proposal raises a matter of sufficiently significant policy.

. . .

2.   Even if Trinity's proposal raises a significant policy issue, does that issue transcend Wal-Mart's ordinary business operations?

To repeat, . . . a shareholder must do more than focus its proposal on a significant policy issue; the subject matter of its proposal must "transcend" the company's ordinary business. . . . Thus, . . . we think the transcendence requirement plays a pivotal role in the social-policy exception calculus. Without it shareholders would be free to submit "proposals dealing with ordinary business matters yet cabined in social policy concern." *Apache Corp. v. New York City Emps.' Ret. Sys.,* 621 F.Supp.2d 444, 451 n. 7 (S.D.Tex.2008) . . . .

For major retailers of myriad products, a policy issue is rarely transcendent if it treads on the meat of management's responsibility: crafting a product mix that satisfies consumer demand. This explains why the Commission's staff, almost as a matter of course, allows retailers to exclude proposals that "concern[ ] the sale of particular products and services." *Rite Aid Corp.*, SEC No-Action Letter, 2015 WL 364996, at *1 (Mar. 24, 2015). On the other hand, if a significant policy issue disengages from the core of a retailer's business (deciding whether to sell certain goods that customers want), it is more likely to transcend its daily business dealings.

To illustrate the distinction, a proposal that asks a supermarket chain to evaluate its sale of sugary sodas because of the effect on childhood obesity should be excludable because, although the proposal raises a significant social policy issue, the request is too entwined with the fundamentals of the daily activities of a supermarket running its business: deciding which food products will occupy its shelves. So too would a proposal that, out of concern for animal welfare, aims to limit which food items a grocer sells. . . .

By contrast, a proposal raising the impropriety of a supermarket's discriminatory hiring or compensation practices generally is not excludable because, even though human resources management is a core business function, it is disengaged from the essence of a supermarket's business. The same goes for proposals asking for information on the environmental effect of constructing stores near environmentally sensitive sites.

With those principles in mind, we turn to Trinity's proposal. Trinity says it focuses on "both corporate policy and social policy"—specifically, the "transcendent policy issue of under what policies and standards and with what Board oversight Wal-Mart handles [ ] merchandising decisions" for products that are "especially dangerous to [the company's] reputation, brand value, or the community." Trinity Br. 44 . . . . "In an age of mass shootings, increased violence, and concerns about product safety," Trinity argues, "the [p]roposal goes to the heart of Wal-Mart's impact on and approach to social welfare as well as the risks such impact and approach may have to Wal-Mart's reputation and brand image and its community." Id. at 43.

But is how a retailer weighs safety in deciding which products to sell too enmeshed with its day-to-day business? We think it is in this instance. As we noted before, the essence of a retailer's business is deciding what products to put on its shelves—decisions made daily that involve a careful balancing of financial, marketing, reputational, competitive and other factors. The emphasis management places on safety to the consumer or the community is fundamental to its role in managing the company in the best interests of its shareholders and cannot, "as a practical matter, be subject to direct shareholder oversight." 1998 Adopting Release, 1998 WL 254809, at *4. Although shareholders perform a valuable service by creating awareness of social issues, they are not well-positioned to opine on basic business choices made by management.

It is thus not surprising that the Corp. Fin. staff consistently allows retailers to omit proposals that address their product menu. For example, it has indicated that a proposal trying to stop a retailer from selling or promoting products that connote negative stereotypes is excludable. It has done the same for proposals aiming to restrict a retailer's promotion of products that pose a threat to public health, as well as those proposals targeting a retailer's approach to product safety.

For further support of the view that a policy issue does not transcend a company's ordinary business operations where it targets day-to-day decision-making, we look to the difference in treatment of stop-selling proposals sent to retailers and those sent to pure-play manufacturers [that is, undiversified]. A policy matter relating to a product is far more likely to transcend a company's ordinary business operations when the product is that of a manufacturer with a narrow line. Here the staff often will decline a no-action request.

But the outcome changes where those same policy proposals are directed at retailers who sell thousands of products.

The reason for the difference, in our view, is that a manufacturer with a very narrow product focus—like a tobacco or gun manufacturer—exists principally to sell the product it manufactures. Its daily business deliberations do not involve whether to continue to sell the product to which it owes its reason for being. As such, a stop-selling proposal generally isn't excludable because it relates to the seller's very existence. Quite the contrary for retailers. They typically deal with thousands of products amid many options for each, precisely the sort of business decisions a retailer makes many times daily. Thus, and in contrast to the manufacturing context, a stop-selling proposal implicates a retailer's ordinary business operations and is in turn excludable. Although Trinity's proposal is not strictly a stop-selling proposal, it still targets the same basic business decision: how to weigh safety risks in the merchandising calculus.

Trinity's claim that its proposal raises a "significant" and "transcendent" corporate policy is likewise insufficient to fit that proposal within the social-policy exception to exclusion. The relevant question to us is whether Wal-Mart's consideration of the risk that certain products pose to its "economic success" and "reputation for good corporate citizenship" is enmeshed with the way it runs its business and the retailer-consumer interaction. We think the answer is yes. Decisions relating to what products Wal-Mart sells in its rural locations versus its urban sites will vary considerably, and these are quintessentially calls made by management. Wal-Mart serves different Americas with different values. Its customers in rural America want different products than its customers in cities, and that management decides how to deal with these differing desires is not an issue typical for its Board of Directors. Indeed, catering to "small-town America" is how Wal-Mart built its business. And whether to put emphasis on brand integrity and brand protection, or none at all, is naturally a decision shareholders as well as directors entrust management to make in the exercise of their experience and business judgment.

. . .

We thus hold that, even if Trinity's proposal raises sufficiently significant social and corporate policy issues, those policies do not transcend the ordinary business operations of Wal-Mart. For a policy issue here to transcend Wal-Mart's business operations, it must target something more than the choosing of one among tens of thousands of products it sells. Trinity's proposal fails that test and is properly excludable under Rule 14a–8(i)(7).

NOTES AND QUESTIONS

1.   In order to discern the true subject matter of a proposal, one must determine the "ultimate consequence" of a proposal. How does one do so?

2.   The court explained that: "In short, so long as the subject matter of the proposal relates—that is, bears on—a company's ordinary business operations, the proposal is excludable unless some other exception to the exclusion applies." How does one determine if the proposal "bears on" "a company's ordinary business operations"?

3.   Should proposals bearing on strategic decisions—such as a proposal that the company sell all or substantially all of the corporation's assets—be excludable under Rule 14a–8(i)(7)?

4.   The court stated that "it is hard to counter that Trinity's proposal doesn't touch the bases of what are significant concerns in our society and corporations in that society." But does the court provide any helpful advice as to how to decide harder cases? What metric should courts use to determine a proposal's significance? How does one determine whether the proposal's significance is sufficient?

On this issue, the federal district court decision in *Austin v. Consolidated Edison Company of New York, Inc.*[17] is both instructive and troubling. The plaintiffs put forward a proposal that the issuer provide more generous pension benefits to its employees. The court authorized the issuer to exclude the proposal as impinging on an ordinary business matter. Acknowledging that shareholder proposals relating to senior executive compensation were not excludable, the court observed that the issue of "enhanced pension rights" for workers "has not yet captured public attention and concern as has the issue of senior executive compensation." Does this mean that the significance of a proposal turns on whether its subject matter has become a routine story for CNBC or CNN?

---

[17]   788 F.Supp. 192 (S.D.N.Y.1992).

5.   In order to be sufficiently significant, a proposal must transcend "day-to-day business matters." Transcend is undefined in the opinion. Instead, the court contrasts a proposal that is not excludable because it transcends the company's ordinary business with one that is excludable because it is "enmeshed with the way it runs its business and the retailer-consumer interaction." Unfortunately, the court also failed to define "enmeshed." The mental images invoked by the dictionary definition—"[t]o mesh; to tangle or interweave in such a manner as not to be easily separated, particularly in a mesh or net like manner—are singularly unhelpful. The same is true of the dictionary definition of transcend, which is "to pass beyond the limits of something." Once again, the question thus is how one determines when a proposal transcends "day-to-day business matters."

6.   If selling sugary sodas is ordinary business, should not making them be so as well?

7.   Is it true that Trinity's proposal "targets the same basic business decision" as would a "stop selling" proposal?

8.   Is it in fact the case that "shareholders perform a valuable service by creating awareness of social issues"? If so, what is that service and to whom is it rendered? Do the costs of providing this service outweigh the benefits it produces?

9.   If "it is neither fair nor reasonable to expect securities experts [like the Commission and its staff] to deduce the prevailing wind on public policy issues that have yet to be addressed by Congress in any decisive fashion," does that not suggest that a proposal's social significance ought to be irrelevant in deciding whether it must be included on the company's proxy statement?

10.   The *Trinity* court stated that "a proposal that, out of concern for animal welfare, aims to limit which food items a grocer sells" can be excluded. Is that consistent with the *Lovenheim* decision?

PROBLEM

Flyers Rights Education Fund submitted the following proposal to American Airlines:

RESOLVED: The shareholders of American Airlines Group, Inc. (the "Company") request that the Board of Directors prepare a report on the regulatory risk and discriminatory effects of smaller cabin seat sizes on overweight, obese, and tall passengers. This report will also analyze the impact of smaller cabin seat sizes on the Company's profit margin and stock price.

SUPPORTING STATEMENT: Average seat width in economy class has dramatically decreased in the past two decades, from 18.5 inches in the early 2000s to 17 inches today. (Seat pitch (leg room) in economy class has similarly declined, "from an average of 35 inches in the early 2000s to 31 inches today—and in an increasing number of cases [. . .] 28 inches." On an American Boeing 737 MAX, the seat width in the main cabin ranges from 16.6 inches to 17.8 inches and seat pitch is 30 inches.

According to the CDC, over 70% of American adults aged 20 and over are overweight or obese. About 4% of adults are also now over 74 inches (6′2″) tall.

Reducing seat size in the face of these trends risks losing loyal customers at best—and discriminates at worst. When the Air Carrier Access Act was enacted, seat width in economy class on American Airlines ranged from 19 inches to 20 inches, while seat pitch in economy class ranged from 31 inches to 33 inches. Those who passed the law could hardly have imagined that a majority of Americans could now be in a position where one seat is insufficient without encroaching on their neighboring seat mate or the aisle.

Some effects of reducing seat size and passenger space are already on display. According to the Association of Professional Flight Attendants, "flights (have) had to divert after passengers got into fights over reclining seats and lack of leg room." Reduced seat pitch has also made "it harder for crew to treat anyone needing medical help."

Reducing seat size and passenger space also exposes the Company to potential regulatory risk. In July 2017 the U.S. Court of Appeals for the D.C. Circuit ordered the FAA to adequately address a petition brought asking the agency "to promulgate rules governing the minimum requirements for seat sizes and spacing on commercial passenger airlines."

Excluding a majority of the population from being able to reliably, comfortably, and safely use the Company's services is highly questionable as a business model for the Company, its revenue, and shareholder interests. Millions of passengers who would otherwise fly are now forced to look to alternate forms of transportation.

We urge shareholders to vote FOR this proposal.[18]

Can the proposal be excluded under Rule 14a–8(i)(7)?

4) ELECTIONS AND NOMINATIONS OF DIRECTORS

AFSCME v. AIG, Inc.
462 F.3d 121 (2d Cir. 2006)

This case raises the question of whether a shareholder proposal requiring a company to include certain shareholder-nominated candidates for the board of directors on the corporate ballot can be excluded from the corporate proxy materials on the basis that the proposal "relates to an election" under Securities Exchange Act Rule 14a–

---

[18] SEC No-Action Letter, Am. Airlines Group Inc., 2018 WL 774824, at *11–12 (Mar. 23, 2018) (citations omitted).

8(i)(8) . . . ("election exclusion" or "Rule 14a–8(i)(8)"). Complicating this question is not only the ambiguity of Rule 14a–8(i)8) itself but also the fact that the [SEC] has ascribed two different interpretations to the Rule's language. The SEC's first interpretation was published in 1976, the same year that it last revised the election exclusion. The Division of Corporation Finance (the "Division"), the group within the SEC that handles investor disclosure matters and issues no-action letters, continued to apply this interpretation consistently for fifteen years until 1990, when it began applying a different interpretation, although at first in an ad hoc and inconsistent manner. The result of this gradual interpretive shift is the SEC's second interpretation, as set forth in its amicus brief to this Court. We believe that an agency's interpretation of an ambiguous regulation made at the time the regulation was implemented or revised should control unless that agency has offered sufficient reasons for its changed interpretation. Accordingly, we hold that a shareholder proposal that seeks to amend the corporate bylaws to establish a procedure by which shareholder-nominated candidates may be included on the corporate ballot does not relate to an election within the meaning of the Rule and therefore cannot be excluded from corporate proxy materials under that regulation.

Background

The American Federation of State, County & Municipal Employees ("AFSCME") is one of the country's largest public service employee unions. Through its pension plan, AFSCME holds 26,965 shares of voting common stock of American International Group ("AIG" or "Company"), a multi-national corporation operating in the insurance and financial services sectors. On December 1, 2004, AFSCME submitted to AIG for inclusion in the Company's 2005 proxy statement a shareholder proposal that, if adopted by a majority of AIG shareholders at the Company's 2005 annual meeting, would amend the AIG bylaws to require the Company, under certain circumstances, to publish the names of shareholder-nominated candidates for director positions together with any candidates nominated by AIG's board of directors ("Proposal"). AIG sought the input of the Division regarding whether AIG could exclude the Proposal from its proxy statement under the election exclusion on the basis that it "relates to an election." The Division issued a no-action letter in which it indicated that it would not recommend an enforcement action against AIG should the Company exclude the Proposal from its proxy statement. . . .

Armed with the no-action letter, AIG then proceeded to exclude the Proposal from the Company's proxy statement. In response, AFSCME brought suit in the United States District Court for the Southern District of New York (Stanton, J.) seeking a court order compelling AIG to include the Proposal in its next proxy statement. . . . [T]he district court entered final judgment denying plaintiff's claims for declaratory and injunctive relief and dismissing plaintiff's complaint.

Discussion

Rule 14a–8(i)(8), also known as "the town meeting rule," regulates what are referred to as "shareholders proposals," that is, "recommendation[s] or requirement[s] that the company and/or its board of directors take [some] action, which [the submitting shareholder(s)] intend to present at a meeting of the company's shareholders," [Rule] 14a–8(a). If a shareholder seeking to submit a proposal meets certain eligibility and procedural requirements, the corporation is required to include the proposal in its proxy statement and identify the proposal in its form of proxy, unless the corporation can prove to the SEC that a given proposal may be excluded based on one of thirteen grounds enumerated in the regulations. . . . One of these grounds, Rule 14a–8(i)(8), provides that a corporation may exclude a shareholder proposal "[i]f the proposal relates to an election for membership on the company's board of directors or analogous governing body."

We must determine whether, under Rule 14a–8(i)(8), a shareholder proposal "relates to an election" if it seeks to amend the corporate bylaws to establish a procedure by which certain shareholders are entitled to include in the corporate proxy materials their nominees for the board of directors ("proxy access bylaw proposal"). . . . The relevant language here—"relates to an election"—is not particularly helpful. AFSCME reads the election exclusion as creating an obvious distinction between proposals addressing a particular seat in a particular election (which AFSCME concedes are excludable) and those, like AFSCME's proposal, that simply set the background rules governing elections generally (which AFSCME claims are not excludable). AFSCME's distinction rests on Rule 14a–8(i)(8)'s use of the article "an," which AFSCME claims "necessarily implies that the phrase 'relates to an election' is intended to relate to proposals that address particular elections, instead of simply 'elections' generally." It is at least plausible that the words "an election" were intended to narrow the scope of the election exclusion, confining its application to proposals relating to "a particular election and not elections generally." It is, however, also plausible that the phrase was intended to create a comparatively broader exclusion, one covering "a particular election or elections generally" since any proposal that relates to elections in general will necessarily relate to an election in particular. The language of Rule 14a8(i)(8) provides no reason to adopt one interpretation over the other.

When the language of a regulation is ambiguous, we typically look for guidance in any interpretation made by the agency that promulgated the regulation in question. . . . We are aware of two statements published by the SEC that offer informal interpretations of Rule 14a–8(i)(8). The first is a statement appearing in the amicus brief that the SEC filed in this case at our request. The second interpretation is contained in a statement the SEC published in 1976, the last time the SEC revised the election exclusion. Neither of these interpretations has the force of law.

But, while agency interpretations that lack the force of law do not warrant deference when they interpret ambiguous statutes, they do normally warrant deference when they interpret ambiguous regulations. . . .

The 1976 Statement clearly reflects the view that the election exclusion is limited to shareholder proposals used to oppose solicitations dealing with an identified board seat in an upcoming election and rejects the somewhat broader interpretation that the election exclusion applies to shareholder proposals that would institute procedures making such election contests more likely. The SEC suggested as much when, four months after its 1976 Statement, it explained that the scope of the election exclusion does not cover shareholder proposals dealing with matters such as cumulative voting and general director requirements, both of which have the potential to increase the likelihood of election contests. . . . That the 1976 statement adopted this narrower view of the election exclusion finds further support in the fact that it was also the view that the Division adopted for roughly sixteen years following publication of the SEC's 1976 Statement. . . . It was not until 1990 that the Division first signaled a change of course by deeming excludable proposals that might result in contested elections, even if the proposal only purports to alter general procedures for nominating and electing directors. . . .

Because the interpretation of Rule 14a–8(i)(8) that the SEC advances in its amicus brief-that the election exclusion applies to proxy access bylaw proposals-conflicts with the 1976 Statement, it does not merit the usual deference we would reserve for an agency's interpretation of its own regulations. . . . The SEC has not provided, nor to our knowledge has it or the Division ever provided, reasons for its changed position regarding the excludability of proxy access bylaw proposals. Although the SEC has substantial discretion to adopt new interpretations of its own regulations in light of, for example, changes in the capital markets or even simply because of a shift in the Commission's regulatory approach, it nevertheless has a "duty to explain its departure from prior norms." *Atchison, T. & S.F. Ry. Co. v. Wichita Bd. of Trade*, 412 U.S. 800, 808, 93 S.Ct. 2367, 37 L.Ed.2d 350 (1973) (citing *Sec. of Agric. v. United States*, 347 U.S. 645, 652–53, 74 S.Ct. 826, 98 L.Ed. 1015 (1954)). . . .

Accordingly, we deem it appropriate to defer to the 1976 Statement, which represents the SEC's interpretation of the election exclusion the last time the Rule was substantively revised. . . .

In deeming proxy access bylaw proposals non-excludable under Rule 14a–8(i)(8), we take no side in the policy debate regarding shareholder access to the corporate ballot. There might be perfectly good reasons for permitting companies to exclude proposals like AFSCME's, just as there may well be valid policy reasons for rendering them non-excludable.

However, Congress has determined that such issues are appropriately the province of the SEC, not the judiciary.

Dodd-Frank § 971

(a) PROXY ACCESS.—Section 14(a) of the Securities Exchange Act of 1934 (15 U.S.C. 78n(a)) is amended—

(1) by inserting "(1)" after "(a)"; and

(2) by adding at the end the following:

"(2) The rules and regulations prescribed by the Commission under paragraph (1) may include—

"(A) a requirement that a solicitation of proxy, consent, or authorization by (or on behalf of) an issuer include a nominee submitted by a shareholder to serve on the board of directors of the issuer; and

"(B) a requirement that an issuer follow a certain procedure in relation to a solicitation described in subparagraph (A).".

(b) REGULATIONS.—The Commission may issue rules permitting the use by a shareholder of proxy solicitation materials supplied by an issuer of securities for the purpose of nominating individuals to membership on the board of directors of the issuer, under such terms and conditions as the Commission determines are in the interests of shareholders and for the protection of investors.

(c) EXEMPTIONS.—The Commission may, by rule or order, exempt an issuer or class of issuers from the requirement made by this section or an amendment made by this section. In determining whether to make an exemption under this subsection, the Commission shall take into account, among other considerations, whether the requirement in the amendment made by subsection (a) disproportionately burdens small issuers.

Subsequent Developments

In 2003, the SEC proposed a new Rule 14a–11 that would permit shareholders, upon the occurrence of certain specified events and subject to various restrictions, to have their nominees placed on the company's proxy statement and ballot. If the rule had been adopted, a shareholder-nominated director thus could be elected to the board in a fashion quite similar to the way shareholder-sponsored proposals are now put to a shareholder vote under SEC Rule 14a–8. The proposal received considerable opposition from the business community, while also being criticized by shareholder activists as not going far enough. The SEC never acted on the proposal, allowing it to die a quiet death.

Shareholder activists such as AFSCME then tried using Rule 14a–8 to bypass the SEC's failure to act by putting forward shareholder proposals adopting bylaws allowing shareholders to nominate directors. In addition, shareholder activists also began putting forward similar proposals to adopt bylaws under which directors would be elected by majority vote rather than the traditional plurality.

In the wake of the AIG decision, the SEC began a rulemaking process to determine whether Rule 14a–8(i)(8) should be amended to permit or deny shareholder access to the corporate ballot. On November 28, 2007, the SEC announced an amendment to Rule 14a–8(i)(8), pursuant to which the Rule would read:

> (i) Question 9: If I have complied with the procedural requirements, on what other bases may a company rely to exclude my proposal? . . .
>
> (8) Relates to election: If the proposal relates to a nomination or an election for membership on the company's board of directors or analogous governing body or a procedure for such nomination or election.

The amendment thus reversed the 1976 statement and effectively overturned the substantive result of the AIG case. At the same time, however, the SEC announced its intention to continue studying the issue.

Proponents of proxy access persuaded Congress to include a provision in the Dodd-Frank financial reform legislation of 2010 affirming that the SEC has authority to adopt a rule along the lines of the 2003 proposal. Section 971 of the Act did not require that the SEC do so. On the other hand, if the SEC chose to do so, § 971 expressed Congress' intent that the SEC "should have wide latitude in setting the terms of such proxy access." In particular, § 971 expressly authorizes the SEC to exempt "an issuer or class of issuers" from any proxy access rule and specifically requires the SEC to "take into account, among other considerations, whether" proxy access "disproportionately burdens small issuers."

Section 971 probably was unnecessary. An SEC rulemaking proceeding on proxy access was well advanced long before Dodd-Frank was adopted, so a shove from Congress was superfluous. As to the question of SEC authority, proxy access almost certainly fell within the disclosure and process sphere over which the SEC has unquestioned authority. By adopting § 971, however, Congress did preempt an expected challenge to any forthcoming SEC regulation.

In any case, the ink was hardly dry on Dodd-Frank when the SEC announced final adoption of new Rule 14a–11. The rule required companies to include in their proxy materials, alongside the nominees of the incumbent board, the nominees of shareholders who own at least 3 percent of the company's shares and have done so continuously for at least the prior three years. A shareholder could only put forward a short slate, consisting of at least 1 nominee or up to 25% of the company's board of directors whichever was greater. Oddly, this entitlement applied even to minority shareholders of a corporation that had a controlling shareholder with sufficient voting power to elect the entire board. Application of the rule to small companies was to be deferred for three years, while the SEC studied its impact.

As was the case with the 2003 proposal, in order for an individual to be eligible to be nominated under Rule 14a–11, that individual would have to satisfy the applicable stock exchange listing standard definition of independence from the company. The 2003 proposal also contemplated that the nominee must satisfy a number of independence criteria (e.g., no family or employment relationships) vis-à-vis the nominating shareholder or group. The SEC at that time clearly was concerned that the proposal would be used to put forward special interest directors who would not broadly represent the shareholders as a whole but rather only the narrow interests of those who nominated them. As adopted, Rule 14a–11 contained no such requirement. Accordingly, there was a very real risk shareholder nominated directors would perceive themselves as representatives of their electoral constituency rather than all shareholders.

Dissidents could not, however, use the rule to bypass a proxy contest for control. Shareholders whose disclosed intent was to seek control of the company could not use the rule to nominate directors. Likewise, shareholders whose disclosed intent was to elect more directors than the number authorized by the rule could not use the rule to nominate directors. In either case, such shareholders would have had to run a traditional proxy contest.

Concurrently, the SEC amended Rule 14a–8(i)(8). As amended, the new rule stated that a proposal may be excluded if it:

> (i) Would disqualify a nominee who is standing for election; (ii) Would remove a director from office before his or her term expired; (iii) Questions the competence, business judgment, or character of one or more nominees or directors; (iv) Seeks to include a specific individual in the company's proxy materials for election to the board of directors; or (v) Otherwise could affect the outcome of the upcoming election of directors.

In adopting these amendments, the SEC explained that proxy access bylaws no longer were automatically excludable. To the contrary, bylaws that expand proxy access rights to a broader group of shareholders or create alternative proxy access rights were expressly authorized. A shareholder proposal to eliminate or restrict proxy access rights, however, was impermissible.

In *Business Roundtable v. SEC*,[19] however, the U.S. Court of Appeals for the District of Columbia struck down Rule 14a–11 in a lawsuit brought by the Business Roundtable and the U.S. Chamber of Commerce.

---

[19]   647 F.3d 1144 (D.C. Cir. 2011).

Even though the SEC clearly had authority to adopt the rule, the court found that the SEC had:

> [A]cted arbitrarily and capriciously for having failed . . . adequately to assess the economic effects of [the] new rule. Here the Commission inconsistently and opportunistically framed the costs and benefits of the rule; failed adequately to quantify the certain costs or to explain why those costs could not be quantified; neglected to support its predictive judgments; contradicted itself; and failed to respond to substantial problems raised by commenters.

The court agreed with those who argue that, if the proxy access rule had been validly adopted, a board often would have not just the right—but the duty—to oppose shareholder nominees:

> [T]he American Bar Association Committee on Federal Regulation of Securities commented: "If the [shareholder] nominee is determined [by the board] not to be as appropriate a candidate as those to be nominated by the board's independent nominating committee . . ., then the board will be compelled by its fiduciary duty to make an appropriate effort to oppose the nominee, as boards now do in traditional proxy contests."

The court also decisively rejected the SEC's claim that shareholder activism is beneficial for corporate performance:

> The petitioners also maintain, and we agree, the Commission relied upon insufficient empirical data when it concluded that Rule 14a–11 will improve board performance and increase shareholder value by facilitating the election of dissident shareholder nominees. . . . The Commission acknowledged the numerous studies submitted by commenters that reached the opposite result. . . . One commenter, for example, submitted an empirical study showing that "when dissident directors win board seats, those firms underperform peers by 19 to 40% over the two years following the proxy contest." . . . . The Commission completely discounted those studies "because of questions raised by subsequent studies, limitations acknowledged by the studies' authors, or [its] own concerns about the studies' methodology or scope."
>
> The Commission instead relied exclusively and heavily upon two relatively unpersuasive studies, one concerning the effect of "hybrid boards" (which include some dissident directors) and the other concerning the effect of proxy contests in general, upon shareholder value. . . . Indeed, the Commission "recognize[d] the limitations of the Cernich (2009) study," and noted "its long-term findings on shareholder value creation are difficult to interpret." . . . In view of the admittedly (and at best) "mixed" empirical evidence, . . . we think the Commission has

not sufficiently supported its conclusion that increasing the potential for election of directors nominated by shareholders will result in improved board and company performance and shareholder value. . . .

Likewise, the Court agreed with those who argue that certain institutional investors—most notably union pension funds and state and local government pension funds—would use proxy access as leverage to extract private gains at the expense of other investors:

> Notwithstanding the ownership and holding requirements, there is good reason to believe institutional investors with special interests will be able to use the rule and, as more than one commenter noted, "public and union pension funds" are the institutional investors "most likely to make use of proxy access." . . . Nonetheless, the Commission failed to respond to comments arguing that investors with a special interest, such as unions and state and local governments whose interests in jobs may well be greater than their interest in share value, can be expected to pursue self-interested objectives rather than the goal of maximizing shareholder value, and will likely cause companies to incur costs even when their nominee is unlikely to be elected.

The D.C. Circuit opinion was not the end of the story. After the D.C. Circuit decision, the SEC put its planned amendments to Rule 14a–8 into effect. Accordingly, shareholders who want proxy access now can put forward proposals under that rule to amend the issuer's bylaws so as to permit shareholder nominees to be included on the proxy card.

NOTES AND QUESTIONS

1.   What policy justification is there, if any, for requiring companies to include shareholder nominees for director elections in company proxy materials, i.e., for making proxy access the default rule?

2.   What policy justification is there, if any, for instead making the default rule for proxy access one that does not allow shareholders to nominate directors?

3.   Under the SEC's current rules, how can shareholders gain the right to place their director nominees on the corporate ballot?

4.   Professor Jill Fisch has proposed an alternative approach to shareholder access:

> Instead of trying to structure proxy access, the SEC should allow state law to determine both the circumstances under which shareholders have the power to nominate director candidates and the appropriate qualifications for nominating shareholders and their nominees. State law can make these determinations in a variety of ways. State statutes can set forth the scope of shareholder nominating power. Similarly, state statutes can, as

Delaware already does, explicitly authorize issuers to adopt individually tailored nominating procedures and to describe the manner for doing so. Under the traditional enabling approach of state law, issuers can establish individually tailored nominating procedures directly, through charter and bylaw provisions, and indirectly, by specifying director qualification requirements, advance notice rules, annual meeting procedures, and so forth. Overreaching by either shareholders or corporate management can be constrained through judicial review—state courts can evaluate the permissible scope of issuer-specific provisions and restrictions consistent with shareholders' statutory voting authority and management's fiduciary obligations. Federal proxy rules should, instead, focus on the SEC's core competency—disclosure.

. . . First, the SEC should amend Regulation 14A to require issuers to disclose in their proxy statements all properly nominated director candidates, whether the nominations are made by a nominating committee, a shareholder, or some other mechanism. State law, including case law, state corporation statutes, and the issuer's governing documents (to the extent those documents are consistent with state law), would determine whether a nomination is proper. This amendment would enable individual issuers to experiment with varying criteria, such as the ownership threshold or holding period, to determine the extent to which their choices affected the quality and quantity of shareholder nominations. It would also allow issuers to experiment with other mechanisms for increasing shareholder input, such as expense reimbursement or shareholder representation on nominating committees. Issuers would also have the power to adopt mechanisms to limit the extent of shareholder input, including imposing qualification requirements and establishing methods for determining priority among director candidates.

In terms of disclosure, federal law would require that the issuer provide comparable disclosure in the proxy statement for all director candidates, including the directors' employment, compensation, other directorships, and qualifications. Nominating shareholders and their nominees would be required to supply this information to the issuer as a condition of inclusion in the proxy statement. Issuers would also be required to disclose, in the proxy statement and for each director candidate, the source of that director's nomination (e.g., issuer nominating committee or shareholder). If the issuer's proxy statement includes a statement in support of any of the board-nominated director candidates, Regulation 14A would require the board to give nominating shareholders the opportunity to include a supporting statement of equal length for their nominees.

Second, consistent with the disclosure in the proxy statement, the SEC should amend Rule 14a–4 to require the issuer's proxy card to give shareholders the opportunity to vote for any of the candidates included in the proxy statement. The proxy card would thus constitute a universal ballot for all properly nominated candidates.

Third, the SEC should adopt exemptions from sections 13(d) and 16(b) for collective shareholder action in connection with the election of directors so long as the shareholders do not, individually or collectively, seek to obtain economic control of the issuer. Specifically, the exemption should provide that collective shareholder action does not, itself, create a group for purposes of 13(d) or result in the aggregation of shareholder holdings for purposes of 13(d) or 16(b). Such exemptions should extend to both the nomination and the election of directors and the collective action associated with proposed bylaw amendments concerning director qualifications, nominating procedures, and similar issues.

Finally, the federal proxy rules should directly facilitate issuer efforts to experiment with different mechanisms for private ordering. In particular, the SEC should extend the disinterested shareholder exemption under Rule 14A–2(b)(1) to exempt shareholders engaging in collective action for the purpose of nominating director candidates pursuant to their issuer's nominating procedures from the notice and filing requirements of the federal proxy rules. This change would remove the important existing impediment to nominating procedures that require a minimum number of shareholders to support or second a nomination.[20]

What advantages, if any, would Fisch's proposal have relative to federal regulation of proxy access?

Exercise: Evaluating Microsoft's Proxy Access Bylaws

Microsoft Corp. Bylaw 1.14. Proxy Access for Director Nominations

(a) The Corporation shall include in its proxy statement and on its form of proxy for an annual meeting of shareholders the name of, and the Additional Information (as defined below) relating to, any nominee for election or reelection to the Board who satisfies the eligibility requirements in this Section 1.14 (a "Shareholder Nominee") and who is identified in a notice that complies with . . . Section 1.14(f) and that is timely delivered pursuant to Section 1.14(g) (the "Shareholder Notice") by a shareholder on behalf of one or more Holders, but in no case more than twenty Holders, who:

---

[20]   Jill E. Fisch, The Destructive Ambiguity of Federal Proxy Access, 61 Emory L.J. 435, 494–97 (2012).

Questions

It has become generally accepted best practice for proxy access bylaws to follow a 3/3/20/20 rule: In order to make use of the rule, the shareholder must own at least 3% of the issuer's common stock. The shareholder must have owned such amount for at least three years. Up to but not more than 20 shareholders acting as a group may aggregate their shares for purposes of holding the requisite percentage of stock (but all must meet the three-year holding period). A shareholder may nominate up to a maximum of 20% of the corporation's board members.

1. Does Microsoft's bylaw follow the 3/3/20/20 rule?

2. What advantages, if any, would Microsoft gain if it raised the ownership requirement to 5%?

(i) elect at the time of delivering the Shareholder Notice to have such Shareholder Nominee included in the Corporation's proxy materials,

(ii) as of the date of the Shareholder Notice, own (as defined below in Section 1.14(c)) a number of shares that represents at least 3% of the outstanding shares of the Corporation entitled to vote in the election of directors (the "Required Shares") and has owned (as defined below in Section 1.14(c)) continuously the Required Shares (as adjusted for any stock splits, stock dividends, or similar events) for at least three years, and

(iii) satisfy the additional requirements in these Bylaws (such Holder or Holders collectively, an "Eligible Shareholder").

(b) For purposes of satisfying the ownership requirement under Section 1.14(a):

(i) the outstanding shares of the Corporation owned by one or more Holders may be aggregated, provided that the number of shareholders and other beneficial owners whose ownership of shares is aggregated for such purpose shall not exceed twenty, and

(ii) a group of any two or more funds shall be treated as one Holder if they are (A) under common management and investment control, or (B) part of a "group of investment companies," as such term is defined in Section 12(d)(1)(G)(ii) of the Investment Company Act of 1940, as amended.

(c) For purposes of this Section 1.14, an Eligible Shareholder "owns" only those outstanding shares of the Corporation as to which the Holder possesses both:

(i) the full voting and investment rights pertaining to the shares and

(ii) the full economic interest in (including the opportunity for profit and risk of loss on) such shares; provided that the number of shares calculated in accordance with clauses (i) and (ii) shall not include any shares:

(A) sold by such Holder or any control person in any transaction that has not been settled or closed,

(B) borrowed by such Holder or any control person for any purposes or purchased by such Holder or any control person pursuant to an agreement to resell, or

(C) subject to any option, warrant, forward contract, swap, contract of sale, other derivative or similar agreement entered into by such Holder or any of its control persons, whether any such instrument or agreement is to be settled with shares or with cash based on the notional amount or value of outstanding shares of the Corporation, in any such case which instrument or agreement has, or is intended to have, the purpose or effect of:

(1) reducing in any manner, to any extent or at any time in the future, such Holder's or any of its control persons' full right to vote or direct the voting of any such shares, and/or

(2) hedging, offsetting, or altering to any degree gain or loss arising from the full economic ownership of such shares by such Holder or control person.

Question

3.   Many companies have drafted their proxy access bylaws to require a nominating shareholder to hold a net long position in the company's stock. Does Microsoft's bylaw have that effect?

A Holder "owns" shares held in the name of a nominee or other intermediary so long as the Holder retains the right to instruct how the shares are voted with respect to the election of directors and possesses the full economic interest in the shares. A Holder's ownership of shares shall be deemed to continue during any period in which the Holder has delegated any voting power by means of a proxy, power of attorney, or other instrument or arrangement that is revocable at any time by the Holder. A Holder's ownership of shares shall be deemed to continue during any period in which the Holder has loaned such shares provided that the Holder has the power to recall such loaned shares on five business days' notice. The terms "owned," "owning" and other variations of the word "own" shall have correlative meanings. Whether outstanding shares of the Corporation are "owned" for these purposes shall be determined by the Board.

(d)   No Holder may be a member of more than one group of Holders constituting an Eligible Shareholder under this Section 1.14.

(e)   For purposes of this Section 1.14, the "Required Information" that the Corporation will include in its proxy statement is:

(i)   the information concerning the Shareholder Nominee and the Eligible Shareholder that is required to be disclosed in the Corporation's proxy statement by the applicable requirements of the Exchange Act and the rules and regulations thereunder; and

(ii)   if the Eligible Shareholder so elects, a written statement of the Eligible Shareholder, not to exceed 500 words, in support of its Shareholder Nominee, which must be provided at the same time as the Shareholder Notice for inclusion in the Corporation's proxy statement for the annual meeting (the "Statement").

Notwithstanding anything to the contrary contained in this Section 1.14, the Corporation may omit from its proxy materials any information or Statement that it, in good faith, believes would violate any applicable law or regulation. Nothing in this Section 1.14 shall limit the Corporation's ability to solicit against and include in its proxy materials its own statements relating to any Eligible Shareholder or Shareholder Nominee.

(f)   The Shareholder Notice shall set forth the information required under Section 1.13(b)(i), (iii), and (v) of these Bylaws and in addition shall set forth:

(i)   the written consent of each Shareholder Nominee to being named in the Corporation's proxy statement as a nominee;

(ii)   a copy of the Schedule 14N that has been or concurrently is filed with the Securities and Exchange Commission under Exchange Act Rule 14a–18; and

(iii)   the written agreement of the Eligible Shareholder (or in the case of a group, each Holder whose shares are aggregated for purposes of constituting an Eligible Shareholder) addressed to the Corporation, setting forth the following additional agreements, representations, and warranties:

> **FYI**
>
> The Schedule 14N is a disclosure document that must be filed by a nominating shareholder. It must contain disclosures about the identity of the nominating shareholder, the voting power of the shares controlled by that shareholder, and the identity of the nominees and some basic biographical information about them. It also must contain a statement that the nominating shareholder intends to retain the minimum necessary shares at least through the date of the annual meeting. Finally, it must contain a written statement of what intentions the nominating shareholder has to continue holding stock after the meeting.

(A) setting forth and certifying to the number of shares of the Corporation it owns and has owned (as defined in Section 1.14(c)) continuously for at least three years as of the date of the Shareholder Notice and agreeing to continue to own such shares through the date of the annual meeting, which statement shall also be included in the written statements set forth in Item 4 of the Schedule 14N filed by the Eligible Shareholder with the Securities and Exchange Commission;

Question

4.   Microsoft does not require that the nominating shareholder continue owning shares after the meeting. Most companies have done likewise, although a few do impose post-meeting holding periods of up to one year. The ISS views such requirements as "especially problematic." What are the pros and cons of such a requirement?

(B) the Eligible Shareholder's agreement to provide written statements from the record holder and intermediaries as required under Section 1.14(h) verifying the Eligible Shareholder's continuous ownership of the Required Shares through and as of the business day immediately preceding the date of the annual meeting;

(C) the   Eligible   Shareholder's   representation   and agreement that the Eligible Shareholder (including each member of any group of shareholders that together is an Eligible Shareholder under this Section 1.14):

(1) acquired the Required Shares in the ordinary course of business and not with the intent to change or influence control at the Corporation, and does not presently have such intent,

(2) has not nominated and will not nominate for election to the Board at the annual meeting any person other than the Shareholder Nominee(s) being nominated pursuant to this Section 1.14,

(3) has not engaged and will not engage in a, and has not been and will not be a "participant" in another person's, "solicitation" within the meaning of Exchange Act Rule 14a–1(*l*), in support of the election of any individual as a director at the annual meeting other than its Shareholder Nominee or a nominee of the Board, and

(4) will not distribute to any shareholder any form of proxy for the annual meeting other than the form distributed by the Corporation; and

> **Question**
>
> 5.   What is the function and purpose
> of subsections (C)(1)–(4)?

(D) the Eligible Shareholder's agreement to:

(1) assume all liability stemming from any legal or regulatory violation arising out of the Eligible Shareholder's communications with the shareholders of the Corporation or out of the information that the Eligible Shareholder provided to the Corporation,

(2) indemnify and hold harmless the Corporation and each of its directors, officers and employees individually against any liability, loss or damages in connection with any threatened or pending action, suit or proceeding, whether legal, administrative or investigative, against the Corporation or any of its directors, officers or employees arising out of the Eligible Shareholder's communications with the shareholders of the Corporation or out of the information that the Eligible Shareholder provided to the Corporation pursuant to this Section 1.14,

(3) comply with all other laws and regulations applicable to any solicitation in connection with the annual meeting,

(4) file all materials described below in Section 1.14(h)(iii) with the Securities and Exchange Commission, regardless of whether any such filing is required under Exchange Act Regulation 14A, or whether any exemption from filing is available for such materials under Exchange Act Regulation 14A, and

(5) provide to the Corporation prior to the annual meeting such additional information as necessary or reasonably requested by the Corporation; and

(iv) in the case of a nomination by a group of shareholders that together is an Eligible Shareholder, the designation by all group members of one group member that is authorized to act on behalf of all such members with respect to the nomination and matters related thereto, including any withdrawal of the nomination.

(g) To be timely under this Section 1.14, the Shareholder Notice must be received by the secretary of the Corporation not later than the close of business on the 120th day nor earlier than the close of business on the 150th day prior to the first anniversary of the date the definitive proxy statement was first released to shareholders in connection with the preceding year's annual meeting of shareholders; provided, however that in the event the date of the Current Year Meeting is more than 30 days before or more than 60 days after such anniversary date, notice by the shareholder to be timely must be so delivered not earlier than the close of business on the 120th day and not later than the close of business on the later of the 90th day prior to the Current Year Meeting or the 10th day following the day on which public announcement of the date of the Current Year Meeting is first made by the Corporation. In no event shall any adjournment or postponement of an annual meeting, or the announcement thereof, commence a new time period for the giving of the Shareholder Notice as described above.

> ### Question
> 6.   Should the notice dates used in this proxy access bylaw be the same as those used in the company's advanced notice bylaw?

(h) An Eligible Shareholder (or in the case of a group, each Holder whose shares are aggregated for purposes of constituting an Eligible Shareholder) must:

(i)   within five business days after the date of the Shareholder Notice, provide one or more written statements from the record holder(s) of the Required Shares and from each intermediary through which the Required Shares are or have been held, in each case during the requisite three-year holding period, verifying that the Eligible Shareholder owns, and has owned continuously for the preceding three years, the Required Shares,

(ii) include in the written statements provided pursuant to Item 4 of Schedule 14N filed with the Securities and Exchange Commission a statement certifying that it owns and continuously has owned, as defined in Section 1.14(c), the Required Shares for at least three years,

(iii) file with the Securities and Exchange Commission any solicitation or other communication relating to the Current Year Meeting, one or more of the Corporation's directors or director nominees or any Shareholder Nominee, regardless of whether any such filing is required under Exchange Act Regulation 14A or whether any exemption from filing is available for such solicitation or other communication under Exchange Act Regulation 14A, and

(iv) as to any group of funds whose shares are aggregated for purposes of constituting an Eligible Shareholder, within five business days after the date of the Shareholder Notice, provide documentation reasonably satisfactory to the Corporation that demonstrates that the funds are under common management and investment control.

(i)   Within the time period specified in Section 1.14(g) for delivery of the Shareholder Notice, a Shareholder Nominee must deliver to the

Secretary of the Corporation the questionnaire, representation and agreement set forth in Section 1.15 below. At the request of the Corporation, the Shareholder Nominee must promptly, but in any event within five business days of such request, submit any additional completed and signed questionnaires required of the Corporation's directors and provide to the Corporation such other information as it may reasonably request. The Corporation may request such additional information as necessary to permit the Board to determine if each Shareholder Nominee is independent under the listing standards of the principal U.S. exchange upon which the shares of the Corporation are listed, any applicable rules of the Securities and Exchange Commission and any publicly disclosed standards used by the Board in determining and disclosing the independence of the Corporation's directors.

(j)   Notwithstanding anything to the contrary contained in this Section 1.14, the Corporation may omit from its proxy statement any Shareholder Nominee, and such nomination shall be disregarded and no vote on such Shareholder Nominee will occur, notwithstanding that proxies in respect of such vote may have been received by the Corporation, if:

(i)   the Secretary of the Corporation receives notice that a shareholder intends to nominate a person for election to the Board which shareholder does not elect to have its nominee(s) included in the Corporation's proxy materials pursuant to this Section 1.14,

---

Question

7.   What is the purpose and effect of subsection (j)(i)?

(ii)   the Eligible Shareholder materially breaches any of its agreements, representations, or warranties set forth in the Shareholder Notice, or if any of the information in the Shareholder Notice was not, when provided, true and correct, or

(iii)   the Shareholder Nominee (A) is not independent under the listing standards of the principal U.S. exchange upon which the shares of the Corporation are listed, any applicable rules of the Securities and Exchange Commission, and any publicly disclosed standards used by the Board in determining and disclosing the independence of the Corporation's directors, (B) does not qualify as independent under the audit committee independence requirements set forth in the rules of the principal U.S. exchange on which shares of the Corporation are listed, as a "non-employee director" under Exchange Act Rule 16b–3, or as an "outside director" for the purposes of Section 162(m) of the Internal Revenue Code (or any successor provision), (C) is or has been, within the past three years, an officer or director of a competitor, as defined in Section 8 of the Clayton Antitrust Act of 1914, as amended, or (D) is a named subject of a pending criminal proceeding (excluding traffic violations and other minor offenses) or has been convicted in a criminal proceeding within the past ten years.

(k) The number of Shareholder Nominees appearing in the Corporation's proxy materials with respect to an annual meeting of shareholders (including any Shareholder Nominee whose name was submitted for inclusion in the Corporation's proxy materials but who is nominated by the Board as a Board nominee), together with any nominees who were previously elected to the Board as Shareholder Nominees at any of the preceding two annual meetings and who are re-nominated for election at such annual meeting by the Board and any Shareholder Nominee who was qualified for inclusion in the Corporation's proxy materials but whose nomination is subsequently withdrawn, shall not exceed the greater of (i) two or (ii) 20% of the number of directors in office as of the last day on which a Shareholder Notice may be delivered pursuant to this Section 1.14 with respect to the annual meeting, or if such amount is not a whole number, the closest whole number below 20%. In the event that the number of Shareholder Nominees submitted by Eligible Shareholders pursuant to this Section 1.14 exceeds this maximum number, each Eligible Shareholder will select one Shareholder Nominee for inclusion in the Corporation's proxy materials until the maximum number is reached, going in order of the number (largest to smallest) of shares of the Corporation each Eligible Shareholder disclosed as owned in its respective Shareholder Notice submitted to the Corporation. If the maximum number is not reached after each Eligible Shareholder has selected one Shareholder Nominee, this selection process will continue as many times as necessary, following the same order each time, until the maximum number is reached.

Question

8.　Why does Microsoft's bylaw count incumbent proxy access director nominees against the current year's permitted number of shareholder nominees?

(*l*)　Any Shareholder Nominee who is included in the Corporation's proxy materials for a particular annual meeting of shareholders but either (i) withdraws from or becomes ineligible or unavailable for election at the annual meeting, or (ii) does not receive a number of votes cast in favor of his or her election equal to at least fifteen percent (15%) of the shares present in person or represented by proxy and entitled to vote in the election of directors, will be ineligible to be a Shareholder Nominee pursuant to this Section 1.14 for the next two annual meetings.

> ### Question
>
> 9.   Most process access bylaws contain a similar prohibition on renomination of failed candidates, but typically only disqualify candidates who receive less than twenty-five percent of the votes. What is the effect does Microsoft's fifteen percent cutoff? Is the Microsoft provision more or less favorable to shareholders?

Microsoft Corp. Bylaw 1.15 Submission of Questionnaire, Representation and Agreement.

To be eligible to be a nominee for election or reelection as a director of the Corporation by a Holder or Eligible Shareholder, a person must complete and deliver (in accordance with the time periods prescribed for delivery of notice under Section 1.13 or 1.14, whichever is applicable) to the Secretary at the principal executive offices of the Corporation a written questionnaire providing the information requested about the background and qualifications of such person and the background of any other person or entity on whose behalf the nomination is being made and a written representation and agreement (the questionnaire, representation, and agreement to be in the form provided by the Secretary upon written request) that such person:

(a)   is not and will not become a party to:

(i)   any agreement, arrangement or understanding with, and has not given any commitment or assurance to, any person or entity as to how the person, if elected as a director of the Corporation, will act or vote on any issue or question (a "Voting Commitment") that has not been disclosed to the Corporation, or

(ii)   any Voting Commitment that could limit or interfere with the person's ability to comply, if elected as a director of the Corporation, with the person's fiduciary duties under applicable law,

> ### Question
>
> 10.   Would a voting commitment that limited or interfered with the director's fiduciary duties be legally enforceable?

(b) is not and will not become a party to any agreement, arrangement or understanding with any person or entity other than the Corporation with respect to any direct or indirect compensation, reimbursement, or indemnification in connection with service or action as a director that has not been disclosed therein, and

Questions

"Activist hedge funds invented the golden leash as a tool for attracting and incentivizing director candidates in a proxy contest. Under the terms of the golden leash, these hedge funds agreed to pay their director nominees millions of dollars if the nominees were successful both in winning board seats and achieving the hedge fund's desired objectives. The golden leash burst onto the scene in 20125 when JANA Partners, LLC (JANA) offered to pay its nominees to the board of Agrium, Inc. . . . $50,000 each [over and above whatever director fees they received from Agrium], if elected, plus a collective total of 2.6% of JANA's net gain on the investment." Matthew D. Cain et. al., How Corporate Governance Is Made: The Case of the Golden Leash, 164 U. Pa. L. Rev. 649, 651 (2016).

11. Does Section 1.15(b) ban all golden leashes?

12. Does it ban any?

13. As a matter of public policy, are golden leashes desirable?

14. ISS vigorously opposes bylaws that restrict golden leashes. Why?

(c)   in the person's individual capacity and on behalf of any person or entity on whose behalf the nomination is being made, would be in compliance, if elected as a director of the Corporation, and will comply with all applicable publicly disclosed corporate governance, conflict of interest, confidentiality, and stock ownership and trading policies and guidelines of the Corporation.

To assess your understanding of the material in this chapter, click here to take a quiz.

CHAPTER 13

ESG ACTIVISM

There has been a longstanding debate over corporate social responsibility (CSR), which can be defined as "the obligations and inclinations, if any, of corporations organized for profit, voluntarily to pursue social ends that conflict with the presumptive shareholder desire to maximize profit."[1] One important school of thought contends corporations should be run so as to maximize shareholder wealth. The other major school of thought argues that directors and managers should consider the interests of all corporate stakeholders in making corporate decisions. Judges and scholars in the latter camp define the "socially responsible firm" as "one that becomes deeply involved in the solution of society's major problems."[2] In particular, they emphasize the corporation's obligation to consider the impact of its actions on nonshareholder corporate constituents, such as employees, customers, suppliers, and local communities.

Although there long have been some investors who preferred to invest in socially responsible corporations, mainstream investors were primarily concerned with profit maximization. In recent years, however, there has been growing investor interest in environmental, social, and governance (ESG) investing. Although that term "resists precise definition," it is generally defined as "an umbrella term that refers to an investment strategy that emphasizes a firm's governance structure or the environmental or social impacts of the firm's products or practices."[3]

Unlike older forms of CSR activism, proponents of ESG activism contend that it is largely grounded on economic rationales:

> The two primary rationales that together form the "business case" for this form of "responsible investment" are the prospect of higher long-term returns, and improved firm-level risk management and portfolio-level risk analysis. For example, the PRI affirms that a focus on ESG matters "may better align investors with the broader objectives of society," but its fundamental rationale is solidly grounded in shareholder primacy—namely, that "consideration of [ESG] issues is part of

---

[1] David L. Engel, An Approach to Corporate Social Responsibility, 32 Stan. L. Rev. 1, 5–6 (1979). "Note that the definition excludes acts beneficial to nonshareholder constituencies which, although detrimental to profits in the short run, lead to long-run profit maximization." Ronald J. Gilson, A Structural Approach to Corporations: The Case Against Defensive Tactics in Tender Offers, 33 Stan. L. Rev. 819, 863 (1981).

[2] Robert D. Hay & Edmund R. Gray, Social Responsibilities of Business Managers, in Managing Corporate Social Responsibility 8, 11 (Archie B. Carroll ed. 1977).

[3] Max M. Schanzenbach, Robert H. Sitkoff, Reconciling Fiduciary Duty and Social Conscience: The Law and Economics of ESG Investing by A Trustee, 72 Stan. L. Rev. 381, 388 (2020).

delivering superior risk-adjusted returns" to investors over the long run.[4]

This Chapter first considers the traditional CSR debate and then turns to the modern ESG controversy.

A. WHAT ARE A BOARD OF DIRECTORS' RESPONSIBILITIES TO SHAREHOLDERS, STAKEHOLDERS, AND SOCIETY?

1) THE LAW

Dodge v. Ford Motor Co.
170 N.W. 668 (Mich. 1919)

The Ford Motor Company is a corporation, organized and existing under Act No. 232 of the Public Acts of 1903 . . . .

The articles of association were executed June 16, 1903, and acknowledged on that day by the parties associating. . . .

The parties . . . who signed the articles, included Henry Ford, whose subscription was for 255 shares, John F. Dodge, Horace E. Dodge, the plaintiffs, Horace H. Rackham and James Couzens, who each subscribed for 50 shares, and several other persons. The company began business in the month of June, 1903. . . .

The business of the company continued to expand. The cars it manufactured met a public demand, and were profitably marketed, so that, in addition to regular quarterly dividends equal to 5 per cent. monthly on the capital stock of $2,000,000, its board of directors declared and the company paid special dividends: December 13, 1911, $1,000,000; May 15, 1912, $2,000,000; July 11, 1912, $2,000,000; June 16, 1913, $10,000,000; May 14, 1914, $2,000,000; June 12, 1914, $2,000,000; July 6, 1914, $2,000,000; July 23, 1914, $2,000,000; August 23, 1914, $3,000,000; May 28, 1915, $10,000,000; October 13, 1915, $5,000,000, a total of $41,000,000 in special dividends. . . .

. . . No special dividend having been paid after October, 1915 . . ., the plaintiffs [i.e., the Dodge Bros., filed suit against the Cord Motor Co., alleging that,] notwithstanding the earnings for the fiscal year ending July 31, 1916, the Ford Motor Company has not since that date declared any special dividends:

'And the said Henry Ford, president of the company, has declared it to be the settled policy of the company not to pay in the future any special dividends, but to put back into the business for the future all of the earnings of the company, other than the regular dividend of five per cent.

---

[4]   Virginia Harper Ho, "Enlightened Shareholder Value": Corporate Governance Beyond the Shareholder-Stakeholder Divide, 36 J. Corp. L. 59, 82 (2010).

(5%) monthly upon the authorized capital stock of the company—two million dollars ($2,000,000).'

This declaration of the future policy, it is charged in the bill, was published in the public press in the city of Detroit and throughout the United States in substantially the following language:

"My ambition,' declared Mr. Ford, 'is to employ still more men; to spread the benefits of this industrial system to the greatest possible number, to help them build up their lives and their homes. To do this, we are putting the greatest share of our profits back into the business."

It is charged further that the said Henry Ford . . . has actually engaged in negotiations looking to carrying such purposes into effect—to invest millions of dollars of the company's money in the purchase of iron ore mines . . .; to acquire by purchase or have built ships for the purpose of transporting such ore to smelters to be erected on the River Rouge adjacent to Detroit . . .; and to construct and install steel manufacturing plants to produce steel products to be used in the manufacture of cars at the factory of said company; and by this means to deprive the stockholders of the company of the fair and reasonable returns upon their investment by way of dividends to be declared upon their stockholding interest in said company.'

. . .

As we regard the testimony . . ., the case for plaintiffs must rest upon the claim, and the proof in support of it, that the proposed expansion of the business of the corporation, involving the further use of profits as capital, ought to be enjoined because inimical to the best interests of the company and its shareholders, and upon the further claim that in any event the withholding of the special dividend asked for by plaintiffs is arbitrary action of the directors requiring judicial interference.

The rule which will govern courts in deciding these questions is not in dispute. This court, in *Hunter v. Roberts, Throp & Co.*, 83 Mich. 63, 71, 47 N. W. 131, 134, recognized the rule in the following language:

> 'It is a well-recognized principle of law that the directors of a corporation, and they alone, have the power to declare a dividend of the earnings of the corporation, and to determine its amount. Courts of equity will not interfere in the management of the directors unless it is clearly made to appear that they are guilty of fraud or misappropriation of the corporate funds, or refuse to declare a dividend when the corporation has a surplus of net profits which it can, without detriment to its business, divide among its stockholders, and when a refusal to do so would amount to such an abuse of discretion as would constitute a fraud, or breach of that good faith which they are bound to exercise towards the stockholders.'

. . .

In Morawetz on Corporations (2d Ed.) § 447, it is stated:

'Profits earned by a corporation may be divided among its shareholders, but it is not a violation of the charter if they are allowed to accumulate and remain invested in the company's business. The managing agents of a corporation are impliedly invested with a discretionary power with regard to the time and manner of distributing its profits. They may apply profits in payment of floating or funded debts, or in development of the company's business; and so long as they do not abuse their discretionary powers, or violate the company's charter, the courts cannot interfere.

. . .

When plaintiffs made their complaint and demand for further dividends, the Ford Motor Company had concluded its most prosperous year of business. The demand for its cars at the price of the preceding year continued. It could make and could market in the year beginning August 1, 1916, more than 500,000 cars. Sales of parts and repairs would necessarily increase. The cost of materials was likely to advance, and perhaps the price of labor; but it reasonably might have expected a profit for the year of upwards of $60,000,000. It had assets of more than $132,000,000, a surplus of almost $112,000,000, and its cash on hand and municipal bonds were nearly $54,000,000. Its total liabilities, including capital stock, was a little over $20,000,000. It had declared no special dividend during the business year except the October, 1915, dividend. It had been the practice, under similar circumstances, to declare larger dividends. Considering only these facts, a refusal to declare and pay further dividends appears to be not an exercise of discretion on the part of the directors, but an arbitrary refusal to do what the circumstances required to be done. These facts and others call upon the directors to justify their action, or failure or refusal to act. In justification, the defendants have offered testimony tending to prove, and which does prove, the following facts: It had been the policy of the corporation for a considerable time to annually reduce the selling price of cars, while keeping up, or improving, their quality. As early as in June, 1915, a general plan for the expansion of the productive capacity of the concern by a practical duplication of its plant had been talked over by the executive officers and directors and agreed upon; not all of the details having been settled, and no formal action of directors having been taken. The erection of a smelter was considered, and engineering and other data in connection therewith secured. In consequence, it was determined not to reduce the selling price of cars for the year beginning August 1, 1915, but to maintain the price and to accumulate a large surplus to pay for the proposed expansion of plant and equipment, and perhaps to build a plant for smelting ore. It is hoped, by Mr. Ford, that eventually 1,000,000 cars will be annually produced. The contemplated changes will permit the increased output.

The plan, as affecting the profits of the business for the year beginning August 1, 1916, and thereafter, calls for a reduction in the selling price of the cars. It is true that this price might be at any time increased, but the plan called for the reduction in price of $80 a car. The capacity of the plant, without the additions thereto voted to be made (without a part of them at least), would produce more than 600,000 cars annually. This number, and more, could have been sold for $440 instead of $360, a difference in the return for capital, labor, and materials employed of at least $48,000,000. In short, the plan does not call for and is not intended to produce immediately a more profitable business, but a less profitable one; not only less profitable than formerly, but less profitable than it is admitted it might be made. The apparent immediate effect will be to diminish the value of shares and the returns to shareholders.

It is the contention of plaintiffs that the apparent effect of the plan is intended to be the continued and continuing effect of it, and that it is deliberately proposed, not of record and not by official corporate declaration, but nevertheless proposed, to continue the corporation henceforth as a semi-eleemosynary institution and not as a business institution. In support of this contention, they point to the attitude and to the expressions of Mr. Henry Ford.

. . .

The record, and especially the testimony of Mr. Ford, convinces that he has to some extent the attitude towards shareholders of one who has dispensed and distributed to them large gains and that they should be content to take what he chooses to give. His testimony creates the impression, also, that he thinks the Ford Motor Company has made too much money, has had too large profits, and that, although large profits might be still earned, a sharing of them with the public, by reducing the price of the output of the company, ought to be undertaken. We have no doubt that certain sentiments, philanthropic and altruistic, creditable to Mr. Ford, had large influence in determining the policy to be pursued by the Ford Motor Company—the policy which has been herein referred to.

It is said by his counsel that—

> 'Although a manufacturing corporation cannot engage in humanitarian works as its principal business, the fact that it is organized for profit does not prevent the existence of implied powers to carry on with humanitarian motives such charitable works as are incidental to the main business of the corporation.'

. . .

. . . We do not draw in question, nor do counsel for the plaintiffs do so, the validity of the general proposition stated by counsel nor the soundness of the opinions delivered in the cases cited. The case presented here is not like any of them. The difference between an incidental humanitarian expenditure of corporate funds for the benefit of the employés, like the building of a hospital for their use and the employment of agencies for the betterment of their condition, and a general purpose and plan to benefit mankind at the expense of others, is obvious. There should be no confusion (of which there is evidence) of the duties which Mr. Ford conceives that he and the stockholders owe to the general public and the duties which in law he and his codirectors owe to protesting, minority stockholders. A business corporation is organized and carried on primarily for the profit of the stockholders. The powers of the directors are to be employed for that end. The discretion of directors is to be exercised in the choice of means to attain that end, and does not extend to a change in the end itself, to the reduction of profits, or to the nondistribution of profits among stockholders in order to devote them to other purposes.

There is committed to the discretion of directors, a discretion to be exercised in good faith, the infinite details of business, including the wages which shall be paid to employés, the number of hours they shall work, the conditions under which labor shall be carried on, and the price for which products shall be offered to the public.

It is said by appellants that the motives of the board members are not material and will not be inquired into by the court so long as their acts are within their lawful powers. As we have pointed out, and the proposition does not require argument to sustain it, it is not within the lawful powers of a board of directors to shape and conduct the affairs of a corporation for the merely incidental benefit of shareholders and for the primary purpose of benefiting others, and no one will contend that, if the avowed purpose of the defendant directors was to sacrifice the interests of shareholders, it would not be the duty of the courts to interfere.

We are not, however, persuaded that we should interfere with the proposed expansion of the business of the Ford Motor Company. In view of the fact that the selling price of products may be increased at any time, the ultimate results of the larger business cannot be certainly estimated. The judges are not business experts. It is recognized that plans must often be made for a long future, for expected competition, for a continuing as well as an immediately profitable venture. The experience of the Ford Motor Company is evidence of capable management of its affairs. . . .

Defendants say, and it is true, that a considerable cash balance must be at all times carried by such a concern. But, as has been stated, there was a large daily, weekly, monthly, receipt of cash. The output was practically continuous and was continuously, and within a few days, turned into cash. Moreover, the contemplated expenditures were not to be immediately made. The large sum appropriated for the smelter plant was payable over a considerable period of time. So that, without going further, it would appear that, accepting and approving the plan of the directors, it was their duty to distribute on or near the 1st of August, 1916, a very large sum of money to stockholders.

. . .

NOTES AND QUESTIONS

1.   Will the interests of shareholders and stakeholders always be in conflict?

2.   Do all stakeholders have the same interests or might their interests sometimes conflict?

3.   In general, whose interests will the board of directors and the C-suite prefer?

4.   A later court explained:

Judges are not business experts, *Dodge v. Ford Motor Co.*, 204 Mich. 459, 170 N.W. 668, 684 (1919), a fact which has become expressed in the so-called "business judgment rule." The essence of that doctrine is that courts are reluctant to substitute their judgment for that of the board of directors unless the board's decisions are unreasonable. No proof was presented that the alleged acts were unreasonable in the sense that they would not have been taken by "an ordinarily prudent man . . . in the management of his own affairs of like magnitude and importance." *Nanfito v. Tekseed Hybrid Co.*, 341 F.Supp. 240, 244 (D.Neb.1972). The proof offered was therefore insufficient to present a question for the trier of fact.[5]

5.   *Shlensky v. Wrigley*[6] offers a useful example of how the business judgment applies to situations analogous to that found in *Dodge*:

Plaintiff is a minority stockholder of defendant corporation, Chicago National League Ball Club (Inc.), a Delaware corporation with its principal place of business in Chicago, Illinois. Defendant corporation owns and operates the major league professional baseball team known as the Chicago Cubs. The corporation also engages in the operation of Wrigley Field, the Cubs' home park, the concessionaire sales during Cubs' home games, television and radio broadcasts of Cubs' home games, the leasing of the field for football games and other events and receives its share, as visiting team, of admission moneys from games played in other National League stadia. The individual defendants are directors of the Cubs and have served for varying periods of years. Defendant Philip K. Wrigley is also president of the corporation and owner of approximately 80% Of the stock therein.

Plaintiff alleges that since night baseball was first played in 1935 nineteen of the twenty major league teams have scheduled night games. In 1966, out of a total of 1620 games in the major leagues, 932 were played at night. Plaintiff alleges that every member of the major leagues, other than the Cubs, scheduled substantially all of its home games in 1966 at night, exclusive of opening days, Saturdays, Sundays, holidays and days prohibited by league rules. Allegedly this has been done for the specific purpose

---

[5]   Alaska Plastics, Inc. v. Coppock, 621 P.2d 270, 278 (Alaska 1980).

[6]   237 N.E.2d 776, 777 (Ill. App. Ct. 1968).

of maximizing attendance and thereby maximizing revenue and income.

The Cubs, in the years 1961–65, sustained operating losses from its direct baseball operations. Plaintiff attributes those losses to inadequate attendance at Cubs' home games. He concludes that if the directors continue to refuse to install lights at Wrigley Field and schedule night baseball games, the Cubs will continue to sustain comparable losses and its financial condition will continue to deteriorate. . . .

The cases in this area are numerous and each differs from the others on a factual basis. However, the courts have pronounced certain ground rules which appear in all cases and which are then applied to the given factual situation. The court in *Wheeler v. Pullman Iron and Steel Company*, 143 Ill. 197, 207, 32 N.E. 420, 423, said:

> 'It is, however, fundamental in the law of corporations, that the majority of its stockholders shall control the policy of the corporation, and regulate and govern the lawful exercise of its franchise and business. * * * Every one purchasing or subscribing for stock in a corporation impliedly agrees that he will be bound by the acts and proceedings done or sanctioned by a majority of the shareholders, or by the agents of the corporation duly chosen by such majority, within the scope of the powers conferred by the charter, and courts of equity will not undertake to control the policy or business methods of a corporation, although it may be seen that a wiser policy might be adopted and the business more successful if other methods were pursued. The majority of shares of its stock, or the agents by the holders thereof lawfully chosen, must be permitted to control the business of the corporation in their discretion, when not in violation of its charter or some public law, or corruptly and fraudulently subversive of the rights and interests of the corporation or of a shareholder.'

The standards set in Delaware are also clearly stated in the cases. In *Davis v. Louisville Gas & Electric Co.*, 16 Del.Ch. 157, 142 A. 654, a minority shareholder sought to have the directors enjoined from amending the certificate of incorporation. The court said on page 659:

> 'We have then a conflict in view between the responsible managers of a corporation and an overwhelming majority of its stockholders on the one hand and a dissenting minority on the other-a conflict touching matters of business policy, such as has occasioned innumerable applications to courts to intervene and determine which of the two conflicting views should prevail. The response which courts make to such applications is that it is not their function to resolve for corporations questions of policy and business management. The directors

are chosen to pass upon such questions and their judgment Unless shown to be tainted with fraud is accepted as final. The judgment of the directors of corporations enjoys the benefit of a presumption that it was formed in good faith and was designed to promote the best interests of the corporation they serve.' . . .

Plaintiff in the instant case argues that the directors are acting for reasons unrelated to the financial interest and welfare of the Cubs. However, we are not satisfied that the motives assigned to Philip K. Wrigley, and through him to the other directors, are contrary to the best interests of the corporation and the stockholders. For example, it appears to us that the effect on the surrounding neighborhood might well be considered by a director who was considering the patrons who would or would not attend the games if the park were in a poor neighborhood. Furthermore, the long run interest of the corporation in its property value at Wrigley Field might demand all efforts to keep the neighborhood from deteriorating. By these thoughts we do not mean to say that we have decided that the decision of the directors was a correct one. That is beyond our jurisdiction and ability. We are merely saying that the decision is one properly before directors and the motives alleged in the amended complaint showed no fraud, illegality or conflict of interest in their making of that decision.

Did the court require Wrigley to show his decision was reasonable? Did the court otherwise conclude that the decision was reasonable? If not, what was the basis of the court's holding that plaintiff's suit should be dismissed?

Your author has elsewhere suggested that:

Two conceptions of the business judgment rule compete in the case law. One treats the rule as a standard of liability. Hence, for example, some courts and commentators argue that the business judgment rule shields directors from liability so long as they act in good faith. Others contend that the rule simply raises the liability bar from mere negligence to, say, gross negligence or recklessness.

Alternatively, however, the business judgment rule can be seen as an abstention doctrine. In this conception, the rule's presumption of good faith does not state a standard of liability but rather establishes a presumption against judicial review of duty of care claims. The court therefore abstains from reviewing the substantive merits of the directors' conduct unless the plaintiff can rebut the business judgment rule's presumption of good faith.[7]

He contends that the latter is the correct view, explaining that:

The claim is not that courts rubberstamp the board's decision. Conceptualizing the business judgment rule as a principle of judicial abstention means that the rule is not a standard of liability;

---

[7]   Stephen M. Bainbridge, The Business Judgment Rule As Abstention Doctrine, 57 Vand. L. Rev. 83, 89 (2004).

it does not preclude the rule from having some aspects of a standard of review. As the quoted passages from [*Shlensky*] make clear, the business judgment rule does not prevent judicial review of director conduct involving fraud or self-dealing. In addition, before the rule comes into play, various prerequisites must be satisfied. It is well established, for example, that directors may only invoke the business judgment rule when they have made a conscious decision. Hence, the business judgment rule does not prevent judicial review of a board's failure to exercise proper oversight of the corporation's management. The good faith and disinterested independence of the directors are also often identified as conditions on which the rule is predicated. Finally, some courts and commentators contend that the business judgment rule does not protect an irrational decision. Instead, what the abstention conception contemplates is that, if the requisite preconditions are satisfied, there is no remaining scope for judicial review of the substantive merits of the board's decision.

The Delaware Supreme Court expressed this point well in *Brehm v. Eisner*, in which the court explicitly rejected, as "foreign to the business judgment rule," the plaintiffs' argument that the rule could be rebutted by a showing that the directors failed to exercise "substantive due care":

> Courts do not measure, weigh or quantify directors' judgments. We do not even decide if they are reasonable in this context. Due care in the decisionmaking context is process due care only. . . .

Thus, directors' decisions will be respected by courts unless the directors are interested or lack independence relative to the decision, do not act in good faith, act in a manner that cannot be attributed to a rational business purpose or reach their decision by a grossly negligent process that includes the failure to consider all material facts reasonably available. Perhaps *Brehm* was not as pure an abstention decision as was *Shlensky*, but note that none of the preconditions set forth by *Brehm* contemplate substantive review of the merits of the board's decision. Even the reference to a rational business purpose requires only the possibility that the decision was actuated by a legitimate business reason, not that directors must prove the existence of such a reason. Absent self dealing or other conflicted interests, or truly egregious process failures, the court will abstain.[8]

Why would courts abstain from reviewing director decisions provided the requisite preconditions are satisfied?

6.   Gordon Smith has argued that the shareholder wealth maximization norm originated as a means for resolving disputes among majority and minority shareholders in closely held corporations:

---

[8]   Id. at 98–100.

One fact about the case that is rarely mentioned is that it involved an oppression claim by minority shareholders (the Dodge brothers) in a closely held corporation (Ford Motor Company). The case involved a refusal by Henry Ford to pay dividends, which is the quintessential squeeze-out technique. . . .

. . . The court never used the words "minority oppression," but the analysis in the opinion leaves no doubt about its focus. . . .

. . . The court did not think it was enunciating a meta-principle of corporate law. Rather, the court thought it was merely deciding a dispute between majority and minority shareholders in a closely held corporation in the same way courts had decided such disputes for nearly a century. In short, *Dodge v. Ford Motor Co.* is best viewed as a minority oppression case. The language of the case convincingly establishes the link between the shareholder primacy norm and the modern doctrine of minority oppression.[9]

Do you agree with Smith that *Dodge* is merely about minority oppression in close corporations? In addition to the text of the opinion, consider also the materials that follow.

7.   In *A. P. Smith Mfg. Co. v. Barlow*,[10] the A.P. Smith Manufacturing Co. ("APS") donated to $1,500 to Princeton University's 1951 Annual Giving campaign. A shareholder questioned the gift, arguing that it was *ultra vires*. APS sued seeking a declaratory judgment. The court upheld that gift as valid, stating:

> There is no suggestion that it was made indiscriminately or to a pet charity of the corporate directors in furtherance of personal rather than corporate ends. On the contrary, it was made to a preeminent institution of higher learning, was modest in amount and well within the limitations imposed by the statutory enactments, and was voluntarily made in the reasonable belief that it would aid the public welfare and advance the interests of the plaintiff as a private corporation and as part of the community in which it operates. We find that it was a lawful exercise of the corporation's implied and incidental powers under common-law principles and that it came within the express authority of the pertinent state legislation.[11]

WHAT'S THAT?

ULTRA VIRES, Black's Law Dictionary (10th ed. 2014): Unauthorized; beyond the scope of power allowed or granted by a corporate charter or by law."

There is much discussion in the opinion about the corporation's role in society, which the court summarized by observing that:

> As has been indicated, there is now widespread belief throughout the nation that free and vigorous non-governmental institutions of learning are vital to our democracy and the system

---

[9]   D. Gordon Smith, The Shareholder Primacy Norm, 23 J. Corp. L. 277 (1998).

[10]   98 A.2d 581 (1953).

[11]   Id. at 590.

of free enterprise and that withdrawal of corporate authority to make such contributions within reasonable limits would seriously threaten their continuance. Corporations have come to recognize this and with their enlightenment have sought in varying measures, as has the plaintiff by its contribution, to insure and strengthen the society which gives them existence and the means of aiding themselves and their fellow citizens. Clearly then, the appellants, as individual stockholders whose private interests rest entirely upon the well-being of the plaintiff corporation, ought not be permitted to close their eyes to present-day realities and thwart the long-visioned [sic] corporate action in recognizing and voluntarily discharging its high obligations as a constituent of our modern social structure.[12]

Despite the court's sweeping endorsement of a corporate social responsibility, is *Barlow* really inconsistent with *Dodge*? How might one seek to reconcile the two cases?

8. The American Law Institute's Principles of Corporate Governance claims that: "Present law . . . cannot be stated with precision, because the case law is evolving and not entirely harmonious, while the statutes cover only some of the relevant issues and leave open significant questions even as to the issues they do cover."[13] Do you agree?

In order to provide clarity, Section 2.01 of the ALI Principles provided that:

(a) [A] corporation should have as its objective the conduct of business activities with a view to enhancing corporate profit and shareholder gain.

(b) Even if corporate profit and shareholder gain are not thereby enhanced, the corporation, in the conduct of its business:

(1) Is obliged, to the same extent as a natural person, to act within the boundaries set by law;

(2) May take into account ethical considerations that are reasonably regarded as appropriate to the responsible conduct of business; and

(3) May devote a reasonable amount of resources to public welfare, humanitarian, educational, and philanthropic purposes.

To explain how § 2.01 would work in practice, the ALI offered a number of illustrations, including:

A. Corporation A is a publicly held corporation with annual earnings in the range of $2–3 million. A has entered into a contract that is unenforceable against it under the Statute of Frauds. Performance of the contract will involve a loss of $70,000. A performs the contract, because the relevant

---

[12] Id.

[13] Principles of Corp. Governance § 2.01 cmt. a (1994).

corporate decisionmaker makes a judgment, in a manner that meets the . . . Duty of Care of Directors and Officers . . ., that the loss is likely to be exceeded by long-run profits from preserving confidence in A's willingness to honor its commitments. A's action does not involve a departure from the economic objective stated in § 2.01(a).

B. F Corporation is a publicly held corporation with annual earnings in the range of $3–5 million. F hopes to be awarded a supply contract by P, a large publicly held corporation. The anticipated profits on the contract are $5 million over a two-year period. A vice-president of P has approached Brown, the relevant corporate decisionmaker of F, with the suggestion that if F pays the vice-president $20,000, F will be awarded the contract. Brown knows such a payment would be illegal, but correctly regards the risk of detection as extremely small. After carefully weighing that risk and the consequences of detection, Brown causes F to pay the $20,000. F's action involves a departure from the principle stated in § 2.01(b)(1).

C. M Cement Company is a publicly held corporation with assets of approximately $125 million and annual earnings in the range of $13–15 million. All of M's facilities are located in the western United States, and the nature of the cement business is such that M cannot practicably make sales outside the region. On the basis solely of philanthropic considerations, M makes an anonymous donation of $3.1 million to a local-history museum in New York City. M's action involves a departure from the principles stated in § 2.01. A contribution equal to approximately 20 percent of M's annual earnings for a use that lacks any meaningful nexus to M's business is not reasonable under § 2.01(b)(3). The contribution cannot be justified under § 2.01(a), because it is not motivated by profit considerations, and given the nature of M's business there would be no basis for concluding that the contribution would increase either short- or long-term profitability.

How would the *Dodge* court have decided these cases? How would the *Shlensky* court have decided the case?

9. To what extent does the law allow directors and C-suite managers to make corporate decisions on the basis of their personal morals and values? Suppose, for example, that a corporation has developed a potentially profitable product, but the board members are concerned that it could be used for what they regard as immoral purposes. If the board refused to market the product, would the board have breached its fiduciary duty to the shareholders? If so, would a shareholder suit against the board be likely to succeed? In general, should the law make it easier or harder for board members to base their decisions on personal morals?

PROBLEM

You are outside counsel to a public corporation engaged in the manufacture and sale of automobile replacement parts. The CEO calls you for advice about having the corporation make a gift of $100,000 to a charitable organization in which a good friend of hers is involved.

The organization operates a private school for poor minority children and has had considerable success over many years in motivating and educating children who might otherwise not have had much of a chance to succeed academically.

The before-tax earnings of your corporation for the current year will be about $20 million.

The CEO says that she is besieged by requests for charitable donations and, to avoid creating ill will with people seeking funds for other causes (some of whom are important customers), wants the corporation's gift to the school to be anonymous. She asks if there is any problem with doing so. Advise her.

NOTE ON DELAWARE LAW

In 2008, Professor Lynn Stout argued that her fellow corporate law professors should stop teaching *Dodge* because:

> *Dodge v. Ford* . . . is bad law, at least when cited for the proposition that the corporate purpose is, or should be, maximizing shareholder wealth. *Dodge v. Ford* is a mistake, a judicial "sport," a doctrinal oddity largely irrelevant to corporate law and corporate practice. What is more, courts and legislatures alike treat it as irrelevant. In the past thirty years, the Delaware courts have cited Dodge v. Ford as authority in only one unpublished case, and then not on the subject of corporate purpose, but on another legal question entirely.[14]

In 2010, however, Delaware Chancellor William Chandler embraced *Dodge* in *eBay Domestic Holdings, Inc. v. Newmark*:[15]

> On June 29, 2007, eBay launched the online classifieds site www.Kijiji.com in the United States. eBay designed Kijiji to compete with www.craigslist.org, the most widely used online classifieds site in the United States, which is owned and operated

---

[14]   Lynn A. Stout, Why We Should Stop Teaching Dodge v. Ford, 3 Va. L. & Bus. Rev. 163, 166 (2008). For similar views, see Margaret M. Blair & Lynn A. Stout, A Team Production Theory of Corporate Law, 85 Va. L. Rev. 247, 308 (1999) (arguing that, in evaluating a target company's board of directors' response to a hostile takeover bid, Delaware law allows the board to consider how the takeover would affect nonshareholder constituencies, such as creditors, customers, employees, and even the general community); Christopher M. Bruner, Corporate Governance Reform in a Time of Crisis, 36 J. Corp. L. 309, 324 (2011) (contending that, under Delaware law, "U.S. boards generally. . .have explicit latitude to consider the interests of other stakeholders, such as employees and creditors, in deciding how to respond to a hostile bid"); Einer Elhauge, Sacrificing Corporate Profits in the Public Interest, 80 N.Y.U. L. Rev. 733, 763–69 (2005) (arguing that Delaware law allows corporate managers to sacrifice corporate profits in order to protect nonshareholder constituencies and the public interest).

[15]   16 A.3d 1 (Del. Ch. 2010).

by craigslist, Inc. ("craigslist" or "the Company"). At the time of Kijiji's launch, eBay owned 28.4% of craigslist and was one of only three craigslist stockholders. The other two stockholders were Craig Newmark ("Craig") and James Buckmaster ("Jim"), who together own a majority of craigslist's shares and dominate the craigslist board.[1]

eBay purchased its stake in craigslist in August 2004 pursuant to the terms of a stockholders' agreement between Jim, Craig, craigslist, and eBay that expressly permits eBay to compete with craigslist in the online classifieds arena. Under the stockholders' agreement, when eBay chose to compete with craigslist by launching Kijiji, eBay lost certain contractual consent rights that gave eBay the right to approve or disapprove of a variety of corporate actions at craigslist. Another consequence of eBay's choice to compete with craigslist, however, was that the craigslist shares eBay owns were freed of the right of first refusal Jim and Craig had held over the shares, and the shares became freely transferable.

Notwithstanding eBay's express right to compete, Jim and Craig were not enthusiastic about eBay's foray into online classifieds. Accordingly, they asked eBay to sell its stake in craigslist, indicating a preference that eBay either sell its craigslist shares back to the Company or to a third party who would be compatible with Jim, Craig, and craigslist's unique corporate culture. When eBay refused to sell, Jim and Craig deliberated with outside counsel for six months about how to respond. Finally, on January 1, 2008, Jim and Craig, acting in their capacity as directors, responded by (1) adopting a rights plan that restricted eBay from purchasing additional craigslist shares and hampered eBay's ability to freely sell the craigslist shares it owned to third parties, (2) implementing a staggered board that made it impossible for eBay to unilaterally elect a director to the craigslist board, and (3) seeking to obtain a right of first refusal in craigslist's favor over the craigslist shares eBay owns by offering to issue one new share of craigslist stock in exchange for every five shares over which any craigslist stockholder granted a right of first refusal in craigslist's favor. As to the third measure, Jim and Craig accepted the right of first refusal offer in their capacity as craigslist stockholders and received new shares; eBay, however, declined the offer, did not receive new shares, and had its ownership in craigslist diluted from 28.4% to 24.9%.

eBay filed this action challenging all three measures on April 22, 2008. eBay asserts that, in approving and implementing each measure, Jim and Craig, as directors and controlling stockholders, breached the fiduciary duties they owe to eBay as a minority stockholder of the corporation. . . .

---

[1]   I use first names for convenience and ease of reference, and not out of disrespect.

Jim and Craig owe fiduciary duties to eBay because they are directors and controlling stockholders of craigslist, and eBay is a minority stockholder of craigslist. All directors of Delaware corporations are fiduciaries of the corporations' stockholders. Similarly, controlling stockholders are fiduciaries of their corporations' minority stockholders. Even though neither Jim nor Craig individually owns a majority of craigslist's shares, the law treats them as craigslist's controlling stockholders because they form a control group, bound together by [a voting agreement], with the power to elect the majority of the craigslist board.

> **FYI**
>
> The agreement between Jim and Craig required them to consult with one another and then vote their shares so as to ensure that they elected a majority of the board under eBay's cumulative voting system. Such vote pooling agreements (a.k.a. shareholder voting agreements) have been routinely upheld by Delaware courts. See, e.g., *Ringling Bros.-Barnum & Bailey Combined Shows v. Ringling*, 53 A.2d 441, 447 (Del.1947) ("Various forms of such pooling agreements, as they are sometimes called, have been held valid . . . .").

Any time a stockholder challenges an action taken by the board of directors, the Court must first determine the appropriate standard of review to use in analyzing the challenged action. . . .

I will review Jim and Craig's adoption of the Rights Plan using the intermediate standard of enhanced scrutiny, typically referred to as the [*Unocal Corporation v. Mesa Petroleum Company*[16]] test. Framed generally, enhanced scrutiny "requires directors to bear the burden to show their actions were reasonable."[83] The directors must "(1) identify the proper corporate objectives served by their actions; and (2) justify their actions as reasonable in relationship to those objectives."[84]

. . .

Promoting, protecting, or pursuing nonstockholder considerations must lead at some point to value for stockholders.[105] When director decisions are reviewed under the business judgment rule, this Court will not question rational judgments about how

---

[16]   493 A.2d 946 (Del.1985).

[83]   Mercier v. Inter-Tel (Delaware), Inc., 929 A.2d 786, 807 (Del.Ch.2007).

[84]   Id.

[105]   E.g., Revlon Inc. v. MacAndrews & Forbes Holdings, Inc., 506 A.2d 173, 183 (Del.1986) ("Although such considerations [of non-stockholder corporate constituencies and interests] may be permissible, there are fundamental limitations upon that prerogative. A board may have regard for various constituencies in discharging its responsibilities, provided there are rationally related benefits accruing to the stockholders."). See also . . . Jonathan Macey, A Close Read of an Excellent Commentary on Dodge v. Ford, 3 VA. L. & Bus. Rev. 177, 179 (2008) (suggesting that boards can take action that may not seem to directly maximize profits, so long as there is some plausible connection to a rational business purpose that ultimately benefits stockholders in some way; the benefit to other constituencies cannot be at the stockholders' expense).

promoting non-stockholder interests—be it through making a charitable contribution, paying employees higher salaries and benefits, or more general norms like promoting a particular corporate culture—ultimately promote stockholder value. Under the *Unocal* standard, however, the directors must act within the range of reasonableness.

. . . Based on all of the evidence, I find . . . that Jim and Craig resented eBay's decision to compete with craigslist and adopted the Rights Plan as a punitive response. They then cloaked this decision in the language of culture and post mortem corporate benefit. Although Jim and Craig (and the psychological culture they embrace) were the only known beneficiaries of the Rights Plan, such a motive is no substitute for their fiduciary duty to craigslist stockholders.

Jim and Craig did prove that they personally believe craigslist should not be about the business of stockholder wealth maximization, now or in the future. As an abstract matter, there is nothing inappropriate about an organization seeking to aid local, national, and global communities by providing a website for online classifieds that is largely devoid of monetized elements. Indeed, I personally appreciate and admire Jim's and Craig's desire to be of service to communities. The corporate form in which craigslist operates, however, is not an appropriate vehicle for purely philanthropic ends, at least not when there are other stockholders interested in realizing a return on their investment. Jim and Craig opted to form craigslist, Inc. as a for-profit Delaware corporation and voluntarily accepted millions of dollars from eBay as part of a transaction whereby eBay became a stockholder. Having chosen a for-profit corporate form, the craigslist directors are bound by the fiduciary duties and standards that accompany that form. Those standards include acting to promote the value of the corporation for the benefit of its stockholders. The "Inc." after the company name has to mean at least that. Thus, I cannot accept as valid for the purposes of implementing the Rights Plan a corporate policy that specifically, clearly, and admittedly seeks not to maximize the economic value of a for-profit Delaware corporation for the benefit of its stockholders—no matter whether those stockholders are individuals of modest means or a corporate titan of online commerce. If Jim and Craig were the only stockholders affected by their decisions, then there would be no one to object. eBay, however, holds a significant stake in craigslist, and Jim and Craig's actions affect others besides themselves.

In a subsequent law review article, Delaware Chief Justice Leo Strine criticized "commentators [who] pretend that corporate directors do not, under corporate law of the most important American jurisdiction— Delaware—have to make stockholder welfare the sole end of corporate governance within the limits of their legal discretion."[17] Instead, Strine contended that:

> Despite attempts [by such commentators] to muddy the doctrinal waters, a clear-eyed look at the law of corporations in Delaware reveals that, within the limits of their discretion, directors must make stockholder welfare their sole end, and that other interests may be taken into consideration only as a means of promoting stockholder welfare.[18]

Strine cited an earlier law review article by former Delaware Chancellor William Allen, which Strine argued interpreted "Delaware law as requiring directors . . . to maximize the value for (hypothetical) stockholders who have entrusted their capital to the firm indefinitely."[19]

Strine continued:

> Of course, it is true that the business judgment rule provides directors with wide discretion, and thus enables directors to justify—by reference to long-run stockholder interests—a number of decisions that may in fact be motivated more by a concern for a charity the CEO cares about, the community in which the corporate headquarters is located, or once in a while, even the company's ordinary workers, rather than long-run stockholder wealth. But that does not alter the reality of what the law is. *Dodge v. Ford* and *eBay* are hornbook law because they make clear that if a fiduciary admits that he is treating an interest other than stockholder wealth as an end in itself, rather than an instrument to stockholder wealth, he is committing a breach of fiduciary duty.[20]

NOTES AND QUESTIONS ON NONSHAREHOLDER CONSTITUENCY STATUTES

Over thirty states have purported to address the corporate social responsibility debate by adopting so-called nonshareholder constituency statutes. Typically, these statutes amend the existing statutory statement of the director's duty of care. They commonly authorize the board of directors, in discharging its duty of care, to consider the impact a decision will have on not only shareholders, but also on a list of other constituency groups, such as employees, suppliers, customers, creditors, and the local communities in which the firm does business. In addition to the laundry list of constituency factors, some statutes more generally authorize directors to consider both the long- and short-term effects of the decision.

---

[17] Leo E. Strine, Jr., The Dangers of Denial: The Need for A Clear-Eyed Understanding of the Power and Accountability Structure Established by the Delaware General Corporation Law, 50 Wake Forest L. Rev. 761, 781 (2015).

[18] Id. at 768.

[19] Id. at 774.

[20] Id. at 776–77. See David G. Yosifon, The Law of Corporate Purpose, 10 Berkeley Bus. L.J. 181, 194 (2013) ("Remarkably, Chandler did not cite a single case, statute, or piece of scholarship to support his conclusion. As with the *Dodge* court in Michigan, the proposition seemed so obvious and fundamental to Chandler that it needed no citation. Those who prefer to have one now have *eBay*.").

Most nonshareholder constituency statutes are permissive. Directors "may," but need not, take nonshareholder interests into account. There are no express constraints on the directors' discretion in deciding whether to consider nonshareholder interests and, if they decide to do so, which constituency groups' interests to consider. As a result, the statutes should not be interpreted as creating new director fiduciary duties running to nonshareholder constituencies and the latter should not have standing under these statutes to seek judicial review of a director's decision.[21]

Beyond this, however, the nonshareholder constituency statutes uniformly are silent on many key issues. Among the issues left open by almost all statutes are such critical questions as: How should directors decide whether particular claimants fall into one of the protected constituent categories, some of which, such as customers and communities, are very amorphous? What weight should directors assign to shareholder and nonshareholder interests? What should directors do when those interests cannot be reconciled? What should directors do when the interests of various nonshareholder constituencies conflict amongst themselves? What standards should courts use in reviewing a director's decision not to consider nonshareholder interests? What standards of review apply to director action claimed to be motivated by concern for nonshareholder constituents? Nor is there, as yet, any significant guidance from the courts. The statutes have rarely been cited outside the takeover setting, and even there they have not received authoritative interpretation. To the contrary, the decisions generally are limited to the not very startling observation that the statutes permit director consideration of stakeholder interests.[22] The waters thus remain quite murky.

Plausible interpretations of nonshareholder constituency statutes fall on a spectrum between two extremes. At one end of the spectrum is a reading that allows directors to ignore shareholder interests in making corporate decisions. At the other end is a reading under which the statutes simply codify the pre-existing common law, including an unmodified shareholder wealth maximization norm. Neither extreme seems likely to emerge as the prevailing interpretation. Instead, we will end up somewhere in the middle. But where?

At a minimum, if the statutes do anything beyond merely codifying present law, they presumably permit directors to select a plan that is second-best from the shareholders' perspective, but which alleviates the decision's impact on the firm's nonshareholder constituencies. In other words, the directors may balance a decision's effect on shareholders against its effect on stakeholders. If the decision would harm stakeholders, the directors may trade-off a reduction in shareholder gains for enhanced stakeholder welfare.

This interpretation is virtually compelled by the statutory language. What purpose is there in giving the directors the right to consider

---

[21] Although most statutes are silent on this point, the New York and Pennsylvania statutes explicitly state that they create no duties towards any party. N.Y. Bus. Corp. Law § 717(b); 15 Pa. Cons. Stat. § 1717.

[22] See, e.g., Keyser v. Commonwealth Nat'l Fin. Corp., 675 F. Supp. 238, 265–66 (M.D. Pa.1987); Baron v. Strawbridge & Clothier, 646 F. Supp. 690, 697 (E.D. Pa.1986).

nonshareholder interests if the directors cannot protect those interests? Without the right to act on their deliberations, the right to include stakeholder interests in those deliberations is rendered nugatory. If the statutes are to have any meaning, they must permit directors to make some trade-offs between their various constituencies.

How then might these statutes change the outcome of specific cases, if at all? Assume the XYZ Company operates a manufacturing plant nearing obsolescence in an economically depressed area. XYZ's board of directors is considering three plans for the plant's future. Plan A will keep the plant open, which will preserve the jobs of two hundred fifty workers, but will reduce earnings per share by ten percent as long as the plant remains open. Plan B will close the plant immediately, which will put the two hundred fifty plant employees out of work in an area where manufacturing jobs are scarce, but will cause earnings per share to rise by ten percent. Plan C contemplates closing the plant, but implementing a job training and relocation program for its workers as a supplement to state-provided programs. Plan C will cause a ten percent reduction in earnings per share for one year.

A shareholder threatens to bring a derivative action against the directors charging breach of their duty of care if they pick any plan other than Plan B.

1.   How would the case be analyzed under the traditional corporate law rules as espoused in cases like *Dodge* and *Shlensky*?

2.   How would the case be analyzed under a nonshareholder constituency statute?

3.   As a practical matter, would the result be any different?

4.   Should states permit directors to consider nonshareholder interests in making corporate decisions? Should states require directors to do so? Put another way, what policy justification is there for Chancellor Chandler's assertion that: "The corporate form in which craigslist operates . . . is not an appropriate vehicle for purely philanthropic ends, at least not when there are other stockholders interested in realizing a return on their investment"?

NOTE AND QUESTIONS ON BENEFIT CORPORATIONS

In 2013 Delaware enacted new provisions to its General Corporation Law allowing the formation of a new hybrid type of entity called a "public benefit corporation" (PBC). A PBC is defined in § 362 as a "for-profit corporation . . . that is intended to produce a public benefit or benefits and to operate in a responsible and sustainable manner." The "public benefit" must be specified in the firm's certificate of incorporation and consist of "a positive effect . . . on one or more categories of persons, entities, communities or interests (other than stockholders in their capacities as stockholders) including, but not limited to, effects of an artistic, charitable, cultural, economic, educational, environmental, literary, medical, religious, scientific or technological nature." Existing for-profit corporations may convert to PBCs only with the approval of 90 percent of outstanding shares, with the dissenting shareholders entitled to appraisal (that is, the right to be cashed out at fair market value). The PBC must, at least biennially, provide its shareholders with a statement that includes "objective factual information . . . regarding [its] success in meeting [its] objectives for promoting [its specified] public benefits and interests."

Other states have adopted similar provisions, with variations, particularly as to public disclosure, and third-party assessment, of the public benefit.

If a case like *Dodge v. Ford Motor Company* were to arise today, would the availability of this type of organization add force to the plaintiffs' argument? What might be the relevance to this question of a provision such as § 368 of the Delaware PBC law, which provides that enactment of the new set of provisions "shall not affect a statute or rule of law that is applicable to a corporation that is not a public benefit corporation"?

2) THEORY

Every couple of decades the corporate social responsibility debate heats up again. While it is almost as old as the corporate form itself, the debate took its modern form in the 1930s in an exchange between Professors Adolf Berle and Merrick Dodd. Today, however, the most famous policy argument relating to corporate social responsibility is that put forward in the New York Times Magazine by economist Milton Friedman.

E. Merrick Dodd, Jr., For Whom Are Corporate Managers Trustees?
45 Harv. L. Rev. 1145 (1932)[23]

. . . Directors and managers of modern large corporations are granted all sorts of novel powers by present-day corporation statutes and charters, and are free from any substantial supervision by stockholders by reason of the difficulty which the modern stockholder has in discovering what is going on and taking effective measures even if he has discovered it. The fact that managers so empowered not infrequently act as though maximum stockholder profit was not the sole object of managerial activities has led some students of corporate problems . . . to advocate an increased emphasis on the doctrine that managerial powers are held in trust for stockholders as sole beneficiaries of the corporate enterprise.

The present writer is thoroughly in sympathy with . . . efforts to establish a legal control which will more effectually prevent corporate managers from diverting profit into their own pockets from those of stockholders, and agrees with many of the specific rules which the latter deduces from his trusteeship principle. He nevertheless believes that it is undesirable, even with the laudable purpose of giving stockholders much-needed protection against self-seeking managers, to give increased

---

23   Reprinted by permission of the Harvard Law Review.

emphasis at the present time to the view that business corporations exist for the sole purpose of making profits for their stockholders. He believes that public opinion, which ultimately makes law, has made and is today making substantial strides in the direction of a view of the business corporation as an economic institution which has a social service as well as a profit-making function, that this view has already had some effect upon legal theory, and that it is likely to have a greatly increased effect upon the latter in the near future.

Several hundred years ago, when business enterprises were small affairs involving the activities of men rather than the employment of capital, our law took the position that business is a public profession rather than a purely private matter, and that the business man, far from being free to obtain all the profits which his skill in bargaining might secure for him, owes a legal duty to give adequate service at reasonable rates. Although a growing belief in liberty of contract and in the efficacy of free competition to prevent extortion led to abandonment of this theory for business as a whole, the theory survived as the rule applicable to the carrier and the innkeeper. In recent years we have seen this carrier law expanded to include a variety of businesses classed as public utilities. Under modern conditions the conduct of such businesses normally involves the use of a substantial amount of property. This fact, together with the accidental circumstance that a passage from Lord Hale was quoted in one of the briefs in the leading case of *Munn v. Illinois*, has led to a change in the conventional legal phraseology. Instead of talking, as the early judges talked, in terms of the duty of one engaged in business activities toward the public who are his customers, it has become the practice since *Munn v. Illinois* to talk of the public duty of one who has devoted his property to public use, the conception being that property employed in certain kinds of business is devoted to public use while property employed in other kinds of business remains strictly private.

This approach to the problem has been justly criticized as attempting to draw an unreasonably clean-cut distinction between businesses which do not differ substantially, and as furnishing no intelligible criterion by which to distinguish those businesses which are private property from those which are property devoted to public use. The phrase does, however, have the merit of emphasizing the fact that business is permitted and encouraged by the law primarily because it is of service to the community rather than because it is a source of profit to its owners. Accordingly, where it appears that unlimited private profit is incompatible with adequate service, the claim of those engaged therein that the business belongs to them in an unqualified sense and can be pursued in such manner as they choose need not be accepted by the legislature. Despite certain recent conservative decisions . . ., it may well be that the law is approaching a point of view which will regard all business as affected with a public interest. . . .

. . . Outside the public utility field there is in the present state of the law little or no attempt to curtail private property in the interest of the customer, it being generally assumed that competition furnishes him adequate protection. On the other hand, the inequality of bargaining power between employer and employee—an inequality which the recent rise of the large corporation has greatly accentuated—has resulted in a considerable amount of legislation designed to protect the health and safety, and even to a slight extent the financial rewards, of the employee.

Recent economic events suggest that the day may not be far distant when public opinion will demand a much greater degree of protection to the worker. There is a widespread and growing feeling that industry owes to its employees not merely the negative duties of refraining from overworking or injuring them, but the affirmative duty of providing them so far as possible with economic security. Concentration of control of industry in a relatively few hands has encouraged the belief in the practicability of methods of economic planning by which such security can be achieved in much greater degree than at present. This belief is no longer confined to radical opponents of the capitalistic system; it has come to be shared by many conservatives who believe that capitalism is worth saving but that it can not permanently survive under modern conditions unless it treats the economic security of the worker as one of its obligations and is intelligently directed so as to attain that object.

It is true that, as many advocates of industrial planning have pointed out, high wages and economic security for workers tend in the main to increase the profits of stockholders, inasmuch as they tend to increase consumption of the things which business corporations produce. It cannot, however, be successfully maintained that the sort of industrial planning which may be found desirable to protect the employee is necessarily under all circumstances in line with the interest of the stockholders of each individual corporation. If contemporary discussion of the need for a planned economic order ultimately results in a more stabilized system of production and employment, we may safely predict that this will involve some further modifications of the maximum-profit-for-the-stockholders-of-the-individual-company formula.

It may, however, be forcibly urged that all these and other past, present, and possible future limitations on the pursuit of stockholder profit in no way alter the theory that the sole function of directors and other corporate managers is to seek to obtain the maximum amount of profits for the stockholders as owners of the enterprise. Ownership of a modern railroad may today be hedged about with restrictions which make such ownership considerably less absolute than was the ownership of a cotton mill at the time when economic and legal theories of laissez faire were most completely accepted. Ownership in the cotton industry tomorrow may be even more restricted in some ways than is ownership in the railroad field today. Regulations imposed in the interest of employees, consumers, or others may increasingly limit the methods which managers of incorporated business enterprises may employ in seeking profits for their stockholders without in any way affecting the proposition that the sole function of such managers is to work for the best interests of the stockholders as their employers or beneficiaries.

If, however, as much recent writing suggests, we are undergoing a substantial change in our public opinion with regard to the obligations of business to the community, it is natural to expect that this change of opinion will have some effect upon the attitude of those who manage business. If, therefore, the managers of modern businesses were also its owners, the development of a public opinion to the effect that business has responsibilities to its employees and its customers would, quite apart from any legal compulsion, tend to affect the conduct of the better type of business man. The principal object of legal compulsion might then be to keep those who failed to catch the new spirit up to the standards which their more enlightened competitors would desire to adopt voluntarily. Business might then become a profession of public service, not primarily because the law had made it such but because a public opinion shared in by businessmen themselves had brought about a professional attitude.

Our present economic system, under which our more important business enterprises are owned by investors who take no part in carrying them on—absentee owners who in many cases have not even seen the property from which they derive their profits—alters the situation materially. That stockholders who have no contact with business other than to derive dividends from it should become imbued with a professional spirit of public service is hardly thinkable. If incorporated business is to become professionalized, it is to the managers, not to the owners, that we must look for the accomplishment of this result.

If we may believe what some of our business leaders and students of business tell us, there is in fact a growing feeling not only that business has responsibilities to the community but that our corporate managers who control business should voluntarily and without waiting for legal compulsion manage it in such a way as to fulfill those responsibilities. Thus, even before the present depression had set many business men thinking about the place of business in society, one of our leading business executives, Mr. Owen D. Young, had expressed himself as follows as to his conception of what a business executive's attitude should be:

> "If there is one thing a lawyer is taught it is knowledge of trusteeship and the sacredness of that position. Very soon he saw rising a notion that managers were no longer attorneys for stockholders; they were becoming trustees of an institution.
>
> If you will pardon me for being personal, it makes a great difference in my attitude toward my job as an executive officer of the General Electric Company whether I am a trustee of the institution or an attorney for the investor. If I am a trustee, who

are the beneficiaries of the trust? To whom do I owe my obligations?

My conception of it is this: That there are three groups of people who have an interest in that institution. One is the group of fifty-odd thousand people who have put their capital in the company, namely, its stockholders. Another is a group of well toward one hundred thousand people who are putting their labor and their lives into the business of the company. The third group is of customers and the general public.

Customers have a right to demand that a concern so large shall not only do its business honestly and properly, but, further, that it shall meet its public obligations and perform its public duties—in a word, vast as it is, that it should be a good citizen.

Now, I conceive my trust first to be to see to it that the capital which is put into this concern is safe, honestly and wisely used, and paid a fair rate of return. Otherwise we cannot get capital. The worker will have no tools.

Second, that the people who put their labor and lives into this concern get fair wages, continuity of employment, and a recognition of their right to their jobs where they have educated themselves to highly skilled and specialized work.

Third, that the customers get a product which is as represented and that the price is such as is consistent with the obligations to the people who put their capital and labor in.

Last, that the public has a concern functioning in the public interest and performing its duties as a great and good citizen should.

I think what is right in business is influenced very largely by the growing sense of trusteeship which I have described. One no longer feels the obligation to take from labor for the benefit of capital, nor to take from the public for the benefit of both, but rather to administer wisely and fairly in the interest of all."

. . . "The only way to defend capitalism is through leadership which accepts social responsibility and meets the sound needs of the great majority of our people. Such leadership will seek to form constructive plans framed not in the interest of capital or capitalism but in the interest of the American people as a whole . . . . The responsibility of capital for leadership is overwhelming. To a large extent in this industrial civilization of ours the potential leadership of the country is concentrated in industry." . . . Assumption of social responsibility by industrial leadership necessarily means assumption of such responsibility by corporate managers.

The view that those who manage our business corporations should concern themselves with the interests of employees, consumers, and the general public, as well as of the stockholders, is thus advanced today by persons whose position in the business world is such as to give them great power of influencing both business opinion and public opinion generally. Little or no attempt seems to have been made, however, to consider how far such an attitude on the part of corporate managers is compatible with the legal duties which they owe the stockholder-owners as the elected representatives of the latter.

No doubt it is to a large extent true that an attempt by business managers to take into consideration the welfare of employees and consumers (and under modern industrial conditions the two classes are largely the same) will in the long run increase the profits of stockholders. . . . If the social responsibility of business means merely a more enlightened view as to the ultimate advantage of the stockholder-owners, then obviously corporate managers may accept such social responsibility without any departure from the traditional view that their function is to seek to obtain the maximum amount of profits for their stockholders.

And yet one need not be unduly credulous to feel that there is more to this talk of social responsibility on the part of corporation managers than merely a more intelligent appreciation of what tends to the ultimate benefit of their stockholders. Modern large-scale industry has given to the managers of our principal corporations enormous power over the welfare of wage earners and consumers, particularly the former. Power over the lives of others tends to create on the part of those most worthy to exercise it a sense of responsibility. The managers, who along with the subordinate employees are part of the group which is contributing to the success of the enterprise by day-to-day efforts, may easily come to feel as strong a community of interest with their fellow workers as with a group of investors whose only connection with the enterprise is that they or their predecessors in title invested money in it, perhaps in the rather remote past. Moreover, the concept that the managers are merely, in Mr. Young's phrase, "attorneys for the investors" leads to-the conclusion that if other classes who are affected by the corporation's activities need protection, that protection must be entrusted to other hands than those of the managers. Desire to retain their present powers accordingly encourages the latter to adopt and disseminate the view that they are guardians of all the interests which the corporation affects and not merely servants of its absentee owners.

Any clash between this point of view and the orthodox theory that the managers are elected by stockholder-owners to serve their interests exclusively has thus far been chiefly potential rather than actual. Judicial willingness—which has increased of late—to allow corporate directors a wide range of discretion as to what policies will best promote the interests of the stockholders, together with managerial disinclination to indulge a sense of social responsibility to a point where it is likely to injure the stockholders, has thus far prevented the issue from being frequently raised in clear-cut fashion in litigation. . . .

It may well be that any substantial assumption of social responsibility by incorporated business through voluntary action on the part of its managers cannot reasonably be expected. Experience may indicate that corporate managers are so closely identified with profit-seeking capital that we must look to other agencies to safeguard the other interests involved, or that the competition of the socially irresponsible makes it impracticable for the more public-spirited managers to act as they would like to do, or that to expect managers to conduct an institution for the combined benefit of classes whose interests are largely conflicting is to impose upon them an impossible task and to endow them with dangerous powers. The question with which this article is concerned is not whether the voluntary acceptance of social responsibility by corporate managers is workable, but whether experiments in that direction run counter to fundamental principles of the law of business corporations.

The view that they do so rests upon two assumptions: that business is private property, and that the directors of an incorporated business are fiduciaries (directly if we disregard the corporate fiction, indirectly in any case) for the stockholder-owners. The first assumption is being rapidly undermined . . . Business—which is the economic organization of society—is private property only in a qualified sense, and society may properly demand that it be carried on in such a way as to safeguard the interests of those who deal with it either as employees or consumers even if the proprietary rights of its owners are thereby curtailed.

The legal recognition that there are other interests than those of the stockholders to be protected does not, as we have seen, necessarily give corporate managers the right to consider those interests, as it is possible to regard the managers as representatives of the stockholding interest only. Such a view means in practice that there are no human beings who are in a position where they can lawfully accept for incorporated business those social responsibilities which public opinion is coming to expect, and that these responsibilities must be imposed on corporations by legal compulsion. This makes the situation of incorporated business so anomalous that we are justified in demanding clear proof that it is a correct statement of the legal situation.

Clear proof is not forthcoming. Despite many attempts to dissolve the corporation into an aggregate of stockholders, our legal tradition is rather in favor of treating it as an institution directed by persons who are primarily fiduciaries for the institution rather than for its members. That lawyers have commonly assumed that the managers must conduct the institution with single-minded devotion to stockholder profit is true; but the assumption is based upon a particular view of the nature of the institution which we call a business corporation, which concept is in turn based upon a particular view of the nature of business as a purely private enterprise. If we recognize that the attitude of law and public opinion toward business is changing, we may then properly modify our ideas as to the nature of such a business institution as the corporation and hence as to the considerations which may properly influence the conduct of those who direct its activities.

QUESTIONS

1.   Law professor Henry Manne once wrote that: "To qualify as socially responsible corporate action, a business expenditure or activity must be one for which the marginal returns to the corporation are less than the returns available from some alternative expenditure, must be purely voluntary, and must be an actual corporate expenditure rather than a conduit for individual largesse." Would Dodd agree?

2.   It is said that a rising tide lifts all boats. Would Dodd agree?

3.   What exactly is Dodd arguing the law should do?

4.   What is the basis for Dodd's argument?

A. A. Berle, Jr., For Whom Corporate Managers Are Trustees: A Note
45 Harv. L. Rev. 1365 (1932)[24]

The administration of corporations—peculiarly, a few hundred large corporations—is now the crux of American industrial life. Upon the securities of these corporations has been erected the dominant part of the property system of the industrial east. A major function of these securities is to provide safety, security, or means of support for that part of the community which is unable to earn its living in the normal channels of work or trade. Under cover of that system, certain individuals may perhaps acquire a disproportionate share of wealth. But this is an incident to the system and not its major premise; statistically, it plays a relatively minor part. Historically, and as a matter of law, corporate managements have been required to run their affairs in the interests of their security holders. From time to time other groups, notably labor, have asserted their claims; and these claims are receiving steadily greater recognition as a cost of industry. If these costs are not met, security holders receive an illusory additional profit. But the security holder's claim was the supposed main objective.

Professor Dodd has challenged the theory. . . . This is a point of view which cannot be ignored.

. . . No one familiar with European or advanced American thought seriously disputes the propositions: first, that the present mode of life entails a high degree of large-scale production; second, that this necessitates an unprecedented degree of financial concentration which

---

[24]   Reprinted by permission of the Harvard Law Review.

has clothed itself in the corporate form; and, third, that the result of such concentration has been, and must be, to pose a few large organisms, the task of whose administrators is, fundamentally, that of industrial government.

In other words, the great industrial managers, their bankers and still more the men composing their silent "control," function today more as princes and ministers than as promoters or merchants. Exclusive profit-making purpose necessarily yields to this analysis.

This is the real justification for Professor Dodd's argument. But it is theory, not practice. The industrial "control" does not now think of himself as a prince; he does not now assume responsibilities to the community; his bankers do not now undertake to recognize social claims; his lawyers do not advise him in terms of social responsibility. Nor is there any mechanism now in sight enforcing accomplishment of his theoretical function.

. . . When the fiduciary obligation of the corporate management and "control" to stockholders is weakened or eliminated, the management and "control" become for all practical purposes absolute. The claims upon the assembled industrial wealth and funneled industrial income which managements are then likely to enforce (they have no need to urge) are their own. . . .

Now I submit that you cannot abandon emphasis on "the view that business corporations exist for the sole purpose of making profits for their stockholders" until such time as you are prepared to offer a clear and reasonably enforceable scheme of responsibilities to someone else. Roughly speaking, there are between five and eight million stockholders in the country (the estimates vary); to which must be added a very large group of bondholders and many millions of individuals who have an interest in corporate securities through the medium of life insurance companies and savings banks. This group, expanded to include their families and dependents, must directly affect not less than half of the population of the country, to say nothing of indirect results. When the fund and income stream upon which this group rely are irresponsibly dealt with, a large portion of the group merely devolves on the community; and there is presented a staggering bill for relief, old age pensions, sickness-aid, and the like. Nothing is accomplished, either as a matter of law or of economics, merely by saying that the claim of this group ought not to be "emphasized." Either you have a system based on individual ownership of property or you do not. If not—and there are at the moment plenty of reasons why capitalism does not seem ideal—it becomes necessary to present a system (none has been presented) of law or government, or both, by which responsibility for control of national wealth and income is so apportioned and enforced that the community as a whole, or at least the great bulk of it, is properly taken care of. Otherwise the economic power now mobilized and massed under the corporate form, in the hands of a few thousand directors, and the few hundred individuals holding "control" is simply handed over, weakly, to the present administrators with a pious wish that something nice will come out of it all.

The only thing that can come out of it, in any long view, is the massing of group after group to assert their private claims by force or threat—to take what each can get, just as corporate managements do. The laborer is invited to organize and strike, the security holder is invited either to jettison his corporate securities and demand relief from the state, or to decline to save money at all under a system which grants to someone else power to take his savings at will. The consumer or patron is left nowhere, unless he learns the dubious art of boycott. This is an invitation not to law or orderly government, but to a process of economic civil war. . . .

    . . .

Unfortunately, the lawyers have not given too good an account of themselves thus far, either in theory or administration. . . . The private property right, though still honored in tradition even when passive property—securities—are involved, has in practice been cut to pieces by them. . . .

Nevertheless, development in the corporate field is more likely to come through lawyers than through any other group. For one thing, they do, approximately, understand the system. They have, however, a function widely divergent from that of the economist or the social theorist. They must meet a series of practical situations from day to day. They are not, accordingly, in a position to relinquish one position—here, the idea of corporate trusteeship for security holdings—leaving the situation in flux until a new order shall emerge. Legal technique does not contemplate intervening periods of chaos; it can only follow out new theories as they become established and accepted by the community at large. It is likely that claims upon corporate wealth and corporate income will be asserted from many directions. The shareholder who now has a primary property right over residual income after expenses are met, may ultimately be conceived of as having an equal participation with a number of other claimants. Or he may emerge, still with a primary property right over residual income, but subordinated to a number of claims by labor, by customers and patrons, by the community and the like, which cut down that residue. It would, as Professor Dodd points out, be unfortunate to leave the law in such shape that these developments could not be recognized as a matter of constitutional or corporation law. But it is one thing to say that the law must allow for such developments. It is quite another to grant uncontrolled power to corporate managers in the hope that they will produce that development.

Most students of corporation finance dream of a time when corporate administration will be held to a high degree of required responsibility— a responsibility conceived not merely in terms of stockholders' rights, but in terms of economic government satisfying the respective needs of investors, workers, customers, and the aggregated community. Indications, indeed, are not wanting that without such readjustment the corporate system will involve itself in successive cataclysms perhaps leading to its ultimate downfall. But apart from occasional and brilliant experiments of men like Mr. Swope and Mr. Young (who after all are the exceptions rather than the rule), we must expect our evolutionary process to be stimulated from quite different quarters.

Unchecked by present legal balances, a social-economic absolutism of corporate administrators, even if benevolent, might be unsafe; and in any case it hardly affords the soundest base on which to construct the economic commonwealth which industrialism seems to require. Meanwhile, as lawyers, we had best be protecting the interests we know, being no less swift to provide for the new interests as they successively appear.

QUESTIONS

1. What exactly is Berle arguing the law should do?

2. What is the basis for Berle's argument?

3. Why is appropriate for an individual to act responsibly but not corporate directors or managers?

4. The so-called nexus of contracts theory visualizes the firm not as an entity, but as an aggregate of various inputs acting together to produce goods or services. Employees provide labor. Creditors provide debt capital. Shareholders initially provide equity capital and subsequently bear the risk of losses and monitor the performance of management. Management monitors the performance of employees and coordinates the activities of all the firm's inputs. The firm is seen as simply a legal fiction representing the complex set of contractual relationships between these inputs. In other words, the firm is treated not as a thing, but rather as a nexus or web of explicit and implicit contracts establishing rights and obligations among the various inputs making up the firm.

Is the shareholder wealth maximization norm itself consistent with contractarian theory?

5. How does corporate social responsibility relate to agency costs? In that regard, consider Berle's claim that "you cannot abandon emphasis on 'the view that business corporations exist for the sole purpose of making profits for their stockholders' until such time as you are prepared to offer a clear and reasonably enforceable scheme of responsibilities to someone else." How does that argument relate to the agency cost perspective?

PROBLEM

The State of California is considering adopting the following provision as an amendment to its corporation statute:

> Directors and officers, in exercising their respective powers with a view to the interests of the corporation, may consider:

(a) The interests of the corporation's employees, suppliers, creditors and customers;

(b) The economy of the state and nation;

(c) The interests of the community and of society; and

(d) The long term as well as short term interests of the corporation and its stockholders, including the possibility that these interests may be best served by the continued independence of the corporation.

This subsection does not create or authorize any causes of action against the corporation or its directors or officers.

You are an advisor to a state legislator. Advise your legislator whether to vote for or against the proposed law.

B. ESG ACTIVISM

As saw in the preceding Chapter, shareholder activists traditionally fell into two camps. The earliest activists were primarily concerned with corporate social responsibility. They were concerned primarily with ensuring that their investments are consistent with their values. They tended to be individuals, charitable and religious organizations, and union or government pension funds. Their primary mode of activism was using non-binding shareholder proposals to request reports on their focus topic, change corporate policy, or ask the board to review corporate policy on their issue. Their issue set evolved over time, but tended to focus on the environment (e.g., climate change), human rights (e.g., divestment and boycott), divestment of certain product lines (e.g., defense, tobacco, nuclear power), affirmative action (e.g., gay rights), animal rights (e.g., no lab experiments), tying executive pay to social benchmarks, and labor rights.

A second generation of activists focused on corporate governance. They were primarily concerned with increasing value the economic value of their investments. They included union or government pension funds and hedge funds. Their issue set included such matters as takeover defenses, board independence, CEO compensation, and separating the CEO and Chairman of the Board positions.

Beginning around 2010, these formerly separate lines of activism began to coalesce into what became known as environmental, social, and governance (ESG) activism. ESG activists include a wide range of individuals, charitable and religious organizations, union or government pension funds, and hedge funds, but also relatively new activists such as mutual funds and exchange traded funds. Blackrock, Inc., an investment management company that is one of the largest institutional investors in the world, with over $7 trillion under management in hundreds of exchange traded funds, is often cited as an example of this new breed of activists. Blackrock's CEO Lawrence Fink for many years has written an annual letter to the CEOs of Blackrock's portfolio companies, setting out

Blackrock's goals. Those letters eventually took on an increasingly strong ESG emphasis. In 2020, for example, Fink's letter focused on climate change issues:

> Investors are increasingly . . . recognizing that climate risk is investment risk. Indeed, climate change is almost invariably the top issue that clients around the world raise with BlackRock. . . .
>
> As a fiduciary, our responsibility is to help clients navigate this transition. Our investment conviction is that sustainability- and climate-integrated portfolios can provide better risk-adjusted returns to investors. And with the impact of sustainability on investment returns increasing, we believe that sustainable investing is the strongest foundation for client portfolios going forward.
>
> In a letter to our clients today, BlackRock announced a number of initiatives to place sustainability at the center of our investment approach, including: making sustainability integral to portfolio construction and risk management; exiting investments that present a high sustainability-related risk, such as thermal coal producers; launching new investment products that screen fossil fuels; and strengthening our commitment to sustainability and transparency in our investment stewardship activities. . . .
>
> We believe that when a company is not effectively addressing a material issue, its directors should be held accountable. Last year BlackRock voted against or withheld votes from 4,800 directors at 2,700 different companies. Where we feel companies and boards are not producing effective sustainability disclosures or implementing frameworks for managing these issues, we will hold board members accountable. Given the groundwork we have already laid engaging on disclosure, and the growing investment risks surrounding sustainability, we will be increasingly disposed to vote against management and board directors when companies are not making sufficient progress on sustainability-related disclosures and the business practices and plans underlying them.

Max M. Schanzenbach & Robert H. Sitkoff, Reconciling Fiduciary Duty and Social Conscience: The Law and Economics of ESG Investing by a Trustee

72 Stan. L. Rev. 381 (2020)[25]

Today's [environmental, social, and governance (ESG)] investing phenomenon traces its roots to [socially responsible investing (SRI)] practices that avoided investment in firms that made antisocial products. In an eighteenth century sermon, John Wesley, the founder of the Methodist Church, called on his followers to avoid profiting from businesses harmful to one's neighbors, particularly the alcohol and slave trades, or to oneself or one's workers, such as the production of dangerous chemicals. Some commentators view this exhortation, in effect an investment screen, as an early instance of SRI. As financial markets developed, some mutual funds applied social screens to their investment programs, providing an investment vehicle that avoided certain businesses on moral grounds. The first SRI fund, Pioneer Investments, began in 1928 as an ecclesiastical investment fund committed to the Christian values of its founder, and it remains in existence today. Pioneer Investments and other early SRI funds, however, emphasized the avoidance of morally questionable investments, not the pursuit of better risk-adjusted returns.

SRI funds that eschewed defense firms gained additional prominence in the 1970s as a consequence of the Vietnam War. During the late 1970s and into the 1980s, the policies of South Africa's apartheid government put SRI more clearly into the spotlight as activists called for a boycott of firms that did business in South Africa. . . .

. . . Investment professionals . . . developed a renewed interest in SRI as investor demand for socially responsible funds increased in the 1990s and the 2000s. Between 1995 and 2005, numerous SRI funds were launched and their assets under management increased substantially, growing by one estimate from 55 funds to 201 funds and from $12 billion to $179 billion. Today such funds are experiencing yearly net inflows in the billions of dollars, with net inflows from the first half of 2019 exceeding full-year net inflows from 2018 by more than $3 billion.

At the same time, SRI advocates have shifted both their investment strategies and their marketing in two related ways. First, SRI funds began explicitly to incorporate corporate governance (the G in ESG) into their investment strategies, tying sound governance to their social mission and rebranding SRI as ESG. Second, SRI funds began appealing to investors' financial interests, as well as their ethical sense, by

---

[25] Reprinted by permission of Max M. Schanzenbach, Robert H. Sitkoff, and the Board of Trustees of the Leland Stanford Junior University, from the Stanford Law Review at 72 Stan. L. Rev. 381 (2020).

asserting that SRI funds could be both morally and financially superior to other funds, offering lower risk and higher returns.

The addition of governance factors in the 1990s, widely accepted as relevant to firm value, brought theoretical and empirical credibility to claims regarding excess return. At the same time, massive corporate bankruptcies such as WorldCom and Enron, tied to misconduct and weak governance, drew further attention to governance factors in investing and were followed by regulatory reforms. . . . A further prod for ESG investing came as a result of the financial crisis of 2007 and the Great Recession, which led to a search for better risk measures, with some suggesting that considering ESG factors improves risk assessment.

The term "ESG investing" is inherently ambiguous as to whether the investor's purpose is collateral benefits (in effect, classic SRI) or improved risk-adjusted returns (rebranded as ESG), and it is widely and confusingly used today to encompass both. For clarity, we will refer to ESG investing motivated by providing a benefit to a third party or otherwise for moral or ethical reasons as *collateral benefits ESG*, and ESG investing to improve risk-adjusted returns as *risk-return ESG*. The distinction turns on the investor's motive. By way of illustration, CalPERS, the prominent California Public Employees' Retirement System, recently responded to criticism that it was undertaking what we would call collateral benefits ESG by arguing that it employed risk-return ESG, that is, it used ESG factors "as an informed investor," "not because [ESG factors] make us feel good but because there is sound economic reasoning to do so."[77]

Collateral benefits ESG often operates as a screen on investment activity, with the investor eschewing firms or industries identified as unethical or falling below a certain ESG threshold. For example, a collateral benefits ESG investment strategy might avoid investment in a fossil fuel company for the collateral benefit of reducing pollution. Collateral benefits ESG can also be implemented via shareholder voting or engagement, with the aim of inducing a firm to change its practices toward providing collateral benefits apart from improvement to investor risk and return.

Risk-return ESG investing, by contrast, entails the use of ESG factors as metrics for assessing expected risk and return with the aim of improved return with less risk. A typical risk-return ESG strategy is to use ESG factors to pick stocks or other securities on the theory that those factors can identify market mispricing and therefore profit opportunities (we'll call this *active investing*). For example, a risk-return ESG analysis of a fossil fuel company might conclude that the company's litigation and regulatory risks are underestimated by its share price, and therefore that reducing or avoiding investment in the company will improve risk-

---

[77]   Slanted "Study" on the Role of ESG Falls Completely Apart, CALPERS (updated Dec. 13, 2017), https://perma.cc/YEZ8-BHA8. . . .

adjusted return. Risk-return ESG investing can also be implemented via shareholder voting or other engagement with management in a manner that improves firm performance and therefore investment returns (we'll call this *active shareholding*; others have called it *stewardship*).

Our taxonomy of collateral benefits ESG versus risk-return ESG is meaningful . . . as a matter of financial economics for at least two reasons. First, a screen or other form of active investing cannot in fact achieve collateral benefits while increasing returns. The theory behind a collateral benefits ESG screen is that by eschewing investment in bad-ESG firms, investors will raise the cost of capital to those firms, inducing them to change their practices. But necessarily this strategy, if successful, entails sacrificing returns (and with reduced diversification to boot), because a higher cost of capital is just another way of saying that the firm offers better returns. In other words, a successful collateral benefits ESG screening strategy depends on low-ESG firms offering better returns.

Second, increasing the cost of capital to a public company is unlikely given the depth and liquidity of modern financial markets. The capital lost to a firm from a screening strategy employed by even a large number of trustees will tend to be replaced by other capital that rushes in to take advantage of the opportunity. In this event, a collateral benefit ESG investor will not achieve any collateral benefit but will still bear a diversification cost.

. . .

There is, to be sure, a rough consensus on core ESG factors. Unhealthy products and poor labor practices are bad social factors. Strong compliance records on environmental and labor regulations are good environmental and social factors. Poorly incentivized and entrenched management are bad governance factors. However, even at this level of abstraction, an investor will have to make subjective judgments about how much weight to give E versus S versus G factors. For example, an environmentally sound firm could have weak corporate governance or mistreat its workforce. On balance, is such a firm a good or a bad ESG bet?

When moving from abstract principles to specific implementation, the inherent subjectivity of the ESG rubric itself becomes even more apparent. As the professional association for Chartered Financial Analysts has explained, "[t]here is no one exhaustive list of ESG issues,"[268] and there is no consistency in the labels used to describe investment strategies that consider ESG factors. There are hundreds of

---

[268] [CFA Inst., Environmental, Social, and Governance Issues in Investing: A Guide for Investment Professionals 4 (2015), https://perma.cc/GU5Q-8L7A.] The extent of a company's ESG disclosure is itself a factor in the ESG scoring of the company by some ratings services. See [Michael T. Dieschbourg & Andrew P. Nussbaum, No Place to Hide Thanks to Morningstar, Bloomberg, MSCI, and Multiple Global Data Providers, Inv. & Wealth Monitor, Nov.–Dec. 2017, at 29, 30.]

ESG ratings services and ESG-themed mutual funds, and they often disagree. For example, the well-known ratings agency Morningstar found that about half of the ESG mutual funds assessed scored as average or worse than non-ESG funds on Morningstar's own "sustainability" assessments.

. . .

Setting aside the subjectivity inherent to the ESG rubric, there are indeed sound theoretical arguments that various ESG factors may be related to firm performance. Some empirical evidence validates these arguments, although the findings are mixed and contextual, and highly dependent on the research design.

Corporate governance (i.e., G) factors have straightforward theoretical relationships to firm performance. The entrenchment of management, executive compensation arrangements, and whether a firm has a controlling shareholder are familiar governance factors routinely considered by active investors. A robust empirical literature confirms that identifiable governance factors can have a significant effect on firm performance.

On the other hand, there is disagreement about the extent to which existing studies have reliably measured the relationship between governance and firm value. Moreover, optimal corporate governance might be contextual, that is, heterogeneity among firms may require heterogeneity in governance. What is a good G factor for one firm may not be good for another. Indeed, the prevailing academic view of corporate law is that it should enable tailor-made governance for a wide variety of contexts.

The contextual nature of optimal governance speaks to the need for subjective judgments in applying G factors within an active investment strategy. For example, there is some evidence that for many firms a classified board is a minus, but for certain kinds of firms it may be a plus. Although investors and academics are generally hostile to poison pills, most acknowledge that there are circumstances in which a pill may be beneficial to shareholders, depending on the design of the pill and the firm's circumstances.

Environmental and social (i.e., E and S) factors, though perhaps less obviously related to firm value than governance factors, may affect firm value through at least two mechanisms. First, environmental and social factors may help identify specific risks. Firms with weak internal controls, poor compliance records, or in socially unpopular or environmentally risky industries may face greater political, regulatory, and litigation risks. Consider the fossil fuel industry, which is disfavored in collateral benefits ESG investing for a variety of reasons. Some supporters of risk-return ESG investing argue that these same environmental factors predict litigation and regulatory risk, such as a catastrophic environmental or the risk of large fixed investments becoming "stranded" following a dramatic regulatory change.

Second, environmental and social factors may serve as proxies for management quality, an important investment consideration that is hard to observe directly. Well-run firms may have better compliance programs, and high-quality managers may be attracted to firms that have pro-environmental or socially responsible policies. A firm that is better at regulatory compliance and managing environmental and social risks may be better managed and governed in general, making environmental and social factors a useful proxy for better management. High-quality managers may be especially concerned about protecting their reputational capital, or perhaps socially and environmentally responsible behavior is correlated with other attributes of sound management.

The theoretical relationship between firm value and environmental and social factors has some empirical support, though not as strong as that in favor of governance factors. In general, studies of firm performance find that firms with high environmental and social scores enjoy higher earnings with lower risk than firms with low environmental and social scores. Moreover, there is evidence that firms can build goodwill through socially responsible activities, which can protect against reputational harm from adverse events.

The favorable empirical results regarding environmental and social factors, however, are not uniform. A significant concern is that managers may invoke ESG factors to enact their own policy preferences at the expense of shareholders—an agency problem for which there is also some empirical evidence. Another concern is that the extent of a firm's regulatory and political risks may not be reflected in its ESG scoring. For example, companies pursuing alternative energy sources may score high on ESG factors but still face significant political and regulatory risk owing to heavy reliance on current government policy. Indeed, one of the Commissioners on the Securities and Exchange Commission (SEC) has suggested that the SEC has not yet taken a position on ESG disclosure in part because defining ESG factors is value laden and would involve confronting contentious political issues.

. . .

Another active strategy is to use shareholder control rights or engagement with management to improve firm value. We call this approach active shareholding, in contrast to active investing via screens or stock picking (others call it stewardship). By way of illustration, a firm's board may become complacent or might propose changes to the corporate structure that would entrench current management (such as a classified board). Voting against lazy directors or entrenchment can protect firm value.

In contrast to stock picking, active shareholding seeks to improve corporate policies or prevent bad decisions, allowing the active shareholder to reap the reward of improved or at least protected share prices later. All that is necessary for active shareholding to improve investment returns is for the expected benefit of the investor's activism to outweigh its monitoring, investigation, voting, or other costs. Additionally, active shareholding does not tend to entail a diversification cost like active investing. Even index fund managers can engage in active shareholding. BlackRock and Vanguard, for example, explicitly identify ESG factors in their proxy voting guidelines.

Active shareholding has increased significantly over the past two decades, in part facilitated by regulatory reforms and increasing institutional ownership that facilitates monitoring and coordination among shareholders. Much of this activity has been focused on governance factors, such as reducing management entrenchment and executive pay. But there is also growing attention to environmental and social factors such as diversity in board composition and "climate risk and the environment." Given the likelihood that market prices will come to reflect ESG factors, prominent advocates of ESG investing, including the chair of the PRI, have argued that ESG-based active shareholding will likely come to supplant active investing strategies.

There is evidence that shareholder activism, even in the form of nonbinding resolutions or withholding votes, can affect corporate policy. Firms commonly adopt shareholder proposals, and incumbent directors often resign if a large number of votes are withheld. Informal engagement, which may be combined with proxy contests, withholding votes, or the threat of either or both, is commonly used and also affects corporate policies.

However, active shareholding has practical and theoretical limits, whether based on ESG factors or otherwise. The core difficulty is that a shareholder receives only a pro rata portion of the benefit of a successful shareholder action, whereas the costs are borne fully by the active shareholder. In consequence, collective action and free-rider difficulties plague active shareholding, as acknowledged by the PRI.

True, some forms of active shareholding can be low cost. For example, an investor might hire a proxy advisory firm, such as Institutional Shareholder Services, to flag votes on matters that the advisory firm anticipates might adversely affect firm value. Or an investor might speak directly with management, threatening to sell the investor's shares or vote against incumbents if specific reforms, ESG or otherwise, are not pursued. There is survey evidence that these forms of active shareholding are common, are generally low cost, and have had some success.

But a low-cost approach may be insufficient to defeat a management proposal, remove a director, or pass a shareholder resolution. An investor could try to coordinate with other shareholders, but this entails more costs and risks triggering securities law disclosure rules or a poison pill. An investor could wage an outright proxy fight, soliciting all shareholders to vote in agreement with the investor. But this involves paying the costs of a proxy contest, and incumbent directors have powerful structural advantages. A more aggressive but more expensive tactic is to increase the investor's voting power such as by borrowing shares from other shareholders and voting with them. Most daringly, an activist shareholder could identify poorly governed firms or firms with high environmental and social risks, purchase a block share, and try to change firm practices. The costs of these more aggressive approaches must be weighed against their expected benefits.

The evidence is mixed on whether active shareholding, even by institutional investors, in fact improves firm value. Successful shareholder proxy fights have been found to improve firm value, but this approach is costly and risky, and unsuccessful fights can decrease firm value. Shareholder proposals and informal negotiations have, at most, very small positive effects on firm performance, with some studies finding negative effects. There is stronger evidence that activist hedge funds may be successful in achieving excess returns, in part because they do not need to be diversified and so can assemble larger stakes, and in part because they are less regulated than other investment vehicles.

A further challenge to active shareholding is that it may undermine a corporate structure or practice that has other, offsetting benefits. Active shareholding by definition disrupts the separation of ownership and control that is characteristic of the corporate form, and it could dull managerial incentives while reducing the quality of managerial decisionmaking. It may also direct scarce managerial resources to implementing shareholder proposals or contesting elections. That even a sophisticated shareholder will be a better decisionmaker than management is hardly a forgone conclusion. Shareholders can be wrong and indeed may be so more often than management. The corporate form, which separates ownership and control, is an efficient form of enterprise organization in part for this very reason.

Susan N. Gary, Values and Value: University Endowments, Fiduciary Duties, and ESG Investing

42 J.C. & U.L. 247 (2016)[26]

In recent years, some investors have begun to focus on the significance of ESG factors in improving returns while reducing risk. . . .

ESG investing uses environmental, social, and governance factors related to a potential investment as part of a decision-making process that includes financial factors. The goals are to improve stock selection by expanding the information considered about a company and to invest

---

[26] Reprinted by permission of Susan N. Gary and the Journal of College & University Law.

in a sustainable and responsible manner. An ESG investor seeks to identify material risks and opportunities related to investment performance that may not be reflected in traditional financial data. The term "ESG investing" is used to distinguish this strategy from some other forms of [socially responsible investing (SRI)] and to emphasize an overall investment strategy that seeks to maximize financial gain. An investor with no interest in addressing social or environmental problems could use ESG investing as a strategy to seek better returns, and as the reporting mechanisms become more useful, more investors will likely consider ESG factors in their overall investment strategies. . . .

The difference between a strategy that depends on negative screens and one that uses ESG investing can be described, simplistically, with two examples. A fund using exclusionary screens might screen out oil and gas companies. The exclusionary screens would reduce the choices the fund manager could make in constructing the portfolio, but many other choices still exist. Whether the fund matches, exceeds or falls below its benchmarks will depend in part on how the oil and gas sector performs and in part on other selections made for the fund. If the oil and gas stocks decline in value more than stocks in other sectors, perhaps due to increased regulation, the fund might outperform its benchmarks. Alternatively, if the oil and gas stocks go up, as they did in 2004, the screened fund might do less well than its benchmarks, depending on its other investments. . . . The important distinction in comparison with the ESG investing strategy described below, is that certain decisions were made for the screened fund without regard to the value of the stocks being excluded, except to the extent that someone had concluded that the entire group of stocks would perform less well.

In contrast, a fund manager using ESG factors might start with her usual process to create a list of potential stocks. For example, a manager whose strategy is to look for undervalued stocks could do so, in whatever sectors the manager or the fund favors (large cap, small cap, etc.). The manager could create a list of stocks that meet her goals in terms of financial data. Then the manager would narrow the initial list by analyzing the companies' ESG ratings. The ESG factors add information that can help the manager identify stocks more likely to perform well. In this scenario no stock is screened out, except based on financial quality. . . .

A question in considering whether the use of ESG factors will improve performance is whether the environmental, social, and governance information that will affect a company's performance is already reflected in the company's financial data. If the market and the financial indicators already reflect all of the potential social and environmental harms or benefits that could affect the company, the ESG factors will contribute no additional information. Under some circumstances, consideration of ESG factors may lead to that information. The two hypotheticals that follow provide examples of the types of information that might not be included in the financial indicators.

Assume that Company A uses international suppliers that keep costs down by allowing employees to work long hours under unsafe conditions. The suppliers have had no dramatic problems, and the supply chain has never been broken. Company B uses suppliers that conform to production standards it imposes. Factories are safe and employees work under conditions that minimize on-the-job accidents. Company B has also faced no dramatic problems. Company B may have a slightly higher cost for the goods produced by its suppliers, and that information could make Company B's financial data look slightly less favorable than Company A's data. What the data will not reflect is the possibility that a catastrophic fire in a factory used by one of Company A's suppliers could kill hundreds of workers. The repercussions for Company A could include a break in the supply chain, loss of consumer goodwill if the company is linked to the supplier, and even a consumer boycott. The financial impact on Company A could be significant, but current financial data probably does not reveal that risk. The risk is a long-term risk, and merely a risk, not a certainty, but in a process that purports to evaluate financial risk, the risk to Company A may be missing if the evaluator uses only traditional financial data.

. . .

The core financial performance claim for SRI is that corporate value depends upon numerous relationships, including those with employees, customers, communities and the natural environment. Companies that manage these relationships well should prosper in the long run, and those that damage them will face obstacles to their long-term success.[183]

. . .

. . . The attention devoted to ESG investing by investment firms reflects both a response to demands of investors and a growing awareness that integrating ESG factors into overall analysis can improve returns, especially on a risk-adjusted basis. The most recent Trends report from the Forum for Sustainable and Responsible Investment shows a growth in investment funds incorporating ESG factors from $12 billion in assets in 1995, when the first Trends report was compiled, to $4,306 billion in 2014. Further, the report identified $6,572.2 billion in assets engaged in sustainable and responsible investing in 2014. A dramatic upward shift in assets engaged in ESG investing began between the 2007 and 2010 Trends reports, and since 2010 the numbers have risen rapidly. . . .

Firms that offer traditional investment services to institutional investors and individuals increasingly tout their sustainability products or ESG approaches. . . .

---

[183] [Adam M. Kanzer, Exposing False Claims about Socially Responsible Investing: A Response to Adler and Kritzman, ADVISOR PERSPECTIVES 3,4 (Jun. 4, 2013).]

In addition to managing and promoting SRI funds to investors interested in social responsibility and sustainability, investment firms increasingly seek extra-financial information disclosed by companies to make better financial decisions. A study published in 2011 by Robert G. Eccles, Michael P. Krzus, and George Serafeim found a high level of market interest in ESG disclosure, based on an analysis of "hits" accessing extra-financial metrics in the Bloomberg database during three bimonthly periods in late 2010 and early 2011. Their report suggests that investors may be interested in transparency concerning ESG performance and policies as a way to understand whether companies are using that extra-financial information. In addition, the authors' hypothesize that the market perceives less risk in transparent companies, because there is less uncertainty about them. The companies are better positioned to deliver on expected performance if they are "using effective ESG management to capture revenue-generating opportunities, achieve cost savings, and minimize the downside of failures, fines, and lawsuits."[295]

Transparency and governance information also appear to be used as a proxy for good management, because "more capable executives are confident in providing more performance information for which they are held accountable."[297] Investors may be relying in part on research that shows the connection between governance and firm performance, and in part on management's ability to address ESG factors to the long-term benefit of the company.

. . .

Investors, customers, and other stakeholders increasingly request extra-financial as well as financial information about companies. In response, the numbers of companies reporting on ESG factors has risen sharply in recent years. . . .

Sustainability reporting refers to reporting by a company about its environmental, social, and economic impacts. Sustainability reporting began in a somewhat piecemeal fashion, but growing interest led to the development of a framework and guidelines. CERES, the Coalition for Environmentally Responsible Economies, working with the Tellus Institute, took the lead. In the early 1990s, advisors connected with CERES began developing a framework for environmental reporting, and in 1997 CERES created the Global Reporting Initiative (GRI). As work on the initiative continued, the scope expanded to include social, governance and economic reporting. GRI issued the first Sustainability Reporting Framework, with Reporting Guidelines, in 2000. . . . GRI has continued to update the Reporting Framework, and issued the most

---

[295] [Robert G. Eccles, Michael P. Krzus & George Serafeim, Market Interest in Nonfinancial Information, (Harv. Bus. School, Working Paper 12-018 at 7, 2011).]

[297] [Id. at 10.]

recent version of its Sustainability Reporting Guidelines, G4, in May 2013.

Integrated reporting is the merging of financial and extra-financial information about a company based on an assumption that both financial and extra-financial information are needed to assess a company's true value. While sustainability reporting focuses on the extra-financial data, integrated reporting presents all data relevant to a company in one report. Integrated reporting can assist those who manage a company to link long-term strategies with environmental, social, and financial objectives. . . .

A company can use the Generally Accepted Accounting Principles (GAAP) for financial information included in an integrated report. For extra-financial information, the Climate Change Reporting Framework developed by the Climate Disclosure Standards Board and the G4 Guidelines provide guidance on disclosures but do not provide reporting standards. The Sustainability Accounting Standards Board (SASB), created in July 2011, has already developed seven standards for sustainability information for seven sectors and will finish the remaining standards by 2016. These standards are industry-specific, and create performance metrics and a process for determining materiality of issues.

. . . The reports assist investors and other stakeholders in understanding a company's progress and overall strategy and assist companies in developing sustainability strategies that can be incorporated into business operations. . . .

Firms that assist companies with preparing financial statements now actively market their ability to assist with integrated reporting. For example, the website of Ernst & Young (now EY) includes information on integrated reporting and sustainable reporting and states: "Integrated reporting has been created to better articulate the broader range of metrics that contribute to long-term value . . . ." EY explains that in order to create sustainable value, organizations must be able to adapt to "challenges and opportunities in their environments" and must demonstrate the ability to manage their intangible assets effectively. Thus, investors will benefit from the information provided, and companies will benefit because by engaging in sustainability reporting a company will be better able to develop "a sustainable strategy (that is, a coherent plan to balance long term viability—for the benefit of both shareholders and society—with demands for short term competitiveness and profitability.)"

NOTES AND QUESTIONS

1. A review of institutional investor voting patterns on ESG-related shareholder proposals found that support for such proposals by the 50 largest mutual fund families had risen from an average of 27% to 46%. The largest fund families, including Vanguard and BlackRock, however, remained

laggards voting against an average of 87% of ESG-related proposals.[27] Given BlackRock CEO Larry Fink's prominence as an advocate for ESG issues, why might Blackrock lag in supporting ESG-related shareholder proposals?

2.   Although most shareholder activism in this space remain favorable to ESG issues, there has been somewhat of a backlash:

> For example, proposals entitled "Greenwashing Audit" were brought at Duke Energy and Exelon Corporation by the same proponent, in each case, requesting an annual report on actual incurred costs and associated benefits to shareholders, public health and the environment of the company's voluntary environment-related activities. In both cases, the companies were unsuccessful in excluding the proposals based on vagueness, ordinary business or substantial implementation grounds, despite a detailed discussion of the board's analysis and, in each case, noting that the proponent is a co-founder of a pro-coal special interest group and runs a website critical of climate change science, which the letters claimed puts the proponent at odds with the views of the majority of the companies' shareholders.[28]

3.   Advocates for ESG activism offer the following best practices for companies responding to shareholder initiatives in this space:

> 1.   Proactive shareholder engagement: A proactive shareholder engagement program enables a public company to understand the issues most important to its institutional investors, including its passive It is no longer enough to center investor outreach around quarterly results and the buy-side/sell-side teams that track them. Shareholder communications should be responsive to the changing investor base and the increased focus on long-term value, including ESG matters. These shareholder engagements, built over years of discussion, are essential to understanding voting policies and expectations, shaping sustainability disclosure, and building a company's activism preparedness.

> 2.   Embrace sustainability—integrate ESG into corporate strategy: The enhanced focus on sustainability and ESG is a priority for many investors and other Leading companies will ensure that sustainability topics relevant to their business are not only on the board's agenda but integrated into company strategy. Successful companies will embrace material environmental and social issues as part of creating a sustainable business strategy, and integral to their governance profile. Similarly, companies should understand how they compare to their peers and investor expectations. Just as well-governed companies have long prepared

---

[27]   Jackie Cook & Jon Hale, 2019 ESG Proxy Voting Trends by 50 U.S. Fund Families, Harv. L. Sch. Forum on Corp. Gov. (Mar. 23, 2020).

[28]   Richard Alsop & Yoon-jee Kim, Shareholder Proposals 2019—ESG No-Action Letter Trends and Strategies, Harv. L. Sch. Forum on Corp. Gov. (Mar. 25, 2020).

'vulnerability assessments' for shareholder activism, companies should now also focus on their ESG vulnerabilities.

3.   Build a 'fit for ESG' board: The job of a director has never been more challenging and time consuming, particularly with the emergence of sustainability and ESG as top Companies need an engaged, 'fit for purpose' board of directors with the expertise and perspectives to provide appropriate oversight, ask difficult questions, and engage with institutional investors during both good and challenging times. It is crucial that boards have the breadth of backgrounds, range of capabilities and adequate capacity to execute their fiduciary duty. Likewise, it is imperative that companies clearly communicate the strength of their board's skills, experiences, and processes.

4.   Enhance your internal ESG governance. Sustainability governance should not be limited to the boardroom, and a well-designed ESG program must embed sustainability-focused controls, key performance indicators (KPIs), and reporting throughout the organization. All levels of management must be involved in incorporating sustainability into the company's day-to-day activities. This requires a company culture where sustainability and purpose is not an afterthought, but core to the company's existence.

5.   Tell your sustainability story. It is no longer the norm to categorically dismiss queries related to sustainability, in any industry. The question now is how to respond, and it is imperative that public companies proactively enhance their disclosure rather than let third-party ratings providers control the narrative. Since there is not yet a regulatory mandate or other universally accepted disclosure standard for sustainability data, crafting this disclosure remains a challenge. However, investors continue to coalesce around the merits of industry-specific standards issued by the Sustainability Accounting Standards Board (SASB) and the climate-related disclosure recommendations of the Task Force on Climate-related Financial Disclosure (TCFD). Companies should look first to these frameworks as they map out their sustainability journey.[29]

4.   Is it possible to develop meaningful ESG analyses given the very wide range of issues encompassed therein, ranging from emission levels, diversity, human rights, labor practices, business ethics, and corporate governance?

5.   If ESG disclosures become routine, should the SEC adopt rules governing the form and content of those disclosures comparable to the existing SEC rules governing other types of disclosure? If so, should the assessments required by SOX § 404 be extended to these new ESG disclosures?

---

[29]   Jessica Strine et al. The Age of ESG, Harv. L. Sch. Forum on Corp. Gov. (Mar. 9, 2020).

6.   If corporate ESG initiatives both improve firm performance and result in more pro-social outcomes, the case for such initiatives seems obvious. Suppose, however, that corporate ESG initiatives tend to reduce firm performance but also result in more pro-social outcomes. Should they still be encouraged?

To assess your understanding of the material in this chapter, click here to take a quiz.

APPENDIX

THE TOOLS OF THE ECONOMIC ANALYSIS OF CORPORATE GOVERNANCE

What is a corporation? Our analysis of that question starts with a classic article by Nobel Prize laureate Ronald Coase, *The Nature of the Firm*.[625] Since Coase's article appeared more than six decades ago, economic analysis has taken on ever-increasing importance within corporate law. Indeed, it is fair to say that the economic theory of the firm is now the dominant paradigm in corporate law and has been for at least two decades.[626] Not only legal scholars, but also judges and lawyers are adept at using economic analysis. Hence, even those who reject economic analysis must respond to those who practice it.

There are three core economic tools used herein:

- The nexus of contracts theory or the contractarian model of the corporation, which describes the corporation as a set of explicit and implicit contracts. The corporation is neither an entity nor a thing capable of being owned. It is simply a legal fiction that encompasses a set of contractual relations.

- An emphasis on transaction costs. We can analogize transaction costs to friction: they are dead weight losses that reduce efficiency. They make transactions more costly and less likely to occur. Although there are many sources and types of transaction costs, the three most important for our purposes are uncertainty, complexity, and opportunism. At the policy level, transaction cost analysis is highly relevant to setting legal rules. Suppose a steam locomotive drives by a field of wheat. Sparks from the engine set crops on fire. Should the railroad company be liable? In a world of zero transaction costs, the initial assignment of rights is irrelevant. If the legal rule we choose is inefficient, the parties can bargain around it. In a world of transaction costs, however, the parties may not be able to bargain. This is likely to be true in our example. The railroad travels past the property of many landowners, who put their property to differing uses and put differing values on those uses. Negotiating an optimal solution will all of

---

[625] Ronald Coase, The Nature of the Firm, 4 Economica (n.s.) 386 (1937).

[626] This verdict was rendered by no less an authority than former Delaware Chancellor William Allen. See William T. Allen, Contracts and Communities in Corporation Law, 50 Wash. & Lee L. Rev. 1395, 1399 (1993).

those owners would be, at best, time consuming and onerous. Hence, choosing the right rule—which is typically the rule the parties would have chosen if they were able to bargain (the so-called hypothetical bargain)—becomes quite important. At the practical level, much of what transactional lawyers do is figure out ways to minimize transaction costs.

- Agency costs, which are defined as the sum of monitoring costs incurred by the principal, plus bonding costs incurred by the agent, plus the residual loss that inevitably falls through the cracks. Because agents have an incentive to shirk, and principals have an incentive to prevent shirking, much of corporate law necessarily is concerned with constraining agency costs.

A. THE CORPORATION AS NEXUS OF CONTRACTS

Contractarians model the corporation not as an entity, but as an aggregate of various inputs acting together to produce goods or services. Employees provide labor. Creditors provide debt capital. Shareholders initially provide equity capital and subsequently bear the risk of losses and monitor the performance of management. Management monitors the performance of employees and coordinates the activities of all the firm's inputs. The firm is a legal fiction representing the complex set of contractual relationships between these inputs. In other words, the firm is not a thing, but rather a nexus or web of explicit and implicit contracts establishing rights and obligations among the various inputs making up the firm.

The name "nexus of contracts," by the way, is somewhat unfortunate. For lawyers, the term carries with it all of the baggage learned in Contracts class during the first year of law school. Among that baggage are two particularly problematic features. First, the focus on legal notions such as consideration and mutuality. Second, the paradigm seems to be transactions on spot markets that are thick and relatively untroubled by asymmetric information.[627] Neither of which has much to do with the internal governance of corporations.

As used by contractarians, however, the term is not limited to those relationships that constitute legal contracts. Instead, recall that New Institutional Economics uses the word contract to refer to any process by which property rights to assets are created, modified, or transferred.

---

[627] A spot market is one where products and services are exchanged by autonomous market actors who may deal with one another only once. Contracts in such markets typically are executed simultaneously with the exchange and do not have on-going features. Commodities exchanges, such as those for livestock or grain, are good examples of spot markets. So are day laborer employment halls.

A thick market is one in which there are many buyers and sellers, typically characterized by goods for which there are ready substitutes.

Perhaps even more important, contractarians are concerned with long-term relationships characterized by asymmetric information, bilateral monopoly, and opportunism. The relationship between shareholders and creditors of a corporation is contractual in this sense, even though there is no single document we could identify as a legally binding contract through which they are in privity.

The nexus of contracts model has important implications for a range of corporate law topics, the most obvious of which is the debate over the proper role of mandatory legal rules. As a positive matter, contractarians contend that corporate law in fact is generally comprised of default rules, from which the parties to the set of contracts making up the corporation are free to depart, rather than mandatory rules. As a normative matter, contractarians argue that this is just as it should be.

Contractarianism also has implications for the way in which we think about intra-corporate relationships. Take, for example, the commonly held assumption that shareholders own the corporation. Under traditional theories, the corporation is a thing, so it can be owned. In other words, traditionalists reify the corporation: they treat the firm as an entity separate from its various constituents. Nexus of contracts theory rejects this basic proposition. Because shareholders are simply one of the inputs bound together by this web of voluntary agreements, ownership is not a meaningful concept in nexus of contracts theory. Someone owns each input, but no one owns the totality. Instead, the corporation is an aggregation of people bound together by a complex web of contractual relationships. (The validity of this insight becomes apparent when one recognizes that buying a few shares of IBM stock does not entitle me to trespass on IBM's property—I do not own the land or even have any ownership-like right to enter its land.)

The implications of the foregoing may not seem as staggering as they actually are. Consider, for example, the traditional corporate law principle of shareholder wealth maximization. According to a significant line of corporate precedents, the principal obligation of corporate directors is to increase the value of the residual claim—i.e., to increase shareholder wealth.[628] In its traditional guise, this shareholder primacy norm derives from a conception of the corporation as a thing capable of being owned. The shareholders own the corporation, while directors are merely stewards of the shareholders' property.

The nexus of contracts model squarely rejects this conception of the corporation. As such, the shareholder wealth maximization norm is transformed from a right incident to private property into a mere bargained-for contract term. The contractarian account of this norm thus rests not on an outmoded reification of the corporation, but on the

---

[628] See, e.g., Revlon, Inc. v. MacAndrews & Forbes Holdings, Inc., 506 A.2d 173 (Del. 1986); Dodge v. Ford Motor Co., 170 N.W. 668 (Mich. 1919).

presumption of validity a free market society accords voluntary contracts.

Taken to its logical extreme, this insight allows us to transform the traditional notion of shareholder primacy into one of director primacy. The latter perspective regards the corporation as a vehicle by which directors hire capital from shareholders and creditors. The implications of this shift will affect our analysis of a host of issues, such as the allocation of decision-making authority within the corporation and the proper scope of fiduciary obligation. Indeed, director primacy figures as the central organizing principle of this treatise.

In the nexus of contracts model, corporations statutes and judicial opinions can be thought of as a standard form contract voluntarily adopted—perhaps with modifications—by the parties. The point of a standard form contract, of course, is to reduce bargaining costs. Parties for whom the default rules are a good fit can take the default rules off the rack, without having to bargain over them. Parties for whom the default rules are inappropriate, in contrast, are free to bargain out of the default rules.

> **CASE IN POINT**
>
> "A corporation is just a nexus of contracts, subject to rearrangement in many ways." *Central States, Southeast and Southwest Areas Pension Fund v. Sherwin-Williams Co.*, 71 F.3d 1338 (7th Cir. 1995).

If transaction costs are zero, the default rules—whether contained in a statute or a private standard form contract—do not matter very much.[629] In the face of positive transaction costs, however, the default rule begins to matter very much. Indeed, if transaction costs are very high, bargaining around the rule becomes wholly impractical, forcing the parties to live with an inefficient rule. In such settings, we cannot depend on private contracting to achieve efficient outcomes. Instead, statutes must function as a substitute for private bargaining. The public corporation—with its thousands of shareholders, managers, employees, and creditors, each with different interests and asymmetrical information—is a very high transaction cost environment indeed.[630]

Identifying the party for whom getting its way has the highest value thus becomes the critical question. In effect, we must perform a thought experiment: "If the parties could costlessly bargain over the question, which rule would they adopt?" In other words, we mentally play out the following scenario: Sit all interested parties down around a conference table before organizing the corporation. Ask the prospective

---

[629] This is simply a straight-forward application of the famous Coase Theorem, which asserts that, in the absence of transaction costs, the initial assignment of a property right will not determine its ultimate use. R. H. Coase, The Problem of Social Cost, 3 J. L. & Econ. 1 (1960).

[630] It should be apparent that the hypothetical bargain methodology is useful even in a relatively low transaction cost environment like a small partnership or close corporation. Although partners can bargain amongst themselves, they cannot do so costlessly. Accordingly, providing partners a standard form contract comprised of the default rules that most parties would select should reduce transaction costs.

shareholders, employees, contract creditors, tort victims, and the like to bargain over what rules they would want to govern their relationships. Adopt that bargain as the corporate law default rule. Doing so reduces transaction costs and therefore makes it more efficient to run a business. Of course, you cannot really do this; but you can draw on your experience and economic analysis to predict what the parties would do in such a situation.

The basic thesis of the hypothetical bargain methodology is that by providing the rule to which the parties would agree if they could bargain (the so-called "majoritarian default"), society facilitates private ordering. In an important series of articles, however, Ian Ayres and his collaborators argued that majoritarian defaults are not always desirable, even if a potentially dominant one can be identified.[631] Among the alternative, non-majoritarian defaults they identify, the most relevant for our purposes are: (1) Tailored defaults, which purport to fill gaps in the contract at bar by giving the litigants precisely the rule for which those litigants (as opposed to the hypothetical majority) would have bargained if they had thought to do so. (2) Muddy defaults, which make contractual obligations contingent on the circumstances in which the parties find themselves by asking the court to apply a rule that is fair or reasonable under those circumstances. Any rule authorizing judges to fill in gaps in incomplete contracts by supplying terms that are reasonable under the circumstances is an example of a muddy default. (3) Penalty defaults, which are designed to impose a penalty on at least one of the parties if they fail to bargain out of the default rule, thereby giving at least the party subject to the penalty an incentive to negotiate a contractual alternative to the penalty default. They force the parties to choose affirmatively the contract provision they prefer. Penalty defaults are appropriate where it is costly for courts to determine what the parties would have wanted. In such cases, it may be more efficient for the parties to negotiate a term ex ante than for courts to determine ex post what the parties would have wanted.[632]

---

[631] See, e.g., Ian Ayres, Making a Difference: The Contractual Contributions of Easterbrook and Fischel, 59 U. Chi. L. Rev. 1391 (1992); Ian Ayres and Robert Gertner, Filling Gaps in Incomplete Contracts: An Economic Theory of Default Rules, 99 Yale L.J. 87 (1989); Ian Ayres and Eric Talley, Solomonic Bargaining: Dividing a Legal Entitlement to Facilitate Coasean Trade, 104 Yale L.J. 1027 (1995).

[632] The penalty, or bargain-forcing, default flips the majoritarian default concept on its head—the terms imposed by bargain-forcing rules are designed to be contrary to those to which the parties likely would agree if they in fact bargained over the issue, thereby forcing them to choose affirmatively the contract provision they prefer. Choosing between majoritarian and penalty defaults requires one to take into account the lessons of behavioral economics, especially the status quo bias. This aspect of behavioral economics posits a systematic decision-making bias pursuant to which people favor maintaining the status quo rather than switching to some alternative state. Selecting a default rule makes it part of the status quo, altering preferences with respect to contract terms by making parties favor the chosen default and, accordingly, making them less likely to bargain out of that default. A series of experiments using law students provides strong empirical support for that thesis. See generally Russell Korobkin, The Status Quo Bias and Contract Default Rules, 83 Cornell L. Rev. 608 (1998) (describing experiment and analyzing results). If this result can be generalized, it argues in favor of majoritarian defaults and against the use of penalty defaults. Default rules will tend to be sticky

For our purposes, tailored defaults are the most important. Much of our attention will be devoted to fiduciary obligations within corporations. While it will often be the case that some form of fiduciary obligation would be the majoritarian default in a particular setting, those defaults are almost always tailored in the sense that fiduciary obligations are stated not as bright-line rules but as rather vague standards.[633] As a result, judges deciding fiduciary obligation cases typically have substantial discretion to tailor the result to the parties and circumstances at bar.

As a matter of intellectual interest, the debate over the contractual nature of the firm is over. This is not to say that the contractarian view has pre-empted the field, as an important group of scholars continues to reject it,[634] but only to say that the debate has been fully played out. Contractarians and non-contractarians no longer have much of interest to say to one another; indeed, they barely speak the same language. To shift metaphors, those who adhere to the nexus of contracts model pass those who do not like two ships in the night, with only an occasional exchange of broadsides to enliven the proceedings. The real action now for contractarians is not in developing the paradigm, but rather in using it as a heuristic for exploring the nooks and crannies of corporate law. In the interests of completeness, however, we consider a few of the most common criticisms of the nexus of contracts theory of the firm.

The Mandatory Rules Red Herring. Some reject the positive contractarian story on grounds that corporate law is pervaded by mandatory rules.[635] But this objection is far from fatal. In the first instance, many mandatory corporate law rules are in fact trivial, in the sense that they are subject to evasion through choice of form or jurisdiction, or to the extent that some rules appear across the spectrum

---

even in low transaction cost settings. Accordingly, penalty defaults will not lead to parties selecting an optimal rule through private ordering. Instead, provided we redefine the concept of majoritarian default as the rule most parties would select in the absence of any controlling legal authority if they could bargain costlessly, lawmakers should strive to provide socially efficient majoritarian defaults.

[633] It is now conventional to distinguish between standards and rules. A requirement that automobile drivers use reasonable care is a standard. A speed limit forbidding drivers to go faster than 30 miles an hour is a rule. In the former case, the court will have substantial discretion to decide whether the driver's conduct was reasonable, balancing competing policies and concerns. In the latter, the driver either was speeding or not.

[634] See, e.g., William W. Bratton, Jr., The "Nexus of Contracts" Corporation: A Critical Appraisal, 74 Cornell L. Rev. 407 (1989); Melvin A. Eisenberg, The Conception That the Corporation is a Nexus of Contracts and the Dual Nature of the Firm, 24 J. Corp. L. 819 (1999); Melvin A. Eisenberg, Contractarianism Without Contracts: A Response to Professor McChesney, 90 Colum. L. Rev. 1321 (1990). For ripostes from contractarian scholars, see, e.g., Stephen M. Bainbridge, Community and Statism: A Conservative Contractarian Critique of Progressive Corporate Law Scholarship, 82 Cornell L. Rev. 856 (1997); Henry N. Butler and Larry Ribstein, Opting Out of Fiduciary Duties: A Response to the Anti-Contractarians, 65 Wash. L. Rev. 1 (1990); Fred S. McChesney, Contractarianism Without Contracts? Yet Another Critique of Eisenberg, 90 Colum. L. Rev. 1332 (1990); Fred S. McChesney, Economics, Law, and Science in the Corporate Field: A Critique of Eisenberg, 89 Colum. L. Rev. 1530 (1989).

[635] See, e.g., Douglas M. Branson, The Death of Contractarianism and the Vindication of Structure and Authority in Corporate Governance and Corporate Law, in Progressive Corporate Law 93, 94–95 (Lawrence E. Mitchell ed. 1995).

of possible organizational forms, they are rules almost everyone would reach in the event of actual bargaining.[636]

In the second, most contractarians probably regard the normative story as being the more important of the two. As such, we cheerfully concede the existence of mandatory rules, while deploring that unfortunate fact. Contractarians assume that default rules are preferable to mandatory rules in most settings.[637] So long as the default rule is properly chosen, of course, most parties will be spared the need to reach a private agreement on the issue in question. Default rules in this sense provide cost savings comparable to those provided by standard form contracts, because both can be accepted without the need for costly negotiation. At the same time, however, because the default rule can be modified by contrary agreement, idiosyncratic parties wishing a different rule can be accommodated. Given these advantages, a fairly compelling case ought to be required before we impose a mandatory rule.[638] Mandatory rules are justifiable only if a default rule would demonstrably create significant negative externalities or, perhaps, if one of the contracting parties is demonstrably unable to protect itself through bargaining.

Lack of bargaining. As already noted, contractarians contend that corporate law consists mainly of default rules. Put another way, in the nexus of contracts model, corporate statutes and decisions amount to a standard form contract voluntarily adopted—perhaps with modifications—by the corporation's various constituencies. Some reject this argument on grounds that the corporation's constituencies do not and cannot actually bargain.

Part of the answer to this criticism derives from the distinction between actual and hypothetical bargaining. Contractarians concede (or at least should do so) that actual bargaining over corporate law rules is precluded by transaction cost barriers, but contend that this is precisely

---

[636] Bernard S. Black, Is Corporate Law Trivial?: A Political and Economic Analysis, 84 Nw. U. L. Rev. 542 (1990).

[637] Probably the best introduction to this debate is Symposium, Contractual Freedom in Corporate Law, 89 Colum. L. Rev. 1395 (1989). See also Robert B. Thompson, The Law's Limits on Contracts in a Corporation, 15 J. Corp. L. 377 (1990). In conjunction with the mid-1990s revisions to the Uniform Partnership Act, there was also a considerable blossoming of contractarian and anti-contractarian scholarship dealing with the central question of the extent to which freedom of contract trumped fiduciary obligation. See, e.g., J. Dennis Hynes, Fiduciary Duties and UPA (1997): An Inquiry Into Freedom of Contract, 58 Law & Contemp. Probs. 29 (1995); Larry Ribstein, Fiduciary Duty Contracts in Unincorporated Firms, 54 Wash. & Lee L. Rev. 537 (1997); Allan W. Vestal, Advancing the Search for a Compromise: A Response to Professor Hynes, 58 Law & Contemp. Probs. 55 (1995); Allan W. Vestal, The Disclosure Obligations of Partners inter se under the Revised Uniform Partnership Act of 1994: Is the Contractarian Revolution Failing?, 36 Wm. & Mary L. Rev. 1559 (1995); Allan W. Vestal, Fundamental Contractarian Error in the Revised Uniform Partnership Act of 1992, 73 B.U. L. Rev. 523 (1993); see also Larry Ribstein, Unlimited Contracting in the Delaware Limited Partnership and its Implications for Corporate Law, 16 J. Corp. L. 299 (1991).

[638] Cf. In re Pace Photographers, Ltd., 525 N.E.2d 713, 718 (N.Y. 1988) ("Participants in business ventures are free to express their understandings in written agreements, and such consensual arrangements are generally favored and upheld by the courts.").

why corporate statutes provide a set of off-the-rack rules amounting to a standard-form contract. Put another way, legal rules function as a substitute for private bargaining.

A related point has to do with the distinction between outcome and process bargaining. A bargain can be understood in two distinct ways: as a process or as an outcome. There is no bargaining process between a shareholder and the public corporations in which he invests, but there is an outcome—the set of organic rules contained in the articles and bylaws as drafted by the corporation's founders or directors—that fairly can be described as a bargain. A bargain involving only an outcome is just as much a contract as a bargain involving both a process and an outcome.

Summation. Despite these and other objections by the nexus of contracts model's critics, there is no doubt that contractarianism is today the dominant theory of the firm in the legal academy. It is also steadily working its way into judicial decisionmaking. Delaware supreme court Chief Justice Veasey, for example, opines: "Although the contract analogy is imperfect, it comes reasonably close to a working hypothesis. I think courts might consider using as a point of departure—but not necessarily a controlling principle—what they perceive to be the investors' reasonable contractual expectations."[639]

B. Transaction Costs

As already noted, transaction costs are the economic equivalent of friction—dead weight losses that increase the cost of transacting and, hence, reduce the number of transactions. Transaction costs are pervasive and, hence, drive the analysis both of market transactions and intra-firm governance. At present, however, the transaction costs most relevant for our purposes are those that explain the emergence and success of the corporation as an economic institution. As we shall see throughout this text, it is those costs that necessarily provide the framework for our analysis.

Why then do firms exist? In capitalist economic systems, there are two basic coordinating mechanisms: markets, in which resources are allocated by the price system, and firms, in which resources are allocated by authoritative direction. This was Ronald Coase's fundamental insight: If a workman moves from department Y to department X he does so not because of change in relative prices, but because he is ordered to do so. Accordingly, Coase opined, firms come into existence when the costs of bargaining are higher than the costs of command-and-control.[640]

Organizing economic activity within a firm, for example, may lower search and other transaction costs associated with bargaining. Consider Adam Smith's classic example: the manufacturing of pins in eighteenth

---

[639] E. Norman Veasey, An Economic Rationale for Judicial Decisionmaking in Corporate Law, 53 Bus. Law. 681 (1998).

[640] Ronald Coase, The Nature of the Firm, 4 Economica (n.s.) 386 (1937).

century England.[641] Smith observed that making a pin involves eighteen distinct operations. A substantial synergistic effect resulted when a team was organized in which each operation was conducted by a separate individual: the team was able to produce thousands of pins a day, while an individual working alone might produce one pin a day at best. In theory, the team could be organized through a decentralized price mechanism; indeed, there are a few historical examples of quasi-assembly line production processes involving independent craftsmen transacting across a small local market. In normal practice, however, team production requires personnel interactions that are too complex to be handled through a price mechanism. The firm solves that problem by acting as a centralized contracting party—some team member is charged with seeking out the necessary inputs and bringing them together for productive labor.

Organizing production within a firm can also lower costs associated with uncertainty, opportunism, and complexity. Uncertainty arises because it is difficult to predict the future. Opportunism arises because parties to a contract are inevitably tempted to pursue their own self-interest at the expense of the collective good, which in market transactions leads to contract breaches requiring resort to costly enforcement mechanisms.[642] Complexity arises when the parties attempt to contractually specify how they will respond to a given situation. As the relationship's term lengthens, it necessarily becomes more difficult to foresee the needs and threats of the future, which in turn presents an ever-growing myriad of contingencies to be dealt with. The more contingencies to be accounted for, and the greater the degree of uncertainty that is present, the more difficult it becomes for the parties to draft completely specified contracts. Indeed, the phenomenon of bounded rationality implies that making complete contracts is costly, at best, and often impossible. Given the limits on cognitive competence implied by bounded rationality, incomplete contracts are the inevitable result of uncertainty and complexity, which in turn leave greater room for opportunistic behavior, and thus inexorably lead to the need for coordination. According to the Coasean theory of the firm, firms arise when it is possible to lower these costs by delegating to a team member the power to direct how the various inputs will be utilized by the firm; in effect, allowing one team member to constantly and, more important, unilaterally rewrite certain terms of the contract between the firm and its various constituents.

Centralized decision making thus emerges as the defining characteristic of the Coasean firm. At first blush, there may appear to be an inconsistency between Coase's command-and-control theory of the

---

[641] Adam Smith, The Wealth of Nations 4–5 (Modern Library ed. 1937).

[642] The transaction cost economics concept of opportunism or strategic behavior is closely related to agency cost economics, which is described in the next section. The two approaches are complementary rather than competing—indeed, agency costs can be thought of as a subset of transaction costs so important that they deserve separate consideration.

firm and the contractarian model embraced above. In a classic article, Armen Alchian and Harold Demsetz rejected Coase's argument that the power of direction was the factor distinguishing firms from markets.[643] They argued that a firm has no power of fiat; instead, an employer's power to direct its employees does not differ from a consumer's power to direct his grocer. Just as a firm can fire a lousy worker, a consumer can "fire" a lousy grocer by patronizing a different store.

Coase may well have erred in treating the firm as a nonmarket institution in which prices and contracts are of relatively little consequence, but there also is something of a disconnect between Alchian and Demsetz's argument and the real world of work. Command-and-control is the norm in most workplaces. In any case, there is no necessary contradiction between a theory of the firm characterized by command-and-control decision making and the contractarian model. The set of contracts making up the firm consists in very large measure of implicit agreements, which by definition are both incomplete and unenforceable. As we have just seen, under conditions of uncertainty and complexity, employees and employers cannot execute a complete contract, so that many decisions must be left for later contractual rewrites imposed by employer fiat. It is precisely the lack of enforceability of implicit corporate contracts that makes it possible for the central decision maker to rewrite them more-or-less freely. The parties to the corporate contract presumably accept this consequence of relying on implicit contracts because the resulting reduction in transaction costs benefits them all. It is thus possible to harmonize the Coasean and contractarian models without having to reject a theory of the firm in which management has the power to direct its workers or in which the corporation is characterized by bureaucratic hierarchies. Instead, the firm's employees voluntarily enter into a relationship in which they agree to obey managerial commands, while reserving the right to disassociate from the firm.

C. AGENCY COSTS

Organizing production within a firm creates certain costs, of which the class known as agency costs is the most important for our purposes. Agency costs are defined as the sum of the monitoring and bonding costs, plus any residual loss, incurred to prevent shirking by agents.[644] In turn, shirking is defined to include any action by a member of a production team that diverges from the interests of the team as a whole. As such, shirking includes not only culpable cheating, but also negligence, oversight, incapacity, and even honest mistakes. In other words, shirking

---

[643]   Armen A. Alchian and Harold Demsetz, Production, Information Costs, and Economic Organization, 62 Am. Econ. Rev. 777 (1972).

[644]   Michael C. Jensen and William H. Meckling, Theory of the Firm: Managerial Behavior, Agency Costs and Ownership Structure, 3 J. Fin. Econ. 305 (1976).

is simply the inevitable consequence of bounded rationality and opportunism within agency relationships.[645]

A sole proprietorship with no agents will internalize all costs of shirking, because the proprietor's optimal trade-off between labor and leisure is, by definition, the same as the firm's optimal trade-off. Agents of a firm, however, will not internalize all of the costs of shirking: the principal reaps part of the value of hard work by the agent, but the agent receives all of the value of shirking. In a classic article, Professors Alchian and Demsetz offered the useful example of two workers who jointly lift heavy boxes into a truck.[646] The marginal productivity of each worker is difficult to measure and their joint output cannot be separated easily into individual components. In such situations, obtaining information about a team member's productivity and appropriately rewarding each team member are very difficult and costly. In the absence of such information, however, the disutility of labor gives each team member an incentive to shirk because the individual's reward is unlikely to be closely related to conscientiousness.

Although agents ex post have strong incentives to shirk, ex ante they have equally strong incentives to agree to a corporate contract containing terms designed to prevent shirking. Bounded rationality, however, precludes firms and agents from entering into the complete contract necessary to prevent shirking by the latter. Instead, there must be some system of ex post governance: some mechanism for detecting and punishing shirking. Accordingly, an essential economic function of management is monitoring the various inputs into the team effort: management meters the marginal productivity of each team member and then takes steps to reduce shirking. (No implication is intended that ex post governance structures are noncontractual.)

The process just described, of course, raises a new question: who will monitor the monitors? In any organization, one must have some ultimate monitor who has sufficient incentives to ensure firm productivity without himself having to be monitored. Otherwise, one ends up with a never ending series of monitors monitoring lower level monitors. Alchian and

---

[645] A simple example of the agency cost problem is provided by the bail upon which alleged criminals are released from jail while they await trial. The defendant promises to appear for trial. But that promise is not very credible: The defendant will be tempted to flee the country. The court could keep track of the defendant—monitor him—by keeping him in jail or perhaps by means of some electronic device permanently attached to the defendant's person. Yet, such monitoring efforts are not free—indeed, keeping someone in jail is quite expensive (food, guards, building the jail, etc.). Alternatively, the defendant could give his promise credibility by bonding it, which is exactly what bail does. The defendant puts up a sum of money that he will forfeit if he fails to appear for trial. (Notice that the common use of bail bonds and the employment of bounty hunters to track fugitives further enhances the credibility of bail as a deterrent against flight.) Of course, despite these precautions, some defendants will escape jail and/or jump bail. Hence, there will always be some residual loss in the form of defendants who escape punishment. Notice, by the way, that this example illustrates how the economic analysis can be extended beyond the traditional agency relationship.

[646] Armen A. Alchian and Harold Demsetz, Production, Information Costs, and Economic Organization, 62 Am. Econ. Rev. 777 (1972).

Demsetz solved this dilemma by consolidating the roles of ultimate monitor and residual claimant. According to Alchian and Demsetz, if the constituent entitled to the firm's residual income is given final monitoring authority, he is encouraged to detect and punish shirking by the firm's other inputs because his reward will vary exactly with his success as a monitor.

Unfortunately, this elegant theory breaks down precisely where it would be most useful. Because of the separation of ownership and control, it simply does not describe the modern publicly held corporation. As the corporation's residual claimants, the shareholders should act as the firm's ultimate monitors. But while the law provides shareholders with some enforcement and electoral rights, these are reserved for fairly extraordinary situations. In general, shareholders of public corporation have neither the legal right, the practical ability, nor the desire to exercise the kind of control necessary for meaningful monitoring of the corporation's agents.

The apparent lack of managerial accountability inherent in the modern corporate structure has troubled legal commentators since at least Adolf Berle's time.[647] To be sure, agency costs are an important component of any viable theory of the firm. A narrow focus on agency costs, however, easily can distort one's understanding of the firm. Corporate managers operate within a pervasive web of accountability mechanisms that substitute for monitoring by residual claimants. Important constraints are provided by a variety of market forces. The capital and product markets, the internal and external employment markets, and the market for corporate control all constrain shirking by firm agents. In addition, the legal system evolved various adaptive responses to the ineffectiveness of shareholder monitoring, establishing alternative accountability structures to punish and deter wrongdoing by firm agents, such as the board of directors.

An even more important consideration, however, is that agency costs are the inevitable consequence of vesting discretion in someone other than the residual claimant. We could substantially reduce, if not eliminate, agency costs by eliminating discretion; that we do not do so suggests that discretion has substantial virtues. A complete theory of the firm thus requires one to balance the virtues of discretion against the need to require that discretion be used responsibly. Neither discretion nor accountability can be ignored, because both promote values essential to the survival of business organizations. Unfortunately, they are ultimately antithetical: one cannot have more of one without also having less of the other. Managers cannot be made more accountable without undermining their discretionary authority. Establishing the proper mix

---

[647] Adolf A. Berle, Jr. and Gardiner C. Means, The Modern Corporation and Private Property 6 (1932) ("The separation of ownership from control produces a condition where the interests of owner and of ultimate manager may, and often do, diverge, and where many of the checks which formerly operated to limit the use of power disappear.").

of discretion and accountability thus emerges as the central corporate governance question,[648] and the one around which this text is largely centered.

---

[648] See generally Michael P. Dooley, Two Models of Corporate Governance, 47 Bus. Law. 461 (1992) (upon which the preceding discussion draws).

INDEX

References are to Pages